W9-BMM-402

SEEING OURSELVES

SEEING OURSELVES

Classic, Contemporary,
and Cross-Cultural Readings
in Sociology

Seventh Edition

Edited by

John J. Macionis
Kenyon College

Nijole V. Benokraitis
University of Baltimore

PEARSON

Prentice
Hall

Upper Saddle River, New Jersey 07458

Library of Congress Cataloging-in-Publication Data

Seeing ourselves : classic, contemporary, and cross-cultural readings in sociology /
edited by John J. Macionis, Nijole V. Benokraitis .—7th ed.
   p. cm.
ISBN 0-13-220491-6
1. Sociology. I. Macionis, John J. II. Benokraitis, Nijole V. (Nijole Vaicaitis)
 HM586.S44 2006
 301

                              2006002751

Editorial Director: Leah Jewell
Editorial Assistant/Supervisor: Christina Walker
Publisher: Nancy Roberts
Editorial Assistant: Lee Peterson
Production Liaison: Joanne Hakim
Director of Marketing: Brandy Dawson
Senior Marketing Manager: Marissa Feliberty
Manufacturing Buyer: Brian Mackey
Cover Art Director: Jayne Conte
Cover Image: Leroux, Georges Paul (1877–1957) © ARS, NY. In the Grande Galerie of the Louvre. Oil on canvas, 89 × 151 cm.
Inv: RF 1974-3. Photographed by Jean Schormans. Louvre, Paris, France. Réunion des Musées Nationaux/Art Resource, NY.
Director, Image Resource Center: Melinda Reo
Manager, Rights and Permissions: Zina Arabia
Manager, Visual Research: Beth Brenzel
Manager, Cover Visual Research & Permissions: Karen Sanatar
Photo Coordinator: Debbie Hewitson
Full-Service Project Management: Jessica Balch/Pine Tree Composition, Inc.
Composition: Laserwords Private Limited
Printer/Binder: Courier Stoughton

Credits and acknowledgments for text borrowed from other sources and reproduced, with permission, in this textbook appear
on appropriate page within text. Photo credits appear on p. 529.

Copyright © 2007, 2004, 2001, 1998, 1995 by Pearson Education, Inc., Upper Saddle River, New Jersey, 07458.
Pearson Prentice Hall. All rights reserved. Printed in the United States of America. This publication is protected by Copyright
and permission should be obtained from the publisher prior to any prohibited reproduction, storage in a retrieval system, or
transmission in any form or by any means, electronic, mechanical, photocopying, recording, or likewise. For information regarding permission(s), write to: Rights and Permissions Department.

Pearson Prentice Hall™ is a trademark of Pearson Education, Inc.
Pearson® is a registered trademark of Pearson plc
Prentice Hall® is a registered trademark of Pearson Education, Inc.

Pearson Education LTD., London
Pearson Education Singapore, Pte. Ltd
Pearson Education, Canada, Ltd
Pearson Education—Japan
Pearson Education Australia PTY, Limited

Pearson Education North Asia Ltd
Pearson Educación de Mexico, S.A. de C.V.
Pearson Education Malaysia, Pte. Ltd
Pearson Education, Upper Saddle River, New Jersey

10 9 8 7 6 5 4 3 2 1
ISBN 0-13-220491-6

Contents

Sexuality

Social Stratification

Gender

Preface

If there is a college course that is more exciting for students than the introduction to sociology, we don't know what it is. Both of us began our careers as students taking the "intro course," and we both found it to be life-changing. Over the (many) years since then, we have received thousands of e-mail messages from students that, in different ways and using different words, say pretty much the same thing: "Sociology has given me a new way to see the world around me. It has changed the way I think about myself and our society. It has given me knowledge and skills that I can use every day."

Why is sociology so exciting? First, understanding how society operates is a source of power, helping us to recognize the opportunities and challenges that frame our lives and to see that society is a human creation that is subject to change. Second, sociology is liberating. It frees us from the belief that we alone are responsible for our life situations and, by showing how society shapes our world, opens the door to new possibilities. Third, sociology is plain fun. Looking at our

families, workplaces, campuses, and local communities with a sociological eye, we suddenly recognize patterns and processes that were always there but went unnoticed. To learn to see sociologically is to have the world around you come alive as it never has before. What could be more fun than that?

Sociology is also a vast and diverse body of knowledge that stretches back more than 150 years. *Seeing Ourselves: Classic, Contemporary, and Cross-Cultural Readings in Sociology* captures this rich legacy, presenting it to readers in the words of the men and women who created it. This collection of readings contains the work of the discipline's founders and others who have made lasting contributions. In addition, it contains important research being done by women and men who are standing on the shoulders of the founders. Finally, it deepens our understanding of our own way of life by making comparisons with other societies and cultural systems.

This reader provides excellent material for use in a wide range of courses. *Seeing Ourselves* is most widely used in introductory sociology, but it is also well suited for courses in social problems, cultural anthropology, social theory, social stratification, American studies, women's studies, and marriage and the family.

Since its introduction a decade ago, *Seeing Ourselves* has been the most popular reader in the discipline. This seventh edition offers eighty-two readings that represent the widest range of material found in any similar text. In short, *Seeing Ourselves* gives instructors the largest selection of articles to consider for their courses. It also gives students the best value for their textbook dollar, costing less per article than competing readers and "custom" readers.

THE THREE C'S: CLASSIC, CONTEMPORARY, AND CROSS-CULTURAL

Seeing Ourselves is the only reader that systematically weaves together three types of selections. For each general topic typically covered in a sociology course, three types of articles are included: *classic, contemporary,* and *cross-cultural.*

Classic articles—30 in all—are sociological statements of recognized importance and lasting significance. Included here are the ideas of sociology's founders and shakers—including Emile Durkheim, Karl Marx, Max Weber, Georg Simmel, Ferdinand Tönnies, as well as Margaret Mead, W. E. B. Du Bois, Louis Wirth, George Herbert Mead, Thomas Robert Malthus, and Charles Horton Cooley. There are also many more recent contributions by Alfred Kinsey, Jessie Bernard, Robert Merton, Erving Goffman, Peter Berger, Kingsley Davis and Wilbert Moore, C. Wright Mills, Talcott Parsons, Leslie White, and Jo Freeman.

We realize that not everyone will agree about precisely which selections should be called "classics." But we hope that instructors will be pleased to see the work of so many outstanding women and men—carefully edited with undergraduate students in mind—available in a single, affordable source.

Twenty-nine *contemporary* selections focus on current sociological issues, controversies, and applications. These articles show sociologists at work and demonstrate the importance of ongoing research. They address many of the issues that concern today's students, providing solid data and reasoned analysis. Among the contemporary selections in *Seeing Ourselves* are Donna Gaines on teenage suicide, Patricia Madoo Lengermann and Jill Niebrugge-Brantley on women founders of sociology, Becky Thompson on our cultural obsession with thinness, Michael Messner on how our society defines "masculine," Jill Kilbourne on the power of mass-media advertising, Paula Rothenberg on privilege that many of us take for granted, George Ritzer on McDonaldization and jobs, Elijah Anderson on the normative system that operates on the streets of some low-income communities, David Rosenhan on diagnosing mental illness, Andrew Hacker on patterns of inequality in the United States, Judith Lorber on the social construction of gender, Patricia Hill Collins on black women's oppression, Karen B. Brodkin on the social construction of race, William Julius Wilson on the rising desperation of some inner-city residents, Thomas Dye on who's at the center of power in the United States, Susan Douglas and Meredith Michaels on motherhood, Naomi Schaefer Riley on student life at religious colleges, Jonathan Kozol on inequality in U.S. public schools, and Eric Schlosser giving an insider look at the fast-food industry.

The twenty-three *cross-cultural* selections offer sociological insights about the striking cultural diversity of the United States and the larger world. Included are well-known works such as "Body Ritual among the Nacirema" by Horace Miner, "India's Sacred Cow" by Marvin Harris, "The Amish: A Small Society" by John Hostetler, J. M. Carrier's "Homosexuality in Cross-Cultural Perspective," and Elaine Leeder's "Domestic Violence: A Cross-Cultural View." Other articles focus on Arab women and social research, learning to be a doctor in Canada, prostitution around the world, the ways in which global inequality benefits rich countries including the United States, the practice of female genital mutilation, how courtship and marriage differ around the world, global population increase, the health of Native American men, the central role played by Japanese mothers in their children's schooling, and differences in the abortion movements that are found in various countries. Cross-cultural selections broaden students' understanding of other cultures and, in the process, sharpen their understanding of our own society.

ORGANIZATION OF THE READER

This reader parallels the chapter sequence common to textbooks used in introductory sociology. Instructors can easily and effectively use these articles in a host of other courses and can assign articles in whatever order they wish. For each of the twenty-three general topics, we present a cluster of three to five articles, including at least one classic, at least one contemporary, and at least one cross-cultural selection. The expansive coverage of these eighty-two articles ensures that instructors can choose readings well suited to their own classes, and at the lowest cost.

The first grouping of articles describes the distinctive sociological perspective, brings to life the promise and pitfalls of sociological research, and demonstrates the discipline's applications to a variety of issues. The selections that follow emphasize key concepts: culture, society, socialization, social interaction, groups and organizations, deviance, and the importance of sexuality to our society. The focus then turns to various dimensions of social inequality, with attention to class, gender, race and ethnicity, and aging. The major social institutions are covered next, including the economy and work; politics, government, and the military; families; religion; education; and health and medicine. The final sets of articles explore dimensions of global transformation—including population growth, urbanization, the natural environment, social movements, and social change.

A NOTE ON LANGUAGE

One of the advantages of using this reader is allowing students to read the exact words of dozens of notable sociologists. The editors have assembled their selections from the sources in their original form; although we have edited some readings for length, we have not altered any author's language. At the same time, we want students and instructors to know that some of the older selections—especially the classics—use male pronouns rather than more contemporary gender-neutral terminology, and one article employs the term "Negro." We have not changed the language in any article, wishing not to violate the historical authenticity of any document. That said, we urge faculty and students, with the original articles in hand, to consider the importance of language and how it has changed in their analysis of the author's ideas.

TEACHING FEATURES

Seeing Ourselves has two features that enhance the learning of students. First, a brief introduction, placed at the beginning of each selection, summarizes the main argument and highlights important issues to keep in mind while reading the article. Second, at the end of each article are at least three critical-thinking questions which develop the significance of the reading, help students evaluate their own learning, and stimulate class discussion.

INTERNET SITES

Readers are also invited to visit our sociology Web sites. At **http://prenhall.com/macionis**, students will find on-line study guides for the Macionis introductory texts (*Sociology* and *Society: The Basics*), including discussion topics, test questions, and Internet links. In addition, **http://www.TheSociologyPage.com** (or **http://www.macionis.com**) provides information about the field of sociology, biographies of key sociologists, recent news of interest to sociologists, and more than fifty links to worthwhile Internet sites.

Also, **www.prenhall.com/benokraitis** offers more than 400 "hot links" to topics such as theory, sociological research, culture, socialization, interaction and communication, sexuality, race and ethnicity, gender roles, aging, work, marriage and the family, health, and social change.

INSTRUCTOR'S MANUAL WITH TEST QUESTIONS

Prentice Hall also supports *Seeing Ourselves* with an Instructor's Manual, prepared by Leda A. Thompson. For each selection, the Instructor's Manual provides a summary of the article's arguments and conclusions, eight multiple-choice questions with answers, and suggested essay questions. The multiple-choice questions are also available on computer disk for both PC and Mac users.

CHANGES TO THE SEVENTH EDITION

We are grateful to our colleagues at hundreds of colleges and universities in the United States and Canada who have made *Seeing Ourselves* a part of their courses. In response to this unparalleled reception, the editors have worked especially hard this time around to prepare what we believe is the best and strongest reader available for our discipline. Here are the key changes:

1. **Fifteen new articles** appear in the seventh edition. This raises the total to eighty-two, an increase of five articles from the last edition, and twice as many selections as in some other readers.
2. **More attention to important contemporary research.** We have made no changes to the *classic* selections, which, after all, stand up well over time. Most of the changes in this edition are new *contemporary* selections and reflect recent scholarship that has attracted a lot of attention both within and beyond the field of sociology.

These new and popular selections include "Teenage Wasteland" by Donna Gaines, "Women and the Birth of Sociology" by Patricia Madoo Lengermann and Jill Niebrugge-Brantley, "Unmarried with Children" by Kathryn Edin and Maria Kefalas, "Boyhood, Organized Sports, and the Construction of Masculinities" by Michael Messner, "Invisible Privilege" by Paula Rothenberg, "'Night to His Day': The Social Construction of Gender" by Judith Lorber, "Who Is Running America?" by Thomas Dye, "The Mommy Myth" by Susan J. Douglas and Meredith W. Michaels, "How Student Life Is Different at Religious Colleges" by Naomi Schaefer Riley, and "The Slaughterhouse: The Most Dangerous Job" from Eric Schlosser's recent book, *Fast Food Nation.*

In addition, this edition of *Seeing Ourselves,* offers five new cross-cultural selections, enriching the anthology's multicultural and global content. The new selections in this category are " 'Even If I Don't Know What I'm Doing, I Can Make It Look Like I Do': Becoming a Doctor in Canada" by Brenda L. Beagan, "Prostitution: A Worldwide Business of Sexual Exploitation" by Melissa Farley, "Domestic Violence: A Cross-Cultural View" by Elaine Leeder, "The Roots of Terrorism" from The 9/11 Commission Report, and "Japanese Mothers as the Best Teachers" by Keiko Hirao.

3. **A greater emphasis on race, class, and gender.** Because so much of the research carried out in sociology deals with the causes, the character, and the consequences of social inequality, this new edition of *Seeing Ourselves* offers more on these vital issues than ever before.

As in the past, we invite faculty and students to share their thoughts and reactions to this reader. Write to John Macionis at **macionis@kenyon.edu** or send a letter to the Department of Sociology, Palme House, Kenyon College, Gambier, Ohio 43022-9623 and to Nijole Benokraitis at **nbenokraitis@.ubalt.edu** or contact her at the Department of Sociology, University of Baltimore, 1420 North Charles Street, Baltimore, Maryland 21201-5779.

ACKNOWLEDGMENTS

The editors are grateful to many people for their generous help in preparing this reader. First, the relationship between writers and publishers is a special mix of friendship, creative tension, and a shared commitment to doing the best job possible. In this regard, two important people at Prentice Hall are Chris DeJohn, former executive editor of sociology, and Nancy Roberts, Publisher for Humanities and Social Sciences. In addition, we acknowledge the timely and skillful work of the production team, including Joanne Hakim of Prentice Hall and Jessica Balch and the staff of Pine Tree Composition.

A number of our colleagues offered critical comments that have improved the final book:

Sharon Abbott, Fairfield University; Rebecca Adams, University of North Carolina at Greensboro; Amy Ansell, Bora College; Jacqueline Bergdahl, Wright State University; Jonathan Cordero, Westmont College; Angela D. Danzi, Farmingdale State University of New York; Virginia Gill, Illinois State University; Pam Hunter-Holmes, Texas A & M University; Charles Jaret, Georgia State University; Todd M. Krohn, University of Georgia; Gail Murphy-Geiss, Colorado College; Thomas Soltis, Westmoreland County Community College; Cynthia Neal Spence, Spelman College; and George Ann Weatherby, Gonzaga University.

We dedicate this edition of *Seeing Ourselves* to students—yours and ours. Their insights, probing questions, and thoughtful observations about society enliven our classrooms and enrich our teaching lives immeasurably.

About the Editors

JOHN J. MACIONIS is Professor and Distinguished Scholar of Sociology at Kenyon College in Gambier, Ohio. Born and raised in Philadelphia, he earned a bachelor's degree from Cornell University and a doctorate in sociology from the University of Pennsylvania. Macionis has authored a number of best-selling sociology textbooks, including *Sociology,* the leading comprehensive text; *Society: The Basics,* the leading brief textbook; and *Social Problems,* the leading text for that course. Professor Macionis has been active in academic programs in other countries, having traveled to more than fifty nations. In 2002, the American Sociological Association honored Macionis for his work with textbooks and for pioneering the use of new technology in sociology by bestowing on him the major Award for Distinguished Contributions to Teaching. At Kenyon, Macionis offers a wide range of upper-level courses, but his favorite course is Introduction to Sociology, which he teaches every year. He enjoys extensive contact with students, making an occasional appearance on campus to play oldies rock and roll, and each term inviting his students to enjoy a home-cooked meal. The Macionis family—John, Amy, and children McLean and Whitney—live on a farm in rural Ohio. In his free time, Macionis enjoys playing the Scottish bagpipes, working for environmental organizations, and sharing an adventure with his two children.

NIJOLE V. BENOKRAITIS is Professor of Sociology at the University of Baltimore. She earned a B.A. at Emmanuel College (Boston), an M.A. at the University of Illinois at Urbana-Champaign, and a doctorate at the University of Texas at Austin. Professor Benokraitis, who immigrated to the United States from Lithuania with her family when she was 6 years old, is bilingual and bicultural and is very empathetic of students who try to balance two cultural worlds. She is the author, co-author, editor, and co-editor of seven books, including *Marriages and Families: Changes, Choices, and Constraints.* Benokraitis has published numerous articles and book chapters on topics such as sexism and institutional racism, has received grants and fellowships from many institutions—including the Ford Foundation and the Administration on Aging—and has made numerous appearances on local radio and television shows. She currently serves on the editorial board of *Women & Criminal Justice* and reviews international fellowship applications for the American Association of University Women's Educational Foundation. Benokraitis and her husband, Vitalius, have two adult children, Gema and Andrius. If she had free time, Benokraitis would read mystery novels, expand her mug collection, have more lunches with her past students, garden, and watch at least two movies every day.

SEEING OURSELVES

CLASSIC

CONTEMPORARY

CROSS-CULTURAL

1 The Sociological Imagination

C. WRIGHT MILLS

To C. Wright Mills, the sociological imagination is a special way to engage the world. To think sociologically is to realize that what we experience as personal problems are often widely shared by others like ourselves. Thus, many personal problems are actually social issues. For Mills, one of sociology's most outspoken activists, the sociological imagination encouraged collective action to change the world in some way.

Nowadays men often feel that their private lives are a series of traps. They sense that within their everyday worlds, they cannot overcome their troubles, and in this feeling, they are often quite correct: What ordinary men are directly aware of and what they try to do are bounded by the private orbits in which they live; their visions and their powers are limited to the close-up scenes of job, family, neighborhood; in other milieux, they move vicariously and remain spectators. And the more aware they become, however vaguely, of ambitions and of threats which transcend their immediate locales, the more trapped they seem to feel.

Source: From *The Sociological Imagination* by C. Wright Mills. Copyright © 2000 by Oxford University Press, Inc. Used by permission of Oxford University Press, Inc.

Alex Colville (1920–), *To Prince Edward Island,* 1965, acrylic emulsion on masonite, 61.9 × 92.5 cm. National Gallery of Canada, Ottawa, © NGC/MBAC.

Underlying this sense of being trapped are seemingly impersonal changes in the very structure of continent-wide societies. The facts of contemporary history are also facts about the success and the failure of individual men and women. When a society is industrialized, a peasant becomes a worker; a feudal lord is liquidated or becomes a businessman. When classes rise or fall, a man is employed or unemployed; when the rate of investment goes up or down, a man takes new heart or goes broke. When wars happen, an insurance salesman becomes a rocket launcher; a store clerk, a radar man; a wife lives alone; a child grows up without a father. Neither the life of an individual nor the history of a society can be understood without understanding both.

Yet men do not usually define the troubles

they endure in terms of historical change and institutional contradiction. The well-being they enjoy, they do not usually impute to the big ups and downs of the societies in which they live. Seldom aware of the intricate connection between the patterns of their own lives and the course of world history, ordinary men do not usually know what this connection means for the kinds of men they are becoming and for the kinds of history-making in which they might take part. They do not possess the quality of mind essential to grasp the interplay of man and society, of biography and history, of self and world. They cannot cope with their personal troubles in such ways as to control the structural transformations that usually lie behind them.

Surely it is no wonder. In what period have so many men been so totally exposed at so fast a pace to such earthquakes of change? That Americans have not known such catastrophic changes as have the men and women of other societies is due to historical facts that are now quickly becoming "merely history." The history that now affects every man is world history. Within this scene and this period, in the course of a single generation, one-sixth of mankind is transformed from all that is feudal and backward into all that is modern, advanced, and fearful. Political colonies are freed; new and less visible forms of imperialism installed. Revolutions occur; men feel the intimate grip of new kinds of authority. Totalitarian societies rise, and are smashed to bits—or succeed fabulously. After two centuries of ascendancy, capitalism is shown up as only one way to make society into an industrial apparatus. After two centuries of hope, even formal democracy is restricted to a quite small portion of mankind. Everywhere in the underdeveloped world, ancient ways of life are broken up and vague expectations become urgent demands. Everywhere in the overdeveloped world, the means of authority and of violence become total in scope and bureaucratic in form. Humanity itself now lies before us, the super-nation at either pole concentrating its most coordinated and massive efforts upon the preparation of World War III.

The very shaping of history now outpaces the ability of men to orient themselves in accordance with cherished values. And which values? Even when they do not panic, men often sense that older ways of feeling and thinking have collapsed and that newer beginnings are ambiguous to the point of moral stasis. Is it any wonder that ordinary men feel they cannot cope with the larger worlds with which they are so suddenly confronted? That they cannot understand the meaning of their epoch for their own lives? That— in defense of selfhood—they become morally insensible, trying to remain altogether private men? Is it any wonder that they come to be possessed by a sense of the trap?

It is not only information that they need—in this Age of Fact, information often dominates their attention and overwhelms their capacities to assimilate it. It is not only the skills of reason that they need—although their struggles to acquire these often exhaust their limited moral energy.

What they need, and what they feel they need, is a quality of mind that will help them to use information and to develop reason in order to achieve lucid summations of what is going on in the world and of what may be happening within themselves. It is this quality, I am going to contend, that journalists and scholars, artists and publics, scientists and editors are coming to expect of what may be called the sociological imagination.

The sociological imagination enables its possessor to understand the larger historical scene in terms of its meaning for the inner life and the external career of a variety of individuals. It enables him to take into account how individuals, in the welter of their daily experience, often become falsely conscious of their social positions. Within that welter, the framework of modern society is sought, and within that framework the psychologies of a variety of men and women are formulated. By such means the personal uneasiness of individuals is focused upon explicit troubles and the indifference of publics is transformed into involvement with public issues.

The first fruit of this imagination—and the first lesson of the social science that embodies it—is the idea that the individual can understand his own experience and gauge his own fate only by locating himself within his period, that he can know his own chances in life by becoming aware of those of all individuals in his circumstances. In many ways it is a terrible lesson; in many ways a magnificent one. We do not know the limits of man's capacities for supreme effort or willing degradation, for agony or glee, for pleasurable brutality or the sweetness of reason. But in our time we have come to know that the limits of "human nature" are frighteningly broad. We have come to know that every individual lives, from one generation to the next, in some society; that he lives out a biography, and that he lives it out within some historical sequence. By the fact of his living he contributes, however minutely, to the shaping of this society and to the course of its history, even as he is made by society and by its historical push and shove.

The sociological imagination enables us to grasp history and biography and the relations between the two within society. That is its task and its promise. To recognize this task and this promise is the mark of the classic social analyst. It is characteristic of Herbert Spencer—turgid, polysyllabic, comprehensive; of E. A. Ross—graceful, muckraking, upright; of Auguste Comte and Emile Durkheim; of the intricate and subtle Karl Mannheim. It is the quality of all that is intellectually excellent in Karl Marx; it is the clue to Thorstein Veblen's brilliant and ironic insight, to Joseph Schumpeter's many-sided constructions of reality; it is the basis of the psychological sweep of W. E. H. Lecky no less than of the profundity and clarity of Max Weber. And it is the signal of what is best in contemporary studies of man and society.

No social study that does not come back to the problems of biography, of history, and of their intersections within a society has completed its intellectual journey. Whatever the specific problems of the classic social analysts, however limited or however broad the features of social reality they have examined, those who have been imaginatively aware of the promise of their work have consistently asked three sorts of questions:

1. What is the structure of this particular society as a whole? What are its essential components, and how are they related to one another? How does it differ from other varieties of social order? Within it, what is the meaning of any particular feature for its continuance and for its change?

2. Where does this society stand in human history? What are the mechanics by which it is changing? What is its place within and its meaning for the development of humanity as a whole? How does any particular feature we are examining affect, and how is it affected by, the historical period in which it moves? And this period—what are its essential features? How does it differ from other periods? What are its characteristic ways of history-making?

3. What varieties of men and women now prevail in this society and in this period? And what varieties are coming to prevail? In what ways are they selected and formed, liberated and repressed, made sensitive and blunted? What kinds of "human nature" are revealed in the conduct and character we observe in this society in this period? And what is the meaning for "human nature" of each and every feature of the society we are examining?

Whether the point of interest is a great power state or a minor literary mood, a family, a prison, a creed—these are the kinds of questions the best social analysts have asked. They are the intellectual pivots of classic studies of man in society—and they are the questions inevitably raised by any mind possessing the sociological imagination. For that imagination is the capacity to shift from one perspective to another—from the political to the psychological; from examination of a single family to comparative assessment of the national budgets of the world; from the theological school to the military establishment; from considerations of an oil industry to studies of contemporary poetry. It is the capacity to range from the most impersonal and remote transformations to the most intimate features of the human self—and to see the relations between the two. Back of its use there is always the urge to know the social and historical meaning of the individual in the society and in the period in which he has his quality and his being.

That, in brief, is why it is by means of the sociological imagination that men now hope to grasp what is going on in the world, and to understand what is happening in themselves as minute points of the intersections of biography and history within society. In large part, contemporary man's self-conscious view of himself as at least an outsider, if not a permanent stranger, rests upon an absorbed realization of social relativity and of the transformative power of history. The sociological imagination is the most fruitful form of this self-consciousness. By its use men whose mentalities have swept only a series of limited orbits often come to feel as if suddenly awakened in a house with which they had only supposed themselves to be familiar. Correctly or incorrectly, they often come to feel that they can now provide themselves with adequate summations, cohesive assessments, comprehensive orientations. Older decisions that once appeared sound now seem to them products of a mind unaccountably dense. Their capacity for astonishment is made lively again. They acquire a new way of thinking, they experience a transvaluation of values: In a word, by their reflection and by their sensibility, they realize the cultural meaning of the social sciences.

Perhaps the most fruitful distinction with which the sociological imagination works is between "the personal troubles of milieu" and "the public issues of social structure." This distinction is an essential tool of the sociological imagination and a feature of all classic work in social science.

Troubles occur within the character of the individual and within the range of his immediate relations with others; they have to do with his self and with those limited areas of social life of which he is directly and personally aware. Accordingly, the statement and the resolution of troubles properly lie within the individual as a biographical entity and within the scope of his immediate milieu—the social setting that is directly open to his personal experience and to some extent his willful activity. A trouble is a private matter: Values cherished by an individual are felt by him to be threatened.

Issues have to do with matters that transcend these local environments of the individual and the range of his inner life. They have to do with the organization of many such milieux into the institutions of an historical society as a whole, with the ways in which various milieux overlap and interpenetrate to form the larger structure of social and historical life. An issue is a public matter: Some value cherished by publics is felt to be threatened. Often there is a debate about what that value really is and about what it is that really threatens it. This debate is often without focus if only because it is the very nature of an issue, unlike even widespread trouble, that it cannot very well be defined in terms of the immediate and everyday environments of ordinary men. An issue, in fact, often involves a crisis in institutional arrangements, and often too it involves what Marxists call "contradictions" or "antagonisms."

In these terms, consider unemployment. When, in a city of 100,000, only one man is unemployed, that is his personal trouble, and for its relief we properly look to the character of the man, his skills, and his immediate opportunities. But when in a nation of 50 million employees, 15 million men are unemployed, that is an issue, and we may not hope to find its solution within the range of opportunities open to any one individual. The very structure of opportunities has collapsed. Both the correct statement of the problem and the range of possible solutions require us to consider the economic and political institutions of the society, and not merely the personal situation and character of a scatter of individuals.

Consider war. The personal problem of war, when it occurs, may be how to survive it or how to die in it with honor; how to make money out of it; how to climb into the higher safety of the military apparatus; or how to contribute to the war's termination. In short, according to one's values, to find a set of milieux and within it to survive the war or make one's death in it meaningful. But the structural issues of war have to do with its causes; with what types of men it throws up into command; with its effects upon economic and political, family and religious institutions; with the unorganized irresponsibility of a world of nation-states.

Consider marriage. Inside a marriage a man and a woman may experience personal troubles, but when the divorce rate during the first four years of marriage is 250 out of every 1,000 attempts, this is an indication of a structural issue having to do with the institutions of marriage and the family and other institutions that bear upon them.

Or consider the metropolis—the horrible, beautiful, ugly, magnificent sprawl of the great city. For many upper-class people, the personal solution to "the problem of the city" is to have an apartment with private garage under it in the heart of the city and, forty miles out, a house by Henry Hill, garden by Garrett Eckbo, on a hundred acres of private land. In these two controlled environments—with a small staff at each end and a private helicopter connection—most people could solve many of the problems of personal milieux caused by the facts of the city. But all this, however splendid, does not solve the public issues that the structural fact of the city poses. What should be done with this wonderful monstrosity? Break it up into scattered units, combining residence and work? Refurbish it as it stands? Or, after evacuation, dynamite it and build new cities according to new plans in new places? What should those plans be? And who is to decide and to accomplish whatever choice is made? These are structural issues; to confront them and to solve them requires us to consider political and economic issues that affect innumerable milieux.

Insofar as an economy is so arranged that slumps occur, the problem of unemployment becomes incapable of personal solution. Insofar as war is inherent in the nation-state system and in the uneven industrialization of the world, the ordinary individual in his restricted milieu will be powerless—with or without psychiatric aid—to solve the troubles this system or lack of system imposes upon him. Insofar as the family as an institution turns women into darling little slaves and men into their chief providers and unweaned dependents, the problem of a satisfactory marriage remains incapable of purely private solution. Insofar as the overdeveloped megalopolis and the overdeveloped automobile are built-in features of the overdeveloped society, the issues of urban living will not be solved by personal ingenuity and private wealth.

What we experience in various and specific milieux, I have noted, is often caused by structural changes. Accordingly, to understand the changes of many personal milieux we are required to look beyond them. And the number and variety of such structural changes increase as the institutions within which we live become more embracing and more intricately connected with one another. To be aware of the idea of social structure and to use it with sensibility is to be capable of tracing such linkages among a great variety of milieux. To be able to do that is to possess the sociological imagination.

CRITICAL-THINKING QUESTIONS

1. Why do people in the United States tend to think of the operation of society in personal terms?

2. What are the practical benefits of the sociological perspective? Are there liabilities?

3. What does Mills have in mind in suggesting that by developing the sociological imagination we learn to assemble *facts* into *social analysis?*

CLASSIC

CONTEMPORARY

CROSS-CULTURAL

2 Invitation to Sociology

PETER L. BERGER

Using the sociological perspective changes how we perceive the surrounding world and even ourselves. Peter Berger compares thinking sociologically to entering a new and unfamiliar society—one in which "things are no longer what they seem." This article should lead you to rethink your social world so that you become aware of issues that you may never before have considered.

It can be said that the first wisdom of sociology is this—things are not what they seem. This too is a deceptively simple statement. It ceases to be simple after a while. Social reality turns out to have many layers of meaning. The discovery of each new layer changes the perception of the whole.

Anthropologists use the term "culture shock" to describe the impact of a totally new culture upon a newcomer. In an extreme instance such shock will be experienced by the Western explorer who is told, halfway through dinner, that he is eating the nice old lady he had been chatting with the previous day—a shock with predictable physiological if not moral consequences. Most explorers no longer encounter cannibalism in their travels today. However, the first encounters with polygamy or with puberty rites or even with the way some nations drive their automobiles can be quite a shock to an American visitor. With the

Source: From *Invitation to Sociology* by Peter L. Berger. Copyright © 1963 by Peter L. Berger, Doubleday Dell Group, Inc. Reprinted with permission.

shock may go not only disapproval or disgust but a sense of excitement that things can *really* be that different from what they are at home. To some extent, at least, this is the excitement of any first travel abroad. The experience of sociological discovery could be described as "culture shock" minus geographical displacement. In other words, the sociologist travels at home—with shocking results. He is unlikely to find that he is eating a nice old lady for dinner. But the discovery, for instance, that his own church has considerable money invested in the missile industry or that a few blocks from his home there are people who engage in cultic orgies may not be drastically different in emotional impact. Yet we would not want to imply that sociological discoveries are always or even usually outrageous to moral sentiment. Not at all. What they have in common with exploration in distant lands, however, is the sudden illumination of new and unsuspected facets of human existence in society. This is the excitement and, as we shall try to show later, the humanistic justification of sociology.

People who like to avoid shocking discoveries, who prefer to believe that society is just what they were taught in Sunday school, who like the safety of the rules and the maxims of what Alfred Schuetz has called the "world-taken-for-granted," should stay away from sociology. People who feel no temptation before closed doors, who have no curiosity about human beings, who are content to admire scenery without wondering about the people who live in those houses on the other side of that river, should probably also stay away from sociology. They will find it unpleasant or, at any rate, unrewarding. People who are interested in human beings only if they can change, convert, or reform them should also be warned, for they will find sociology much less useful than they hoped. And people whose interest is mainly in their own conceptual constructions will do just as well to turn to the study of little white mice. Sociology will be satisfying, in the long run, only to those who can think of nothing more entrancing than to watch men and to understand things human. . . .

To ask sociological questions, then, presupposes that one is interested in looking some distance beyond the commonly accepted or officially defined goals of human actions. It presupposes a certain awareness that human events have different levels of meaning, some of which are hidden from the consciousness of everyday life. It may even presuppose a measure of suspicion about the way in which human events are officially interpreted by the authorities, be they political, juridical, or religious in character. If one is willing to go as far as that, it would seem evident that not all historical circumstances are equally favorable for the development of sociological perspective.

It would appear plausible, in consequence, that sociological thought would have the best chance to develop in historical circumstances marked by severe jolts to the self-conception, especially the official and authoritative and generally accepted self-conception of a culture. It is only in such circumstances that perceptive men are likely to be motivated to think beyond the assertions of this self-conception and, as a result, question the authorities. . . .

Sociological perspective can then be understood in terms of such phrases as "seeing through," "looking behind," very much as such phrases would be employed in common speech—"seeing through his game," "looking behind the scenes"—in other words, "being up on all the tricks."

. . . We could think of this in terms of a common experience of people living in large cities. One of the fascinations of a large city is the immense variety of human activities taking place behind the seemingly anonymous and endlessly undifferentiated rows of houses. A person who lives in such a city will time and again experience surprise or even shock as he discovers the strange pursuits that some men engage in quite unobtrusively in houses that, from the outside, look like all the others on a certain street. Having had this experience once or twice, one will repeatedly find oneself walking down a street, perhaps late in the evening, and wondering what may be going on under the bright lights showing through a line of drawn curtains. An ordinary family engaged in pleasant talk with guests? A scene of desperation amid illness or death? Or a scene of debauched pleasures? Perhaps a strange cult or a dangerous conspiracy? The facades of the houses cannot tell us, proclaiming nothing but an architectural conformity to the tastes of some group or class that may not even inhabit the street any longer. The social mysteries lie behind the facades. The wish to penetrate these mysteries is an analogon to sociological curiosity. In some cities that are suddenly struck by calamity this wish may be abruptly realized. Those who have experienced wartime bombings know of the sudden encounters with unsuspected (and sometimes unimaginable) fellow tenants in the air-raid shelter of one's apartment building. Or they can recollect the startling morning sight of a house hit by a bomb during the night, neatly sliced in half, the facade torn away and the previously hidden interior mercilessly revealed in the daylight. But in most cities that one may normally live in, the facades must be penetrated by one's own inquisitive intrusions. Similarly, there are historical situations in which the facades of society are violently torn apart and all but the most incurious are forced to see that there was a reality behind the facades all along. Usually this does not happen, and the facades continue to confront us with seemingly rocklike permanence. The perception of the reality behind the facades then demands a considerable intellectual effort.

A few examples of the way in which sociology "looks behind" the facades of social structures might serve to make our argument clearer. Take, for instance, the political organization of a community. If one wants to find out how a modern American city is governed, it is very easy to get the official information about this subject. The city will have a charter, operating under the laws of the state. With some advice from informed individuals, one may look up various statutes that define the constitution of the city. Thus one may find out that this particular community has a city-manager form of administration, or that party affiliations do not appear on the ballot in municipal elections, or that the city government participates in a regional water district. In similar fashion, with the help of some newspaper reading, one may find out the officially recognized political problems of the community. One may read that the city plans to annex a certain suburban area, or that there has been a change in the zoning ordinances to facilitate industrial development in another area, or even that one of the members of the city council has been accused of using his office for personal gain. All such matters still occur on the, as it were, visible, official, or public level of political life. However, it would be an exceedingly naive person who would believe that this kind of information gives him a rounded picture of the political reality of that community. The sociologist will want to know above all the constituency of the "informal power structure" (as it has been called by Floyd Hunter, an American sociologist interested in such studies), which is a configuration of men and their

power that cannot be found in any statutes, and probably cannot be read about in the newspapers. The political scientist or the legal expert might find it very interesting to compare the city charter with the constitutions of other similar communities. The sociologist will be far more concerned with discovering the way in which powerful vested interests influence or even control the actions of officials elected under the charter. These vested interests will not be found in city hall, but rather in the executive suites of corporations that may not even be located in that community, in the private mansions of a handful of powerful men, perhaps in the offices of certain labor unions, or even, in some instances, in the headquarters of criminal organizations. When the sociologist concerns himself with power, he will "look behind" the official mechanisms that are supposed to regulate power in the community. This does not necessarily mean that he will regard the official mechanisms as totally ineffective or their legal definition as totally illusionary. But at the very least he will insist that there is another level of reality to be investigated in the particular system of power. In some cases he might conclude that to look for real power in the publicly recognized places is quite delusional. . . .

Let us take one further example. In Western countries, and especially in America, it is assumed that men and women marry because they are in love. There is a broadly based popular mythology about the character of love as a violent, irresistible emotion that strikes where it will, a mystery that is the goal of most young people and often of the not-so-young as well. As soon as one investigates, however, which people actually marry each other, one finds that the lightning-shaft of Cupid seems to be guided rather strongly within very definite channels of class, income, education, [and] racial and religious background. If one then investigates a little further into the behavior that is engaged in prior to marriage under the rather misleading euphemism of "courtship," one finds channels of interaction that are often rigid to the point of ritual.

The suspicion begins to dawn on one that, most of the time, it is not so much the emotion of love that creates a certain kind of relationship, but that carefully predefined and often planned relationships eventually generate the desired emotion. In other words, when certain conditions are met or have been constructed, one allows oneself "to fall in love." The sociologist investigating our patterns of "courtship" and marriage soon discovers a complex web of motives related in many ways to the entire institutional structure within which an individual lives his life—class, career, economic ambition, aspirations of power and prestige. The miracle of love now begins to look somewhat synthetic. Again, this need not mean in any given instance that the sociologist will declare the romantic interpretation to be an illusion. But, once more, he will look beyond the immediately given and publicly approved interpretations. . . .

We would contend, then, that there is a debunking motif inherent in sociological consciousness. The sociologist will be driven time and again, by the very logic of his discipline, to debunk the social systems he is studying. This unmasking tendency need not necessarily be due to the sociologist's temperament or inclinations. Indeed, it may happen that the sociologist, who as an individual may be of a conciliatory disposition and quite disinclined to disturb the comfortable assumptions on which he rests his own social existence, is nevertheless compelled by what he is doing to fly in the face of what those around him take for granted. In other words, we would contend that the roots of the debunking motif in sociology are not psychological but methodological. The sociological frame of reference, with its built-in procedure of looking for levels of reality other than those given in the official interpretations of society, carries with it a logical imperative to unmask the pretensions and the propaganda by which men cloak their actions with each other. This unmasking imperative is one of the characteristics of sociology particularly at home in the temper of the modern era.

CRITICAL-THINKING QUESTIONS

1. How can we explain the fact that people within any society tend to take their own way of life for granted?
2. What does Berger think is the justification for studying sociology?
3. What is involved in sociological "debunking"? How are others likely to respond to sociological insights?

CLASSIC

CONTEMPORARY

CROSS-CULTURAL

3 Teenage Wasteland

DONNA GAINES

The power of the sociological imagination lies in showing that even the most personal decision people might make have social causes. In this article, Donna Gaines explains how the 1987 suicide of four teenagers in Bergenfield, New Jersey, is the result of a society that provides many working-class young men and women with little meaning and little opportunity.

In Bergenfield, New Jersey, on the morning of March 11, 1987, the bodies of four teenagers were discovered inside a 1977 rust-colored Chevrolet Camaro. The car, which belonged to Thomas Olton, was parked in an unused garage in the Foster Village garden apartment complex, behind the Foster Village Shopping Center. Two sisters, Lisa and Cheryl Burress, and their friends, Thomas Rizzo and Thomas Olton, had died of carbon monoxide poisoning.

Lisa was sixteen, Cheryl was seventeen, and the boys were nineteen—they were suburban teens, turnpike kids like the ones in the town I live in. And thinking about them made me remember how it felt being a teenager too. I was horrified that it had come to this. I believed I understood why they did it, although it wasn't a feeling I could have put into words.

You could tell from the newspapers that they were rock and roll kids. The police had found a

cassette tape cover of AC/DC's *If You Want Blood, You've Got It* near the bodies. Their friends were described as kids who listened to thrash metal, had shaggy haircuts, wore lots of black and leather. "Dropouts," "druggies," the papers called them. Teenage suburban rockers whose lives revolved around their favorite bands and their friends. Youths who barely got by in school and at home and who did not impress authority figures in any remarkable way. Except as fuck-ups.

My friends, most of whom were born in the 1950s, felt the same way about the kids everyone called "burnouts." On the weekend following the suicides, a friend's band, the Grinders, were playing at My Father's Place, a Long Island club. That night the guys dedicated a song, "The Kids in the Basement," to the four teens from Bergenfield—"This is for the suicide kids." In the weeks following the suicide pact, a number of bands in the tri-state area also dedicated songs to them. Their deaths had hit close to home. . . .

By the beginning of the 1980s, . . . I went back to school. I spent the next few years working on a

From *Teenage Wasteland* by Donna Gaines. Random House, 1990. Used with permission.

doctorate in sociology, commuting a few days a week from my neighborhood to the State University of New York at Stony Brook, teaching, doing consulting work, and freelancing as a journalist. In my free time I stayed involved with the Grinders, but was now also interested in the West Coast–based hardcore bands like Black Flag, MDC, and Flipper. By 1987, the young people in my life were either my students, my neighbors, or people I met at shows.

A week or two after the suicide pact, *The Village Voice* assigned me to go to Bergenfield. . . . [My editor] knew my background—that I knew suburbia, that I could talk to kids. By now I fully embraced the sociologist's ethical commitment to the "rights of the researched," and the social worker's vow of client confidentiality. As far as suicidal teenagers were concerned, I felt that if I couldn't help them, I didn't want to bother them.

But I was really pissed off at what I kept reading. How people in Bergenfield openly referred to the four kids as "troubled losers." Even after they were dead, nobody cut them any slack. "Burnouts," "druggies," "dropouts." Something was wrong. So I took the opportunity.

From the beginning, I believed that the Bergenfield suicides symbolized a tragic defeat for young people. Something was happening in the larger society that was not yet comprehended. Scholars spoke ominously of "the postmodern condition," "societal upheaval," "decay," "anomie." Meanwhile, American kids kept losing ground, showing all the symptoms of societal neglect. Many were left to fend for themselves, often with little success. The news got worse. Teenage suicides continued, and still nobody seemed to be getting the point.

Now, in trying to understand this event, I might have continued working within the established discourse on teenage suicide. I might have carried on the tradition of obscuring the bigger picture, psychologizing the Bergenfield suicide pact, interviewing the parents of the four youths, hounding their friends for the gory details. I might have spent my time probing school records, tracking down their teachers and shrinks for insights, focusing on their personal histories and intimate relationships. I might have searched out the individual motivations behind the words left in the note written and signed by each youth on the brown paper bag found with their bodies on March 11. But I did not.

Because the world has changed for today's kids. We also engaged in activities that adults called self-destructive. But for my generation, "doing it" meant having sex; for them, it means committing suicide.

"Teenage suicide" was a virtually nonexistent category prior to 1960. But between 1950 and 1980 it nearly tripled, and at the time of the Bergenfield suicide pact it was the second leading cause of death among America's young people; "accidents" were the first. The actual suicide rate among people aged fifteen to twenty-four—the statistical category for teenage suicide—is estimated to be even higher, underreported because of social stigma. Then there are the murky numbers derived from drug overdoses and car crashes, recorded as accidents. To date, there are more than 5,000 teen suicides annually, accounting for 12 percent of youth mortalities. An estimated 400,000 adolescents attempt suicide each year. While youth suicide rates leveled off by 1980, by mid-decade they began to increase again. Although they remained lower than adult suicide rates, the acceleration at which youth suicide rates increased was alarming. By 1987, we had books and articles detailing "copycat" and "cluster" suicides. Teenage suicide was now described as an epidemic.

Authors, experts, and scholars compiled the lists of kids' names, ages, dates, and possible motives. They generated predictive models: Rural and suburban white kids do it more often. Black kids in America's urban teenage wastelands are more likely to kill each other. Increasingly, alcohol and drugs are involved. In some cases adults have tried to identify the instigating factor as a lyric or a song—Judas Priest, Ozzy Osbourne. Or else a popular film about the subject—the suicide of a celebrity; too much media attention or not enough.

Some kids do it violently: drowning, hanging, slashing, jumping, or crashing. Firearms are still the most popular. Others prefer to go out more peacefully, by gas or drug overdose. Boys do it more than girls, though girls try it more often than boys. And it does not seem to matter if kids are rich or poor.

Throughout the 1980s, teenage suicide clusters appeared across the country—six or seven deaths, sometimes more, in a short period of time in a single community. In the boomtown of Plano, Texas. The fading factory town of Leominster, Massachusetts. At Bryan High School in a white, working-class suburb of Omaha, Nebraska. A series of domino suicides among Arapaho Indian youths at the Wind River Reservation in Wyoming. Six youth suicides in the county of Westchester, New York, in 1984; five in 1985 and seven in 1986.

Sometimes they were close friends who died together in pacts of two. In other cases, one followed shortly after the other, unable to survive apart. Then there were strangers who died alone, in separate incidents timed closely together.

The Bergenfield suicide pact of March 11 was alternately termed a "multiple-death pact," a "quadruple suicide," or simply a "pact," depending on where you read about it. Some people actually called it a *mass* suicide because the Bergenfield case reminded them of Jonestown, Guyana, in 1978, where over nine hundred followers of Jim Jones poisoned themselves, fearing their community would be destroyed.

As experts speculated over the deaths in Bergenfield, none could recall a teenage suicide pact involving four people dying together; *it was historically unique.*

I wondered, did the "burnouts" see themselves as a community under siege? . . . Were the "burnouts" of Bergenfield choosing death over surrender? Surrender to what? Were they martyrs? If so, what was their common cause?

Because the suicide pact was a *collective act,* it warrants a social explanation—a portrait of the "burnouts" in Bergenfield as actors within a particular social landscape.

For a long time now, the discourse of teenage suicide has been dominated by atomizing psychological and medical models. And so the larger picture of American youth as members of a distinctive generation with a unique collective biography, emerging at a particular moment in history, has been lost.

The starting-off point for this [analysis] then, is a teenage suicide pact in an "upper-poor" white ethnic suburb in northern New Jersey. But, of course, the story did not begin and will not end in Bergenfield. . . .

This was a suicide pact that involved close friends who were by no accounts obsessed, star-crossed lovers. What would make four people want to die together? Why would they ask, in their collective suicide note, to be waked and buried together? Were they part of a suicide cult?

If not, what was the nature of the *social* bond that tied them so closely? What could be so intimately binding that in the early morning hours of March 11 not one of them could stop, step back from the pact they had made to say, "Wait, I can't do this"? Who were these kids that everybody called "burnouts"? . . .

From the beginning, I decided I didn't want to dwell too much on the negatives. I wanted to understand how alienated kids survived, as well as how they were defeated. How did they maintain their humanity against what I now felt were impossible odds? I wondered. What keeps young people together when the world they are told to trust no longer seems to work? What motivates them to be decent human beings when nobody seems to respect them or take them seriously? . . .

Somewhat like a nervous breakdown, burnout involves a change in your ability to function, to "perform." You numb out, hoping to lower anxiety by shutting down, denying access to your feelings. The body, the organism, is overwhelmed. Burnout is a way of slipping out the back door with your body still present. You can still go through the motions of living, but you feel dead.

The burned-out individual protects the self for the moment, but in the long run the self is estranged. The ability to relate in any way at all is compromised. You are living at half speed in a world you cannot handle—shut down, tuned out; you're gone.

This estrangement from feeling, this disowning and disengaging from feeling, is a form of *alienation.* According to Marx, in the process of laboring, human beings enjoy the creative activity of transforming the world. If the product of this pleasure is taken from you, alienated (as in the process of capitalist production), you experience deep loss. You become detached from your world because your connection to that world, your power to create and transform in that world *through your own efforts,* has been taken from you. So you are living in the world in a state of detachedness; you no longer feel viable.

Powerless, useless, ineffectual, you are only remotely connected to life around you. The most you can hope for is to get through the day—at home, at work, in school. Drugs and alcohol will help to kill the pain, protect you from things that would, if fully perceived, drive you crazy. But then you have to deal with the secondary effects of your anodyne solution. Either way, you know you're not well.

It is not surprising that the Alcoholics Anonymous doctrine advises never to let yourself get too hungry, too tired, or too lonely. Being emotionally strung out often leads to desperate self-medicating. The active alcoholic, overworked professional, and emotionally overwhelmed kid all appear to be wasted. Often, they are. Whether stressful life experiences or excessive drug taking has wasted you is unimportant—a burned-out soul feels empty, the spirit seems depleted.

For a bored, ignored, lonely kid, drug oblivion may offer immediate comfort; purpose and adventure in the place of everyday ennui. But soon it has a life of its own—at a psychic and a social level, the focus of your life becomes *getting high* (or *well* as some people describe it). Ironically, the whole miserable process often begins as a positive act of self-preservation. . . .

So they end up stranded in teenage wasteland. They devote their lives to their bands, to their friends, to partying; they live in the moment. They're going down in flames, taking literally the notion that "rust never sleeps," that it is "better to burn out than fade away."

Such wasted suburban kids are typically not politically "correct," nor do they constitute an identifiable segment of the industrial working class. They are not members of a specific racial or ethnic minority.

Small in numbers, isolated in decaying suburbs, they aren't visible on any national scale until they are involved in something that really horrifies us, like a suicide pact, or parricide, or incest, or "satanic" sacrifice. For the most part, burnouts and dirtbags are anomic small town white boys and girls, just trying to get through the day. Their way of fighting back is to have enough fun to kill themselves before everything else does.

CRITICAL-THINKING QUESTIONS

1. What is it about the society in which the four young people lived that contributed to their suicide?

2. Do you think teen suicide is an issue all across the United States? Explain your view.

3. What might be done to prevent deaths like this?

CLASSIC

CONTEMPORARY

CROSS-CULTURAL

4 Women and the Birth of Sociology

PATRICIA MADOO LENGERMANN
AND JILL NIEBRUGGE-BRANTLEY

Most beginning students of sociology know about Karl Marx, Max Weber, and Emile Durkheim; but Harriet Martineau, Ida Wells-Barnett, Anna Julia Cooper, Charlotte Perkins Gilman, and other women were also important founders of the discipline.

The history of sociology's theories is conventionally told as a history of white male agency—an account of the theoretical contributions of a "founding" generation of men, Auguste Comte, Herbert Spencer, and Karl Marx, writing in the middle of the nineteenth century, expanded by a second, "classic" generation of men, Emile Durkheim, Max Weber, Georg Simmel, George Herbert Mead, and Robert E. Park, who wrote between 1890 and 1930. This history is presented as an account of the natural way things occurred, a chronicle beyond the powers of human tellers to change. In contrast, we portray this history as a social construction arising out of the discipline's power arrangements, and like all histories, reflecting an ongoing conflict between exclusionary and inclusionary values and practices (Becker, 1971; Lemert, 1995; D. Smith, 1987). . . .

The claim that a group has been "written out" of history is different from the claim that a group has been "invisible." "Invisibility" suggests not

From *The Women Founders: Sociology and Theory, 1830–1930,* by Patricia Madoo Lengermann and Jill Niebrugge-Brantley. Copyright © 1998 by McGraw-Hill, Inc.

being seen, that is, never having one's presence acknowledged as significant—a concept applied by many African Americans to their experience of marginalization (e.g., Collins, 1990; Cooper, 1892; Du Bois, 1903; Ellison, 1952; Lorde, 1984; Rollins, 1985). "Being written out" suggests having once been seen as a presence in a community and then having been erased from its record. For several reasons, the case of the fifteen women sociologists treated in this volume is an instance of erasure rather than invisibility. First, almost all these women were well-known public figures in their lifetime, larger than the fledgling discipline of sociology they helped create; like the work of Marx, Max Weber, or Durkheim, their work has relevance for all the social sciences. Second, they created social theory and did sociology in the same times and places as the male founders (see Figure 1). Third, they were widely recognized by their contemporaries, including male sociologists, as significant social analysts. Fourth, they all acted as members of a sociological community, meeting at least one of the following criteria: employment as a sociologist, membership in a national sociological association, publication

FIGURE 1 Lifelines of Women and Men Founders of Sociology

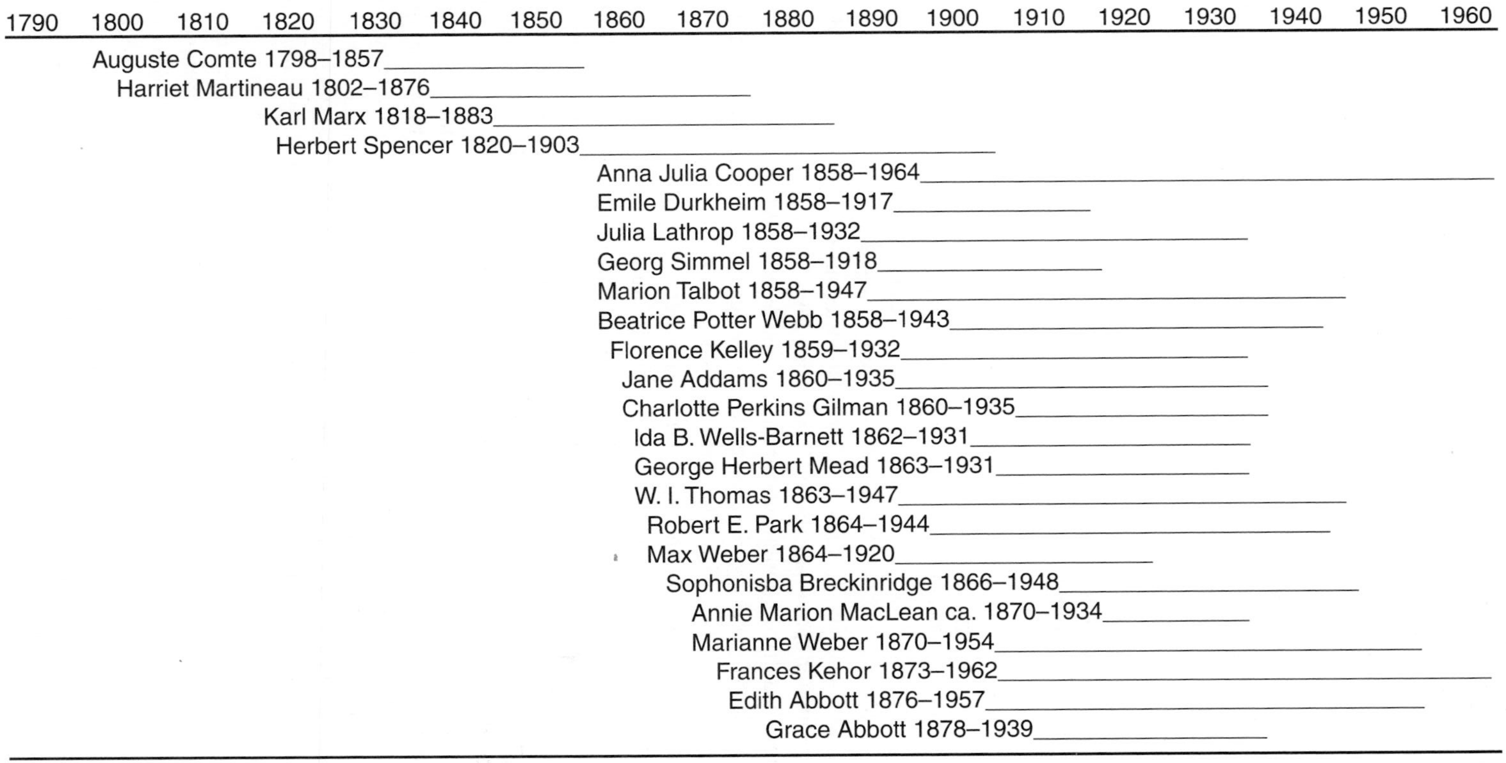

1790	1800	1810	1820	1830	1840	1850	1860	1870	1880	1890	1900	1910	1920	1930	1940	1950	1960

Auguste Comte 1798–1857
Harriet Martineau 1802–1876
Karl Marx 1818–1883
Herbert Spencer 1820–1903
Anna Julia Cooper 1858–1964
Emile Durkheim 1858–1917
Julia Lathrop 1858–1932
Georg Simmel 1858–1918
Marion Talbot 1858–1947
Beatrice Potter Webb 1858–1943
Florence Kelley 1859–1932
Jane Addams 1860–1935
Charlotte Perkins Gilman 1860–1935
Ida B. Wells-Barnett 1862–1931
George Herbert Mead 1863–1931
W. I. Thomas 1863–1947
Robert E. Park 1864–1944
Max Weber 1864–1920
Sophonisba Breckinridge 1866–1948
Annie Marion MacLean ca. 1870–1934
Marianne Weber 1870–1954
Frances Kehor 1873–1962
Edith Abbott 1876–1957
Grace Abbott 1878–1939

15

framed by an explicit concern with sociological principles, self-identification as a sociologist and recognition by contemporaries as a sociologist (Käsler, 1981; Deegan, 1991). We introduce some of the evidence for these claims in the brief descriptions of the women that follow. . . .

Martineau—whose *Illustrations of Political Economy* (1832–1834) outsold even Charles Dickens (Hoecker-Drysdale 1992)—was Britain's preeminent woman of letters until her death, writing social analysis, journalism, history, novels, children's stories, and travel books. Long identified in the history of sociology for her 1853 translation and abridgement of Comte, she was herself writing sociology as early as 1834, drafting what would become the first major statement of method, *How to Observe Morals and Manners* (1838b) and testing her methodology in her classic study *Society in America* (1836). Addams was the founder of Hull-House, the famous Chicago social settlement; a major spokesperson for Progressive reform on behalf of immigrants, trade unions, women, children, working-class people, and African Americans; and consistently named in public opinion polls as one of the most admired Americans (Davis, 1973; Daniel Levine, 1971). At Hull-House, she administered a major research institution, drawing on her experiences there to formulate a social theory in eight major books and some 200 articles. She self-identified as a sociologist; taught sociology; was a member of the American Sociological Society (ASS)—until 1959 the name of the American Sociological Association (ASA); published in the *American Journal of Sociology (AJS)*; and had significant relationships with Mead, Park, W. I. Thomas, Albion Small, and Ernest Burgess (Deegan, 1988). Gilman was widely regarded as the leading feminist intellectual of her day. *Her Women and Economics* (1898) went through nine printings by 1920, was translated into seven languages, and was the bible of many women's college student bodies (Ceplair, 1991). Besides the classic feminist novella *The Yellow Wallpaper* (1892) and some 2,000 pieces of journalism, poetry, and

prose, she wrote six significant works of formal social theory, including *Women and Economics, Human Work* (1904), and *The Man-Made World* (1911). She also published in the *AJS,* was a member of the ASS, and maintained intellectual relationships with Lester Ward and E. A. Ross.

Wells-Barnett spearheaded national and international anti-lynching campaigns, writing major analyses of lynching—*Southern Horrors* (1892) and *A Red Record* (1895)—and carrying the battle to Britain, where she often spoke to crowds in the thousands. She was an active organizer for African American civil rights, helping to found the National Association for the Advancement of Colored People (NAACP). Cooper's major book *A Voice from the South* (1892) received superlative reviews from black and white publications alike, establishing her as a prominent intellectual and spokesperson for African American women; she was one of two women to address the world's first Pan-African Conference in London in 1900. Cooper and Wells-Barnett created a genuine American non-Marxian conflict theory in which they spoke of the sociological framing of their argument; but American racism made tentative any relationship between them and white professional sociology, although both knew and worked with black sociologist W. E. B. Du Bois. Marianne Weber lived at the center of German sociological circles and debated the ideas of both Simmel and her husband Max in her own writings. She was a leading figure in the German feminist movement, the first woman to be elected to a German parliament, and the author of nine books of social analysis and sociology including her monumental work on the legal position of women, *Ehefrau und Mutter in der Rechtsentwicklung (Marriage, Motherhood, and the Law)* (1907), and her collected essays, *Frauenfragen und Frauengedanken (Reflections on Women and Women's Issues)* (1919). She secured Max's position within sociology after his death by editing and publishing ten volumes of his work and writing her important interpretive biography of him.

Webb was tutored by Spencer, self-identified as a sociologist, taught sociology, worked as a social investigator on the major empirical study of her age (Charles Booth's *Life and Labour of the People of London*), and did her own independent investigations, leading to the socialist reform classic *The Co-operative Movement in Great Britain* (1891). With her husband Sidney, she researched and co-authored eleven voluminous works of empirical sociology that formed the blueprint for the British welfare state. All the members of the Chicago Women's School of Sociology (hereafter referred to as the Chicago Women's School or the Chicago Women) wrote prolifically as social analysis, all publishing in the *AJS*. Many were prominent public figures: Kelley headed the National Consumers' League (1899–1932); Lathrop (1912–20), and then Grace Abbott (1920–34), served as chief of the Children's Bureau, the highest-ranking woman in the federal government at that time; Edith Abbott and Breckinridge founded the University of Chicago's School of Social Service Administration (1922); Talbot was dean of women at the University of Chicago (1893–1925); Kellor was a founder and executive officer of the American Arbitration League (1926–53). Kelley knew Friedrich Engels, maintained a correspondence with him until his death, and did the first English translation of *The Condition of the Working Class in England in 1844:* MacLean studied with Small, Mead, and Charles Henderson; Kellor also studied with Henderson; Edith Abbott, Grace Abbott, and Breckinridge are all referenced in Park and Burgess's *Introduction to the Science of Sociology;* Talbot served as an associate editor of the *AJS* from its founding by Small to her retirement in 1925.

These women knew each other or each other's work. Gilman, Webb, Weber, and Wells-Barnett all visited Hull-House, which was, of course, the working base for Addams and most of the Chicago Women. Many of them read Gilman's *Women and Economics*—Webb, Weber, Addams, Kelley, Lathrop, and Talbot. Addams published with Wells-Barnett on lynching on at least two occasions, one of which was in a remarkable issue of *Survey* in February of 1913 in which Addams, Wells-Barnett, Breckinridge, and Du Bois all analyze the problem of race.[1] Addams, Wells-Barnett, Kelley, and Breckinridge participated in the founding of the NAACP. Hull-House residents, including Addams, Lathrop, and Kelley, used Webb's *The Co-operative Movement in Great Britain* in preparation for their own venture into cooperative housing for working women. The persons most outside this network are Martineau, a full generation earlier than the rest of the women, and Cooper, whose life course rarely took her to Chicago. Yet Edith Abbott knew and responded to Martineau's work on women's employment in America, and Gilman refers to Martineau's struggle to overcome gender barriers to her career as a social analyst. And Cooper spoke in Chicago in 1893 at the white feminist Women's Congress, was active, as was Wells-Barnett, in the National Federation of Colored Women's Clubs and the African American settlement house movement, and wrote a sympathetic response to Gilman's suicide.

These women knew that they were part of a larger movement to create a science of society and had their own sense of what that science should be: a project of social critique in which research and theory had as a morally necessary focus the description, analysis, and correction of social inequality. The women vary in terms of the particular inequality focused on—gender, class, race, ethnicity, age, or combinations thereof; the relative balance between research and theory, and the choice of research strategy and theoretical method. Working out this commitment to critical social theory, these women engaged with sociology and the sociological community at the moment in which the discipline was itself emerging. Their varying relationships to that community thus reflect both the instability of sociology's emerging identity and the effects of gender, class, and race on access to what would become a formal academic enterprise, the province of educated white men.

But at the moment these women were writing, sociology was as much their intellectual project as the men's; it is only in the retelling that they have disappeared.

CRITICAL-THINKING QUESTIONS

1. What does it mean to say that women have been "written out" of sociology's history? Why did this happen?
2. What issues or ideas did sociology's women founders have in common?
3. What is the importance today of recognizing the contributions of sociology's women founders?

NOTE

1. The *Survey* was a magazine founded in the merger of several social work journals; it was edited by Paul U. Kellogg, and Addams served on its editorial board. This magazine served as a major vehicle for social reformers who saw themselves as engaged in sociology. It also offered a more popular version, *Survey Graphic*, because its editorial board took communication with a general public as a primary duty.

REFERENCES

BECKER, ERNEST. 1971. *The Lost Science of Man.* New York: Braziller.

CEPLAIR, LARRY (ed.). 1991. *Charlotte Perkins Gilman: A Non-Fiction Reader.* New York: Columbia University Press.

COLLINS, RANDALL. 1975. *Conflict Sociology.* New York: Academic Press.

COOPER, ANNA JULIA. 1892. *A Voice from the South by a Black Woman from the South.* Xenia, OH: Aldine Press.

DAVIS, ALLEN F. 1973. *American Heroine.* New York: Oxford University Press.

DEEGAN, MARY JO. 1988. *Jane Addams and the Men of the Chicago School, 1892–1918.* New Brunswick, N.J. Transaction Books.

———— (ed.). 1991. *Women in Sociology: A Bio-Bibliographical Sourcebook.* Westport, CT: Greenwood Press.

DU BOIS, W. E. B. 1903/1989. *The Souls of Black Folks.* New York: Bantam.

ELLISON, RALPH. 1952/1972. *Invisible Man.* New York: Vintage Books.

GILMAN, CHARLOTTE PERKINS. 1892/1973. *The Yellow Wallpaper 1892–1973.* New York: Feminist Press.

————. 1898. *Women and Economics.* Boston: Small and Maynard.

————. 1904. *Human Work.* New York: McClure and Phillips.

————. 1911. *The Man-Made World, or Our Androcentric Culture.* New York. Charlton Company.

HOECKER-DRYSDALE, SUSAN. 1992. *Harriet Martineau: First Woman Sociologist.* Oxford, England: Berg Publishers, Inc.

KÄSLER, DIRK. 1981. "Methodological Problems of a Sociological History of Early German Sociology." Paper presented at the Department of Education, University of Chicago, November 5.

LEMERT, CHARLES. 1995. *Sociology after the Crisis.* Boulder, CO: Westview Press.

LEVINE, DANIEL. 1971. *Jane Addams and the Liberal Tradition.* Madison: State Historical Society of Wisconsin.

LORDE, AUDRE. 1984. *Sister Outsider.* Trumansburg, NY: Crossings Press.

MARTINEU, HARRIET. 1832–34. *Illustrations of Political Economy.* 9 vols. London: Charles Fox.

————. 1836/1837. *Society in America.* 2 vols. New York: Saunders and Otley.

————. 1838b. *How to Observe Morals and Manners.* London: Charles Knight and Company.

ROLLINS, JUDITH. 1985. *Between Women: Domestics and Their Employers.* Philadelphia: Temple University Press.

SMITH, DOROTHY E. 1979. "A Sociology for Women." In *The Prism of Sex: Essays in the Sociology of Knowledge,* ed. J. A. Sherman and E. T. Beck, pp. 135–87. Madison: University of Wisconsin Press.

————. 1987. *The Everyday World as Problematic: A Feminist Sociology.* Boston: Northeastern University Press.

WEBER, MARIANNE. 1907. *Ehefrau und Mutter in der Rechtsentwicklung.* Tübingen: J. C. B. Mohr.

————. 1919. *Frauenfragen und Frauengedanken,* Tübingen: J. C. B. Mohr.

WELLS-BARNETT, IDA B. 1892/1969. *Southern Horrors.* Reprinted in *On Lynchings,* New York: Arno.

————. 1895. *A Red Record.* Chicago: Donohue and Henneberry.

CLASSIC

CONTEMPORARY

CROSS-CULTURAL

5 Body Ritual among the Nacirema

HORACE MINER

Most people take their life for granted; when they think about society at all, it is usually viewed as both natural and good. To help us step back from our society, anthropologist Horace Miner describes the Nacirema, a peculiar people living in North America (whose lives should strike you as familiar). Miner's intellectual sleight-of-hand illustrates how the sociological perspective involves detachment, so that everyday life becomes something new and unusual.

The anthropologist has become so familiar with the diversity of ways in which different peoples behave in similar situations that he is not apt to be surprised by even the most exotic customs. In fact, if all of the logically possible combinations of behavior have not been found somewhere in the world, he is apt to suspect that they must be present in some yet undescribed tribe. This point has, in fact, been expressed with respect to clan organization by Murdock (1949:71). In this light, the magical beliefs and practices of the Nacirema present such unusual aspects that it seems desirable to describe them as an example of the extremes to which human behavior can go.

Professor Linton first brought the ritual of the Nacirema to the attention of anthropologists twenty years ago (1936:326), but the culture of this people is still very poorly understood. They are a North American group living in the territory between the Canadian Cree, the Yaqui and Tarahumare of Mexico, and the Carib and Arawak of the Antilles. Little is known of their origin, although tradition states that they came from the east. According to Nacirema mythology, their nation was originated by a culture hero, Notgnihsaw, who is otherwise known for two great feats of strength—the throwing of a piece of wampum across the river Pa-To-Mac and the chopping down of a cherry tree in which the Spirit of Truth resided.

Nacirema culture is characterized by a highly developed market economy which has evolved in a rich natural habitat. While much of the people's time is devoted to economic pursuits, a large part of the fruits of these labors and a considerable portion of the day are spent in ritual activity. The focus of this activity is the human body, the appearance and health of which loom as a dominant concern in the ethos of the people. While such concern is certainly not unusual, its ceremonial aspects and associated philosophy are unique.

Source: "Body Ritual among the Nacirema" by Horace Miner. Reprinted courtesy of the American Anthropological Association from *American Anthropologist,* vol. 58, no. 3, June, 1956.

19

The fundamental belief underlying the whole system appears to be that the human body is ugly and that its natural tendency is to debility and disease. Incarcerated in such a body, man's only hope is to avert these characteristics through the use of the powerful influences of ritual and ceremony. Every household has one or more shrines devoted to this purpose. The more powerful individuals in this society have several shrines in their houses, and, in fact, the opulence of a house is often referred to in terms of the number of such ritual centers it possesses. Most houses are of wattle and daub construction, but the shrine rooms of the more wealthy are walled with stone. Poorer families imitate the rich by applying pottery plaques to their shrine walls.

While each family has at least one such shrine, the rituals associated with it are not family ceremonies but are private and secret. The rites are normally only discussed with children, and then only during the period when they are being initiated into these mysteries. I was able, however, to establish sufficient rapport with the natives to examine these shrines and to have the rituals described to me.

The focal point of the shrine is a box or chest which is built into the wall. In this chest are kept the many charms and magical potions without which no native believes he could live. These preparations are secured from a variety of specialized practitioners. The most powerful of these are the medicine men, whose assistance must be rewarded with substantial gifts. However, the medicine men do not provide the curative potions for their clients, but decide what the ingredients should be and then write them down in an ancient and secret language. This writing is understood only by the medicine men and by the herbalists who, for another gift, provide the required charm.

The charm is not disposed of after it has served its purpose, but is placed in the charm-box of the household shrine. As these magical materials are specific for certain ills, and the real or imagined maladies of the people are many, the charm-box is usually full to overflowing. The magical packets are so numerous that people forget what their purposes were and fear to use them again. While the natives are very vague on this point, we can only assume that the idea in retaining all the old magical materials is that their presence in the charm-box, before which the body rituals are conducted, will in some way protect the worshipper.

Beneath the charm-box is a small font. Each day every member of the family, in succession, enters the shrine room, bows his head before the charm-box, mingles different sorts of holy water in the font, and proceeds with a brief rite of ablution. The holy waters are secured from the Water Temple of the community, where the priests conduct elaborate ceremonies to make the liquid ritually pure.

In the hierarchy of magical practitioners, and below the medicine men in prestige, are specialists whose designation is best translated "holy-mouth-men." The Nacirema have an almost pathological horror of and fascination with the mouth, the condition of which is believed to have a supernatural influence on all social relationships. Were it not for the rituals of the mouth, they believe that their teeth would fall out, their gums bleed, their jaws shrink, their friends desert them, and their lovers reject them. They also believe that a strong relationship exists between oral and moral characteristics. For example, there is a ritual ablution of the mouth for children which is supposed to improve their moral fiber.

The daily body ritual performed by everyone includes a mouth-rite. Despite the fact that these people are so punctilious about care of the mouth, this rite involves a practice which strikes the uninitiated stranger as revolting. It was reported to me that the ritual consists of inserting a small bundle of hog hairs into the mouth, along with certain magical powders, and then moving the bundle in a highly formalized series of gestures.

In addition to the private mouth-rite, the people seek out a holy-mouth-man once or twice a year. These practitioners have an impressive set of paraphernalia, consisting of a variety of augers, awls, probes, and prods. The use of these objects in the exorcism of the evils of the mouth involves almost unbelievable ritual torture of the client. The holy-mouth-man opens the client's mouth and, using the above-mentioned tools, enlarges any holes which decay may have created in the teeth. Magical materials are put into these holes. If there are no naturally occurring holes in the teeth, large sections of one or more teeth are gouged out so that the supernatural substance can be applied. In the client's view, the purpose of these ministrations is to arrest decay and to draw friends. The extremely sacred and traditional character of the rite is evident in the fact that the natives return to the holy-mouth-man year after year, despite the fact that their teeth continue to decay.

It is to be hoped that, when a thorough study of the Nacirema is made, there will be careful inquiry into the personality structure of these people. One has but to watch the gleam in the eye of a holy-mouth-man, as he jabs an awl into an exposed nerve, to suspect that a certain amount of sadism is involved. If this can be established, a very interesting pattern emerges, for most of the population shows definite masochistic tendencies. It was to these that Professor Linton referred in discussing a distinctive part of the daily body ritual which is performed only by men. This part of the rite involves scraping and lacerating the surface of the face with a sharp instrument. Special women's rites are performed only four times during each lunar month, but what they lack in frequency is made up in barbarity. As part of this ceremony, women bake their heads in small ovens for about an hour. The theoretically interesting point is that what seems to be a preponderantly masochistic people have developed sadistic specialists.

The medicine men have an imposing temple, or *latipso,* in every community of any size. The more elaborate ceremonies required to treat very sick patients can only be performed at this temple. These ceremonies involve not only the thaumaturge but a permanent group of vestal maidens who move sedately about the temple chambers in distinctive costume and headdress.

The *latipso* ceremonies are so harsh that it is phenomenal that a fair proportion of the really sick natives who enter the temple ever recover. Small children whose indoctrination is still incomplete have been known to resist attempts to take them to the temple because "that is where you go to die." Despite this fact, sick adults are not only willing but eager to undergo the protracted ritual purification, if they can afford to do so. No matter how ill the supplicant or how grave the emergency, the guardians of many temples will not admit a client if he cannot give a rich gift to the custodian. Even after one has gained admission and survived the ceremonies, the guardians will not permit the neophyte to leave until he makes still another gift.

The supplicant entering the temple is first stripped of all his or her clothes. In everyday life the Nacirema avoids exposure of his body and its natural functions. Bathing and excretory acts are performed only in the secrecy of the household shrine, where they are ritualized as part of the body-rites. Psychological shock results from the fact that body secrecy is suddenly lost upon entry into the *latipso.* A man, whose own wife has never seen him in an excretory act, suddenly finds himself naked and assisted by a vestal maiden while he performs his natural functions into a sacred vessel. This sort of ceremonial treatment is necessitated by the fact that the excreta are used by a diviner to ascertain the course and nature of the client's sickness. Female clients, on the other hand, find their naked bodies are subjected to the scrutiny, manipulation, and prodding of the medicine men.

Few supplicants in the temple are well enough to do anything but lie on their hard beds. The daily ceremonies, like the rites of the holy-mouth-men, involve discomfort and torture. With ritual precision, the vestals awaken their miserable charges each dawn and roll them about on their beds of pain while performing ablutions, in the formal movements of which the maidens are highly trained. At other times they insert magic wands in the supplicant's mouth or force him to eat substances which are supposed to be healing. From time to time the medicine men come to their clients and jab magically treated needles into their flesh. The fact that these temple ceremonies may not cure, and may even kill, the neophyte, in no way decreases the people's faith in the medicine men.

There remains one other kind of practitioner, known as a "listener." This witch-doctor has the power to exorcise the devils that lodge in the heads of people who have been bewitched. The Nacirema believe that parents bewitch their own children. Mothers are particularly suspected of putting a curse on children while teaching them the secret body rituals. The counter-magic of the witch-doctor is unusual in its lack of ritual. The patient simply tells the "listener" all his troubles and fears, beginning with the earliest difficulties he can remember. The memory displayed by the Nacirema in these exorcism sessions is truly remarkable. It is not uncommon for the patient to bemoan the rejection he felt upon being weaned as a babe, and a few individuals even see their troubles going back to the traumatic effects of their own birth.

In conclusion, mention must be made of certain practices which have their base in native esthetics but which depend upon the pervasive aversion to the natural body and its functions. There are ritual fasts to make fat people thin and ceremonial feasts to make thin people fat. Still other rites are used to make women's breasts larger if they are small, and smaller if they are large. General dissatisfaction with breast shape is symbolized in the fact that the ideal form is virtually outside the range of human variation. A few women afflicted with almost inhuman hyper-mammary development are so idolized that they make a handsome living by simply going from village to village and permitting the natives to stare at them for a fee.

Reference has already been made to the fact that excretory functions are ritualized, routinized, and relegated to secrecy. Natural reproductive functions are similarly distorted. Intercourse is taboo as a topic and scheduled as an act. Efforts are made to avoid pregnancy by the use of magical materials or by limiting intercourse to certain phases of the moon. Conception is actually very infrequent. When pregnant, women dress so as to hide their condition. Parturition takes place in secret, without friends or relatives to assist, and the majority of women do not nurse their infants.

Our review of the ritual life of the Nacirema has certainly shown them to be a magic-ridden people. It is hard to understand how they have managed to exist so long under the burdens which they have imposed upon themselves. But even such exotic customs as these take on real meaning when they are viewed with the insight provided by Malinowski when he wrote (1948:70):

Looking from far and above, from our high places of safety in the developed civilization, it is easy to see all the crudity and irrelevance of magic. But without its power and guidance early man could not have mastered his practical difficulties as he has done, nor could man have advanced to the higher stages of civilization.

CRITICAL-THINKING QUESTIONS

1. Did you understand that Miner is describing the American—"Nacirema" spelled backwards? Why do we not recognize this right away?

2. Using Miner's approach, describe a baseball game, an auction, shoppers in a supermarket, or a college classroom.

3. What do we gain from being able to "step back" from our way of life as Miner has done here?

REFERENCES

LINTON, R. 1936. *The study of man.* New York: Appleton-Century.

MALINOWSKI, B. 1948. *Magic, science and religion.* Glencoe, Ill.: Free Press.

MURDOCK, G. P. 1949. *Social structure.* New York: Macmillan.

CLASSIC

CONTEMPORARY

CROSS-CULTURAL

6 The Case for Value-Free Sociology

MAX WEBER

The following is part of a lecture given in 1918 at Germany's Munich University by Max Weber, one of sociology's pioneers. Weber lived in politically turbulent times, in which the government and other organizations were demanding that university faculty teach the "right" ideas. Weber responded to these pressures by encouraging everyone to be politically involved as citizens; yet, he maintained that the teachers and scholars should prize dispassionate analysis rather than political advocacy. This selection stimulates critical thinking about the mix of fact and value that is found in all sociological research.

Let us consider the disciplines close to me: sociology, history, economics, political science, and those types of cultural philosophy that make it their task to interpret the sciences. It is said, and I agree, that politics is out of place in the lecture-room. It does not belong there on the part of the students. . . . Neither does [it] belong in the lecture-room on the part of the [instructors], and when the [instructor] is scientifically concerned with politics, it belongs there least of all.

Source: Excerpts from *From Max Weber: Essays in Sociology* by Max Weber, edited by H. H. Gerth and C. Wright Mills, translated by H. H. Gerth and C. Wright Mills, copyright © 1946, 1958 by H. H. Gerth and C. Wright Mills. Used by permission of Oxford University Press.

To take a practical stand is one thing, and to analyze political structures and party positions is another. When speaking in a political meeting about democracy, one does not hide one's personal standpoint; indeed, to come out clearly and take a stand is one's damned duty. The words one uses in such a meeting are not means of scientific analysis but means of canvassing votes and winning over others. They are not plowshares to loosen the soil of contemplative thought; they are swords against the enemies: Such words are weapons. It would be an outrage, however, to use words in this fashion in a lecture or in the lecture-room. If, for instance, "democracy" is under discussion, one considers its various forms, analyzes them in the way they function, determines what results for the conditions of life the one form has as compared with the other. Then one confronts the forms of democracy with nondemocratic forms of political order and endeavors to come to a position where the student may find the point from which, in terms of his ultimate ideals, he can take a stand. But the true teacher will beware of imposing from the platform any political position upon the student, whether it is expressed or suggested. "To let the facts speak for themselves" is the most unfair way of putting over a political position to the student.

Why should we abstain from doing this? I state in advance that some highly esteemed colleagues are of the opinion that it is not possible to carry through this self-restraint and that, even if it were possible, it would be a whim to avoid declaring oneself. Now one cannot demonstrate scientifically what the duty of an academic teacher is. One can only demand of the teacher that he have the intellectual integrity to see that it is one thing to state facts, to determine mathematical or logical relations or the internal structure of cultural values, while it is another thing to answer questions of the *value* of culture and its individual contents and the question of how one should act in the cultural community and in political associations. These are quite heterogeneous problems. If he asks further why he should not deal with both types of problems in the lecture-room, the answer is: because the prophet and the demagogue do not belong on the academic platform.

To the prophet and the demagogue, it is said: "Go your ways out into the streets and speak openly to the world," that is, speak where criticism is possible. In the lecture-room we stand opposite our audience, and it has to remain silent. I deem it irresponsible to exploit the circumstance that for the sake of their career the students have to attend a teacher's course while there is nobody present to oppose him with criticism. The task of the teacher is to serve the students with his knowledge and scientific experience and not to imprint upon them his personal political views. It is certainly possible that the individual teacher will not entirely succeed in eliminating his personal sympathies. He is then exposed to the sharpest criticism in the forum of his own conscience. And this deficiency does not prove anything; other errors are also possible, for instance, erroneous statements of fact, and yet they prove nothing against the duty of searching for the truth. I also reject this in the very interest of science. I am ready to prove from the works of our historians that whenever the man of science introduces his personal value judgment, a full understanding of the facts *ceases.* . . .

The primary task of a useful teacher is to teach his students to recognize "inconvenient" facts—I mean facts that are inconvenient for their party opinions. And for every party opinion there are facts that are extremely inconvenient, for my own opinion no less than for others. I believe the teacher accomplishes more than a mere intellectual task if he compels his audience to accustom itself to the existence of such facts. I would be so immodest as even to apply the expression "moral achievement," though perhaps this may sound too grandiose for something that should go without saying.

CRITICAL-THINKING QUESTIONS

1. Why does Weber seek to set the campus apart from society as an "ivory tower"?

2. How is the classroom a distinctive setting in terms of political neutrality? If instructors cannot be entirely free from value positions, why should they strive to point out "inconvenient facts" to their students?

3. Do you see arguments *for* instructors presenting passionate advocacy of issues that are of great political and moral significance?

7 The Importance of Social Research

EARL BABBIE

How do we know what we know? Tradition, religion, laws, the media, personal experiences, and people in authority shape our everyday beliefs and behaviors. In this selection, Earl Babbie argues that social problems such as poverty could be diminished if policymakers and the general public based their responses on rigorous social science research results rather than on emotions and stereotypes.

We can't solve our social problems until we understand how they come about, persist. Social science research offers a way to examine and understand the operation of human social affairs. It provides points of view and technical procedures that uncover things that would otherwise escape our awareness. Often, as the cliché goes, things are not what they seem; social science research can make that clear. One example illustrates this fact.

Poverty is a persistent problem in the United States, and none of its intended solutions is more controversial than *welfare*. Although the program is intended to give the poor a helping hand while they reestablish their financial viability, many complain that it has the opposite effect.

Source: From *Practice of Social Research* (with InfoTrac), 8th edition, by E. R. Babbie, copyright © 1998. Reprinted by permission of Wadsworth, a division of Thomson Learning: *www.thomsonrights.com.* Fax (800) 730–2215.

Part of the public image of welfare in action was crystallized by Susan Sheehan (1976) in her book, *A Welfare Mother,* which describes the situation of a three-generation welfare family, suggesting that the welfare system trapped the poor rather than liberat[ed] them. Martin Anderson (1978:56) agreed with Sheehan's assessment and charged that the welfare system had established a caste system in America, "perhaps as much as one-tenth of this nation—a caste of people almost totally dependent on the state, with little hope or prospect of breaking free. Perhaps we should call them the Dependent Americans."

George Gilder (1990) has spoken for many who believe the poor are poor mainly because they refuse to work, saying the welfare system saps their incentive to take care of themselves. Ralph Segalman and David Marsland (1989:6–7) support the view that welfare has become an intergenerational way of life for the poor in welfare systems around the world. Children raised in welfare families, they assert, will likely live their adult lives on welfare:

This conflict between the intent of welfare as a temporary aid (as so understood by most of the public) and welfare as a permanent right (as understood by the welfare bureaucracy and welfare state planners) has serious implications. The welfare state nations, by and large, have given up on the concept of client rehabilitation for self-sufficiency, an intent originally supported by most welfare state proponents. What was to have been a temporary condition has become a permanent cost on the welfare state. As a result, welfare discourages productivity and self-sufficiency and establishes a new mode of approved behaviour in the society—one of acceptance of dependency as the norm.

These negative views of the effects of the welfare system are widely shared by the general public, even among those basically sympathetic to the aims of the program. Greg Duncan (1984: 2–3) at the University of Michigan's Survey Research Center points out that census data would seem to confirm the impression that a hard core of the poor have become trapped in their poverty. Speaking of the percentage of the population living in poverty at any given time, he says,

Year-to-year changes in these fractions are typically less than 1 percent, and the Census survey's other measures show little change in the characteristic of the poor from one year to the next. They have shown repeatedly that the individuals who are poor are more likely to be in families headed by a woman, by someone with low education, and by blacks.

Evidence that one-eighth of the population was poor in two consecutive years, and that those poor shared similar characteristics, is consistent with an inference of absolutely no turnover in the poverty population. Moreover, the evidence seems to fit the stereotype that those families that are poor are likely to remain poor, and that there is a hard-core population of poor families for whom there is little hope of self-improvement.

Duncan continues, however, to warn that such snapshots of the population can conceal changes taking place. Specifically, an unchanging percentage of the population living in poverty does not necessarily mean the *same* families are poor from year to year. Theoretically, it could be a totally different set of families each year.

To determine the real nature of poverty and welfare, the University of Michigan undertook a "Panel Study of Income Dynamics" in which they followed the economic fate of 5,000 families from 1969 to 1978, or ten years, the period supposedly typified by Sheehan's "welfare mother." At the beginning, the researchers found that in 1978, 8.1 percent of these families were receiving some welfare benefits and 3.5 percent depended on welfare for more than half their income. Moreover, these percentages did not differ drastically over the ten-year period (Duncan 1984:75).

Looking beyond these surface data, however, the researchers found something you might not have expected. During the ten-year period, about one-fourth of the 5,000 families received welfare benefits at least once. However, only 8.7 percent of the families were ever dependent on welfare for more than half their income. *"Only a little over one-half of the individuals living in poverty in one year are found to be poor in the next, and considerably less than one-half of those who experience poverty remain persistently poor over many years"* (Duncan 1984:3; emphasis original).

Only 2 percent of the families received welfare each of the ten years, and less than 1 percent were continuously dependent on welfare for the ten years. Table 1 summarizes these findings.

These data paint a much different picture of poverty than people commonly assume. In a summary of his findings, Duncan (1984:4–5) says:

While nearly one-quarter of the population received income from welfare sources at least once in the decade, only about 2 percent of all the population could be characterized as dependent upon this income for extended periods of time. Many families receiving welfare benefits at any given time were in the early stages of recovering from an economic crisis caused by the death, departure, or disability of a husband, a recovery that often lifted them out of welfare when they found full-time employment, or remarried, or both. Furthermore, most of the children raised in welfare families did not themselves receive welfare benefits after they left home and formed their own households.

TABLE 1   Incidence of Short- and Long-Run Welfare Receipt and Dependence, 1969–1978

	Percent of U.S. Population:	
	Receiving Any Welfare Income	*Dependent on Welfare for More than 50% of Family Income*
Welfare in 1978	8.1%	3.5%
Welfare in 1 or more years, 1969–78	25.2	8.7
Welfare in 5 or more years, 1969–78	8.3	3.5
Welfare in all 10 years, 1969–78	2.0	0.7
"Persistent welfare" (welfare in 8 or more years), 1969–78	4.4	2.0

Source: Greg J. Duncan, *Years of Poverty, Years of Plenty: The Changing Fortunes of American Workers and Families* (Ann Arbor: University of Michigan, 1984), 75.

Many of the things social scientists study—including [the issue of welfare] you've just read about—generate deep emotions and firm convictions in most people. This makes effective inquiry into the facts difficult at best; all too often, researchers manage only to confirm their initial prejudices. The special value of social science research methods is that they offer a way to address such issues with logical and observational rigor. They let us all pierce through our personal viewpoints and take a look at the world that lies beyond our own perspectives. And it is that "world beyond" that holds the solutions to the social problems we face today.

At a time of increased depression and disillusionment, we are continually tempted to turn away from confronting social problems and retreat into the concerns of our own self-interest. Social science research offers an opportunity to take on those problems and discover the experience of making a difference after all. The choice is yours; I invite you to take on the challenge.

CRITICAL-THINKING QUESTIONS

1. What does Babbie mean when he says that "things are not what they seem" when we read about controversial issues such as welfare?

2. Many people believe that welfare has become an intergenerational way of life. What data does Babbie present that challenge such beliefs?

3. In the classic selection ("The Case for Value-Free Sociology"), Max Weber asserts, "The primary task of a useful teacher is to teach [her/his] students to recognize 'inconvenient' facts—I mean facts that are inconvenient for their party opinions." Do you think some instructors (and students) feel pressure to conform to approved points of view, whether religious or political? Should faculty and students ignore research findings that contradict such perspectives?

REFERENCES

ANDERSON, MARTIN. 1978. *Welfare: The political economy of welfare reform in the United States.* Stanford, Calif.: Hoover Institution Press.

DUNCAN, GREG J., with RICHARD D. COE, et al. 1984. *Years of poverty, years of plenty: The changing fortunes of American workers and families.* Ann Arbor: Survey Research Center Institute.

GILDER, GEORGE. 1990. The nature of poverty. In *The American polity reader,* eds. A. Serow, W. Shannon, and E. Ladd, 658–63. New York: Norton.

SEGALMAN, RALPH, and DAVID MARSLAND. 1989. *Cradle to grave: Comparative perspectives on the state of welfare.* New York: St. Martin's Press.

SHEEHAN, SUSAN. 1976. *A welfare mother.* New York: Mentor.

CLASSIC

CONTEMPORARY

CROSS-CULTURAL

8 Arab Women in the Field

SORAYA ALTORKI

Social scientists often rely on ethnography—*the study of people using observation or interviews—to provide detailed descriptions of groups, organizations, and communities. Such fieldwork, like other data collection methods, has both strengths and limitations. As Soraya Altorki shows, a major advantage of studying one's own culture includes a familiarity with the people and the environment. The researcher also encounters a number of problems. One of Altorki's challenges, for example, involved resocializing herself into her culture, having been abroad for a number of years. She also had to overcome the informants' reluctance to address sensitive questions about their religious practices and family life to an "outsider."*

AT HOME IN THE FIELD

Having been socialized many years in Egypt and identifying with its people, I had regarded it, on one level, to be my home. On another level, however, I had been brought up in a Saudi Arabian family committed in great measure to that country's cultural heritage and the observance of its cultural norms, even while selectively observing certain Egyptian values and practices. Throughout my college days, I had been reminded that I could not do what my Egyptian girlfriends could do, because "our" traditions were different and for "us" such behavior was unacceptable.

Besides, it was not only the constraining elements of Saudi Arabian culture that molded my

Source: "At Home in the Field," by Soraya Altorki, in *Arab Women in the Field: Studying Your Own Society,* eds. Soraya Altorki and Camillia Fawzi El-Solh, pp. 51–59. New York: Syracuse University Press, 1998. Reprinted by permission.

growing-up experiences in Egypt, but also the rich rewards that I reaped from kinship support and shared cultural knowledge. These provided for me the security of a closure that was not attainable in Egypt. Thus, Saudi Arabia was home for me on a more fundamental level.

Arriving in Jiddah [Saudi Arabia], my native city, I knew I wanted to study urban life. Although the entire northern portion of the Arabian Peninsula was virtually unknown to social scientists, yet early travelers and even scholars avoided its study in favor of the nomad and the camel. Barring Hürgrouje and Burton, almost nothing was known about urban life. In retrospect, I believe that my choice to focus on urban society was partly a reaction to the stereotypical view of Saudi Arabia as a society of nomads and oil wells.

There were also social constraints to my choice. I knew that, as an unmarried woman, I could neither travel alone in the country nor wander around with the nomads. Living alone, anywhere in the country, was out of the question. Thus, for many considerations, an urban-based study seemed most appropriate, and the city of Jiddah the most convenient.

The realities of being an unmarried woman in many ways dictated my field of research, although it did not determine my choice of research topic within that field (Altorki, 1986). This essentially meant that I could work with women and that I had limited access to men. Within these bounds, my choice was absolutely free. . . .

INSIDER/OUTSIDER

Being literally at home in Jiddah, I was spared having to worry about the problems of settling in that most anthropologists face when entering the field. Furthermore, I needed no research permit (or if I did, I never bothered to find out) and no letters of guarantee. Neither was I required to make commitments to local authorities and research institutes concerning the conduct of my work and the use and distribution of my data.

The people I studied saw me as one of themselves. Some of them had ties of kinship and friendship to my family. Others knew my family members by name. This state of affairs provided me with significant advantages. Others, working in their own society, have observed similar benefits in knowing the culture and consequently being able to select their research agenda in consonance with what is most expedient for the research task and what is most feasible within the limits of what will be allowed by the subjects under investigation (see Stephenson and Greer 1981:126).

However, some facets of my life concerned my informants. Why, for example, was I not a married woman with children, like all my peers? And why was I still living abroad rather than residing in Jiddah, awaiting marriage? My unmarried status at the age of twenty-two made me somewhat of an anomaly. More distressing to the older women among whom I worked was the conclusion that I was more interested in following my studies than in settling down to married life. Although the role of an educated woman had come to be accepted by the community at large and the elite in particular, the problem was in the priorities this role took over what was perceived to be the more important aspect of gender role, namely the status that marriage and motherhood bring. According to both men and women, it is these dimensions of womanhood that are primary. In fact, given the segregation of Saudi Arabian women from men, and their isolation from public life, marriage and motherhood become a woman's avenues to maturity, security, and greater prestige. Being a member of the society, I anticipated this and was well prepared to deal with its consequences.

Although women come of age with marriage, and prestige for them is attained by motherhood, my status within the community had to rest on other things: It relied greatly on my education. Lacking husband and child, I predicated my adulthood on education and depended on the community's acceptance of it as a legitimate goal for women to attain. Men and women alike respected this, although never failing to remind me of the fundamentals of my role as a woman. As one older woman put it to me: "Education is good, but women are weak. No matter how much money they have, no matter their education, they cannot manage without men. May Allah save your father and your brother. But you have to start your own family." That statement accurately reflects the dependence of women on men, a dependence that also correlates with their segregation in Saudi Arabian society. But my role as a Saudi Arabian woman, educated abroad, permitted me more flexibility and autonomy. For one thing, my interaction with men who were not my relatives was tolerated.

My long absence abroad was an additional factor leading to more mobility. While abroad, I had been immersed in a different way of life, and hence women and men alike did not expect me to conform totally to the cultural norms governing the relationship of men and women in Saudi Arabian society. My absence had a complex effect on my reentry into my own community. On the one hand, it allowed more maneuverability in my role as an unmarried woman, and, on the other hand, it made conformity especially expedient in strengthening my ties to my informants.

Repeatedly, men and women expressed their surprise and approval when my behavior showed conformity to Saudi Arabian culture. They were, for example, delighted that my many years in Egypt had not changed my accent to Egyptian. Whenever I showed observance of norms that young people my age had begun to modify, members of the older generation were astonished and particularly delighted. Those of the younger generation, however, saw such conformity as awkward and continued to remind me that times had changed: "Nobody is observing such things these days."

For example, norms of deference to older siblings necessitate that they be addressed in specific terms. To an older brother and kinsmen his age the term is *sidi,* which means "my master." My use of these terms of address was welcomed by all, barring girls of my age who by then were seeking to substitute as equivalent for the term *sidi* those of *akhuya* (my brother) and the sobriquet *abu flan* (father of). In doing this, I took my cues from young men who had obtained their college education abroad, sometimes through graduate school, and who continued to use traditional terms of reference in addressing older female siblings and other kinswomen in their age group.

It was in the same spirit that I observed some norms of modesty, particularly those related to veiling. Such practices were changing at the time of my fieldwork, so that the families I studied showed the whole spectrum of veiling practices, from those who had considerably modified its use to leave the face bare, to those who still observed the traditional practice of covering the face as well. While visiting the homes of the latter,

I made sure to conform and to cover my face carefully. This gesture of respect did not go unnoticed: Women and men alike commented that my many years abroad had not made me behave like a "foreigner."

The years abroad had been spent as a student, and now I had come back as a researcher with the intention of recording a way of life that had not previously been studied. Everyone understood that role. Female education was not a novelty. Girls were sent to *faqihas* (informal traditional schools) as far back as older informants could remember; and formal girls' schools were opened by the government in 1960. By the time I went to the field, the first women's university had already opened in Jiddah. College education was thoroughly acceptable for women; indeed, it had become greatly valued.

Thus, I had no problem in defining part of my role to the subjects of my research. I wanted to study social life, family organization, rituals, beliefs, and customs, and to document how these have changed for the younger people in the study. In another way, my role was more ascribed. My return to Jiddah meant taking my place in a family and getting involved in the various ramifications of family life. It also meant belonging to a class with the task of conforming to the behavior of that class. I was aware that I could in fact not conform to that behavior, but I had little choice with regard to involvement in family life.

The ascribed aspects of my role, i.e., gender, age, and kinship, were more fundamental in people's perception of me, which may be unavoidable in doing research among one's own people. My education was important in allowing me to explore areas of social life (e.g., more access to the world of men) that other women could not undertake. Despite my research objective, known and accepted to all the families, I remained primarily a Saudi Arabian woman. As such, I was known to some as the daughter or a sister of a friend, while to others as a member of a lineage they knew from other mutual friends. These considerations were always present in my interaction with others. While criteria centering on the individual are not without relevance in structuring relations, the world of these elite families was in the first instance structured by consanguineous and marital ties, and in the second place by friendship and business networks.

Within this world an individual—whether man or woman—is deeply embedded in the *'aila* (family). One's status is, to a considerable degree, ascribed by the status of the *'aila*. Individual achievement is an avenue to mobility, but clearly it is the achievement of men and not of women that is associated with family prestige. Recent changes in the wider society have introduced more emphasis on individuality and an increase of distance from the *'aila*. This is evidenced in neolocal residence patterns, more individual involvement in marriage choice, relative reduction of parental authority, independent career choices for men, and less observance of traditional obligations to kinsmen (Altorki, 1986).

On the whole, I experienced no problems in establishing rapport—that quality in the relationship between the ethnographer and the host community that the introductions to ethnographic monographs rarely fail to mention, but which probably involves the most enigmatic aspect of our methodological trademark: participant observation. I spoke the language, and the trademark itself had no special meaning for me, although, as I will explain, it had very special implications in my case.

In short, I found practical advantages in my particular field situation: Unencumbered by bureaucratic impediments, comfortably set up in my family's home, fluent in the vernacular, and personally known in some of the households I was to study, I could begin my research under very auspicious circumstances—or so it seemed until I realized the implications of being an indigenous anthropologist. I discovered that almost every one of the advantages had its negative side.

In a very real sense, my fieldwork experience was a process of resocialization into my own society. Although I was raised in a Saudi Arabian family, my long years of residence abroad had established considerable distance between me and my society. The advantages were that much of the culture was not so familiar that it could easily escape my notice. This problem in the collection of data has been observed by other ethnographers working under similar conditions (cf. Spradley and McCurdy, 1972; Ablon, 1977; Stephenson and Greer, 1981), but it is one that can be overcome by rigorous training. The researcher can counteract familiarity by close observation, meticulous recording of ethnographic scenes, and detailed probing to uncover the "taken-for-granted" world he or she may share with members of the community being studied.

Living at home meant that I had to assume the role expected of a family member in my position within the household group. The ordinary field situation reversed itself in my case. I became what may best be described as an observant participant. My primary duty was to participate. To observe became an incidental privilege.

My status did not afford me immunity from observing all the taboos and attending to all the obligations my culture prescribed for me—an immunity usually granted to foreign anthropologists. I had to accept severe restrictions on my movements and on my interaction with other people. For example, I had no freedom to move in public on my own, and challenging any norms of conduct would have jeopardized my relationships with the families I had decided to study. Had I not conformed, I would have risked ostracism and termination of my research. Persistently, if slowly, I achieved a precarious balance of roles that allowed me mobility and freedom to do my research as well as to be accepted and taken seriously. I became a conscious witness to my own resocialization as an Arab woman in my society and thus learned and comprehended many aspects of this role in the best possible manner.

This, perhaps, is one of the hidden advantages of being an insider. For example, veiling norms can be observed and described by an outsider, and one can also learn about the meaning of veiling by soliciting relevant information from informants. Yet the participant charged with the task of abiding by the norms experiences the constraints, to be sure, but also the rewards of these norms on a more basic level. In that sense, my resocialization generated data on an experiential level different from that to which an outsider could bear witness. This point has also been observed as a merit of indigenous research elsewhere. Aguilar, for example, summarizing the pros and cons of this kind of research, mentions that its advocates insist "that the covert culture of the insider has the heuristic value of lending psychological reality (or cultural reality) to ethnographic analyses" (1981:16).

My status affected my research in another way. Restricted possibilities for movement outside the house and pervasive segregation of men and women in public confined the research predominantly to the world of women. These realities affected the choice of topic for investigation. I could not study market or political relations, for example. Neither could I investigate any other subject in which men, rather than women, are the dominant actors. Family organization seemed the most accessible for a female researcher, and elites became my focus. Within that, my emphasis was on how ideology and practice affect and are influenced by one another. But, as noted elsewhere, elites are the least accessible to inquiry, especially through the technique of prolonged participant observation. The families I elected to study formed closed groups, and although the observation of and participation in their daily lives was possible for me as a member of the group, even I could gain their confidence only through patient approaches along the lines of friendship.

Although generous hospitality is highly valued behavior, there remain degrees of formality that the families must always maintain vis-à-vis the whole community. Only with considerable caution can a nonmember see their lives as they live them, as opposed to how they want the rest of the community to perceive them. For example, it takes a long time,

coupled with intensive interaction, before people allow a friend to move within their home free of the facade of formality exhibited to outsiders. Indeed, it took between six and eight months before I could develop the friendships that made close observation of their daily lives possible to the degree that my presence was more or less ignored.

Being an insider has even more serious consequences for research. Information may be withheld when it relates to behavior that must be concealed from public knowledge. If one is outside the system, one's awareness of goings-on may not be problematical. But as a participant, the researcher constitutes a threat of exposure and judgment. Lewis (1973:588) explains this situation very well:

> There is a growing fear that the information collected by an outsider, someone not constrained by group values and interests, will expose the group to outside manipulation and control. . . . The insider, on the other hand, is accountable; s/he must remain in the community and take responsibility for her/his actions. Thus, s/he is forced through self-interest to exercise discretion.

This was one of the hardest areas to overcome in doing research among one's own people. For example, family solidarity and cohesion are greatly valued. Verbally, men and women endorse the ideal of love and support between siblings; respect and obedience in filial relations; and honoring family duties of financial support to the needy and maintenance of elderly parents. In practice, the older generations approximated many of these ideals (Altorki, 1986).

But family conflict does occur, and younger generation members have begun to modify family obligations in general. Differences over inheritance constitute the most serious threat to family solidarity—a threat that mounts as the stakes become higher and people's wealth increases. The ideal remains that such differences must be kept out of the public eye and should be reconciled between family members without recourse to the courts. So important is this family ideal that information about conflict, especially that considered to be serious, was at first not revealed to me. I learned about such conflicts indirectly from domestic servants working in these homes who, by coincidence, happened to be related to women working in my family's household. On other occasions, I obtained relevant information from women with whom I had established such strong ties of friendship that we had come to be considered "sisters." This family idiom symbolized our enclosure in the same kinship group and, by implication, showed our interest in protecting that group and shielding it from public criticism.

On one point, my learning about family conflicts was fortuitous. Is it conceivable that I would have returned from the field with the belief that the ideal of family solidarity was the reality? By being an insider, and from my own kinship network, I "experienced" the fact that reality was different and that disagreement can escalate to conflicts between family members. The problem, however, was in collecting data about conflict from the other families to uncover patterns in its expression and management. What, for example, were the patterns for the expression of intrafamily conflict? How was it managed, and what are the patterns for its resolution?

In this respect, my status as an insider prevented people from divulging such information for fear of having it exposed to the wider community. Obviously, disseminating information about intrafamilial conflict to the community also implies that the disseminator, i.e., the indigenous anthropologist, has judged it negatively and is now taking an active role in censoring the behavior it bespeaks. While the question of exposure to the public can be bridged by trust and confidence in the researcher, the threat of judgment is harder to overcome. Being a participating family member implies, of course, subscribing to the cultural norms and values of the group and to the sanctions that follow a breach of valued behavior.

These considerations are different for a foreign anthropologist. As an outsider investigating family organization and interfamilial conflict, she or he must gain the confidence of the people and be trusted not to expose family differences to the community. But outsider status does not imply shared cultural knowledge, and thus protects the outsider from applying the same moral judgments. The nonindigenous researcher is outside the system, and for this very reason people may not conceal family differences to the same degree as they would from a member of their own group. In collecting relevant data, the indigenous researcher is twice bound and must be able to overcome barriers to confidence and to potential value judgment.

Other social scientists have made similar observations. Aguilar, for example, highlights the constraints indigenous status may place on access to data (1981:21), although, as he points out, other anthropologists claim the opposite (1981:18). However, the Saudi Arabian case indicates that while confidence can be established, a morally neutral judgment is harder to demonstrate. An effective strategy is to be drawn into the same closure that allows sharing of such delicate information. In my case, the idiom of kinship and the ties of close friendships provided such a closure.

My general familiarity with these families had another irksome drawback. My informants presumed that I knew my own culture, and for a long time they either misinterpreted my questions as implying an unbecoming skepticism or failed to appreciate that I truly did not know what I had asked them to explain. This was especially true for knowledge of religious beliefs and rituals, which for me was a difficult area to explore. Such knowledge is essential to an adult Muslim, and any queries about it reveal a lapse in religious duties. Fed up with my questions, an older woman put it to me this way: "Are you not ashamed that you do not know how to pray at your age? What then did they teach you abroad?"

This revealed to me the cultural givens of the community and the cultural repertoire indispensable to membership in it. The best research strategy to circumvent this role was to openly admit my ignorance and to blame it all on my long absence abroad. Women and men patiently explained matters to me in a desire to resocialize me as a Muslim Arab woman. In fact, it was especially pleasing to the older women, often illiterate, to instruct me despite my higher formal education.

These considerations have been well described by Stephenson and Greer. They note that while familiarity with the culture under study can be a bonus, prior knowledge of the people studied provides no guaranteed advantage. The expectations people may have of the investigator could make it more difficult for her or him to break out of fixed patterns and thus serve to restrict the work at hand (1981:129). The role that the community attributes to the researcher may inhibit other relationships and bias the researcher's thoughts. Moreover, the role ascribed by kinship to the indigenous anthropologist may forcefully draw that person into factionalism within the community and thereby limit the work that can be accomplished. Sometimes, such problems can be circumvented by conscious strategy. As Stephenson and Greer observe, "the researcher can mitigate the effects of already established roles by emphasizing some over others" (1981:127).

CRITICAL-THINKING QUESTIONS

1. How did Altorki's sex and background influence her decisions about where and how to conduct her research on Arab society?

2. Field researchers must often balance the advantages and disadvantages of playing "insider" and "outsider" roles. How did being an insider both benefit and limit Altorki's research? What barriers did she have to overcome?

3. What strengths and weaknesses did Altorki encounter as an outsider? Is it possible for researchers who are outsiders to offer information and valid insights about the societies they study? Explain your answer.

REFERENCES

ABLON, J. 1977. Field methods in working with middle class Americans: New issues of values, personality and reciprocity. *Human Organization,* 36(1): 69–72.

AGUILAR, J. 1981. Insider research: An ethnography of a debate. In *Anthropologists at home in North America: Methods and issues in the study of one's own society,* ed. D. A. Messerschmidt. Cambridge: Cambridge University Press.

ALTORKI, S. 1986. *Women in Saudi Arabia: Ideology and behavior among the elite.* New York: Columbia University Press.

LEWIS, D. 1973. Anthropology and colonialism. *Current Anthropology,* 14(12): 581–602.

SPRADLEY, J. P., and D. W. McCURDY. 1972. *The cultural experience.* Chicago: Science Research Association.

STEPHENSON, J. B., and L. S. GREER. 1981. Ethnographers in their own cultures: Two Appalachian cases. *Human Organization,* 40(2): 123–30.

CLASSIC

CONTEMPORARY

CROSS-CULTURAL

9 Symbol: The Basic Element of Culture

LESLIE A. WHITE

Leslie A. White, a noted anthropologist, argues in this selection that the key to human existence is the ability to use symbols. While all animals are capable of complex behavior, only humanity depends on symbolic activity. This is the special power that underlies our autonomy as the only creatures who live according to meanings we set for ourselves. Thus symbols convert our animal species into humanity, in the process transforming social behavior into true civilization.

All human behavior originates in the use of symbols. It was the symbol which transformed our anthropoid ancestors into men and made them human. All civilizations have been generated, and are perpetuated, only by the use of symbols. It is the symbol which transforms an infant of *Homo sapiens* into a human being; deaf mutes who grow up without the use of symbols are not human beings. All human behavior consists of, or is dependent upon, the use of symbols. Human behavior is symbolic behavior; symbolic behavior is human behavior. The symbol is the universe of humanity. . . .

Source: From "The Symbol: The Origin and the Basis of Human Behavior," in *The Science of Culture: A Study of Man and Civilization* by Leslie White. Copyright © 1949 by Leslie White. Copyright renewed by Crocker National Bank. Reprinted by permission of Farrar, Straus & Giroux, Inc.

That there are numerous and impressive similarities between the behavior of man and that of ape is fairly obvious; it is quite possible that chimpanzees and gorillas in zoos have noted and appreciated them. Fairly apparent, too, are man's behavioral similarities to many other kinds of animals. Almost as obvious, but not easy to define, is a difference in behavior which distinguishes man from all other living creatures. I say "obvious" because it is quite apparent to the common man that the nonhuman animals with which he is familiar do not and cannot enter, and participate in, the world in which he, as a human being, lives. It is impossible for a dog, horse, bird, or even an ape, to have *any* understanding of the meaning of the sign of the cross to a Christian, or of the fact that black (white among the Chinese) is the color of mourning. No chimpanzee or laboratory rat can appreciate the difference between Holy water and distilled water, or grasp the meaning of *Tuesday, 3,* or *sin.* No animal save man can distinguish a cousin from an uncle, or a cross cousin from a parallel cousin. Only man can commit the crime of incest or adultery; only he can remember the Sabbath and keep it Holy. It is not, as we well know, that the lower animals can do these things but to a lesser degree than ourselves; they cannot perform these acts of appreciation and distinction *at all.* It is, as Descartes said long ago, "not only that the brutes have less Reason than man, but that they have none at all." . . .

A symbol may be defined as a thing the value or meaning of which is bestowed upon it by those who use it. I say "thing" because a symbol may have any kind of physical form; it may have the form of a material object, a color, a sound, an odor, a motion of an object, a taste.

The meaning, or value, of a symbol is in no instance derived from or determined by properties intrinsic in its physical form: The color appropriate to mourning may be yellow, green, or any other color; purple need not be the color of royalty; among the Manchu rulers of China it was yellow. . . . The meaning of symbols is derived from and determined by the organisms who use them; meaning is bestowed by human organisms upon physical things or events which thereupon become symbols. Symbols "have their signification," to use John Locke's phrase, "from the arbitrary imposition of men."

All symbols must have a physical form; otherwise they could not enter our experience. . . . But the meaning of a symbol cannot be discovered by mere sensory examination of its physical form. One cannot tell by looking at an *x* in an algebraic equation what it stands for; one cannot ascertain with the ears alone the symbolic value of the phonetic compound *si;* one cannot tell merely by weighing a pig how much gold he will exchange for; one cannot tell from the wavelength of a color whether it stands for courage or cowardice, "stop" or "go"; nor can one discover the spirit in

a fetish by any amount of physical or chemical examination. The meaning of a symbol can be grasped only by nonsensory, symbolic means. . . .

Thus Darwin says: "That which distinguishes man from the lower animals is not the understanding of articulate sounds, for as everyone knows, dogs understand many words and sentences."[1] . . .

The man differs from the dog—and all other creatures—in that *he can and does play an active role in determining what value the vocal stimulus is to have, and the dog cannot.* The dog does not and cannot play an active part in determining the value of the vocal stimulus. Whether he is to roll over or go fetch at a given stimulus, or whether the stimulus for roll over be one combination of sounds or another is a matter in which the dog has nothing whatever to "say." He plays a purely passive role and can do nothing else. He learns the meaning of a vocal command just as his salivary glands may learn to respond to the sound of a bell. But man plays an active role and thus becomes a creator: Let *x* equal three pounds of coal and it does equal three pounds of coal; let removal of the hat in a house of worship indicate respect and it becomes so. This creative faculty, that of freely, actively, and arbitrarily bestowing value upon things, is one of the most commonplace as well as *the* most important characteristic of man. Children employ it freely in their play: "Let's pretend that this rock is a wolf." . . .

All culture (civilization) depends upon the symbol. It was the exercise of the symbolic faculty that brought culture into existence, and it is the use of symbols that makes the perpetuation of culture possible. Without the symbol there would be no culture, and man would be merely an animal, not a human being.

Articulate speech is the most important form of symbolic expression. Remove speech from culture and what would remain? Let us see.

Without articulate speech we would have no *human* social organization. Families we might have, but this form of organization is not peculiar to man; it is not, *per se,* human. But we would have no prohibitions of incest, no rules prescribing exogamy and endogamy, polygamy, monogamy. How could marriage with a cross cousin be prescribed, marriage with a parallel cousin proscribed, without articulate speech? How could rules which prohibit plural mates possessed simultaneously, but permit them if possessed one at a time, exist without speech?

Without speech we would have no political, economic, ecclesiastic, or military organization; no codes of etiquette or ethics; no laws; no science, theology, or literature; no games or music, except on an ape level. Rituals and ceremonial paraphernalia would be meaningless without articulate speech. Indeed, without articulate speech we would be all but toolless: We would have only the occasional and insignificant use of the tool such as we find today among the higher apes, for it was articulate speech that transformed the non-progressive tool-using of the ape into the progressive, cumulative tool-using of man, the human being.

In short, without symbolic communication in some form, we would have no culture. "In the Word was the beginning" of culture—and its perpetuation also.

To be sure, with all his culture man is still an animal and strives for the same ends that all other living creatures strive for: the preservation of the individual and the perpetuation of the [species]. In concrete terms these ends are food, shelter from the elements, defense from enemies, health, and offspring. The fact that man strives for these ends just as all other animals do has, no doubt, led many to declare that there is "no fundamental difference between the behavior of man and of other creatures." But man does differ, not in *ends* but in *means*. Man's means are cultural means: Culture is simply the human animal's way of living. And, since these means, culture, are dependent upon a faculty possessed by man alone, the ability to use symbols, the difference between the behavior of man and of all other creatures is not merely great, but basic and fundamental.

The behavior of man is of two distinct kinds: symbolic and nonsymbolic. Man yawns, stretches, coughs, scratches himself, cries out in pain, shrinks with fear, "bristles" with anger, and so on. Nonsymbolic behavior of this sort is not peculiar to man; he shares it not only with the other primates but with many other animal species as well. But man communicates with his fellows with articulate speech, uses amulets, confesses sins, makes laws, observes codes of etiquette, explains his dreams, classifies his relatives in designated categories, and so on. This kind of behavior is unique; only man is capable of it; it is peculiar to man because it consists of, or is dependent upon, the use of symbols. The nonsymbolic behavior of *Homo sapiens* is the behavior of man the animal; the symbolic behavior is that of man the human being. It is the symbol which has transformed man from a mere animal to a human animal. . . .

The infant of the species *Homo sapiens* becomes human only when and as he exercises his symbol faculty. Only through articulate speech—not necessarily vocal—can he enter the world of human beings and take part in their affairs. The questions asked earlier may be repeated now. How could a growing child know and appreciate such things as social organization, ethics, etiquette, ritual, science, religion, art, and games without symbolic communication? The answer is of course that he could know nothing of these things and have no appreciation of them at all. . . .

Children who have been cut off from human intercourse for years by blindness and deafness but who have eventually effected communication with their fellows on a symbolic level are exceedingly illuminating. The case of Helen Keller is exceptionally instructive. . . .

Helen Keller was rendered blind and deaf at an early age by illness. She grew up as a child without symbolic contact with anyone. Descriptions of her at the age of seven, the time at which her teacher, Miss Sullivan, came to her home, disclosed no *human* attributes of Helen's behavior at all. She was a headstrong, undisciplined, and unruly little animal.

Within a day or so after her arrival at the Keller home, Miss Sullivan taught Helen her first word, spelling it into her hand. But this word was merely a sign, not a symbol. A week later Helen knew several words but, as Miss Sullivan reports, she had "no idea how to use them or that everything has a name." Within three weeks Helen knew eighteen nouns and three verbs. But she was still on the level of signs; she still had no notion "that everything has a name."

Helen confused the word signs for "mug" and "water" because, apparently, both were associated with drinking. Miss Sullivan made a few attempts to clear up this confusion but without success. One morning, however, about a month after Miss Sullivan's arrival, the two went out to the pump in the garden. What happened then is best told in their own words:

I made Helen hold her mug under the spout while I pumped. As the cold water gushed forth, filling the mug, I spelled "w-a-t-e-r" into Helen's free hand. The word coming so close upon the sensation of cold water rushing over her hand seemed to startle her. She dropped the mug and stood as one transfixed. A new light came into her face. She spelled "water" several times. Then she dropped on the ground and asked for its name and pointed to the pump and the trellis, and suddenly turning round she asked for my name. . . . *In a few hours she had added thirty new words to her vocabulary.*

But these words were now more than mere signs as they are to a dog and as they had been to Helen up to then. They were *symbols.* Helen had at last grasped and turned the key that admitted her for the first time to a new universe: the world of human beings. Helen describes this marvelous experience herself:

We walked down the path to the well-house, attracted by the fragrance of the honeysuckle with which it was covered. Someone was drawing water and my teacher placed my hand under the spout. As the cool stream gushed over one hand she spelled into the other the word *water,* first slowly, then rapidly. I stood still, my whole attention fixed upon the motion of her fingers.

Suddenly I felt a misty consciousness as of something forgotten—a thrill of returning thought; and somehow *the mystery of language was revealed to me.* I knew then that "w-a-t-e-r" meant the wonderful cool something that was flowing over my hand. That living word awakened my soul, gave it light, hope, joy, set it free!

Helen was transformed on the instant by this experience. Miss Sullivan had managed to touch Helen's symbol mechanism and set it in motion. Helen, on her part, grasped the external world with this mechanism that had lain dormant and inert all these years, sealed in dark and silent isolation by eyes that could not see and ears that heard not. But now she had crossed the boundary and entered a new land. Henceforth the progress would be rapid.

"I left the well-house," Helen reports, "eager to learn. Everything had a name, and each name gave birth to a new thought. As we returned to the house every object which I touched seemed to quiver with life. That was because I saw everything with the strange new sight that had come to me."

Helen became humanized rapidly. "I see an improvement in Helen from day to day," Miss Sullivan wrote in her diary, "*almost from hour to hour.* Everything must have a name now. . . . She drops the signs and pantomime she used before as soon as she has words to supply their place. . . . We notice her face grows more expressive each day. . . ."

A more eloquent and convincing account of the significance of symbols and of the great gulf between the human mind and that of minds without symbols could hardly be imagined.

The natural processes of biologic evolution brought into existence in man, and man alone, a new and distinctive ability; the ability to use symbols. The most important form of symbolic expression is articulate speech. Articulate speech means communication of ideas; communication means preservation—tradition—and preservation means accumulation and progress. The emergence of the faculty of symboling has resulted in the genesis of a new order of phenomena: an extrasomatic, cultural order. All civilizations are born of, and are perpetuated by, the use of symbols. A culture, or civilization, is but a particular kind of form which the biologic, life-perpetuating activities of a particular animal, man, assume.

Human behavior is symbolic behavior; if it is not symbolic, it is not human. The infant of the genus *Homo* becomes a human being only as he is introduced into and participates in that order of phenomena which is culture. And the key to this world and the means of participation in it is—the symbol.

CRITICAL-THINKING QUESTIONS

1. Why does White argue that a deaf mute unable to communicate symbolically is not fully human? What opposing argument might be made? What position would White take in the pro-choice versus pro-life abortion controversy?

2. Because the reality we experience is based on a particular system of symbols, how do we tend to view members of other cultures? What special efforts are needed to overcome the tendency to treat people of different cultures as less worthy than we are?

3. How did gaining the capacity to use symbols transform Helen Keller? How did this ability alter her capacity for further learning?

NOTE

1. Charles Darwin, *The Descent of Man,* chap. 3.

CLASSIC

CONTEMPORARY

CROSS-CULTURAL

10 Manifest and Latent Functions

ROBERT K. MERTON

Robert Merton made a major contribution to structural-functional theory by pointing out that social patterns have both manifest and latent functions. Manifest functions are those consequences that are familiar, planned, and generally recognized. Latent functions, on the other hand, are unfamiliar, unplanned, and widely overlooked. For this reason, Merton argued, comprehending latent functions is a special responsibility of sociologists. Merton illustrates this process by offering observations about the pattern of conspicuous consumption.

. . . Armed with the concept of latent function, the sociologist extends his inquiry in those very directions which promise most for the theoretic development of the discipline. He examines the familiar (or planned) social practice to ascertain the latent, and hence generally unrecognized, functions (as well, of course, as the manifest functions). He considers, for example, the consequences of the new wage plan for, say, the trade union in which the workers are organized or the consequences of a propaganda program, not only for increasing its avowed purpose of stirring up patriotic fervor, but also for making large numbers of people reluctant to speak their minds when they differ with official policies, etc. In short, it is suggested that the *distinctive*

intellectual contributions of the sociologist are found primarily in the study of unintended consequences (among which are latent functions) of social practices, as well as in the study of anticipated consequences (among which are manifest functions).

[Illustration]: The Pattern of Conspicuous Consumption. The manifest purpose of buying consumption goods is, of course, the satisfaction of the needs for which these goods are explicitly designed. Thus, automobiles are obviously intended to provide a certain kind of transportation; candles, to provide light; choice articles of food to provide sustenance; rare art products to provide aesthetic pleasure. Since these products *do* have these uses, it was largely assumed that these encompass the range of socially significant functions. Veblen indeed suggests that this was ordinarily the prevailing view (in the pre-Veblenian era, of course): "The end of acquisition and accumulation is conventionally held to be the

Source: Reprinted with the permission of The Free Press, a Division of Simon & Schuster Adult Publishing Group, from *Social Theory and Social Structure,* revised and enlarged edition by Robert K. Merton. Copyright © 1967, 1968 by Robert K. Merton.

consumption of the goods accumulated. . . . This is at least felt to be the economically legitimate end of acquisition, *which alone it is incumbent on the theory to take account of.*"[1]

However, says Veblen in effect, as sociologists we must go on to consider the latent functions of acquisition, accumulation, and consumption, and these latent functions are remote indeed from the manifest functions. "But, it is only when taken in a sense of far removed from its naive meaning [i.e., manifest function] that the consumption of goods can be said to afford the incentive from which accumulation invariably proceeds." And among these latent functions, which help explain the persistence and the social location of the pattern of conspicuous consumption, is [the fact that] . . . it results in a *heightening or reaffirmation of social status.*

The Veblenian paradox is that people buy expensive goods not so much because they are superior but because they are expensive. For it is the latent equation ("costliness = mark of higher social status") which he singles out in his functional analysis, rather than the manifest equation ("costliness = excellence of the goods"). Not that he denies manifest functions *any* place in buttressing the pattern of conspicuous consumption. These, too, are operative. . . . *It is only that these direct, manifest functions do not fully account for the prevailing patterns of consumption. Otherwise put, if the latent functions of status-enhancement or status-reaffirmation were removed from the patterns of conspicuous consumption, these patterns would undergo severe changes of a sort which the "conventional" economist could not foresee.*

CRITICAL-THINKING QUESTIONS

1. Why, according to Merton, is the study of latent functions one of the important tasks of sociologists?

2. Distinguish between the manifest and latent functions of owning designer clothing, a fine car, or a large home.

3. According to Thorstein Veblen, whom Merton cites in his analysis, does the higher cost of various goods typically reflect their higher quality? Why or why not?

4. Identify some of the manifest and latent functions of (a) a primary school spelling bee, (b) sports, and (c) attending college.

NOTE

1. Thorstein Veblen, *Theory of the Leisure Class* (1899) (New York: Vanguard Press, 1928), p. 25.

11 Cultural Obsessions with Thinness: African American, Latina, and White Women

BECKY W. THOMPSON

According to the American Anorexia/Bulimia Association, 7 million women and 1 million men, ages ten to early twenties, suffer from eating disorders. An estimated 1,000 women die from anorexia every year. From an early age, girls are bombarded with messages that being thin will make them popular and happy and will attract a successful man. In this selection, Becky W. Thompson challenges the widely accepted belief that eating problems are largely limited to white, middle- and upper-class, heterosexual women. Instead of assuming that women are anorexic and bulimic because we live in a "culture of thinness," Thompson argues, eating problems may also be a response to poverty, sexual abuse, racism, heterosexism, social class inequality, and acculturation.

EXISTING RESEARCH ON EATING PROBLEMS

There are three theoretical models used to explain the epidemiology, etiology, and treatment of eating problems. The biomedical model offers important scientific research about possible physiological causes of eating problems and the physiological dangers of purging and starvation (Copeland, 1985; Spack, 1985). However, this model adopts medical treatment strategies that may disempower and traumatize women (Garner, 1985; Orbach, 1985). In addition, this model ignores many social, historical, and cultural factors that influence women's eating patterns. The

Source: Becky W. Thompson, "A Way Outa No Way: Eating Problems among African American, Latina, and White Women," pp. 52–69, in Esther Ngan-Ling Chow, Doris Wilkinson, and Maxine Baca Zinn, eds. *Race, Class & Gender: Common Bonds, Different Voices.* Copyright © 1996 by Sage Publications, Inc. Reprinted by permission of Sage Publications, Inc.

psychological model identifies eating problems as "multidimensional disorders" that are influenced by biological, psychological, and cultural factors (Garfinkel & Garner, 1982). While useful in its exploration of effective therapeutic treatments, this model, like the biomedical one, tends to neglect women of color, lesbians, and working-class women.

The third model, offered by feminists, asserts that eating problems are gendered. This model explains why the vast majority of people with eating problems are women, how gender socialization and sexism may relate to eating problems, and how masculine models of psychological development have shaped theoretical interpretations. Feminists offer the *culture of thinness model* as a key reason why eating problems predominate among women. According to this model, thinness is a culturally, socially, and economically enforced requirement for female beauty.

This imperative makes women vulnerable to cycles of dieting, weight loss, and subsequent weight gain, which may lead to anorexia nervosa and bulimia (Chernin, 1981; Orbach, 1978, 1985; Smead, 1984).

Feminists have rescued eating problems from the realm of individual psychopathology by showing how the difficulties are rooted in systematic and pervasive attempts to control women's body sizes and appetites. However, researchers have yet to give significant attention to how race, class, and sexuality influence women's understanding of their bodies and appetites. The handful of epidemiological studies that include African American women and Latinas casts doubt on the accuracy of the normative epidemiological portrait. The studies suggest that this portrait reflects which particular populations of women have been studied rather than actual prevalence (Anderson & Hay, 1985; Gray, Ford, & Kelly, 1987; Hsu, 1987; Nevo, 1985; Silber, 1986).

More important, this research shows that bias in research has consequences for women of color. Tomas Silber (1986) asserts that many well-trained professionals have either misdiagnosed or delayed their diagnoses of eating problems among African American and Latina women due to stereotypical thinking that these problems are restricted to white women. As a consequence, when African American women or Latinas are diagnosed, their eating problems tend to be more severe due to extended processes of starvation prior to intervention. In her autobiographical account of her eating problems, Retha Powers (1989), an African American woman, describes being told not to worry about her eating problems since "fat is more acceptable in the Black community" (p. 78). Stereotypical perceptions held by her peers and teachers of the "maternal Black woman" and the "persistent mammy–brickhouse Black woman image" (p. 134) made it difficult for Powers to find people who took her problems with food seriously.

Recent work by African American women reveals that eating problems often relate to women's struggles against a "simultaneity of oppressions" (Clarke, 1982; Naylor, 1985; White, 1991). Byllye

Avery (1990), the founder of the National Black Women's Health Project, links the origins of eating problems among African American women to the daily stress of being undervalued and overburdened at home and at work. In Evelyn C. White's (1990) anthology, *The Black Woman's Health Book: Speaking for Ourselves,* Georgiana Arnold (1990) links her eating problems partly to racism and racial isolation during childhood.

Recent feminist research also identifies factors that are related to eating problems among lesbians (Brown, 1987; Dworkin, 1989; Iazzetto, 1989; Schoenfielder & Wieser, 1983). In her clinical work, Brown (1987) found that lesbians who have internalized a high degree of homophobia are more likely to accept negative attitudes about fat than are lesbians who have examined their internalized homophobia. Autobiographical accounts by lesbians have also indicated that secrecy about eating problems among lesbians partly reflects their fear of being associated with a stigmatized illness ("What's Important," 1988).

Attention to African American women, Latinas, and lesbians paves the way for further research that explores the possible interface between facing multiple oppressions and the development of eating problems. In this way, this study is part of a larger feminist and sociological research agenda that seeks to understand how race, class, gender, nationality, and sexuality inform women's experiences and influence theory production.

METHODOLOGY

I conducted eighteen life history interviews and administered lengthy questionnaires to explore eating problems among African American, Latina, and white women. I employed a snowball sample, a method in which potential respondents often first learn about the study from people who have already participated. . . .

Demographics of the Women in the Study

The eighteen women I interviewed included five African American women, five Latinas, and eight white women. Of these women, twelve are lesbian and six are heterosexual. Five women are Jewish, eight are Catholic, and five are Protestant. Three women grew up outside of the United States. The women represented a range of class backgrounds (both in terms of origin and current class status) and ranged in age from nineteen to forty-six years old (with a median age of 33.5 years).

The majority of the women reported having had a combination of eating problems (at least two of the following: bulimia, compulsive eating, anorexia nervosa, and/or extensive dieting). In addition, the particular types of eating problems often changed during a woman's life span. . . .

Two-thirds of the women have had eating problems for more than half of their lives, a finding that contradicts the stereotype of eating problems as transitory. The weight fluctuation among the women varied from 16 to 160 pounds, with an average fluctuation of 74 pounds. This drastic weight change illustrates the degree to which the women adjusted to major changes in body size at least once during their lives as they lost, gained, and lost weight again. The average age of onset was eleven years old, meaning that most of the women developed eating problems prior to puberty. Almost all of the women (88 percent) considered themselves as still having a problem with eating, although the majority believed they were well on the way to recovery.

THE INTERFACE OF TRAUMA AND EATING PROBLEMS

One of the most striking findings in this study was the range of traumas the women associated with the origins of their eating problems, including racism, sexual abuse, poverty, sexism, emotional or physical abuse, heterosexism, class injuries, and acculturation.[1] The particular constellation of eating problems among the women did not vary with race, class, sexuality, or nationality. Women from various race and class backgrounds attributed the origins of their eating problems to sexual abuse, sexism, and emotional

and/or physical abuse. Among some of the African American and Latina women, eating problems were also associated with poverty, racism, and class injuries. Heterosexism was a key factor in the onset of bulimia, compulsive eating, and extensive dieting among some of the lesbians. These oppressions are not the same nor are the injuries caused by them. And certainly, there are a variety of potentially harmful ways that women respond to oppression (such as using drugs, becoming a workaholic, or committing suicide). However, for all these women, eating was a way of coping with trauma.

Sexual Abuse

Sexual abuse was the most common trauma that the women related to the origins of their eating problems. Until recently, there has been virtually no research exploring the possible relationship between these two phenomena. Since the mid-1980s, however, researchers have begun identifying connections between the two, a task that is part of a larger feminist critique of traditional psychoanalytic symptomatology (DeSalvo, 1989; Herman, 1981; Masson, 1984). Results of a number of incidence studies indicate that between one-third and two-thirds of women who have eating problems have been abused (Oppenheimer et al., 1985; Root & Fallon, 1988). In addition, a growing number of therapists and researchers have offered interpretations of the meaning and impact of eating problems for survivors of sexual abuse (Bass & Davis, 1988; Goldfarb, 1987; Iazzetto, 1989; Swink & Leveille, 1986). . . .

Among the women I interviewed, 61 percent were survivors of sexual abuse (eleven of the eighteen women), most of whom made connections between sexual abuse and the beginning of their eating problems. Binging was the most common method of coping identified by the survivors. Binging helped women "numb out" or anesthetize their feelings. Eating sedated, alleviated anxiety, and combated loneliness. Food was something that they could trust and was accessible whenever they needed it. Antonia (a pseudonym) is an Italian American woman who was first sexually abused by a male relative when she was four years old. Retrospectively, she knows that binging was a way she coped with the abuse. When the abuse began, and for many years subsequently, Antonia often woke up during the middle of the night with anxiety attacks or nightmares and would go straight to the kitchen cupboards to get food. Binging helped her block painful feelings because it put her back to sleep.

Like other women in the study who began binging when they were very young, Antonia was not always fully conscious as she binged. She described eating during the night as "sleepwalking. It was mostly desperate—like I had to have it." Describing why she ate after waking up with nightmares, Antonia said, "What else do you do? If you don't have any coping mechanisms, you eat." She said that binging made her "disappear," which made her feel protected. Like Antonia, most of the women were sexually abused before puberty; four of them before they were five years old. Given their youth, food was the most accessible and socially acceptable drug available to them. Because all of the women endured the psychological consequences alone, it is logical that they coped with tactics they could use alone as well.

One reason Antonia binged (rather than dieted) to cope with sexual abuse is that she saw little reason to try to be the small size girls were supposed to be. Growing up as one of the only Italian Americans in what she described as a "very WASP town," Antonia felt that everything from her weight and size to having dark hair on her upper lip were physical characteristics she was supposed to hide. From a young age she knew she "never embodied the essence of the good girl. I don't like her. I have never acted like her. I can't be her. I sort of gave up." For Antonia, her body was the physical entity that signified her outsider status. When the sexual abuse occurred, Antonia felt she had lost her body. In her mind, the body she lived in after the abuse was not really hers. By the time Antonia was eleven, her mother put her on diet pills. Antonia began to eat behind closed doors as she continued to cope with the psychological consequences of sexual abuse and feeling like a cultural outsider.

Extensive dieting and bulimia were also ways in which women responded to sexual abuse. Some women thought that the men had abused them because of their weight. They believed that if they were smaller, they might not have been abused. For example, when Elsa, an Argentine woman, was sexually abused at the age of eleven, she thought her chubby size was the reason the man was abusing her. Elsa said, "I had this notion that these old perverts liked these plump girls. You heard adults say this too. Sex and flesh being associated." Looking back on her childhood, Elsa believes she made fat the enemy partly due to the shame and guilt she felt about the incest. Her belief that fat was the source of her problems was also supported by her socialization. Raised by strict German governesses in an upper-class family, Elsa was taught that a woman's weight was a primary criterion for judging her worth. Her mother "was socially conscious of walking into places with a fat daughter and maybe people staring at her." Her father often referred to Elsa's body as "shot to hell." When asked to describe how she felt about her body when growing up, Elsa described being completely alienated from her body. She explained,

Remember in school when they talk about the difference between body and soul? I always felt like my soul was skinny. My soul was free. My soul sort of flew. I was tied down by this big bag of rocks that was my body. I had to drag it around. It did pretty much what it wanted and I had a lot of trouble controlling it. It kept me from doing all the things that I dreamed of.

As is true for many women who have been abused, the split that Elsa described between her body and soul was an attempt to protect herself from the pain she believed her body caused her. In her mind, her fat body was what had "bashed in her dreams." Dieting became her solution but, as is true for many women in the study, this strategy soon led to cycles of binging and weight fluctuation.

Ruthie, a Puerto Rican woman who was sexually abused from twelve until sixteen years of age, described bulimia as a way she responded to sexual abuse. As a child, Ruthie liked her body. Like many Puerto Rican women of her mother's generation, Ruthie's mother did not want skinny children, interpreting that as a sign that they were sick or being fed improperly. Despite her mother's attempts to make her gain weight, Ruthie remained thin through puberty. When a male relative began sexually abusing her, Ruthie's sense of her body changed dramatically. Although she weighed only one hundred pounds, she began to feel fat and thought her size was causing the abuse. She had seen a movie on television about Romans who made themselves throw up and so she began doing it, in hopes that she could look like the "little kid" she was before the abuse began. Her symbolic attempt to protect herself by purging stands in stark contrast to the psychoanalytic explanation of eating problems as an "abnormal" repudiation of sexuality. In fact, her actions and those of many other survivors indicate a girl's logical attempt to protect herself (including her sexuality) by being a size and shape that does not seem as vulnerable to sexual assault. . . .

Poverty

Like sexual abuse, poverty is another injury that may make women vulnerable to eating problems. One woman I interviewed attributed her eating problems directly to the stress caused by poverty. Yolanda is a Black Cape Verdean mother who began eating compulsively when she was 27 years old. After leaving an abusive husband in her early twenties, Yolanda was forced to go on welfare. As a single mother with small children and few financial resources, she tried to support herself and her children on $539 a month. Yolanda began binging in the evenings after putting her children to bed. Eating was something she could do alone. It would calm her, help her deal with loneliness, and make her feel safe.

Food was an accessible commodity that was cheap. She ate three boxes of macaroni and cheese when nothing else was available. As a single mother with little money, Yolanda felt as if her body was the only thing she had left. As she described it,

I am here, [in my body] 'cause there is no where else for me to go. Where am I going to go? This is all I got . . . that probably contributes to putting on so much weight cause staying in your body, in your home, in yourself, you don't go out. You aren't around other people. . . . You hide and as long as you hide you don't have to face . . . nobody can see you eat. You are safe.

When she was eating, Yolanda felt a momentary reprieve from her worries. Binging not only became a logical solution because it was cheap and easy but also because she had grown up amid positive messages about eating. In her family, eating was a celebrated and joyful act. However, in adulthood, eating became a double-edged sword. While comforting her, binging also led to weight gain. During the three years Yolanda was on welfare, she gained seventy pounds.

Yolanda's story captures how poverty can be a precipitating factor in eating problems and highlights the value of understanding how class inequalities may shape women's eating problems. As a single mother, her financial constraints mirrored those of most female heads of households. The dual hazards of a race- and sex-stratified labor market further limited her options (Higginbotham, 1986). In an article about Black women's health, Byllye Avery quotes a Black woman's explanation about why she eats compulsively (1990:7). The woman told Avery,

I work for General Electric making batteries, and I know it's killing me. My old man is an alcoholic. My kids got babies. Things are not well with me. And one thing I know I can do when I come home is cook me a pot of food and sit down in front of the TV and eat it. And you can't take that away from me until you're ready to give me something in its place.

Like Yolanda, this woman identifies eating compulsively as a quick, accessible, and immediately satisfying way of coping with the daily stress caused by conditions she could not control. Connections between poverty and eating problems also show the limits of portraying eating problems as maladies of upper-class adolescent women.

The fact that many women use food to anesthetize themselves, rather than other drugs (even when they gained access to alcohol, marijuana, and other illegal drugs), is partly a function of gender socialization and the competing demands that women face. One of the physiological consequences of binge eating is a numbed state similar to that experienced by drinking. Troubles and tensions are covered over as a consequence of the body's defensive response to massive food intake. When food is eaten in that way, it effectively works like a drug with immediate and predictable effects. Yolanda said she binged late at night rather than getting drunk because she could still get up in the morning, get her children ready for school, and be clearheaded for the college classes she attended. By binging, she avoided the hangover or sickness that results from alcohol or illegal drugs. In this way, food was her drug of choice, since it was possible for her to eat while she continued to care for her children, drive, cook, and study. Binging is also less expensive than drinking, a factor that is especially significant for poor women. . . .

Heterosexism

The life history interviews also uncovered new connections between heterosexism and eating problems. One of the most important recent feminist contributions has been identifying compulsory heterosexuality as an institution which truncates opportunities for heterosexual and lesbian women (Rich, 1986). All of the women interviewed for this study, both lesbian and heterosexual, were taught that heterosexuality was compulsory, although the versions of this enforcement were shaped by race and class. Expectations about heterosexuality were partly taught through messages that girls learned about eating and their bodies. In some homes, boys were given

more food than girls, especially as teenagers, based on the rationale that girls need to be thin to attract boys. As the girls approached puberty, many were told to stop being athletic, begin wearing dresses, and watch their weight. For the women who weighed more than was considered acceptable, threats about their need to diet were laced with admonitions that being fat would ensure becoming an "old maid."

While compulsory heterosexuality influenced all of the women's emerging sense of their bodies and eating patterns, the women who linked heterosexism directly to the beginning of their eating problems were those who knew they were lesbians when very young and actively resisted heterosexual norms. One working-class Jewish woman, Martha, began compulsively eating when she was eleven years old, the same year she started getting clues of her lesbian identity. In junior high school, as many of her female peers began dating boys, Martha began fantasizing about girls, which made her feel utterly alone. Confused and ashamed about her fantasies, Martha came home every day from school and binged. Binging was a way she drugged herself so that being alone was tolerable. Describing binging, she said, "It was the only thing I knew. I was looking for a comfort." Like many women, Martha binged because it softened painful feelings. Binging sedated her, lessened her anxiety, and induced sleep.

Martha's story also reveals ways that trauma can influence women's experience of their bodies. Like many other women, Martha had no sense of herself as connected to her body. When I asked Martha whether she saw herself as fat when she was growing up she said, "I didn't see myself as fat. I didn't see myself. I wasn't there. I get so sad about that because I missed so much." In the literature on eating problems, *body image* is the term that is typically used to describe a woman's experience of her body. This term connotes the act of imagining one's physical appearance. Typically, women with eating problems are assumed to have difficulties with their body image. However, the term body image does not adequately capture the complexity and range of bodily responses to trauma experienced by the women. Exposure to trauma did much more than distort the women's visual image of themselves. These traumas often jeopardized their capacity to consider themselves as having bodies at all. . . .

Racism and Class Injuries

For some of the Latinas and African American women, racism coupled with the stress resulting from class mobility related to the onset of their eating problems. Joselyn, an African American woman, remembered her white grandmother telling her she would never be as pretty as her cousins because they were lighter skinned. Her grandmother often humiliated Joselyn in front of others, as she made fun of Joselyn's body while she was naked and told her she was fat. As a young child, Joselyn began to think that although she could not change her skin color, she could at least try to be thin. When Joselyn was young, her grandmother was the only family member who objected to Joselyn's weight. However, her father also began encouraging his wife and daughter to be thin as the family's class standing began to change. When the family was working class, serving big meals, having chubby children, and keeping plenty of food in the house was a sign the family was doing well. But, as the family became mobile, Joselyn's father began insisting that Joselyn be thin. She remembered, "When my father's business began to bloom and my father was interacting more with white businessmen and seeing how they did business, suddenly thin became important. If you were a truly well-to-do family, then your family was slim and elegant."

As Joselyn's grandmother used Joselyn's body as territory for enforcing her own racism and prejudice about size, Joselyn's father used her body as the territory through which he channeled the demands he faced in the white-dominated business world. However, as Joselyn was pressured to diet, her father still served her large portions and bought

treats for her and the neighborhood children. These contradictory messages made her feel confused about her body. As was true for many women in this study, Joselyn was told she was fat beginning when she was very young even though she was not overweight. And, like most of the women, Joselyn was put on diet pills and diets before even reaching puberty, beginning the cycles of dieting, compulsive eating, and bulimia.

The confusion about body size expectations that Joselyn associated with changes in class paralleled one Puerto Rican woman's association between her eating problems and the stress of assimilation as her family's class standing moved from poverty to working class. When Vera was very young, she was so thin that her mother took her to a doctor who prescribed appetite stimulants. However, by the time Vera was eight years old, her mother began trying to shame Vera into dieting. Looking back on it, Vera attributed her mother's change of heart to competition among extended family members that centered on "being white, being successful, being middle class, . . . and it was always, 'Ay Bendito. She is so fat. What happened?'"

The fact that some of the African American and Latina women associated the ambivalent messages about food and eating to their family's class mobility and/or the demands of assimilation while none of the eight white women expressed this (including those whose class was stable and changing) suggests that the added dimension of racism was connected to the imperative to be thin. In fact, the class expectations that their parents experienced exacerbated standards about weight that they inflicted on their daughters.

EATING PROBLEMS AS SURVIVAL STRATEGIES

My research permits a reevaluation of many assumptions about eating problems. First, this work challenges the theoretical reliance on the culture-of-thinness model. Although all of the women I interviewed were manipulated and hurt by this imperative at some point in their lives, it is not the primary source of their problems. Even in the instances in which a culture of thinness was a precipitating factor in anorexia, bulimia, or binging, this influence occurred in concert with other oppressions.

Attributing the etiology of eating problems primarily to a woman's striving to attain a certain beauty ideal is also problematic because it labels a common way that women cope with pain as essentially appearance-based disorders. One blatant example of sexism is the notion that women's foremost worry is about their appearance. By focusing on the emphasis on slenderness, the eating problems literature falls into the same trap of assuming that the problems reflect women's "obsession" with appearance. Some women were raised in families and communities in which thinness was not considered a criterion for beauty. Yet they still developed eating problems. Other women were taught that women should be thin but their eating problems were not primarily in reaction to this imperative. Their eating strategies began as logical solutions to problems rather than problems themselves as they tried to cope with a variety of traumas.

Establishing links between eating problems and a range of oppressions invites a rethinking of both the groups of women who have been excluded from research and those whose lives have been the basis of theory formation. The construction of bulimia and anorexia nervosa as appearance-based disorders is rooted in a notion of femininity in which white middle- and upper-class women are portrayed as frivolous, obsessed with their bodies, and overly accepting of narrow gender roles. This portrayal fuels women's tremendous shame and guilt about eating problems—as signs of self-centered vanity. This construction of white middle- and upper-class women is intimately linked to the portrayal of working-class white women and women of color as their opposite: as somehow exempt from accepting the dominant standards of beauty or as one step away from being hungry and therefore not susceptible to eating problems.

Identifying that women may binge to cope with poverty contrasts the notion that eating problems are class bound. Attending to the intricacies of race, class, sexuality, and gender pushes us to rethink the demeaning construction of middle-class femininity and establishes bulimia and anorexia nervosa as serious responses to injustices.

CRITICAL-THINKING QUESTIONS

1. How do the biomedical, psychological, and feminist models differ in explaining eating disorders?

2. Why does Thompson argue that eating problems are survival strategies to cope with sexism; heterosexism; and emotional, sexual, or physical abuse?

3. Thompson maintains that women's eating problems are a response to poverty, racism, acculturation, and social class inequality. How, then, might we explain the low rates of eating disorders among Black, ethnic, and low-income men?

NOTE

1. By trauma I mean a violating experience that has long-term emotional, physical, and/or spiritual consequences that may have immediate or delayed effects. One reason the term *trauma* is useful conceptually is its association with the diagnostic label Post Traumatic Stress Disorder (PTSD) (American Psychological Association, 1987). PTSD is one of the few clinical diagnostic categories that recognizes social problems (such as war or the Holocaust) as responsible for the symptoms identified (Trimble, 1985). This concept adapts well to the feminist assertion that a woman's symptoms cannot be understood as solely individual, considered outside of her social context, or prevented without significant changes in social conditions.

REFERENCES

AMERICAN PSYCHOLOGICAL ASSOCIATION. 1987. *Diagnostic and statistical manual of mental disorders.* 3rd ed. rev. Washington, D.C.: American Psychological Association.

ANDERSEN, ARNOLD, and ANDY HAY. 1985. Racial and socioeconomic influences in anorexia nervosa and bulimia. *International Journal of Eating Disorders* 4: 479–87.

ARNOLD, GEORGIANA. 1990. Coming home: One Black woman's journey to health and fitness. In *The Black women's health book: Speaking for ourselves,* ed. Evelyn C. White. Seattle, Wash. Seal Press.

AVERY, BYLLYE Y. 1990. Breathing life into ourselves: The evolution of the National Black Women's Health Project. In *The Black women's health book: Speaking for ourselves,* ed. Evelyn C. White. Seattle, Wash.: Seal Press.

BASS, ELLEN, and LAURA DAVIS. 1988. *The courage to heal: A guide for women survivors of child sexual abuse.* New York: Harper & Row.

BROWN, LAURA S. 1987. Lesbians, weight and eating: New analyses and perspectives. In *Lesbian psychologies,* ed. Boston Lesbian Psychologies Collective. Champaign: University of Illinois Press.

CHERNIN, KIM. 1981. *The obsession: Reflections on the tyranny of slenderness.* New York: Harper & Row.

CLARKE, CHERYL. 1982. *Narratives.* New Brunswick, N.J.: Sister Books.

COPELAND, PAUL M. 1985. Neuroendocrine aspects of eating disorders. In *Theory and treatment of anorexia nervosa and bulimia: Biomedical, sociocultural and psychological perspectives,* ed. Steven Wiley Emmett. New York: Brunner/Mazel.

DESALVO, LOUISE. 1989. *Virginia Woolf: The impact of childhood sexual abuse on her life and work.* Boston: Beacon.

DWORKIN, SARI H. 1989. Not in man's image: Lesbians and the cultural oppression of body image. In *Loving boldly: Issues facing lesbians,* ed. Ester D. Rothblum and Ellen Close. New York: Harrington Park.

GARFINKEL, PAUL E., and DAVID M. GARNER. 1982. *Anorexia nervosa: A multidimensional perspective.* New York: Brunner/Mazel.

GARNER, DAVID. 1985. Iatrogenesis in anorexia nervosa and bulimia nervosa. *International Journal of Eating Disorders* 4: 701–26.

GOLDFARB, LORI. 1987. Sexual abuse antecedent to anorexia nervosa, bulimia and compulsive overeating: Three case reports. *International Journal of Eating Disorders* 6: 675–80.

GRAY, JAMES, KATHRYN FORD, and LILY M. KELLY. 1987. The prevalence of bulimia in a Black college population. *International Journal of Eating Disorders* 6: 733–40.

HERMAN, JUDITH. 1981. *Father–daughter incest.* Cambridge, Mass.: Harvard University Press.

HIGGINBOTHAM, ELIZABETH. 1986. We were never on a pedestal: Women of color continue to struggle with poverty, racism and sexism. In *For crying out loud,* ed. Rochelle Lefkowitz and Ann Withorn. Boston: Pilgrim.

HSU, GEORGE. 1987. Are eating disorders becoming more common in Blacks? *International Journal of Eating Disorders* 6: 13–24.

IAZZETTO, DEMETRIA. 1989. When the body is not an easy place to be: Women's sexual abuse and eating problems. Ph.D. diss., Union for Experimenting Colleges and Universities, Cincinnati.

MASSON, JEFFREY. 1984. *The assault on the truth: Freud's suppression of the seduction theory.* New York: Farrar, Strauss & Giroux.

NAYLOR, GLORIA. 1985. *Linden Hills.* New York: Ticknor & Fields.

NEVO, SHOSHANA. 1985. Bulimic symptoms: Prevalence and ethnic differences among college women. *International Journal of Eating Disorders* 4: 151–68.

OPPENHEIMER, R., K. HOWELLS, R. L. PALMER, and D. A. CHALONER. 1985. Adverse sexual experience in childhood and clinical eating disorders: A preliminary description. *Journal of Psychiatric Research* 19: 357–61.

ORBACH, SUSIE. 1978. *Fat is a feminist issue.* New York: Paddington.

———. 1985. Accepting the symptom: A feminist psychoanalytic treatment of anorexia nervosa. In *Handbook of psychotherapy for anorexia nervosa and bulimia,* ed. David M. Garner and Paul E. Garfinkel. New York: Guilford.

POWERS, RETHA. 1989. Fat is a Black women's issue. *Essence* (October): 75, 78, 134, 136.

RICH, ADRIENNE. 1986. Compulsory heterosexuality and lesbian existence. In *Blood, bread and poetry.* New York: Norton.

ROOT, MARIA P. P., and PATRICIA FALLON. 1988. The incidence of victimization experiences in a bulimic sample. *Journal of Interpersonal Violence* 3: 161–73.

SCHOENFIELDER, LISA, and BARBARA WIESER, eds. 1983. *Shadow on a tightrope: Writings by women about fat liberation.* Iowa City: Aunt Lute Book Co.

SILBER, TOMAS. 1986. Anorexia nervosa in Blacks and Hispanics. *International Journal of Eating Disorders* 5: 121–28.

SMEAD, VALERIE. 1984. Eating behaviors which may lead to and perpetuate anorexia nervosa, bulimarexia, and bulimia. *Women and Therapy* 3: 37–49.

SPACK, NORMAN. 1985. Medical complications of anorexia nervosa and bulimia. In *Theory and treatment of anorexia nervosa and bulimia: Biomedical, sociocultural and psychological perspectives,* ed. Steven Wiley Emmett. New York: Brunner/Mazel.

SWINK, KATHY, and ANTOINETTE E. LEVEILLE. 1986. From victim to survivor: A new look at the issues and recovery process for adult incest survivors. *Women and Therapy* 5: 119–43.

TRIMBLE, MICHAEL. 1985. Post-traumatic stress disorder: History of a concept. In *Trauma and its wake: The study and treatment of post-traumatic stress disorder,* ed. C. R. Figley. New York: Brunner/Mazel.

What's important is what you look like. 1988. *Gay Community News* (July): 24–30.

WHITE, EVELYN C., ed. 1990. *The Black women's health book: Speaking for ourselves.* Seattle, Wash.: Seal Press.

———. 1991. Unhealthy appetites. *Essence* (September): 28, 30.

12 India's Sacred Cow

MARVIN HARRIS

Anthropologist Marvin Harris uses the approach of cultural ecology to investigate how exotic and seemingly inexplicable cultural patterns may turn out to be everyday strategies for human survival in a particular natural environment. In this article, he offers his own favorite example: Why do people in India—many of whom are hungry—refuse to eat beef from the "sacred cows" that are found most everywhere?

Whenever I get into discussions about the influence of practical and mundane factors on lifestyles, someone is sure to say, "But what about all those cows the hungry peasants in India refuse to eat?" The picture of a ragged farmer starving to death alongside a big fat cow conveys a reassuring sense of mystery to Western observers. In countless learned and popular allusions, it confirms our deepest conviction about how people with inscrutable Oriental minds ought to act. It is comforting to know—somewhat like "there will always be an England"—that in India spiritual values are more precious than life itself. And at the same time it makes us feel sad. How can we ever hope to understand people so different from ourselves? Westerners find the idea that there might be a practical explanation for Hindu love of the cow more upsetting than Hindus do. The sacred cow—how else can I say it?—is one of our favorite sacred cows.

Source: From *Cows, Pigs, Wars, and Witches: The Riddles of Culture* by Marvin Harris. Copyright © 1974 by Marvin Harris, Random House. Reprinted with permission of Random House, Inc.

Hindus venerate cows because cows are the symbol of everything that is alive. As Mary is to Christians the mother of God, the cow to Hindus is the mother of life. So there is no greater sacrilege for a Hindu than killing a cow. Even the taking of human life lacks the symbolic meaning, the unutterable defilement, that is evoked by cow slaughter.

According to many experts, cow worship is the number one cause of India's hunger and poverty. Some Western-trained agronomists say that the taboo against cow slaughter is keeping 100 million "useless" animals alive. They claim that cow worship lowers the efficiency of agriculture because the useless animals contribute neither milk nor meat while competing for croplands and food-stuff with useful animals and hungry human beings. . . .

It does seem that there are enormous numbers of surplus, useless, and uneconomic animals, and that this situation is a direct result of irrational Hindu doctrines. Tourists on their way through Delhi, Calcutta, Madras, Bombay, and other Indian cities are astonished at the liberties enjoyed

51

by stray cattle. The animals wander through the streets, browse off the stalls in the market place, break into private gardens, defecate all over the sidewalks, and snarl traffic by pausing to chew their cuds in the middle of busy intersections. In the countryside, the cattle congregate on the shoulders of every highway and spend much of their time taking leisurely walks down the railroad tracks.

To Western observers familiar with modern industrial techniques of agriculture and stock raising, cow love seems senseless, even suicidal. The efficiency expert yearns to get his hands on all those useless animals and ship them off to a proper fate. And yet one finds certain inconsistencies in the condemnation of cow love. When I began to wonder if there might be a practical explanation for the sacred cow, I came across an intriguing government report. It said that India had too many cows but too few oxen. With so many cows around, how could there be a shortage of oxen? Oxen and male water buffalo are the principal source of traction for plowing India's fields. For each farm of ten acres or less, one pair of oxen or water buffalo is considered adequate. A little arithmetic shows that as far as plowing is concerned, there is indeed a shortage rather than a surplus of animals. India has 60 million farms, but only 80 million traction animals. If each farm had its quota of two oxen or two water buffalo, there ought to be 120 million traction animals—that is, 40 million more than are actually available.

The shortage may not be quite so bad, since some farmers rent or borrow oxen from their neighbors. But the sharing of plow animals often proves impractical. Plowing must be coordinated with the monsoon rains, and by the time one farm has been plowed, the optimum moment for plowing another may already have passed. Also, after plowing is over, a farmer still needs his own pair of oxen to pull his oxcart, the mainstay of the bulk transport throughout rural India. Quite possibly private ownership of farms, livestock, plows, and oxcarts lowers the efficiency of Indian agriculture, but this, I soon realized, was not caused by cow love.

The shortage of draft animals is a terrible threat that hangs over most of India's peasant families. When an ox falls sick a poor farmer is in danger of losing his farm. If he has no replacement for it, he will have to borrow money at usurious rates. Millions of rural households have in fact lost all or part of their holdings and have gone into sharecropping or day labor as a result of such debts. Each year hundreds of thousands of destitute farmers end up migrating to the cities, which already teem with unemployed and homeless persons.

The Indian farmer who can't replace his sick or deceased ox is in much the same situation as an American farmer who can neither replace nor repair his broken tractor. But there is an important difference: Tractors are made by factories, but oxen are made by cows. A farmer who owns a cow owns a factory for making oxen. With or without cow love, this is a good reason for him not to be too anxious to sell his cow to the slaughterhouse. One also begins to see why Indian farmers might be willing to tolerate cows that give only 500 pounds of milk per year. If the main economic function of the zebu cow is to breed male traction animals, then there's no point in comparing her with specialized American dairy animals, whose main function is to produce milk. Still, the milk produced by zebu cows plays an important role in meeting the nutritional needs of many poor families. Even small amounts of milk products can improve the health of people who are forced to subsist on the edge of starvation.

Agriculture is part of a vast system of human and natural relationships. To judge isolated portions of this "ecosystem" in terms that are relevant to the conduct of American agribusiness leads to some very strange impressions. Cattle figure in the Indian ecosystem in ways that are easily overlooked or demeaned by observers from industrialized, high-energy societies. In the United States, chemicals have almost completely replaced animal manure as the principal source of farm fertilizer. American farmers stopped using manure when they began to plow with tractors rather than mules or horses. Since tractors excrete poisons rather than fertilizers, a commitment to large-scale machine farming is almost of necessity a commitment to the use of chemical fertilizers. And around the world today there has in fact grown up a vast integrated petrochemical-tractor-truck industrial complex that produces farm machinery, motorized transport, oil and gasoline, and chemical fertilizers and pesticides upon which new high-yield production techniques depend.

For better or worse, most of India's farmers cannot participate in this complex, not because they worship their cows, but because they can't afford to buy tractors. Like other underdeveloped nations, India can't build factories that are competitive with the facilities of the industrialized nations nor pay for large quantities of imported industrial products. To convert from animals and manure to tractors and petrochemicals would require the investment of incredible amounts of capital. Moreover, the inevitable effect of substituting costly machines for cheap animals is to reduce the number of people who can earn their living from agriculture and to force a corresponding increase in the size of the average farm. We know that the development of large-scale agribusiness in the United States has meant the virtual destruction of the small family farm. Less than 5 percent of U.S. families now live on farms, as compared with 60 percent about a hundred years ago. If agribusiness were to develop along similar lines in India, jobs and housing would soon have to be found for a quarter of a billion displaced peasants.

Since the suffering caused by unemployment and homelessness in India's cities is already intolerable, an additional massive build-up of the urban population can only lead to unprecedented upheavals and catastrophes.

With this alternative in view, it becomes easier to understand low-energy, small-scale, animal-based systems. As I have already pointed out, cows and oxen provide low-energy substitutes for tractors and tractor factories. They also should be credited with carrying out the functions of a petrochemical industry. India's cattle annually excrete about 700 million tons of recoverable manure. Approximately half of this total is used as fertilizer, while most of the remainder is burned to provide heat for cooking. The annual quantity of heat liberated by this dung, the Indian housewife's main cooking fuel, is the thermal equivalent of 27 million tons of kerosene, 35 million tons of coal, or 68 million tons of wood. Since India has only small reserves of oil and coal and is already the victim of extensive deforestation, none of these fuels can be considered practical substitutes for cow dung. The thought of dung in the kitchen may not appeal to the average American, but Indian women regard it as a superior cooking fuel because it is finely adjusted to their domestic routines. Most Indian dishes are prepared with clarified butter known as *ghee*, for which cow dung is the preferred source of heat since it burns with a clean, slow, long-lasting flame that doesn't scorch the food. This enables the Indian housewife to start cooking her meals and to leave them unattended for several hours while she takes care of the children, helps out in the fields, or performs other chores. American housewives achieve a similar effect through a complex set of electronic controls that come as expensive options on late-model stoves.

Cow dung has at least one other major function. Mixed with water and made into a paste, it is used as a household flooring material. Smeared over a dirt floor and left to harden into a smooth surface, it keeps the dust down and can be swept clean with a broom.

Because cattle droppings have so many useful properties, every bit of dung is carefully collected. Village small fry are given the task of following the family cow around and of bringing home its daily petrochemical output. In the cities, sweeper castes enjoy a monopoly on the dung deposited by strays and earn their living by selling it to housewives. . . .

During droughts and famines, farmers are severely tempted to kill or sell their livestock.

Those who succumb to this temptation seal their doom, even if they survive the drought, for when the rains come, they will be unable to plow their fields. I want to be even more emphatic: Massive slaughter of cattle under the duress of famine constitutes a much greater threat to aggregate welfare than any likely miscalculation by particular farmers concerning the usefulness of their animals during normal times. It seems probable that the sense of unutterable profanity elicited by cow slaughter has its roots in the excruciating contradiction between immediate needs and long-term conditions of survival. Cow love with its sacred symbols and holy doctrines protects the farmer against calculations that are "rational" only in the short term. To Western experts it looks as if "the Indian farmer would rather starve to death than eat his cow." . . . They don't realize that the farmer would rather eat his cow than starve, but that he will starve if he does eat it. . . .

Do I mean to say that cow love has no effect whatsoever on . . . the agricultural system? No. What I am saying is that cow love is an active element in a complex, finely articulated material and cultural order. Cow love mobilizes the latent capacity of human beings to persevere in a low-energy ecosystem in which there is little room for waste or indolence. Cow love contributes to the adaptive resilience of the human population by preserving temporarily dry or barren but still useful animals; by discouraging the growth of an energy-expensive beef industry; by protecting cattle that fatten in the public domain or at landlord's expense; and by preserving the recovery potential of the cattle population during droughts and famines. . . .

Wastefulness is more a characteristic of modern agribusiness than of traditional peasant economies. . . .

Automobiles and airplanes are faster than oxcarts, but they do not use energy more efficiently. In fact, more calories go up in useless heat and smoke during a single day of traffic jams in the United States than is wasted by all the cows of India during an entire year. The comparison is even less favorable when we consider the fact that the stalled vehicles are burning up irreplaceable reserves of petroleum that it took the earth tens of millions of years to accumulate. If you want to see a real sacred cow, go out and look at the family car.

CRITICAL-THINKING QUESTIONS

1. What evidence does Harris offer to support his argument that defining the cow as sacred is a necessary strategy for human survival in India?

2. If survival strategies make sense when we take a close look at them, why do they become so "encased" in elaborate cultural explanations?

3. Does India's recognition of the sacred cow help or hurt that nation's natural environment?

4. Following Harris's logic, can you think of reasons that people in some parts of the world (the Middle East, for instance) do not eat pork?

CLASSIC

CONTEMPORARY

CROSS-CULTURAL

13 Manifesto of the Communist Party

KARL MARX AND FRIEDRICH ENGELS

Karl Marx, collaborating with Friedrich Engels, produced the "Manifesto" in 1848. This document is a well-known statement about the origin of social conflict in the process of material production. The ideas of Marx and Engels have been instrumental in shaping the political lives of more than one-fifth of the world's population, and, of course, they have been instrumental in the development of the social-conflict paradigm in sociology.

BOURGEOIS AND PROLETARIANS[1]

The history of all hitherto existing society[2] is the history of class struggles.

Freeman and slave, patrician and plebeian, lord and serf, guild-master[3] and journeyman, in a word, oppressor and oppressed, stood in constant opposition to one another, carried on an uninterrupted, now hidden, now open fight, a fight that each time ended, either in a revolutionary reconstitution of society at large, or in the common ruin of the contending classes.

In the earlier epochs of history, we find almost everywhere a complicated arrangement of society into various orders, a manifold gradation of social rank. In ancient Rome we have patricians, knights, plebeians, slaves; in the Middle Ages, feudal lords,

Source: From *Manifesto of the Communist Party,* Part I, by Karl Marx and Friedrich Engels.

vassals, guild-masters, journeymen, apprentices, serfs; in almost all of these classes, again, subordinate gradations.

The modern bourgeois society that has sprouted from the ruins of feudal society has not done away with class antagonisms. It has but established new classes, new conditions of oppression, new forms of struggle in place of the old ones.

Our epoch, the epoch of the bourgeoisie, possesses, however, this distinctive feature; it has simplified the class antagonisms. Society as a whole is more and more splitting up into two great hostile camps, into two great classes directly facing each other: Bourgeoisie and Proletariat.

From the serfs of the Middle Ages sprang the chartered burghers of the earliest towns. From these burgesses the first elements of the bourgeoisie were developed.

The discovery of America, the rounding of the Cape, opened up fresh ground for the rising bourgeoisie. The East Indian and Chinese markets, the [colonization] of America, trade with the colonies, the increase in the means of exchange and in commodities generally, gave to commerce, to navigation, to industry, an impulse never before known, and thereby, to the revolutionary element in the tottering feudal society, a rapid development.

The feudal system of industry, under which industrial production was monopolized by close guilds, now no longer sufficed for the growing wants of the new markets. The manufacturing system took its place. The guild-masters were pushed on one side by the manufacturing middle class; division of labor between the different corporate guilds vanished in the face of division of labor in each single workshop.

Meantime the markets kept ever growing, the demand, ever rising. Even manufacture no longer sufficed. Thereupon, steam and machinery revolutionized industrial production. The place of manufacture was taken by the giant, Modern Industry, the place of the industrial middle class, by industrial millionaires, the leaders of whole industrial armies, the modern bourgeois.

Modern industry has established the world-market, for which the discovery of America paved the way. This market has given an immense development to commerce, to navigation, to communication by land. This development has, in its turn, reacted on the extension of industry; and in proportion as industry, commerce, navigation, railways extended, in the same proportion the bourgeoisie developed, increased its capital, and pushed into the background every class handed down from the Middle Ages.

We see, therefore, how the modern bourgeoisie is itself the product of a long course of development, of a series of revolutions in the modes of production and of exchange.

Each step in the development of the bourgeoisie was accompanied by a corresponding political advance of that class. An oppressed class under the sway of the feudal nobility, an armed and self-governing association in the mediaeval commune,[4] here independent urban republic (as in Italy and Germany), there taxable "third estate" of the monarchy (as in France), afterwards, in the period of manufacture proper, serving either the semi-feudal or the absolute monarchy as a counterpoise against the nobility, and, in fact, cornerstone of the great monarchies in general, the bourgeoisie has at last, since the establishment of modern industry and of the world-market, conquered for itself, in the modern representative State, exclusive political sway. The executive of the modern State is but a committee for managing the common affairs of the whole bourgeoisie.

The bourgeoisie, historically, has played a most revolutionary part.

The bourgeoisie, wherever it has got the upper hand, has put an end to all feudal, patriarchal, idyllic relations. It has pitilessly torn asunder the motley feudal ties that bound man to his "natural superiors," and has left remaining no other nexus between man and man than naked self-interest, than callous "cash payment." It has drowned the most heavenly ecstasies of religious fervour, of chivalrous enthusiasm, of philistine sentimentalism, in the icy water of egotistical calculation. It has resolved personal worth into exchange value, and in place of the numberless indefeasible chartered freedoms, has set up that single, unconscionable freedom—Free Trade. In one word, for exploitation, veiled by religious and political illusions, it has substituted naked, shameless, direct, brutal exploitation.

The bourgeoisie has stripped of its halo every occupation hitherto honoured and looked up to with reverent awe. It has converted the physician, the lawyer, the priest, the poet, the man of science, into its paid [wage-laborers].

The bourgeoisie has torn away from the family its sentimental veil, and has reduced the family relation to a mere money relation.

The bourgeoisie has disclosed how it came to pass that the brutal display of vigour in the Middle Ages, which reactionists so much admire, found its fitting complement in the most slothful indolence. It has been the first to show what man's activity can bring about. It has accomplished wonders far surpassing Egyptian pyramids, Roman aqueducts, and Gothic cathedrals; it has conducted expeditions that put in the shade all former Exoduses of nations and crusades.

The bourgeoisie cannot exist without constantly revolutionizing the instruments of production, and thereby the relations of production, and with them the whole relations of society. Conservation of the old modes of production in unaltered form, was, on the contrary, the first condition of existence for all earlier industrial classes. Constant revolutionizing of production, uninterrupted disturbance of all social conditions, everlasting uncertainty and agitation distinguish the bourgeois epoch from all earlier ones. All fixed, fast-frozen relations, with their train of ancient and venerable prejudices and opinions, are swept away, all new-formed ones become antiquated before they can ossify. All that is solid melts into air, all that is holy is profaned, and man is at last compelled to face with sober senses, his real conditions of life, and his relations with his kind.

The need of a constantly expanding market for its products chases the bourgeoisie over the whole surface of the globe. It must nestle everywhere, settle everywhere, establish [connections] everywhere.

The bourgeoisie has through its exploitation of the world-market given a cosmopolitan character to production and consumption in every country. To the great chagrin of reactionists, it has drawn from under the feet of industry the national ground on which it stood. All old-established national industries have been destroyed or are daily being destroyed. They are dislodged by new industries, whose introduction becomes a life and death question for all civilised nations, by industries that no longer work up indigenous raw material, but raw material drawn from the remotest zones; industries whose products are consumed, not only at home, but in every quarter of the globe. In place of the old wants, satisfied by the productions of the country, we find new wants, requiring for their satisfaction the products of distant lands and climes. In place of the old local and national seclusion and self-sufficiency, we have intercourse in every direction, universal interdependence of nations. And as in material, so also in intellectual production. The intellectual creations of individual nations become common property. National one-sidedness and narrow-mindedness become more and more impossible, and from the numerous national and local literatures there arises a world-literature.

The bourgeoisie, by the rapid improvement of all instruments of production, by the immensely facilitated means of communication, draws all, even the most barbarian, nations into civilization. The cheap prices of its commodities are the heavy artillery with which it batters down all Chinese walls, with which it forces the barbarians' intensely obstinate hatred of foreigners to capitulate. It compels all nations, on pain of extinction, to adopt the bourgeois mode of production; it compels them to introduce what it calls civilization into their midst, i.e., to become bourgeois themselves. In a word, it creates a world after its own image.

The bourgeoisie has subjected the country to the rule of the towns. It has created enormous cities, has greatly increased the urban population as compared with the rural, and has thus rescued a considerable part of the population from the idiocy of rural life. Just as it has made the country dependent on the towns, so it has made barbarian and semi-barbarian countries dependent on the civilised ones, nations of peasants on nations of bourgeois, the East on the West.

The bourgeoisie keeps more and more doing away with the scattered state of the population, of the means of production, and of property. It has agglomerated population, centralized means of production, and has concentrated property in a few hands. The necessary consequence of this was political centralization. Independent, or but loosely connected provinces, with separate interests, laws, governments and systems of taxation, became lumped together in one nation, with one government, one code of laws, one national class-interest, one frontier and one customs-tariff.

The bourgeoisie, during its rule of scarce one hundred years, has created more massive and more colossal productive forces than have all preceding generations together. Subjection of Nature's forces to man, machinery, application of chemistry to industry and agriculture, steam-navigation, railways, electric telegraphs, clearing of whole continents for cultivation, canalization of rivers, whole populations conjured out of the ground—what earlier century had even a presentiment that such productive forces slumbered in the lap of social labor?

We see then: The means of production and of exchange on whose foundation the bourgeoisie built itself up, were generated in feudal society. At a certain stage in the development of these means of production and of exchange, the conditions under which feudal society produced and exchanged, the feudal organization of agriculture and manufacturing industry, in one word, the feudal relations of property became no longer compatible with the already developed productive forces; they became so many fetters. They had to burst asunder; they were burst asunder.

Into their places stepped free competition, accompanied by a social and political constitution adapted to it, and by the economical and political sway of the bourgeois class.

A similar movement is going on before our own eyes. Modern bourgeois society with its relations of production, of exchange and of property, a society that has conjured up such gigantic means of production and of exchange, is like the sorcerer, who is no longer able to control the powers of the nether world whom he has called up by his spells. For many a decade past the history of industry and commerce is but the history of the revolt of modern productive forces against modern conditions of production, against the property relations that are the conditions for the existence of the bourgeoisie and of its rule. It is enough to mention the commercial crises that by their periodical return put on its trial, each time more threateningly, the existence of the entire bourgeois society. In these crises a great part not only of the existing products, but also of the previously created productive forces, are periodically destroyed. In these crises there breaks out an epidemic that, in all earlier epochs, would have seemed an absurdity—the epidemic of overproduction. Society suddenly finds itself put back into a state of momentary barbarism; it appears as if a famine, a universal war of devastation had cut off the supply of every means of subsistence; industry and commerce seem to be destroyed; and why? Because there is too much civilization, too much means of subsistence, too much industry, too much commerce. The productive forces at the disposal of society no longer tend to further the development of the conditions of bourgeois property; on the contrary, they have become too powerful for these conditions, by which they are fettered, and so soon as they overcome these fetters, they bring disorder into the whole of bourgeois society, endanger the existence of bourgeois property. The conditions of bourgeois society are too narrow to comprise the wealth created by them. And how does the bourgeoisie get over these crises? On the one hand by enforced destruction of a mass of productive forces; on the other, by the conquest of new markets, and by the more thorough exploitation of the old ones. That is to say, by paving the way for more extensive and more destructive crises, and by diminishing the means whereby crises are prevented.

The weapons with which the bourgeoisie felled feudalism to the ground are now turned against the bourgeoisie itself.

But not only has the bourgeoisie forged the weapons that bring death to itself; it has also called into existence the men who are to wield those weapons—the modern working class—the proletarians.

In proportion as the bourgeoisie, i.e., capital, is developed, in the same proportion is the proletariat, the modern working class, developed, a class of laborers, who live only so long as they find work, and who find work only so long as their labor increases capital. These laborers, who must sell themselves piecemeal, are a commodity, like every other article of commerce, and are consequently exposed to all the vicissitudes of competition, to all the fluctuations of the market.

Owing to the extensive use of machinery and to division of labor, the work of the proletarians has lost all individual character, and, consequently, all charm for the workman. He becomes an appendage of the machine, and it is only the most simple, most monotonous and most easily acquired knack that is required of him. Hence, the cost of production of a workman is restricted, almost entirely, to the means of subsistence that he requires for his maintenance, and for the propagation of his race. But the price of a commodity, and also of labor, is equal to its cost of production. In proportion, therefore, as the repulsiveness of the work increases, the wage decreases. Nay more, in proportion as the use of machinery and division of labor increases, in the same proportion the burden of toil also increases, whether by prolongation of the working hours, by increase of the work enacted in a given time, or by increased speed of the machinery, etc.

Modern industry has converted the little workshop of the patriarchal master into the great factory of the industrial capitalist. Masses of laborers, crowded into the factory, are organized like soldiers. As privates of the industrial army they are placed under the command of a perfect hierarchy of officers and sergeants. Not only are they the slaves of the bourgeois class, and of the bourgeois State, they are daily and hourly enslaved by the machine, by the over-looker, and, above all, by the individual bourgeois manufacturer himself. The more openly this despotism proclaims gain to be its end and aim, the more petty, the more hateful and the more embittering it is.

The less the skill and exertion or strength implied in manual labor, in other words, the more modern industry becomes developed, the more is the labor of men superseded by that of women. Differences of age and sex have no longer any distinctive social validity for the working class. All are instruments of labor, more or less expensive to use, according to their age and sex.

No sooner is the exploitation of the laborer by the manufacturer, so far, at an end, that he receives his wages in cash, than he is set upon by the other portions of the bourgeoisie, the landlord, the shopkeeper, the pawnbroker, etc.

The lower strata of the middle class—the small tradespeople, shopkeepers, and retired tradesmen generally, the handicraftsmen and peasants—all these sink gradually into the proletariat, partly because their diminutive capital does not suffice for the scale on which Modern Industry is carried on, and is swamped in the competition with the large capitalists, partly because their specialised skill is rendered worthless by new methods of production. Thus the proletariat is recruited from all classes of the population.

The proletariat goes through various stages of development. With its birth begins its struggle with the bourgeoisie. At first the contest is carried on by individual laborers, then by the workpeople of a factory, then by the operatives of one trade, in one locality, against the individual bourgeois who directly exploits them. They direct their attacks not against the bourgeois conditions of production, but against the instruments of production themselves; they destroy imported wares that compete with their labor, they smash to pieces machinery, they set factories ablaze, they seek to restore by force the vanished status of the workman of the Middle Ages.

At this stage the laborers still form an incoherent mass scattered over the whole country, and broken up by their mutual competition. If anywhere they unite to form more compact bodies, this is not yet the consequence of their own active union, but of the union of the bourgeoisie, which class, in order to attain its own political ends, is compelled to set the whole proletariat in motion, and is moreover yet, for a time, able to do so. At this stage, therefore, the proletarians do not fight their enemies, but the enemies of their enemies, the remnants of absolute monarchy, the landowners, the non-industrial bourgeois, the petty bourgeoisie. Thus the whole historical movement is concentrated in the hands of the bourgeoisie; every victory so obtained is a victory for the bourgeoisie.

But with the development of industry the proletariat not only increases in number, it becomes concentrated in greater masses, its strength grows, and it feels that strength more. The various interests and conditions of life within the ranks of the proletariat are more and more equalized, in proportion as machinery obliterates all distinctions of labor, and nearly everywhere reduces wages to the same low level. The growing competition among the bourgeois, and the resulting commercial crises, make the wages of the workers ever more fluctuating. The unceasing improvement of machinery, ever more rapidly developing, makes their livelihood more and more precarious; the collisions between individual workmen and individual bourgeois take more and more the character of collisions between two classes. Thereupon the workers begin to form combinations (Trades' Unions) against the bourgeois; they club together in order to keep up the rate of wages; they found permanent associations in order to make provision beforehand for these occasional revolts. Here and there the contest breaks out into riots.

Now and then the workers are victorious, but only for a time. The real fruit of their battles lies, not in the immediate result, but in the ever expanding union of the workers. This union is helped on by the improved means of communication that are created by modern industry, and that place the workers of different localities in contact with one another. It was just this contact that was needed to centralize the numerous local struggles, all of the same character, into one national struggle between classes. But every class struggle is a political struggle. And that union, to attain which the burghers of the Middle Ages, with their miserable highways, required centuries, the modern proletarians, thanks to railways, achieve in a few years.

This organization of the proletarians into a class, and consequently into a political party, is continually being upset again by the competition between the workers themselves. But it ever rises up again, stronger, firmer, mightier. It compels legislative recognition of particular interests of the workers, by taking advantage of the divisions among the bourgeoisie itself. Thus the ten-hours'-bill in England was carried.

Altogether collisions between the classes of the old society further, in many ways, the course of development of the proletariat. The bourgeoisie finds itself involved in a constant battle. At first with the aristocracy; later on, with those portions of the bourgeoisie itself, whose interests have become antagonistic to the progress of industry; at all times, with the bourgeoisie of foreign countries. In all these battles it sees itself compelled to appeal to the proletariat, to ask for its help, and thus, to drag it into the political arena. The bourgeoisie itself, therefore, supplies the proletariat with its own elements of political and general education, in other words, it furnishes the proletariat with weapons for fighting the bourgeoisie.

Further, as we have already seen, entire sections of the ruling classes are, by the advance of industry, precipitated into the proletariat, or are at least threatened in their conditions of existence. These also supply the proletariat with fresh elements of enlightenment and progress.

Finally, in times when the class-struggle nears the decisive hour, the process of dissolution going on within the ruling class, in fact within the whole range of old society, assumes such a violent, glaring character, that a small section of the ruling class cuts itself adrift, and joins the revolutionary class, the class that holds the future in its hands. Just as, therefore, at an earlier period, a section of the nobility went over to the bourgeoisie, so now a portion of the bourgeoisie goes over to the proletariat, and in particular, a portion of the bourgeois ideologists, who have raised themselves to the level of comprehending theoretically the historical movements as a whole.

Of all the classes that stand face to face with the bourgeoisie today, the proletariat alone is a really revolutionary class. The other classes decay and finally disappear in the face of modern industry; the proletariat is its special and essential product.

The lower-middle class, the small manufacturer, the shopkeeper, the artisan, the peasant, all these fight against the bourgeoisie, to save from extinction their existence as fractions of the middle class. They are therefore not revolutionary, but conservative. Nay more, they are reactionary, for they try to roll back the wheel of history. If by chance they are revolutionary, they are so, only in view of their impending transfer into the proletariat, they thus defend not their present, but their future interests, they desert their own standpoint to place themselves at that of the proletariat.

The "dangerous class," the social scum, that passively rotting mass thrown off by the lowest layers of old society, may, here and there, be swept into the movement by a proletarian revolution; its conditions of life, however, prepare it far more for the part of a bribed tool of reactionary intrigue.

In the conditions of the proletariat, those of old society at large are already virtually swamped. The proletarian is without property; his relation to his wife and children has no longer anything in common with the bourgeois family-relations; modern industrial labor, modern subjection to capital, the same in England as in France, in America as in Germany, has stripped him of every trace of national character. Law, morality, religion, are to him so many bourgeois prejudices, behind which lurk in ambush just as many bourgeois interests.

All the preceding classes that got the upper hand sought to fortify their already acquired status by subjecting at large to their conditions of appropriation. The proletarians cannot become masters of the productive forces of society, except by abolishing their own previous mode of appropriation, and thereby also every other previous mode of appropriation. They have nothing of their own to secure and to fortify; their mission is to destroy all previous securities for, and insurances of, individual property.

All previous historical movements were movements of minorities, or in the interest of minorities. The proletarian movement is the self-conscious, independent movement of the immense majority, in the interest of the immense majority. The proletariat, the lowest stratum of our present society, cannot stir, cannot raise itself up, without the whole superincumbent strata of official society being sprung into the air.

Though not in substance, yet in form, the struggle of the proletariat with the bourgeoisie is at first a national struggle. The proletariat of each country must, of course, first of all settle matters with its own bourgeoisie.

In depicting the most general phases of the development of the proletariat, we traced the more or less veiled civil war, raging within existing society, up to the point where that war breaks out into open revolution, and where the violent overthrow of the bourgeoisie, lays the foundation for the sway of the proletariat.

Hitherto, every form of society has been based, as we have already seen, on the antagonism of oppressing and oppressed classes. But in order to oppress a class, certain conditions must be assured to it under which it can, at least, continue its slavish existence. The serf, in the period of serfdom, raised himself to membership in the commune, just as the petty bourgeois, under the yoke of feudal absolutism, managed to develop into a bourgeois. The modern laborer, on the contrary, instead of rising with the progress of industry, sinks deeper and deeper below the conditions of existence of his own class. He becomes a pauper, and pauperism develops more rapidly than population and wealth. And here it becomes evident, that the bourgeoisie is unfit any longer to be the ruling class in society, and to impose its conditions of existence upon society as an overriding law. It is unfit to rule, because it is incompetent to assure an existence to its slave within his slavery, because it cannot help letting him sink into such a state, that it has to feed him, instead of being fed by him. Society can no longer live under this bourgeoisie, in other words, its existence is no longer compatible with society.

The essential condition for the existence, and for the sway of the bourgeois class, is the formation and augmentation of capital; the condition for capital is wage-labor. Wage-labor rests exclusively on competition between the laborers. The advance of industry, whose involuntary promoter is the bourgeoisie, replaces the isolation of the laborers, due to competition, by their involuntary combination, due to association. The development of modern industry, therefore, cuts from under its feet the very foundation on which the bourgeoisie produces and appropriates products. What the bourgeoisie therefore produces, above all, are its own grave-diggers. Its fall and the victory of the proletariat are equally inevitable.

CRITICAL-THINKING QUESTIONS

1. What are the distinguishing factors of "class conflict"? How does this differ from other kinds of conflict, as between individuals or nations?

2. Why do Marx and Engels argue that understanding society in the present requires investigating the society of the past?

3. On what grounds did Marx and Engels *praise* industrial capitalism? On what grounds did they *condemn* the system?

NOTES

1. By *bourgeoisie* is meant the class of modern capitalists, owners of the means of social production and employers of wage-labor. By *proletariat,* the class of modern wage-laborers who, having no means of production of their own, are reduced to selling their labor-power in order to live.

2. That is, all written history. In 1847, the prehistory of society, the social organization existing previous to recorded history, was all but unknown. Since then, Haxthausen discovered common ownership of land in Russia. Maurer proved it to be the social foundation from which all Teutonic races started in history, and by and by village communities were found to be, or to have been, the primitive form of society everywhere from India to Ireland. The inner organization of this primitive Communistic society was laid bare, in its typical form, by Morgan's crowning discovery of the true nature of the gens and its relation to the tribe. With the dissolution of these primaeval communities society begins to be differentiated into separate and finally antagonistic classes. I have attempted to retrace this process of dissolution in "Der Ursprung der Familie, des Privateigenthums und des Staats," 2d ed. Stuttgart 1886.

3. Guild-master, that is, a full member of a guild, a master within, not a head of, a guild.

4. "Commune" was the name taken, in France, by the nascent towns even before they had conquered from their feudal lords and masters, local self-government and political rights as "the Third Estate." Generally speaking, for the economical development of the bourgeoisie, England is here taken as the typical country, for its political development, France.

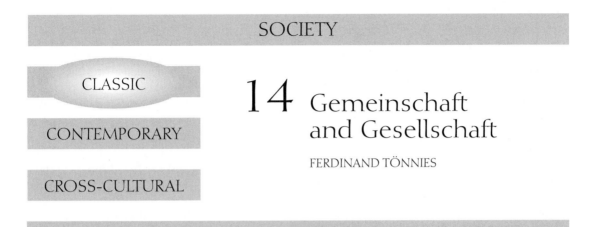

SOCIETY

CLASSIC

CONTEMPORARY

CROSS-CULTURAL

14 Gemeinschaft and Gesellschaft

FERDINAND TÖNNIES

The German sociologist Ferdinand Tönnies (1855–1936) described patterns of change by contrasting two types of social living: Gemeinschaft and Gesellschaft. In simple terms, Gemeinschaft is rooted in the rural, kinship-based life of the past; Gesellschaft, by contrast, finds its clearest expression in the commercial world of today's large, anonymous cities.

[A] relationship . . . and also the resulting association is conceived of either as real and organic life—this is the essential characteristic of the Gemeinschaft (community); or as imaginary and mechanical structure—this is the concept of Gesellschaft (society). . . .

All intimate, private, and exclusive living together, so we discover, is understood as life in Gemeinschaft (community). Gesellschaft (society) is public life—it is the world itself. In Gemeinschaft with one's family, one lives from birth on, bound to it in weal and woe. One goes into Gesellschaft as one goes into a strange country. A young man is warned against bad Gesellschaft, but the expression bad Gemeinschaft violates the meaning of the word. Lawyers may speak of domestic (*häusliche*) Gesellschaft, thinking only of the legalistic concept of social association; but the domestic Gemeinschaft, or home life with its immeasurable influence upon

Source: From *Community and Society* by Ferdinand Tönnies. Copyright © 1957 Michigan State University Press. Reprinted with permission.

the human soul, has been felt by everyone who ever shared it. Likewise, a bride or groom knows that he or she goes into marriage as a complete Gemeinschaft of life (*communio totius vitae*). A Gesellschaft of life would be a contradiction in and of itself. One keeps or enjoys another's Gesellschaft, but not his Gemeinschaft in this sense. One becomes a part of a religious Gemeinschaft; religious Gesellschaften (associations or societies), like any other groups formed for given purposes, exist only in so far as they, viewed from without, take their places among the institutions of a political body or as they represent conceptual elements of a theory; they do not touch upon the religious Gemeinschaft as such. There exists a Gemeinschaft of language, of folkways or mores, or of beliefs; but, by way of contrast, Gesellschaft exists in the realm of business, travel, or sciences. So of special importance are the commercial Gesellschaften; whereas, even though a certain familiarity and Gemeinschaft may exist among business partners, one could indeed hardly speak of commercial Gemeinschaft.

To make the word combination "joint-stock Gemeinschaft" would be abominable. On the other hand, there exists a Gemeinschaft of ownership in fields, forest, and pasture. The Gemeinschaft of property between man and wife cannot be called Gesellschaft of property. Thus many differences become apparent.

Gemeinschaft is old; Gesellschaft is new as a name as well as a phenomenon. . . . [S]ays Bluntschli (*Staatswörterbuch IV*), "Wherever urban culture blossoms and bears fruits, Gesellschaft appears as its indispensable organ. The rural people know little of it." On the other hand, all praise of rural life has pointed out that the Gemeinschaft among people is stronger there and more alive; it is the lasting and genuine form of living together. In contrast to Gemeinschaft, Gesellschaft is transitory and superficial. Accordingly, Gemeinschaft should be understood as a living organism, Gesellschaft as a mechanical aggregate and artifact. . . .

The Gemeinschaft by blood, denoting unity of being, is developed and differentiated into Gemeinschaft of locality, which is based on a common habitat. A further differentiation leads to the Gemeinschaft of mind, which implies only cooperation and coordinated action for a common goal. Gemeinschaft of locality may be conceived as a community of physical life, just as Gemeinschaft of mind expresses the community of mental life. In conjunction with the others, this last type of Gemeinschaft represents the truly human and supreme form of community. Kinship Gemeinschaft signifies a common relation to, and share in, human beings themselves, while in Gemeinschaft of locality such a common relation is established through collective ownership of land; and, in Gemeinschaft of mind, the common bond is represented by sacred places and worshiped deities. All three types of Gemeinschaft are closely interrelated in space as well as in time. They are, therefore, also related in all such single phenomena and in their development, as well as in general human culture and its history.

Wherever human beings are related through their wills in an organic manner and affirm each other, we find one or another of the three types of Gemeinschaft. Either the earlier type involves the later one, or the later type has developed to relative independence from some earlier one. It is, therefore, possible to deal with (1) kinship, (2) neighborhood, and (3) friendship as definite and meaningful derivations of these original categories. . . .

The theory of the Gesellschaft deals with the artificial construction of an aggregate of human beings which superficially resembles the Gemeinschaft in so far as the individuals live and dwell together peacefully. However, in the Gemeinschaft they remain essentially united in spite of all separating factors, whereas in the Gesellschaft they are essentially separated in spite of all uniting factors. In the Gesellschaft, as contrasted with the Gemeinschaft, we find no actions that can be derived from a priori and necessarily existing unity; no actions, therefore, which manifest the will and the spirit of the unity even if performed by the individual; no actions which, in so far as they are performed by the individual, take place on behalf of those united with him. In the Gesellschaft such actions do not exist. On the contrary, here everybody is by himself and isolated, and there exists a condition of tension against all others. Their spheres of activity and power are sharply separated, so that everybody refuses to everyone else contact with and admittance to his sphere; i.e., intrusions are regarded as hostile acts. Such a negative attitude toward one another becomes the normal and always underlying relation of these power-endowed individuals, and it characterizes the Gesellschaft in the condition of rest; nobody wants to grant and produce anything for another individual, nor will he be inclined to give ungrudgingly to another individual, if it be not in exchange for a gift or labor equivalent that he considers at least equal to what he has given. . . .

. . . In Gesellschaft every person strives for that which is to his own advantage and he affirms the actions of others only in so far as and as long as they can further his interest. Before and outside of convention and also before and outside of each special contract, the relation of all to all may therefore be conceived as potential hostility or latent war. Against this condition, all agreements of the will stand out as so many treaties and peace pacts. This conception is the only one which does justice to all facts of business and trade where all rights and duties can be reduced to mere value and definitions of ability to deliver. Every theory of pure private law or law of nature understood as pertaining to the Gesellschaft has to be considered as being based upon this conception.

CRITICAL-THINKING QUESTIONS

1. Describe the essential features of Gemeinschaft and Gesellschaft in order to clearly distinguish the two organizational types.

2. Why does Tönnies link Gemeinschaft to kinship, neighborhood, and friendship? How is Gesellschaft linked to commerce?

3. Based on reading this selection, do you think Tönnies found one type of social organization preferable to the other? If so, which one? Why?

CLASSIC

CONTEMPORARY

CROSS-CULTURAL

15 Unmarried with Children

KATHRYN EDIN AND MARIA KEFALAS

Since the late 1980s, one of the major changes in U.S. society has been a dramatic in-crease of unmarried mothers, especially at lower socioeconomic levels. Have these women given up on marriage, as most male, white, and middle-class observers have con-cluded? According to Kathryn Edin and Maria Kefalas, many of the single women who have children believe in marriage. They are still waiting for the right partner to fulfill their dreams of having a middle-class home with a devoted husband and father.

Jen Burke, a white tenth-grade dropout who is seventeen years old, lives with her stepmother, her sister, and her sixteen-month-old son in a cramped but tidy row home in Philadelphia's beleaguered Kensington neighborhood. She is broke, on welfare, and struggling to complete her GED. Wouldn't she and her son have been better off if she had finished high school, found a job, and married her son's father first?

In 1950, when Jen's grandmother came of age, only one in twenty American children was born to an unmarried mother. Today, that rate is one in three—and they are usually born to those least likely to be able to support a child on their own. In our book, *Promises I Can Keep: Why Poor Women Put Motherhood Before Marriage,*[1] we discuss the lives of 162 white, African American, and Puerto Rican low-income single mothers living in eight destitute neighborhoods across

Philadelphia and its poorest industrial suburb, Camden. We spent five years chatting over kitchen tables and on front stoops, giving mothers like Jen the opportunity to speak to the question so many affluent Americans ask about them: Why do they have children while still young and un-married when they will face such an uphill strug-gle to support them?

ROMANCE AT LIGHTNING SPEED

Jen started having sex with her twenty-year-old boyfriend Rick just before her fifteenth birthday. A month and a half later, she was pregnant. "I didn't want to get pregnant," she claims. "*He* wanted me to get pregnant." "As soon as he met me, he wanted to have a kid with me," she ex-plains. Though Jen's college-bound suburban peers would be appalled by such a declaration, on the streets of Jen's neighborhood, it is something of a badge of honor. "All those other girls he was with, he didn't want to have a baby with any of them," Jen boasts. "I asked him, 'Why did you

Source: Kathryn Edin and Maria Kefalas, "Unmarried with Children," *Contexts* 4 (Spring, 2005): 16–22 by the American Sociological Association.

choose me to have a kid when you could have a kid with any one of them?' He was like, 'I want to have a kid with *you*.'" Looking back, Jen says she now believes that the reason "he wanted me to have a kid that early is so that I didn't leave him."

In inner-city neighborhoods like Kensington, where child-bearing within marriage has become rare, romantic relationships like Jen and Rick's proceed at lightning speed. A young man's avowal, "I want to have a baby by you," is often part of the courtship ritual from the beginning. This is more than idle talk, as their first child is typically conceived within a year from the time a couple begins "kicking it." Yet while poor couples' pillow talk often revolves around dreams of shared children, the news of a pregnancy—the first indelible sign of the huge changes to come—puts these still-new relationships into overdrive. Suddenly, the would-be mother begins to scrutinize her mate as never before, wondering whether he can "get himself together"—find a job, settle down, and become a family man—in time.

Jen began pestering Rick to get a real job instead of picking up day-labor jobs at nearby construction sites. She also wanted him to stop hanging out with his ne'er-do-well friends, who had been getting him into serious trouble for more than a decade. Most of all, she wanted Rick to shed what she calls his "kiddie mentality"—his habit of spending money on alcohol and drugs rather than recognizing his growing financial obligations at home.

Rick did not try to deny paternity, as many would-be fathers do. Nor did he abandon or mistreat Jen, at least intentionally. But Rick, who had been in and out of juvenile detention since he was eight years old for everything from stealing cars to selling drugs, proved unable to stay away from his unsavory friends. At the beginning of her seventh month of pregnancy, an escapade that began as a drunken lark landed Rick in jail on a carjacking charge. Jen moved back home with her step-mother, applied for welfare, and spent the last two-and-a-half months of her pregnancy without Rick.

Rick sent penitent letters from jail. "I thought he changed by the letters he wrote me. I thought he changed a lot," she says. "He used to tell me that he loved me when he was in jail. . . . It was always gonna be me and him and the baby when he got out." Thus, when Rick's alleged victim failed to appear to testify and he was released just days before Colin's birth, the couple's reunion was a happy one. Often, the magic moment of childbirth calms the troubled waters of such relationships. New parents typically make amends and resolve to stay together for the sake of their child. When surveyed just after a child's birth, eight in ten unmarried parents say they are still together, and most plan to stay together and raise the child.

Promoting marriage among the poor has become the new war on poverty, Bush style. And it is true that the correlation between marital status and child poverty is strong. But poor single mothers already believe in marriage. Jen insists that she will walk down the aisle one day, though she admits it might not be with Rick. And demographers still project that more than seven in ten women who had a child outside of marriage will eventually wed someone. First, though, Jen wants to get a good job, finish school, and get her son out of Kensington.

Most poor, unmarried mothers and fathers readily admit that bearing children while poor and unmarried is not the ideal way to do things. Jen believes the best time to become a mother is "after you're out of school and you got a job, at least, when you're like twenty-one. . . . When you're ready to have kids, you should have everything ready, have your house, have a job, so when that baby comes, the baby can have its own room." Yet given their already limited economic prospects, the poor have little motivation to time their births as precisely as their middle-class counterparts do. The dreams of young people like Jen and Rick center on children at a time of life when their more affluent peers plan for college and careers. Poor girls coming of age in the inner city value children highly, anticipate them eagerly, and believe strongly that they are up to the job of mothering—even in difficult circumstances. Jen, for example, tells us, "People outside the neighborhood, they're like, 'You're fifteen! You're pregnant?' I'm like, it's not none of their business. I'm gonna be able to take care of my kid. They have nothing to worry about." Jen says she has concluded that "some people . . . are better at having kids at a younger age. . . . I think it's better for some people to have kids younger."

WHEN I BECAME A MOM

When we asked mothers like Jen what their lives would be like if they had not had children, we expected them to express regret over foregone opportunities for school and careers. Instead, most believe their children "saved" them. They describe their lives as spinning out of control before becoming pregnant—struggles with parents and peers, "wild," risky behavior, depression, and school failure. Jen speaks to this poignantly. "I was just real bad. I hung with a real bad crowd. I was doing pills. I was really depressed. . . . I was drinking. That was before I was pregnant." "I think," she reflects, "if I never had a baby or anything, . . . I would still be doing the things I was doing. I would probably still be doing drugs. I'd probably still be drinking." Jen admits that when she first became pregnant, she was angry that she "couldn't be out no more. Couldn't be out with my friends. Couldn't do nothing." Now, though, she says, "I'm glad I have a son . . . because I would still be doing all that stuff."

Children offer poor youth like Jen a compelling sense of purpose. Jen paints a before-and-after picture of her life that was common among the mothers we interviewed. "Before, I didn't have nobody to take care of. I didn't have nothing left to go home for. . . . Now I have my son to take care of. I have him to go home for. . . . I don't have to go buy weed or drugs with my money. I could buy my son stuff with my money! . . . I have something to look up to now." Children

also are a crucial source of relational intimacy, a self-made community of care. After a nasty fight with Rick, Jen recalls, "I was crying. My son came in the room. He was hugging me. He's sixteen months and he was hugging me with his little arms. He was really cute and happy, so I got happy. That's one of the good things. When you're sad, the baby's always gonna be there for you no matter what." Lately she has been thinking a lot about what her life was like back then, before the baby. "I thought about the stuff before I became a mom, what my life was like back then. I used to see pictures of me, and I would hide in every picture. This baby did so much for me. My son did a lot for me. He helped me a lot. I'm thankful that I had my baby."

Around the time of the birth, most unmarried parents claim they plan to get married eventually. Rick did not propose marriage when Jen's first child was born, but when she conceived a second time, at seventeen, Rick informed his dad, "It's time for me to get married. It's time for me to straighten up. This is the one I wanna be with. I had a baby with her, I'm gonna have another baby with her." Yet despite their intentions, few of these couples actually marry. Indeed, most break up well before their child enters preschool.

I'D LIKE TO GET MARRIED, BUT . . .

The sharp decline in marriage in impoverished urban areas has led some to charge that the poor have abandoned the marriage norm. Yet we found few who had given up on the idea of marriage. But like their elite counterparts, disadvantaged women set a high financial bar for marriage. For the poor, marriage has become an elusive goal—one they feel ought to be reserved for those who can support a "white picket fence" lifestyle: a mortgage on a modest row home, a car and some furniture, some savings in the bank, and enough money left over to pay for a "decent" wedding. Jen's views on marriage provide a perfect case in point. "If I was gonna get married, I would want to be married like my Aunt Nancy and my Uncle

Pat. They live in the mountains. She has a job. My Uncle Pat is a state trooper; he has lots of money. They live in the [Poconos]. It's real nice out there. Her kids go to Catholic school. . . . That's the kind of life I would want to have. If I get married, I would have a life like [theirs]." She adds, "And I would wanna have a big wedding, a real nice wedding."

Unlike the women of their mothers' and grandmothers' generations, young women like Jen are not merely content to rely on a man's earnings. Instead, they insist on being economically "set" in their own right before taking marriage vows. This is partly because they want a partnership of equals, and they believe money buys say-so in a relationship. Jen explains, "I'm not gonna just get into marrying him and not have my own house! Not have a job! I still wanna do a lot of things before I get married. He [already] tells me I can't do nothing. I can't go out. What's gonna happen when I marry him? He's gonna say he owns me!"

Economic independence is also insurance against a marriage gone bad. Jen explains, "I want to have everything ready, in case something goes wrong. . . . If we got a divorce, that would be my house. I bought that house, he can't kick me out or he can't take my kids from me." "That's what I want in case that ever happens. I know a lot of people that happened to. I don't want it to happen to me." These statements reveal that despite her desire to marry, Rick's role in the family's future is provisional at best. "We get along, but we fight a lot. If he's there, he's there, but if he's not, that's why I want a job . . . a job with computers . . . so I could afford my kids, could afford the house. . . . I don't want to be living off him. I want my kids to be living off me."

Why is Jen, who describes Rick as "the love of my life," so insistent on planning an exit strategy before she is willing to take the vows she firmly believes ought to last "forever?" If love is so sure, why does mistrust seem so palpable and strong? In relationships among poor couples like Jen and Rick, mistrust is often spawned by chronic violence and infidelity, drug and alcohol abuse, criminal activity, and the threat of imprisonment. In these tarnished corners of urban America, the stigma of a failed marriage is far worse than an out-of-wedlock birth. New mothers like Jen feel they must test the relationship over three, four, even five years' time. This is the only way, they believe, to ensure that their marriages will last.

Trust has been an enormous issue in Jen's relationship with Rick. "My son was born December 23rd, and [Rick] started cheating on me again . . . in March. He started cheating on me with some girl—Amanda. . . . Then it was another girl, another girl, another girl after. I didn't wanna believe it. My friends would come up to me and be like, 'Oh yeah, your boyfriend's cheating on you with this person.' I wouldn't believe it. . . . I would see him with them. He used to have hickies. He used to make up some excuse that he was drunk—that was always his excuse for everything." Things finally came to a head when Rick got another girl pregnant. "For a while, I forgave him for everything. Now, I don't forgive him for nothing." Now we begin to understand the source of Jen's hesitancy. "He wants me to marry him, [but] I'm not really sure. . . . If I can't trust him, I can't marry him, 'cause we would get a divorce. If you're gonna get married, you're supposed to be faithful!" she insists. To Jen and her peers, the worst thing that could happen is "to get married just to get divorced."

Given the economic challenges and often perilously low quality of the romantic relationships among unmarried parents, poor women may be right to be cautious about marriage. Five years after we first spoke with her, we met with Jen again. We learned that Jen's second pregnancy ended in a miscarriage. We also learned that Rick was out of the picture—apparently for good. "You know that bar [down the street?] It happened in that bar. . . . They were in the bar, and this guy was like badmouthing [Rick's friend] Mikey, talking stuff to him or whatever. So Rick had to go get involved in it and start with this guy. . . . Then he goes outside and fights the guy [and] the guy dies of head trauma. They were all on drugs, they were all drinking, and things just got out of control, and that's what happened. He got fourteen to thirty years."

THESE ARE CARDS I DEALT MYSELF

Jen stuck with Rick for the first two and a half years of his prison sentence, but when another girl's name replaced her own on the visitors' list, Jen decided she was finished with him once and for all. Readers might be asking what Jen ever saw in a man like Rick. But Jen and Rick operate in a partner market where the better-off men go to the better-off women. The only way for someone like Jen to forge a satisfying relationship with a man is to find a diamond in the rough or improve her own economic position so that she can realistically compete for more upwardly mobile partners, which is what Jen is trying to do now. "There's this kid, Donny, he works at my job. He works on C shift. He's a supervisor! He's funny, three years older, and he's not a geek or anything, but he's not a real preppy good boy either. But he's not [a player like Rick] and them. He had a job, you know, so that's good. He doesn't do drugs or anything. And he asked my dad if he could take me out!"

These days, there is a new air of determination, even pride, about Jen. The aimless high school dropout pulls ten-hour shifts entering data at a warehouse distribution center Monday through Thursday. She has held the job for three years, and her aptitude and hard work have earned her a series of raises. Her current salary is higher than anyone in her household commands—$10.25 per hour, and she now gets two weeks of paid vacation, four personal days, sixty hours of sick time, and medical benefits. She has saved up the necessary $400 in tuition for a high school completion program that offers evening and weekend classes. Now all that stands between her and a diploma is a passing grade in mathematics, her least favorite subject. "My plan is to start college in January. [This month] I take my math test . . . so I can get my diploma," she confides.

Jen clearly sees how her life has improved since Rick's dramatic exit from the scene. "That's when I really started [to get better] because I didn't have to worry about what *he* was doing, didn't have to worry about him cheating on me, all this stuff. [It was] then I realized that I had to do what I had to do to take care of my son. . . . When he was there, I think that my whole life revolved around him, you know, so I always messed up somehow because I was so busy worrying about what *he* was doing. Like I would leave the [GED] programs I was in just to go home and see what he was doing. My mind was never concentrating." Now, she says, "a lot of people in my family look up to me now, because all my sisters dropped out from school, you know, nobody went back to school. I went back to school, you know? . . . I went back to school, and I plan to go to college, and a lot of people look up to me for that, you know? So that makes me happy . . . because five years ago nobody looked up to me. I was just like everybody else."

Yet the journey has not been easy. "Being a young mom, being fifteen, it's hard, hard, hard, you know." She says, "I have no life. . . . I work from 6:30 in the morning until 5:00 at night. I leave here at 5:30 in the morning. I don't get home until about 6:00 at night." Yet she measures her worth as a mother by the fact that she has managed to provide for her son largely on her own. "I don't depend on nobody. I might live with my dad and them, but I don't depend on them, you know." She continues, "There [used to] be days when I'd be so stressed out, like, 'I can't do this!' And I would just cry and cry and cry. . . . Then I look at Colin, and he'll be sleeping, and I'll just look at him and think I don't have no [reason to feel sorry for myself]. The cards I have I've dealt myself so I have to deal with it now. I'm older. I can't change anything. He's my responsibility—he's nobody else's but mine—so I have to deal with that."

Becoming a mother transformed Jen's point of view on just about everything. She says, "I thought hanging on the corner drinking, getting high—I thought that was a good life, and I thought I could live that way for eternity, like sitting out with my friends. But it's not as fun once you have your own kid. . . . I think it changes [you]. I think, 'Would I want Colin to do that? Would I want my son to be like that . . .?' It was fun to me but it's not fun anymore. Half the people I hung with are either . . . Some have died from drug overdoses, some are in jail, and some people are just out there living the same life that they always lived, and they don't look really good. They look really bad." In the end, Jen believes, Colin's birth has brought far more good into her life than bad. "I know I could have waited [to have a child], but in a way I think Colin's the best thing that could have happened to me. . . . So I think I had my son for a purpose because I think Colin changed my life. He *saved* my life, really. My whole life revolves around Colin!"

PROMISES I CAN KEEP

There are unique themes in Jen's story—most fathers are only one or two, not five years older than the mothers of their children, and few fathers have as many glaring problems as Rick—but we heard most of these themes repeatedly in the stories of the 161 other poor, single mothers we came to know. Notably, poor women do not reject marriage; they revere it. Indeed, it is the conviction that marriage is forever that makes them think that divorce is worse than having a baby outside of marriage. Their children, far from being liabilities, provide crucial social-psychological resources—a strong sense of purpose and a profound source of intimacy. Jen and the other mothers we came to know are coming of age in an America that is profoundly unequal—where the gap between rich and poor continues to grow.

This economic reality has convinced them that they have little to lose and, perhaps, something to gain by a seemingly "ill-timed" birth.

The lesson one draws from stories like Jen's is quite simple: Until poor young women have more access to jobs that lead to financial independence—until there is reason to hope for the rewarding life pathways that their privileged peers pursue—the poor will continue to have children far sooner than most Americans think they should, while still deferring marriage. Marital standards have risen for all Americans, and the poor want the same things that everyone now wants out of marriage. The poor want to marry too, but they insist on marrying well. This, in their view, is the only way to avoid an almost certain divorce. Like Jen, they are simply not willing to make promises they are not sure they can keep.

CRITICAL-THINKING QUESTIONS

1. Why does romance among many low-income women not result in marriage? How do these women differ from most middle-class women who have an out-of-wedlock baby?

2. Why is marriage for many low-income women an "elusive goal"? Consider, especially, the economic factors that these mothers describe as well as their expectations for a family provider in the future.

3. Do you agree or not with the women in this study that it's better to raise children as a single parent rather than marry a man who's not "marriage material"? Do you know any middle-class women (including yourself, your mother, relatives, or friends) who have made the same decisions?

NOTE

1. Kathryn Edin and Maria Kefalas. *Promises I Can Keep: Why Poor Women Put Motherhood Before Marriage* (University of California Press, 2005).

CLASSIC

CONTEMPORARY

CROSS-CULTURAL

16 The Amish: A Small Society

JOHN A. HOSTETLER

Some 100,000 Old Order Amish live in the rolling farmland of Pennsylvania, Ohio, Indiana, and southern Ontario. These descendants of sixteenth-century Germans, who fled persecution for their religious beliefs, constitute a distinctive "small society" that keeps the larger world at arm's length. This description of the Amish suggests the extent of cultural diversity within North America and raises questions about why some people would reject the "advantages" that many others take for granted.

Small communities, with their distinctive character—where life is stable and intensely human—are disappearing. Some have vanished from the face of the earth, others are dying slowly, but all have undergone changes as they have come into contact with an expanding machine civilization. The merging of diverse peoples into a common mass has produced tension among members of the minorities and the majority alike.

The Old Order Amish, who arrived on American shores in colonial times, have survived in the modern world in distinctive, viable, small communities. They have resisted the homogenization process more successfully than others. In planting and harvest time one can see their bearded men working the fields with horses and their women hanging out the laundry in neat rows to dry. Many American people have seen Amish families, with the men wearing broad-brimmed black hats and the women in bonnets and long dresses, in railway depots or bus terminals. Although the Amish have lived with industrialized America for over two and a half centuries, they have moderated its influence on their personal lives, their families, communities, and their values.

The Amish are often perceived by other Americans to be relics of the past who live an austere, inflexible life dedicated to inconvenient and archaic customs. They are seen as renouncing both modern conveniences and the American dream of success and progress. But most people have no quarrel with the Amish for doing things the old-fashioned way. Their conscientious objection was tolerated in wartime, for after all, they are meticulous farmers who practice the virtues of work and thrift.

. . . The Amish are a church, a community, a spiritual union, a conservative branch of Christianity, a religion, a community whose members practice simple and austere living, a familistic entrepreneuring system, and an adaptive human community. . . .

Source: From *Amish Society*, 3rd ed., by John A. Hostetler (Baltimore: The Johns Hopkins University Press, 1980), pp. 3–12. Reprinted with permission.

The Amish are in some ways a little commonwealth, for their members claim to be ruled by the law of love and redemption. The bonds that unite them are many. Their beliefs, however, do not permit them solely to occupy and defend a particular territory. They are highly sensitive in caring for their own. They will move to other lands when circumstances force them to do so.

Commonwealth implies a place, a province, which means any part of a national domain that geographically and socially is sufficiently unified to have a true consciousness of its unity. Its inhabitants feel comfortable with their own ideas and customs, and the "place" possesses a sense of distinction from other parts of the country. Members of a commonwealth are not foot-loose. They have a sense of productivity and accountability in a province where "the general welfare" is accepted as a day-to-day reality. Commonwealth has come to have an archaic meaning in today's world, because when groups and institutions become too large, the sense of commonwealth or the common good is lost. Thus it is little wonder that the most recent dictionaries of the American English language render the meaning of commonwealth as "obsolescent." In reality, the Amish are in part a commonwealth. There is, however, no provision for outcasts.

It may be argued that the Amish have retained elements of wholesome provincialism, a saving power to which the world in the future will need more and more to appeal. Provincialism need not turn to ancient narrowness and ignorance, confines from which many have sought to escape. A sense of province or commonwealth, with its cherished love of people and self-conscious dignity, is a necessary basis for relating to the wider world community. Respect for locality, place, custom, and local idealism can go a long way toward checking the monstrous growth of consolidation in the nation and thus help to save human freedom and individual dignity.

. . . Anthropologists, who have compared societies all over the world, have tended to call semi-isolated peoples "folk societies," "primitives," or merely "simple societies." These societies constitute an altogether different type in contrast to the industrialized, or so-called civilized, societies.

The "folk society," as conceptualized by Robert Redfield,[1] is a small, isolated, traditional, simple, homogeneous society in which oral communication and conventionalized ways are important factors in integrating the whole life. In such an ideal-type society, shared practical knowledge is more important than science, custom is valued more than critical knowledge, and associations are personal and emotional rather than abstract and categoric.

Folk societies are uncomfortable with the idea of change. Young people do what the old people did when they were young. Members communicate intimately with one another, not only by word of mouth but also through custom and symbols that reflect a strong sense of belonging to one another. A folk society is *Gemeinschaft*-like; there is a strong sense of "we-ness." Leadership is personal rather than institutionalized. There are no gross economic inequalities. Mutual aid is characteristic of the society's members. The goals of life are never stated as matters of doctrine, but neither are they questioned. They are implied by the acts that constitute living in a small society. Custom tends to become sacred. Behavior is strongly patterned, and acts as well as cultural objects are given symbolic meaning that is often pervasively religious. Religion is diffuse and all-pervasive. In the typical folk society, planting and harvesting are as sacred in their own ways as singing and praying.

The folk model lends itself well to understanding the tradition-directed character of Amish society. The heavy weight of tradition can scarcely be explained in any other way. The Amish, for example, have retained many of the customs and small-scale technologies that were common in rural society in the nineteenth century. Through a process of syncretism, Amish religious values have been fused with an earlier period of simple country living when everyone farmed with horses and on a scale where family members could work together. The Amish exist as a folk or "little" community in a rural subculture within the modern state. . . . The outsider who drives through an Amish settlement cannot help but recognize them by their clothing, farm homes, furnishings, fields, and other material traits of culture. Although they speak perfect English with outsiders, they speak a dialect of German among themselves.

Amish life is distinctive in that religion and custom blend into a way of life. The two are inseparable. The core values of the community are religious beliefs. Not only do the members worship a deity they understand through the revelation of Jesus Christ and the Bible, but their patterned behavior has a religious dimension. A distinctive way of life permeates daily life, agriculture, and the application of energy to economic ends. Their beliefs determine their conceptions of the self, the universe, and man's place in it. The Amish world view recognizes a certain spiritual worth and dignity in the universe in its natural form. Religious considerations determine hours of work and the daily, weekly, seasonal, and yearly rituals associated with life experience. Occupation, the means and destinations of travel, and choice of friends and mate are determined by religious considerations. Religious and work attitudes are not far distant from each other. The universe includes the divine, and Amish society itself is considered divine insofar as the Amish recognize themselves as "a chosen people of God." The Amish do not seek to master nature or to work against the elements, but try to work with them. The affinity between Amish society and nature in the form of land, terrain, and vegetation is expressed in various degrees of intensity.

Religion is highly patterned, so one may properly speak of the Amish as a tradition-directed group. Though allusions to the Bible play an important role in determining their outlook on the world, and on life after death, these beliefs have been fused with several centuries of struggling to survive in [a] community. Out of intense religious experience, societal conflict, and intimate agrarian experience, a mentality has developed that prefers the old rather than the new. While the principle seems to apply especially to religion, it has also become a charter for social behavior. "The old is the best, and the new is of the devil" has become a prevalent mode of thought. By living in closed communities where custom and a strong sense of togetherness prevail, the Amish have formed an integrated way of life and a folklike culture. Continuity of conformity and custom is assured and the needs of the individual from birth to death are met within an integrated and shared system of meanings. Oral tradition, custom, and conventionality play an important part in maintaining the group as a functioning whole. To the participant, religion and custom are inseparable. Commitment and culture are combined to produce a stable human existence.

. . . A century ago, hardly anyone knew the Amish existed. A half-century ago they were viewed as an obscure sect living by ridiculous customs, as stubborn people who resisted education and exploited the labor of their children. Today the Amish are the unwilling objects of a thriving tourist industry on the eastern seaboard. They are revered as hard-working, thrifty people with enormous agrarian stamina, and by some, as islands of sanity in a culture gripped by commercialism and technology run wild.

CRITICAL-THINKING QUESTIONS

1. Does this description of the Amish way of life make you think about your own way of life in different terms? How?

2. Why would the Amish reject technological advances, which most members of our society hold to be invaluable?

3. What might the majority of the U.S. population learn from the Amish?

NOTE

1. Robert Redfield, "The Folk Society," *American Journal of Sociology,* 52 (Jan. 1947), 293–308. See also his book *The Little Community* (Chicago: University of Chicago Press, 1955).

CLASSIC

CONTEMPORARY

CROSS-CULTURAL

17 The Self

GEORGE HERBERT MEAD

The self is not the body but arises in social experience. Explaining this insight is perhaps the greatest contribution of George Herbert Mead. Mead argues that the basic shape of our personalities is derived from the social groupings in which we live. Note, too, that even the qualities that distinguish each of us from others emerge only within a social community.

In our statement of the development of intelligence we have already suggested that the language process is essential for the development of the self. The self has a character which is different from that of the physiological organism proper. The self is something which has a development; it is not initially there, at birth, but arises in the process of social experience and activity, that is, develops in the given individual as a result of his relations to that process as a whole and to other individuals within that process. . . .

We can distinguish very definitely between the self and the

Source: From *Mind, Self and Society: From the Standpoint of a Social Behaviorist* by George Herbert Mead (Chicago: University of Chicago Press, 1934), pp. 135–42, 144, 149–56, 158, 162–64. Copyright © 1934 by The University of Chicago Press. Reprinted with permission of the University of Chicago Press.

body. The body can be there and can operate in a very intelligent fashion without there being a self involved in the experience. The self has the characteristic that it is an object to itself, and that characteristic distinguishes it from other objects and from the body. It is perfectly true that the eye can see the foot, but it does not see the body as a whole. We cannot see our backs; we can feel certain portions of them, if we are agile, but we cannot get an experience of our whole body. There are, of course, experiences which are somewhat vague and difficult of location, but the bodily experiences are for us organized about a self. The foot and hand belong to the self. We can see our feet, especially if we look at them from the wrong end of an opera glass, as strange things which we have difficulty in recognizing as our own. The parts of the body are quite distinguishable from the self. We can lose parts of the body without any serious invasion of the self. The mere ability to experience different parts of the body is not different from the experience of a table. The table presents a different feel from what the hand does when one hand feels another, but it is an experience of something with which we come definitely into contact. The body does not experience itself as a whole, in the sense in which the self in some way enters into the experience of the self.

It is the characteristic of the self as an object to itself that I want to bring out. This characteristic is represented in the word "self," which is a reflexive, and indicates that which can be both subject and object. This type of object is essentially different from other objects, and in the past it has been distinguished as conscious, a term which indicates an experience with, an experience of, one's self. It was assumed that consciousness in some way carried this capacity of being an object to itself. In giving a behavioristic statement of consciousness we have to look for some sort of experience in which the physical organism can become an object to itself.[1]

When one is running to get away from someone who is chasing him, he is entirely occupied in this action, and his experience may be swallowed up in the objects about him, so that he has, at the time being, no consciousness of self at all. We must be, of course, very completely occupied to have that take place, but we can, I think, recognize that sort of a possible experience in which the self does not enter. We can, perhaps, get some light on that situation through those experiences in which in very intense action there appear in the experience of the individual, back of this intense action, memories and anticipations. Tolstoi as an officer in the war gives an account of having pictures of his past experience in the midst of his most intense action. There are also the pictures that flash into a person's mind when he is drowning. In such instances there is a contrast between an experience that is absolutely wound

up in outside activity in which the self as an object does not enter, and an activity of memory and imagination in which the self is the principal object. The self is then entirely distinguishable from an organism that is surrounded by things and acts with reference to things, including parts of its own body. These latter may be objects like other objects, but they are just objects out there in the field, and they do not involve a self that is an object to the organism. This is, I think, frequently overlooked. It is that fact which makes our anthropomorphic reconstructions of animal life so fallacious. How can an individual get outside himself (experientially) in such a way as to become an object to himself? This is the essential psychological problem of selfhood or of self-consciousness; and its solution is to be found by referring to the process of social conduct or activity in which the given person or individual is implicated. The apparatus of reason would not be complete unless it swept itself into its own analysis of the field of experience; or unless the individual brought himself into the same experiential field as that of the other individual selves in relation to whom he acts in any given social situation. Reason cannot become impersonal unless it takes an objective, noneffective attitude toward itself; otherwise we have just consciousness, not *self*-consciousness. And it is necessary to rational conduct that the individual should thus take an objective, impersonal attitude toward himself, that he should become an object to himself. For the individual organism is obviously an essential and important fact or constituent element of the empirical situation in which it acts; and without taking objective account of itself as such, it cannot act intelligently, or rationally.

The individual experiences himself as such, not directly, but only indirectly, from the particular standpoints of other individual members of the same social group, or from the generalized standpoint of the social group as a whole to which he belongs. For he enters his own experience as a self or individual, not directly or immediately, not by becoming a subject to himself, but only insofar as he first becomes an object to himself just as other individuals are objects to him or in his experience; and he becomes an object to himself only by taking the attitudes of other individuals toward himself within a social environment or context of experience and behavior in which both he and they are involved.

The importance of what we term "communication" lies in the fact that it provides a form of behavior in which the organism or the individual may become an object to himself. It is that sort of communication which we have been discussing— not communication in the sense of the cluck of the hen to the chickens, or the bark of a wolf to the pack, or the lowing of a cow, but communication in the sense of significant symbols, communication which is directed not only to others but also to the individual himself. So far as that type of communication is a part of behavior it at least introduces a self. Of course, one may hear without listening; one may see things that he does not realize; do things that he is not really aware of. But it is where one does respond to that which he addresses to another and where that response of his own becomes a part of his conduct, where he not only hears himself but responds to himself, talks and replies to himself as truly as the other person replies to him, that we have behavior in which the individuals become objects to themselves. . . .

The self, as that which can be an object to itself, is essentially a social structure, and it arises in social experience. After a self has arisen, it in a certain sense provides for itself its social experiences, and so we can conceive of an absolutely solitary self. But it is impossible to conceive of a self arising outside of social experience. When it has arisen we can think of a person in solitary confinement for the rest of his life, but who still has himself as a companion, and is able to think and to converse with himself as he had communicated with others. That process to which I have just referred, of responding to one's self as another responds to it, taking part in one's own conversation with others, being aware of what one is saying and using that awareness of what one is saying to determine what one is going to say thereafter—that is a process with which we are all familiar. We are continually following up our own address to other persons by an understanding of what we are saying, and using that understanding in the direction of our continued speech. We are finding out what we are going to say, what we are going to do, by saying and doing, and in the process we are continually controlling the process itself. In the conversation of gestures what we say calls out a certain response in another and that in turn changes our own action, so that we shift from what we started to do because of the reply the other makes. The conversation of gestures is the beginning of communication. The individual comes to carry on a conversation of gestures with himself. He says something, and that calls out a certain reply in himself which makes him change what he was going to say. One starts to say something, we will presume an unpleasant something, but when he starts to say it he realizes it is cruel. The effect on himself of what he is saying checks him; there is here a conversation of gestures between the individual and himself. We mean by significant speech that the action is one that affects the individual himself, and that the effect upon the individual himself is part of the intelligent carrying-out of the conversation with others. Now we, so to speak, amputate that social phase and dispense with it for the time being, so that one is talking to one's self as one would talk to another person.[2]

This process of abstraction cannot be carried on indefinitely. One inevitably seeks an audience, has to pour himself out to somebody. In reflective intelligence one thinks to act, and to act solely so that this action remains a part of a social process. Thinking becomes preparatory to social action. The very process of thinking is, of course, simply an inner conversation that goes on, but it is a conversation of gestures which in its completion implies the expression of that which one thinks to an audience. One separates the significance of what he is saying to others from the actual speech and gets it ready before saying it. He thinks it out, and perhaps writes it in the form of a book; but it is still a part of social intercourse in which one is addressing other persons and at the same time addressing one's self, and in which one controls the address to other persons by the response made to one's own gesture. That the person should be responding to himself is necessary to the self, and it is this sort of social conduct which provides behavior within which that self appears. I know of no other form of behavior than the linguistic in which the individual is an object to himself, and, so far as I can see, the individual is not a self in the reflexive sense unless he is an object to himself. It is this fact that gives a critical importance to communication, since this is a type of behavior in which the individual does so respond to himself.

We realize in everyday conduct and experience that an individual does not mean a great deal of what he is doing and saying. We frequently say that such an individual is not himself. We come away from an interview with a realization that we have left out important things, that there are parts of the self that did not get into what was said. What determines the amount of the self that gets into communication is the social experience itself. Of course, a good deal of the self does not need to get expression. We carry on a whole series of different relationships to different people. We are one thing to one man and another thing to another. There are parts of the self which exist only for the self in relationship to itself. We divide ourselves up in all sorts of different selves with reference to our acquaintances. We discuss politics with one and religion with another. There are all sorts of different selves answering to all sorts of different social reactions. It is the social process itself that is responsible for the appearance of the self; it is not there as a self apart from this type of experience.

A multiple personality is in a certain sense normal, as I have just pointed out. . . .

The unity and structure of the complete self reflects the unity and structure of the social process

as a whole; and each of the elementary selves of which it is composed reflects the unity and structure of one of the various aspects of that process in which the individual is implicated. In other words, the various elementary selves which constitute, or are organized into, a complete self are the various aspects of the structure of that complete self answering to the various aspects of the structure of the social process as a whole; the structure of the complete self is thus a reflection of the complete social process. The organization and unification of a social group is identical with the organization and unification of any one of the selves arising within the social process in which that group is engaged, or which it is carrying on.[3]

. . . Another set of background factors in the genesis of the self is represented in the activities of play and the game. . . . We find in children . . . imaginary companions which a good many children produce in their own experience. They organize in this way the responses which they call out in other persons and call out also in themselves. Of course, this playing with an imaginary companion is only a peculiarly interesting phase of ordinary play. Play in this sense, especially the stage which precedes the organized games, is a play at something. A child plays at being a mother, at being a teacher, at being a policeman; that is, it is taking different roles, as we say. We have something that suggests this in what we call the play of animals: A cat will play with her kittens, and dogs play with each other. Two dogs playing with each other will attack and defend, in a process which if carried through would amount to an actual fight. There is a combination of responses which checks the depth of the bite. But we do not have in such a situation the dogs taking a definite role in the sense that a child deliberately takes the role of another. This tendency on the part of children is what we are working with in the kindergarten where the roles which the children assume are made the basis for training. When a child does assume a role he has in himself the stimuli which call out that particular response or group of responses. He may, of course, run away when he is chased, as the dog does, or he may turn around and strike back just as the dog does in his play. But that is not the same as playing at something. Children get together to "play Indian." This means that the child has a certain set of stimuli that call out in itself the responses that they would call out in others, and which answer to an Indian. In the play period the child utilizes his own responses to these stimuli which he makes use of in building a self. The response which he has a tendency to make to these stimuli organizes them. He plays that he is, for instance, offering himself something, and he buys it; he gives a letter to himself and takes it away; he addresses himself as a parent, as a teacher; he arrests himself as a policeman. He has a set of stimuli which call out in himself the sort of responses they call out in others. He takes this group of responses and organizes them into a certain whole. Such is the simplest form of being another to one's self. It involves a temporal situation. The child says something in one character and responds in another character, and then his responding in another character is a stimulus to himself in the first character, and so the conversation goes on. A certain organized structure arises in him and in his other which replies to it, and these carry on the conversation of gestures between themselves.

If we contrast play with the situation in an organized game, we note the essential difference that the child who plays in a game must be ready to take the attitude of everyone else involved in that game, and that these different roles must have a definite relationship to each other. Taking a very simple game such as hide-and-seek, everyone with the exception of the one who is hiding is a person who is hunting. A child does not require more than the person who is hunted and the one who is hunting. If a child is playing in the first sense he just goes on playing, but there is no basic organization gained. In that early stage he passes from one to another just as a whim takes him. But in a game where a number of individuals are involved, then the child taking one role must be ready to take the role of everyone else. If he gets in a ball game he must have the responses of each position involved in his own position. He must know what everyone else is going to do in order to carry out his own play. He has to take all of these roles. They do not all have to be present in consciousness at the same time, but at some moments he has to have three or four individuals present in his own attitude, such as the one who is going to throw the ball, the one who is going to catch it, and so on. These responses must be, in some degree, present in his own make-up. In the game, then, there is a set of responses of such others so organized that the attitude of one calls out the appropriate attitudes of the other.

This organization is put in the form of the rules of the game. Children take a great interest in rules. They make rules on the spot in order to help themselves out of difficulties. Part of the enjoyment of the game is to get these rules. Now, the rules are the set of responses which a particular attitude calls out. You can demand a certain response in others if you take a certain attitude. These responses are all in yourself as well. There you get an organized set of such responses as that to which I have referred, which is something more elaborate than the roles found in play. Here there is just a set of responses that follow on each other indefinitely. At such a stage we speak of a child as not yet having a fully developed self. The child responds in a fairly intelligent fashion to the immediate stimuli that come to him, but they are not organized. He does not organize his life as we would like to have him do, namely, as a whole. There is just a set of responses of the type of play. The child reacts to a certain stimulus, and the reaction is in himself that is called out in others, but he is not a whole self. In his game he has to have an organization of these roles; otherwise he cannot play the game. The game represents the passage in the life of the child from taking the role of others in play to the organized part that is essential to self-consciousness in the full sense of the term.

. . . The fundamental difference between the game and play is that in the former the child must have the attitude of all the others involved in that game. The attitudes of the other players which the participant assumes organize into a sort of unit, and it is that organization which controls the response of the individual. The illustration used was of a person playing baseball. Each one of his own acts is determined by his assumption of the action of the others who are playing the game. What he does is controlled by his being everyone else on that team, at least insofar as those attitudes affect his own particular response. We get then an "other" which is an organization of the attitudes of those involved in the same process.

The organized community or social group which gives to the individual his unity of self may be called "the generalized other." The attitude of the generalized other is the attitude of the whole community.[4] Thus, for example, in the case of such a social group as a ball team, the team is the generalized other insofar as it enters—as an organized process or social activity—into the experience of any one of the individual members of it.

If the given human individual is to develop a self in the fullest sense, it is not sufficient for him merely to take the attitudes of other human individuals toward himself and toward one another within the human social process, and to bring that social process as a whole into his individual experience merely in these terms: He must also, in the same way that he takes the attitudes of other individuals toward himself and toward one another, take their attitudes toward the various phases or aspects of the common social activity or set of social undertakings in which, as members of an organized society or social group, they are all engaged; and he must then, by generalizing these individual attitudes of that organized society or social group itself, as a whole, act toward different social projects which at any given time it is carrying out, or toward the various larger phases of the general social process which constitutes its life and of which these projects are specific manifestations. This getting of the broad activities of any given social whole or organized society as such within the experiential field of any one of the individuals involved or included in that whole is, in other words, the essential basis and prerequisite of the fullest development of that individual's self: Only insofar as he takes the attitudes of the organized social group to which he belongs toward the organized, cooperative social activity or set of such activities in which that group as such is engaged, does he develop a complete self or possess the sort of complete self he has developed. And on the other hand, the complex cooperative processes and activities and institutional functionings of organized human society are also possible only insofar as every individual involved in them or belonging to that society can take the general attitudes of all other such individuals with reference to these processes and activities and institutional functionings, and to the organized social whole of experiential relations and interactions thereby constituted—and can direct his own behavior accordingly.

It is in the form of the generalized other that the social process influences the behavior of the individuals involved in it and carrying it on, i.e., that the community exercises control over the conduct of its individual members; for it is in this form that the social process or community enters as a determining factor into the individual's thinking. In abstract thought the individual takes the attitude of the generalized other[5] toward himself, without reference to its expression in any particular other individuals; and in concrete thought he takes that attitude insofar as it is expressed in the attitudes toward his behavior of those other individuals with whom he is involved in the given social situation or act. But only by taking the attitude of the generalized other toward himself, in one or another of these ways, can he think at all; for only thus can thinking—or the internalized conversation of gestures which constitutes thinking—occur. And only through the taking by individuals of the attitude or attitudes of the generalized other toward themselves is the existence of a universe of discourse, as that system of common or social meanings which thinking presupposes at its context, rendered possible.

. . . I have pointed out, then, that there are two general stages in the full development of the self. At the first of these stages, the individual's self is considered simply by an organization of the particular attitudes of other individuals toward himself and toward one another in the specific social acts in which he participates with them. But at the second stage in the full development of the individual's self that self is constituted not only by an organization of these particular individual attitudes, but also by an organization of the social attitudes of the generalized other or the social group as a whole to which he belongs. . . . So the self reaches its full development by organizing these individual attitudes of others into the organized social or group attitudes, and by thus becoming an individual reflection of the general systematic pattern of social or group behavior in which it and the others are all involved—a pattern which enters as a whole into the individual's experience in terms of these organized group attitudes which, through the mechanism of his central nervous system, he takes toward himself, just as he takes the individual attitudes of others.

. . . A person is a personality because he belongs to a community, because he takes over the institutions of that community into his own conduct. He takes its language as a medium by which he gets his personality, and then through a process of taking the different roles that all the others furnish he comes to get the attitude of the members of the community. Such, in a certain sense, is the structure of a man's personality. There are certain common responses which each individual has toward certain common things, and insofar as those common responses are awakened in the individual when he is affecting other persons he arouses his own self. The structure, then, on which the self is built is this response which is common to all, for one has to be a member of a community to be a self. Such responses are abstract attitudes, but they constitute just what we term a man's character. They give him what we term his principles, the acknowledged attitudes of all members of the community toward what are the values of that community. He is putting himself in the place of the generalized other, which represents the organized responses of all the members of the group. It is that which guides conduct controlled by principles, and a person who has such an organized group of responses is a man who we say has character, in the moral sense.

. . . I have so far emphasized what I have called the structures upon which the self is constructed, the framework of the self, as it were. Of course we are not only what is common to all: Each one of the selves is different from everyone else; but there has to be such a common structure as I have sketched in order that we may be members of a community at all. We cannot be ourselves unless we are also members in whom there is a community of attitudes which control the attitudes of all. We cannot have rights unless we have common attitudes. That which we have acquired as self-conscious persons makes us such members of society and gives us selves. Selves can only exist in definite relationships to other selves. No hard-and-fast line can be drawn between our own selves and the selves of others, since our own selves exist and enter as such into our experience only insofar as the selves of others exist and enter as such into our experience also. The individual possesses a self only in relation to the selves of the other members of his social group; and the structure of his self expresses or reflects the general behavior pattern of this social group to which he belongs, just as does the structure of the self of every other individual belonging to this social group.

CRITICAL-THINKING QUESTIONS

1. How does Mead distinguish between body and the self? What makes this a radically *social* view of the self?

2. How is the self both a subject and an object to itself? How is the ability to assume "the role of the other" vital to our humanity?

3. The idea that socialization produces conformity is easy to understand, but how does Mead argue that individual distinctiveness is also a result of social experience?

NOTES

1. Man's behavior is such in his social group that he is able to become an object to himself, a fact which constitutes him a more advanced product of evolutionary development than are the lower animals. Fundamentally it is this social fact—and not his alleged possession of a soul or mind with which he, as an individual, has been mysteriously and supernaturally endowed, and with which the lower animals have not been endowed—that differentiates him from them.

2. It is generally recognized that the specifically social expressions of intelligence, or the exercise of what is often called "social intelligence," depend upon the given individual's ability to take the roles of, or "put himself in the place of," the other individuals implicated with him in given social situations; and upon his consequent sensitivity to their attitudes toward himself and toward one another. These specifically social expressions of intelligence, of course, acquire unique significance in terms of our view that the whole nature of intelligence is social to the very core—that this putting of one's self in the places of others, this taking by one's self of their roles or attitudes, is not merely one of the various aspects or expressions of intelligence or intelligent behavior, but is the very essence of its character. Spearman's "X factor" in intelligence—the unknown factor which, according to him, intelligence contains—is simply (if our social theory of intelligence is correct) this ability of the intelligent individual to take the attitude of the other, or the attitudes of others, thus realizing the significations or grasping the meanings of the symbols or gestures in terms of which thinking proceeds; and thus being able to carry on with himself the internal conversation with these symbols or gestures which thinking involves.

3. The unity of the mind is not identical with the unity of the self. The unity of the self is constituted by the unity of the entire relational pattern of social behavior and experience in which the individual is implicated, and which is reflected in the structure of the self; but many of the aspects or features of this entire pattern do not enter into consciousness, so that the unity of the mind is in a sense an abstraction from the more inclusive unity of the self.

4. It is possible for inanimate objects, no less than for other human organisms, to form parts of the generalized and organized—the completely socialized—other for any given human individual, insofar as he responds to such objects socially or in a social fashion (by means of the mechanism of thought, the internalized conversation of gestures). Any thing—any object or set of objects, whether animate or inanimate, human or animal, or merely physical—toward which he acts, or to which he responds, socially, is an element in what for him is the generalized other; by taking the attitudes of which toward himself he becomes conscious of himself as an object or individual, and thus develops a self or personality. Thus, for example, the cult, in its primitive form, is merely the social embodiment of the relation between the given social group or community and its physical environment—an organized social means, adopted by the individual members of that group or community, of entering into social relations with that environment, or (in a sense) of carrying on conversations with it; and in this way that environment becomes part of the total generalized other for each of the individual members of the given social group or community.

5. We have said that the internal conversation of the individual with himself in terms of words or significant gestures—the conversation which constitutes the process or activity of thinking—is carried on by the individual from the standpoint of the "generalized other." And the more abstract that conversation is, the more abstract thinking happens to be, the further removed is the generalized other from any connection with particular individuals. It is especially in abstract thinking, that is to say, that the conversation involved is carried on by the individual with the generalized other, rather than with any particular individuals. Thus it is, for example, that abstract concepts are concepts stated in terms of the attitudes of the entire social group or community; they are stated on the basis of the individual's consciousness of the attitudes of the generalized other toward them, as a result of his taking these attitudes of the generalized other and then responding to them. And thus it is also that abstract propositions are stated in a form which anyone—any other intelligent individual—will accept.

18 Boyhood, Organized Sports, and the Construction of Masculinities

MICHAEL A. MESSNER

Many people still believe that gender roles—especially men's participation and interest in sports—are biological. Instead, Michael Messner argues, sports teach boys to be "masculine" and stigmatize those who aren't very interested or successful in athletics. He claims that masculinity is learned rather than innate.

I view gender identity not as a "thing" that people "have," but rather as a *process of construction* that develops, comes into crisis, and changes as a person interacts with the social world. Through this perspective, it becomes possible to speak of "gendering" identities rather than "masculinity" or "femininity" as relatively fixed identities or statuses.

. . . Levinson (1978) has argued that masculine identity is neither fully "formed" by the social context, nor is it "caused" by some internal dynamic put into place during infancy. Instead, it is shaped and constructed through the interaction between the internal and the social. The internal gendering identity may set developmental "tasks," may create thresholds of anxiety and ambivalence, yet it is only through a concrete examination of people's interactions with others within social institutions that we can begin to understand both the similarities and differences in the construction of gender identities.

Source: Michael A. Messner, 1990. "Boyhood, Organized Sports and the Construction of Masculinities." *Journal of Contemporary Ethnography* 18 (January): 416–444.

In this study I explore and interpret the meanings that males themselves attribute to their boyhood participation in organized sport. In what ways do males construct masculine identities within the institution of organized sports? In what ways do class and racial differences mediate this relationship and perhaps lead to the construction of different meanings, and perhaps different masculinities? And what are some of the problems and contradictions within these constructions of masculinity?

DESCRIPTION OF RESEARCH

Between 1983 and 1985, I conducted interviews with thirty male former athletes. Most of the men I interviewed had played the (U.S.) "major sports"—football, basketball, baseball, track. At the time of the interview, each had been retired from playing organized sports for at least five years. Their ages ranged from twenty-one to forty-eight, with the median, thirty-three, fourteen were black, fourteen were white, and two were Hispanic; fifteen of the sixteen black and Hispanic men had come from poor or working-class families, while the majority (nine of fourteen of the white men) had come from middle-class or professional families. All had at some time in their lives based their identities largely on their roles as athletes and could therefore be said to have had "athletic careers." Twelve had played organized sports through high school, eleven through college, and seven had been professional athletes. Though the sample was not randomly selected, an effort was made to see that the sample had a range of difference in terms of race and social class backgrounds, and that there was some variety in terms of age, types of sports played, and levels of success in athletic careers. Without exception, each man contacted agreed to be interviewed.

The tape-recorded interviews were semistructured and took from one and one-half to six hours, with most taking about three hours. I asked each man to talk about four broad eras in his life: (1) his earliest experiences with sports in boyhood, (2) his athletic career, (3) retirement or disengagement from the athletic career, and (4) life after the athletic career. In each era, I focused the interview on the meanings of "success and failure," and on the boy's/man's relationships with family, with other males, with women, and with his own body.

In collecting what amounted to life histories of these men, my overarching purpose was to use feminist theories of masculine gender identity to explore how masculinity develops and changes as boys and men interact within the socially constructed world of organized sports. In addition to using the data to move toward some generalizations about the relationship between "masculinity and sport," I was also concerned with sorting out some of the variations among boys, based on class and racial inequalities, that led them to relate differently to athletic careers. I divided my sample into two comparison groups. The first group was made up of ten men from higher-status backgrounds, primarily white, middle-class, and professional families. The second group was made up of twenty men from lower-status backgrounds, primarily minority, poor, and working-class families.

BOYHOOD AND THE PROMISE OF SPORTS

Zane Grey once said, "All boys love baseball. If they don't they're not real boys" . . . . This is, of course, an ideological statement; in fact, some boys do *not* love baseball, or any other sports, for that matter. There are millions of males who at an early age are rejected by, become alienated from, or lose interest in organized sports. Yet all boys are, to a greater or lesser extent, judged according to their ability, or lack of ability, in competitive sports (Eitzen, 1975; Sabo, 1985). In this study I focus on those males who did become athletes—males who eventually poured thousands of hours into the development of specific physical skills. It is in boyhood that we can discover the roots of their commitment to athletic careers.

How did organized sports come to play such a central role in these boys' lives? When asked to recall how and why they initially got into playing sports, many of the men interviewed for this study seemed a bit puzzled: after all, playing sports was "just the thing to do." A forty-two-year-old black man who had played college basketball put it this way:

It was just what you did. It's kind of like, you went to school, you played athletics, and if you didn't, there was something wrong with you. It was just like brushing your teeth: it's just what you did. It's part of your existence.

Spending one's time playing sports with other boys seemed as natural as the cycle of the seasons: baseball in the spring and summer, football in the fall, basketball in the winter—and then it was time to get out the old baseball glove and begin again. As a black thirty-five-year-old former professional football star said:

I'd say when I wasn't in school, 95% of the time was spent in the park playing. It was the only thing to do. It just came as natural.

And a black, thirty-four-year-old professional basketball player explained his early experiences in sports:

My principal and teacher said, "Now if you work at this you might be pretty damned good." So it was more or less a community thing—everybody in the community said, "Boy, if you work hard and keep your nose clean, you gonna be good." Cause it was natural instinct.

"It was natural instinct." "I was a natural." Several athletes used words such as these to explain their early attraction to sports. But certainly there is nothing "natural" about throwing a ball through a hoop, hitting a ball with a bat, or jumping over hurdles. A boy, for instance, may have amazingly dexterous inborn hand–eye coordination, but this does not predispose him to a career of hitting baseballs any more than it predisposes him to a life as a brain surgeon. When one listens closely to what these men said about their early experiences in sports, it becomes clear that their adoption of the self-definition of "natural athlete" was the result of what Connell (1990) has called "a collective practice" that constructs masculinities. The boyhood development of masculine identity and status—truly problematic in a society that offers no official rite of passage into adulthood—results from a process of interaction with people and social institutions. Thus, in discussing early motivations in sports, men commonly talk of the importance of relationships with family members, peers, and the broader community.

FAMILY INFLUENCES

Though most of the men in this study spoke of their mothers with love, respect, even reverence, their descriptions of their earliest experiences in sports are stories of an exclusively male world. The existence of older brothers or uncles who served as teachers and athletic role models—as well as sources of competition for attention and status within the family—was very common. An older brother, uncle, or even close friend of the family who was a successful athlete appears to have acted as a sort of standard of achievement against whom to measure oneself. A thirty-four-year-old black man who had been a three-sport star in high school said:

My uncles—my Uncle Harold went to the Detroit Tigers, played pro ball—all of 'em, everybody played sports, so I wanted to be better than anybody else. I knew that everybody in this town knew them—their names were something. I wanted my name to be just like theirs.

Similarly, a black forty-one-year-old former professional football player recalled:

I was the younger of three brothers and everybody played sports, so consequently I was more or less forced into it. 'Cause one brother was always better than the next brother and then I came along and had to show them that I was just as good as them. My oldest brother was an all-city ballplayer, then my other brother comes along he's all-city and all-state, and then I have to come along.

For some, attempting to emulate or surpass the athletic accomplishments of older male family members created pressures that were difficult to deal with. A thirty-three-year-old white man explained that he was a good athlete during boyhood, but the constant awareness that his two older brothers had been better made it difficult for him to feel good about himself, or to have fun in sports:

I had this sort of reputation that I followed from the playgrounds through grade school, and through high school. I followed these guys who were all-conference and all-state.

Most of these men, however, saw their relationships with their athletic older brothers and uncles in a positive light; it was within these relationships that they gained experience and developed motivations that gave them a competitive "edge" within their same-aged peer group. As a thirty-three-year-old black man describes his earliest athletic experiences:

My brothers were role models. I wanted to prove—especially to my brothers—that I had heart, you know, that I was a man.

When asked, "What did it mean to you to be 'a man' at that age?" he replied:

Well, it meant that I didn't want to be a so-called scaredy-cat. You want to hit a guy even though he's bigger than you to show that, you know, you've got this macho image. I remember that at that young an age, that feeling was exciting to me. And that carried over, and as I got older, I got better and I began to look around me and see, well hey! I'm competitive with these guys, even though I'm younger, you know? And then of course all the compliments come—and I began to notice a change, even in my parents—especially in my father—he was proud of that, and that was very important to me. He was extremely important . . . he showed me more affection, now that I think of it.

As this man's words suggest, if men talk of their older brothers and uncles mostly as role models, teachers, and "names" to emulate, their talk of their relationships with their fathers is more deeply layered and complex. Athletic skills and competition for status may often be learned from older brothers, but it is in boys' relationships with fathers that we find many of the keys to the emotional salience of sports in the development of masculine identity.

RELATIONSHIPS WITH FATHERS

The fact that boys' introductions to organized sports are often made by fathers who might otherwise be absent or emotionally distant adds a powerful emotional charge to these early experiences (Osherson, 1986). Although playing organized sports eventually came to feel "natural" for all of the men interviewed in this study, many needed to be "exposed" to sports, or even gently "pushed" by their fathers to become involved in activities like Little League baseball. A white, thirty-three-year-old man explained:

I still remember it like it was yesterday—Dad and I driving up in his truck, and I had my glove and my hat and all that—and I said, "Dad, I don't want to do it." He says, "What?" I says, "I don't want to do it." I was nervous. That I might fail. And he says, "Don't be silly. Lookit: There's Joey and Petey and all your friends out there." And so Dad says, "You're gonna do it, come on." And in my memory he's never said that about anything else; he just knew I needed a little kick in the pants and I'd do it. And once you're out there and you see all the other kids making errors and stuff,

and you know you're better than those guys, you know: Maybe I *do* belong here. As it turned out, Little League was a good experience.

Some who were similarly "pushed" by their fathers were not so successful as the aforementioned man had been in Little League baseball, and thus the experience was not altogether a joyous affair. One thirty-four-year-old white man, for instance, said he "inherited" his interest in sports from his father, who started playing catch with him at the age of four. Once he got into Little League, he felt pressured by his father, one of the coaches, who expected him to be the star of the team:

I'd go zero-for-four sometimes, strike out three times in a Little League game, and I'd dread the ride home. I'd come home and he'd say, "Go in the bathroom and swing the bat in the mirror for an hour," to get my swing level . . . It didn't help much, though, I'd go out and strike out three or four times again the next game too [laughs ironically].

When asked if he had been concerned with having his father's approval, he responded:

Failure in his eyes? Yeah, I always thought that he wanted me to get some kind of [athletic] scholarship. I guess I was afraid of him when I was a kid. He didn't hit that much, but he had a rage about him—he'd rage, and that voice would just rattle you.

Similarly, a twenty-four-year-old black man described his awe of his father's physical power and presence, and his sense of inadequacy in attempting to emulate him:

My father had a voice that sounded like rolling thunder. Whether it was intentional on his part or not, I don't know, but my father gave me a sense, an image of him being the most powerful being on earth, and that no matter what I ever did I would never come close to him . . . There were definite feelings of physical inadequacy that I couldn't work around.

It is interesting to note how these feelings of physical inadequacy relative to the father lived on as part of this young man's permanent internalized image. He eventually became a "feared" high school football player and broke school records in weight-lifting, yet,

As I grew older, my mother and friends told me that I had actually grown to be a larger man than my father. Even though in time I required larger clothes than he, which should have been a very concrete indication, neither my brother nor I could ever bring ourselves to say that I was bigger. We simply couldn't conceive of it.

Using sports activities as a means of identifying with and "living up to" the power and status of one's father was not always such a painful and difficult task for the men I interviewed. Most did not describe fathers who "pushed" them to become sports stars. The relationship between their athletic strivings and their identification with their fathers was more subtle. A forty-eight-year-old black man, for instance, explained that he was not pushed into sports by his father, but was aware from an early age of the community status his father had gained through sports. He saw his own athletic accomplishments as a way to connect with and emulate his father:

I wanted to play baseball because my father had been quite a good baseball player in the Negro leagues before baseball was integrated, and so he was kind of a model for me. I remember, quite young, going to a baseball game he was in—this was before the war and all—I remember being in the stands with my mother and seeing him on first base, and being aware of the crowd . . . I was aware of people's confidence in him as a serious baseball player. I don't think my father ever said anything to me like "play sports" . . . [But] I knew he would like it if I did well. His admiration was important . . . he mattered.

Similarly, a twenty-four-year-old white man described his father as a somewhat distant "role model" whose approval mattered:

My father was more of an example . . . he definitely was very much in touch with and still had very fond memories of being an athlete and talked about it, bragged about it. . . . But he really didn't do that much to teach me skills, and didn't always go to every game I played like some parents. But he approved and that was important, you know. That was important to get his approval. I always knew that playing sports was important to him, so I knew implicitly that it was good and there was definitely a value on it.

First experiences in sports might often come through relationships with brothers or older male relatives, and the early emotional salience of sports was often directly related to a boy's relationship with his father. The sense of commitment that these young boys eventually made to the development of athletic careers is best explained as a process of development of masculine gender identity and status in relation to same-sex peers.

MASCULINE IDENTITY AND EARLY COMMITMENT TO SPORTS

When many of the men in this study said that during childhood they played sports because "it's just what everybody did," they of course meant that it was just what *boys* did. They were introduced to organized sports by older brothers and fathers, and once involved, found themselves playing within an exclusively male world. Though the separate (and unequal) gendered worlds of boys and girls came to appear as "natural," they were in fact socially constructed. Thorne's observations of children's activities in schools indicated that rather than "naturally" constituting "separate gendered cultures," there is considerable interaction between boys and girls in classrooms and on playgrounds. When adults set up legitimate contact between boys and girls, Thorne observed, this usually results in "relaxed interactions." But when activities in the classroom or on the playground are presented to children as sex-segregated activities and gender is marked by teachers and other adults ("boys line up here, girls over there"), "gender boundaries are heightened, and mixed-sex interaction becomes an explicit arena of risk" (Thorne, 1986; 70). Thus sex-segregated activities such as organized sports as structured by adults, provide the context in which gendered identities and separate "gendered cultures" develop and come to appear natural. For the boys in this study, it became "natural" to equate masculinity with competition, physical strength, and skills. Girls simply did not (could not, it was believed) participate in these activities.

Yet it is not simply the separation of children, by adults, into separate activities that explains why many boys came to feel such a strong connection with sports activities, while so few girls did. As I listened to men recall their earliest experiences in organized sports, I heard them talk of insecurity, loneliness, and especially a need to connect with other people as a primary motivation in their early sports strivings. As a forty-two-year-old white man stated, "The most important thing was just being out there with the rest of the guys—being friends." Another thirty-two-year-old interviewee was born in Mexico and moved to the United States at a fairly young age. He never knew his father, and his mother died when he was only nine years old. Suddenly he felt rootless, and threw himself into sports. His initial motivations, however, do not appear to be based on a need to compete and win:

Actually, what I think sports did for me is it brought me into kind of an instant family. By being on a Little League team, or even just playing with all kinds of different kids in the neighborhood, it brought what I really wanted, which was some kind of closeness. It was just being there, and being friends.

Clearly, what these boys needed and craved was that which was most problematic for them: connection and unity with other people. But why do these young males find *organized sports* such an attractive context in which to establish "a kind of closeness" with others? Comparative observations of young boys' and girls' game-playing behaviors yield important insights into this question. Piaget (1965) and Lever (1976) both observed that girls tend to have more "pragmatic" and "flexible" orientations to the rules of games; they are more prone to make exceptions and innovations in the middle of a game in order to make the game more "fair." Boys, on the other hand, tend to have a more firm, even inflexible orientation to the rules of a game; to them, the rules are what protects any fairness. This difference, according to Gilligan (1982), is based on the fact that early developmental experiences

have yielded deeply rooted differences between males' and females' developmental tasks, needs, and moral reasoning. Girls, who tend to define themselves primarily through connection with others, experience highly competitive situations (whether in organized sports or in other hierarchical institutions) as threats to relationships, and thus to their identities. For boys, the development of gender identity involves the construction of positional identities, where a sense of self is solidified through separation from others (Chodorow, 1978). Yet feminist psychoanalytic theory has tended to oversimplify the internal lives of men (Lichterman, 1986). Males do appear to develop positional identities, yet despite their fears of intimacy, they also retain a human need for closeness and unity with others. This ambivalence toward intimate relationships is a major thread running through masculine development throughout the life course. Here we can conceptualize what Craib (1987) calls the "elective affinity" between personality and social structure: For the boy who both seeks and fears attachment with others, the rule-bound structure of organized sports can promise to be a safe place in which to seek nonintimate attachment with others within a context that maintains clear boundaries, distance, and separation.

COMPETITIVE STRUCTURES AND CONDITIONAL SELF-WORTH

Young boys may initially find that sports gives them the opportunity to experience "some kind of closeness" with others, but the structure of sports and athletic careers often undermines the possibility of boys learning to transcend their fears of intimacy, thus becoming able to develop truly close and intimate relationships with others (Kidd, 1990; Messner, 1987). The sports world is extremely hierarchical, and an incredible amount of importance is placed on winning, on "being number one." For instance, a few years ago I observed a basketball camp put on for boys by a professional basketball coach and his staff. The youngest boys, about eight years old (who could barely reach the basket with their shots) played a brief scrimmage. Afterwards, the coaches lined them up in a row in front of the older boys who were sitting in the grandstands. One by one, the coach would stand behind each boy, put his hand on the boy's head (much in the manner of a priestly benediction), and the older boys in the stands would applaud and cheer, louder or softer, depending on how well or poorly the young boy was judged to have performed. The two or three boys who were clearly the exceptional players looked confident that they would receive the praise they were due. Most of the boys, though, had expressions ranging from puzzlement to thinly disguised terror on their faces as they awaited the judgments of the older boys.

This kind of experience teaches boys that it is not "just being out there with the guys—being friends," that ensures the kind of attention and connection that they crave; it is being *better* than the other guys—*beating* them—that is the key to acceptance. Most of the boys in this study did have some early successes in sports, and thus their ambivalent need for connection with others was met, at least for a time. But the institution of sport tends to encourage the development of what Schafer (1975) has called "conditional self-worth" in boys. As boys become aware that acceptance by others is contingent upon being good—a "winner"—narrow definitions of success, based upon performance and winning become increasingly important to them. A thirty-three-year-old black man said that by the time he was in his early teens:

It was expected of me to do well in all my contests—I mean by my coaches, my peers, and my family. So I in turn expected to do well, and if I didn't do well, then I'd be very disappointed.

The man from Mexico, discussed above, who said that he had sought "some kind of closeness" in his early sports experiences began to notice in his early teens that if he played well, was a *winner,* he would get attention from others:

It got to the point where I started realizing, noticing that people were always there for me, backing me all the time—sports got to be really fun because I always had some people there backing me. Finally my oldest brother started going to all my games, even though I had never really seen who he was [laughs]—after the game, you know, we never really saw each other, but he was at all my baseball games, and it seemed like we shared a kind of closeness there, but only in those situations. Off the field, when I wasn't in uniform, he was never around.

By high school, he said, he felt "up against the wall." Sports hadn't delivered what he had hoped it would, but he thought if he just tried harder, won one more championship trophy, he would get the attention he truly craved. Despite his efforts, this attention was not forthcoming. And, sadly, the pressures he had put on himself to excel in sports had taken most of the fun out of playing.

For many of the men in this study, throughout boyhood and into adolescence, this conscious striving for successful achievement became the primary means through which they sought connection with other people (Messner, 1987). But it is important to recognize that young males' internalized ambivalences about intimacy do not fully determine the contours and directions of their lives. Masculinity continues to develop through interaction with the social world—and because boys from different backgrounds are interacting with substantially different familial, educational, and other institutions, these differences will lead them to make different choices and define situations in different ways. Next, I examine the differences in the ways that boys from higher- and lower-status families and communities related to organized sports.

STATUS DIFFERENCES AND COMMITMENTS TO SPORTS

In discussing early attractions to sports, the experiences of boys from higher- and lower-status backgrounds are quite similar. Both groups indicate the importance of fathers and older brothers in introducing them to sports. Both groups speak of the joys of receiving attention and acceptance among family and peers for early successes in sports. Note the similarities, for instance, in the following descriptions of boyhood athletic experiences of two men. First, a man born in a white, middle-class family:

I loved playing sports so much from a very early age because of early exposure. A lot of the sports came easy at an early age, and because they did, and because you were successful at something, I think that you're inclined to strive for that gratification. It's like, if you're good, you like it, because it's instant gratification. I'm doing something that I'm good at and I'm gonna keep doing it.

Second, a black man from a poor family:

Fortunately I had some athletic ability, and, quite naturally, once you start doing good in whatever it is—I don't care if it's jacks—you show off what you do. That's your ability, that's your blessing, so you show it off as much as you can.

For boys from both groups, early exposure to sports, the discovery that they had some "ability," shortly followed by some sort of family, peer, and community recognition, all eventually led to the commitment of hundreds and thousands of hours of playing, practicing, and dreaming of future stardom. Despite these similarities, there are also some identifiable differences that begin to explain the tendency of males from lower-status backgrounds to develop higher levels of commitment to sports careers. The most clear-cut difference was that while men from higher-status backgrounds are likely to describe their earliest athletic experiences and motivations almost exclusively in terms of immediate family, men from lower-status backgrounds more commonly describe the importance of a broader community context. For instance, a forty-six-year-old man who grew up in a "poor working class" black family in a small town in Arkansas explained:

In that community, at the age of third or fourth grade, if you're a male, they expect you to show some kind of inclination, some kind of skill in football or basketball.

It was an expected thing, you know? My mom and my dad, they didn't push at all. It was the general environment.

A forty-eight-year-old man describes sports activities as a survival strategy in his poor black community:

Sports protected me from having to compete in gang stuff, or having to be good with my fists. If you were an athlete and got into the fist world, that was your business, and that was okay—but you didn't have to if you didn't want to. People would generally defer to you, give you your space away from trouble.

A thirty-five-year-old man who grew up in "a poor black ghetto" described his boyhood relationship to sports similarly:

Where I came from, either you were one of two things: you were in sports or you were out on the streets being a drug addict, or breaking into places. The guys who were in sports, we had it a little easier, because we were accepted by both groups. . . . So it worked out to my advantage, cause I didn't get into a lot of trouble—some trouble, but not a lot.

The fact that boys in lower-status communities faced these kinds of realities gave salience to their developing athletic identities. In contrast, sports were important to boys from higher-status backgrounds, yet the middle-class environment seemed more secure, less threatening, and offered far more options. By the time most of these boys got into junior high or high school, many had made conscious decisions to shift their attentions away from athletic careers to educational and (nonathletic) career goals. A thirty-two-year-old white college athletic director told me that he had seen his chance to pursue a pro baseball career as "pissing in the wind," and instead, focused on education. Similarly, a thirty-three-year-old white dentist who was a three-sport star in high school, decided not to play sports in college, so he could focus on getting into dental school. As he put it,

I think I kind of downgraded the stardom thing. I thought it was small potatoes. And sure, that's nice in high school and all that, but on a broad scale, I didn't think it amounted to all that much.

This statement offers an important key to understanding the construction of masculine identity within a middle-class context. The status that this boy got through sports had been *very* important to him, yet he could see that "on a broad scale," this sort of status was "small potatoes." This sort of early recognition is more than a result of the oft-noted middle-class tendency to raise "future-oriented" children (Rubin, 1976; Sennett and Cobb, 1973). Perhaps more important, it is that the *kinds* of future orientations developed by boys from higher-status backgrounds are consistent with the middle-class context. These men's descriptions of their boyhoods reveal that they grew up immersed in a wide range of institutional frameworks, of which organized sports was just one. And—importantly—they could see that the status of adult males around them was clearly linked to their positions within various professions, public institutions, and bureaucratic organizations. It was clear that access to this sort of institutional status came through educational achievement, not athletic prowess. A thirty-two-year-old black man who grew up in a professional-class family recalled that he had idolized Wilt Chamberlain and dreamed of being a pro basketball player, yet his father discouraged his athletic strivings:

He knew I liked the game. I *loved* the game. But basketball was not recommended; my dad would say, "That's a stereotyped image for black youth. . . . When your basketball is gone and finished, what are you gonna do? One day, you might get injured. What are you gonna look forward to?" He stressed education.

Similarly, a thirty-two-year-old man who was raised in a white, middle-class family, had found in sports a key means of gaining acceptance and connection in his peer group. Yet he was simultaneously developing an image of himself as a "smart student," and becoming aware of a wide range of nonsports life options:

My mother was constantly telling me how smart I was, how good I was, what a nice person I was, and giving me all sorts of positive strokes, and those positive strokes became a self-motivating kind of thing. I had this image of myself as smart, and I lived up to that image.

It is not that parents of boys in lower-status families did not also encourage their boys to work hard in school. Several reported that their parents "stressed books first, sports second." It's just that the broader social context—education, economy, and community—was more likely to *narrow* lower-status boys' perceptions of real-life options, while boys from higher-status backgrounds faced an expanding world of options. For instance, with a different socioeconomic background, one thirty-five-year-old black man might have become a great musician instead of a star professional football running back. But he did not. When he was a child, he said, he was most interested in music:

I wanted to be a drummer. But we couldn't afford drums. My dad couldn't go out and buy me a drum set or a guitar even—it was just one of those things; he was just trying to make ends meet.

But he *could* afford, as could so many in his socioeconomic condition, to spend countless hours at the local park, where he was told by the park supervisor

that I was a natural—not only in gymnastics or baseball—whatever I did, I was a natural. He told me I shouldn't waste this talent, and so I immediately started watching the big guys then.

In retrospect, this man had potential to be a musician or any number of things, but his environment limited his options to sports, and he made the best of it. Even within sports, he, like most boys in the ghetto, was limited:

We didn't have any tennis courts in the ghetto—we used to have a lot of tennis balls, but no racquets. I wonder today how good I might be in tennis if I had gotten a racquet in my hands at an early age.

It is within this limited structure of opportunity that many lower-status young boys found sports to be *the* place, rather than *a* place, within which to construct masculine identity, status, the relationships. A thirty-six-year-old white man explained that his father left the family when he was very young and his mother faced a very difficult struggle to make ends meet. As his words suggest, the more limited a boy's options, and the more insecure his family situation, the more likely he is to make an early commitment to an athletic career:

I used to ride my bicycle to Little League practice—if I'd waited for someone to pick me up and take me to the ball park I'd have never played. I'd get to the ball park and all the other kids would have their dad bring them to practice or games. But I'd park my bike to the side and when it was over I'd get on it and go home. Sports was the way for me to move everything to the side—family problems, just all the embarrassments—and think about one thing, and that was sports . . . In the third grade, when the teacher went around the classroom and asked everybody, "What do you want to be when you grow up?," I said, "I want to be a major league baseball player," and everybody laughed their heads off.

This man eventually did enjoy a major league baseball career. Most boys from lower-status backgrounds who make similar early commitments to athletic careers are not so successful. As stated earlier, the career structure of organized sports is highly competitive and hierarchical. In fact, the chances of attaining professional status in sports are approximately 4:100,000 for a white man, 2:100,000 for a black man, and 3:1 million for a Hispanic man in the United States (Leonard and Reyman, 1988). Nevertheless, the immediate rewards (fun, status, attention), along with the constricted (nonsports) structure of opportunity, attract disproportionately large numbers of boys from lower-status backgrounds to athletic careers as their major means of constructing a masculine identity. These are the boys who later, as young men, had to struggle with "conditional self-worth," and, more often than not, occupational dead ends. Boys from higher-status backgrounds, on the other hand, bolstered their boyhood, adolescent, and early adult status through their athletic accomplishments. Their wider range of experiences and life chances led to an early shift away from sports careers as the major basis of identity (Messner, 1989).

CONCLUSION

The conception of the masculinity–sports relationship developed here begins to illustrate the idea of an "elective affinity" between social structure and personality. Organized sports is a "gendered institution"—an institution constructed by gender relations. As such, its structure and values (rules, formal organization, sex composition, etc.), reflect dominant conceptions of masculinity and femininity. Organized sports is also a "gendering institution"—an institution that helps to construct the current gender order. Part of this construction of gender is accomplished through the "masculinizing" of male bodies and minds.

Yet boys do not come to their first experiences in organized sports as "blank slates," but arrive with already "gendering" identities due to early developmental experiences and previous socialization. I have suggested here that an important thread running through the development of masculine identity is males' ambivalence toward intimate unity with others. Those boys who experience early athletic successes find in the structure of organized sport an affinity with this masculine ambivalence toward intimacy: The rule-bound, competitive, hierarchical world of sport offers boys an attractive means of establishing an emotionally distant (and thus "safe") connection with others. Yet as boys begin to define themselves as "athletes," they learn that in order to be accepted (to have connection) through sports, they must be winners. And in order to be winners, they must construct relationships with others (and with themselves) that are consistent with the competitive and hierarchical values and structure of the sports world. As a result, they often develop a "conditional self-worth" that leads them to construct more instrumental relationships with themselves and others. This ultimately exacerbates their difficulties in constructing intimate relationships with others. In effect, the interaction between the young male's preexisting internalized ambivalence toward intimacy with the competitive hierarchical institution of sport has resulted in the construction of a masculine personality that is characterized by instrumental rationality, goal-orientation, and difficulties with intimate connection and expression (Messner, 1987).

This theoretical line of inquiry invites us not simply to examine how social institutions "socialize" boys, but also to explore the ways that boys' already-gendering identities interact with social institutions (which, like organized sport, are themselves the product of gender relations). This study has also suggested that it is not some singular "masculinity" that is being constructed through athletic careers. It may be correct, from a psychoanalytic perspective, to suggest that all males bring ambivalences toward intimacy to their interactions with the world, but "the world" is a very different place for males from different racial and socioeconomic backgrounds. Because males have substantially different interactions with the world, based on class, race, and other differences and inequalities, we might expect the construction of masculinity to take on different meanings for boys and men from differing backgrounds (Messner, 1989). Indeed, this study has suggested that boys from higher-status backgrounds face a much broader range of options than do their lower-status counterparts. As a result, athletic careers take on different meanings for these boys. Lower-status boys are likely to see athletic careers as *the* institutional context for the construction of their masculine status and identities, while higher-status males make an early shift away from athletic careers toward other institutions (usually education and nonsports careers). A key line of inquiry for future studies might begin by exploring this irony of sports careers: Despite the fact that "the athlete" is currently an example of an exemplary form of masculinity in public ideology, the vast majority of boys who become most committed to athletic careers are never well-rewarded for their efforts. The fact that class and racial dynamics lead boys from higher-status backgrounds, unlike their lower-status counterparts, to move into nonsports careers illustrates how the construction of different kinds of masculinities is a key component of the overall construction of the gender order.

CRITICAL-THINKING QUESTIONS

1. If masculinity is innate, as many people believe, why aren't all boys and men jocks? And why are many girls and women successful athletes, while also being very "feminine"?
2. How would you explain the rise of female athletes during the last few decades?
3. How do factors such as family influence, a father's role, and social class shape a boy's interest in sports and his identity as "masculine"?

REFERENCES

CHODOROW, N. 1978. *The reproduction of mothering.* Berkeley: Univ. of California Press.

CONNELL, R. W. 1987. *Gender and power.* Stanford, Calif.: Stanford Univ. Press.

————. 1990. An iron man: the body and some contradictions of hegemonic masculinity. In M. A. Messner and D. F. Sabo (eds.). *Sport, men and the gender order: Critical feminist perspectives.* Champaign, Ill.: Human Kinetics.

CRAIB, I. 1987. Masculinity and male dominance. *Soc. Rev.* 38: 721–43.

EITZEN, D. S. 1975. Athletics in the status system of male adolescents: a replication of Coleman's *The Adolescent Society. Adolescence* 10: 268–76.

GILLIGAN, C. 1982. *In a different voice: Psychological theory and women's development.* Cambridge, Mass.: Harvard Univ. Press.

KIDD, B. 1987. Sports and masculinity. In *Beyond patriarchy: Essays by men on pleasure, power, and change,* ed. M. Kaufman. Toronto: Oxford Univ. Press.

————. 1990. The men's cultural centre: sports and the dynamic of women's oppression/men's repression. In *Sport, men and the gender order: Critical feminist perspectives,* eds. M. A. Messner and D. F. Sabo. Champaign, Ill.: Human Kinetics.

LEONARD, W. M. II. and J. M. REYMAN. 1988. The odds of attaining professional athlete status: refining the computations. *Sociology of Sport J.* 5: 162–69.

LEVER, J. 1976. Sex differences in the games children play. *Social Problems* 23: 478–87.

LEVINSON, D. J. et al. 1978. *The seasons of a man's life.* New York: Ballantine.

LICHTERMAN, P. 1986. Chodorow's psychoanalytic sociology: a project half-completed. *California Sociologist* 9: 147–66.

MESSNER, M. 1987. The meaning of success: the athletic experience and the development of male identity. In *The making of masculinities: The new men's studies,* ed. H. Brod. Boston: Allen and Unwin.

———. 1989. Masculinities and athletic careers. *Gender and Society* 3: 71–88.

OSHERSON, S. 1986. *Finding our fathers: How a man's life is shaped by his relationship with his father.* New York: Fawcett Columbine.

PIAGET, J. H. 1965. *The moral judgment of the child.* New York: Free Press.

RUBIN, L. B. 1976. *Worlds of pain: Life in the working class family.* New York: Basic Books.

SABO, D. 1985. Sport, patriarchy and male identity: new questions about men and sport. *Arena Rev.* 9: 2.

SCHAFER, W. E. 1975. Sport and male sex role socialization. *Sport Sociology Bull.* 4: 47–54.

SENNETT, R., and J. COBB. 1973. *The Hidden Injuries of Class.* New York: Random House.

THOME, B. 1986. Girls and boys together . . . but mostly apart: gender arrangements in elementary schools. In *Relationships and development,* eds. W. W. Hartup and Z. Rubin. Hillsdale, N.J.: Lawrence Erlbaum.

CLASSIC

CONTEMPORARY

CROSS-CULTURAL

19 Socialization and the Power of Advertising

JEAN KILBOURNE

Can parents just turn off the TV to protect their kids from the negative impact of advertising? No, claims Jean Kilbourne. Because advertising permeates our environment, she claims, "We cannot escape it." Advertisers customize ads for subscribers of the same magazine, attract children to Web sites with games and prizes, and bombard us with products on billboards, public transportation systems, and the sides of buildings, trucks, and shopping carts. As a result, Kilbourne argues, advertising continues to persuade people of all ages that the way to be happy is to buy, buy, buy.

If you're like most people, you think that advertising has no influence on you. This is what advertisers want you to believe. But, if that were true, why would companies spend over $200 billion a year on advertising? Why would they be willing to spend over $250,000 to produce an average television commercial and another $250,000 to air it? If they want to broadcast their commercial during the Super Bowl, they will gladly spend over a million dollars to produce it and over one and a half million to air it. After all, they might have the kind of success that Victoria's Secret did during the 1999 Super Bowl. When they paraded bra-and-panty-clad models across TV screens for a mere thirty seconds, 1 million people turned away from the game to log on to the Web site promoted in the ad. No influence? . . .

Source: Reprinted with the permission of The Free Press, a Division of Simon & Schuster Adult Publishing Group, from *Deadly Persuasion: Why Women and Girls Must Fight the Addictive Power of Advertising* by Jean Kilbourne. Copyright © 1999 by Jean Kilbourne.

Through focus groups and depth interviews, psychological researchers can zero in on very specific target audiences—and their leaders. "Buy this twenty-four-year-old and get all his friends absolutely free," proclaims an ad for MTV directed to advertisers. MTV presents itself publicly as a place for rebels and nonconformists. Behind the scenes, however, it tells potential advertisers that its viewers are lemmings who will buy whatever they are told to buy.

The MTV ad gives us a somewhat different perspective on the concept of "peer pressure." Advertisers, especially those who advertise tobacco and alcohol, are forever claiming that advertising doesn't influence anyone, that kids smoke and drink because of peer pressure. Sure, such pressure exists and is an important influence, but a lot of it is created by advertising. Kids who exert peer pressure don't drop into high schools like Martians. They are kids who tend to be leaders, whom other kids follow for good or for bad. And they themselves are mightily influenced by advertising, sometimes very deliberately, as in the MTV ad. As an ad for *Seventeen* magazine, picturing a group of attractive young people, says, "Hip doesn't just happen. It starts at the source: *Seventeen.*" In the global village, the "peers" are very much the same, regardless of nationality, ethnicity, culture. In the eyes of the media, the youths of the world are becoming a single, seamless, soulless target audience—often cynically labeled Generation X, or, for the newest wave of teens, Generation Y. "We're helping a soft drink company reach them, even if their parents can't," says [a newspaper ad] featuring a group of young people. The ad continues, "If you think authority figures have a hard time talking to Generation X, you should try being an advertiser," and goes on to suggest placing ads in the television sections of newspapers. . . .

Home pages on the World Wide Web hawk everything from potato chips to cereal to fast food—to drugs. Alcohol and tobacco companies, chafing under advertising restrictions in other media, have discovered they can find and woo young people without any problem on the Web. Indeed, children are especially vulnerable on the Internet, where advertising manipulates them, invades their privacy, and transforms them into customers without their knowledge. Although there are various initiatives pending, there are as yet no regulations against targeting children online. Marketers attract children to Web sites with games and contests, and then extract from them information that can be used in future sales pitches to the child and the child's family. They should be aware that this information might be misleading. My daughter recently checked the "less than $20,000" household income box because she was thinking of her allowance.

Some sites offer prizes to lure children into giving up the email addresses of their friends too. Online advertising targets children as young as four in an attempt to develop "brand loyalty" as early as possible. Companies unrelated to children's products have Web sites for children, such as Chevron's site, which features games, toys,

and videos touting the importance of—surprise!—the oil industry. In this way, companies can create an image early on and can also gather marketing data. As one ad says to advertisers, "Beginning this August, Kidstar will be able to reach every kid on the planet. And you can, too."

The United States is one of the few industrialized nations in the world that thinks that children are legitimate targets for advertisers. Belgium, Denmark, Norway, and the Canadian province of Quebec ban all advertising to children on television and radio, and Sweden and Greece are pushing for an end to all advertising aimed at children throughout the European Union. An effort to pass similar legislation in the United States in the 1970s was squelched by a coalition of food and toy companies, broadcasters, and ad agencies. Children in America appear to have value primarily as new consumers. As an ad for juvenile and infant bedding and home accessories says, "Having children is so rewarding. You get to buy childish stuff and pretend it's for them." Our public policy—or lack thereof—on every children's issue, from education to drugs to teen suicide to child abuse, leaves many to conclude that we are a nation that hates its children.

However, the media care about them. The Turner Cartoon Network tells advertisers, "Today's kids influence over $130 billion of their parent's spending annually. Kids also spend $8 billion of their own money. That makes these little consumers big business." Not only are children influencing a lot of spending in the present, they are developing brand loyalty and the beginnings of an addiction to consumption that will serve corporations well in the future. According to Mike Searles, president of Kids 'R' Us, "If you own this child at an early age, you can own this child for years to come. Companies are saying, 'Hey, I want to own the kid younger and younger.'" No wonder Levi Strauss & Co. finds it worthwhile to send a direct mailing to seven- to twelve-year-old girls to learn about them when they are starting to form brand opinions. According to the senior advertising manager, "This is more of a long-term relationship that we're trying to explore." There may not seem much harm in this until we consider that the tobacco and alcohol industries are also interested in long-term relationships beginning in childhood—and are selling products that can indeed end up "owning" people.

Advertisers are willing to spend a great deal on psychological research that will help them target children more effectively. Nintendo U.S. has a research center which interviews at least fifteen hundred children every week. Kid Connection, a unit of the advertising agency Saatchi & Saatchi, has commissioned what the company calls "psychocultural youth research" studies from cultural anthropologists and clinical psychologists. In a recent study, psychologists interviewed young people between the ages of six and twenty and then analyzed their dreams, drawings, and reactions to symbols. Meanwhile, the anthropologists spent over five hundred hours watching other children use the Internet.

Children are easily influenced. Most little children can't tell the difference between the shows and the commercials (which basically means they are smarter than the rest of us). The toys sold during children's programs are often based on characters in the programs. Recently, the Center for Media Education asked the Federal Trade Commission to examine "kidola," a television marketing strategy in which toy companies promise to buy blocks of commercial time if a local broadcast station airs programs associated with their toys.

One company has initiated a program for advertisers to distribute samples, coupons, and promotional materials to a network of twenty-two thousand day care centers and 2 million preschool children. The editor-in-chief of *KidStyle,* a kids' fashion magazine that made its debut in 1997, said, "It's not going to be another parenting magazine. This will be a pictorial magazine focusing on products."

Perhaps most troubling, advertising is increasingly showing up in our schools, where ads are emblazoned on school buses, scoreboards, and book covers, where corporations provide "free" material for teachers, and where many children are a captive audience for the commercials on Channel One, a marketing program that gives video equipment to desperate schools in exchange for the right to broadcast a "news" program studded with commercials to all students every morning. Channel One is hardly free, however—it is estimated that it costs taxpayers $1.8 billion in lost classroom time. But it certainly is profitable for the owners who promise advertisers "the largest teen audience around" and "the undivided attention of millions of teenagers for twelve minutes a day." Another ad for Channel One boasts, "Our relationship with 8.1 million teenagers lasts for six years [rather remarkable considering most of theirs last for . . . like six days]." Imagine the public outcry if a political or religious group offered schools an information package with ten minutes of news and two minutes of political or religious persuasion. Yet we tend to think of commercial persuasion as somehow neutral, although it certainly promotes beliefs and behavior that have significant and sometimes harmful effects on the individual, the family, the society, and the environment.

"Reach him at the office," says an ad featuring a small boy in a business suit, which continues, "His first day job is kindergarten. Modern can put your sponsored educational materials in the lesson plan." Advertisers are reaching nearly 8 million public-school students each day.

Cash-strapped and underfunded schools accept this dance with the devil. And they are not alone. As many people become less and less willing to pay taxes to support public schools and other institutions and services, corporations are only too eager to pick up the slack—in exchange for a captive audience, of course. As one good corporate citizen, head of an outdoor advertising agency, suggested, "Perhaps fewer libraries would be closing their doors or reducing their services if they wrapped their buildings in tastefully done outdoor ads."

According to the Council for Aid to Education, the total amount corporations spend on "educational" programs from kindergarten through high school has increased from $5 million in 1965 to about $500 million today. The Seattle School Board recently voted to aggressively pursue advertising and corporate sponsorship. "There can be a Nike concert series and a Boeing valedictorian," said the head of the task force. We already have market-driven educational materials in our schools, such as Exxon's documentary on the beauty of the Alaskan coastline or the Mc-Donald's Nutrition Chart and a kindergarten curriculum that teaches children to "Learn to Read through Recognizing Corporate Logos."

No wonder so many people fell for a "news item" in *Adbusters* (a Canadian magazine that critiques advertising and commercialism) about a new program called "Tattoo You Too!", which pays schools a fee in exchange for students willing to be tattooed with famous corporate logos, such as the Nike "swoosh" and the Guess question mark. Although the item was a spoof, it was believable enough to be picked up by some major media. I guess nothing about advertising seems unbelievable these days.

There are penalties for young people who resist this commercialization. In the spring of 1998 Mike Cameron, a senior at Greenbrier High School in Evans, Georgia, was suspended from school. Why? Did he bring a gun to school? Was he smoking in the boys' room? Did he assault a teacher? No. He wore a Pepsi shirt on a school-sponsored Coke day, an entire school day dedicated to an attempt to win ten thousand dollars in a national contest run by Coca-Cola.

Coke has several "partnerships" with schools around the country in which the company gives several million dollars to the school in exchange for a longterm contract giving Coke exclusive rights to school vending machines. John Bushey, an area superintendent for thirteen schools in Colorado Springs who signs his correspondence "The Coke Dude," urged school officials to "get next year's volume up to 70,000 cases" and suggested letting students buy Coke throughout the day and putting vending machines "where they are accessible all day." Twenty years ago, teens drank almost twice as much milk as soda. Today they drink twice as much soda as milk. Some data suggest this contributes to broken bones while they are still teenagers and to osteoporosis in later life. . . .

ADVERTISING IS OUR ENVIRONMENT

Advertisers like to tell parents that they can always turn off the TV to protect their kids from any of the negative impact of advertising. This is like telling us that we can protect our children from air pollution by making sure they never breathe. Advertising is our *environment.* We swim in it as fish swim in water. We cannot escape it. Unless, of course, we keep our children home from school and blindfold them whenever they are outside of the house. And never let them play with other children. Even then, advertising's messages are inside our intimate relationships, our homes, our hearts, our heads.

Advertising not only appears on radio and television, in our magazines and newspapers, but also surrounds us on billboards, on the sides of buildings, plastered on our public transportation. Buses now in many cities are transformed into facsimiles of products, so that one boards a bus masquerading as a box of Dunkin' Donuts (followed, no doubt, by a Slimfast bus). The creators of this atrocity proudly tell us in their ad in *Advertising Age,* "In your face . . . all over the place!" Indeed.

Trucks carry advertising along with products as part of a marketing strategy. "I want every truck we have on the road making folks thirsty for Bud Light," says an ad in *Advertising Age,* which refers to a truck as a "valuable moving billboard." Given that almost half of all automobile crashes are alcohol-related, it's frightening to think of people becoming thirsty for Bud Light while driving their cars. A Spanish company has paid the drivers of seventy-five cars in Madrid to turn their cars into Pall Mall cigarette packages, and hopes to expand its operation throughout

Spain. Imagine cars disguised as bottles of beer zipping along our highways. If we seek to escape all this by taking a plane, we become a captive audience for in-flight promotional videos.

Ads are on the videos we rent, the shopping carts we push through stores, the apples and hot dogs we buy, the online services we use, and the navigational screens of the luxury cars we drive. A new device allows advertisers to print their messages directly onto the sand of a beach. "This is my best idea ever—5,000 imprints of Skippy Peanut Butter jars covering the beach," crowed the inventor. Added the promotion director, "I'm here looking at thousands of families with kids. If they're on the beach thinking of Skippy, that's just what we want." Their next big idea is snow imprinting at ski resorts. In England the legendary white cliffs of Dover now serve as the backdrop for a laser-projected Adidas ad. American consumers have recently joined Europeans in being offered free phone calls if they will also listen to commercials. Conversations are interrupted by brief ads, tailored to match the age and social profiles of the conversants. And beer companies have experimented with messages posted over urinals, such as "Time for more Coors" or "Put used Bud here."

The average American is exposed to at least three thousand ads every day and will spend three years of his or her life watching television commercials. Advertising makes up about 70 percent of our newspapers and 40 percent of our mail. Of course, we don't pay direct attention to very many of these ads, but we are powerfully influenced, mostly on an unconscious level, by the experience of being immersed in an advertising culture, a market-driven culture, in which all our institutions, from political to religious to educational, are increasingly for sale to the highest bidder. According to Rance Crain, editor-in-chief of *Advertising Age,* the major publication of the advertising industry, "Only eight percent of an ad's message is received by the conscious mind; the rest is worked and reworked deep within the recesses of the brain, where a product's positioning

and repositioning takes shape." It is in this sense that advertising is subliminal: not in the sense of hidden messages embedded in ice cubes, but in the sense that we aren't consciously aware of what advertising is doing.

Commercialism has no borders. There is barely any line left between advertising and the rest of the culture. The prestigious Museum of Fine Arts in Boston puts on a huge exhibit of Herb Ritts, fashion photographer, and draws one of the largest crowds in its history. In 1998 the museum's Monet show was the most popular exhibit in the world. Museum officials were especially pleased by results of a survey showing 74 percent of visitors recognized that the show's sponsor was Fleet Financial Group, which shelled out $1.2 million to underwrite the show.

Bob Dole plays on his defeat in the presidential election in ads for Air France and Viagra, while Ed Koch, former mayor of New York City, peddles Dunkin' Donuts' bagels. Dr. Jane Goodall, doyenne of primatology, appears with her chimpanzees in an ad for Home Box Office, and Sarah Ferguson, the former duchess of York, gets a million dollars for being the official spokeswoman for Weight Watchers (with a bonus if she keeps her weight down). . . .

The unintended effects of advertising are far more important and far more difficult to measure than those effects that are intended. The important question is not "Does this ad sell the product?" but rather "What else does this ad sell?" An ad for Gap khakis featuring a group of acrobatic swing dancers probably sold a lot of pants, which, of course, was the intention of the advertisers. But it also contributed to a rage for swing dancing. This is an innocuous example of advertising's powerful unintended effects. Swing dancing is not binge drinking, after all.

Advertising often sells a great deal more than products. It sells values, images, and concepts of love and sexuality, romance, success, and, perhaps most important, normalcy. To a great extent, it tells us who we are and who we should be. We are increasingly using brand names to create our identities. James Twitchell argues that the label of our shirt, the make of our car, and our favorite laundry detergent are filling the vacuum once occupied by religion, education, and our family name.

CRITICAL-THINKING QUESTIONS

1. Advertisers maintain that people rely on commercials and ads to make informed decisions about the products and services they buy. Using the material in this chapter, discuss whether you agree or disagree with advertisers' claims that they are providing a service to consumers by educating them about their market choices.

2. What does Kilbourne mean when she says that advertising "sells much more than products"? How, for example, does advertising influence our values and lifestyles? What about children's and adolescents' attitudes about tobacco, alcohol, food, and their self-image?

3. Belgium, Denmark, Norway, and other countries ban all television and radio advertising directed at children. Should the United States pass similar legislation?

REFERENCES

ANGIER, N. 1996. Who needs this ad most? *New York Times* (November 24): 4E.

ASSOCIATED PRESS. 1998. Pepsi prank goes flat. *Boston Globe* (March 26): A3.

AUSTEN, I. 1999. But first, another word from our sponsors. *New York Times* (February 18): E1, E8.

BIDLAKE, S. 1997. Commercials support free phone calls. *Advertising Age International* (September): 147, 149.

CARROLL, J. 1996. Adventures into new territory. *Boston Globe* (November 24): D1, D5.

CORTISSOZ, A. 1998. For young people, swing's the thing. *Boston Globe* (July 25): A2, A10.

CRAIN, R. 1997. Who knows what ads lurk in the hearts of consumers? The inner mind knows. *Advertising Age* (June 9): 25.

FOREMAN, J. 1999. Sugar's "empty calories" pile up. *Boston Globe* (March 1): C1, C4.

GRUNWALD, M. 1997. Megamall sells stimulation. *Boston Globe* (December 9): A1, A26.

HARRIS, R. 1989. Children who dress for excess: Today's youngsters have become fixated with fashion. *Los Angeles Times* (November 12): A1.

JACOBSON, M. F., and L. A. MAZUR. 1995. *Marketing madness: A survival guide for a consumer society.* Boulder, Colo.: Westview Press.

JHALLY, S. 1998. *Advertising and the end of the world* (a video). Northampton, Mass.: Media Education Foundation.

KERWIN, A. M. 1997. "KidStyle" crafts customized ad opportunities. *Advertising Age* (April 28): 46.

KORANTENG, J. 1999. Sweden presses EU for further ad restrictions. *Advertising Age International* (April 12): 2.

KROL, C. 1998. Levi's reaches girls as they develop opinions on brands. *Advertising Age* (April 20): 29.

LEWIS, M. 1997. Royal scam. *New York Times Magazine* (February 9): 22.

LIU, E. 1999. Remember when public space didn't carry brand names? *USA Today* (March 25): 15A.

McCARTHY, C. 1990. In thingdom, laying waste our powers. *Washington Post* (November 11): F3.

McLAREN, C. 1997. The babysitter's club. *Stay Free!* (Spring): 8–11.

MOHL, B. 1999. Lend them your ear, and your call is free. *Boston Globe* (January 13): AI, A10.

Monet show sets world record 1999. *Boston Globe* (February 2): E2.

Not for Sale! 1997. Oakland, Calif.: Center for Commercial-Free Public Education. (Spring).

Not for Sale! 1999. Oakland, Calif.: Center for Commercial-Free Public Education. (Winter).

ORLANDO, S. 1999. A material world: Defining ourselves by consumer goods. [Online]. Available: *http://www.sciencedaily.com/releases/1999/05/990518114815.htm*.

Reading, Writing . . . and TV commercials. 1999. *Enough!* 7(10) (Spring).

RICH, F. 1997. howdydoody.com. *New York Times* (June 8): E15.

ROSENBERG, A. S. 1999. Ad ideas etched in sand. *Boston Globe* (February 1): A3.

SHARKEY, J. 1998. Beach-blanket babel: Another reason to stay at the pool. *New York Times* (July 5): 2.

TWITCHELL, J. B. 1996. *Adcult USA: The triumph of advertising in American culture.* New York: Columbia University Press.

U.S. Department of Transportation. 1999. National Highway Traffic Safety Administration. [Online]. Available: *http://www.nhtsa.dot.gov/people/ncsa/FactPreve/alc96.html*.

WALLACE, D. F. 1996. *Infinite jest.* Boston: Little Brown.

WEBER, J. 1997. Selling to kids: At what price? *Boston Globe* (May 18): F4.

CLASSIC

CONTEMPORARY

CROSS-CULTURAL

20 Parents' Socialization of Children in Global Perspective

D. TERRI HEATH

One of the most important functions of the family worldwide is the socialization of children. Although parents might receive help from others (such as relatives, neighbors, and professional caregivers), most communities expect parents themselves to raise their children to be productive and responsible adults. Across vastly different cultural environments, D. Terri Heath shows the universal importance of closeness with parents in affecting "the academic achievement, psychological well-being, substance use and juvenile delinquency, and general behavior of children worldwide."

THE BENEFITS OF CLOSE PARENT–YOUTH RELATIONSHIPS IN ADOLESCENCE

This article . . . [describes] how a positive relationship between parents and children later enhances the life satisfaction and psychological well-being of older youths and protects them from juvenile delinquency and substance abuse. As the cross-cultural examples illustrate, youth who perceive a close relationship with their parents exhibit more positive outcomes in each of these four areas. Life satisfaction and psychological well-being are described first, followed by illustrative cross-cultural examples. Next is a description of the impact of close parent-child relationships and their protective value on the substance abuse and juvenile delinquency of

Source: From *Families in Multicultural Perspective,* eds. Bron B. Ingoldsby and Suzanna Smith, pp. 161–86. Copyright © 1995 Guilford Press, NY. Reprinted with permission.

adolescents. Relevant, illustrative cross-cultural examples conclude this section.

Life satisfaction is a subjective measure of an individual's perception of his/her quality of life. Rather than objective measures of income, education, accumulation of wealth, and home ownership, life satisfaction is the level of individual satisfaction each person perceives in his/her own life: that which is privately known and privately evaluated. A multitude of factors influence life satisfaction, and because it is a personal evaluation, these factors differ for individuals. A study of life satisfaction among Hong Kong adolescents illustrates the profound effects peers and parents can exert on an adolescent's life satisfaction.

Psychological well-being is a measure of multiple submissions: self-esteem, locus of control, anxiety, loneliness, and sociability. Persons who exhibit high self-esteem, an internal locus of control, low anxiety and loneliness, and high sociability are considered to have strong psychological well-being. Just as with life satisfaction, many

101

factors can influence psychological well-being, but this section focuses specifically on the association between strong relationships with parents and positive outcomes for youth and young adults.

Hong Kong

Adolescence is a transitional period in the life cycle. Associations with family and peers are changing, and adolescents often feel increased pressure to succeed in social relationships outside their families. Their level of attachment, identification, and frequency of consultation with parents relative to that with peers influences the life satisfaction of adolescents in general and, specifically, their satisfaction with school, family, and others. Hong Kong, on the south coast of China, is heavily influenced by current political and economic changes in China. Chinese culture, with its emphasis on family and community over individual independence, continues to play a significant role in the culture of Hong Kong. Because the orientation of adolescents toward their peers and parents has important implications for their satisfaction with life, Hong Kong offers a unique look at this relationship in a rapidly developing society. In a study of 1,906 students, ages thirteen to sixteen, adolescents who were more oriented toward their parents, as well as those who were more oriented toward their peers, were equally satisfied with school, their acceptance by others, the government, and the media. However, those adolescents who are most oriented toward their parents were additionally satisfied with life in general, their families, and the environment (Man, 1991). Man (1991) concludes that "in a predominantly Chinese society like Hong Kong, the family remains a highly important determinant of the adolescents' life satisfaction" (p. 363).

Iran

Parents continue to influence the lives of their children as young adults through parental interactions, guidance, and shared history. When young adults are dissatisfied with their parents, their adult psychological well-being appears to be negatively influenced. When Iranian students, ages seventeen to thirty-nine, studying at universities in Iran and the United States, were asked about their childhood dissatisfactions with their parents, an interesting pattern emerged. Those adults who perceived the most childhood dissatisfaction with parents were most likely to experience current loneliness, anxiety, external locus of control, misanthropy, neurosis, and psychosis when compared to adults who scored low on the dissatisfaction scale. They were also more likely to experience lower self-esteem and lower sociability, as well as decreased satisfaction with peer relationships, than were adults who had perceptions of childhood satisfaction with parents (Hojat, Borenstein, & Shapurian, 1990). There were no differences between the Iranian students studying at U.S. universities and those studying at Iranian institutions. The authors conclude that when a child's needs for closeness, attachment, and intimacy are not fulfilled to the child's satisfaction in early childhood, the result can be adult dissatisfactions with peer relationships and decreased psychological well-being in adulthood.

Puerto Rico

Can a child's need for closeness and intimacy be adequately fulfilled when the parents of the child are either alcohol dependent or mentally ill? By comparing three groups of children—those with an alcoholic parent, with a mentally ill parent, and with other parents without obvious diagnoses—researchers in Puerto Rico believe that children and adolescents, ages four to sixteen, with alcoholic or mentally ill parents are more likely than other children to be exposed to adverse family environments, such as stressful life events, marital discord, and family dysfunction. In addition, the children in these families were more maladjusted than were children in families without a diagnosed parent, according to reports by psychiatrists, parents, and the children themselves (Rubio-Stipec et al., 1991). (However, the teachers of these three groups of children were unable to detect differences in child behavior, probably because 43 percent of them rated their familiarity with the child as "not good.") It appears from this research that children of alcoholic or mentally ill parents suffer negative consequences during childhood, and these consequences are readily apparent to psychiatrists, their parents, and even the children themselves.

In many cultures, adolescence is a period of rapid psychological growth and a shift in orientation from parents to peers. Adolescents move through this period from childhood at the beginning to adulthood at the end. Most choose educational and career paths during this period. Many choose marriage partners. They move from residing with their parents to residing with peers, with spouses, or by themselves. Because this is a time of such change, some adolescents cope with the transitions by engaging in problematic behaviors (e.g., drug and alcohol abuse and juvenile delinquency). This section presents some of the factors that contribute to problematic behaviors for youth in Canada and three subcultures in the United States: Native American, white, and Hispanic.

Canada

Social control theorists contend that adolescent alcohol consumption is influenced by the degree to which youth are influenced by peers more than parents. A study of alcohol consumption by Canadian eleventh and twelfth graders demonstrates this relationship (Mitic, 1990). Students were divided into three groups: (1) those who drank only with their parents, (2) those who drank only with their peers, and (3) those who drank both with and without their parents. The consumption rates of this last group were further divided into the amount of drinking with and without parents. As might be expected, students who drank only with parents consumed the least amount of alcohol. Those who drank with both parents and peers consumed the most alcohol and drank more heavily when they were with peers. It

appears that what parents model for their children regarding alcohol consumption has only a small influence in the youths' consumption behaviors when the parents are not present.

Hispanics and Whites in the United States

Researchers found that Hispanic and white youth (ages nine to seventeen) in the United States are also significantly influenced in their drug and alcohol consumption by their relationships with friends and parents. For white and Hispanic adolescents who used either licit substances (e.g., cigarettes and alcohol), marijuana, or other illicit substances (e.g., cocaine, heroin, and prescription drugs used for recreational purposes), the single most important influence was the percentage of friends who used marijuana. Those youths who had higher percentages of friends who used marijuana were more likely to use each category of drug (licit, marijuana, and other illicit) than were youths who had fewer friends who used marijuana; this is equally true for both Hispanic and white youth. Although both users and abstainers were more affiliated with their parents than their peers, users were more strongly influenced by their peers; more likely to disregard parental objections to their friends; more likely to believe that their friends, rather than their parents, understand them best; and more likely to respect the ideas of their friends in difficult situations. The only cultural difference was that, in general, Hispanic youths respected their parents' views more than did white youths, regardless of whether they used or abstained from drugs and alcohol (Coombs, Paulson, & Richardson, 1991). Coombs et al. conclude that "youths having viable relationships with parents are less involved with drugs and drug-oriented peers" (p. 87).

Ojibway Native Americans

Delinquent behavior represents a dysfunctional response to stressors and strains in adolescence.

On Native American reservations in the United States, an orientation toward parents and tribal elders appears to protect some youth from these negative behaviors. High percentages of Native American Ojibway adolescents, ages twelve to eighteen, reported inappropriate or illegal activities, such as using alcohol (85 percent), stealing something (70 percent), skipping school (64 percent), smoking marijuana (53 percent), and intentional damage to property (45 percent). However, those who spent more time with their family in chores, recreation, family discussions, and meals were less involved in negative behaviors. As expected, those youth who spent more time in activities away from their families—such as listening alone to the radio, and partying with drugs and alcohol—were at greatest risk for delinquent behaviors and court adjudications (Zitzow, 1990). Ojibway youths who spent more time in activities with parents and tribal elders were less likely to engage in delinquent behaviors resulting in court adjudications.

Summary

This last section focuses on how close parent-youth relationships are associated with the life satisfaction, psychological well-being, lack of substance use, and absence of delinquent behavior in adolescents. Without exception, adolescents in all six studies benefit from increased involvement with healthy parents. Parental involvement enhanced life satisfaction among adolescents in Hong Kong and contributed to psychological well-being among Iranian college students and Puerto Rican youths. The presence of parents was associated with less alcohol consumption among Canadian adolescents, a strong bond with parents was associated with less drug consumption by Hispanic and white youth in the United States, and spending time with parents and tribal elders was associated with less involvement in delinquent behaviors for Native American adolescents in the United States.

CONCLUSION

In reviewing the literature on cross-cultural research on parent-child relations for this chapter, a clear trend became increasingly apparent. When parents are more involved and/or have greater expectations of their children's behavior, children demonstrate better outcomes. As is apparent from the illustrative examples, greater parental involvement is an active involvement, not a passive one. It is acquired not simply by the amount of time parents and children spend together but rather by how the time is spent. An involved parent is not one who spends the majority of the day near his/her child but rarely interacting with the child. It is, instead, the parent who uses opportunities to share activities such as teaching the child a local trade, reading together, or fostering a close, supportive relationship through companionship. This active, involved parent appears much more likely to rear a successful child. Illustrative cross-cultural examples presented here of high-quality interaction between parents and children, such as spending time reading together in Great Britain, establishing firm limits and offering support in China, and engaging adolescents in activities with parents and tribal elders in the United States, has been associated with better child outcomes. These patterns emerged even when examining parent-son versus parent-daughter relations, relationships among family members in developing versus developed countries, or parent-child relationships in families that resided in Western cultures versus Eastern ones.

CRITICAL-THINKING QUESTIONS

1. According to Heath, are there greater differences or similarities across cultures in the relationship between parent-child closeness and adolescent behavior?

2. What are some of the factors that contribute to the problematic behavior of adolescents both cross-culturally and within subcultures in the United States?

3. What does Heath mean by "parental involvement"? What other variables might also have an impact on parent–child relationships that are not discussed in this selection?

REFERENCES

COOMBS, R. H., M. J. PAULSON, and M. A. RICHARDSON. 1991. Peer versus parental influence in substance use among Hispanic and Anglo children and adolescents. *Journal of Youth and Adolescence,* 20(1): 73–88.

HOJAT, M., B. D. BORENSTEIN, and R. SHAPURIAN. 1990. Perception of childhood dissatisfaction with parents and selected personality traits in adulthood. *Journal of General Psychology,* 117(3): 241–53.

MAN, P. 1991. The influence of peers and parents on youth life satisfaction in Hong Kong. *Social Indicators Research,* 24(4): 347–65.

MITIC, W. 1990. Parental versus peer influence on adolescents' alcohol consumption. *Psychological Reports,* 67: 1273–74.

RUBIO-STIPEC, M., H. BIRD, G. CANINO, and M. ALEGRIA. 1991. Children of alcoholic parents in the community. *Journal of Studies on Alcohol,* 52(1): 78–88.

ZITZOW, D. 1990. Ojibway adolescent time spent with parents/ elders as related to delinquency and court adjudication experiences. *American Indian and Alaska Native Mental Health Research,* 4(1): 53–63.

CLASSIC

CONTEMPORARY

CROSS-CULTURAL

21 The Dyad and the Triad

GEORG SIMMEL

Sometimes called the Freud of sociology, Georg Simmel explored many of the intricate details of everyday life with a keen perceptiveness. In this selection, Simmel describes the distinctive qualities of human relationships with two members (the dyad) and three members (the triad).

THE DYAD

Everyday experiences show the specific character that a relationship attains by the fact that only two elements participate in it. A common fate or enterprise, an agreement or secret between two persons, ties each of them in a very different manner than if even only three have a part in it. This is perhaps most characteristic of the secret. General experience seems to indicate that this minimum of two, with which the secret ceases to be the property of the one individual, is at the same time the maximum at which its preservation is relatively secure. . . .

The social structure here rests immediately on the one and on the other of the

Source: Reprinted and abridged with the permission of The Free Press, a Division of Simon & Schuster Adult Publishing Group, from *The Sociology of Georg Simmel,* translated and edited by Kurt H. Wolff. Copyright © 1950, copyright renewed 1978 by The Free Press.

two, and the secession of either would destroy the whole. The dyad, therefore, does not attain that super-personal life which the individual feels to be independent of himself. As soon, however, as there is a sociation of three, a group continues to exist even in case one of the members drops out.

. . . Neither of the two members can hide what he has done behind the group, nor hold the group responsible for what he has failed to do. Here the forces with which the group surpasses the individual—indefinitely and partially, to be sure, but yet quite perceptibly—cannot compensate for individual inadequacies, as they can in larger groups. There are many respects in which two united individuals accomplish more than two isolated individuals. Nevertheless, the decisive characteristic of the dyad is that each of the two must actually accomplish something, and that in

case of failure only the other remains—not a super-individual force, as prevails in a group even of three.

. . . Precisely the fact that each of the two knows that he can depend only upon the other and on nobody else, gives the dyad a special consecration—as is seen in marriage and friendship, but also in more external associations, including political ones, that consist of two groups. In respect to its sociological destiny and in regard to any other destiny that depends on it, the dyadic element is much more frequently confronted with All or Nothing than is the member of the larger group.

THE TRIAD VERSUS THE DYAD

This peculiar closeness between two is most clearly revealed if the dyad is contrasted with the triad. For among three elements, each one operates as an intermediary between the other two, exhibiting the twofold function of such an organ, which is to unite and to separate. Where three elements, A, B, C, constitute a group, there is, in addition to the direct relationship between A and B, for instance, their indirect one, which is derived from their common relation to C. . . . Discords between two parties which they themselves cannot remedy are accommodated by the third or by absorption in a comprehensive whole.

Yet the indirect relation does not only strengthen the direct one. It may also disturb it. No matter how close a triad may be, there is always the occasion on which two of the three members regard the third as an intruder. The reason may be the mere fact that he shares in certain moods which can unfold in all their intensity and tenderness only when two can meet without distraction: The sensitive union of two is always irritated by the spectator. It may also be noted how extraordinarily difficult and rare it is for three people to attain a really uniform mood—when visiting a museum, for instance, or looking at a landscape—and how much more easily such a mood emerges between two. . . .

The sociological structure of the dyad is characterized by two phenomena that are absent from it. One is the intensification of relation by a third element, or by a social framework that transcends both members of the dyad. The other is any disturbance and distraction of pure and immediate reciprocity. In some cases it is precisely this absence which makes the dyadic relationship more intensive and strong. For, many otherwise undeveloped, unifying forces that derive from more remote psychical reservoirs come to life in the feeling of exclusive dependence upon one another and of hopelessness that cohesion might come from anywhere but immediate interaction. Likewise, they carefully avoid many disturbances and dangers into which confidence in a third party and in the triad itself might lead the two. This intimacy, which is the tendency of relations between two persons, is the reason why the dyad constitutes the chief seat of jealousy.

CRITICAL-THINKING QUESTIONS

1. Why do most people find their greatest experience of intimacy in a dyad?
2. What features of the dyad make this form of interaction unstable?
3. What are the characteristic strengths of the triad? What about weaknesses?
4. How might Simmel explain the common observation that "two's company; three's a crowd"?

CLASSIC

CONTEMPORARY

CROSS-CULTURAL

22 The Presentation of Self

ERVING GOFFMAN

Face-to-face interaction is a complex process by which people both convey and receive information about each other. In this selection, Erving Goffman presents basic observations about how everyone tries to influence how others perceive them. In addition, he suggests ways in which people can evaluate how honestly others present themselves.

When an individual enters the presence of others, they commonly seek to acquire information about him or to bring into play information about him already possessed. They will be interested in his general socioeconomic status, his conception of self, his attitude toward them, his competence, his trustworthiness, etc. Although some of this information seems to be sought almost as an end in itself, there are usually quite practical reasons for acquiring it. Information about the individual helps to define the situation, enabling others to know in advance what he will expect of them and what they may expect of him. Informed in these ways, the others will know how best to act in order to call forth a desired response from him.

For those present, many sources of information become accessible and many carriers (or "sign-vehicles") become available for conveying this information. If unacquainted with the individual, observers can glean clues from his

conduct and appearance which allow them to apply their previous experience with individuals roughly similar to the one before them or, more important, to apply untested stereotypes to him. They can also assume from past experience that only individuals of a particular kind are likely to be found in a given social setting. They can rely on what the individual says about himself or on documentary evidence he provides as to who and what he is. If they know, or know of, the individual by virtue of experience prior to the interaction, they can rely on assumptions as to the persistence and generality of psychological traits as a means of predicting his present and future behavior.

However, during the period in which the individual is in the immediate presence of the others, few events may occur which directly provide the others with the conclusive information they will need if they are to direct wisely their own activity. Many crucial facts lie beyond the time and place of interaction or lie concealed within it. For example, the "true" or "real" attitudes, beliefs, and emotions of the individual can be ascertained only indirectly, through his avowals or through what

Source: From *The Presentation of Self in Everyday Life* by Erving Goffman, copyright © 1959 by Erving Goffman, Bantam Doubleday Dell Publishing Group, Inc. Reprinted with permission.

appears to be involuntary expressive behavior. Similarly, if the individual offers the others a product or service, they will often find that during the interaction there will be no time and place immediately available for eating the pudding that the proof can be found in. They will be forced to accept some events as conventional or natural signs of something not directly available to the senses. In Ichheiser's terms,[1] the individual will have to act so that he intentionally or unintentionally *expresses* himself, and the others will in turn have to be *impressed* in some way by him.

The expressiveness of the individual (and therefore his capacity to give impressions) appears to involve two radically different kinds of sign activity: the expression that he *gives*, and the expression that he *gives off*. The first involves verbal symbols or their substitutes which he uses admittedly and solely to convey the information that he and the others are known to attach to these symbols. This is communication in the traditional and narrow sense. The second involves a wide range of action that others can treat as symptomatic of the actor, the expectation being that the action was performed for reasons other than the information conveyed in this way. As we shall have to see, this distinction has an only initial validity. The individual does of course intentionally convey misinformation by means of both of these types of communication, the first involving deceit, the second feigning.

. . . Let us now turn from the others to the point of view of the individual who presents himself before them. He may wish them to think highly of him, or to think that he thinks highly of them, or to perceive how in fact he feels toward them, or to obtain no clear-cut impression; he may wish to ensure sufficient harmony so that the interaction can be sustained, or to defraud, get rid of, confuse, mislead, antagonize, or insult them. Regardless of the particular objective which the individual has in mind and of his motive for having this objective, it will be in his interests to control the conduct of the others, especially their responsive treatment of him. This control is achieved largely by influencing

the definition of the situation which the others come to formulate, and he can influence this definition by expressing himself in such a way as to give them the kind of impression that will lead them to act voluntarily in accordance with his own plan. Thus, when an individual appears in the presence of others, there will usually be some reason for him to mobilize his activity so that it will convey an impression to others which it is in his interests to convey. Since a girl's dormitory mates will glean evidence of her popularity from the calls she receives on the phone, we can suspect that some girls will arrange for calls to be made, and Willard Waller's finding can be anticipated:

It has been reported by many observers that a girl who is called to the telephone in the dormitories will often allow herself to be called several times, in order to give all the other girls ample opportunity to hear her paged.[2]

Of the two kinds of communication—expressions given and expressions given off—this report will be primarily concerned with the latter, with the more theatrical and contextual kind, the nonverbal, presumably unintentional kind, whether this communication be purposely engineered or not. As an example of what we must try to examine, I would like to cite at length a novelistic incident in which Preedy, a vacationing Englishman, makes his first appearance on the beach of his summer hotel in Spain:

But in any case he took care to avoid catching anyone's eye. First of all, he had to make it clear to those potential companions of his holiday that they were of no concern to him whatsoever. He stared through them, round them, over them—eyes lost in space. The beach might have been empty. If by chance a ball was thrown his way, he looked surprised; then let a smile of amusement lighten his face (Kindly Preedy), looked round dazed to see that there *were* people on the beach, tossed it back with a smile to himself and not a smile *at* the people, and then resumed carelessly his nonchalant survey of space.

But it was time to institute a little parade, the parade of the Ideal Preedy. By devious handlings he gave any who wanted to look a chance to see the title of his book—a Spanish translation of Homer, classic thus, but not daring, cosmopolitan too—and then gathered together his beach-wrap and bag into a neat sand-resistant pile (Methodical and Sensible Preedy), rose slowly to stretch at ease his huge frame (Big-Cat Preedy), and tossed aside his sandals (Carefree Preedy, after all).

The marriage of Preedy and the sea! There were alternative rituals. The first involved the stroll that turns into a run and a dive straight into the water, thereafter smoothing into a strong splashless crawl towards the horizon. But of course not really to the horizon. Quite suddenly he would turn on to his back and thrash great white splashes with his legs, somehow thus showing that he could have swum further had he wanted to, and then would stand up a quarter out of water for all to see who it was.

The alternative course was simpler, it avoided the cold-water shock and it avoided the risk of appearing too high-spirited. The point was to appear to be so used to the sea, the Mediterranean, and this particular beach, that one might as well be in the sea as out of it. It involved a slow stroll down and into the edge of the water—not even noticing his toes were wet, land and water all the same to *him!*—with his eyes up at the sky gravely surveying portents, invisible to others, of the weather (Local Fisherman Preedy).[3]

The novelist means us to see that Preedy is improperly concerned with the extensive impressions he feels his sheer bodily action is giving off to those around him. We can malign Preedy further by assuming that he has acted merely in order to give a particular impression, that this is a false impression, and that the others present receive either no impression at all, or, worse still, the impression that Preedy is affectedly trying to cause them to receive this particular impression. But the important point for us here is that the kind of impression Preedy thinks he is making is in fact the kind of impression that others correctly and incorrectly glean from someone in their midst. . . .

There is one aspect of the others' response that bears special comment here. Knowing that the individual is likely to present himself in a light that is favorable to him, the others may divide what they witness into two parts; a part that is relatively easy for the individual to manipulate at will, being chiefly his verbal assertions, and a part in regard to which he seems to have little concern or control, being chiefly derived from the expressions he gives off. The others may then use what are considered to be the ungovernable aspects of his expressive behavior as a check upon the validity of what is conveyed by the governable aspects. In this a fundamental asymmetry is demonstrated in the communication process, the individual presumably being aware of only one stream of his communication, the witnesses of this stream and one other. For example, in Shetland Isle one crofter's wife, in serving native dishes to a visitor from the mainland of Britain, would listen with a polite smile to his polite claims of liking what he was eating; at the same time she would take note of the rapidity with which the visitor lifted his fork or spoon to his mouth, the eagerness with which he passed food into his mouth, and the gusto expressed in chewing the food, using these signs as a check on the stated feelings of the eater. The same woman, in order to discover what one acquaintance (A) "actually" thought of another acquaintance (B), would wait until B was in the presence of A but engaged in conversation with still another person (C). She would then covertly examine the facial expressions of A as he regarded B in conversation with C. Not being in conversation with B, and not being directly observed by him, A would sometimes relax usual constraints and tactful deceptions, and freely express what he was "actually" feeling about B. This Shetlander, in short, would observe the unobserved observer.

Now given the fact that others are likely to check up on the more controllable aspects of behavior by means of the less controllable, one can expect that sometimes the individual will try to exploit this very possibility, guiding the impression he makes through behavior felt to be reliably informing.[4] For example, in gaining admission to a tight social circle, the participant observer may not only wear an accepting look while listening to an informant, but may also be careful to wear the same look when observing the informant talking to others; observers of the observer will then not as easily discover where he actually stands. A specific illustration may be cited from Shetland Isle. When a neighbor dropped in to have a cup of tea, he would ordinarily wear at least a hint of an expectant warm smile as he passed through the door into the cottage. Since lack of physical obstructions outside the cottage and lack of light within it usually made it possible to observe the visitor unobserved as he approached the house, islanders sometimes took pleasure in watching the visitor drop whatever expression he was manifesting and replace it with a sociable one just before reaching the door. However, some visitors, in appreciating that this examination was occurring, would blindly adopt a social face a long distance from the house, thus ensuring the projection of a constant image.

This kind of control upon the part of the individual reinstates the symmetry of the communication process, and sets the stage for a kind of information game—a potentially infinite cycle of concealment, discovery, false revelation, and rediscovery. It should be added that since the others are likely to be relatively unsuspicious of the presumably unguided aspects of the individual's conduct, he can gain much by controlling it. The others of course may sense that the individual is manipulating the presumably spontaneous aspects of his behavior, and seek in this very act of manipulation some shading of conduct that the individual has not managed to control. This again provides a check upon the individual's behavior, this time his presumably uncalculated behavior, thus re-establishing the asymmetry of the communication process. Here I would like only to add the suggestion that the arts of piercing an individual's effort at calculated unintentionality seem better developed than our capacity to manipulate our own behavior, so that regardless of how many steps have occurred in the information game, the witness is likely to have the advantage over the actor, and the initial asymmetry of the communication process is likely to be retained. . . .

In everyday life, of course, there is a clear understanding that first impressions are important. Thus, the work adjustment of those in service occupations will often hinge upon a capacity to seize and hold the initiative in the service relation, a capacity that will require subtle aggressiveness on the part of the server when he is of lower socioeconomic status than his client. W. F. Whyte suggests the waitress as an example:

The first point that stands out is that the waitress who bears up under pressure does not simply respond to her customers. She acts with some skill to control their behavior. The first question to ask when we look at the customer relationship is, "Does the waitress get the jump on the customer, or does the customer get the jump on the waitress?" The skilled waitress realizes the crucial nature of this question. . . .

The skilled waitress tackles the customer with confidence and without hesitation. For example, she may find that a new customer has seated himself before she could clear off the dirty dishes and change the cloth. He is now leaning on the table studying the menu. She greets him, says, "May I change the cover, please?" and, without waiting for an answer, takes his menu away from him so that he moves back from the table, and she goes about her work. The relationship is handled politely but firmly, and there is never any question as to who is in charge.[5]

When the interaction that is initiated by "first impressions" is itself merely the initial interaction in an extended series of interactions involving the same participants, we speak of "getting off on the right foot" and feel that it is crucial that we do so. Thus, one learns that some teachers take the following view:

You can't ever let them get the upper hand on you or you're through. So I start out tough. The first day I get a new class in, I let them know who's boss. . . . You've got to start off tough, then you can ease up as you go along. If you start out easy-going, when you try to get tough, they'll just look at you and laugh.[6]

. . . In stressing the fact that the initial definition of the situation projected by an individual tends to provide a plan for the cooperative activity that follows—in stressing this action point of view—we must not overlook the crucial fact that any projected definition of the situation also has a distinctive moral character. It is this moral character of projections that will chiefly concern us in this report. Society is organized on the principle that any individual who possesses certain social characteristics has a moral right to expect that others will value and treat him in an appropriate way. Connected with this principle is a second, namely that an individual who implicitly or explicitly signifies that he has certain social characteristics ought in fact to be what he claims he is. In consequence, when an individual projects a definition of the situation and thereby makes an implicit or explicit claim to be a person of a particular kind, he automatically exerts a moral demand upon the others, obliging them to value and treat him in the manner that persons of his kind have a right to expect. He also implicitly foregoes all claims to be things he does not appear to be[7] and hence foregoes the treatment that would be appropriate for such individuals. The others find, then, that the individual has informed them as to what is and as to what they *ought* to see as the "is."

One cannot judge the importance of definitional disruptions by the frequency with which they occur, for apparently they would occur more frequently were not constant precautions taken. We find that preventive practices are constantly employed to avoid these embarrassments and that corrective practices are constantly employed to compensate for discrediting occurrences that have not been successfully avoided. When the individual employs these strategies and tactics to protect his own projections, we may refer to them as "defensive practices"; when a participant employs them to save the definition of the situation projected by another, we speak of "protective practices" or "tact." Together, defensive and protective practices comprise the techniques employed to safeguard the impression fostered by an individual during his presence before others. It should be added that while we may be ready to see that no fostered impression would survive if defensive practices were not employed, we are less ready perhaps to see that few impressions could survive if those who received the impression did not exert tact in their reception of it.

In addition to the fact that precautions are taken to prevent disruption of projected definitions, we may also note that an intense interest in these disruptions comes to play a significant role in the social life of the group. Practical jokes and social games are played in which embarrassments which are to be taken unseriously are purposely engineered.[8] Fantasies are created in which devastating exposures occur. Anecdotes from the past—real, embroidered, or fictitious—are told and retold, detailing disruptions which occurred, almost occurred, or occurred and were admirably resolved. There seems to be no grouping which does not have a ready supply of these games, reveries, and cautionary tales, to be used as a source of humor, a catharsis for anxieties, and a sanction for inducing individuals to be modest in their claims and reasonable in their projected expectations. The individual may tell himself through dreams of getting into impossible positions. Families tell of the time a guest got his dates mixed and arrived when neither the house nor anyone in it was ready for him. Journalists tell of times when an all-too-meaningful misprint occurred, and the paper's assumption of objectivity or decorum was humorously discredited. Public servants tell of times a client ridiculously misunderstood form instructions, giving answers which implied an unanticipated and bizarre definition of the situation.[9] Seamen, whose home away from home is rigorously he-man, tell stories of coming back home and inadvertently asking mother to "pass the fucking butter."[10] Diplomats tell of the time a near-sighted queen asked a republican ambassador about the health of his king.[11]

To summarize, then, I assume that when an individual appears before others he will have many motives for trying to control the impression they receive of the situation.

CRITICAL-THINKING QUESTIONS

1. How does the "presentation of self" contribute to a definition of a situation in the minds of participants? How does this definition change over time?

2. Apply Goffman's approach to the classroom. What are the typical elements of the instructor's presentation of self? A student's presentation of self?

3. Can we evaluate the validity of people's presentations? How?

NOTES

1. Gustav Ichheiser, "Misunderstandings in Human Relations," supplement to *The American Journal of Sociology* 55 (Sept., 1949), 6–7.

2. Willard Waller, "The Rating and Dating Complex," *American Sociological Review* 2 (1937), 730.

3. William Sansom, *A Contest of Ladies* (London: Hogarth, 1956), pp. 230–32.

4. The widely read and rather sound writings of Stephen Potter are concerned in part with signs that can be engineered to give a shrewd observer the apparently incidental cues he needs to discover concealed virtues the gamesman does not in fact possess.

5. W. F. Whyte, "When Workers and Customers Meet," chap. 7, *Industry and Society,* ed. W. F. Whyte (New York: McGraw-Hill, 1946), pp. 132–33.

6. Teacher interview quoted by Howard S. Becker, "Social Class Variations in the Teacher-Pupil Relationship," *Journal of Educational Sociology* 25, p. 459.

7. This role of the witness in limiting what it is the individual can be has been stressed by Existentialists, who see it as a basic threat to individual freedom. See Jean-Paul Sartre, *Being and Nothingness,* trans. Hazel E. Barnes (New York: Philosophical Library, 1956), pp. 365ff.

8. Goffman, op. cit., pp. 319–27.

9. Peter Blau, "Dynamics of Bureaucracy" (Ph.D. dissertation, Department of Sociology, Columbia University, forthcoming, University of Chicago Press), pp. 127–29.

10. Walter M. Beattie, Jr., "The Merchant Seaman" (unpublished M.A. Report, Department of Sociology, University of Chicago, 1950), p. 35.

11. Sir Frederick Ponsonby, *Recollections of Three Reigns* (New York: Dutton, 1952), p. 46.

CLASSIC

CONTEMPORARY

CROSS-CULTURAL

23 Invisible Privilege

PAULA S. ROTHENBERG

In this article, mother and feminist scholar Paula Rothenberg explains how class and race affect friendship in the life of her daughter.

Perhaps it will be instructive to tell the story of the friendship between my daughter, Andrea, who is white and her onetime friend, Jewel, who is Black. Although it is simply the story of two little girls who managed to be best friends for a very brief time and is highly specific to them, it sheds light on the complex nature of relations across race/ethnicity and class in the suburbs.

Jewel and Andrea met in kindergarten and were kindred spirits from the start. Both were smart and spunky, and both loved to be silly. The girls wanted to play together after school, but that was easier said than done. They managed to trade phone numbers, but whenever I called Jewel's house her grandmother answered and said that Jewel's parents were not available and she was not able to make arrangements for a play date in their absence.

After several weeks of fruitless calls, persistence finally paid off; one day, Jewel's mother, Carol, called back. Yes, Jewel could play at our house after school as long as I didn't mind keeping

her until after dinner. Her mother worked late and wouldn't be able to come by until 7:30 or so. Since that was no problem, I picked up both girls at school the very next day. What I remember about the visit was Jewel's amazement as she explored our house for the first time and discovered that we had more than one bathroom.

After a series of other play dates and several conversations over coffee, Carol told me what I suspected. It was so difficult to reach her and so hard to coordinate play dates for the girls because Carol and her husband did not live in Montclair and Jewel managed to go to the Montclair public schools by claiming her grandmother's house as her residence.

This practice is not uncommon. Taxes in Montclair are very high, and many African-Americans who were raised in town and whose parents still live here can't afford either the price of a house or the taxes they would have to pay as residents. A common solution is to live in East Orange or some other surrounding community in a neighborhood where the schools are inferior but the taxes and property values are much lower and use a parent's or relative's address to claim residency and gain access to the Montclair school system.

From *Invisible Privilege: A Memoir about Race, Class, and Gender* by Paula S. Rothenberg, University Press of Kansas, 2000.

Obviously people react to this subterfuge in different ways, depending largely on their race and their class. Many whites in town are angered by the fact that some children, mostly Black, who don't actually live in town attend the public schools, thereby raising their tax burden, while many Blacks see nothing very wrong with the practice. They question why education should be funded by local property taxes in the first place instead of on a statewide basis, which could ensure equal education for all children. Besides, having grown up here, they think of themselves as part of the town—quite apart from the technicality of their legal residence. While many of the white homeowner/tax payers are recent arrivals to Montclair, many of the African-Americans who resort to the subterfuge are members of families that have lived in the town for several generations. In many cases, they attended the same schools that their children now attend. What seems like a gross violation of law and justice to some of the whites, who focus on whether the parents of the children actually live in town, hardly seems that way to many of the African-Americans whose sense of family is much more inclusive. Children and grandchildren, cousins and nieces are understood to be part of the extended family of the relatives who are Montclair residents and taxpayers. These relatives care for the children at their homes on a regular basis, often having the children spend nights as well as days with them. The children's parents and other family members see the house itself as part of their extended residence, frequently eating and socializing with one another there, dropping in to use the phone or to help with home repairs. Legal residency often seems like a procedural technicality rather than an accurate indicator of who is part of town life. In fact, according to some criteria, these Black Montclairions, whose roots are firmly planted in the town, have more claim to being part of it than the newly arrived white professionals who simply sleep here, commuting to work in New York each day and spending their weekends playing golf at the country club in Glen Ridge.

When Carol finally gave me the family's address and phone number in another town, it was a real sign of trust. The first priority in her life was keeping Jewel in a good school system, arranging afternoon play dates with a white classmate was low on the list. But as the girls' friendship blossomed, Carol, like me, was eager to let them enjoy time together.

And then the inevitable happened. During one of the periodic efforts that the town officials make to track down children who are attending public school illegally, Jewel's illegal status was discovered. Carol never asked whether I had provided the school officials with the information—of course, I had not—but it's difficult to imagine that the idea didn't cross her mind. How could she ever be sure? Through some special arrangement, Jewel was allowed to finish up the school year, which was almost over. During the summer, her family moved out of their apartment and into a small house on the outskirts of Newark, about twenty minutes away. The following September, Jewel began attending parochial school. For her family, as for others like them, parochial school provided the only viable alternative to the inferior and dangerous public school near their home.

Jewel attended Andrea's birthday party that September, as she had in the past, and in January, Carol called to invite Andrea to Jewel's birthday party a week later. Andrea was thrilled with the prospect of seeing Jewel again and of visiting Jewel's house for the first time. She could talk of nothing else.

Jewel's new house was located in a fairly rundown Black neighborhood of small, single-family, urban-style homes. In spite of its appearance, I knew that it would be classified as a middle-class neighborhood by other Black families, since definitions of what counts as "middle class" are themselves race specific, and it is informal residential segregation that often determines how neighborhoods are defined and who gets to live in them. The front door of the house opened into a tiny living room that, in turn, opened into a larger, but still small, dining alcove. Sitting around a large wood table, filling all the space in the room, was a gaggle of aunts and uncles, grandparents and cousins. Apart from Jewel's young cousins, Andrea was the only child present, and she and I were the only white people. Conversation among the adults was friendly, if labored, with everyone trying hard to make us feel welcome. I tried hard not to cramp their good time.

But Andrea was very uncomfortable. Many of the social cues that she counted on to negotiate such events were missing, and she had not had the opportunity to learn the ones that were in place. People talked to each other in unfamiliar ways, and, at times, what I recognized as affectionate teasing must have sounded to her like sharp criticism or argument. She was frightened by how dark the house was and couldn't understand why only one lightbulb was burning on such a dark day. Coming from a world where people have enough money to use lighting as much for decoration as to be functional, she couldn't know that for most of the world, electric lights are a luxury or at least a carefully conserved resource.

A special point of pride for Jewel was the second toilet—literally a water closet—her dad had rigged up in the basement of the house to supplement the full bath upstairs. It consisted of a four-sided wooden cabinet set on a platform in the middle of a dark basement. The cabinet itself had no electric light, but some open space had been left between the ceiling and one side of the cabinet to allow light to enter. Jewel's pride was my daughter's terror. She went to the bathroom only after it was clear that one more postponement would have dire consequences, and she could use the bathroom at all only because I stayed in the cabinet with her.

As we drove home, I knew it was unlikely that the girls would continue their friendship. And in fact, they did not. It was just too difficult. Although Carol and I had tried to help the girls be friends, perhaps because we wanted the possibility of friendship for ourselves as well, the odds against it were too overwhelming and the differences separating the girls were just too great to bridge. In the end, personal relations occur within

social contexts, and, in this case, it was unreasonable to expect two eight-year-old girls to be able to negotiate each other's worlds.

Different people will make different things out of this story. Some will see class as the villain here and argue, along with William Julius Wilson and others, that it is class, not race, that separates whites and Blacks today. This I think is an oversimplification. Jewel and Andrea carried with them the combined history of three hundred years of race, class, and gender oppression and privilege, and the differences created by them were just too great to overcome. For example, why was I able to live in the town and have legitimate access to the schools for my children while Jewel's mother, who had grown up there, could no longer claim access to her own community? Both Jewel's mother and I worked full time, but my job as a college teacher allowed me flexible hours with good pay. Carol worked in the accounting department of a large supermarket corporation in a job that often required her to stay until 11 P.M. Although both she and her husband worked full time, as did Andrea's father and I, their combined income was a fraction of ours. This was not surprising, since statistics indicate that in 1996 annual income for the typical Black family was about half of the $47,000 a year enjoyed by white families. In fact, according to a report issued by the White House's Council of Economic Advisers, Black and Hispanic family incomes are farther behind those of whites today than they were twenty years ago.* For so many years, while I was fortunate enough to be paying off a mortgage on a home I obtained because my in-laws could afford to provide a down payment, Carol and her husband were paying rent and working overtime to save up for a house. Their down payment ultimately bought them a poorly constructed home in a marginal urban neighborhood with inadequate schools, dirty streets, and food stores that overcharge. Some little white

---

New York Times, February 17, 1998, A18.

girl, a mirror image of my long-ago self, drives through those streets today, and her parents caution her to roll up her window and lock her door. They shake their heads over the way some people choose to live when nothing more than hard work and ability are required to earn us all a piece of the American dream. They do not know that for Jewel's family, this *is* their piece of the American dream and they have had to work very hard to achieve it. They do not understand that those of us who have more have drawn on the privileges of our race, our class, our gender, or some combination of them and have done so at the expense of the very people we denigrate.

CRITICAL-THINKING QUESTIONS

1. Why is privilege often invisible? What categories of people are more and less likely to be aware of privilege?

2. Why was Andrea so uncomfortable in Jewel's Newark home? Do you think people can overcome the type of social differences described here? Explain.

3. Can you identify elements of privilege in your own life? How have they affected your relationships with others?

CLASSIC

CONTEMPORARY

CROSS-CULTURAL

24 You Just Don't Understand: Women and Men in Conversation

DEBORAH TANNEN

Many men and women complain with frustration that they communicate on different "wave lengths." Deborah Tannen, a sociolinguist, explains why men and women often talk past each other in a host of everyday situations.

I was sitting in a suburban living room, speaking to a women's group that had invited men to join them for the occasion of my talk about communication between women and men. During the discussion, one man was particularly talkative, full of lengthy comments and explanations. When I made the observation that women often complain that their husbands don't talk to them enough, this man volunteered that he heartily agreed. He gestured toward his wife, who had sat silently beside him on the couch throughout the evening, and said, "She's the talker in our family."

Everyone in the room burst into laughter. The man looked puzzled and hurt. "It's true," he explained. "When I come home from work, I usually have nothing to say, but she never runs out. If it weren't for her, we'd spend the whole evening in silence." Another woman expressed a similar paradox about her husband: "When we go out, he's the life of the party. If I happen to be in another room, I can always hear his voice above the others. But when we're home, he doesn't have that much to say. I do most of the talking."

Who talks more, women or men? According to the stereotype, women talk too much. Linguist Jennifer Coates notes some proverbs:

A woman's tongue wags like a lamb's tail.
Foxes are all tail and women are all tongue.
The North Sea will sooner be found wanting in water than a woman be at a loss for a word.

Throughout history, women have been punished for talking too much or in the wrong way. Linguist Connie Eble lists a variety of physical punishments used in Colonial America: Women were strapped to ducking stools and held underwater until they nearly drowned, put into the stocks with signs pinned to them, gagged, and silenced by a cleft stick applied to their tongues.

Though such institutionalized corporal punishments have given way to informal, often psychological ones, modern stereotypes are not much different from those expressed in the old proverbs. Women are believed to talk too much. Yet study after study finds that it is men who talk more at meetings, in mixed-group discussions, and in classrooms where girls or young women sit next to

Source: Pp. 279–88 from *You Just Don't Understand* by Deborah Tannen. Copyright © 1990 by Deborah Tannen. Reprinted by permission of HarperCollins Publishers, Inc./William Morrow.

boys or young men. For example, communications researchers Barbara and Gene Eakins tape recorded and studied seven university faculty meetings. They found that, with one exception, men spoke more often and, without exception, spoke for a longer time. The men's turns ranged from 10.66 to 17.07 seconds, while the women's turns ranged from 3 to 10 seconds. In other words, the women's longest turns were still shorter than the men's shortest turns.

When a public lecture is followed by questions from the floor, or a talk show host opens the phones, the first voice to be heard asking a question is almost always a man's. And when they ask questions or offer comments from the audience, men tend to talk longer. Linguist Marjorie Swacker recorded question-and-answer sessions at academic conferences. Women were highly visible as speakers at the conferences studied; they presented 40.7 percent of the papers at the conferences studied and made up 42 percent of the audiences. But when it came to volunteering and being called on to ask questions, women contributed only 27.4 percent. Furthermore, the women's questions, on the average, took less than half as much time as the men's. (The mean was 23.1 seconds for women, 52.7 for men.) This happened, Swacker shows, because men (but not women) tended to preface their questions with statements, ask more than one question, and follow up the speaker's answer with another question or comment.

I have observed this pattern at my own lectures, which concern issues of direct relevance to women. Regardless of the proportion of women and men in the audience, men almost invariably ask the first question, more questions, and longer questions. In these situations, women often feel that men are talking too much. I recall one discussion period following a lecture I gave to a group assembled in a bookstore. The group was composed mostly of women, but most of the discussion was being conducted by men in the audience. At one point, a man sitting in the middle was talking at such great length that several women in the front rows began shifting in their seats and rolling their eyes at me. Ironically,

what he was going on about was how frustrated he feels when he has to listen to women going on and on about topics he finds boring and unimportant.

RAPPORT-TALK AND REPORT-TALK

Who talks more, then, women or men? The seemingly contradictory evidence is reconciled by the difference between what I call *public* and *private speaking*. More men feel comfortable doing "public speaking," while more women feel comfortable doing "private speaking." Another way of capturing these differences is by using the terms *report-talk* and *rapport-talk*.

For most women, the language of conversation is primarily a language of rapport: a way of establishing connections and negotiating relationships. Emphasis is placed on displaying similarities and matching experiences. From childhood, girls criticize peers who try to stand out or appear better than others. People feel their closest connections at home, or in settings where they *feel* at home—with one or a few people they feel close to and comfortable with—in other words, during private speaking. But even the most public situations can be approached like private speaking.

For most men, talk is primarily a means to preserve independence and negotiate and maintain status in a hierarchical social order. This is done by exhibiting knowledge and skill, and by holding center stage through verbal performance such as storytelling, joking, or imparting information. From childhood, men learn to use talking as a way to get and keep attention. So they are more comfortable speaking in larger groups made up of people they know less well—in the broadest sense, "public speaking." But even the most private situations can be approached like public speaking, more like giving a report than establishing rapport.

PRIVATE SPEAKING: THE WORDY WOMAN AND THE MUTE MAN

What is the source of the stereotype that women talk a lot? Dale Spender suggests that most people feel instinctively (if not consciously) that women, like children, should be seen and not heard, so any amount of talk from them seems like too much. Studies have shown that if women and men talk equally in a group, people think the women talked more. So there is truth to Spender's view. But another explanation is that men think women talk a lot because they hear women talking in situations where men would not: on the telephone; or in social situations with friends, when they are not discussing topics that men find inherently interesting; or, like the couple at the women's group, at home alone—in other words, in private speaking.

Home is the setting for an American icon that features the silent man and the talkative woman. And this icon, which grows out of the different goals and habits I have been describing, explains why the complaint most often voiced by women about the men with whom they are intimate is "He doesn't talk to me"—and the second most frequent is "He doesn't listen to me."

A woman who wrote to Ann Landers is typical:

My husband never speaks to me when he comes home from work. When I ask, "How did everything go today?" he says, "Rough . . ." or "It's a jungle out there." (We live in Jersey and he works in New York City.)

It's a different story when we have guests or go visiting. Paul is the gabbiest guy in the crowd—a real spellbinder. He comes up with the most interesting stories. People hang on every word. I think to myself, "Why doesn't he ever tell *me* these things?"

This has been going on for thirty-eight years. Paul started to go quiet on me after ten years of marriage. I could never figure out why. Can you solve the mystery?

—The Invisible Woman

Ann Landers suggests that the husband may not want to talk because he is tired when he comes home from work. Yet women who work come home tired too, and they are nonetheless eager to tell their partners or friends everything that happened to them during the day and what these fleeting, daily dramas made them think and feel.

Sources as lofty as studies conducted by psychologists, as down to earth as letters written to advice columnists, and as sophisticated as movies and plays come up with the same insight: Men's silence at home is a disappointment to women. Again and again, women complain, "He seems to have everything to say to everyone else, and nothing to say to me."

The film *Divorce American Style* opens with a conversation in which Debbie Reynolds is claiming that she and Dick Van Dyke don't communicate, and he is protesting that he tells her everything that's on his mind. The doorbell interrupts their quarrel, and husband and wife compose themselves before opening the door to greet their guests with cheerful smiles.

Behind closed doors, many couples are having conversations like this. Like the character played by Debbie Reynolds, women feel men don't communicate. Like the husband played by Dick Van Dyke, men feel wrongly accused. How can she be convinced that he doesn't tell her anything, while he is equally convinced he tells her everything that's on his mind? How can women and men have such different ideas about the same conversations?

When something goes wrong, people look around for a source to blame: either the person they are trying to communicate with ("You're demanding, stubborn, self-centered") or the group that the other person belongs to ("All women are demanding"; "All men are self-centered"). Some generous-minded people blame the relationship ("We just can't communicate"). But underneath, or overlaid on these types of blame cast outward, most people believe that something is wrong with them.

If individual people or particular relationships were to blame, there wouldn't be so many different people having the same problems. The real problem is conversational style. Women and men have different ways of talking. Even with the best intentions, trying to settle the problem through talk can only make things worse if it is ways of talking that are causing trouble in the first place. . . .

"TALK TO ME!"

Women's dissatisfaction with men's silence at home is captured in the stock cartoon setting of a breakfast table at which a husband and wife are sitting: He's reading a newspaper; she's glaring at the back of the newspaper. In a Dagwood strip, Blondie complains, "Every morning all he sees is the newspaper! I'll bet you don't even know I'm here!" Dagwood reassures her, "Of course I know you're here. You're my wonderful wife and I love you very much." With this, he unseeingly pats the paw of the family dog, which the wife has put in her place before leaving the room. The cartoon strip shows that Blondie is justified in feeling like the woman who wrote to Ann Landers: invisible.

Another cartoon shows a husband opening a newspaper and asking his wife, "Is there anything you would like to say to me before I begin reading the newspaper?" The reader knows that there isn't—but that as soon as he begins reading the paper, she will think of something. The cartoon highlights the difference in what women and men think talk is for: To him, talk is for information. So when his wife interrupts his reading, it must be to inform him of something that he needs to know. This being the case, she might as well tell him what she thinks he needs to know before he starts reading. But to her, talk is for interaction. Telling things is a way to show involvement, and listening is a way to show interest and caring. It is not an odd coincidence that she always thinks of things to tell him when he is reading. She feels the need for verbal interaction most keenly when he is (unaccountably, from her point of view) buried in the newspaper instead of talking to her.

Yet another cartoon shows a wedding cake that has, on top, in place of the plastic statues of bride and groom in tuxedo and gown, a breakfast scene in which an unshaven husband reads a newspaper across the table from his disgruntled wife. The cartoon reflects the enormous gulf between the romantic expectations of marriage, represented by the plastic couple in traditional wedding costume, and the often disappointing reality represented by the two sides of the newspaper at the breakfast table—the front, which he is reading, and the back, at which she is glaring.

These cartoons, and many others on the same theme, are funny because people recognize their own experience in them. What's not funny is that many women are deeply hurt when men don't talk to them at home, and many men are deeply frustrated by feeling they have disappointed their partners, without understanding how they failed or how else they could have behaved.

Some men are further frustrated because, as one put it, "When in the world am I supposed to read the morning paper?" If many women are incredulous that many men do not exchange personal information with their friends, this man is incredulous that many women do not bother to read the morning paper. To him, reading the paper is an essential part of his morning ritual, and his whole day is awry if he doesn't get to read it. In his words, reading the newspaper in the morning is as important to him as putting on makeup in the morning is to many women he knows. Yet many women, he observed, either don't subscribe to a paper or don't read it until they get home in the evening. "I find this very puzzling," he said. "I can't tell you how often I have picked up a woman's morning newspaper from her front door in the evening and handed it to her when she opened the door for me."

To this man (and I am sure many others), a woman who objects to his reading the morning paper is trying to keep him from doing something essential and harmless. It's a violation of his independence—his freedom of action. But when a woman who expects her partner to talk to her is disappointed that he doesn't, she perceives his behavior as a failure of intimacy: He's keeping things from her; he's lost interest in her; he's pulling away. A woman I will call Rebecca, who is generally quite happily married, told me that this is the one source of serious dissatisfaction with her husband, Stuart. Her term for his taciturnity is *stinginess of spirit.* She tells him what she is thinking, and he listens silently. She asks him what he is thinking, and he takes a long time to answer, "I don't know." In frustration she challenges, "Is there nothing on your mind?"

For Rebecca, who is accustomed to expressing her fleeting thoughts and opinions as they come to her, *saying* nothing means *thinking* nothing. But Stuart does not assume that his passing thoughts are worthy of utterance. He is not in the habit of uttering his fleeting ruminations, so just as Rebecca "naturally" speaks her thoughts, he "naturally" dismisses his as soon as they occur to him. Speaking them would give them more weight and significance than he feels they merit. All her life she has had practice in verbalizing her thoughts and feelings in private conversations with people she is close to; all his life he has had practice in dismissing his and keeping them to himself. . . .

PUBLIC SPEAKING: THE TALKATIVE MAN AND THE SILENT WOMAN

So far I have been discussing the private scenes in which many men are silent and many women are talkative. But there are other scenes in which the roles are reversed. Returning to Rebecca and Stuart, we saw that when they are home alone, Rebecca's thoughts find their way into words effortlessly, whereas Stuart finds he can't come up with anything to say. The reverse happens when they are in other situations. For example, at a meeting of the neighborhood council or the parents' association at their children's school, it is Stuart who stands up and speaks. In that situation, it is Rebecca who is silent, her tongue tied by an acute awareness of all the negative reactions people could have to what she might say, all the mistakes she might make in trying to express her ideas. If she musters her courage and prepares to say something, she needs time to formulate it and then waits to be recognized by the chair. She cannot just jump up and start talking the way Stuart and some other men can.

Eleanor Smeal, president of the Fund for the Feminist Majority, was a guest on a call-in radio talk show, discussing abortion. No subject could be of more direct concern to women, yet during the hour-long show, all the callers except two were men. Diane Rehm, host of a radio talk show, expresses puzzlement that although the audience for her show is evenly split between women and men, 90 percent of the callers to the show are men. I am convinced that the reason is not that women are uninterested in the subjects discussed on the show. I would wager that women listeners are bringing up the subjects they heard on *The Diane Rehm Show* to their friends and family over lunch, tea, and dinner. But fewer of them call in because to do so would be putting themselves on display, claiming public attention for what they have to say, catapulting themselves onto center stage.

I myself have been the guest on innumerable radio and television talk shows. Perhaps I am unusual in being completely at ease in this mode of display. But perhaps I am not unusual at all, because although I am comfortable in the role of invited expert, I have never called in to a talk show I was listening to, although I have often had ideas to contribute. When I am the guest, my position of authority is granted before I begin to speak. Were I to call in, I would be claiming that right on my own. I would have to establish my credibility by explaining who I am, which might seem self-aggrandizing, or not explain who I am and risk having my comments ignored or not valued. For similar reasons, though I am comfortable lecturing to groups numbering in the thousands, I rarely ask questions following another lecturer's talk, unless I know both the subject and the group very well.

My own experience and that of talk show hosts seems to hold a clue to the difference in women's and men's attitudes toward talk: Many men are more comfortable than most women in using talk to claim attention. And this difference lies at the heart of the distinction between report-talk and rapport-talk.

CRITICAL-THINKING QUESTIONS

1. In general, who talks more, men or women? Who talks longer?

2. What is the difference between "report-talk" and "rapport-talk"? Between "private speaking" and "public speaking"?

3. In your opinion, is it possible to avoid some of the conflicts between report-talk and rapport-talk by developing a *shared* conversational style between men and women? Or is this unlikely?

CLASSIC

CONTEMPORARY

CROSS-CULTURAL

25 The DOs and TABOOs of Body Language Around the World

ROGER E. AXTELL

In a world that grows smaller every year, it is easy to offend others simply by being ourselves—gestures that we take as innocent may be seen by someone else as deeply insulting. This selection suggests the extent of the problem and, in an age of global business dealings, the need to cultivate cultural sensitivity.

THREE GREAT GAFFES OR ONE COUNTRY'S GOOD MANNERS, ANOTHER'S GRAND FAUX PAS

In Washington they call protocol "etiquette with a government expense account." But diplomacy isn't just for diplomats. How you behave in other people's countries reflects on more than you alone. It also brightens—or dims—the image of where you come from and whom you work for. The Ugly American about whom we used to read so much may be dead, but here and there the ghost still wobbles out of the closet.

Three well-traveled Americans tell how even an old pro can sometimes make the wrong move in the wrong place at the wrong time.

A Partner in One of New York's Leading Private Banking Firms

When the board chairman is Lo Win Hao, do you smile brightly and say, "How do you do, Mr. Hao?" or "Mr. Lo"? Or "Mr. Win"?

I traveled nine thousand miles to meet a client and arrived with my foot in my mouth. Determined to do things right, I'd memorized the names of the key men I was to see in Singapore. No easy job, inasmuch as the names all came in threes. So, of course, I couldn't resist showing off that I'd done my homework. I began by addressing top man Lo Win Hao with plenty of well placed Mr. Hao's—and sprinkled the rest of my remarks with a Mr. Chee this and a Mr. Woon that. Great show. Until a note was passed to me from one man I'd met before, in New York. Bad news. "Too friendly too soon, Mr. Long," it said. Where diffidence is next to godliness, there I was, calling a roomful of VIPs, in effect, Mr. Ed and Mr. Charlie. I'd remembered everybody's name—but forgotten that in Chinese the surname comes *first* and the given name *last*.

An Associate in Charge of Family Planning for an International Human Welfare Organization

The lady steps out in her dazzling new necklace and everybody dies laughing. (Or what not to wear to Togo on a Saturday night.)

Source: "The DOs and TABOOs of Body Language around the World," by Roger E. Axtell, from *The DOs and TABOOs around the World,* 3rd ed., by Roger E. Axtell. Copyright © 1993 by Parker Pen Company. A Benjamin Book distributed by John Wiley & Sons, Inc. This material is used by permission of John Wiley & Sons, Inc.

From growing up in Cuba to joining the Peace Corps to my present work, I've spent most of my life in the Third World. So nobody should know better than I how to dress for it. Certainly one of the silliest mistakes an outsider can make is to dress up in "native" costume, whether it's a sari or a sombrero, unless you really know what you're doing. Yet, in Togo, when I found some of the most beautiful beads I'd ever seen, it never occurred to me not to wear them. While I was up-country, I seized the first grand occasion to flaunt my new find. What I didn't know is that locally the beads are worn not at the neck but at the waist—to hold up a sort of loincloth under the skirt. So, into the party I strutted, wearing around my neck what to every Togolese eye was part of a pair of underpants.

An Account Executive at an International Data Processing and Electronics Conglomerate

Even in a country run by generals, would you believe a runny nose could get you arrested?

A friend and I were coming into Colombia on business after a weekend in the Peruvian mountains touring Machu Picchu. What a sight that had been. And what a head cold the change in temperature had given my friend. As we proceeded through customs at the airport, he was wheezing and blowing into his handkerchief like an active volcano. Next thing I knew, two armed guards were lockstepping him through a door. I tried to intercede before the door slammed shut, but my spotty Spanish failed me completely. Inside a windowless room with the guards, so did his. He shouted in English. They shouted in Spanish. It was beginning to look like a bad day in Bogotá when a Colombian woman who had seen what happened burst into the room and finally achieved some bilingual understanding. It seems all that sniffling in the land of the infamous coca leaf had convinced the guards that my friend was waltzing through their airport snorting cocaine.

CUDDLY ETHNOCENTRICS

If only the world's customs inspectors could train their German shepherds to sniff out the invisible baggage we all manage to slip with us into foreign countries. They are like secret little land mines of the mind. Set to go off at the slightest quiver, they can sabotage a five-minute stroll down the Champs-Élysées or a $5 million tractor sale to Beijing. Three of our most popular national take-alongs:

Why Don't They Speak English?   For the same reason we don't speak Catalan or Urdu. The wonder, in fact, is that so many people do speak so many languages. Seldom is a Continental European fluent in fewer than three, often more. Africans grow up with language of the nation that once colonized theirs plus half a dozen different tribal dialects. Japan has three distinct Japanese languages, which even the lowliest street sweeper can understand. Middle Eastern businesspeople shift effortlessly from their native tongue(s) to Oxford English to Quai d'Orsay French. Yet most of the English-speaking world remains as cheerfully monolingual as Queen Victoria's parakeet. If there are any complaints, then, it is clear they should not be coming from the American/English-speaking traveler.

Take Me to Your Burger King.   In Peoria a Persian does not go looking for pot-au-feu. Alone among travelers, Americans seem to embark like astronauts—sealed inside a cozy life-support system from home. Scrambled eggs. Rent-a-cars. Showers. TV. Nothing wrong with any of it back home, but to the rest of the universe it looks sadly like somebody trying to read a book with the cover closed. Experiment! Try the local specialties.

American Know-How to the Rescue!   Our brightest ideas have taken root all over the world—from assembling lines in Düsseldorf to silicon chips in Osaka to hybrid grains that are helping to nourish the Third World. Nonetheless, bigger, smarter, and faster do not inevitably add up to better. Indeed, the desire to take on shiny new American ways has been the downfall of nations whose cultures were already rich in art and technology when North America was still a glacier. As important as the idea itself is the way it is presented.

A U.S. doctor of public health recently back from West Africa offers an example of how to make the idea fit the ideology. "I don't just pop over and start handing out antimalarial pills on the corner," she says. "First I visit with the village chief. After he gives his blessing, I move in with the local witch doctor. After she shows me her techniques and I show her mine—and a few lives are saved—maybe then we can get the first native to swallow the first pill."

This is as true at the high-tech level as at the village dispensary. "What is all this drinking of green tea before the meeting with Mitsubishi?" The American way is to get right down to business. Yet if you look at Mitsubishi's bottom line, you have to wonder if green tea is such a bad idea after all.

It should come as no surprise that people surrounded by oceans rather than by other people end up ethnocentric. Even our biggest fans admit that America often strikes the rest of the world as a sweet-but-spoiled little darling, wanting desperately to please, but not paying too much attention to how it is done. Ever since the Marshall Plan, we seemed to believe that *our* games and *our* rules were the only ones in town. Any town. And that all else was the Heart of Darkness.

Take this scene in a Chinese cemetery. Watching a Chinese reverently placing fresh fruit on a grave, an American visitor asked, "When do you expect your ancestors to get up and eat the fruit?" The Chinese replied, "As soon as your ancestors get up and smell the flowers."

HANDS ACROSS THE ABYSS

Our bad old habits are giving way to a new when-in-Rome awareness. Some corporations take it so seriously that they put employees into a crash course of overseas cultural immersion. AT&T, for instance, encourages—and pays for—the whole family of an executive on the way to a foreign assignment to enroll in classes given by experts in the mores and manners of other lands.

Among the areas that cry out loudest for international understanding are how to say people's names, eat, dress, and talk. Get those four basics right and the rest is a piece of kuchen.

Basic Rule #1: What's in a Name?

. . . The first transaction between even ordinary citizens—and the first chance to make an impression for better or worse—is, of course, an exchange of names. In America there usually is not very much to get wrong. And even if you do, so what?

Not so elsewhere. Especially in the Eastern Hemisphere, where name frequently denotes social rank or family status, a mistake can be an outright insult. So can switching to a given name without the other person's permission, even when you think the situation calls for it.

"What would you like me to call you?" is always the opening line of one overseas deputy director for an international telecommunications corporation. "Better to ask several times," he advises, "than to get it wrong." Even then, "I err on the side of formality until asked to 'Call me Joe.'" Another frequent traveler insists his company provide him with a list of key people he will meet, country by country, surnames underlined, to be memorized on the flight over.

Don't Trust the Rules. Just when you think you have broken the international name code, they switch the rules on you. Take Latin America. Most people's names are a combination of the father's and mother's, with only the father's name used in conversation. In the Spanish-speaking countries the father's name comes first. Hence, Carlos Mendoza-Miller is called Mr. Mendoza. *But* in Portuguese-speaking Brazil it is the other way around, with the mother's name first.

In the Orient the Chinese system of surname first, given name last does not always apply. The Taiwanese, many of whom were educated in missionary schools, often have a Christian first name, which comes before any of the others—as in Tommy Ho Chin, who should be called Mr. Ho or, to his friends, Tommy Ho. Also, given names are often officially changed to initials, and a Y.Y. Lang is Y.Y.; never mind what it stands for. In Korea, which of a man's names takes a Mr. is determined by whether he is his father's first or second son. Although in Thailand names run backwards, Chinese style, the Mr. is put with the *given* name, and to a Thai it is just as important to be called by his given name as it is for a Japanese to be addressed by his surname. With the latter, incidentally, you can in a very friendly relationship respond to his using *your* first name by dropping the Mr. and adding *san* to his last name, as in Ishikawa-san.

Hello. Are you still there? Then get ready for the last installment of the name game, which is to disregard all of the above—sometimes. The reason is that many Easterners who deal regularly with the West are now changing the order of their names to un-confuse us. So, while to one another their names remain the same, to us the given name may come before the surname. Then again, it may not.

The safest course remains: Ask.

Basic Rule #2: Eat, Drink, and Be Wary

. . . [M]ealtime is no time for a thanks-but-no-thanks response. Acceptance of what is on your plate is tantamount to acceptance of host, country, and company. So, no matter how tough things may be to swallow, swallow. Or, as one veteran globe-girdler puts it, "Travel with a cast-iron stomach and eat everything everywhere."

Tastiness Is in the Eye of the Beholder. Often, what is offered constitutes your host country's proudest culinary achievements. What would we Americans think of a Frenchman who refused a bite of homemade apple pie or sizzling sirloin? Squeamishness comes not so much from the thing itself as from our unfamiliarity with it. After all, an oyster has remarkably the same look and consistency as a sheep's eye, and at first encounter a lobster would strike almost anybody as more a creature from science fiction than something you dip in melted butter and pop into your mouth.

Incidentally, in Saudi Arabia sheep's eyes are a delicacy, and in China it's bear's paw soup.

Perhaps the ultimate in exotic dining abroad befell a family planning expert on a trip for an international human welfare organization. It was a newly emerged African country where the national dish—in fact, the *only* dish eleven months of the year—is yam. The visitor's luck, however, was to be there the *other* month, when gorillas come in from the bush to steal the harvest. Being the only available protein, gorilla meat is as prized as sirloin is over here, and the village guest of honor was served a choice cut. Proudly, a platter of the usual mashed yams was placed before her—but with a roast gorilla hand thrusting artfully up from the center.

Is there any polite way out besides the back door?

Most experienced business travelers say no, at least not before taking at least a few bites. It helps, though, to slice whatever the item is very thin. This way, you minimize the texture—gristly, slimy, etc.—and the reminder of whence it came. Or, "Swallow it quickly," as one traveler recommends. "I still can't tell you what sheep's eyeballs taste like." As for dealing with taste, the old canard that "it tastes just like chicken" is often mercifully true. Even when the "it" is rodent, snake—or gorilla.

Another useful dodge is not knowing what you are eating. What's for dinner? Don't ask. Avoid poking around in the kitchen or looking at English-language menus. Your host will be flattered that you are following his lead, and who knows? Maybe it really is chicken in that stew. . . .

Bottoms Up—or Down? Some countries seem to do it deliberately, some inadvertently, except for Islam, where they don't do it at all. Either way, getting visitors as tipsy as possible as fast as possible stands as a universal sign of hospitality, and refusal to play your part equals rebuff. Wherever you go, toasts are as reciprocal as handshakes: If one does, all do. "I don't drink, thank you" rarely gets you off gracefully. Neither does protesting that you must get up early. (So must everyone else.)

"I try to wangle a glass of wine instead of the local firewater," one itinerant American says. "The only trouble is, the wine is usually stronger than the hard stuff." Mao-tai, Chinese wine made from sorghum, is notorious for leaving the unsuspecting thoroughly shanghaied. The Georgian wine so popular in Russia is no ladylike little Chablis either. In Nordic lands proper form for the toast is to raise the glass in a sweeping arc from belt buckle to lips while locking stares with your host. It takes very few akvavit-with-beer-chasers before you both start seeing northern lights.

In Africa, where all the new countries were once old European colonies, it is often taken for granted that if you are white you must have whiskey or gin or whatever the colonials used to like. A traveler to a former French possession describes the dilemma of being served a large gourdful of Johnnie Walker Red at nine in the morning. The host was simply remembering how the French had always loved their Scotch. *When* they drank it and *how much* were details he had never noticed. Yet there was no saying no without giving offense. A few sips had to be taken and a promise made to finish the rest later.

Basic Rule #3: Clothes Can Also *Un*make the Man

. . . Wherever you are, what you wear among strangers should not look strange to *them.* Which does not mean, "When in Morocco wear djellabas," etc. It means wear what you look natural in—and know how to wear—that also fits in with your surroundings.

For example, a woman dressed in a tailored suit, even with high heels and flowery blouse, looks startlingly masculine in a country full of diaphanous saris. More appropriate, then, is a silky, loose-fitting dress in a bright color—as opposed to blue serge or banker's gray.

In downtown Nairobi, a safari jacket looks as out of place as in London. With a few exceptions (where the weather is just too steamy for it), the general rule everywhere is that for business, for eating out, even for visiting people at home, you should be very buttoned up: conservative suit and tie for men, dress or skirt-suit for women. To be left in the closet until you go on an outdoor sight-seeing trek:

jeans, however haute couture
jogging shoes
tennis and T-shirts
tight-fitting sweaters (women)
open-to-the-navel shirts (men)
funny hats (both)

Where you *can* loosen up, it is best to do it the way the indigines do. In the Philippines men wear the barong tagalog—a loose, frilly, usually white or cream-colored shirt with tails out, no jacket or tie. In tropical Latin American countries the counterpart to the barong is called a *guayabera* and, except for formal occasions, is acceptable business attire. In Indonesia they wear *Batiks*—brightly patterned shirts that go tieless and jacketless everywhere. In Thailand the same is true for the collarless Thai silk shirt. In Japan dress is at least as formal as in Europe (dark suit and tie for a man, business suit or tailored dress for a woman) except at country inns (called *ryokans*), where even big-city corporations sometimes hold meetings. Here you are expected to wear a kimono. Not to daytime meetings but to dinner, no matter how formal. (Don't worry—the inn always provides the kimono.)

One thing you notice wherever you go is that polyester is the mark of the tourist. The less drip-dry you are, the more you look as if you have come to do serious business, even if it means multiple dry-cleaning bills along the way.

Take It Off or Put It On—Depending. What you do or do not wear can be worse than bad taste—ranging from insulting to unhygienic to positively sinful. Shoes are among the biggest offenders in the East, even if you wear a 5AAA. They are forbidden within Muslim mosques and Buddhist temples. Never wear them into Japanese homes or restaurants unless the owner insists, and in Indian and Indonesian homes, if the host goes shoeless, do likewise. And wherever you take your shoes off, remember to place them neatly together facing the door you came in. This is particularly important in Japan. . . .

In certain conservative Arab countries, the price for wearing the wrong thing can hurt more than feelings. Mullahs have been known to give a sharp whack with their walking sticks to any woman whom they consider immodestly dressed. Even at American-style hotels there, do not wear shorts, skirts above the knee, sleeveless blouses, or low necklines—much less a bikini at the pool.

CRITICAL-THINKING QUESTIONS

1. Historically, people in the United States have been rather indifferent to the dangers of inadvertently offending others. Why do you think this has been the case?

2. Have you ever offended others—or been offended—in the way depicted by Axtell? If so, how? How did you and others respond?

3. Can the type of cultural conflict Axtell describes occur right here in the United States? How?

26 Primary Groups

CHARLES HORTON COOLEY

Charles Horton Cooley argues that human nature is a social nature and is clearly expressed in group life. Cooley describes primary groups as "spheres of intimate association and cooperation" that are vital to the process of socialization.

By primary groups I mean those characterized by intimate face-to-face association and cooperation. They are primary in several senses, but chiefly in that they are fundamental in forming the social nature and ideals of the individual. The result of intimate association, psychologically, is a certain fusion of individualities in a common whole, so that one's very self, for many purposes at least, is the common life and purpose of the group. Perhaps the simplest way of describing this wholeness is by saying that it is a "we"; it involves the sort of sympathy and mutual identification for which "we" is the natural expression. One lives in the feeling of the whole and finds the chief aims of his will in that feeling.

It is not to be supposed that the unity of the primary group is one of mere

Source: From *Social Organization: A Study of the Larger Mind* by Charles Horton Cooley (New York: Schocken Books, a subsidiary of Pantheon Books, 1962; orig. 1909), pp. 23–31). Reprinted with permission.

harmony and love. It is always a differentiated and usually a competitive unity, admitting of self-assertion and various appropriative passions; but these passions are socialized by sympathy, and come, or tend to come, under the discipline of a common spirit. The individual will be ambitious, but the chief object of his ambition will be some desired place in the thought of the others, and he will feel allegiance to common standards of service and fair play. So the boy will dispute with his fellows a place on the team, but above such disputes will place the common glory of his class and school.

The most important spheres of this intimate association and cooperation—though by no means the only ones—are the family, the play-group of children, and the neighborhood or community group of elders. These are practically universal, belonging to all times and all stages of development; and are accordingly a chief basis

of what is universal in human nature and human ideals. The best comparative studies of the family, such as those of Westermarck[1] or Howard,[2] show it to us as not only a universal institution, but as more alike the world over than the exaggeration of exceptional customs by an earlier school had led us to suppose. Nor can anyone doubt the general prevalence of play-groups among children or of informal assemblies of various kinds among their elders. Such association is clearly the nursery of human nature in the world about us, and there is no apparent reason to suppose that the case has anywhere or at any time been essentially different.

As regards play, I might, were it not a matter of common observation, multiply illustrations of the universality and spontaneity of the group discussion and cooperation to which it gives rise. The general fact is that children, especially boys after about their twelfth year, live in fellowships in which their sympathy, ambition, and honor are engaged even more often than they are in the family. Most of us can recall examples of the endurance by boys of injustice and even cruelty, rather than appeal from their fellows to parents or teachers—as, for instance, in the hazing so prevalent at schools, and so difficult, for this very reason, to suppress. And how elaborate the discussion, how cogent the public opinion, how hot the ambitions in these fellowships.

Nor is this facility of juvenile association, as is sometimes supposed, a trait peculiar to English and American boys; since experience among our immigrant population seems to show that the offspring of the more restrictive civilizations of the continent of Europe form self-governing play-groups with almost equal readiness. Thus Miss Jane Addams, after pointing out that the "gang" is almost universal, speaks of the interminable discussion which every detail of the gang's activity receives, remarking that "in these social folk-motes, so to speak, the young citizen learns to act upon his own determination."[3]

Of the neighborhood group it may be said, in general, that from the time men formed permanent settlements upon the land, down, at least, to the rise of modern industrial cities, it has played a main part of the primary, heart-to-heart life of the people. Among our Teutonic forefathers the village community was apparently the chief sphere of sympathy and mutual aid for the commons all through the "Dark" and Middle Ages, and for many purposes it remains so in rural districts at the present day. In some countries we still find it with all its ancient vitality, notably in Russia, where the *mir,* or self-governing village group, is the main theatre of life, along with the family, for perhaps fifty million peasants.

In our own life the intimacy of the neighborhood has been broken up by the growth of an intricate mesh of wider contacts which leaves us strangers to people who live in the same house. And even in the country the same principle is at work, though less obviously, diminishing our economic and spiritual community with our neighbors. How far this change is a healthy development, and how far a disease, is perhaps still uncertain.

Besides these almost universal kinds of primary association, there are many others whose form depends upon the particular state of civilization; the only essential thing, as I have said, being a certain intimacy and fusion of personalities. In our own society, being little bound by place, people easily form clubs, fraternal societies and the like, based on congeniality, which may give rise to real intimacy. Many such relations are formed at school and college, and among men and women brought together in the first instance by their occupations—as workmen in the same trade, or the like. Where there is a little common interest and activity, kindness grows like weeds by the roadside.

But the fact that the family and neighborhood groups are ascendant in the open and plastic time of childhood makes them even now incomparably more influential than all the rest.

Primary groups are primary in the sense that they give the individual his earliest and completest experience of social unity, and also in the sense that they do not change in the same degree as more elaborate relations, but form a comparatively permanent source out of which the latter are ever springing. Of course they are not independent of the larger society, but to some extent reflect its spirit; as the German family and the German school bear somewhat distinctly the print of German militarism. But this, after all, is like the tide setting back into creeks, and does not commonly go very far. Among the German, and still more among the Russian, peasantry are found habits of free cooperation and discussion almost uninfluenced by the character of the state; and it is a familiar and well-supported view that the village commune, self-governing as regards local affairs and habituated to discussion, is a very widespread institution in settled communities, and the continuator of a similar autonomy previously existing in the clan. "It is man who makes monarchies and establishes republics, but the commune seems to come directly from the hand of God."[4]

In our own cities the crowded tenements and the general economic and social confusion have sorely wounded the family and the neighborhood, but it is remarkable, in view of these conditions, what vitality they show; and there is nothing upon which the conscience of the time is more determined than upon restoring them to health.

These groups, then, are springs of life, not only for the individual but for social institutions. They are only in part moulded by special traditions, and, in larger degree, express a universal nature. The religion or government of other civilizations may seem alien to us, but the children or the family group wear the common life, and with them we can always make ourselves at home.

By human nature, I suppose, we may understand those sentiments and impulses that are human in being superior to those of lower animals, and also in the sense that they belong to mankind at large, and not to any particular race or time. It means, particularly, sympathy and the innumerable sentiments into which sympathy enters, such as love, resentment, ambition, vanity, hero-worship, and the feeling of social right and wrong.

Human nature in this sense is justly regarded as a comparatively permanent element in society. Always and everywhere men seek honor and dread ridicule, defer to public opinion, cherish their goods and their children, and admire courage, generosity, and success. It is always safe to assume that people are and have been human. . . .

To return to primary groups: The view here maintained is that human nature is not something existing separately in the individual, but a *group-nature* or *primary phase of society,* a relatively simple and general condition of the social mind. It is something more, on the one hand, than the mere instinct that is born in us—though that enters into it—and something else, on the other, than the more elaborate development of ideas and sentiments that makes up institutions. It is the nature which is developed and expressed in those simple, face-to-face groups that are somewhat alike in all societies; groups of the family, the playground, and the neighborhood. In the essential similarity of these is to be found the basis, in experience, for similar ideas and sentiments in the human mind. In these, everywhere, human nature comes into existence. Man does not have it at birth; he cannot acquire it except through fellowship, and it decays in isolation.

If this view does not recommend itself to common sense I do not know that elaboration will be of much avail. It simply means the application at this point of the idea that society and individuals are inseparable phases of a common whole, so that wherever we find an individual fact we may look for a social fact to go with it. If there is a universal nature in persons there must be something universal in association to correspond to it.

What else can human nature be than a trait of primary groups? Surely not an attribute of the separate individual—supposing there were any such thing—since its typical characteristics, such as affection, ambition, vanity, and resentment, are inconceivable apart from society. If it belongs, then, to man in association, what kind or degree of association is required to develop it? Evidently nothing elaborate, because elaborate phases of society are transient and diverse, while human nature is comparatively stable and universal. In short the family and neighborhood life is essential to its genesis and nothing more is.

Here as everywhere in the study of society we must learn to see mankind in psychical wholes, rather than in artificial separation. We must see and feel the communal life of family and local groups as immediate facts, not as combinations of something else. And perhaps we shall do this best by recalling our own experience and extending it through sympathetic observation. What, in our life, is the family and the fellowship; what do we know of the we-feeling? Thought of this kind may help us to get a concrete perception of that primary group-nature of which everything social is the outgrowth.

CRITICAL-THINKING QUESTIONS

1. Are primary groups necessarily devoid of conflict? How does Cooley address this issue?

2. Why does Cooley employ the term *primary* in his analysis? What are the characteristics of the implied opposite of primary groups: "secondary groups"?

3. What is Cooley's view of human nature? Why does he think that society cannot be reduced to the behavior of many distinct individuals?

NOTES

1. *The History of Human Marriage.*
2. *A History of Matrimonial Institutions.*
3. *Newer Ideals of Peace,* p. 177.
4. De Tocqueville, *Democracy in America,* vol. 1, chap 5.

CLASSIC

CONTEMPORARY

CROSS-CULTURAL

27 The Characteristics of Bureaucracy

MAX WEBER

According to Max Weber, human societies have historically been oriented by tradition of one kind or another. Modernity, in contrast, is marked by a different form of human consciousness: a rational world view. For Weber, there is no clearer expression of modern rationality than bureaucracy. In this selection, Weber identifies the characteristics of this organizational form.

Modern officialdom functions in the following specific manner:

I. There is the principle of fixed and official jurisdictional areas, which are generally ordered by rules, that is, by laws or administrative regulations. (1) The regular activities required for the purposes of the bureaucratically governed structure are distributed in a fixed way as official duties. (2) The authority to give the commands required for the discharge of these duties is distributed in a stable way and is strictly delimited by rules concerning the coercive means, physical, sacerdotal, or otherwise, which may be placed at the disposal of officials. (3) Methodical provision is made for the regular and continuous fulfillment of these duties and for the execution of the corresponding rights; only persons who have the generally regulated qualifications to serve are employed.

Source: From *From Max Weber: Essays in Sociology,* by Max Weber, edited by H. H. Gerth and C. Wright Mills, translated by H. H. Gerth and C. Wright Mills. Copyright © 1946, 1958 by H. H. Gerth and C. Wright Mills. Used by permission of Oxford University Press.

In public and lawful government these three elements constitute "bureaucratic authority." In private economic domination, they constitute bureaucratic "management." Bureaucracy, thus understood, is fully developed in political and ecclesiastical communities only in the modern state, and, in the private economy, only in the most advanced institutions of capitalism. Permanent and public office authority, with fixed jurisdiction, is not the historical rule but rather the exception. This is so even in large political structures such as those of the ancient Orient, the Germanic, and Mongolian empires of conquest, or of many feudal structures of state. In all these cases, the ruler executes the most important measures through personal trustees, table-companions, or court-servants. Their commissions and authority are not precisely delimited and are temporarily called into being for each case.

II. The principles of office hierarchy and of levels of graded authority mean a firmly ordered system of super- and subordination in which there is a supervision of the lower offices by the higher ones. Such a system offers the governed the possibility of appealing the decision of a lower office to its higher authority, in a definitely regulated manner. With the full development of the bureaucratic type, the office hierarchy is monocratically organized. The principle of hierarchical office authority is found in all bureaucratic structures: in state and ecclesiastical structures as well as in large party organizations and private enterprises. It does not matter for the character of bureaucracy whether its authority is called "private" or "public."

When the principle of jurisdictional "competency" is fully carried through, hierarchical subordination—at least in public office—does not mean that the "higher" authority is simply authorized to take over the business of the "lower." Indeed, the opposite is the rule. Once established and having fulfilled its task, an office tends to continue in existence and be held by another incumbent.

III. The management of the modern office is based upon written documents ("the files"), which are preserved in their original or draft form. There is, therefore, a staff of subaltern officials and scribes of all sorts. The body of officials actively engaged in a "public" office, along with the respective apparatus of material implements and the files, make up a "bureau." In private enterprise, "the bureau" is often called "the office."

In principle, the modern organization of the civil service separates the bureau from the private domicile of the official, and, in general, bureaucracy segregates official activity as something distinct from the sphere of private life. Public monies and equipment are divorced from the private property of the official. . . . In principle, the executive office is separated from the household, business from private correspondence, and business assets from private fortunes. The more consistently the modern type of business management has been carried through, the more are these separations the case. The beginnings of this process are to be found as early as the Middle Ages.

It is the peculiarity of the modern entrepreneur that he conducts himself as the "first official" of his enterprise, in the very same way in which the ruler of a specifically modern bureaucratic state spoke of himself as "the first servant" of the state. The idea that the bureau activities of the state are intrinsically different in character from the management of private economic offices is a continental European notion and, by the way of contrast, is totally foreign to the American way.

IV. Office management, at least all specialized office management—and such management is distinctly modern—usually presupposes a thorough and expert training. This increasingly holds for the modern executive and employee of private enterprises, in the same manner as it holds for the state official.

V. When the office is fully developed, official activity demands the full working capacity of the official, irrespective of the fact that his obligatory time in the bureau may be firmly delimited. In the normal case, this is only the product of a long development, in the public as well as in the private office. Formerly, in all cases, the normal state of affairs was reversed: Official business was discharged as a secondary activity.

VI. The management of the office follows general rules, which are more or less stable, more or less exhaustive, and which can be learned. Knowledge of these rules represents a special technical learning which the officials possess. It involves jurisprudence, or administrative or business management.

VII. The reduction of modern office management to rules is deeply embedded in its very nature. The theory of modern public administration, for instance, assumes that the authority to order certain matters by decree—which has been legally granted to public authorities—does not entitle the bureau to regulate the matter by commands given for each case, but only to regulate the matter abstractly. This stands in extreme contrast to the regulation of all relationships through individual privileges and bestowals of favor, which is absolutely dominant in patrimonialism, at least insofar as such relationships are not fixed by sacred tradition.

All this results in the following for the internal and external position of the official.

I. Office holding is a "vocation." This is shown, first, in the requirement of a firmly prescribed course of training, which demands the entire capacity for work for a long period of time, and in the generally prescribed and special examinations which are prerequisites of employment. Furthermore, the position of the official is in the nature of a duty. This determines the internal structure of his relations, in the following manner: Legally and actually, office holding is not considered a source to be exploited for rents or emoluments, as was normally the case during the Middle Ages and frequently up to the threshold of recent times. . . . Entrances into an office, including one in the private economy, is considered an acceptance of a specific obligation of faithful management in return for a secure existence. It is decisive for the specific nature of modern loyalty to an office that, in the pure type, it does not establish a relationship to a *person,* like the vassal's or disciple's faith in feudal or in patrimonial relations and authority. Modern loyalty is devoted to impersonal and functional purposes. . . .

II. The personal position of the official is patterned in the following way:

(1) Whether he is in a private office or a public bureau, the modern official always strives and usually enjoys a distinct *social esteem* as compared with the governed. His social position is guaranteed by the prescriptive rules of rank order and, for the political official, by special definitions of the criminal code against "insults of officials" and "contempt" of state and church authorities.

The actual social position of the official is normally highest where, as in old civilized countries, the following conditions prevail: a strong demand for administration by trained experts; a strong and stable social differentiation, where the official predominantly derives from socially and economically privileged strata because of the social distribution of power; or where the costliness of the required training and status conventions are binding upon him. The possession of educational certificates—to be discussed elsewhere—are usually linked with qualification for office. Naturally, such certificates or patents enhance the "status element" in the social position of the official. . . .

Usually the social esteem of the officials as such is especially low where the demand for expert administration and the dominance of status conventions are weak. This is especially the case in the United States; it is often the case in new settlements by virtue of their wide fields for profit-taking and the great instability of their social stratification.

(2) The pure type of bureaucratic official is *appointed* by a superior authority. An official elected by the governed is not a purely bureaucratic figure. Of course, the formal existence of an election does not by itself mean that no appointment hides behind the election—in the state, especially, appointment by party chiefs. Whether or not this is the case does not depend upon legal statutes but upon the way in which the party mechanism functions. Once firmly organized, the parties can turn a formally free election into the mere acclamation of a candidate designated by the party chief. As a rule, however, a formally free election is turned into a fight, conducted according to definite rules, for votes in favor of one of two designated candidates. . . .

(3) Normally, the position of the official is held for life, at least in public bureaucracies; and this is increasingly the case for all similar structures. As a factual rule, *tenure for life* is presupposed, even where the giving of notice or periodic reappointment occurs. In contrast to the worker in a private enterprise, the official normally holds tenure. Legal or actual life-tenure, however, is not recognized as the official's right to the possession of office, as was the case with many structures of authority in the past. Where legal guarantees against arbitrary dismissal of transfer are developed, they

merely serve to guarantee a strictly objective discharge of specific office duties free from all personal considerations. . . .

(4) The official receives the regular *pecuniary* compensation of a normally fixed *salary* and the old age security provided by a pension. The salary is not measured like a wage in terms of work done, but according to "status," that is, according to the kind of function (the "rank") and, in addition, possibly, according to the length of service. The relatively great security of the official's income, as well as the rewards of social esteem, make the office a sought-after position. . . .

(5) The official is set for a "*career*" within the hierarchical order of the public service. He moves from the lower, less important, and lower paid to the higher positions. The average official naturally desires a mechanical fixing of the conditions of promotion: if not of the offices, at least of the salary levels. He wants these conditions fixed in terms of "seniority," or possibly according to grades achieved in a developed system of expert examinations.

CRITICAL-THINKING QUESTIONS

1. In what respects is bureaucracy impersonal? What are some of the advantages and disadvantages of this impersonality?

2. Through most of human history, kinship has been the foundation of social organization. Why is kinship missing from Weber's analysis of bureaucracy? On what other basis are people selected for bureaucratic positions?

3. Why does bureaucracy take a hierarchical form? Do you think formal organization must be hierarchical?

CLASSIC

CONTEMPORARY

CROSS-CULTURAL

28 McJobs: McDonaldization and the Workplace

GEORGE RITZER

About a decade ago, George Ritzer coined the term "McDonaldization" to refer to a set of organizational principles—including efficiency, uniformity, predictability, and control—that play an important part in today's society. Here, he describes the way McDonald's and similar organizations control not just their workers, but also their customers.

In recent years the spread of McDonaldized systems has led to the creation of an enormous number of jobs. Unfortunately, the majority of them can be thought of as McDonaldized jobs, or "McJobs." While we usually associate these types of positions with fast-food restaurants, and in fact there are many such jobs in that setting (over 2.5 million people worked in that industry in the United States in 1992 [Van Giezen, 1994]), McJobs have spread throughout much of the economy with the growing impact of McDonaldization on work settings which had previously experienced relatively little rationalization.

It is worth outlining some of the basic realities of employment in the fast-food industry in the United States since those jobs serve as a model for employment in other McDonaldized settings (Van Giezen, 1994). The large number of people employed in fast-food restaurants accounts for over 40 percent of the approximately six million people employed in restaurants of all types.

Fast-food restaurants rely heavily on teenage employees—almost 70 percent of their employees are twenty years of age or younger. For many, the fast-food restaurant is likely to be their first employer. It is estimated that the first job for one of every fifteen workers was at McDonald's; one of every eight Americans has worked at McDonald's at some time in his or her life. The vast majority of employees are part-time workers: The average work week in the fast-food industry is 29.5 hours. There is a high turnover rate: Only slightly more than half the employees remain on the job for a year or more. Minorities are overrepresented in these jobs—almost two-thirds of employees are women and nearly a quarter are non-white. These are low-paid occupations, with many earning the minimum wage, or slightly more. As a result, these jobs are greatly affected by changes in the minimum wage: An upward revision has an important effect on the income of these workers. However, there is a real danger that many workers would lose their positions as a result of such increases, especially in economically marginal fast-food restaurants.[1]

Source: From *The McDonaldization Thesis: Explorations and Extensions,* by George Ritzer, pp. 59–65, 68. Copyright © 1998 Sage Publications. Reprinted with permission.

Although the McDonaldization of society is manifest at all levels and in all realms of the social world, the work world has played a particularly pivotal role in this. On the one hand, it is the main source of many of the precursors of McDonaldization, including bureaucracies, scientific management, assembly lines, and so on. More contemporaneously, the kinds of jobs, work procedures, and organizing principles that have made McDonald's so successful have affected the way in which many businesses now organize much of their work. In fact, it could well be argued that the primary root of the McDonaldization of the larger society is the work world. On the other hand, the McDonaldization of the larger society has, in turn, served to further rationalize the work world. We thus have a self-reinforcing and enriching process that is speeding the growth and spread of McDonaldization.

The process of McDonaldization is leading to the creation of more and more McJobs.[2] The service sector, especially at its lower end, is producing an enormous number of jobs, most of them requiring little or no skill. There is no better example of this than the mountain of jobs being produced by the fast-food industry. However, new occupational creation is not the only source of McJobs: Many extant low-level jobs are being McDonaldized. More strikingly, large numbers of middle-level jobs are also being deskilled and transformed into McJobs.

McJobs are characterized by the five dimensions of McDonaldization. The jobs tend to involve a series of simple tasks in which the emphasis is on performing each as efficiently as possible. Second, the time associated with many of the tasks is carefully calculated and the emphasis on the quantity of time a task should take tends to diminish the quality of the work from the point of view of the worker. That is, tasks are so simplified and streamlined that they provide little or no meaning to the worker. Third, the work is predictable: employees do and say essentially the same things hour after hour, day after day. Fourth, many nonhuman technologies are employed to control workers and

reduce them to robotlike actions. Some technologies are in place, and others are in development, that will lead to the eventual replacement of many of these "human robots" with computerized robots. Finally, the rationalized McJobs lead to a variety of irrationalities, especially the dehumanization of work. The result is the extraordinarily high turnover rate described above and difficulty in maintaining an adequate supply of replacements.[3]

The claim is usually made by spokespeople for McDonaldized systems that they are offering a large number of entry-level positions that help give employees basic skills they will need in order to move up the occupational ladder within such systems (and many of them do). This is likely to be true in the instances in which the middle-level jobs to which they move—for example, shift leader, assistant manager, or manager of a fast-food restaurant—are also routinized and scripted. In fact, it turns out that this even holds for the positions held by the routinized and scripted instructors at [McDonald's training program at] Hamburger University who teach the managers, who teach the employees, and so on. However, the skills acquired in McJobs are not likely to prepare one for, help one to acquire, or help one to function well in, the far more desirable postindustrial occupations which are highly complex and require high levels of skill and education. Experience in routinized actions and scripted interactions do not help much when occupations require thought and creativity. . . .

At the cultural level, large numbers of people in the United States, and increasingly throughout much of the rest of the world, have come to value McDonaldization in general, as well as its fundamental characteristics. McDonaldization, as well as its various principles, has become part of our value system. That value system has, in turn, been translated into a series of principles that have been exported to, adopted by, and adapted to, a wide range of social settings. . . .

. . .For example, the behavior of customers at fast-food restaurants is being affected in much the same way as the behavior of those who work in those restaurants. . . .

The constraints on the behavior of employees and customers in McDonaldized systems are of both a structural and a cultural nature. Employees and customers find themselves in a variety of McDonaldized structures that demand that they behave in accord with the dictates of those structures. For example, the drive-through window associated with the fast-food restaurant (as well as other settings such as banks) structures both what customers in their cars and employees in their booths can and cannot do. They can efficiently exchange money for food, but their positions (in a car and a booth) and the press of other cars in the queue make any kind of personal interaction virtually impossible. Of course, many other kinds of behavior are either made possible, or prohibited, by such structures. In Giddens's (1984) terms, such structures are both enabling and constraining.

At a cultural level, both employees and customers are socialized into, and have internalized, the norms and values of working and living in a McDonaldized society. Employees are trained by managers or owners who are likely, themselves, to have been trained at an institution like McDonald's Hamburger University (Schaaf, 1994). Such institutions are as much concerned with inculcating norms and values as they are with the teaching of basic skills. For their part, customers are not required to attend Hamburger University, but they are "trained" by the employees themselves, by television advertisements, and by their own children who are often diligent students, teachers, and enforcers of the McDonald's way. This "training," like that of those employees who attend Hamburger University, is oriented not only to teaching the "skills" required to be a customer at a fast-food restaurant (e.g., how to queue up in order to order food), but also the norms and values of such settings as they apply to customers (e.g., customers are expected to dispose of their own debris; they are not expected to linger after eating). As a result of such formal and informal training, both employees and customers can be relied on to do what they are supposed to, and what is expected of them, with little or no personal supervision. . . .

. . . McJobs are not simply the deskilled jobs of our industrial past in new settings; they are jobs that have a variety of new and distinctive characteristics. . . . Industrial and McDonaldized jobs both tend to be highly routinized in terms of what people do on the job. However, one of the things that is distinctive about McDonaldized jobs, especially since so many of them involve work that requires interaction and communication, especially with consumers, is that what people *say* on the job is also highly routinized. To put this another way, McDonaldized jobs are tightly scripted: They are characterized by *both* routinized actions (for example, the way McDonald's hamburgers are to be put down on the grill and flipped [Love, 1986: 141–2]) and scripted interactions (examples include "May I help you?"; "Would you like a dessert to go with your meal?"; "Have a nice day!"). Scripts are crucial because, as Leidner (1993) points out, many of the workers in McDonaldized systems are interactive service workers. This means that they not only produce goods and provide services, but they often do so in interaction with customers.

The scripting of interaction leads to new depths in the deskilling of workers. Not only have employee actions been deskilled; employees' ability to speak and interact with customers is now being limited and controlled. There are not only scripts to handle general situations, but also a range of subscripts to deal with a variety of contingencies. Verbal and interactive skills are being taken away from employees and built into the scripts in much the same way that manual skills were taken and built into various technologies. At one time distrusted in their ability to *do* the right thing, workers now find themselves no longer trusted to *say* the right thing. Once able to create distinctive interactive styles, and to adjust them to different circumstances, employees are now asked to follow scripts as mindlessly as possible. . . .

One very important, but rarely noted, aspect of the labor process in the fast-food restaurant and other McDonaldized systems is the extent to which customers are being led, perhaps even almost required, to perform a number of tasks without pay that were formerly performed by paid employees. For example, in the modern gasoline station the driver now does various things for free (pumps gas, cleans windows, checks oil, even pays through a computerized credit card system built into the pump) that were formerly done by paid attendants. In these and many other settings, McDonaldization has brought the customer *into* the labor process: The customer *is* the laborer! This has several advantages for employers, such as lower (even nonexistent) labor costs, the need for fewer employees, and less trouble with personnel problems: Customers are far less likely to complain about a few seconds or minutes of tedious work than employees who devote a full work day to such tasks. Because of its advantages, as well as because customers are growing accustomed to and accepting of it, I think customers are likely to become even more involved in the labor process.

This is the most revolutionary development, at least as far as the labor process is concerned, associated with McDonaldization. As a result of this dramatic change, the analysis of the labor process must be extended to what customers do in McDonaldized systems. The distinction between customer and employee is eroding, or in postmodern terms "imploding," and one can envision more and more work settings in which customers are asked to do an increasing amount of "work." More dramatically, it is also likely that we will see more work settings in which there are no employees at all! In such settings customers, in interaction with nonhuman technologies, will do *all* of the human labor. A widespread example is the ATM in which customers (and the technology) do all of the work formerly done by bank tellers. More strikingly, we are beginning to see automated loan machines which dispense loans as high as $10,000 (Singletary, 1996). Again, customers and technologies do the work and, in the process, many loan-officer positions are eliminated. Similarly, the new automated gasoline pumps allow (or force)

customers to do all of the required tasks; in some cases and at certain times (late at night) no employees at all are present.

In a sense, a key to the success of McDonaldized systems is that they have been able to supplement the exploitation of employees with the exploitation of customers. Lest we forget, Marx "put at the heart of his sociology—as no other sociology does—the theme of exploitation" (Worsley, 1982:115). In Marxian theory, the capitalists are seen as simply paying workers less than the value produced by the workers, and as keeping the rest for themselves. This dynamic continues in contemporary society, but capitalists have learned that they can ratchet up the level of exploitation not only by exploiting workers more, but also by exploiting a whole new group of people—consumers. In Marxian terms, customers create value in the tasks they perform for McDonaldized systems. And they are not simply paid less than the value they produce, they are paid *nothing at all.* In this way, customers are exploited to an even greater degree than workers. . . .

While no class within society is immune to McDonaldization, the lower classes are the most affected. They are the ones who are most likely to go to McDonaldized schools, live in inexpensive, mass-produced tract houses, and work in McDonaldized jobs. Those in the upper classes have much more of a chance of sending their children to non-McDonaldized schools, living in custom-built homes, and working in occupations in which they impose McDonaldization on others while avoiding it to a large degree themselves.

Also related to the social class issue . . . is the fact that the McDonaldization of a significant portion of the labor force does not mean that all, or even most, of the labor force is undergoing this process. In fact, the McDonaldization of some of the labor force is occurring at the same time that another large segment is moving in a postindustrial, that is, more highly skilled, direction (Hage & Powers, 1992). Being created in this sector of society are relatively high-status, well-paid occupations requiring high levels of education and training. In the main, these are far from McJobs and lack most, or all, of the dimensions discussed at the beginning of this [reading]. The growth of such postindustrial occupations parallels the concern in the labor process literature with flexible specialization occurring side by side with the deskilling of many other jobs. This points to a bifurcation in the class system. In spite of appearances, there is no contradiction here; McDonaldization and postindustrialization tend to occur in different sectors of the labor market. However, the spread of McJobs leads us to be dubious of the idea that we have moved into a new postindustrial era and have left behind the kind of deskilled jobs we associate with industrial society.

CRITICAL-THINKING QUESTIONS

1. Describe ways in which McDonaldization is evident in a number of familiar settings (not just the workplace, but perhaps shopping malls and even the college campus). What elements of McDonaldization can you find?

2. In what ways does a McDonaldized setting control not just workers but customers as well? Why do organizations want to control customers?

3. Why does McDonaldization seem to appeal to many people? Do you think this process is good for society as a whole or harmful? Why?

NOTES

This chapter combines a paper, "McJobs," published in Rich Feller and Garry Walz (eds.), *Career Transitions in Turbulent Times* (Greensboro, N.C.: ERIC/CASS Publications, 1996) and the Invited Plenary Address, International Labour Process Conference, Blackpool, England, April, 1995.

1. Although a study by Katz and Krueger (1992) indicates an employment *increase* accompanying a rise in the minimum wage.

2. As we will see below, other kinds of high-status, high-paying postindustrial occupations are also growing.

3. There are, of course, many other factors involved in turnover.

REFERENCES

GIDDENS, ANTHONY. 1984. *The constitution of society: Outline of the theory of structuration.* Berkeley, Calif.: University of California Press.

HAGE, JERALD, and CHARLES H. POWERS. 1992. *Post-industrial lives: Roles and relationships in the 21st century.* Newbury Park, Calif.: Sage.

LEIDNER, ROBIN. 1993. *Fast food, fast talk: Service work and the routinization of everyday life.* Berkeley, Calif.: University of California Press.

LOVE, JOHN. 1986. *McDonald's: Behind the arches.* Toronto: Bantam Books.

SCHAAF, DICK. 1994. Inside Hamburger University. *Training,* December: 18–24.

SINGLETARY, MICHELLE. 1996. Borrowing by the touch. *Washington Post,* 30 March: C1, C2.

VAN GIEZEN, ROBERT W. 1994. Occupational wages in the fast-food restaurant industry. *Monthly Labor Review,* August: 24–30.

WORSLEY, PETER. 1982. *Marx and Marxism.* Chichester: Ellis Horwood.

CLASSIC

CONTEMPORARY

CROSS-CULTURAL

29 "Even If I Don't Know What I'm Doing, I Can Make It Look Like I Do": Becoming a Doctor in Canada

BRENDA L. BEAGAN

Sociologists use the term social structure *to refer to the relatively stable patterns of social interaction and organized relationships that persist over time. Brenda Beagan's article shows how medical students who are trained at Canadian universities are socialized to fit into existing social structures rather than to change them. Notice how medical students incorporate their new professional identity as they move through their studies.*

When students enter medical school they are lay people with some science background. When they leave four years later they have become physicians; they have acquired specialized knowledge and taken on a new identity of medical professional. What happens in those four years? What processes of socialization go into the making of a doctor?

Most of what we know about how students come to identify as future-physicians derives from research conducted when students were almost exclusively male, white, middle- or upper-class, young and single—for example, the classics *Boys in White* (Becker, Geer, Strauss, & Hughes, 1961) and *Student Physician* (Morton, Reader, & Kendall, 1957). When women and students of colour were present in this research it was in token numbers. Even when women and non-traditional students were present, as in Sinclair's (1997) recent ethnography, their impact on processes of

professional identity formation and the potentially distinct impact of professional socialization on these students have been largely unanalysed. What does becoming a doctor look like in a medical school of the late 1990s, where many students are female, are of diverse racial and cultural backgrounds, are working-class, gay, and/or parents?

This study draws on survey and interview data from students and faculty at one Canadian medical school to examine the processes of professional identity formation and how they are experienced by diverse undergraduate medical students in the late 1990s. As the results will show, the processes are remarkably unchanged from the processes documented forty years ago.

RESEARCH METHODS AND PARTICIPANTS

The research employed three complementary research strategies: A survey of a third-year class (123 students) at one medical school, interviews with twenty-five students from that class, and

Source: Brenda L. Beagan. 2001. "Even if I don't know what I'm doing I can make it look like I know what I'm doing": Becoming a doctor in the 1990s. *The Canadian Review of Sociology and Anthropology* 38(3): 275–92.

143

interviews with twenty-three faculty members from the same school.[1] Third-year students were chosen because in a traditional medical curriculum the third year is a key point for students, an important transition as they move out of the classroom to spend the majority of their time working with patients—patients who may or may not call them "doctor," treat them as doctors, and reflect them back to themselves as doctors (cf. Coombs, 1978; Haas & Shaffir, 1987). . . .

Survey respondents also identified faculty members who they believed were "especially interested in medical education." Twenty-three faculty interviews were conducted. All interviews took sixty to ninety minutes following a semi-structured interview guide, and were tape-recorded and transcribed. The interview transcripts were coded inductively using broad categories such as "pressures toward conformity," and "conflicts experienced," and using codes such as "language of medicine" derived from the literature. Initial broad codes were later subdivided into narrower codes.

. . . [T]he students who completed the survey were evenly divided by gender and were heterogeneous in "race"/ethnicity, as well as in self-identified social class background.[2] Twenty students (28%) self-identified as members of "minority groups," all identifying racial or cultural groups. The students interviewed were slightly less heterogeneous in "race"/ethnicity and first language, and were somewhat more likely to be in committed relationships. The purposive sample of faculty members and administrators was predominately male, English-speaking and of European origin—reflective of the school's faculty more generally.

FIRST EXPERIENCES BECOME COMMONPLACE

When identifying how they came to think of themselves as medical students, participants described a process whereby what feels artificial and unnatural initially comes to feel natural simply through repetition. For many students, a series of "first times" were transformative moments.

Denise:[3] I think there are sort of seminal experiences. The first cut in anatomy, the first time you see a patient die, first time you see a treatment that was really aggressive and didn't work. . . . First few procedures that I conducted myself, first time I realized that I really did have somebody's life in my hands. . . . It seems like a whole lot of first times. The first time you take a history, the first time you actually hear the murmur. There are a lot of "Ah-ha!" sort of experiences.

Part of the novelty is the experience of being entitled—even required—to violate conventional social norms, touching patients' bodies, inquiring about bodily functions, probing emotional states: "You have to master a sense that you're invading somebody, and to feel like it's all right to do that, to invade their personal space. . . ."

CONSTRUCTING A PROFESSIONAL APPEARANCE

Students are quite explicitly socialized to adopt a professional appearance: "When people started to relax the dress code a letter was sent to everybody's mailbox, commenting that we were not to show up in jeans, and a tie is appropriate for men." Most students, however, do not require such reminders; they have internalized the requisite standards.

Dressing neatly and appropriately is important to convey respect to patients, other medical staff, and the profession. It probably also helps in patients taking students seriously (survey comment).

Asked whether or not they ever worry about their appearance or dress at the hospital, 41 percent of the survey respondents said they do not, while 59 percent said they do.

There were no statistically significant differences by gender, class background or "minority" status, yet gendered patterns emerged when students detailed their concerns in an open-ended question. Most of the men satisfied their concerns about professional appearance with a shave and a collared shirt, perhaps adding a tie: "I do make sure that I am dressed appropriately when I see patients i.e. well-groomed, collared shirt (but no tie)."

Women, on the other hand, struggled with the complex messages conveyed by their clothing, trying to look well-dressed yet not convey sexual messages. For women, "dressed up" normally means feminine while a professional image is intended to convey competence. Striking a balance at the intersection can be difficult: "Is it professional enough? Competent looking?. . . I do not want to appear 'sexy' on the job." As one student noted, while both men and women sometimes violate standards of professional dress, men's violations tend to involve being too informal; women's may involve dressing too provocatively, thereby sexualizing a doctor-patient encounter.

CHANGES IN LANGUAGE, THINKING AND COMMUNICATION SKILLS

Acquiring a huge vocabulary of new words and old words with new meanings—what one student called "medical-ese"—is one of the central tasks facing medical students, and one of the major bases for examining them (Sinclair, 1997). Students were well aware of adopting the formal language of medicine.

Dawna: All of a sudden all I can think of is this lingo that people won't understand. My brother told me the other day, "Sometimes I just don't understand what you are talking about anymore." I don't realize it! I'll use technical terms that I didn't think that other people wouldn't know.

The language of medicine is the basis for constructing a new social reality. Even as it allows communication, language constructs "zones of meaning that are linguistically circumscribed" (Berger & Luckmann, 1966: 39). Medical language encapsulates and constructs a worldview wherein reducing a person to body parts, tissues, organs and systems becomes normal, natural, "the only reasonable way to think" (Good & Good, 1993: 98–9). Students described this as learning to pare away "extraneous" information about a patient's life to focus on what is clinically relevant.

Becky: I see how it happens. . . . The first day of medicine we're just people. We relate by asking everything about a person, just like you'd have a conversation with anybody. And then that sort of changes and you become focussed on the disease. . . because right now there's just too much. It's overwhelming. I'm hoping that as I learn more and become more comfortable with what I know and I can apply it without having to consciously go through every step in my mind, that I'll be able to focus on the *person* again.

In part through the language of medicine students learn a scientific gaze that reduces patients to bodies, allowing them to concentrate on what is medically important—disease, procedures, and techniques (Haas & Shaffir, 1987).

Not surprisingly, students may simultaneously lose the communication abilities they had upon entering medical school.

Dr. W.: Their ability to talk to people becomes corrupted by the educational process. They learn the language of medicine but they give up some of the knowledge that they brought in. . . . The knowledge of how to listen to somebody, how to be humble, how to hear somebody else's words. . . . It gets overtaken by the agenda of medical interviewing.

Another faculty member noted that students' communication skills improved significantly during their first term of first year, but "by the end of fourth year they were worse than they had been before medical school."

LEARNING THE HIERARCHY

Key to becoming a medical student is learning to negotiate the complex hierarchy within medicine, with students positioned at the bottom. A few faculty saw this hierarchy as a fine and important tradition facilitating students' learning.

Dr. U.: You're always taught by the person above you. Third-year medical students taught by the fourth-year student. . . . Fourth-year student depends on the resident to go over his stuff. Resident depends on maybe the senior or the chief resident or the staff person. So they all get this hierarchy which is wonderful for learning because the attendings can't deal with everybody.

Students, and most faculty, were far less accepting of this traditional hierarchy—particularly of students' place in it.

Both faculty and students pointed out the compliance the hierarchical structure inculcates in students, discouraging them from questioning those above them.

Dr. G.: If they don't appear compliant and so on they will get evaluated poorly. And if you get evaluated poorly then you might not get a good residency position. There's that sort of thing over their shoulders all of the time . . . the fear.

For students being a "good medical student" means not challenging clinicians.

Valerie: If I ever saw something blatantly sexist or racist or wrong I hope that I would say something. But you get so caught up in basically clamming up, shutting up, and just taking it. . . . Is it going to ruin my career, am I going to end up known as the fink, am I going to not get the [residency] spot that I want because I told?

Though virtually every student described seeing things on the wards that they disagreed with, as long as there was no direct harm to a patient they stayed silent and simply field away the incident in their collection of "things not to do when I am a doctor."

Other researchers have noted that medical students develop an approach geared to getting along with faculty, pleasing them whatever their demands (Becker et al., 1961: 281; Bloom, 1973: 20; Sinclair, 1997: 29). Some students, however, had *internalized* the norm of not criticizing clinicians, adopting an unspoken "code of silence" not just to appease faculty, but as part of being a good physician. In particular, one should never critique a colleague in front of patients.

Mark: As students we all critique the professors and our attendings. . . . But I don't think we'd ever do that in front of a patient. It's never been told to us not to. But most of us wouldn't do that. Even if a patient describes something their doctor has prescribed to them or a treatment they've recommended which you know is totally wrong, maybe even harmful, I think most of us, unless it was really harmful, would tend to ignore it and just accept, "This is the doctor and his patient. What happens between them is okay."

These students had developed a sense of alliance with other members of the profession rather than with lay people and patients—a key to professional socialization. Several faculty referred to good medical students as "good team players" (cf. Sinclair, 1997), invoking a notion of belonging.

Dr. M.: That sense of belonging, I think, is a sense of belonging to the profession. . . . You're part of the process of health care. . . . I mean, you haven't a lot of the responsibility, but at least you're connected with the team.

For some students, too, the desire to present a united front for patients was expressed as being a good team player: "You have to go along with some things . . . in front of the patient. For teams it wouldn't be good to have the ranks arguing amongst themselves about the best approach for patient care." To remain good team players, many students, residents and physicians learn to say nothing even when they see colleagues and superiors violating the ethics and standards of the profession; such violations are disregarded as matters of personal style (Light, 1988).

RELATIONSHIP TO PATIENTS

As students are learning their place in the hierarchy within medicine, they are simultaneously learning an appropriate relationship to patients. Within the medical hierarchy students feel powerless at the bottom. Yet in relation to patients even students hold a certain amount of power. In the interviews there were widely diverging views on the degree of professional authority physicians and student-physicians should display.

Some faculty drew a very clear connection between professionalism and the "emotional distancing" Fox documented in medicine in 1957, describing students developing a "hard shell" as a "way of dealing with feelings" to prevent over-identifying with patients. Emotional involvement and over-identification are seen as dangerous; students must strike a balance between empathy and objectivity, learning to overcome or master their emotions (Conrad, 1988; Haas & Shaffir, 1987): "I only become of use if I can create some distance so that I can function."

Dr. E.: Within the professional job that you have to do, one can be very nice to patients but there's a distancing that says you're not their friend, you're their doctor.

In contrast, several faculty members rejected the "emotional distancing" approach to medicine in favour of one based in egalitarian connection.

Dr. V.: I reject that way of dealing with it. . . . When I'm seeing a patient I have to try to get into understanding what's bothering them. And in fact it's a harder job, I mean I need to understand well enough so I can help them to understand. 'Cause the process of healing is self-understanding.

These faculty members talked about recognizing and levelling power or sharing power. They saw professional distancing as the loss of humanitarianism, the adoption of a position of superiority, aloofness, emphasizing that clinicians need to know their patients as something more than a diagnosis. Women were slightly over-represented among those expressing the egalitarian perspective, but several male clinicians also advocated this position.

PLAYING A ROLE GRADUALLY BECOMES REAL

Along with emotional distancing, Fox (1957) identified "training for uncertainty" as key to medical socialization, including the uncertainty arising from not knowing everything, and not knowing enough. Alongside gathering the knowledge and experience that gradually reduces feelings of uncertainty, students also grow to simply tolerate high levels of uncertainty. At the same time they face routine expectations of certainty—from patients who expect them "to know it all" and faculty who often expect them to know far more than they do and who evaluate the students' competence (Haas & Shaffir, 1987). Students quickly learn it is risky to display lack of certainty; impression management becomes a central feature

of clinical learning (Conrad, 1988). Haas and Shaffir (1987: 110) conclude that the process of professionalization involves *above all* the successful adoption of a cloak of competence such that audiences are convinced of the legitimacy of claims to competence.

Robert Coombs argues that medical professional socialization is partly a matter of *playing* the role of doctor, complete with the props of white coat, stethoscope, name tag, and clipboard (1978: 222). The symbols mark medical students off as distinct from lay people and other hospital staff, differentiating between We and They. Students spoke of "taking on a role" that initially made them feel like "total frauds," "impostors."

Erin: It was really role-playing. You were doing all these examinations on these patients which were not going to go into their charts, were not going to ever be read by anybody who was treating the people so it really was just practice. Just play-acting.

They affirmed the importance of the props to successful accomplishment of their role play—even as it enhanced the feeling of artifice: "During third year when we got to put the little white coat on and carry some instruments around the hospital, have a name tag . . . it definitely felt like role-playing."

Despite feeling fraudulent, the role play allows students to meet a crucial objective: demonstrating to faculty, clinical instructors, nurses and patients that they know something. They quickly learn to at least look competent.

Nancy: Even if I don't know what I'm doing I can make it *look* like I know what I'm doing. . . . It was my acting in high school. . . . I get the trust of the patient. . . .

RESPONSES FROM OTHERS

The more students are treated by others as if they really were doctors the more they feel like doctors (cf. Coombs, 1978). In particular, the response from other hospital personnel and patients can help confirm the student's emerging medical professional identity.

Rina: The more the staff treats you as someone who actually belongs there, that definitely adds to your feeling like you do belong there. . . . It's like, "Wow! This nurse is paging me and wants to know *my* opinion on why this patient has no urine output?!"

For many students, patients were the single most important source of confirmation for their emerging identity as physicians. With doctors and nurses, students feel they can easily be caught out for what they don't know; with patients they feel fairly certain they can pull off a convincing performance, and they often realize they *do* know more than the average person.

One response from others that has tremendous impact is simply being called doctor by others (Konner, 1987; Shapiro, 1987). Survey results show 68 percent (*n* = 48) of students had been called doctor at least occasionally by people other than family or friends. All but two fully recalled the first time they were called doctor and how they felt about it. *Not* being called doctor—especially when your peers *are*—can be equally significant. In previous accounts, being white and being male have greatly improved a medical student's chances of being taken for a doctor (Dickstein, 1993; Gamble, 1990; Kirk, 1994; Lenhart, 1993). In this study, although social class background, minority status and first language made no difference, significantly more men than women were *regularly* called doctor and significantly more women had *never* been called doctor.[4]

These data suggest a lingering societal assumption that the doctor is a man. According to the interviews, women medical students and physicians are still often mistaken for nurses. Two of the male students suggested the dominant assumption that a doctor is a man facilitates their establishing rapport with patients and may ease their relationships with those above them in the medical hierarchy: "I've often felt because I fit like a stereotypical white male, that patients might see me as a bit more trustworthy. A bit more what they'd like to see. Who they want to see." Goffman notes that the part of a social performance intended to impress others, which he calls the

"front," and which includes clothing, gender, appearance and manner, is predetermined: "When an actor takes on an established social role, usually he finds that a particular front has already been established for it" (1959: 27). In this case it appears that the role doctor, or medical student, still carries an attached assumption of maleness.

SECONDARY SOCIALIZATION: SUBSUMING THE FORMER SELF?

The fact that roles carry with them established expectations heightens the potential for clashes with the identity characteristics of new incumbents. Education processes, inevitably processes of secondary socialization, must always contend with individuals' already formed and persistent selves, selves established through primary socialization. As Berger and Luckmann (1966: 129) note, "Whatever new contents are now to be internalized must somehow be superimposed upon this already present reality."

In his study of how medical students put together identities as spouses, parents, and so on with their developing identities as physicians, Broadhead (1983) stresses the need for individuals to "articulate" their various identities to one another, sorting out convergences and divergences of attitudes, assumptions, activities and perspectives that accompany different subject positions.

In this research, most students indicated that medicine had largely taken over the rest of their lives, diminishing their performance of other responsibilities. While 55 percent of survey respondents thought they were doing a good job of being a medical student, many thought they were doing a poor to very poor job of being a spouse (26 percent) or family member (37 percent); 46 percent gave themselves failing grades as friends. Fewer than a quarter of respondents thought they were doing a good job of being an informed citizen (18 percent) or member of their religion, if they had one (17 percent).

What emerged from most interviews and from the survey was a picture of medical school dominating all other aspects of daily life. Overwhelmingly, students talked about sacrifice.

Lew: You just sacrifice so much. I don't know about people who don't have children, but I value my family more than anything, and, and I cannot—I didn't know you had to sacrifice that much.

Many students had given things up, at least temporarily: musical instruments, art, writing, sports activities, volunteer activities. Some students spoke of putting themselves on hold, taking on new medical-student identities by subsuming former identities.

This sacrifice of self-identity can be quite serious. Several faculty and students suggested students from non-Western, non-Caucasian cultural backgrounds need to assimilate: "Students from other cultures leave behind a lot of their culture in order to succeed. There's a trade-off." Similarly, faculty and students suggested gay and lesbian students frequently become more "closeted" as they proceed through undergraduate training. One clinician said of a lesbian fourth-year student, "Now all of a sudden her hair's cut very business-like and the clothes are different. . . . She's fitting into medicine. Medicine isn't becoming a component of her, she's becoming a component of the machine." Some faculty suggested women in medicine may need to relinquish their identity as women in order to fit in as physicians.

Dr. Q.: The women who are in those positions are white men. You just have to look at the way they dress. They're wearing power suits often with ties, you know, they're really trying to fit the image. [One of the women here] recently retired and in the elevator in the hospital they talked about her as one of the boys. So the perception of the men is that this is not a woman, this is one of the boys.

Women, they argued, become more-or-less men during medical training, "almost hypermasculine in their interactions," "much more like men in terms of thought processes and interactions with people."

In addition to letting go of gender identity, sexual identity and cultural identity, some students described losing connections to their families and old friends after entering medical school. Often this was due to time constraints and diverging interests, but for some there was also a growing social distance as they moved into a new social status and education level. Lance was disconnecting from his working-class family:

Lance: My family actually were very unsupportive [when I got into medicine]. They didn't even know what I was doing. And there's still this huge gap between them and myself because they don't want to understand what's going on in my world, and their world seems quite simple, simplistic to me. . . . I see that gap getting larger over time.

Relationships with family, friends from outside of medicine, and anyone else who cannot relate to what students are doing every day are put "on the back burner." Intimate relationships are frequent casualties of medical school.

Thus some students do not or cannot integrate their medical student identities with their former sense of self; rather they let go of parts of themselves, bury them, abandon them, or put them aside, at least for a while. Another option for students who experience incongruities between their medical-student identities and other aspects of themselves is to segregate their lives. Because human beings have the ability to reflect on our own actions, it becomes possible to experience a segment of the self as distinct, to "detach a part of the self and its concomitant reality as relevant only to the role-specific situation in question" (Berger & Luckmann, 1966: 131). In this research 31 percent of survey respondents felt they are one person at school and another with friends and family. Perhaps as a consequence, many students maintain quite separate groups of friends, within medicine and outside medicine. Indeed, some faculty stressed the importance of maintaining strong outside connections to make it through medical school without losing part of yourself.[5]

DIFFERENCE AS A BASIS FOR RESISTANCE

Elsewhere I have argued that intentional and unintentional homogenizing influences in medical education neutralize the impact of social differences students bring into medicine (Beagan, 2001). Students come to believe that the social class, "race," ethnicity, gender and sexual orientation of a physician is not—and should not be relevant during physician-patient interactions. Nonetheless, at the same time those social differences can provide a basis for critique of and resistance to aspects of medical professional socialization. A study of medical residents found that those most able to resist socialization pressures minimized contact and interaction with others in medicine; maintained outside relationships that supported an alternative orientation to the program; and entered their programs with a "relatively strong and well-defined orientation" (Shapiro & Jones, 1979: 243). Complete resocialization requires "an intense concentration of all significant interaction within the [new social] group" (Berger & Luckmann, 1966: 145); it is also facilitated by minimal contradictions between the previous social world and the new world.

In this research, age played a clear role in students' ability to resist some aspects of professional socialization. Older students usually had careers before medicine, which helped put medical school in a different perspective. Often medicine was one of a range of possible things they could be doing with their lives—important, but not worth sacrificing for: "There are other things that are more important to me than this, so if at any point this conflicted too much with those things, I would give it up." One student suggested that being older entering medicine meant she had her goals and self-identity more clearly established. Most older students were in committed relationships with non-medical partners and had clear priorities about maintaining non-medical activities and connections, rather than abandoning them under the onslaught of medical school demands.

Robin: I resolved that I wouldn't let my close friends go by the wayside. . . . My partner is important to me, and I wouldn't always make him take a back seat to what I was doing. . . . It was like an ultimatum. If this program won't allow me to do those things, which I thought were reasonable things, then I just wasn't willing to do it.

These outside commitments helped them minimize interactions with their new social group.

The strongest basis for resisting professional socialization, however, came from having a working-class or impoverished family background. Most of the working-class students said they are not seen as particularly praiseworthy within their families—if anything they are somewhat suspect. They expressed a sustained antielitism that keeps them from fully identifying with other medical professionals. Janis, for example, insisted that she is not "one of Them," that she came from the other side of the tracks and still belongs there, that she could never fit in at medical school, could never be "a proper med student." She feels very uncomfortable with social functions at school and sees herself as utterly different from her classmates and preceptors: "Let's just say I don't share Dr. Smith's interest in yachting in the Caribbean, you know what I mean? (laughing)."

Lance, who spent his summers working on fishing boats to pay for medical school, described most of his classmates as "the pampered elite." He resists the required dress code because it epitomizes elitism.

Lance: A lot of people, the first thing they did when we started seeing patients was throw on a nice pair of shoes and grab the tie and button up. I've never worn a tie. And I never will. . . . To me, it symbolizes everything that sets the doctor and the patient apart. It's like . . . 'I'm somewhat better than everyone else.' . . . It gets in the way of good communication. I think you want a level of respect there, but you don't want that B.S. that goes with it.

Although the number of working class students was small, the data showed quite clearly that they tended to be among the least compliant with the processes of secondary socialization encountered in medical school.

Lance: I think I'm very much different from my class-mates . . . more outspoken, definitely. . . . Other people tend to say the right thing because they're a little afraid of the consequences. I don't care. . . . It comes from my background, you know, fishing. I've seen these tough, hard guys, think they're pretty something, but they're puking their guts out being seasick. It kind of reduces to the common denominator.

CONCLUSION

What is perhaps most remarkable about these findings is how little has changed since the publication of *Boys in White* (Becker et al., 1961) and *Student Physician* (Merton et al., 1957), despite the passage of forty years and the influx of a very different student population. The basic processes of socializing new members into the profession of medicine remain remarkably similar, as students encounter new social norms, a new language, new thought processes, and a new world view that will eventually enable them to become full-fledged members of "the team" taking the expected role in the medical hierarchy.

Yet, with the differences in the 1990s student population, there are also some important differences in experiences. The role of medical student continues to carry with it certain expectations of its occupant. At a time when medical students were almost exclusively white, heterosexually identified, upper- or middle-class men, the identity may have "fit" more easily than it does for students who are women, who are from minority racial groups, who identify as gay or lesbian or working-class. If role-playing competence and being reflected back to yourself as "doctor" are as central to medical socialization as Haas and Shaffir (1987) suggest, what does it mean that women students are less likely than their male peers to be called doctor? This research has indicated the presence of a lingering societal assumption that Doctor = Man. Women students struggle to construct a professional appearance that male students find a straightforward accomplishment. Women search for ways to be in a relationship with their patients that are unmarked by gender. Despite the fact that they make up half

of all medical students in Canada, women's experiences of medical school remain different. In this research, almost half (six of fourteen) of the women students interviewed indicated that they do not identify themselves as medical students in casual social settings outside school lest they be seen as putting on airs; none of the male students indicated this. It remains for future research to determine whether gender differences in the "fit" of the physician role make a difference to medical practice.

Interestingly, it is commonly assumed that the source of change in medical education will be the next generation of physicians—in other words, the current crop of medical students and residents (cf. Sinclair, 1997: 323–24). Over and over again I heard the refrain, "Surely the new generation of doctors will do things differently." This was the response to the hierarchy that stifles questioning or dissent through fear; to the inhumane hours expected of student interns and residents; to the need to show deference to superiors; to the need to pretend competence and confidence; to the need to sacrifice family, friends and outside interests to succeed in medicine. Yet, there have been many new generations of doctors in the past forty years . . . with remarkably little change. Why should we expect change now? Students, residents and junior physicians have very little power in the hierarchy to bring about change. Moreover, if they have been well socialized, why would we expect them to facilitate change? As one physician suggested, those who fit in well in medical school, who thrive on the competition and succeed, those are the students who return as physicians to join the faculty of the medical school. The ones who did not fit in, the ones who hated medical school, the ones who barely made it through—they are unlikely to be involved enough in medical education to bring about change.

Medical training has not always been good for patients (see Beagan, 2001). Nor has it been particularly good for medical students in many ways. Yet efforts at change on a structural level seem to have made little overall difference. In fact medical schools have a history of revision and reform without change (Bloom, 1988). Sinclair suggests moves toward entire new educational processes, such as the move to problem-based learning in medical schools throughout North America, simply "realign existing elements in the traditional training" (1997: 325). Furthermore, additions of new and very different components of the curriculum—such as classes on social and cultural aspects of health and illness, communication courses, and courses critiquing the social relations of the medical profession—are often seriously undermined in clinical teaching (Sinclair, 1997). Again, further empirical research should investigate the impact of such curriculum changes on professional socialization.

Finally, this research shows that the same sources of differentiation that mark some students as not quite fitting in also serve as sources of resistance against medical socialization. Older students, gay students who refuse to be closeted, and students who come from poverty or from working-class backgrounds, may be more likely than others to "do medical student" differently. Whether that translates into "doing doctor" differently is a matter for further empirical research. Future research needs to examine how these "different" students, these resisting students, experience residency and professional practice, whether and how they remain in medical practice.

CRITICAL THINKING QUESTIONS

1. One new experience for medical students is learning *medical-ese*. Have you faced a similar process during your college education? Explain.

2. Why do you think that the traditional hierarchy in medical schools (i.e., faculty at the top, students at the bottom) is seen by many as a good thing?

3. Which groups of students were most likely to resist professional socialization? Why would this be the case?

NOTES

1. In order to gain access to the research site, it was agreed that the medical school would remain unnamed. The school in question was in a large Canadian city with a racially and ethnically diverse population. It followed a traditional undergraduate curriculum.

2. At this medical school classes have been 40 percent–50 percent female for about fifteen years (Association of Canadian Medical Colleges, 1996: 16); the class studied here was 48 percent female. Using subjective assessment of club photos, over the past fifteen years about 30 percent of each class would be considered "visible minority" students, mainly of Asian and South Asian heritage.

3. All names are pseudonyms.

4. Never been called doctor, 14 percent of women, 0 percent of men; occasionally or regularly, 57 percent of women, 78 percent of men (Cramer's V = 0.32).

5. All of the gay/lesbian faculty and students described themselves as leading highly segregated lives during medical school.

REFERENCES

Association of Canadian Medical Colleges. 1996. *Canadian medical education statistics,* Vol. 18.

———. 2000. Neutralizing differences: Producing neutral doctors for (almost) neutral patients. *Social Science & Medicine,* 51(8): 1253–65.

BEAGAN, B. L. 2001. Micro inequities and everyday inequalities: "Race," gender, sexuality and class in medical school. *Canadian Journal of Sociology,* 26 (Fall): 583–610.

BECKER, H. S., B. GEER, A. L. STRAUSS, and F. C. HUGHES. 1961. *Boys "in" white: Student culture in medical school.* Chicago: University of Chicago Press.

BERGER, P. L., and T. LUCKMANN. 1966. *The social construction of reality: A treatise in the sociology of knowledge.* New York: Doubleday and Co.

BLOOM, S. W. 1973. *Power and dissent in the medical school.* New York: The Free Press.

———. 1988. Structure and ideology in medical education: An analysis of resistance to change. *Journal of Health and Social Behavior,* 29: 294–306.

BROADHEAD, R. 1983. *The private lives and professional identities of medical students.* New Brunswick, N.J.: Transaction.

CONRAD, E. 1988. Learning to doctor: Reflections on recent accounts of the medical school years. *Journal of Health and Social Behavior,* 29: 323–32.

COOLEY, C. H. 1964. *Human nature and the social order.* New York: Schocken.

COOMBS, R. H. 1978. *Mastering medicine.* New York: Free Press.

DICKSTEIN, L. J. 1993. Gender bias in medical education: Twenty vignettes and recommended responses. *Journal of the American Medical Women's Association,* 48(5): 152–62.

FOX, R. C. 1957. Training for uncertainty. In *The student-physician: Introduction studies in the sociology of medical education,* eds. R. K. Merton, G. G. Reader, and E. L. Kendall, 207–44. Cambridge, Mass.: Harvard University Press.

GAMBLE, V. N. 1990. On becoming a physician: A dream not deferred. In *The black women's health book: Speaking for ourselves,* ed. E. C. White, 52–64. Seattle: Seal Press.

GOFFMAN, E. 1959. *The presentation of self in everyday life.* New York: Doubleday.

GOOD, B. J., and M. J. DELVECCHIO GOOD. 1993. "Learning medicine." The constructing of medical knowledge at Harvard medical school. In *Knowledge, power, and practice: The anthropology of medicine and everyday life,* eds. S. Lindbaum, and M. Lock, 81–107. Berkeley: University of California Press.

HAAS, J., and W. SHAFFIR. 1987. *Becoming doctors: The adoption of a cloak of competence.* Greenwich, Conn.: JAI Press.

HOJAT, M., J. S. GONNELLA, and G. XU. 1995. Gender comparisons of young physicians' perceptions of medical education, professional life, and practice: A follow-up study of Jefferson college graduates. *Academic Medicine,* 70: 305–12.

HOSTLER, S. L., and R. P. GRESSARD. 1993. Perceptions of the gender fairness of the medical education environment. *Journal of the American Medical Women's Association,* 48: 51–4.

KIRK, J. 1994. A feminist analysis of women in medical schools. In *Health, illness, and health care in Canada,* 2nd ed., eds. B. S. Bolaria, and H. D. Dickenson, 158–82. Toronto: Harcourt Brace.

KONNER, M. 1987. *Becoming a doctor: A journey of initiation in medical school.* New York: Viking.

LENHART, S. 1993. Gender discrimination: A health and career development problem for women physicians. *Journal of the American Medical Women's* Association, 48(5): 155–59.

LIGHT, D. W. 1988. Toward a new sociology of medical education. *Journal of Health and Social Behavior,* 29: 307–22.

MEAD, G. H. 1934. *Mind, self, and society: From the standpoint of a social behaviorist.* Chicago: University of Chicago Press.

MERTON, R. K., G. G. READER, and P. L. KENDALL 1957. *The student physician: Introductory studies in the sociology of medical education.* Cambridge, Mass.: Harvard University Press.

SHAPIRO, E. C., and A. B. JONES. 1979. Women physicians and the exercise of power and authority in health care. In *Becoming a physician: Development of values and attitudes in medicine,* eds. E. Shapiro, and L. Lowenstein, 237–45. Cambridge: Bellinger.

SHAPIRO, M. 1987. *Getting doctored: Critical reflections on becoming a physician.* Toronto: Between the Lines.

SINCLAIR, S. 1997. *Making doctors: An institutional apprenticeship.* New York: Berg.

CLASSIC

CONTEMPORARY

CROSS-CULTURAL

30 The Functions of Crime

EMILE DURKHEIM

Common sense leads us to view crime, and all kinds of deviance, as pathological—*that is, as harmful to social life. Despite the obvious social costs of crime, however, Durkheim argues that crime is normal because it is part of all societies. Furthermore, he claims that crime makes important contributions to the operation of a social system.*

Crime is present not only in the majority of societies of one particular species but in all societies of all types. There is no society that is not confronted with the problem of criminality. Its form changes; the acts thus characterized are not the same everywhere; but, everywhere and always, there have been men who have behaved in such a way as to draw upon themselves penal repression. . . . There is, then, no phenomenon that presents more indisputably all the symptoms of normality, since it appears closely connected with the conditions of all collective life. To

Source: Reprinted with permission of The Free Press, a Division of Simon & Schuster Adult Publishing Group, from *The Rules of Sociological Method* by Emile Durkheim, translated by Sarah A. Solovay and John H. Mueller. Edited by George E. G. Catlin. Copyright © 1938 by George E. G. Catlin; copyright renewed 1966 by Sarah A. Solovay, John H. Mueller, and George E. G. Catlin.

make of crime a form of social morbidity would be to admit that morbidity is not something accidental, but, on the contrary, that in certain cases it grows out of the fundamental constitution of the living organism; it would result in wiping out all distinction between the physiological and the pathological. No doubt it is possible that crime itself will have abnormal forms, as, for example, when its rate is unusually high. This excess is, indeed, undoubtedly morbid in nature. What is normal, simply, is the existence of criminality. . . .

Here we are, then, in the presence of a conclusion in appearance quite paradoxical. Let us make no mistake. To classify crime among the phenomena of normal sociology is not to say merely that it is an inevitable, although regrettable, phenomenon, due to the incorrigible wickedness of men; it is to affirm that it is a factor in public health, an integral part of all healthy societies. This result is, at first glance, surprising enough to have puzzled even ourselves for a long time. Once this first surprise has been overcome, however, it is not difficult to find reasons explaining this normality and at the same time confirming it.

In the first place crime is normal because a society exempt from it is utterly impossible. Crime . . . consists of an act that offends certain very strong collective sentiments. In a society in which criminal acts are no longer committed, the sentiments they offend would have to be found without exception in all individual consciousnesses, and they must be found to exist with the same degree as sentiments contrary to them. Assuming that this condition could actually be realized, crime would not thereby disappear; it would only change its form, for the very cause which would thus dry up the sources of criminality would immediately open up new ones.

Indeed, for the collective sentiments which are protected by the penal law of a people at a specified moment of its history to take possession of the public conscience or for them to acquire a stronger hold where they have an insufficient grip, they must acquire an intensity greater than that which they had hitherto had. The community as a whole must experience them more vividly, for it can acquire from no other source the greater force necessary to control these individuals who formerly were the most refractory. For murderers to disappear, the horror of bloodshed must become greater in those social strata from which murderers are recruited; but, first it must become greater throughout the entire society. Moreover, the very absence of crime would directly contribute to produce this horror; because any sentiment seems much more respectable when it is always and uniformly respected.

One easily overlooks the consideration that these strong states of the common consciousness cannot be thus reinforced without reinforcing at the same time the more feeble states, whose violation previously gave birth to mere infraction of convention—since the weaker ones are only the prolongation, the attenuated form, of the stronger. Thus robbery and simple bad taste injure the same single altruistic sentiment, the respect for that which is another's. However, this same sentiment is less grievously offended by bad taste than by robbery; and since, in addition, the average consciousness has not sufficient intensity to react keenly to the bad taste, it is treated with greater tolerance. That is why the person guilty of bad taste is merely blamed, whereas the thief is punished. But, if this sentiment grows stronger, to the point of silencing in all consciousnesses the inclination which disposes man to steal, he will become more sensitive to the offenses which, until then, touched him but lightly. He will react against them, then, with more energy; they will be the object of greater opprobrium, which will transform certain of them from the simple moral faults that they were and give them the quality of crimes. For example, improper contracts, or contracts improperly executed, which only incur public blame or civil damages, will become offenses in law.

Imagine a society of saints, a perfect cloister of exemplary individuals. Crimes, properly so called, will there be unknown; but faults which appear venial to the layman will create there the same scandal that the ordinary offense does in ordinary consciousnesses. If, then, this society has the power to judge and punish, it will define these acts as criminal and will treat them as such. For the same reason, the perfect and upright man judges his smallest failings with a severity that the majority reserve for acts more truly in the nature of an offense. Formerly, acts of violence against persons were more frequent than they are today, because respect for individual dignity was less strong. As this has increased, these crimes have become more rare; and also, many acts violating this sentiment have been introduced into the penal law which were not included there in primitive times. . . .[1]

Crime is, then, necessary; it is bound up with the fundamental conditions of all social life, and by that very fact it is useful, because these conditions of which it is a part are themselves indispensable to the normal evolution of morality and law.

Indeed, it is no longer possible today to dispute the fact that law and morality vary from one social type to the next, nor that they change within the same type if the conditions of life are modified. But, in order that these transformations may be possible, the collective sentiments at the basis of morality must not be hostile to change, and consequently must have but moderate energy. If they were too strong, they would no longer be plastic. Every pattern is an obstacle to new patterns, to the extent that the first pattern is inflexible. The better a structure is articulated, the more it offers a healthy resistance to all modification; and this is equally true of functional, as of anatomical, organization. If there were no crimes, this condition could not have been fulfilled; for such a hypothesis presupposes that collective sentiments have arrived at a degree of intensity unexampled in history. Nothing is good indefinitely and to an unlimited extent. The authority which the moral conscience enjoys must not be excessive; otherwise no one would dare criticize it, and it would too easily congeal into an immutable form. To make progress, individual originality must be able to express itself. In order that the originality of the idealist whose dreams transcend his century may find expression, it is necessary that the originality of the criminal, who is below the level of his time, shall also be possible. One does not occur without the other.

Nor is this all. Aside from this indirect utility, it happens that crime itself plays a useful role in this evolution. Crime implies not only that the way remains open to necessary changes but that in certain cases it directly prepares these changes. Where crime exists, collective sentiments are sufficiently flexible to take on a new form, and crime sometimes helps to determine the form they will take. How many times, indeed, it is only an anticipation of future morality—a step toward what will be! According to Athenian law, Socrates was a criminal, and his condemnation was no more than just. However, his crime, namely, the independence of his thought, rendered a service not only to humanity but to his country. . . .

From this point of view the fundamental facts of criminality present themselves to us in an entirely new light. Contrary to current ideas, the criminal no longer seems a totally unsociable being, a sort of parasitic element, a strange and unassimilable body, introduced into the midst of society. On the contrary, he plays a definite role in social life.

CRITICAL-THINKING QUESTIONS

1. On what grounds does Durkheim argue that crime should be considered a "normal" element of society?
2. Why is a society devoid of crime an impossibility?
3. What are the functional consequences of crime and deviance?

NOTE

1. Calumny, insults, slander, fraud, etc.

CLASSIC

CONTEMPORARY

CROSS-CULTURAL

31 On Being Sane in Insane Places

DAVID L. ROSENHAN*

How do we know precisely what constitutes "normality" or mental illness? Conventional wisdom suggests that specially trained professionals have the ability to make reasonably accurate diagnoses. In this research, however, David Rosenhan provides evidence to challenge this assumption. What is—or is not—"normal" may have much to do with the labels that are applied to people in particular settings.

If sanity and insanity exist, how shall we know them?

The question is neither capricious nor itself insane. However much we may be personally convinced that we can tell the normal from the abnormal, the evidence is simply not compelling. It is commonplace, for example, to read about murder trials wherein eminent psychiatrists for the defense are contradicted by equally eminent psychiatrists for the prosecution on the matter of the defendant's sanity. More generally, there are a great deal of conflicting data on the reliability, utility, and meaning of such terms as "sanity," "insanity," "mental illness," and "schizophrenia." Finally, as early as 1934, [Ruth] Benedict suggested that normality and abnormality are not universal.[1] What is viewed as normal in one culture may be

seen as quite aberrant in another. Thus, notions of normality and abnormality may not be quite as accurate as people believe they are.

To raise questions regarding normality and abnormality is in no way to question the fact that some behaviors are deviant or odd. Murder is deviant. So, too, are hallucinations. Nor does raising such questions deny the existence of the personal anguish that is often associated with "mental illness." Anxiety and depression exist. Psychological suffering exists. But normality and abnormality, sanity and insanity, and the diagnoses that flow from them may be less substantive than many believe them to be.

At its heart, the question of whether the sane can be distinguished from the insane (and whether degrees of insanity can be distinguished from each other) is a simple matter: Do the salient characteristics that lead to diagnoses reside in the patients themselves or in the environments and contexts in which observers find them? From Bleuler, through Kretchmer, through the formulators of the recently revised *Diagnostic and Statistical Manual* of the American Psychiatric Association, the belief has

*I thank W. Mischel, E. Orne, and M. S. Rosenhan for comments on an earlier draft of this manuscript.

Source: Reprinted with permission from American Association for the Advancement of Science. Copyright © 1973 American Association for the Advancement of Science.

been strong that patients present symptoms, that those symptoms can be categorized, and, implicitly, that the sane are distinguishable from the insane. More recently, however, this belief has been questioned. Based in part on theoretical and anthropological considerations, but also on philosophical, legal, and therapeutic ones, the view has grown that psychological categorization of mental illness is useless at best and downright harmful, misleading, and pejorative at worst. Psychiatric diagnoses, in this view, are in the minds of the observers and are not valid summaries of characteristics displayed by the observed.

Gains can be made in deciding which of these is more nearly accurate by getting normal people (that is, people who do not have, and have never suffered, symptoms of serious psychiatric disorders) admitted to psychiatric hospitals and then determining whether they were discovered to be sane and, if so, how. If the sanity of such pseudopatients were always detected, there would be prima facie evidence that a sane individual can be distinguished from the insane context in which he is found. Normality (and presumably abnormality) is distinct enough that it can be recognized wherever it occurs, for it is carried within the person. If, on the other hand, the sanity of the pseudopatients were never discovered, serious difficulties would arise for those who support traditional modes of psychiatric diagnosis. Given that the hospital staff was not incompetent, that the pseudopatient had been behaving as sanely as he had been outside of the hospital, and that it had never been previously suggested that he belonged in a psychiatric hospital, such an unlikely outcome would support the view that psychiatric diagnosis betrays little about the patient but much about the environment in which an observer finds him.

This article describes such an experiment. Eight sane people gained secret admission to twelve different hospitals. Their diagnostic experiences constitute the data of the first part of this article; the remainder is devoted to a description of their experiences in psychiatric institutions. Too few psychiatrists and psychologists, even

those who have worked in such hospitals, know what the experience is like. They rarely talk about it with former patients, perhaps because they distrust information coming from the previously insane. Those who have worked in psychiatric hospitals are likely to have adapted so thoroughly to the settings that they are insensitive to the impact of that experience. And while there have been occasional reports of researchers who submitted themselves to psychiatric hospitalization, these researchers have commonly remained in the hospitals for short periods of time, often with the knowledge of the hospital staff. It is difficult to know the extent to which they were treated like patients or like research colleagues. Nevertheless, their reports about the inside of the psychiatric hospital have been valuable. This article extends those efforts.

PSEUDOPATIENTS AND THEIR SETTINGS

The eight pseudopatients were a varied group. One was a psychology graduate student in his twenties. The remaining seven were older and "established." Among them were three psychologists, a pediatrician, a psychiatrist, a painter, and a housewife. Three pseudopatients were women, five were men. All of them employed pseudonyms, lest their alleged diagnoses embarrass them later. Those who were in mental health professions alleged another occupation in order to avoid the special attentions that might be accorded by staff, as a matter of courtesy or caution, to ailing colleagues.[2] With the exception of myself (I was the first pseudopatient and my presence was known to the hospital administrator and chief psychologist and, so far as I can tell, to them alone), the presence of pseudopatients and the nature of the research program was not known to the hospital staffs.[3]

The settings were similarly varied. In order to generalize the findings, admission into a variety of hospitals was sought. The twelve hospitals in the sample were located in five different states on the East and West coasts. Some were old and shabby, some were quite new. Some were research-oriented, others not. Some had good staff-patient ratios, others were quite understaffed. Only one was a strictly private hospital. All of the others were supported by state or federal funds or, in one instance, by university funds.

After calling the hospital for an appointment, the pseudopatient arrived at the admissions office complaining that he had been hearing voices. Asked what the voices said, he replied that they were often unclear, but as far as he could tell they said "empty," "hollow," and "thud." The voices were unfamiliar and were of the same sex as the pseudopatient. The choice of these symptoms was occasioned by their apparent similarity to existential symptoms. Such symptoms are alleged to arise from painful concerns about the perceived meaninglessness of one's life. It is as if the hallucinating person were saying, "My life is empty and hollow." The choice of these symptoms was also determined by the *absence* of a single report of existential psychoses in the literature.

Beyond alleging the symptoms and falsifying name, vocation, and employment, no further alterations of person, history, or circumstances were made. The significant events of the pseudopatient's life history were presented as they had actually occurred. Relationships with parents and siblings, with spouse and children, with people at work and in school, consistent with the aforementioned exceptions, were described as they were or had been. Frustrations and upsets were described along with joys and satisfactions. These facts are important to remember. If anything, they strongly biased the subsequent results in favor of detecting sanity, since none of their histories or current behaviors were seriously pathological in any way.

Immediately upon admission to the psychiatric ward, the pseudopatient ceased simulating *any* symptoms of abnormality. In some cases, there was a brief period of mild nervousness and anxiety, since none of the pseudopatients really believed that they would be admitted so easily. Indeed, their shared fear was that they would be immediately exposed as frauds and greatly embarrassed. Moreover,

many of them had never visited a psychiatric ward; even those who had, nevertheless had some genuine fears about what might happen to them. Their nervousness, then, was quite appropriate to the novelty of the hospital setting, and it abated rapidly.

Apart from that short-lived nervousness, the pseudopatient behaved on the ward as he "normally" behaved. The pseudopatient spoke to patients and staff as he might ordinarily. Because there is uncommonly little to do on a psychiatric ward, he attempted to engage others in conversation. When asked by staff how he was feeling, he indicated that he was fine, that he no longer experienced symptoms. He responded to instructions from attendants, to calls for medication (which was not swallowed), and to dining-hall instructions. Beyond such activities as were available to him on the admissions ward, he spent his time writing down his observations about the ward, its patients, and the staff. Initially these notes were written "secretly," but as it soon became clear that no one much cared, they were subsequently written on standard tablets of paper in such public places as the dayroom. No secret was made of these activities.

The pseudopatient, very much as a true psychiatric patient, entered a hospital with no foreknowledge of when he would be discharged. Each was told that he would have to get out by his own devices, essentially by convincing the staff that he was sane. The psychological stresses associated with hospitalization were considerable, and all but one of the pseudopatients desired to be discharged almost immediately after being admitted. They were, therefore, motivated not only to behave sanely, but to be paragons of cooperation. That their behavior was in no way disruptive is confirmed by nursing reports, which have been obtained on most of the patients. These reports uniformly indicate that the patients were "friendly," "cooperative," and "exhibited no abnormal indications."

THE NORMAL ARE NOT DETECTABLY SANE

Despite their public "show" of sanity, the pseudopatients were never detected. Admitted, except in one case, with a diagnosis of schizophrenia,[4] each was discharged with a diagnosis of schizophrenia "in remission." The label "in remission" should in no way be dismissed as a formality, for at no time during any hospitalization had any question been raised about any pseudopatient's simulation. Nor are there any indications in the hospital records that the pseudopatient's status was suspect. Rather, the evidence is strong that, once labeled schizophrenic, the pseudopatient was stuck with that label. If the pseudopatient was to be discharged, he must naturally be "in remission"; but he was not sane, nor, in the institution's view, had he ever been sane.

The uniform failure to recognize sanity cannot be attributed to the quality of the hospitals, for, although there were considerable variations among them, several are considered excellent. Nor can it be alleged that there was simply not enough time to observe the pseudopatients. Length of hospitalization ranged from seven to fifty-two days, with an average of nineteen days. The pseudopatients were not, in fact, carefully observed, but this failure clearly speaks more to traditions within psychiatric hospitals than to lack of opportunity.

Finally, it cannot be said that the failure to recognize the pseudopatients' sanity was due to the fact that they were not behaving sanely. While there was clearly some tension present in all of them, their daily visitors could detect no serious behavioral consequences—nor, indeed, could other patients. It was quite common for the patients to "detect" the pseudopatients' sanity. During the first three hospitalizations, when accurate counts were kept, thirty-five of a total of 118 patients on the admissions ward voiced their suspicions, some vigorously. "You're not crazy. You're a journalist, or a professor [referring to the continual note-taking]. You're checking up on the hospital." While most of the patients were reassured by the pseudopatient's insistence that he had been sick before he came in but was fine now, some continued to believe that the pseudopatient was sane throughout his hospitalization. The fact that the patients often recognized normality when staff did not raises important questions.

Failure to detect sanity during the course of hospitalization may be due to the fact that physicians operate with a strong bias toward what statisticians call the type 2 error. This is to say that physicians are more inclined to call a healthy person sick (a false positive, type 2) than a sick person healthy (a false negative, type 1). The reasons for this are not hard to find: It is clearly more dangerous to misdiagnose illness than health. Better to err on the side of caution, to suspect illness even among the healthy.

But what holds for medicine does not hold equally well for psychiatry. Medical illnesses, while unfortunate, are not commonly pejorative. Psychiatric diagnoses, on the contrary, carry with them personal, legal, and social stigmas. It was therefore important to see whether the tendency toward diagnosing the sane insane could be reversed. The following experiment was arranged at a research and teaching hospital whose staff had heard these findings but doubted that such an error could occur in their hospital. The staff was informed that at some time during the following three months, one or more pseudopatients would attempt to be admitted into the psychiatric hospital. Each staff member was asked to rate each patient who presented himself at admissions or on the ward according to the likelihood that the patient was a pseudopatient. A ten-point scale was used, with a 1 and 2 reflecting high confidence that the patient was a pseudopatient.

Judgments were obtained on 193 patients who were admitted for psychiatric treatment. All staff who had had sustained contact with or primary responsibility for the patient—attendants, nurses, psychiatrists, physicians, and psychologists—were asked to make judgments. Forty-one patients were alleged, with high confidence, to be pseudopatients by at least one member of the staff. Twenty-three were considered suspect by at least one psychiatrist. Nineteen were suspected by one psychiatrist *and* one other staff member. Actually, no genuine pseudopatient (at least from my group) presented himself during this period.

The experiment is instructive. It indicates that the tendency to designate sane people as insane can be reversed when the stakes (in this case, prestige and diagnostic acumen) are high. But what can be said of the nineteen people who were suspected of being "sane" by one psychiatrist and another staff member? Were these people truly "sane," or was it rather the case that in the course of avoiding the type 2 error the staff tended to make more errors of the first sort—calling the crazy "sane"? There is no way of knowing. But one thing is certain: Any diagnostic process that lends itself so readily to massive errors of this sort cannot be a very reliable one.

THE STICKINESS OF PSYCHODIAGNOSTIC LABELS

Beyond the tendency to call the healthy sick—a tendency that accounts better for diagnostic behavior on admission than it does for such behavior after a lengthy period of exposure—the data speak to the massive role of labeling in psychiatric assessment. Having once been labeled schizophrenic, there is nothing the pseudopatient can do to overcome the tag. The tag profoundly colors others' perceptions of him and his behavior.

From one viewpoint, these data are hardly surprising, for it has long been known that elements are given meaning by the context in which they occur. Gestalt psychology made this point vigorously, and Asch[5] demonstrated that there are "central" personality traits (such as "warm" versus "cold") which are so powerful that they markedly color the meaning of other information in forming an impression of a given personality. "Insane," "schizophrenic," "manic-depressive," and "crazy" are probably among the most powerful of such central traits. Once a person is designated abnormal, all of his other behaviors and characteristics are colored by that label. Indeed, that label is so powerful that many of the pseudopatients' normal behaviors were overlooked entirely or profoundly misinterpreted. Some examples may clarify this issue.

Earlier I indicated that there were no changes in the pseudopatient's personal history and current status beyond those of name, employment, and, where necessary, vocation. Otherwise, a veridical description of personal history and circumstances was offered. Those circumstances were not psychotic. How were they made consonant with the diagnosis of psychosis? Or were those diagnoses modified in such a way as to bring them into accord with the circumstances of the pseudopatient's life, as described by him?

As far as I can determine, diagnoses were in no way affected by the relative health of the circumstances of a pseudopatient's life. Rather, the reverse occurred: The perception of his circumstances was shaped entirely by the diagnosis. A clear example of such translation is found in the case of a pseudopatient who had had a close relationship with his mother but was rather remote from his father during his early childhood. During adolescence and beyond, however, his father became a close friend, while his relationship with his mother cooled. His present relationship with his wife was characteristically close and warm. Apart from occasional angry exchanges, friction was minimal. The children had rarely been spanked. Surely there is nothing especially pathological about such a history. Indeed, many readers may see a similar pattern in their own experiences, with no markedly deleterious consequences. Observe, however, how such a history was translated in the psychopathological context, this from the case summary prepared after the patient was discharged:

This white thirty-nine-year-old male . . . manifests a long history of considerable ambivalence in close relationships, which begins in early childhood. A warm relationship with his mother cools during his adolescence. A distant relationship to his father is described as becoming very intense. Affective stability is absent. His attempts to control emotionality with his wife and children are punctuated by angry outbursts and, in the case of the children, spankings. And while he says that he has several good friends, one senses considerable ambivalence embedded in those relationships also. . . .

The facts of the case were unintentionally distorted by the staff to achieve consistency with a popular theory of the dynamics of a schizophrenic reaction. Nothing of an ambivalent nature had been described in relations with parents, spouse, or friends. To the extent that ambivalence could be inferred, it was probably not greater than is found in all human relationships. It is true the pseudopatient's relationships with his parents changed over time, but in the ordinary context that would hardly be remarkable—indeed, it might very well be expected. Clearly, the meaning ascribed to his verbalizations (that is, ambivalence, affective instability) was determined by the diagnosis: schizophrenia. An entirely different meaning would have been ascribed if it were known that the man was "normal."

All pseudopatients took extensive notes publicly. Under ordinary circumstances, such behavior would have raised questions in the minds of observers, as, in fact, it did among patients. Indeed, it seemed so certain that the notes would elicit suspicion that elaborate precautions were taken to remove them from the ward each day. But the precautions proved needless. The closest any staff member came to questioning these notes occurred when one pseudopatient asked his physician what kind of medication he was receiving and began to write down the response. "You needn't write it," he was told gently. "If you have trouble remembering, just ask me again."

If no questions were asked of the pseudopatients, how was their writing interpreted? Nursing records for three patients indicate that the writing was seen as an aspect of their pathological behavior. "Patient engages in writing behavior" was the daily nursing comment on one of the pseudopatients who was never questioned about his writing. Given that the patient is in the hospital, he must be psychologically disturbed. And given that he is disturbed, continuous writing must be a behavioral manifestation of that disturbance, perhaps a subset of the compulsive behaviors that are sometimes correlated with schizophrenia.

One tacit characteristic of psychiatric diagnosis is that it locates the sources of aberration within the individual and only rarely within the complex of stimuli that surrounds him. Consequently, behaviors that are stimulated by the environment are commonly misattributed to the patient's disorder. For example, one kindly nurse found a pseudopatient pacing the long hospital corridors. "Nervous, Mr. X?" she asked. "No, bored," he said.

The notes kept by pseudopatients are full of patient behaviors that were misinterpreted by well-intentioned staff. Often enough, a patient would go "berserk" because he had, wittingly or unwittingly, been mistreated by, say, an attendant. A nurse coming upon the scene would rarely inquire even cursorily into the environmental stimuli of the patient's behavior. Rather, she assumed that his upset derived from his pathology, not from his present interactions with other staff members. Occasionally, the staff might assume that the patient's family (especially when they had recently visited) or other patients had stimulated the outburst. But never were the staff found to assume that one of themselves or the structure of the hospital had anything to do with a patient's behavior. One psychiatrist pointed to a group of patients who were sitting outside the cafeteria entrance half an hour before lunchtime. To a group of young residents he indicated that such behavior was characteristic of the oral-acquisitive nature of the syndrome. It seemed not to occur to him that there were very few things to anticipate in a psychiatric hospital besides eating.

A psychiatric label has a life and an influence of its own. Once the impression has been formed that the patient is schizophrenic, the expectation is that he will continue to be schizophrenic. When a sufficient amount of time has passed, during which the patient has done nothing bizarre, he is considered to be in remission and available for discharge. But the label endures beyond discharge, with the unconfirmed expectation that he will behave as a schizophrenic again. Such labels, conferred by mental health professionals, are as influential on the patient as they are on his relatives and friends, and it should not surprise anyone that the diagnosis acts on all of them as a self-fulfilling prophecy. Eventually, the patient himself accepts the diagnosis, with all of its surplus meanings and expectations, and behaves accordingly.

The inferences to be made from these matters are quite simple. Much as Zigler and Phillips have demonstrated that there is enormous overlap in the symptoms presented by patients who have been variously diagnosed,[6] so there is enormous overlap in the behaviors of the sane and the insane. The sane are not "sane" all of the time. We lose our tempers "for no good reason." We are occasionally depressed or anxious, again for no good reason. And we may find it difficult to get along with one or another person—again for no reason that we can specify. Similarly, the insane are not always insane. Indeed, it was the impression of the pseudopatients while living with them that they were sane for long periods of time—that the bizarre behaviors upon which their diagnoses were allegedly predicated constituted only a small fraction of their total behavior. If it makes no sense to label ourselves permanently depressed on the basis of an occasional depression, then it takes better evidence than is presently available to label all patients insane or schizophrenic on the basis of bizarre behaviors or cognitions. It seems more useful, as Mischel[7] has pointed out, to limit our discussions to *behaviors,* the stimuli that provoke them, and their correlates.

It is not known why powerful impressions of personality traits, such as "crazy" or "insane," arise. Conceivably, when the origins of and stimuli that give rise to a behavior are remote or unknown, or when the behavior strikes us as immutable, trait labels regarding the *behaver* arise. When, on the other hand, the origins and stimuli are known and available, discourse is limited to the behavior itself. Thus, I may hallucinate because I am sleeping, or I may hallucinate because I have ingested a peculiar drug. These are termed sleep-induced hallucinations, or dreams, and drug-induced hallucinations, respectively. But when the stimuli to my hallucinations are unknown, that is called craziness, or schizophrenia—

as if that inference were somehow as illuminating as the others.

THE EXPERIENCE OF PSYCHIATRIC HOSPITALIZATION

The term "mental illness" is of recent origin. It was coined by people who were humane in their inclinations and who wanted very much to raise the station of (and the public's sympathies toward) the psychologically disturbed from that of witches and "crazies" to one that was akin to the physically ill. And they were at least partially successful, for the treatment of the mentally ill *has* improved considerably over the years. But while treatment has improved, it is doubtful that people really regard the mentally ill in the same way that they view the physically ill. A broken leg is something one recovers from, but mental illness allegedly endures forever. A broken leg does not threaten the observer, but a crazy schizophrenic? There is by now a host of evidence that attitudes toward the mentally ill are characterized by fear, hostility, aloofness, suspicion, and dread. The mentally ill are society's lepers.

That such attitudes infect the general population is perhaps not surprising, only upsetting. But that they affect the professionals—attendants, nurses, physicians, psychologists, and social workers—who treat and deal with the mentally ill is more disconcerting, both because such attitudes are self-evidently pernicious and because they are unwitting. Most mental health professionals would insist that they are sympathetic toward the mentally ill, that they are neither avoidant nor hostile. But it is more likely that an exquisite ambivalence characterizes their relations with psychiatric patients, such that their avowed impulses are only part of their entire attitude. Negative attitudes are there too and can easily be detected. Such attitudes should not surprise us. They are the natural offspring of the labels patients wear and the places in which they are found.

Consider the structure of the typical psychiatric hospital. Staff and patients are strictly segregated.

Staff have their own living space, including their dining facilities, bathrooms, and assembly places. The glassed quarters that contain the professional staff, which the pseudopatients came to call "the cage," sit out on every dayroom. The staff emerge primarily for caretaking purposes—to give medication, to conduct a therapy or group meeting, to instruct or reprimand a patient. Otherwise, staff keep to themselves, almost as if the disorder that afflicts their charges is somehow catching.

So much is patient–staff segregation the rule that, for four public hospitals in which an attempt was made to measure the degree to which staff and patients mingle, it was necessary to use "time out of the staff cage" as the operational measure. While it was not the case that all time spent out of the cage was spent mingling with patients (attendants, for example, would occasionally emerge to watch television in the dayroom), it was the only way in which one could gather reliable data on time for measuring.

The average amount of time spent by attendants outside of the cage was 11.3 percent (range, 3 to 52 percent). This figure does not represent only time spent mingling with patients, but also includes time spent on such chores as folding laundry, supervising patients while they shave, directing ward cleanup, and sending patients to off-ward activities. It was the relatively rare attendant who spent time talking with patients or playing games with them. It proved impossible to obtain a "percent mingling time" for nurses, since the amount of time they spent out of the cage was too brief. Rather, we counted instances of emergence from the cage. On the average, daytime nurses emerged from the cage 11.5 times per shift, including instances when they left the ward entirely (range, 4 to 39 times). Late afternoon and night nurses were even less available, emerging on the average 9.4 times per shift (range, 4 to 41 times). Data on early morning nurses, who arrived usually after midnight and departed at 8 A.M., are not available because patients were asleep during most of this period.

Physicians, especially psychiatrists, were even less available. They were rarely seen on the wards. Quite commonly, they would be seen only when they arrived and departed, with the remaining time being spent in their offices or in the cage. On the average, physicians emerged on the ward 6.7 times per day (range, 1 to 17 times). It proved difficult to make an accurate estimate in this regard, since physicians often maintained hours that allowed them to come and go at different times.

The hierarchical organization of the psychiatric hospital has been commented on before, but the latent meaning of that kind of organization is worth noting again. Those with the most power have least to do with patients, and those with the least power are most involved with them. Recall, however, that the acquisition of role-appropriate behaviors occurs mainly through the observation of others, with the most powerful having the most influence. Consequently, it is understandable that attendants not only spend more time with patients than do any other members of the staff—that is required by their station in the hierarchy—but also, insofar as they learn from their superiors' behavior, spend as little time with patients as they can. Attendants are seen mainly in the cage, which is where the models, the action, and the power are.

I turn now to a different set of studies, these dealing with staff response to patient-initiated contact. It has long been known that the amount of time a person spends with you can be an index of your significance to him. If he initiates and maintains eye contact, there is reason to believe that he is considering your requests and needs. If he pauses to chat or actually stops and talks, there is added reason to infer that he is individuating you. In four hospitals, the pseudopatient approached the staff member with a request which took the following form: "Pardon me, Mr. [or Dr. or Mrs.] X, could you tell me when I will be eligible for grounds privileges?" (or ". . . when I will be presented at the staff meeting?" or ". . . when I am likely to be discharged?"). While the content of the question varied according to the appropriateness of the target and the pseudopatient's (apparent) current needs, the form was always a courteous and relevant request for information. Care was taken never to approach a particular member of the staff more than once a day, lest the staff member become suspicious or irritated. . . . [R]emember that the behavior of the pseudopatients was neither bizarre nor disruptive. One could indeed engage in good conversation with them.

. . . Minor differences between these four institutions were overwhelmed by the degree to which staff avoided continuing contacts that patients had initiated. By far, their most common response consisted of either a brief response to the question, offered while they were "on the move" and with head averted, or no response at all.

The encounter frequently took the following bizarre form: (pseudopatient) "Pardon me, Dr. X. Could you tell me when I am eligible for grounds privileges?" (physician) "Good morning, Dave. How are you today?" (Moves off without waiting for a response.) . . .

POWERLESSNESS AND DEPERSONALIZATION

Eye contact and verbal contact reflect concern and individuation; their absence, avoidance and depersonalization. The data I have presented do not do justice to the rich daily encounters that grew up around matters of depersonalization and avoidance. I have records of patients who were beaten by staff for the sin of having initiated verbal contact. During my own experience, for example, one patient was beaten in the presence of other patients for having approached an attendant and [telling] him, "I like you." Occasionally, punishment meted out to patients for misdemeanors seemed so excessive that it could not be justified by the most radical interpretations of psychiatric canon. Nevertheless, they appeared to go unquestioned. Tempers were often short. A patient who had not heard a call for medication would be roundly excoriated, and the morning attendants would often wake patients with, "Come on, you m—f—s, out of bed!"

Neither anecdotal nor "hard" data can convey the overwhelming sense of powerlessness which invades the individual as he is continually exposed to the depersonalization of the psychiatric hospital. It hardly matters *which* psychiatric hospital—the excellent public ones and the very plush private hospital were better than the rural and shabby ones in this regard, but again, the features that psychiatric hospitals had in common overwhelmed by far their apparent differences.

Powerlessness was evident everywhere. The patient is deprived of many of his legal rights by dint of his psychiatric commitment. He is shorn of credibility by virtue of his psychiatric label. His freedom of movement is restricted. He cannot initiate contact with the staff, but may only respond to such overtures as they make. Personal privacy is minimal. Patient quarters can be entered and possessions examined by any staff member, for whatever reason. His personal history and anguish is available to any staff member (often including the "grey lady" and "candy striper" volunteer) who chooses to read his folder, regardless of their therapeutic relationship to him. His personal hygiene and waste evacuation are often monitored. The water closets may have no doors.

At times, depersonalization reached such proportions that pseudopatients had the sense that they were invisible, or at least unworthy of account. Upon being admitted, I and other pseudopatients took the initial physical examinations in a semipublic room, where staff members went about their own business as if we were not there.

On the ward, attendants delivered verbal and occasionally serious physical abuse to patients in the presence of other observing patients, some of whom (the pseudopatients) were writing it all down. Abusive behavior, on the other hand, terminated quite abruptly when other staff members were known to be coming. Staff are credible witnesses. Patients are not.

A nurse unbuttoned her uniform to adjust her brassiere in the presence of an entire ward of viewing men. One did not have the sense that she was being seductive. Rather, she didn't notice us. A group of staff persons might point to a patient in the dayroom and discuss him animatedly, as if he were not there.

One illuminating instance of depersonalization and invisibility occurred with regard to medications. All told, the pseudopatients were administered nearly 2,100 pills, including Elavil, Stelazine, Compazine, and Thorazine, to name but a few. (That such a variety of medications should have been administered to patients presenting identical symptoms is itself worthy of note.) Only two were swallowed. The rest were either pocketed or deposited in the toilet. The pseudopatients were not alone in this. Although I have no precise records on how many patients rejected their medications, the pseudopatients frequently found the medications of other patients in the toilet before they deposited their own. As long as they were cooperative, their behavior and the pseudopatients' own in this matter, as in other important matters, went unnoticed throughout.

Reactions to such depersonalization among pseudopatients were intense. Although they had come to the hospital as participant-observers and were fully aware that they did not "belong," they nevertheless found themselves caught up in and fighting the process of depersonalization. Some examples: A graduate student in psychology asked his wife to bring his textbooks to the hospital so he could "catch up on his homework"—this despite the elaborate precautions taken to conceal his professional association. The same student, who had trained for quite some time to get into the hospital, and who had looked forward to the experience, "remembered" some drag races that he had wanted to see on the weekend and insisted that he be discharged by that time. Another pseudopatient attempted a romance with a nurse. Subsequently, he informed the staff that he was applying for admission to graduate school in psychology and was very likely to be admitted, since a graduate professor was one of his regular hospital visitors. The same person began to engage in psychotherapy with other patients—all of this as a way of becoming a person in an impersonal environment.

THE SOURCES OF DEPERSONALIZATION

What are the origins of depersonalization? I have already mentioned two. First are attitudes held by all of us toward the mentally ill—including those who treat them—attitudes characterized by fear, distrust, and horrible expectations on the one hand, and benevolent intentions on the other. Our ambivalence leads, in this instance as in others, to avoidance.

Second, and not entirely separate, the hierarchical structure of the psychiatric hospital facilitates depersonalization. Those who are at the top have least to do with patients, and their behavior inspires the rest of the staff. Average daily contact with psychiatrists, psychologists, residents and physicians combined ranged from 3.9 to 25.1 minutes, with an overall mean of 6.8 (six pseudopatients over a total of 129 days of hospitalization). Included in this average are time spent in the admissions interview, ward meetings in the presence of a senior staff member, group and individual psychotherapy contacts, case presentation conferences, and discharge meetings. Clearly, patients do not spend much time in interpersonal contact with doctoral staff. And doctoral staff serve as models for nurses and attendants.

There are probably other sources. Psychiatric installations are presently in serious financial straits. Staff shortages are pervasive, staff time at a premium. Something has to give, and that something is patient contact. Yet, while financial stresses are realities, too much can be made of them. I have the impression that the psychological forces that result in depersonalization are much stronger than the fiscal ones and that the addition of more staff would not correspondingly improve patient care in this regard. The incidence of staff meetings and the enormous amount of recordkeeping on patients, for example, have not been as substantially reduced as has patient contact. Priorities exist, even during hard times. Patient contact is not a significant priority in the traditional psychiatric hospital, and fiscal pressures do not account for this. Avoidance and depersonalization may.

Heavy reliance upon psychotropic medication tacitly contributes to depersonalization by convincing staff that treatment is indeed being conducted and that further patient contact may not be necessary. Even here, however, caution needs to be exercised in understanding the role of psychotropic drugs. If patients were powerful rather than powerless, if they were viewed as interesting individuals rather than diagnostic entities, if they were socially significant rather than social lepers, if their anguish truly and wholly compelled our sympathies and concerns, would we not *seek* contact with them, despite the availability of medications? Perhaps for the pleasure of it all?

THE CONSEQUENCES OF LABELING AND DEPERSONALIZATION

Whenever the ratio of what is known to what needs to be known approaches zero, we tend to invent "knowledge" and assume that we understand more than we actually do. We seem unable to acknowledge that we simply don't know. The needs for diagnosis and remediation of behavioral and emotional problems are enormous. But rather than acknowledge that we are just embarking on understanding, we continue to label patients "schizophrenic," "manic-depressive," and "insane," as if in those words we had captured the essence of understanding. The facts of the matter are that we have known for a long time that diagnoses are often not useful or reliable, but we have nevertheless continued to use them. We now know that we cannot distinguish insanity from sanity. It is depressing to consider how that information will be used.

Not merely depressing, but frightening. How many people, one wonders, are sane but not recognized as such in our psychiatric institutions? How many have been needlessly stripped of their privileges of citizenship, from the right to vote and drive to that of handling their own accounts? How many have feigned insanity in order to avoid the criminal consequences of their behavior, and, conversely, how many would rather stand trial than live interminably in a psychiatric hospital—but are wrongly thought to be mentally ill? How many have been stigmatized by well-intentioned, but nevertheless erroneous, diagnoses? On the last point, recall again that a type 2 error in psychiatric diagnosis does not have the same consequences it does in medical diagnosis. A diagnosis of cancer that has been found to be in error is cause for celebration. But psychiatric diagnoses are rarely found to be in error. The label sticks, a mark of inadequacy forever.

Finally, how many patients might be "sane" outside the psychiatric hospital but seem insane in it—not because craziness resides in them, as it were, but because they are responding to a bizarre setting, one that may be unique to institutions which harbor nether people? Goffman[8] calls the process of socialization to such institutions "mortification"—an apt metaphor that includes the processes of depersonalization that have been described here. And while it is impossible to know whether the pseudopatients' responses to these processes are characteristic of all inmates—they were, after all, not real patients—it is difficult to believe that these processes of socialization to a psychiatric hospital provide useful attitudes or habits of response for living in the "real world."

SUMMARY AND CONCLUSIONS

It is clear that we cannot distinguish the sane from the insane in psychiatric hospitals. The hospital itself imposes a special environment in which the meanings of behavior can easily be misunderstood. The consequences to patients hospitalized in such an environment—the powerlessness, depersonalization, segregation, mortification, and self-labeling—seem undoubtedly countertherapeutic.

I do not, even now, understand this problem well enough to perceive solutions. But two matters seem to have some promise. The first concerns the proliferation of community mental health facilities, of crisis intervention centers, of the human potential movement, and of behavior therapies that, for all of their own problems, tend to avoid psychiatric labels, to focus on specific problems and behaviors, and to retain the individual in a relatively nonpejorative environment. Clearly, to the extent that we refrain from sending the distressed to insane places, our impressions of them are less likely to be distorted. (The risk of distorted perceptions, it seems to me, is always present, since we are much more sensitive to an individual's behaviors and verbalizations than we are to the subtle contextual stimuli that often promote them. At issue here is a matter of magnitude. And, as I have shown, the magnitude of distortion is exceedingly high in the extreme context that is a psychiatric hospital.)

The second matter that might prove promising speaks to the need to increase the sensitivity of mental health workers and researchers to the catch-22 position of psychiatric patients. Simply reading materials in this area will be of help to some such workers and researchers. For others, directly experiencing the impact of psychiatric hospitalization will be of enormous use. Clearly, further research into the social psychology of such total institutions will both facilitate treatment and deepen understanding.

I and the other pseudopatients in the psychiatric setting had distinctly negative reactions. We do not pretend to describe the subjective experiences of true patients. Theirs may be different from ours, particularly with the passage of time and the necessary process of adaptation to one's environment. But we can and do speak to the relatively more objective indices of treatment within the hospital. It could be a mistake, and a very unfortunate one, to consider that what happened to us derived from malice or stupidity on the part of the staff. Quite the contrary, our overwhelming impression of them was of people who really cared, who were committed, and who were uncommonly intelligent. Where they failed, as they sometimes did painfully, it would be more accurate to attribute those failures to the environment in which they, too, found themselves than to personal callousness. Their perceptions and behavior were controlled by the situation, rather than being motivated by a malicious disposition. In a more benign environment, one that was less attached to global diagnosis, their behaviors and judgments might have been more benign and effective.

CRITICAL-THINKING QUESTIONS

1. How does this research illustrate the basic ideas of labeling theory in sociology?
2. Once the "patients" were admitted to the hospitals, how was their subsequent behavior understood in terms of the label "mentally ill"? Did the label of mental illness disappear at the point at which the "patients" were discharged from the hospitals?
3. What, if any, ethical issues are raised by the way in which this research was conducted?

NOTES

1. R. Benedict, *Journal of General Psychology* 10 (1934), 59.

2. Beyond the personal difficulties that the pseudopatient is likely to experience in the hospital, there are legal and social ones that, combined, require considerable attention before entry. For example, once admitted to a psychiatric institution, it is difficult, if not impossible, to be discharged on short notice, state law to the contrary notwithstanding. I was not sensitive to these difficulties at the outset of the project, nor to the personal and situational emergencies that can arise, but later a writ of habeas corpus was prepared for each of the entering pseudopatients and an attorney was kept "on call" during every hospitalization. I am grateful to John Kaplan and Robert Bartels for legal advice and assistance in these matters.

3. However distasteful such concealment is, it was a necessary first step to examining these questions. Without concealment, there would have been no way to know how valid these experiences were; nor was there any way of knowing whether whatever detections occurred were a tribute to the diagnostic acumen of the staff or to the hospital's rumor network. Obviously, since my concerns are general ones that cut across individual hospitals and staffs, I have respected their anonymity and have eliminated clues that might lead to their identification.

4. Interestingly, of the twelve admissions, eleven were diagnosed as schizophrenic and one, with the identical symptomatology, as manic-depressive psychosis. This diagnosis has a more favorable prognosis, and it was given by the only private hospital in our sample. On the relations between social class and psychiatric diagnosis, see A. B. Hollingshead and F. C. Redlich, *Social Class and Mental Illness: A Community Study* (New York: John Wiley, 1958).

5. S. E. Asch, *Journal of Abnormal Social Psychology* 41(1946); *Social Psychology* (Englewood Cliffs, N.J.: Prentice-Hall, 1952).

6. E. Zigler and L. Phillips, *Journal of Abnormal Social Psychology* 63 (1961), 69. See also R. K. Freudenberg and J. P. Robertson, *American Medical Association Archives of Neurological Psychiatry* 76 (1956), 14.

7. W. Mischel, *Personality and Assessment* (New York: John Wiley, 1968).

8. E. Goffman, *Asylums* (Garden City, N.Y.: Doubleday, 1961).

32 The Code of the Streets

ELIJAH ANDERSON

In this reading, sociologist Elijah Anderson explores the cultural differences that exist in our inner cities. Alongside mainstream cultural values, he explains, exists a "code of the streets," which leads some young people to engage in crime and violence. From this point of view, crime is not so much a matter of breaking the rules as it is playing by a different set of rules.

Of all the problems besetting the poor inner-city black community, none is more pressing than that of interpersonal violence and aggression. It wreaks havoc daily with the lives of community residents and increasingly spills over into downtown and residential middle-class areas. Muggings, burglaries, carjackings, and drug-related shootings, all of which may leave their victims or innocent bystanders dead, are now common enough to concern all urban and many suburban residents. The inclination to violence springs from the circumstances of life among the ghetto poor—the lack of jobs that pay a living wage, the stigma of race, the fallout from rampant drug use and drug trafficking, and the resulting alienation and lack of hope for the future.

Simply living in such an environment places young people at special risk of falling victim to aggressive behavior. Although there are often forces

Source: From *Code of the Street: Decency, Violence, and the Moral Life of the Inner City* by Elijah Anderson. Copyright © 1999 by Elijah Anderson. Used by permission of W.W. Norton & Co., Inc.

in the community which can counteract the negative influences, by far the most powerful being a strong, loving, "decent" (as inner-city residents put it) family committed to middle-class values, the despair is pervasive enough to have spawned an oppositional culture, that of "the streets," whose norms are often consciously opposed to those of mainstream society. These two orientations—decent and street—socially organize the community, and their coexistence has important consequences for residents, particularly children growing up in the inner city. Above all, this environment means that even youngsters whose home lives reflect mainstream values—and the majority of homes in the community do—must be able to handle themselves in a street-oriented environment.

This is because the street culture has evolved what may be called a code of the streets, which amounts to a set of informal rules governing interpersonal public behavior, including violence. The rules prescribe both a proper comportment and a proper way to respond if challenged. They regulate the use of violence and so allow those who are inclined to aggression to precipitate violent encounters in an approved way. The rules have been established and are enforced mainly by the street-oriented, but on the streets the distinction between street and decent is often irrelevant; everybody knows that if the rules are violated, there are penalties. Knowledge of the code is thus largely defensive; it is literally necessary for operating in public. Therefore, even though families with a decency orientation are usually opposed to the values of the code, they often reluctantly encourage their children's familiarity with it to enable them to negotiate the inner-city environment.

At the heart of the code is the issue of respect—loosely defined as being treated "right," or granted the deference one deserves. However, in the troublesome public environment of the inner city, as people increasingly feel buffeted by forces beyond their control, what one deserves in the way of respect becomes more and more problematic and uncertain. This in turn further opens the issue of respect to sometimes intense interpersonal negotiation. In the street culture, especially among young people, respect is viewed as almost an external entity that is hard-won but easily lost, and so must constantly be guarded. The rules of the code in fact provide a framework for negotiating respect. The person whose very appearance—including his clothing, demeanor, and way of moving—deters transgressions feels that he possesses, and may be considered by others to possess, a measure of respect. With the right amount of respect, for instance, he can avoid "being bothered" in public. If he is bothered, not only may he be in physical danger but he has been disgraced or "dissed" (disrespected). Many of the forms that dissing can take might seem petty to middle-class people (maintaining eye contact for too long, for example), but to those invested in the street code, these actions become serious indications of the other person's intentions. Consequently, such people become very sensitive to advances and slights, which could well serve as warnings of imminent physical confrontation.

This hard reality can be traced to the profound sense of alienation from mainstream society and its institutions felt by many poor inner-city black people, particularly the young. The code of the streets is actually a cultural adaptation to a profound lack of faith in the police and the judicial system. The police are most often seen as representing the dominant white society and not caring to protect inner-city residents. When called, they may not respond, which is one reason many residents feel they must be prepared to take extraordinary measures to defend themselves and their loved ones against those who are inclined to aggression. Lack of police accountability has in fact been incorporated into the status system: The person who is believed capable of "taking care of himself" is accorded a certain deference, which translates into a sense of physical and psychological control. Thus the street code emerges where the influence of the police ends and personal responsibility for one's safety is felt to begin. Exacerbated by the proliferation of drugs and easy access to guns, this volatile situation results in the ability of the street-oriented minority (or those who effectively "go for bad") to dominate the public spaces.

DECENT AND STREET FAMILIES

Although almost everyone in poor inner-city neighborhoods is struggling financially and therefore feels a certain distance from the rest of America, the decent and the street family in a real sense represent two poles of value orientation, two contrasting conceptual categories. The labels "decent" and "street," which the residents themselves use, amount to evaluative judgments that confer status on local residents. The labeling is often the result of a social contest among individuals and families of the neighborhood. Individuals of the two orientations often coexist in the same extended family. Decent residents judge themselves to be so while judging others to be of the street, and street individuals often present themselves as decent, drawing distinctions between themselves and other people. In addition, there is quite a bit of circumstantial behavior—that is, one person may at different times exhibit both decent and street orientations, depending on the circumstances. Although these designations result from so much social jockeying, there do exist concrete features that define each conceptual category.

Generally, so-called decent families tend to accept mainstream values more fully and attempt to instill them in their children. Whether married couples with children or single-parent (usually female) households, they are generally "working poor" and so tend to be better off financially than their street-oriented neighbors. They value hard work and self-reliance and are willing to sacrifice for their children. Because they have a certain amount of faith in mainstream society, they harbor hopes for a better future for their children, if not for themselves. Many of them go to church and take a strong interest in their children's schooling. Rather than dwelling on the real hardships and inequities facing them, many such decent people, particularly the increasing number of grandmothers raising grandchildren, see their difficult situation as a test from God and derive great support from their faith and from the church community.

Extremely aware of the problematic and often dangerous environment in which they reside, decent parents tend to be strict in their child-rearing practices, encouraging children to respect authority and walk a straight moral line. They have an almost obsessive concern about trouble of any kind and remind their children to be on the lookout for people and situations that might lead to it. At the same time, they are themselves polite and considerate of others, and teach their children to be the same way. At home, at work, and in church, they strive hard to maintain a positive mental attitude and a spirit of cooperation.

So-called street parents, in contrast, often show a lack of consideration for other people and have a rather superficial sense of family and community. Though they may love their children, many of them are unable to cope with the physical and emotional demands of parenthood, and

find it difficult to reconcile their needs with those of their children. These families, who are more fully invested in the code of the streets than the decent people are, may aggressively socialize their children into it in a normative way. They believe in the code and judge themselves and others according to its values.

In fact the overwhelming majority of families in the inner-city community try to approximate the decent-family model, but there are many others who clearly represent the worst fears of the decent family. Not only are their financial resources extremely limited, but what little they have may easily be misused. The lives of the street-oriented are often marked by disorganization. In the most desperate circumstances people frequently have a limited understanding of priorities and consequences, and so frustrations mount over bills, food, and, at times, drink, cigarettes, and drugs. Some tend toward self-destructive behavior; many street-oriented women are crack-addicted ("on the pipe"), alcoholic, or involved in complicated relationships with men who abuse them. In addition, the seeming intractability of their situation, caused in large part by the lack of well-paying jobs and the persistence of racial discrimination, has engendered deep-seated bitterness and anger in many of the most desperate and poorest blacks, especially young people. The need both to exercise a measure of control and to lash out at somebody is often reflected in the adults' relations with their children. At the least, the frustrations of persistent poverty shorten the fuse in such people—contributing to a lack of patience with anyone, child or adult, who irritates them.

In these circumstances a woman—or a man, although men are less consistently present in children's lives—can be quite aggressive with children, yelling at and striking them for the least little infraction of the rules she has set down. Often little if any serious explanation follows the verbal and physical punishment. This response teaches children a particular lesson. They learn that to solve any kind of interpersonal problem one must quickly resort to hitting or other violent behavior. Actual peace and quiet, and also the appearance of calm, respectful children conveyed to her neighbors and friends, are often what the young mother most desires, but at times she will be very aggressive in trying to get them. Thus she may be quick to beat her children, especially if they defy her law, not because she hates them but because this is the way she knows to control them. In fact, many street-oriented women love their children dearly. Many mothers in the community subscribe to the notion that there is a "devil in the boy" that must be beaten out of him or that socially "fast girls need to be whupped." Thus much of what borders on child abuse in the view of social authorities is acceptable parental punishment in the view of these mothers.

Many street-oriented women are sporadic mothers whose children learn to fend for themselves when necessary, foraging for food and money any way they can get it. The children are sometimes employed by drug dealers or become addicted themselves. These children of the street, growing up with little supervision, are said to "come up hard." They often learn to fight at an early age, sometimes using short-tempered adults around them as role models. The street-oriented home may be fraught with anger, verbal disputes, physical aggression, and even mayhem. The children observe these goings-on, learning the lesson that might makes right. They quickly learn to hit those who cross them, and the dog-eat-dog mentality prevails. In order to survive, to protect oneself, it is necessary to marshal inner resources and be ready to deal with adversity in a hands-on way. In these circumstances physical prowess takes on great significance.

In some of the most desperate cases, a street-oriented mother may simply leave her young children alone and unattended while she goes out. The most irresponsible women can be found at local bars and crack houses, getting high and socializing with other adults. Sometimes a troubled woman will leave very young children alone for days at a time. Reports of crack addicts abandoning their children have become common in drug-infested inner-city communities. Neighbors or relatives discover the abandoned children, often hungry and distraught over the absence of their mother.

After repeated absences, a friend or relative, particularly a grandmother, will often step in to care for the young children, sometimes petitioning the authorities to send her, as guardian of the children, the mother's welfare check, if the mother gets one. By this time, however, the children may well have learned the first lesson of the streets: Survival itself, let alone respect, cannot be taken for granted; you have to fight for your place in the world.

CAMPAIGNING FOR RESPECT

These realities of inner-city life are largely absorbed on the streets. At an early age, often even before they start school, children from street-oriented homes gravitate to the streets, where they "hang"—socialize with their peers. Children from these generally permissive homes have a great deal of latitude and are allowed to "rip and run" up and down the street. They often come home from school, put their books down, and go right back out the door. On school nights eight- and nine-year-olds remain out until nine or ten o'clock (and teenagers typically come in whenever they want to). On the streets they play in groups that often become the source of their primary social bonds. Children from decent homes tend to be more carefully supervised and are thus likely to have curfews and to be taught how to stay out of trouble.

When decent and street kids come together, a kind of social shuffle occurs in which children have a chance to go either way. Tension builds as a child comes to realize that he must choose an orientation. The kind of home he comes from influences but does not determine the way he will ultimately turn out—although it is unlikely that a child from a thoroughly street-oriented family will easily absorb decent values on the streets. Youths who emerge from street-oriented families but develop a decency orientation almost always learn those values in another setting—in school, in a youth group, in church. Often it is the result of their involvement with a caring "old head" (adult role model).

In the street, through their play, children pour their individual life experiences into a common knowledge pool, affirming, confirming, and elaborating on what they have observed in the home and matching their skills against those of others. And they learn to fight. Even small children test one another, pushing and shoving, and are ready to hit other children over circumstances not to their liking. In turn, they are readily hit by other children, and the child who is toughest prevails. Thus the violent resolution of disputes, the hitting and cursing, gains social reinforcement. The child in effect is initiated into a system that is really a way of campaigning for respect.

In addition, younger children witness the disputes of older children, which are often resolved through cursing and abusive talk, if not aggression or outright violence. They see that one child succumbs to the greater physical and mental abilities of the other. They are also alert and attentive witnesses to the verbal and physical fights of adults, after which they compare notes and share their interpretations of the event. In almost every case the victor is the person who physically won the altercation, and this person often enjoys the esteem and respect of onlookers. These experiences reinforce the lessons the children have learned at home: Might makes right, and toughness is a virtue, while humility is not. In effect they learn the social meaning of fighting. When it is left virtually unchallenged, this understanding becomes an ever more important part of the child's working conception of the world. Over time the code of the streets becomes refined.

Those street-oriented adults with whom children come in contact—including mothers, fathers, brothers, sisters, boyfriends, cousins, neighbors, and friends—help them along in forming this understanding by verbalizing the messages they are getting through experience: "Watch your back." "Protect yourself." "Don't punk out." "If somebody messes with you, you got to pay them back." "If someone disses you, you got to straighten them out." Many parents actually impose sanctions if a child is not sufficiently aggressive. For example, if a child loses a fight and comes home upset, the parent might respond, "Don't you come in here crying that somebody beat you up; you better get back out there and whup his ass. I didn't raise no punks! Get back out there and whup his ass. If you don't whup his ass, I'll whup your ass when you come home." Thus the child obtains reinforcement for being tough and showing nerve.

While fighting, some children cry as though they are doing something they are ambivalent about. The fight may be against their wishes, yet they may feel constrained to fight or face the consequences—not just from peers but also from caretakers or parents, who may administer another beating if they back down. Some adults recall receiving such lessons from their own parents and justify repeating them to their children as a way to toughen them up: Looking capable of taking care of oneself as a form of self-defense is a dominant theme among both street-oriented and decent adults who worry about the safety of their children. There is thus at times a convergence in their child-rearing practices; although the rationales behind them may differ.

SELF-IMAGE BASED ON "JUICE"

By the time they are teenagers, most youths have either internalized the code of the streets or at least learned the need to comport themselves in accordance with its rules, which chiefly have to do with interpersonal communication. The code revolves around the presentation of self. Its basic requirement is the display of a certain predisposition to violence. Accordingly, one's bearing must send the unmistakable if sometimes subtle message to "the next person" in public that one is capable of violence and mayhem when the situation requires it, that one can take care of oneself. The nature of this communication is largely determined by the demands of the circumstances but can include facial expressions, gait, and verbal expressions—all of which are geared mainly to deterring aggression. Physical appearance, including clothes, jewelry, and grooming, also plays an important part in how a person is viewed; to be respected, it is important to have the right look.

Even so, there are no guarantees against challenges, because there are always people around looking for a fight to increase their share of respect—or "juice," as it is sometimes called on the street. Moreover, if a person is assaulted, it is important, not only in the eyes of his opponent but also in the eyes of his "running buddies," for him to avenge himself. Otherwise he risks being "tried" (challenged) or "moved on" by any number of others. To maintain his honor he must show he is not someone to be "messed with" or "dissed." In general, the person must "keep himself straight" by managing his position of respect among others; this involves in part his self-image, which is shaped by what he thinks others are thinking of him in relation to his peers.

Objects play an important and complicated role in establishing self-image. Jackets, sneakers, gold jewelry, reflect not just a person's taste, which tends to be tightly regulated among adolescents of all social classes, but also a willingness to possess things that may require defending. A boy wearing a fashionable, expensive jacket, for example, is vulnerable to attack by another who covets the jacket and either cannot afford to buy one or wants the added satisfaction of depriving someone else of his. However, if the boy forgoes the desirable jacket and wears one that isn't "hip," he runs the risk of being teased and possibly even assaulted as an unworthy person. To be allowed to hang with certain prestigious crowds, a boy must wear a different set of expensive clothes—sneakers and athletic suit—every day. Not to be able to do so might make him appear socially deficient. The youth comes to covet such items—especially when he sees easy prey wearing them.

In acquiring valued things, therefore, a person shores up his identity—but since it is an identity based on having things, it is highly precarious.

This very precariousness gives a heightened sense of urgency to staying even with peers, with whom the person is actually competing. Young men and women who are able to command respect through their presentation of self—by allowing their possessions and their body language to speak for them—may not have to campaign for regard but may, rather, gain it by the force of their manner. Those who are unable to command respect in this way must actively campaign for it—and are thus particularly alive to slights.

One way of campaigning for status is by taking the possessions of others. In this context, seemingly ordinary objects can become trophies imbued with symbolic value that far exceeds their monetary worth. Possession of the trophy can symbolize the ability to violate somebody—to "get in his face," to take something of value from him, to "dis" him, and thus to enhance one's own worth by stealing someone else's. The trophy does not have to be something material. It can be another person's sense of honor, snatched away with a derogatory remark. It can be the outcome of a fight. It can be the imposition of a certain standard, such as a girl's getting herself recognized as the most beautiful. Material things, however, fit easily into the pattern. Sneakers, a pistol, even somebody else's girlfriend, can become a trophy. When a person can take something from another and then flaunt it, he gains a certain regard by being the owner, or the controller, of that thing. But this display of ownership can then provoke other people to challenge him. This game of who controls what is thus constantly being played out on inner-city streets, and the trophy—extrinsic or intrinsic, tangible or intangible—identifies the current winner.

An important aspect of this often violent give-and-take is its zero-sum quality. That is, the extent to which one person can raise himself up depends on his ability to put another person down. This underscores the alienation that permeates the inner-city ghetto community. There is a generalized sense that very little respect is to be had, and therefore everyone competes to get what affirmation he can of the little that is available. The craving for respect that results gives people thin skins. Shows of deference by others can be highly soothing, contributing to a sense of security, comfort, self-confidence, and self-respect. Transgressions by others which go unanswered diminish these feelings and are believed to encourage further transgressions. Hence one must be ever vigilant against the transgressions of others or even *appearing* as if transgressions will be tolerated. Among young people, whose sense of self-esteem is particularly vulnerable, there is an especially heightened concern with being disrespected. Many inner-city young men in particular crave respect to such a degree that they will risk their lives to attain and maintain it.

The issue of respect is thus closely tied to whether a person has an inclination to be violent, even as a victim. In the wider society people may not feel required to retaliate physically after an attack, even though they are aware that they have been degraded or taken advantage of. They may feel a great need to defend themselves *during* an attack, or to behave in such a way as to deter aggression (middle-class people certainly can and do become victims of street-oriented youths), but they are much more likely than street-oriented people to feel that they can walk away from a possible altercation with their self-esteem intact. Some people may even have the strength of character to flee, without any thought that their self-respect or esteem will be diminished.

In impoverished inner-city black communities, however, particularly among young males and perhaps increasingly among females, such flight would be extremely difficult. To run away would likely leave one's self-esteem in tatters. Hence people often feel constrained not only to stand up and at least attempt to resist during an assault but also to "pay back"—to seek revenge—after a successful assault on their person. This may include going to get a weapon or even getting relatives involved. Their very identity and self-respect, their honor, is often intricately tied up with the way they perform on the streets during and after such encounters. This outlook reflects the circumscribed opportunities of the inner-city poor. Generally people outside the ghetto have other ways of gaining status and regard, and thus do not feel so dependent on such physical displays.

BY TRIAL OF MANHOOD

On the street, among males these concerns about things and identity have come to be expressed in the concept of "manhood." Manhood in the inner city means taking the prerogatives of men with respect to strangers, other men, and women—being distinguished as a man. It implies physicality and a certain ruthlessness. Regard and respect are associated with this concept in large part because of its practical application: If others have little or no regard for a person's manhood, his very life and those of his loved ones could be in jeopardy. But there is a chicken-and-egg aspect to this situation: One's physical safety is more likely to be jeopardized in public *because* manhood is associated with respect. In other words, an existential link has been created between the idea of manhood and one's self-esteem, so that it has become hard to say which is primary. For many inner-city youths, manhood and respect are flip sides of the same coin; physical and psychological well-being are inseparable, and both require a sense of control, of being in charge.

The operating assumption is that a man, especially a real man, knows what other men know—the code of the streets. And if one is not a real man, one is somehow diminished as a person, and there are certain valued things one simply does not deserve. There is thus believed to be a certain justice to the code, since it is considered that everyone has the opportunity to know it. Implicit in this is that everybody is held responsible for being familiar with the code. If the victim of a mugging, for example, does not know the code and so responds "wrong," the perpetrator may feel justified even in killing him and may feel no remorse. He may think, "Too bad, but it's his fault. He should have known better."

So when a person ventures outside, he must adopt the code—a kind of shield, really—to prevent others from "messing with" him. In these circumstances it is easy for people to think they are being tried or tested by others even when this is not the case. For it is sensed that something extremely valuable is at stake in every interaction, and people are encouraged to rise to the occasion, particularly with strangers. For people who are unfamiliar with the code—generally people who live outside the inner city—the concern with respect in the most ordinary interactions can be frightening and incomprehensible. But for those who are invested in the code, the clear object of their demeanor is to discourage strangers from even thinking about testing their manhood. And the sense of power that attends the ability to deter others can be alluring even to those who know the code without being heavily invested in it—the decent inner-city youths. Thus a boy who has been leading a basically decent life can, in trying circumstances, suddenly resort to deadly force.

Central to the issue of manhood is the widespread belief that one of the most effective ways of gaining respect is to manifest "nerve." Nerve is shown when one takes another person's possessions (the more valuable the better), "messes with" someone's woman, throws the first punch, "gets in someone's face," or pulls a trigger. Its proper display helps on the spot to check others who would violate one's person and also helps to build a reputation that works to prevent future challenges. But since such a show of nerve is a forceful expression of disrespect toward the person on the receiving end, the victim may be greatly offended and seek to retaliate with equal or greater force. A display of nerve, therefore, can easily provoke a life-threatening response, and the background knowledge of that possibility has often been incorporated into the concept of nerve.

True nerve exposes a lack of fear of dying. Many feel that it is acceptable to risk dying over the principle of respect. In fact, among the hard-core street-oriented, the clear risk of violent death may be preferable to being "dissed" by another. The youths who have internalized this attitude and convincingly display it in their public bearing are among the most threatening people of all, for it is commonly assumed that they fear no man. As the people of the community say, "They are the baddest dudes on the street." They often lead an existential life that may acquire meaning only when they are faced with the possibility of imminent death. Not to be afraid to die is by implication to have few compunctions about taking another's life. Not to be afraid to die is the quid pro quo of being able to take somebody else's life—for the right reasons, if the situation demands it. When others believe this is one's position, it gives one a real sense of power on the streets. Such credibility is what many inner-city youths strive to achieve, whether they are decent or street-oriented, both because of its practical defensive value and because of the positive way it makes them feel about themselves. The difference between the decent and the street-oriented youth is often that the decent youth makes a conscious decision to appear tough and manly; in another setting—with teachers, say, or at his part-time job—he can be polite and deferential. The street-oriented youth, on the other hand, has made the concept of manhood a part of his very identity; he has difficulty manipulating it—it often controls him.

GIRLS AND BOYS

Increasingly, teenage girls are mimicking the boys and trying to have their own version of "manhood." Their goal is the same—to get respect, to be recognized as capable of setting or maintaining a certain standard. They try to achieve this end in the ways that have been established by the boys, including posturing, abusive language, and the use of violence to resolve disputes, but the issues for the girls are different. Although conflicts over turf and status exist among the girls, the majority of disputes seem rooted in assessments of beauty (which girl in a group is "the cutest"), competition over boyfriends, and attempts to regulate other people's knowledge of and opinions about a girl's behavior or that of someone close to her, especially her mother.

A major cause of conflicts among girls is "he say, she say." This practice begins in the early school years and continues through high school.

It occurs when "people," particularly girls, talk about others, thus putting their "business in the streets." Usually one girl will say something negative about another in the group, most often behind the person's back. The remark will then get back to the person talked about. She may retaliate or her friends may feel required to "take up for" her. In essence this is a form of group gossiping in which individuals are negatively assessed and evaluated. As with much gossip, the things said may or may not be true, but the point is that such imputations can cast aspersions on a person's good name. The accused is required to defend herself against the slander, which can result in arguments and fights, often over little of real substance. Here again is the problem of low self-esteem, which encourages youngsters to be highly sensitive to slights and to be vulnerable to feeling easily "dissed." To avenge the dissing, a fight is usually necessary.

Because boys are believed to control violence, girls tend to defer to them in situations of conflict. Often if a girl is attacked or feels slighted, she will get a brother, uncle, or cousin to do her fighting for her. Increasingly, however, girls are doing their own fighting and are even asking their male relatives to teach them how to fight. Some girls form groups that attack other girls or take things from them. A hard-core segment of inner-city girls inclined toward violence seems to be developing. As one thirteen-year-old girl in a detention center for youths who have committed violent acts told me, "To get people to leave you alone, you gotta fight. Talking don't always get you out of stuff." One major difference between girls and boys: Girls rarely use guns. Their fights are therefore not life-or-death struggles. Girls are not often willing to put their lives on the line for "manhood." The ultimate form of respect on the male-dominated inner-city street is thus reserved for men.

"GOING FOR BAD"

In the most fearsome youths such a cavalier attitude toward death grows out of a very limited view of life. Many are uncertain about how long they are going to live and believe they could die violently at any time. They accept this fate; they live on the edge. Their manner conveys the message that nothing intimidates them; whatever turn the encounter takes, they maintain their attack—rather like a pit bull, whose spirit many such boys admire. The demonstration of such tenacity "shows heart" and earns their respect.

This fearlessness has implications for law enforcement. Many street-oriented boys are much more concerned about the threat of "justice" at the hands of a peer than at the hands of the police. Moreover, many feel not only that they have little to lose by going to prison but that they have something to gain. The toughening-up one experiences in prison can actually enhance one's reputation on the streets. Hence the system loses influence over the hard core who are without jobs, with little perceptible stake in the system. If mainstream society has done nothing *for* them, they counter by making sure it can do nothing *to* them.

At the same time, however, a competing view maintains that true nerve consists in backing down, walking away from a fight, and going on with one's business. One fights only in self-defense. This view emerges from the decent philosophy that life is precious, and it is an important part of the socialization process common in decent homes. It discourages violence as the primary means of resolving disputes and encourages youngsters to accept nonviolence and talk as confrontational strategies. But "if the deal goes down," self-defense is greatly encouraged. When there is enough positive support for this orientation, either in the home or among one's peers, then nonviolence has a chance to prevail. But it prevails at the cost of relinquishing a claim to being bad and tough; and therefore sets a young person up as at the very least alienated from street-oriented peers and quite possibly a target of derision or even violence.

Although the nonviolent orientation rarely overcomes the impulse to strike back in an encounter, it does introduce a certain confusion and so can prompt a measure of soul-searching, or even profound ambivalence. Did the person back down with his respect intact or did he back down only to be judged a "punk"—a person lacking manhood? Should he or she have acted? Should he or she have hit the other person in the mouth? These questions beset many young men and women during public confrontations. What is the "right" thing to do? In the quest for honor, respect, and local status—which few young people are uninterested in—common sense most often prevails, which leads many to opt for the tough approach, enacting their own particular versions of the display of nerve. The presentation of oneself as rough and tough is very often quite acceptable until one is tested. And then that presentation may help the person pass the test, because it will cause fewer questions to be asked about what he did and why. It is hard for a person to explain why he lost the fight or why he backed down. Hence many will strive to appear to "go for bad," while hoping they will never be tested. But when they are tested, the outcome of the situation may quickly be out of their hands, as they become wrapped up in the circumstances of the moment.

AN OPPOSITIONAL CULTURE

The attitudes of the wider society are deeply implicated in the code of the streets. Most people in inner-city communities are not totally invested in the code, but the significant minority of hard-core street youths who have to maintain the code in order to establish reputations, because they have—or feel they have—few other ways to assert themselves. For these young people the standards of the street code are the only game in town. The extent to which some children—particularly those who through upbringing have become most alienated and those lacking in strong and conventional social support—experience, feel, and internalize racist rejection and contempt from mainstream society may strongly encourage them to express contempt for the more conventional society in turn. In dealing with this contempt and rejection, some youngsters will consciously invest themselves and their considerable mental resources in what amounts to an oppositional culture to preserve themselves and their self-respect. Once they do, any respect they might be able to garner in the wider system pales in comparison with the respect available in the local system; thus they often lose interest in even attempting to negotiate the mainstream system.

At the same time, many less alienated young blacks have assumed a street-oriented demeanor as a way of expressing their blackness while really embracing a much more moderate way of life; they, too, want a nonviolent setting in which to live and raise a family. These decent people are trying hard to be part of the mainstream culture, but the racism, real and perceived, that they encounter helps to legitimate the oppositional culture. And so on occasion they adopt street behavior. In fact, depending on the demands of the situation, many people in the community slip back and forth between decent and street behavior.

A vicious cycle has thus been formed. The hopelessness and alienation many young inner-city black men and women feel, largely as a result of endemic joblessness and persistent racism, fuels the violence they engage in. This violence serves to confirm the negative feelings many whites and some middle-class blacks harbor toward the ghetto poor, further legitimating the oppositional culture and the code of the streets in the eyes of many poor young blacks. Unless this cycle is broken, attitudes on both sides will become increasingly entrenched, and the violence, which claims victims black and white, poor and affluent, will only escalate.

CRITICAL-THINKING QUESTIONS

1. Describe the major elements of what Anderson calls "the code of the streets." How does this "code" oppose mainstream values?

2. How is "the code of the streets" a product of the disadvantages, social isolation, and racism faced by many inner-city people?

3. Why do most inner-city people—even those who are poor—reject the street code?

CLASSIC

CONTEMPORARY

CROSS-CULTURAL

33 Prostitution: A Worldwide Business of Sexual Exploitation

MELISSA FARLEY

Some prostitutes and academic feminists contend that prostitution should be legalized: "Sex workers" would have greater autonomy over their earnings, they could report violence from pimps (men who economically benefit from a prostitute's earnings) and johns (customers), and international sex trafficking would decrease. Others, like Melissa Farley, argue that legalizing prostitution would legitimize and increase women's sexual exploitation around the world.

Prostitution is many kinds of violence against women, but it is often not clearly understood as such. Because prostitution/trafficking is so profitable, the factors that propel women into sex businesses, such as sexism, racism, poverty, and child abuse, are sometimes concealed. This article reviews evidence for the extreme violence that occurs in prostitution and the physical and psychological harm that results from that violence.

DENIAL

Institutions such as prostitution and slavery, which have existed for thousands of years, are so deeply embedded in cultures that they become invisible. In Mauritania, for example, there are 90,000 Africans enslaved by Arabs. Human rights activists travel to Mauritania to report on slavery,

but because they do not observe precisely the stereotype of what they think slavery should look like (for example, if they do not see bidding for shackled people on auction blocks), then they conclude that the Africans working in the fields in front of them are voluntary laborers who are receiving food and shelter as salary.

In a similar way, if observers do not see exactly what the stereotype of "harmful" prostitution is, for example, if they do not see a girl being trafficked at gunpoint from one state to another, or if all they see is a streetwise teenager who says, "I like this job, and besides, I'm making a lot of money," then they do not see the harm. Prostitution tourists go to the prostitution zones of Amsterdam, Atlanta, Phnom Penh, Moscow, or Havana and see smiling girls waving at them from glass cages or strip clubs. The customers decide that prostitution is a free choice.

If we describe women as "sex workers" then we are accepting conditions that in other employment would be correctly described as sexual harassment, sexual exploitation, or rape. If prostitution

Source: Melissa Farley. 2001. "Prostitution: The Business of Sexual Exploitation." *Encyclopedia of Women and Gender,* Vol. 2, pp. 879–91. New York: Academic Press.

is transformed into "commercial sex work," then the brutal exploitation of those prostituted by pimps becomes an employer–employee relationship. And the predatory, pedophiliac purchase of a human being by the john becomes just an everyday business transaction.

The myth that prostitution is a free choice is a major obstacle to understanding the harm of prostitution. Most people in prostitution have few or no other options for obtaining the necessities of life. One woman, interviewed by Ine Vanwesenbeeck in the Netherlands, described prostitution as "volunteer slavery," clearly articulating both the appearance of choice and the overwhelming coercion behind that choice. Sexual exploitation seems to happen with the "consent" of those involved. But real consent involves the option to make other choices. In prostitution, the conditions necessary for choice—physical safety, information, equal power with customers, and real alternatives—are absent. Women in prostitution tend to be the ones who have the fewest options.

The social and legal refusal to acknowledge the harm of prostitution is stunning. Normalization of prostitution by researchers, public health agencies, and the media is a significant barrier to addressing the harm of prostitution. In 1988, for example, the World Health Organization described prostitution as "dynamic and adaptive sex work, involving a transaction between seller and buyer of a sexual service." Continuing this trend a decade later, the International Labor Organization normalized prostitution as the "sex sector" of Asian economies despite citing surveys that indicated that, for example, in Indonesia, 96 percent of those interviewed wanted to leave prostitution if they could. Lin Lim commented, "many groups, sometimes including government officials, have an interest in maintaining the sex sector." Libertarian ideology obfuscates the harm of prostitution, defining it as a form of sex.

In the social sciences as well, the harm of prostitution becomes invisible. The psychological literature of the 1980s blamed battered women for their victimization, describing them as "masochistic," a theoretical perspective that was later rejected for lack of evidence. However, the notion that prostituted women (who are also battered women) have personality characteristics that lead to their victimization is still promoted. Karl Abraham saw prostitution as a woman's act of hostility against her father, based on an oedipal fixation. And the sexologists, from Alfred Kinsey to Havelock Ellis to Masters and Johnson, formulated their theories of human sexuality by observing johns with prostitutes, thus normalizing prostitution-like sexuality.

Since the 1980s, there has been huge growth in socially legitimized pimping in the United States: strip clubs, nude dancing, escort services, tanning salons, massage parlors, phone sex, and computer sex. Many people do not realize that these permutations of the commercial sex industry are, in fact, prostitution. The lines between prostitution and nonprostitution have become blurred. New employees may assume they are going to dance, waitress, or tend bar, but find that the real money comes from prostituting after work. Lisa Sanchez has pointed out that the amount of physical contact between dancers and customers has escalated since the 1980s, although earnings have decreased. In addition to watching a stage show, in most strip clubs, customers can buy either a table dance performance by the dancer directly in front of them or a lap dance where the dancer sits on the customer's lap while she wears few or no clothes and grinds her genitals against his. Although he is clothed, he usually expects ejaculation. Sometimes the table dance or lap dance is in front of the customer on the main floor of the club. It may also take place behind a curtain or in a private room. The more private the sexual performance, the more it costs, and the more likely that violent sexual harassment or rape will occur. Although the typical lap-dancing scenario does not involve skin-to-skin sexual contact, for a larger tip, some dancers allow customers to touch their genitals or they masturbate or fellate johns. Used condoms are often found in lap dance clubs.

Different kinds of exploitation and abuse overlap and combine to harm women. Catharine

MacKinnon has pointed out that "a great many instances of sexual harassment in essence amount to solicitation for prostitution." The words used to humiliate prostituted women are the same verbal abuse used by men when they are beating up or raping nonprostituting women. Racially constructed ideas about women in sex tourism have a greater and greater effect on the ways women of color are treated at home. For example, Asian American women reported rapes after men viewed pornography of Asian women. A vast range of abuse makes up a continuum of violence in which women are first hurt in early childhood.

CHILD ABUSE AND PROSTITUTION

The prostitution of children is aggressively made invisible. For example, commenting that the connection between childhood sexual abuse and prostitution has been "exaggerated," Peter Davies and Rayah Feldman described the prostituted boys they interviewed in the United Kingdom as having an average age of under 18, with 97 percent of them younger than the legal age of consent. In other words, their interviewees were legally minors.

Another example of this invisibility is the common belief in Taiwan that the island's 100,000 child prostitutes want to prostitute because it pays for their "expensive tastes" in clothes and jewelry. Pimps are considered the children's bodyguards. Prejudice against indigenous people in Taiwan bolsters this denial of harm to their children, who comprise most of the children in prostitution.

In many parts of the world, a younger rather than older person is a preferred commodity, for several reasons. First, the culturally advocated pedophiliac sexuality in some countries (the Netherlands, India, the United States) channels men's sexual desire to younger and younger girls. Second, children are more easily controlled than adults by pimps and are more easily coerced by johns into behaviors that adults might resist. Third, there is the widespread but mistaken belief in some locales that younger children are safer for the customer since they are believed to be less likely to have HIV (Thailand, Zambia).

Most women over the age of 18 in prostitution began prostituting when they were adolescents. Adele du Plessis, a social worker who worked with homeless and prostituted children in Johannesburg, South Africa, reported that she could not refuse her agency's services to 21-year-olds because she understood them to be grownup child prostitutes. Estimates regarding the age of recruitment into prostitution vary, but early adolescence is the most frequently reported age of entry into any type of prostitution. Researcher Debra Boyer interviewed sixty women prostituting in escort, street, strip club, phone sex, and massage parlors (brothels) in Seattle, Washington. All of them began prostituting between the ages of 12 and 14. In another study, 89 percent had begun prostitution before the age of 16. Of 200 adult women in prostitution interviewed by Mimi Silbert, 78 percent began prostituting as juveniles and 68 percent began when they were younger than 16.

The artificial distinction between child and adult prostitution obscures the continuity between the two. On a continuum of violence and relative powerlessness, the prostitution of a 12-year-old is more horrific than the prostitution of a 20-year-old, not because the crimes committed against her are different, but because the younger person has less power. In other respects, the experiences of sexual exploitation, rape, verbal abuse, and social contempt are the same, whether the person being prostituted is the legal age of a child or the legal age of an adult. The antecedent poverty and attempts to escape from unbearable living conditions (violence at home or the economic violence of globalization) are similar in child and adult prostitution.

One woman interviewed by Boyer said, "We've all been molested. Over and over, and raped. We were all molested and sexually abused as children, don't you know that? We ran to get away. They didn't want us in the house anymore. We were thrown out, thrown away. We've been on the street since we were 12, 13, 14."

The chronic, systematic nature of violence against girls and women may be seen more clearly when incest is understood as child prostitution. Use of a child for sex by adults, with or without payment, is prostitution of the child. When a child is incestuously assaulted, the perpetrator's objectification of the child victim and his rationalization and denial are the same as those of the john in prostitution. Incest and prostitution cause similar physical and psychological symptoms in the victim.

Child sexual abuse is a primary risk factor for prostitution. Familial sexual abuse functions as a training ground for prostitution. One young woman told Mimi Silbert and Ayala Pines, "I started turning tricks to show my father what he made me." Andrea Dworkin described sexual abuse of children as "boot camp" for prostitution. Research and clinical reports have documented the widespread occurrence of childhood sexual abuse and chronic traumatization among prostituted women. From 60 percent to 90 percent of those in prostitution were sexually assaulted in childhood.

Multiple perpetrators of sexual abuse were common, as was physical abuse in childhood. Sixty-two percent of women in prostitution reported a history of physical abuse as children. Evelina Giobbe found that 90 percent of prostituted women had been physically battered in childhood; 74 percent were sexually abused in their families, with 50 percent also having been sexually abused by someone outside the family. Of 123 survivors of prostitution at the Council for Prostitution Alternatives in Portland, 85 percent reported a history of incest, 90 percent a history of physical abuse, and 98 percent a history of emotional abuse.

In the 1980s, Silbert and Pines published a number of groundbreaking studies that documented the role of child sexual abuse as an antecedent to prostitution. These authors and others have noted the role of pornography in the recruitment of children into prostitution and in teaching them how to act as prostitutes. Eighty percent of a group of prostituted women and girls in Vancouver, Canada, reported that while working as prostitutes, they had been upset by someone trying to coerce them into imitating pornography.

Prostituting adolescents grow up in neglectful, often violent families. Although not all sexually abused girls are recruited into prostitution, most of those in prostitution have a history of sexual abuse as children, usually by several people. For example, in a pilot study of prostituted women in Vancouver, Melissa Farley and Jackie Lynne reported that 88 percent of 40 women had been sexually assaulted as children, by an average of five perpetrators. This latter statistic (those assaulted by an average of five perpetrators) did not include those who responded to the question "If there was unwanted sexual touching or sexual contact between you and an adult, how many people in all?" with "tons" or "I can't count that high" or "I was too young to remember." Sixty-three percent of those whose experiences were recorded in this study were First Nations women.

Survivors directly link physical, sexual, and emotional abuse as children to later prostitution. Seventy percent of the adult women in prostitution in one study stated that their childhood sexual abuse affected their decision to become prostitutes. They described family abuse and neglect as not only causing direct physical and emotional harm, but also creating a cycle of victimization that affected their futures. For example, one woman interviewed by Joanna Phoenix stated that by the time she was 17, "all I knew was how to be raped, and how to be attacked, and how to be beaten up, and that's all I knew. So when he put me on the game [pimped her] I was too down in the dumps to do anything. All I knew was abuse."

When she is sexually abused, the child is reinforced via attention, food, and money for behaving sexually in the way the perpetrator wishes. The perpetrator's seductive manipulation of the child causes immense psychological harm. In addition, many children are threatened with violence if they do not perform sexually.

Angela Browne and David Finkelhor described traumatic sexualization as the inappropriate conditioning of the child's sexual responsiveness and the socialization of the child into faulty beliefs and assumptions about sexuality. Traumatic sexualization leaves the girl vulnerable to additional sexual exploitation and is a critical component of the grooming process for subsequent prostitution. Some of the consequences of childhood sexual abuse are behaviors that are prostitution-like; a common symptom of sexually abused children is sexualized behavior.

Sexual abuse may result in different behaviors at different stages of the child's development. Sexualized behaviors are likely to be prominent among sexually abused preschool-age children, submerge during the latency years, and then reemerge during adolescence as behavior described as promiscuity, prostitution, or sexual aggression.

Sexual abuse causes extreme damage to children's self-esteem. Frank Putnam noted that the child may incorporate the perpetrator's perspective, eventually viewing herself as good for nothing but sex, which is to say, she may adopt the perpetrator's view that she is a prostitute. According to John Briere, this constricted sense of self of the sexually abused child and the coercive refusal of the perpetrator to respect the child's physical boundaries may result in her subsequent difficulties in asserting boundaries, in impaired self-protection, and a greater likelihood of being further sexually victimized, including becoming involved in prostitution.

The powerlessness of having been sexually assaulted as a child may be related to the frequent discussions of control and power by women who are prostituting. The emotional and physical helplessness of the sexually abused child may be reenacted in the prostitution transaction, with vigilant attention to the tiniest shard of control. Payment of money for an unwanted sex act in prostitution may make the girl or woman feel more in control when compared to the same experience with no payment of money. For example, one woman said that at age 17, she felt safer and more in control turning tricks on the street than she did in her home with her stepfather who raped her.

Children commonly run away from homes in which they are being sexually abused. If there is no safe place to escape to, the child or adolescent is left extremely vulnerable to further sexual exploitation and assault. Mimi Silbert reported that 96 percent of the adults she interviewed had been runaway children before they began prostituting. Louie and colleagues found that more than half of fifty prostituting Asian girls aged 11 to 16 ran away because of family problems.

Children in prostitution are recruited from runaway and homeless populations. For example, John Lowman described the average Canadian prostitute as having entered prostitution between the ages of 13 and 19, usually after running away from home. Pimps exploit the vulnerability of runaway or thrown-out children in recruiting them to prostitution. In Vancouver, 46 percent of homeless girls had received offers of "assistance to help them work in prostitution." One 13-year old who had run away from home was given housing by a pimp, but only in exchange for prostituting.

A survey of 500 homeless youths by Barbara Lucas and Lena Hackett in Indianapolis found that at first only 14 percent acknowledged that they were "working as prostitutes." This survey reveals the importance of the wording of questions about prostitution. When the Indiana adolescents were later asked nonjudgmental questions about specific behaviors, they responded as follows: 32 percent said that they had sex to get money; 21 percent said they had sex for a place to stay overnight; 12 percent exchanged sex for food; 10 percent exchanged sex for drugs; and 6 percent exchanged sex for clothes. In other words, a total of 81 percent, not 14 percent of these 500 homeless adolescents, were prostituting. The following wordings for inquiry about prostitution are suggested: "Have you ever exchanged sex for money or clothes, food, housing, or drugs?" or "Have you ever worked in the commercial sex industry: dancing, escort, massage, prostitution, pornography, video, internet, or phone sex?"

Like heterosexual adolescent girls, gay male adolescents' prostitution behavior is likely to be a reenactment of earlier sexual abuse. Homophobia also plays a role in the prostituting of gay young men. Gay youth may have been thrown out of their homes because of their sexual orientation. Furthermore, in many cities, prostitution was the only available entry into the gay community; it was an activity where boys could "practice" being gay. Thus gay adolescent boys may develop an identity that links their sexual orientation to prostitution.

SOCIOECONOMIC CONTRIBUTION TO ENTRY INTO PROSTITUTION

According to Julia Davidson, "Prostitution is an institution in which one person has the social and economic power to transform another human being into the living embodiment of a masturbation fantasy." In addition to gender, poverty is a precondition for prostitution. The economic vulnerability and limited career options of poor women are significant factors in their recruitment into prostitution. Of 854 people in prostitution from nine countries (Canada, Colombia, Germany, Mexico, South Africa, Thailand, Turkey, United States, and Zambia), Melissa Farley and colleagues found that 75 percent were currently or previously homeless. PROMISE, a California agency serving women in prostitution, reported that 67 percent of those requesting services were currently or formerly homeless.

Lack of education was frequently a precursor to entering prostitution. Seventy percent of West Bengal Indian women wanted to escape prostitution, but the cultural and economic factors that channeled them into prostitution prevented that: a 6 percent literacy rate, beatings, starvation, rape by family members, and sexual exploitation at their jobs. As reported by Molly Chattopadhyay and her colleagues, women in most jobs in West Bengal, India, were required to permit sexual exploitation in order to stay employed. The most frequent reason given by these women for leaving

their last job was that prostitution would provide "better pay for what they had to do anyway."

RACISM AND COLONIALISM IN PROSTITUTION

Women in prostitution are purchased for their appearance, including skin color and characteristics based on ethnic stereotyping. Throughout history, women have been enslaved and prostituted based on race and ethnicity, as well as gender and class.

Entire communities are affected by the racism that is entrenched in prostitution. For example, legal prostitution, such as strip clubs and stores that sell pornography (that is, pictures of women in prostitution) tends to be zoned into poor neighborhoods, which in many urban areas in the United States also tend to be neighborhoods of people of color. The insidious trauma of racism continually wears away at people of color and makes them vulnerable to stress disorders. Families who have been subjected to race and class discrimination may interface with street networks that normalize hustling for economic survival. Sex businesses create a hostile environment in which girls and women are continually harassed by pimps and johns. Women and girls are actively recruited by pimps and are harassed by johns driving through their neighborhoods. As Vednita Nelson pointed out, there is a sameness between the abduction into prostitution of African women by slavers and today's cruising of African American neighborhoods by johns searching for women to buy.

Compared to their numbers in the United States as a whole, women of color are overrepresented in prostitution. For example, in Minneapolis, a city that is 96 percent White European American, more than half of the women in strip club prostitution are women of color. Furthermore, African American women are arrested for prostitution solicitation at a higher rate than others charged with this crime.

Colonialism exploits not only natural resources, but also the people whose land contains those resources. Especially vulnerable to violence from wars or economic devastation, indigenous women are brutally exploited in prostitution (for example, Mayan women in Mexico City, Hmong women in Minneapolis, Karen women in Bangkok, and First Nations women in Vancouver).

Once in prostitution, women of color face barriers that prevent escape. Among these is an absence of culturally sensitive advocacy services. Other barriers faced by all women escaping prostitution are the lack of services that address emergency needs (for example, shelters, drug/alcohol detoxification, and treatment of acute posttraumatic stress disorder, or PTSD). There is a similar lack of services that address long-term needs, such as treatment of depression and chronic posttraumatic stress disorder (PTSD), vocational training, and long-term housing.

TRAFFICKING IS INTERNATIONAL PROSTITUTION

Prostitution always involves marketing, and trafficking is the marketing of prostitution. Women in prostitution are transported to the most lucrative market. The United Nations estimated that two million women, girls, and boys were trafficked into prostitution in 1999. Trafficking (moving girls and women across international borders) can not exist without an acceptance of prostitution in the receiving country. Many governments protect commercial sex businesses because of the massive profits (estimated at $56 billion per year). For example, the International Labor Organization called on poor countries to take economic advantage of "the sex sector," that is, prostitution and trafficking. Governments frequently have chosen to protect the demand for prostitution, rather than adopting complex solutions, which would involve prevention through community education programs and penalization of traffickers, pimps, and customers. Governments have failed to address the root cause of prostitution, which is the unequal status of women.

In 1999, Thailand, Vietnam, China, Mexico, Russia, Ukraine, and the Czech Republic were primary source countries for trafficking of women into the United States. Source countries vary according to the economic desperation of women, promotion of prostitution/trafficking by corrupt government officials who issue passports and visas, and criminal connections in both the sending and the receiving country such as gang-controlled massage parlors and the lack of laws to protect women who immigrate. The economic interdependence of countries and multinational corporations (globalization) promotes prostitution and trafficking by creating conditions for women to sell their own sexual exploitation at far better rates of pay than other forms of labor, according to Tanya Hernandez. Pimps and traffickers take advantage of the unequal status of women and girls in the source country by exploiting sexist and racist stereotypes of women as property, commodities, servants, and sexual objects.

Researcher Donna M. Hughes analyzed the ways in which economic devastation in Russia exacerbated preexisting gender inequality, promoting sex businesses including trafficking. Russian women have been scapegoated for keeping jobs that some believe they should have given up to men (the Russian Minister of Labor Melikyan stated that all women should be unemployed before a single man lost his job); domestic violence is at epidemic proportions; and sexual harassment on the job is commonplace. Under these conditions, almost any opportunity to leave Russia, even one that involves trafficking/prostitution, seems tolerable.

International prostitution includes prostitution tourism ("sex tourism"), arranged marriages with foreign women who are sexually objectified and kept in domestic servitude ("mail-order brides"), and recently, promotion of sexual exploitation by internet pimping and online prostitution, as described by Hughes.

The interconnectedness of racism and sexism in prostitution is vividly apparent in sex tourism. Colonialism in Asia and the Caribbean, according to Hernandez, promoted a view of women of color as natural-born sex workers, sexually promiscuous and immoral by nature. Over time, women of color came to be viewed as "exotic others," defined as inherently hypersexual on the basis of race and gender. The prostitution tourist, reading between the lines of travel brochures, denies the racist exploitation of women in "native cultures," as in Ryan Bishop and Lillian Robinson's analysis of the Thai sex business: "Indigenous Thai people are seen as Peter-Pan-like children who are sensual and never grow up. Thus travel brochures assure sex tourists that they are simply partaking of the Thai culture, which just happens to be 'overtly sexual.' "

PERVASIVE VIOLENCE IN PROSTITUTION

Prostitution is like rape. It's like when I was fifteen years old and I was raped. I used to experience leaving my body. I mean that's what I did when that man raped me. I looked up at the ceiling and I went to the ceiling and I numbed myself . . . because I didn't want to feel what I was feeling. I was very frightened. And while I was a prostitute I used to do that all the time. I would numb my feelings. I wouldn't even feel like I was in my body. I would actually leave my body and go somewhere else with my thoughts and with my feelings until he got off and it was over with. I don't know how else to explain it except that it felt like rape. It was rape to me. (Giobbe, 1991, p. 144)

Sexual violence and physical assault are normative experiences for women in prostitution. Silbert and Pines reported that 70 percent of women in prostitution were raped. The Council for Prostitution Alternatives in Portland reported that prostituted women were raped an average of once a week. According to Ine Vanwesenbeeck, in the Netherlands, 60 percent of prostituted women suffered physical assaults, 70 percent experienced verbal threats of physical assault, 40 percent experienced sexual violence, and 40 percent had been forced into prostitution and/or sexual abuse by acquaintances. Most young women in prostitution were abused or beaten by pimps as well as johns. Eighty-five percent of women interviewed by Ruth Parriott had been raped in prostitution.

Of 854 people in prostitution in nine countries, 71 percent had experienced physical assaults in prostitution, and 62 percent had been raped in prostitution, according to Farley and colleagues.

According to Jody Miller, 94 percent of those in street prostitution had experienced sexual assault and 75 percent had been raped by one or more johns. In spite of these reports of extreme violence, there is a widespread belief that the concept of rape does not apply to prostitutes. Some people assume that when a prostituted woman was raped, it was part of her job and that she deserved or even asked for the rape. Nothing could be farther from the truth.

Like battering, prostitution is domestic violence. Giobbe compared pimps and batterers and found similarities in the ways they used extreme physical violence to control women, the ways they forced women into social isolation, used minimization and denial, threats, intimidation, verbal and sexual abuse, and had an attitude of ownership. The techniques of physical violence used by pimps are often the same as those used by batterers and torturers.

The level of harassment and physical abuse of women in strip club prostitution has drastically increased in the past 20 years. Touching, grabbing, pinching, and fingering of dancers removes any boundary that previously existed between dancing, stripping, and prostitution. In 1998, Kelly Holsopple summarized the verbal, physical, and sexual abuse experienced by women in strip club prostitution, which included being grabbed on the breasts, buttocks, and genitals, as well as being kicked, bitten, slapped, spit on, and penetrated vaginally and anally during lap dancing.

TRAUMA SYMPTOMS AMONG WOMEN IN PROSTITUTION

Recruitment into prostitution begins with what Kathleen Barry has called seasoning: brutal violence designed to break the victim's will. After control is established, pimping tactics shift to brainwashing and other forms of psychological control. Pimps establish emotional dependency as quickly as possible, beginning with changing a girl's name. This obliterates her identity, separates her from her past, and isolates her from her community. The purpose of pimps' violence is to convince women of their worthlessness and social invisibility, as well as physically controlling them.

Escape from prostitution becomes more and more difficult as the woman is repeatedly overwhelmed with terror. She is forced to commit acts that are sexually humiliating and that cause her to betray her own principles. The contempt and violence aimed at her are eventually internalized, resulting in a virulent self-hate that then makes it even more difficult to defend herself. Survivors report a sense of contamination, of being different from others, and self-loathing, which lasts many years after getting out of prostitution. Judith Herman and Lenore Terr have each described the complexity of repetitive behaviors found in survivors of chronic trauma. Traumatic reenactments of abuse are common, along with psychobiological dysfunction, including self-destructive thoughts and behaviors, self-contempt, feelings of shame and worthlessness, substance abuse, eating disorders, and sexual aversions or compulsions.

Dissociation is the psychological process of banishing traumatic events from consciousness. It is an emotional shutting down, which occurs during extreme stress among prisoners of war who are being tortured, among children who are being sexually assaulted, and among women who are being battered, raped, or prostituted. The emotional distancing necessary to survive rape and prostitution is the same technique used to endure familial sexual assault. Most women report that they cannot engage in prostitution unless they dissociate. Being drunk or high has been described as chemical dissociation.

One woman described the link between johns' behavior and her dissociation while she was prostituting in a strip club:

You start changing yourself to fit a fantasy role of what they think a woman should be. In the real world, these women don't exist. They're not really looking at you. You become this empty shell. You're not you. You're not even there. (Farley, unpublished interview, 1998)

People in prostitution also suffer from posttraumatic stress disorder (PTSD). Symptoms of PTSD include anxiety, depression, insomnia, irritability, flashbacks, emotional numbing, and hyperalertness. Farley and colleagues found that 68 percent of 854 people in prostitution from nine countries met diagnostic criteria for PTSD, suggesting that the traumatic consequences of prostitution were similar across different cultures. The following are two examples of PTSD.

Saundra Sturdevant and Brenda Stolzfus interviewed an Okinawan woman who had been purchased by U.S. military personnel during the Vietnam War. Many years later, she still became extremely agitated and had visions of sexual assault and persecution on the 15th and 30th of each month, the days that had been Army paydays. Another woman who spoke to Farley described symptoms of PTSD that were a consequence of violence in prostitution: "I wonder why I keep going to therapists and telling them I can't sleep, and I have nightmares. They pass right over the fact that I was a prostitute and I was beaten with two-by-four boards, I had my fingers and toes broken by a pimp, and I was raped more than 30 times. Why do they ignore that?"

Over time, the violence of prostitution, the constant humiliation, the social indignity, and the misogyny result in personality changes that Judith Herman has described as complex posttraumatic stress disorder (CPTSD). Symptoms of CPTSD include changes in consciousness and self-concept, changes in the ability to regulate emotions, shifts in systems of meaning, such as loss of faith, and an unremitting sense of despair. Sexual feelings are severely damaged in prostitution. Once out of prostitution, 76 percent of a group of women interviewed by Ruth Parriott reported that they had great difficulty with intimate relationships.

PHYSICAL HEALTH CONSEQUENCES OF PROSTITUTION

Chronic health problems result from physical abuse and neglect in childhood, sexual assault, battering, untreated health problems, and overwhelming stress. Prostituted women suffer from all of these. Many of the chronic physical symptoms of women in prostitution are similar to the physical consequences of torture. In a 1985 study by the Canadian government, the death rate of those in prostitution was found to be 40 times higher than that of the general population.

A lack of attention to pervasive physical and sexual violence has resulted in failures of the health care system for all women. Those in prostitution lacked access to social and medical services that were available to other women. Fear of arrest and social contempt made it difficult for prostituted women to seek emergency shelter or medical treatment.

Although the majority of research on prostituted women's health from 1980 to 2000 focused exclusively on HIV or other sexually transmitted diseases (STDs), some research has addressed non-HIV-related health problems. Prostituted women had an increased risk of cervical cancer and chronic hepatitis. Incidence of abnormal Pap screens was several times higher than the state average in a Minnesota study of prostituted women's health. Childhood rape was associated with increased incidence of cervical dysplasia in Ann Coker and colleagues' study of women prisoners, many of whom had been in prostitution.

Half of the women interviewed in San Francisco in 1998 by Farley and Barkan reported physical health problems, including joint pain, cardiovascular symptoms, respiratory symptoms, neurological problems, and HIV (8 percent). Seventeen percent stated that, if it were accessible, they would request immediate hospital admission for drug addiction or emotional problems. Many acute and chronic problems were directly related to violence. In addition to poor nutrition, gastrointestinal problems, and pneumonia, Eleanor Miller reported that women in prostitution had bruises, broken bones, cuts, and abrasions that resulted from beatings and sexual assaults. One woman said about her health:

I've had three broken arms, nose broken twice, [and] I'm partially deaf in one ear. . . . I have a small fragment of a bone floating in my head that gives me migraines. I've had a fractured skull. My legs ain't worth shit no more; my toes have been broken. My feet, bottom of my feet, have been burned; they've been whopped with a hot iron and clothes hanger . . . the hair on my pussy had been burned off at one time. . . . I have scars. I've been cut with a knife, beat with guns, two by fours. There hasn't been a place on my body that hasn't been bruised somehow, some way, some big, some small. (Giobbe, 1992, p. 126)

Frida Spiwak reported that 70 percent of 100 prostituted girls and women in Bogota had physical health problems. In addition to STDs, their diseases were those of poverty and despair: allergies, respiratory problems, and blindness caused by glue sniffing, migraines, symptoms of premature aging, dental problems, and complications from abortion. Adolescent girls and boys in prostitution surveyed by D. Kelly Weisberg reported STDs, hepatitis, pregnancies, sore throats, flu, and repeated suicide attempts. Women who serviced more customers in prostitution reported more severe physical symptoms. The longer women were in prostitution, the more they suffered symptoms of STDs.

Globally, the incidence of HIV seropositivity among prostituted women and children is devastating. Homeless children are at highest risk for HIV, for example, in Romania and Colombia. Peter Piot noted that half of new AIDS cases are in the under-25 age group, and that girls are likely to become infected at a much younger age than boys, in part because of the acceptance of violence against women and girls in most cultures. . . .

CRIMINAL JUSTICE RESPONSES TO PROSTITUTION

It is commonly assumed that the greater the legal tolerance of prostitution, the easier it is to control public health. Public health in this context refers primarily to STDs in johns rather than to the psychological and physical health of prostituted women.

Legalized prostitution involves state, county, or city ordinances that regulate prostitution, for example, issuing zoning permits, requiring STD tests, and collecting taxes. In effect, the state operates as the pimp. In Nevada, state regulations determine geographic location and size of brothels, as well as activities of women outside the brothel. Prostituted women are only allowed into nearby towns from 1 to 4 p.m., are restricted to certain locations, and are even prohibited from talking to certain persons. Respondents in South Africa and Zambia were asked whether they thought they would be safer from sexual and physical assault if prostitution were legal. A significant majority (68 percent) said "no." The implication was that regardless of the legal status of prostitution, those in it knew that they would continue to experience violence.

The HIV epidemic has brought with it the advocacy of another legal approach to prostitution: decriminalization, or the cessation of enforcement of all laws against prostitution. Decriminalization of prostitution has been promoted by sex businesses as a way to remove the social stigma associated with prostitution. Decriminalization would normalize commercial sex, but it would not reduce the trauma and the humiliation of being prostituted. Compared to illegal prostitution, decriminalization would facilitate men's access to women and children.

Stating that "prostitution is not a desirable social phenomenon," the Swedish government in 1999 criminalized the behavior of pimps and johns but not those who were prostituting. Noting that "it is not reasonable to punish the person who sells a sexual service [because] in the majority of cases this person is a weaker partner who is exploited," the Swedish government allocated social welfare monies to "motivate prostitutes to seek help to leave their way of life." This progressive interventionist approach reflects the Swedish interest in counteracting growth of commercial sex businesses.

In the United States, although there is legislative concern about forced trafficking, there are few legal remedies for women who enter prostitution because of educational neglect, emotional abuse, or lack of economic alternatives. Some women in prostitution do not appear to have been forced or coerced. Public policies that offer legal, financial, and social assistance only to those who can prove violent force, or who are under age eighteen, or who crossed international borders, do not address the core of violence that is present in all types of prostitution. Legal responses to prostitution are inadequate if they fail to include johns, as well as pimps and traffickers, as perpetrators.

The state of Florida passed a remarkably progressive law that addresses some of the forces propelling girls and women into prostitution. The Florida law specifically prohibits inducement into prostitution by sexual abuse, by pornography, or by exploiting the need for food, shelter, safety, or affection.

CONCLUSION

Commercial sex businesses are a multibillion dollar global market that includes strip clubs, massage parlors, phone sex, online prostitution, internet pimping of women and children, adult and child pornography, street, brothel, and escort prostitution. One's political perspective will determine whether prostitution is viewed primarily as a public health issue, as an issue of zoning and property values (which parts of town should house strip clubs and pornography stores?), as vocational choice, as sexual liberation, as freedom of speech (does the webmaster have the right to sell internet photographs of prostituted women being raped?), as petty crime, as domestic violence, or as human rights violation.

For the vast majority of the world's prostituted women, prostitution is the experience of being hunted, dominated, harassed, assaulted, and battered. Intrinsic to prostitution are numerous violations of human rights: sexual harassment, economic servitude, educational deprivation, job discrimination, domestic violence, racism, classism, vulnerability to frequent physical and sexual assault, and being subjected to body invasions that are equivalent to torture.

Demand creates supply in prostitution. Because men want to buy sex, prostitution is assumed to be inevitable, therefore "normal." Men's ambivalence about the purchase of women, however, is reflected in the scarcity of research interviews with johns and in their desire to remain hidden. In a series of interviews with johns conducted by women prostituting in message parlors, Elizabeth Plumridge noted that, on the one hand, the men believed that commercial sex was a mutually pleasurable exchange, and on the other hand, they asserted that payment of money removed all social and ethical obligations. A john interviewed by Neil McKeganey and Marina Barnard said: "It's like going to have your car done, you tell them what you want done, they don't ask, you tell them you want so and so done."

Programs that assist women in prostitution can not succeed in the long run unless social systems that keep women subordinate also change. Jacquelyn White and Mary Koss observed that violent behaviors against women have been associated with attitudes that promote men's beliefs that they are entitled to sexual access to women, that they are superior to women, and that they have a license for sexual aggression. Prostitution myths are a component of attitudes that normalize sexual violence. Martin Monto found that johns' acceptance of commodified sexuality was strongly associated with their acceptance of rape myths, violent sex, and less frequent use of condoms with women in prostitution. A widespread acceptance among men of what has been described as nonrelational sexuality may be a contributing factor to the normalization of prostitution. According to sociologist Kathleen Barry, in today's culture we do not distinguish sex that is exploitative or coercive from sex that is a positive human experience. This blurring results in what Barry has called the prostitution of human sexuality.

Prostitution must be exposed for what it really is: a particularly lethal form of male violence against women. The focus of research, prevention, and law enforcement in the next decades must be on the demand side of prostitution.

CRITICAL-THINKING QUESTIONS

1. Many people believe that prostitution is a free choice. Farley argues that this belief is false. Why? What is your view of this issue?

2. How does prostitution reflect an intersection of race, sex, and class oppression?

3. In terms of the legal status of prostitution, how do decriminalization and legalization differ? Why is Farley opposed to both? Do you agree or disagree with her position?

REFERENCES

ABRAHAM, K. 1953. *Selected papers on psychoanalysis.* New York: Basic Books.

BALDWIN, M. A. 1999. A million dollars and an apology: Prostitution and public benefits claims. *Hastings Women's Law Journal,* Winter 1999, 189–224.

BARRY, K. 1995. *The prostitution of sexuality.* New York: New York University Press.

BISHOP, R., and L. S. ROBINSON. 1998. *Night market: Sexual cultures and the Thai economic miracle.* New York and London: Routledge.

BOYER, D., L. CHAPMAN, and B. K. MARSHALL. 1993. Survival sex in King County: Helping women out. Seattle: *Report submitted to King County Women's Advisory Board, March 31, 1993.* Northwest Resource Associates.

BRIERE, J. 1992. *Child abuse trauma: Theory and treatment of the lasting effects.* Newbury Park: Sage.

BROWNE, A., and D. FINKLEHOR. 1986. Impact of child sexual abuse: A review of the research. *Psychological Bulletin* 99(1): 66–77.

BURKETT, E. 1997. God created me to be a slave. *New York Times Magazine* 12: 56–60.

CHATTOPADHYAY, M., S. BANDYOPADHYAY, and C. DUTTAGUPTA. 1994. Biosocial factors influencing women to become prostitutes in India, *Social Biology* 41(3–4): 252–259.

COKER, A., N. PATEL, S. KRISHNASWAMI, W. SCHMIDT, and D. RICHTER. 1998. Childhood forced sex and cervical dysplasia among women prison inmates. *Violence Against Women* 4(5): 595–608.

CROWELL, N. A., and A. W. BURGESS (eds.). 1996. *Understanding violence against women.* Washington, D.C.: National Academy Press.

DAVIDSON, J. O. 1998. *Prostitution, power, and freedom.* Ann Arbor: University of Michigan Press.

DAVIS, N. 1993. *Prostitution: An international handbook on trends, problems, and policies.* London: Greenwood Press.

DWORKIN, A. 1997. *Prostitution and male supremacy in life and death.* New York: Free Press.

FARLEY, M., and H. BARKAN. 1998. Prostitution, violence and posttraumatic stress disorder. *Women & Health 27*(3): 37–49.

FARLEY, M., I., BARAL, M., KIREMIRE, and U. SEZGIN, 1998. Prostitution in five countries: Violence and posttraumatic stress disorder. *Feminism & Psychology* 8(4): 415–26.

FINSTAD, L., and C. HOIGARD, 1993. Norway. In *Prostitution: An international handbook on trends, problems, and policies,* ed. N. Davis. London: Greenwood Press.

GIOBBE, E. 1991. Prostitution: Buying the right to rape. In *Rape and sexual assault III: A research handbook,* ed. A. W. Burgess. New York: Garland Press.

GIOBBE, E. 1992. Juvenile prostitution: Profile of recruitment. In *Child trauma: Issues & research,* ed. A. W. Burgess. New York: Garland Press.

GIOBBE, E. 1993. An analysis of individual, institutional and cultural pimping. *Michigan Journal of Gender & Law* 1: 33–57.

GIOBBE, E., M., HARRIGAN, J. RYAN, and D. GAMACHE. 1990. *Prostitution: A matter of violence against women.* Minneapolis, Minn.: WHISPER.

HERMAN, J. L. 1992. *Trauma and recovery.* New York: Basic Books.

HERNANDEZ, T. K. 2001. Sexual harassment and racial disparity: The mutual construction of gender and race. *Journal of Gender, Race & Justice* 4: 183.

HOIGARD, C., and L. FINSTAD. 1986. *Backstreets: Prostitution, money and love.* University Park, Penn.: Pennsylvania State University Press.

HOLSOPPLE, K. 1998. Stripclubs according to strippers: Exposing workplace violence. Unpublished paper.

HUGHES, D. M. 2000. The "Natasha" trade: The transnational shadow market of trafficking in women. *Journal of International Affairs* 53(2): 625–51.

HUGHES, DONNA M. 1999. *Pimps and predators on the Internet—Globalizing the sexual exploitation of women and children.* Kingston, Rhode Island: The Coalition Against Trafficking in Women.

HUNTER, S. K. 1994. Prostitution is cruelty and abuse to women and children. *Michigan Journal of Gender and Law* 1: 1–14.

LIM, L. L., ed. 1998. *The sex sector: The economic and social bases of prostitution in Southeast Asia.* Geneva: International Labor Organization.

LOUIE, L., K. JOE, M. LUU, and B. TONG. 1991. Chinese American adolescent runaways. Paper presented at Annual Convention of the Asian American Psychological Association, San Francisco. August 1991.

LOWMAN, J. 1992. Canada. In *Prostitution: An international handbook on trends, problems, and policies,* ed. N. Davis, Westport, Conn.: Greenwood Press.

LUCAS, B., and L. HACKERR. 1995. *Street youth: On their own in Indianapolis.* Health Foundation of Greater Indianapolis, Ind.

MACKINNON, C. A. 1993. Prostitution and civil rights. *Michigan Journal of Gender and Law* 1: 13–31.

MACKINNON, C. A., and A. DWORKIN, 1997. *In harm's way: The pornography civil rights hearings.* Cambridge: Harvard University Press.

MCKEGANEY, N., and M. BARNARD. 1996. *Sex work on the streets: Prostitutes and their clients.* Buckingham, Scotland: Milton Keynes Open University Press.

MILLER, E. M. 1986. *Street woman.* Philadelphia: Temple University Press.

Ministry of Labour in cooperation with the Ministry of Justice and the Ministry of Health and Social Affairs, Government of Sweden. (1998). Fact Sheet. Secretariat for Information and Communication, Ministry of Labour. Tel +46-8-405 11 55, Fax +46-8-405 12 98. Artiklne, A98.004.

MONTO, M. 1999. *Prostitution and human commodification: A study of arrested clients of female street prostitutes.* Chicago: American Sociological Association.

MURPHY, P. (1993). *Making the connections: Women, work and abuse: Dramatic insight into the lives of abuse victims and practical recommendations for their successful return to work.* Orlando, Fla.: Paul M. Deutsch Press.

NELSON, V. 1993. Prostitution: Where racism and sexism intersect. *Michigan Journal of Gender & Law* 1: 81–89.

PARRIOTT, R. 1994. *Health experiences of twin cities women used in prostitution.* Minneapolis, Minn.: Unpublished survey initiated by WHISPER.

PIOT, P. 1999. Remarks at United Nations Commission on the Status of Women, United Nations Press Release, March 3, New York.

PLUMRIDGE, E. W., J. W. CHETWYND, A. REED, and S. J. GIFFORD. 1997. Discourses of emotionality in commercial sex: The missing client voice. *Feminism & Psychology* 7(2): 165–81.

PUTNAM, F. 1990. Disturbances of "self" in victims of childhood sexual abuse. In *Incest-related syndromes of adult psychopathology,* ed. R. Kluft, pp. 113–31. Washington, D.C: American Psychiatric Press.

ROOT, M. 1996. Women of color and traumatic stress in "domestic captivity": Gender and race as disempowering statuses. In *Ethnocultural aspects of posttraumatic stress disorder: Issues, research, and clinical applications.* eds. A. J. Mirsella, M. J. Friedman, E. T. Gerrity, and R. M. Scurfield. Washington, D.C.: American Psychological Assn.

SANCHEZ, L. 1998. Boundaries of legitimacy: Sex, violence, citizenship, and community in a local sexual economy. *Law and Social Inquiry* 22: 543–80.

SILBERT, M. H., and A. M. PINES. 1983. Early sexual exploitation as an influence in prostitution. *Social Work* 28: 285–89.

SILBERT, M. H., and A. M. PINES. 1984. Pornography and sexual abuse of women. *Sex Roles* 10(11–12): 857–68.

Special Committee on Pornography and Prostitution. 1985. *Pornography and Prostitution in Canada* 350.

STURDEVANT, S., and B. STOLZFUS. 1992. *Let the good times roll: Prostitution and the US military in Asia.* New York: The New Press.

TERR, L. C. 1991. Childhood traumas: An outline and overview. *American Journal of Psychiatry* 148: 10–20.

VANWESENBEECK, I. 1994. *Prostitutes' well-being and risk.* Amsterdam: VU Boekhandel/Uitgeverij Press.

WEISBERG, D. 1985. *Children of the night: A study of adolescent prostitution.* Lexington, Mass.: Lexington Books.

WHITE, J. W., and M. P. KOSS. 1993. Adolescent sexual aggression within heterosexual relationships: Prevalence, characteristics, and causes. In *The juvenile sex offender.* eds. H. E. Barbaree, W. L. Marshall, and D. R. Laws. New York: Guilford Press.

CLASSIC

CONTEMPORARY

CROSS-CULTURAL

34 Understanding Sexual Orientation

ALFRED C. KINSEY, WARDELL B. POMEROY, AND CLYDE E. MARTIN

In 1948, Alfred Kinsey and his colleagues published the first modern study of sexuality in the United States—and raised plenty of eyebrows. For the first time, people began talking openly about sex, questioning many common stereotypes. Here Kinsey reports his finding that sexual orientation is not a matter of clear-cut differences between heterosexuals and homosexuals, but is better described as a continuum by which most people combine elements of both.

THE HETEROSEXUAL-HOMOSEXUAL BALANCE

Concerning patterns of sexual behavior, a great deal of the thinking done by scientists and laymen alike stems from the assumption that there are persons who are "heterosexual" and persons who are "homosexual," that these two types represent antitheses in the sexual world, and that there is only an insignificant class of "bisexuals" who occupy an intermediate position between the other groups. It is implied that every individual is innately—inherently—either heterosexual or homosexual. It is further

Source: From *Sexual Behavior in the Human Male* by Alfred C. Kinsey, Wardell B. Pomeroy, and Clyde E. Martin. (Philadelphia: W. B. Saunders Company, 1948), pp. 636–39 Reprinted by permission of The Kinsey Institute.

implied that from the time of birth one is fated to be one thing or the other, and that there is little chance for one to change his pattern in the course of a lifetime.

It is quite generally believed that one's preference for a sexual partner of one or the other sex is correlated with various physical and mental qualities, and with the total personality which makes a homosexual male or female physically, psychically, and perhaps spiritually distinct from a heterosexual individual. It is generally thought that these qualities make a homosexual person obvious and recognizable to anyone who has a sufficient understanding of such matters. Even psychiatrists discuss "the homosexual personality" and many of them believe that preferences for sexual partners of a particular sex

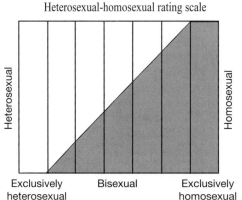

Heterosexual-homosexual rating scale

Heterosexual · Homosexual

Exclusively heterosexual   Bisexual   Exclusively homosexual are merely secondary manifestations of something that lies much deeper in the totality of that intangible which they call the personality.

It is commonly believed, for instance, that homosexual males are rarely robust physically, are uncoordinated or delicate in their movements, or perhaps graceful enough but not strong and vigorous in their physical expression. Fine skins, high-pitched voices, obvious hand movements, a feminine carriage of the hips, and peculiarities of walking gaits are supposed accompaniments of a preference for a male as a sexual partner. It is commonly believed that the homosexual male is artistically sensitive, emotionally unbalanced, temperamental to the point of being unpredictable, difficult to get along with, and undependable in meeting specific obligations. In physical characters there have been attempts to show that the homosexual male has a considerable crop of hair and less often becomes bald, has teeth which are more like those of the female, a broader pelvis, larger genitalia, and a tendency toward being fat, and that he lacks a linea alba. The homosexual male is supposed to be less interested in athletics, more often interested in music and the arts, more often engaged in such occupations as bookkeeping, dress design, window display, hairdressing, acting, radio work, nursing, religious service, and social work. The converse to all of these is supposed to represent the typical heterosexual male. Many a clinician attaches considerable weight to these things in diagnosing the basic heterosexuality or homosexuality of his patients. The characterizations are so distinct that they seem to leave little room for doubt that homosexual and heterosexual represent two very distinct types of males. . . .

It should be pointed out that scientific judgments on this point have been based on little more than the same sorts of impressions which the general public has had concerning homosexual persons. But before any sufficient study can be made of such possible correlations between patterns of sexual behavior and other qualities in the individual, it is necessary to understand the incidences and frequencies of the homosexual in the population as a whole, and the relation of the homosexual activity to the rest of the sexual pattern in each individual's history.

The histories which have been available in the present study make it apparent that the heterosexuality or homosexuality of many individuals is not an all-or-none proposition. It is true that there are persons in the population whose histories are exclusively heterosexual, both in regard to their overt experience and in regard to their psychic reactions. And there are individuals in the population whose histories are exclusively homosexual, both in experience and in psychic reactions. But the record also shows that there is a considerable portion of the population whose members have combined, within their individual histories, both homosexual and heterosexual experience and/or psychic responses. There are some whose heterosexual experiences predominate, there are some whose homosexual experiences predominate, there are some who have had quite equal amounts of both types of experience.

Some of the males who are involved in one type of relation at one period in their lives may have only the other type of relation at some later period. There may be considerable fluctuation of patterns from time to time. Some males may be involved in both heterosexual and homosexual activities within the same period of time. For instance, there are some who engage in both heterosexual and homosexual activities in the same year, or in the same month or week, or even in the same day. There are not a few individuals who engage in group activities in which they may make simultaneous contact with partners of both sexes.

Males do not represent two discrete populations, heterosexual and homosexual. The world is not to be divided into sheep and goats. Not all things are black nor all things white. It is a fundamental of taxonomy that nature rarely deals with discrete categories. Only the human mind invents categories and tries to force facts into separated pigeon-holes. The living world is a continuum in each and every one of its aspects. The sooner we learn this concerning human sexual behavior the sooner we shall reach a sound understanding of the realities of sex.

CRITICAL-THINKING QUESTIONS

1. Why do you think people have long thought of heterosexuality and homosexuality as opposite and mutually exclusive (that is, only in terms of "exclusively heterosexual" or "exclusively homosexual" in the figure on page 194)?

2. Kinsey suggests that anyone's sexual orientation may well change over time. Do you agree? Why or why not?

3. Why do people tend to label someone with any degree of homosexual experience as a "homosexual"? (After all, we don't do the same in the case of any heterosexual experience.)

CLASSIC

CONTEMPORARY

CROSS-CULTURAL

35 Sex in America: How Many Partners Do We Have?

ROBERT T. MICHAEL, JOHN H. GAGNON,
EDWARD O. LAUMANN, AND GINA KOLATA

Sex is a topic at once very familiar and little understood. This selection is part of a broad study of sexuality in the United States that produced some surprising findings. Despite the common belief that our society has become "free and easy" when it comes to sex, the typical individual has fewer sexual partners than most people think.

Sometimes, the myths about sex contain a grain of truth. The common perception is that Americans today have more sexual partners than they did just a decade or two ago. That, it turns out, is correct. A third of Americans who are over age fifty have had five or more sexual partners in their lifetime. But half of all Americans aged thirty to fifty have had five or more partners even though being younger, they had fewer years to accumulate them.

Still, when we ask older or younger people how many partners they had in the past year, the usual reply is zero or one. Something must have changed to make younger people accumulate more partners over a lifetime, yet sustain a pattern of having no partners or only one in any one year. The explanation is linked to one of our most potent social institutions and how it has changed.

That institution is marriage, a social arrangement so powerful that nearly everyone participates.

About 90 percent of Americans have married by the time they are thirty, and a large majority spends much of their adulthood as part of a wedded couple. And marriage, we find, regulates sexual behavior with remarkable precision. No matter what they did before they wed, no matter how many partners they had, the sexual lives of married people are similar. Despite the popular myth that there is a great deal of adultery in marriage, our data and other reliable studies do not find it. Instead, a vast majority are faithful while the marriage is intact. . . .

So, yes, many young people probably are having sexual intercourse with a fair number of partners. But that stops with marriage. The reason that people now have more sexual partners over their lifetimes is that they are spending a longer period sexually active, but unmarried. The period has lengthened from both ends and in the middle. The average age at which people have their first sexual intercourse has crept down and the average age at which people marry for the first time has edged up. And people are more likely to divorce now, which means they have time between marriages when they search for new partners once again.

Source: From *Sex in America: A Definitive Survey* by Robert Michael et al. Copyright © 1994 by CSG Enterprises, Inc. Edward O. Laumann, Robert T. Michael, and Gina Kolata. By permission of Little, Brown and Company, Inc.

To draw these conclusions, we looked at our respondents' replies to a variety of questions. First, we asked people when they first had heterosexual intercourse. Then, we asked what happens between the time when people first have intercourse and when they finally marry. How many partners do they have? Do they have more than one partner at any one time or do they have their partners in succession, practicing serial monogamy? We asked how many people divorced and how long they remained unmarried. Finally, we asked how many partners people had in their lifetimes.

In our analyses of the numbers of sex partners, we could not separately analyze patterns for gay men and lesbians. That is because homosexuals are such a small percentage of our sample that we do not have enough people in our survey to draw valid conclusions about this aspect of sexual behavior.

If we are going to look at heterosexual partners from the beginning, from the time that people first lose their virginity, we plunge headfirst into the maelstrom of teenage sex, always a turbulent subject, but especially so now, in the age of AIDS.

While society disputes whether to counsel abstinence from sexual intercourse or to pass out condoms in high schools, it also must grapple with a basic question: Has sexual behavior among teenagers changed? Are more having sexual intercourse and at younger ages, or is the overheated rhetoric a reaction to fears, without facts? The answer is both troubling and reassuring to the majority of adults who prefer teenagers to delay their sexual activity—troubling because most teenagers are having intercourse, but reassuring because sexual intercourse tends to be sporadic during the teen years.

We saw a steadily declining age at which teenagers first had sexual intercourse. Men and women born in the decade 1933–1942 had sex at an average age of about eighteen. Those born twenty to thirty years later have an average age at first intercourse that is about six months younger, as seen in Figure 1. The figure also indicates that the men report having sex at younger ages than

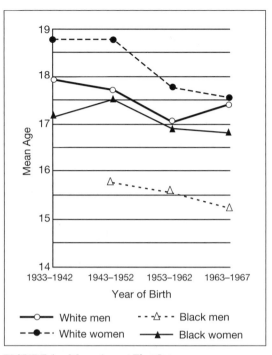

FIGURE 1   Mean Age at First Intercourse

Note: This includes respondents who had vaginal intercourse no later than age twenty-five and who have reached their twenty-fifth birthday by the date of the interview. Missing line segments indicate insufficient number of cases for a particular category (less than thirty). Whites computed from cross-section sample; blacks computed from cross-section and the over-sample.

the women. It also shows that blacks report a younger age at first intercourse than whites.

Another way to look at the age at first intercourse is illustrated in Figure 2. The figure shows the proportions of teenagers and young adults who experienced sexual intercourse at each age from twelve to twenty-five. To see at what age half the people had intercourse, for example, follow the horizontal line that corresponds to a cumulative frequency of 50 percent. It shows that half of all black men had intercourse by the time they were fifteen, half of all Hispanic men had intercourse by the time they were about sixteen and a half, half of all black women had intercourse by the time they were nearly seventeen,

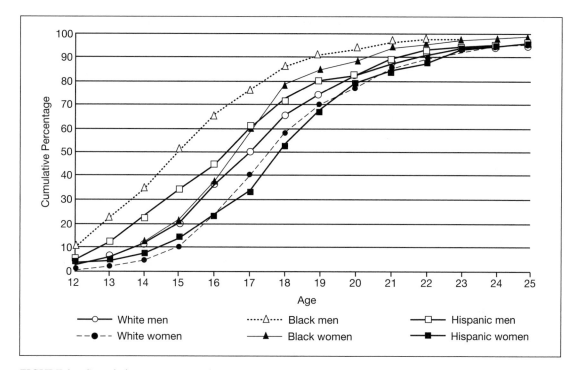

FIGURE 2   Cumulative Percentage Who Have Had Intercourse

Note: Cumulative percentage indicates the proportion of respondents of a given group at a given age. This figure only includes respondents who have reached their twenty-fifth birthday by the date of the interview.

and half the white women and half the Hispanic women had intercourse by the time they were nearly eighteen. By age twenty-two, about 90 percent of each group had intercourse.

The patterns are crystal clear. About half the teenagers of various racial and ethnic groups in the nation have begun having intercourse with a partner in the age range of fifteen to eighteen, and at least four out of five have had intercourse by the time their teenage years are over. Since the average age of marriage is now in the mid-twenties, few Americans wait until they marry to have sex.

Our data, in fact, show that the proportion of women who were either virgins when they turned twenty or had had sexual intercourse with only one person declined from 84 percent, among women born in 1933 to 1942, to about 50 percent for those born after 1953. . . .

The proportion of women who were virgins has traditionally been somewhat higher than the proportion of men who had had no sexual intercourse by age twenty, but that gender difference has disappeared. . . .

It's a change that built up for years, making it sometimes hard to appreciate just how profound it is. Stories of what sex among the unmarried was like decades ago can be startling. Even people who were no longer teenagers, and who were engaged, felt overwhelming social pressure to refrain from intercourse before marriage. . . .

In addition to having intercourse at younger ages, many people also are marrying later—a change that is the real legacy of the late 1960s and early 1970s. This period was not, we find, a sexual revolution, a time of frequent sex with many partners for all. Instead, it was the beginning of a profound change in the sexual life course, providing the second reason why Americans have accumulated more partners now than in decades past.

Since the 1960s, the route to the altar is no longer so predictable as it used to be. In the first half of the twentieth century, almost everyone who married followed the same course: dating, love, a little sexual experimentation with one partner, sometimes including intercourse, then marriage and children. It also was a time when there was a clear and accepted double standard—men were much more likely to have had intercourse with several women before marrying than women were to have had intercourse with several men.

At the dawn of the millennium, we are left with a nation that still has this idealized heterosexual life course but whose actual course has fragmented in the crucial years before marriage. Some people still marry at eighteen, others at thirty, leading to very different numbers of sexual partners before marriage. Social class plays a role, with less-educated people marrying earlier than better-educated people. Blacks tend to marry much later than whites, and a large number of blacks do not marry at all.

But a new and increasingly common pattern has emerged: affection or love and sex with a number of partners, followed by affection, love, and cohabitation. This cycles back to the sexual marketplace, if the cohabitation breaks up, or to marriage. Pregnancy can occur at any of these points, but often occurs before either cohabitation or marriage. The result is that the path toward marriage, once so straight and narrow, has begun to meander and to have many side paths, one of which is being trodden into a well-traveled lane.

That path is the pattern of living together before marriage. Like other recent studies, ours shows a marked shift toward living together rather than marriage as the first union of couples. With an increase in cohabitation, the distinctions among having a steady sexual partner, a live-in sexual partner, and a marriage have gotten more fuzzy. This shift began at the same time as talk of a sexual revolution. Our study shows that people who came of age before 1970 almost invariably

got married without first living together, while the younger people seldom did. But, we find, the average age at which people first move in with a partner—either by marrying, or living together—has remained nearly constant, around age twenty-two for men and twenty for women. The difference is that now that first union is increasingly likely to be a cohabitation. . . .

With the increase in cohabitation, people are marrying later, on average. The longer they wait, however, the more likely they are to live with a sexual partner in the meantime. Since many couples who live together break up within a short time and seek a new partner, the result has been an increase in the average number of partners that people have before they marry. . . .

Finally, we can look at divorce rates, another key social change that began in the 1960s and that has led to increasing numbers of partners over a lifetime. Our data show this divorce pattern, as do many other data sets in the United States. For example, we can look at how likely it is that a couple will be divorced by the tenth anniversary of their marriage. For people born between 1933 and 1942, the chance was about one in five. For those born between 1943 and 1952, the chance was one in three. For those born between 1953 and 1962, the chance was closer to 38 percent. Divorced people as a group have more sexual partners than people who remain married and they are more likely, as a group, to have intercourse with a partner and live with a partner before they marry again.

These three social trends—earlier first intercourse, later marriage, and more frequent divorce—help explain why people now have more sexual partners over their lifetimes.

To discern the patterns of sexual partnering, we asked respondents how many sexual partners they had. We could imagine several scenarios. People could find one partner and marry. Or they could have sex with several before marrying. Or they could live with their partners first and then marry. Or they could simply have lots of casual sex, never marrying at all or marrying but also having extramarital sex.

Since our respondents varied in age from eighteen to fifty-nine, the older people in the study, who married by their early twenties, would have been married by the time the turbulent 1960s and 1970s came around. Their premarital behavior would be a relic from the past, telling us how much intercourse people had in the days before sex became so public an issue. The younger people in our study can show us whether there is a contrast between the earlier days and the decades after a sexual revolution was proclaimed. We can ask if they have more partners, if they have more than one sexual partner at a time, and if their sexual behavior is markedly different from that of the older generations that preceded them.

Most young people today show no signs of having very large numbers of partners. More than half the men and women in America who were eighteen to twenty-four in 1992 had just one sex partner in the past year and another 11 percent had none in the last year. In addition, studies in Europe show that people in the United Kingdom, France, and Finland have sexual life courses that are virtually the same as the American life course. The picture that emerges is strikingly different from the popular image of sexuality running out of control in our time.

In fact, we find, nearly all Americans have a very modest number of partners, whether we ask them to enumerate their partners over their adult lifetime or in the past year. The number of partners varies little with education, race, or religion. Instead, it is determined by marital status or by whether a couple is living together. Once married, people tend to have one and only one partner, and those who are unmarried and living together are almost as likely to be faithful.

Our data for the United States are displayed in Table 1.

The right-hand portion of Table 1 tells how many sexual partners people had since they turned eighteen. Very few, just 3 percent, had no partners, and few, just 9 percent, had a total of more than twenty partners.

The oldest people in our study, those aged fifty-five to fifty-nine, were most likely to have had just one sexual partner in their lifetimes—40 percent said they had had only one. This reflects the earlier age of marriage in previous generations and the low rate of divorce among these older couples. Many of the men were married by age twenty-two and the women by age twenty.

The left-hand portion of Table 1 shows the number of sexual partners that people had in the past twelve months. These are the data that show how likely people are to remain faithful to their sexual partner, whether or not they are married. Among married people, 94 percent had one partner in the past year. Couples who were living together were almost as faithful. Seventy-five percent of people who had never married but were living together had one partner in the past year. Eighty percent of people who were previously married and were cohabiting when we questioned them had one partner in the past year. Two-thirds of the single people who were not living with a partner had no partners or only one in the past year. Only a few percent of the population had as many as five partners for sexual intercourse in the past year, and many of these were people who were never married and were not living with anyone. They were mostly young and mostly male. . . .

One way to imagine the patterns of sexual partners is to think of a graph, with the vertical axis showing numbers of partners and the horizontal axis showing a person's age. The graph will be a series of blips, as the person finds partners, interspersed with flat regions where the person has no partners or when the person has just one steady partner. When the person marries, the line flattens out at a height of one, indicating that the individual has only one partner. If the marriage breaks up, the graph shows a few more blips until the person remarries, and then it flattens out again.

For an individual, the graph is mostly flat, punctuated by a few areas of blips. But if we superimposed everyone's graph on top of each other, we would have a sort of supergraph that looked like it

TABLE 1   Number of Sex Partners in Past Twelve Months and since Age Eighteen

	Sex Partners Past Twelve Months				Sex Partners Since Age Eighteen					
	0	*1*	*2 to 4*	*5+*	*0*	*1*	*2 to 4*	*5 to 10*	*11 to 20*	*21+*
Total	12%	71%	14%	3%	3%	26%	30%	22%	11%	9%
Gender										
Men	10	67	18	5	3	20	21	23	16	17
Women	14	75	10	2	3	31	36	20	6	3
Age										
18–24	11	57	24	9	8	32	34	15	8	3
25–29	6	72	17	6	2	25	31	22	10	9
30–34	9	73	16	2	3	21	29	25	11	10
35–39	10	77	11	2	2	19	30	25	14	11
40–44	11	75	13	1	1	22	28	24	14	12
45–49	15	75	9	1	2	26	24	25	10	14
50–54	15	79	5	0	2	34	28	18	9	9
55–59	32	65	4	0	1	40	28	15	8	7
Marital status										
Never married, noncohabiting	25	38	28	9	12	15	29	21	12	12
Never married, cohabiting	1	75	20	5	0	25	37	16	10	13
Married	2	94	4	1	0	37	28	19	9	7
Divorced, separated, widowed, noncohabiting	31	41	26	3	0	11	33	29	15	12
Divorced, separated, widowed, cohabiting	1	80	15	3	0	0	32	44	12	12
Education										
Less than high school	16	67	15	3	4	27	36	19	9	6
High school graduate or equivalent	11	74	13	3	3	30	29	20	10	7
Some college, vocational	11	71	14	4	2	24	29	23	12	9
Finished college	12	69	15	4	2	24	26	24	11	13
Master's/advanced degree	13	74	10	3	4	25	26	23	10	13
Current Religion										
None	11	68	13	7	3	16	29	20	16	16
Mainline Protestant	11	73	13	2	2	23	31	23	12	8
Conservative Protestant	13	70	14	3	3	30	30	20	10	7
Catholic	12	71	13	3	4	27	29	23	8	9
Jewish	3	75	18	3	0	24	13	30	17	17
Other religion	15	70	12	3	3	42	20	16	8	13
Race/Ethnicity										
White	12	73	12	3	3	26	29	22	11	9
Black	13	60	21	6	2	18	34	24	11	11
Hispanic	11	69	17	2	4	35	27	17	8	9
Asian	15	77	8	0	6	46	25	14	6	3
Native American	12	76	10	2	5	28	35	23	5	5

Note: Row percentages total 100 percent.

was all blips. That, in essence, is what has led to the widespread impression that everyone is having lots of partners. We see the total picture—lots of sex in the population—without realizing that each individual spends most of his or her life with only one partner.

These findings give no support to the idea of a promiscuous society or of a dramatic sexual revolution reflected in huge numbers of people with multiple casual sex partners. The finding on which our data give strong and quite amazing evidence is not that most people do, in fact, form a partnership, or that most people do, in fact, ultimately get married. That fact also was well documented in many previous studies. Nor is it news that more recent marriages are much less stable than marriages that began thirty years ago. That fact, too, was reported by others before us. But we add a new fact, one that is not only important but that is striking.

Our study clearly shows that no matter how sexually active people are before and between marriages, no matter whether they lived with their sexual partners before marriage or whether they were virgins on their wedding day, marriage is such a powerful social institution that, essentially, married people are nearly all alike—they are faithful to their partners as long as the marriage is intact. It does not matter if the couple were high-school sweethearts who married after graduation day or whether they are in their thirties, marrying after each had lived with several others. Once married, the vast majority have no other sexual partner; their past is essentially erased. Marriage remains the great leveler.

We see this, for example, when we ask about fidelity in marriage. More than 80 percent of women and 65 to 85 percent of men of every age report that they had no partners other than their spouse while they were married. . . .

The marriage effect is so dramatic that it swamps all other aspects of our data. When we report that more than 80 percent of adult Americans age eighteen to fifty-nine had zero or one sexual partner in the past year, the figure might sound ludicrous to some young people who know that they and their friends have more than one partner in a year. But the figure really reflects the fact that most Americans in that broad age range are married and are faithful. And many of the others are cohabiting, and they too are faithful. Or they are without partners altogether, a situation that is especially likely for older women. . . . We find only 3 percent of adults had five or more partners in the past year. Half of all adult Americans had three or fewer partners over their lifetimes.

CRITICAL-THINKING QUESTIONS

1. What single factor seems to do more than any other to limit the typical person's number of sexual partners?

2. Were you surprised that half of U.S. adults have had three or fewer sexual partners over their lifetimes? Why do we tend to think of our society as much more sexually active?

3. What has changed with regard to sexuality in the United States over the course of the last fifty years? What has stayed pretty much the same?

CLASSIC

CONTEMPORARY

CROSS-CULTURAL

36 Homosexual Behavior in Cross-Cultural Perspective

J. M. CARRIER*

Although sexuality is a biological process, the meaning *of sexuality is culturally variable. Carrier shows that attitudes toward homosexuality are far from uniform around the world. Some societies are quite accommodating about sexual practices that other societies punish harshly.*

The available cross-cultural data clearly show that the ways in which individuals organize their sexual behavior vary considerably between societies (Westermarck, 1908; Ford & Beach, 1951; Broude & Greene, 1976). Although biological and psychological factors help explain variations of sexual behavior between individuals within a given society, intercultural variations in patterns of human sexual behavior are mainly related to social and cultural differences occurring between societies around the world. The purpose of this chapter is to consider what kinds of variations in homosexual behavior occur between societies, and to determine which sociocultural factors appear to account for the variance of the behavior cross-culturally.[1]

*The author is particularly indebted to Evelyn Hooker for her invaluable comments and criticism; and to the Gender Identity Research Group at UCLA for an early critique of the ideas presented in this paper.

Source: From *Homosexual Behavior: A Modern Reappraisal,* ed. Judd Marmor, copyright © 1980, by Basic Books, Inc. Reprinted with permission.

THE CROSS-CULTURAL DATA

Data available on homosexual behavior in most of the world's societies, past or present, are meager. Much is known about the dominant middle-class white populations of the United States, England, and northern European countries where most scientific research on human sexual behavior has been done, but very little is known about homosexual behavior in the rest of the world. The lack of knowledge stems from the irrational fear and prejudice surrounding the study of human sexual behavior and from the difficulties associated with the collection of information on a topic that is so personal and highly regulated in most societies.

Most of the cross-cultural information on sexual behavior has been gathered by Western anthropologists. The quality of the information collected and published, however, varies considerably. Based on a survey of the literature, Marshall and Suggs (1971) report that "sexual behavior is occasionally touched upon in anthropological publications but is seldom the topic of either articles or monographs by anthropologists." Broude and Greene (1976), after coding the sexual attitudes and practices in 186 societies using the Human Relations Area Files, note:[2]

. . . information of any sort on sexual habits and beliefs is hard to come by. . . . when data do exist concerning sexual attitudes and practices, they are often sketchy and vague; what is more, such information is usually suspect in terms of its reliability, either because of distortions on the part of the subjects or because of biases introduced by the ethnographer. . . .

Cross-cultural data on homosexual behavior is further complicated by the prejudice of many observers who consider the behavior unnatural, dysfunctional, or associated with mental illness, and by the fact that in many of the societies studied the behavior is stigmatized and thus not usually carried out openly. Under these circumstances, the behavior is not easily talked about. At the turn of the twentieth century such adjectives as disgusting, vile, and detestable were still being used to describe homosexual behavior; and even in the mid-1930s some anthropologists continued to view the behavior as unnatural. In discussing sodomy with some of his New Guinea informants, Williams (1936), for example, asked them if they "had ever been subjected to an unnatural practice." With the acceptance of the view in the mid-1930s that homosexual behavior should be classified as a mental illness (or at best dysfunctional), many anthropologists replaced "unnatural" with the medical model. This model still finds adherents among researchers at present, especially those in the branch of anthropology referred to as psychological anthropology.

Because of the prejudice with which many researchers and observers approached the subject, statements about the reported absence of homosexual behavior, or the limited extent of the behavior where reported, should be viewed with some skepticism. Mead (1961) suggests that statements of this kind "can only be accepted with the greatest caution and with very careful analysis of the personality and training of the investigator." She further notes that "denials of a practice cannot be regarded as meaningful if that practice is verbally recognized among a given people, even though a strong taboo exists against it."

This chapter will mainly utilize the published research findings of empirical studies which have considered homosexual behavior in some detail. It will examine homosexual behavior in preliterate, peasant, and complex modern societies in all the major geographical regions of the world.[3] Where necessary, these findings will be supplemented with information found in accounts given by travelers, missionaries, and novelists.

SOCIOCULTURAL FACTORS

A number of sociocultural factors help explain variations of homosexual behavior between societies. Two of the most important are cultural attitudes and proscriptions related to cross-gender behavior, and availability of sexual partners.[4] The latter is in turn related to such variables as segregation of sexes prior to marriage, expectations with respect to virginity, age at marriage, and available economic resources and/or distribution of income.

Cross-Gender and Homosexual Behavior

Different expectations for male persons as opposed to female persons are culturally elaborated from birth onward in every known society. Although behavioral boundaries between the sexes may vary culturally, male persons are clearly differentiated from female persons; and progeny is assured by normative societal rules which correlate male and female gender roles with sexual behavior, marriage, and the family. There is a general expectation in every society that a majority of adult men and women will cohabit and produce the next generation. Social pressure is thus applied in the direction of marriage. The general rule is that one should not remain single.

The cross-cultural data on human sexual behavior suggest that a significant relationship exists between much of the homosexual behavior reported cross culturally and the continuing need of societies to deal with cross-gender behavior. Feminine male behavior, and the set of anxieties associated with its occurrence in the male part of the population, appears to have brought about more elaborate cultural responses temporally and spatially than has masculine female behavior. There are no doubt many reasons why this is so, but it appears to be related in general to the higher status accorded men than women in most societies; and, in particular, to the defense role that men have historically played in protecting women and children from outsiders.

Societies in which homosexual behavior can be linked to cultural responses to cross-gender behavior may be categorized according to the type of response made. Three major cultural types have been identified: those societies which make a basic accommodation to cross-gender behavior, those societies which outlaw the behavior as scandalous and/or criminal, and those societies which neither make an accommodation to such behavior nor outlaw it but instead have a cultural formulation which tries to ensure that cross-gender behavior does not occur.

Accommodating Societies

Societies making an accommodation to cross-gender behavior in one form or another have been reported in many different parts of the world. Munroe et al. (1969), for example, put together a list of societies having what they call "institutionalized male transvestism . . . the permanent adoption by males of aspects of female dress and/or behavior in accordance with customary expectations within a given society." Their list includes Indian societies in North and South America, island societies in Polynesia and Southeast Asia, and preliterate and peasant societies in mainland Asia and Africa. Although reported for both sexes, male cross-gender behavior appears in the literature more often than female.

A folk belief exists in some of these societies that in every generation a certain number of individuals will play the gender role of the opposite sex, usually beginning at or prior to puberty and often identified at a very early age. The Mohave Indians of the American Southwest, for example, used to hold the following belief—typical of many Indian societies in North America—about cross-gender behavior of both sexes:

Ever since the world began at the magic mountain . . . it was said that there would be transvestites. In the beginning, if they were to become transvestites, the process started during their intrauterine life. When they grew up they were given toys according to their sex. They did not like these toys however. (Devereux, 1937)

In southern Mexico one group of Zapotec Indians believes that "effeminate males" are born, not made: "Typical comments include, But what can we do; he was born that way; he is like God made him. A related belief also exists that . . . it is a thing of the blood" (Royce, 1973). In Tahiti, the belief exists that there is at least one cross-gender behaving male, called a *māhū*, in all villages: "When one dies then another substitutes . . . God arranges it like this. It isn't allowed (that there should be) two *māhū*, in one place" (Levy, 1973).

Cross-gender behavior is accepted in other societies because it is believed that some supernatural event makes people that way prior to birth, or that the behavior is acquired through some mystical force or dream after birth. In India, for example, the following belief exists about the *Hijadās,* cross-gender behaving males thought to be impotent at birth who later have their genitals removed:

When we ask a *Hijadā* or an ordinary man in Gujarat "Why does a man become a *Hijadā?*" the usual reply is "One does not become a *Hijadā* by one's own will; it is only by the command of the *mātā* that one becomes a *Hijadā*." The same idea is found in a myth about the origin of the *Hijadās*. It is said that one receives the *mātā's* command either in dreams or when one sits in meditation before her image. (Shah, 1961)

Among the Chukchee of northeastern Asia, a role reversal was accepted because of an unusual dream or vision:

Transformation takes place by the command of the *ka'let* (spirits) usually at the critical age of early youth when shamanistic inspiration first manifests itself. (Bogores, 1904)

Among the Lango in Africa:

A number of Lango men dress as women, simulate menstruation, and become one of the wives of other males. They are believed to be impotent and to have been afflicted by some supernatural agency. (Ford & Beach, 1951)

Although not necessarily accepted gladly, the various folk beliefs make the behavior acceptable, and a certain number of cross-gender behaving individuals are to be expected in every generation. Expectations about the extent to which the opposite gender role is to be played, however, appear to have changed over time with acculturation. Affected individuals in the past often were required to make a public ritualized change of gender and cross-dress and behave in accordance with their new identity. Among the Mohave, for example, there was an initiation ceremony and it was important for the initiate "to duplicate the behavior pattern of his adopted sex and make 'normal' individuals of his anatomic sex feel toward him as though he truly belonged to his adopted sex" (Devereux, 1937). The *māhū* in Tahiti were described in the latter part of the eighteenth century as follows:

These men are in some respects like the Eunichs [sic] in India but are not castrated. They never cohabit with women but live as they do. They pick their beard out and dress as women, dance and sing with them and are as effeminate in their voice. (Morrison, 1935)

Affected individuals in most societies at present are allowed a choice as to the extent they want to play the role; e.g., how far they want to identify with the opposite sex, whether they want to cross-dress or not, etc. Levy (1973) notes, for example, that in Tahiti, "Being a *māhū* does not now usually entail actually dressing as a woman." The North American Indian societies who used to have initiation ceremonies discontinued them long ago; and, although expectations about cross-gender behaving individuals persist, only remnants of the original belief system are remembered currently. They continue, however, to be tolerant and "there apparently is no body of role behavior aimed at humiliating

boys who are feminine or men who prefer men sexually" (Stoller, 1976).

The link between cross-gender behavior and homosexual behavior is the belief that there should be concordance between gender role and sexual object choice. When a male behaves like a female, he should be expected therefore to want a male sexual partner and to play the female sex role—that is, to play the insertee role in anal intercourse or fellatio. The same concordance should be expected when a female behaves like a male. As a result of beliefs about concordance, it is important to note that a society may not conceptualize the sexual behavior or its participants as "homosexual."

There is some evidence in support of this linking of gender role and homosexual behavior in societies making an accommodation and providing a social role for cross-gender behaving individuals. Kroeber (1940), for example, concluded from his investigations that "In most of primitive northern Asia and North America, men of homosexual trends adopted women's dress, work, and status, and were accepted as nonphysiological but institutionalized women." Devereux's Mohave informants said that the males who changed their gender role to female had male husbands and that both anal intercourse and fellatio were practiced, with the participants playing the appropriate gender sex role. The informants noted the same concordance for females who behaved like males.

Unfortunately, the anthropological data do not always make clear whether cultural expectations in a given society were for concordance between gender role and erotic object; or, in terms of actual behavior, how many cross-gender behaving individuals chose same sex, opposite sex, or both sexes as erotic objects. In the paper I just quoted, Kroeber also concluded, "How far invert erotic practices accompanied the status is not always clear from the data, and it probably varied. At any rate, the North American attitude toward the berdache stresses not his erotic life but his social status; born a male, he became accepted as a woman socially."

Many anthropologists and other observers confounded their findings by assuming an equivalence between "transvestite" and "homosexual."[5] Thus, when an informant described cross-gender behavior, they may have concluded without foundation that a same-sex erotic object choice was part of the behavior being described, and that they were eliciting information on "homosexuals." Angelino and Shedd (1955) provide supporting evidence. They reviewed the literature on an often used anthropological concept, berdache, and concluded that the "term has been used in an exceedingly ambiguous way, being used as a synonym for homosexualism, hermaphroditism, transvestism, and effeminism." They also note that the meaning of berdache changed over time, going from kept boy/male prostitute, to individuals who played a passive role in sodomy, to males who played a passive sex role and cross-dressed.

In spite of the confusion between "transvestite" and "homosexual," the available data suggest that in many of the societies providing a social role for cross-gender behavior, the selection of sexual partners was based on the adopted gender role; and, though they might be subjected to ridicule, neither partner in the sexual relationship was penalized for the role played.

The *māhū* role in Tahiti provides a contemporary look at how one Polynesian society continues to provide a social role for cross-gender behavior. According to Levy (1973), villagers in his area of study do not agree on the sexual behavior of the *māhū*—some "believe that *māhū* do not generally engage in homosexual intercourse." Information from both *māhū* and *non-māhū* informants, however, leads to the conclusion that probably a majority of the *māhūs* prefer adolescent males with whom they perform "ote moa" (literally, "penis sucking"). The following are some aspects of the role and the community response to it:

It is said to be exclusive. Its essential defining characteristic is "doing woman's work," that is, a role reversal which is *publicly demonstrated*—either through clothes or through other public aspects of women's role playing. Most villagers approve of, and are pleased by, the role reversal. But homosexual behavior is a covert part of the role, and it is disapproved by many villagers. Men who have sexual relations with the *māhū* . . . do not consider themselves abnormal. Villagers who know of such activities may disapprove, but they do not label the partners as unmanly. The *māhū* is considered as a substitute woman for the partner. A new word, *raerae,* which reportedly originated in Papeete, is used by some to designate nontraditional types of homosexual behavior. (Levy, 1973)

It should also be noted that in Levy's village of study *māhūs* were the only adult men reported to be engaging in homosexual intercourse.

Another contemporary example of a social role for cross-gender behavior is the *Hijadā* role provided cross-gender behaving males in northwestern India. Given slightly different names by different observers (*Hijarās, Hinjrās,* and *Hijirās*), these males appear to be playing the same role. There is general agreement on the fact that they cross-dress, beg alms, and collect dues at special ceremonies where they dance and sing as women. There is a considerable difference of opinion, however, as to whether they engage in homosexual intercourse or in any sexual activity for that matter. From the available data, it appears that they live mostly in towns in communes, with each commune having a definite jurisdiction of villages and towns "where its members can beg alms and collect dues" (Shah, 1961). They are also reported to live separately by themselves. From the findings of Carstairs (1956) and Shah (1961), one can at least conclude that the *Hijadās* living alone are sexually active:

Carstairs is wrong in considering all the Hijadās as homosexual, but there seems to be some truth in his information about the homosexuality of the Deoli Hijadā (Note: Deoli is the village of Carstairs' study.) Faridi and Mehta also note that some Hijadās practice "sodomy." This, however, is not institutionalized homosexuality. (Shah, 1961)

The finding by Opler (1960) that "they cannot carry on sexual activities and do not marry" may apply to the majority of *Hijadās* living in communes. The question of what kind of sexual behavior the *Hijadās* practice, if any, cannot be answered definitively with the data available. That they are still a viable group in India is confirmed by a recent Associated Press release:

About 2000 eunuchs dressed in brightly colored saris and other female garb were converging on this northern town from all over India this weekend for a private convention of song, dance and prayer.

Local reaction to the gathering was mixed. "They're perverts," commented a local peanut vendor. "We should have nothing to do with them. They should be run out of town."

A New Delhi social worker . . . said they sometimes supplement their income as paid lovers of homosexuals. (Excerpts from AP, February 6, 1979)

Disapproving Societies

Societies in which cross-gender behavior produces strong emotional negative reactions in large segments of the population tend to have the following commonalities: (1) negative reactions produced by the behavior are essentially limited to the male part of the population and relate mainly to effeminate males; (2) cross-gender behavior is controlled by laws which prohibit cross-dressing, and by laws and public opinion which consider other attributes associated with the behavior as scandalous; (3) gender roles are sharply dichotomized; and (4) a general belief exists that anyone demonstrating cross-gender behavior is homosexual.

A number of complex modern and peasant societies in the Middle East, North Africa, southern Europe, and Central and South America have the commonalities listed. The author's research in Mexico (Carrier, 1976 and 1977) illustrates how homosexual behavior in these societies appears to be linked to social responses to cross-gender behavior. The comments that follow are limited to male homosexual behavior. Female homosexuality is known to exist in these societies, but too little is known about the behavior to be included in the discussion.

Mexican Homosexual Behavior. The Mexican mestizo culture places a high value on manliness. One of the salient features of the society is

thus a sharp delimitation between the roles played by males and females. Role expectations in general are for the male to be dominant and independent and for the female to be submissive and dependent. The continued sharp boundary between male and female roles in Mexico appears to be due in part to a culturally defined hypermasculine ideal model of manliness, referred to under the label *machismo.* The ideal female role is generally believed to be the reciprocal of the macho (male) role.[6]

As a consequence of the high status given manliness, Mexican males from birth onward are expected to behave in as manly a way as possible. Peñalosa (1968) sums it up as follows: "Any signs of feminization are severely repressed in the boy." McGinn (1966) concludes: "The young Mexican boy may be severely scolded for engaging in feminine activities, such as playing with dolls or jacks. Parents verbally and physically punish feminine traits in their male children." The importance of manly behavior continues throughout the life span of Mexican males.

One result of the sharp dichotomization of male and female gender roles is the widely held belief that effeminate males basically prefer to play the female role rather than the male. The link between male effeminacy and homosexuality is the additional belief that as a result of this role preference effeminate males are sexually interested only in masculine males with whom they play the passive sex role. Although the motivations of males participating in homosexual encounters are without question diverse and complex, the fact remains that in Mexico cultural pressure is brought to bear on effeminate males to play the passive insertee role in sexual intercourse, and a kind of de facto cultural approval is given (that is, no particular stigma is attached to) masculine males who want to play the active insertor role in homosexual intercourse.

The beliefs linking effeminate males with homosexuality are culturally transmitted by a vocabulary which provides the appropriate labels, by homosexually oriented jokes and word games (*albures*), and by the mass media. The links are established at a very early age. From early childhood on, Mexican males are made aware of the labels used to denote male homosexuals and the connection is always clearly made that these homosexual males are guilty of unmanly effeminate behavior.

The author's data also support the notion that prior to puberty effeminate males in Mexico are targeted as sexual objects for adolescent and adult males, and are expected to play the passive insertee sex role in anal intercourse. Following the onset of puberty, they continue to be sexual targets for other males because of their effeminacy. The consensus of my effeminate respondents in Mexico is that regardless of whether they are at school, in a movie theater, on the downtown streets, in a park, or in their own neighborhood, they are sought out and expected to play the anal passive sex role by more masculine males. As one fourteen-year-old respondent put it, in response to the question of where he had looked for sexual contacts during the year prior to the interview: "I didn't have to search for them . . . they looked for me."

The other side of the coin is represented by masculine male participants in homosexual encounters. Given the fact that effeminate males in Mexico are assumed homosexual and thus considered available as sexual outlets, how do the cultural factors contribute to the willingness of masculine males to play the active insertor sex role? The available data suggest that, insofar as the social variables are concerned, their willingness to participate in homosexual encounters is due to the relatively high level of sexual awareness that exists among males in the society, to the lack of stigmatization of the insertor sex role, and to the restraints that may be placed on alternative sexual outlets by available income and/or by marital status. The only cultural proscriptions are that "masculine" males should not play the passive sex role and should not be exclusively involved with homosexual intercourse.

The passive sex role is by inference—through the cultural equivalence of effeminacy with homosexuality—prescribed for "effeminate" males. It becomes a self-fulfilling prophecy of the society that effeminate males (a majority?) are eventually, if not from the beginning, pushed toward exclusively homosexual behavior. Some do engage in heterosexual intercourse, and some marry and set up households; but these probably are a minority of the identifiably effeminate males among the mestizos of the Mexican population.

Brazilian Homosexual Behavior.

Both Young (1973) and Fry (1974) note the relationship between cross-gender behavior and homosexuality in Brazil:

Brazilians are still pretty hung-up about sexual roles. Many Brazilians believe in the *bicha/bofe* (femme/butch) dichotomy and try to live by it. In Brazil, the average person doesn't even recognize the existence of the masculine homosexual. For example, among working-class men, it is considered all right to fuck a *bicha,* an accomplishment of sorts, just like fucking a woman. (Young, 1973)

In the simplest of terms, a male is a man until he is assumed or proved to have "given" in which case he becomes a *bicha.* With very few exceptions, males who "eat" *bichas* are not classified as anything other than "real men." Under this classificatory scheme they differ in no way from males who restrict themselves to "eating" females. (Note: the male who gives is an insertee, the one who eats is an insertor.) (Fry, 1974)

Southern European Homosexual Behavior.

Contemporary patterns of male homosexual behavior in Greece appear similar to those observed by the author in Mexico. An American anthropologist who collected data on homosexual behavior in Greece while working there on an archaeological project (Bialor, 1975) found, for example, that preferences for playing one sex role or the other (anal insertor or anal insertee) appear to be highly developed among Greek males. Little or no stigma is attached to the masculine male who plays the active insertor role. The social setting in modern Greece also appears to be strikingly similar to that in modern Mexico. Karlen (1971) describes it as follows:

The father spends his spare time with other men in cafes; society is a male club, and there all true companionship lies. Women live separate, sequestered lives. Girls' virginity is carefully protected, and the majority of homicides are committed over the "honor" of daughters and sisters. In some Greek villages a woman does not leave her home unaccompanied by a relative between puberty and old age. Women walk the street, even in Athens, with their eyes down; a woman who looks up when a man speaks to her is, quite simply, a whore. The young male goes to prostitutes and may carry on homosexual connections; it is not unusual for him to marry at thirty having had no sexual experience save with prostitutes and male friends. (p. 16)

In an evaluation of the strategy of Turkish boys' verbal dueling rhymes, Dundes, Leach, and Ozkok (1972) make the following observations about homosexual behavior in Turkey:

It is extremely important to note that the insult refers to *passive* homosexuality, not to homosexuality in general. In this context there is nothing insulting about being the active homosexual. In a homosexual relationship, the active phallic aggressor gains status; the passive victim of such aggression loses status. It is important to play the active role in a homosexual relationship; it is shameful and demeaning to be forced to take the passive role.

Moroccan Homosexual Behavior. The author does not know of any formal studies of homo-sexual behavior in Morocco. The available information suggests, however, that contemporary patterns of homosexual behavior in Morocco are similar to those in Mexico; that is, as long as Moroccan males play the active, insertor sex role in the relationship, there is never any question of their being considered homosexual. Based on his field work in Morocco shortly after the turn of the century, Westermarck (1908) believed that "a very large proportion of the men" in some parts of the country were involved in homosexual activity. He also noted that "in Morocco active pederasty is regarded with almost complete indifference, whilst the passive sodomite, if a grown-up individual, is spoken of with scorn. Dr. Polak says the same of the Persians." Contemporary patterns of homosexual behavior in the Islamic Arab countries of North Africa are probably similar to those in Morocco. . . .

DISCUSSION

Heterosexual intercourse, marriage, and the creation of a family are culturally established as primary objectives for adults living in all of the societies discussed above. Ford and Beach (1951) concluded from their cross-cultural survey that "all known cultures are strongly biased in favor of copulation between males and females as contrasted with alternative avenues of sexual expression." They further note that this viewpoint is biologically adaptive in that it favors perpetuation of the species and social group, and that societies favoring other nonreproductive forms of sexual expression for adults would not be likely to survive for many generations.

Homosexual intercourse appears to be the most important alternative form of sexual expression utilized by people living around the world. All cultures have established rules and regulations that govern the selection of a sexual partner or partners. With respect to homosexual behavior, however, there appear to be greater variations of the rules and regulations. And male homosexual behavior generally appears to be more regulated by cultures than female homosexual behavior. This difference may be the result of females being less likely than males to engage in homosexual activity; but it may also just be the result of a lack of data on female as compared with male homosexual behavior cross-culturally.

Exclusive homosexuality, however, because of the cultural dictums concerning marriage and the family, appears to be generally excluded as a sexual option even in those societies where homosexual behavior is generally approved. For example, the two societies where all male individuals are free to participate in homosexual activity if they choose, Siwan and East Bay, do not sanction exclusive homosexuality.[7] Although nearly all male members of these two societies are reported to engage in extensive homosexual activities, they are not permitted to do so exclusively over their adult life span. Davenport (1965) reports that "East Bay is a society which permits men to be either heterosexual or bisexual in their behavior, but denies the possibility of the exclusively homosexual man." He notes that "they have no concept and therefore no word for the exclusive homosexual." There are not much data available on the Siwans, but it has been reported that whether single or married, Siwan males "are expected to have both homosexual and heterosexual affairs" (Ford & Beach, 1951).

In East Bay there are two categories of homosexual relationships. One category appears similar to that found in a number of Melanesian societies; an older man plays the active (insertor) sex role in anal intercourse with younger boys "from seven to perhaps eleven years of age." Davenport notes:

The man always plays the active role, and it is considered obligatory for him to give the boy presents in return for accommodating him. A man would not engage his own son in such a relationship, but fathers do not object when friends use their young sons in this way, provided the adult is kind and generous. (p. 200)

The other category is between young single men of the same age group who play both sex roles in anal intercourse. The young men, however, "are not regarded as homosexual lovers. They are simply friends or relatives, who, understanding each other's needs and desires, accommodate one another thus fulfilling some of the obligations of kinship and friendship." This category may be related to several social factors which limit heterosexual contacts of young single men. First, the population is highly masculine with a male/female ratio of 120:100 in the fifteen- to twenty-five-year-old age group. Second, females have historically been brought in as wives for those who could afford the bride price. Third, sexual relations between unmarried individuals and adultery are forbidden. Both relationships are classed as larcenies and "only murder carries a more severe punishment." At first marriage a bride is expected to be a virgin. Chastity is highly valued in that it indicates adultery is less likely to occur after marriage. And fourth, there is "an extensive system for separating the sexes by what amounts to a general social avoidance between men and women in all but a few situations." From early adolescence on, unmarried men and boys sleep and eat in the men's house; and married men spend much of their time there during the day. Davenport notes that both masturbation and anal copulation are socially approved and regarded as substitutes for heterosexual intercourse by members of the society. Female homosexual activity is not reported in East Bay.

Among Siwan males the accepted homosexual relationship is "between a man and a boy but not between adult men or between two young boys" (Bullough, 1976). They are reported to practice anal intercourse with the adult man always playing the active (insertor) sex role. In this society, boys are more valued than girls. Allah (1917) reports that

. . . bringing up of a boy costs very little whereas the girl needs ornaments, clothing, and stains. Moreover the boy is a very fruitful source of profit for the father, not for the work he does, but because he is hired by his father to another man to be used as a catamite. Sometimes two men exchange their sons. If they are asked about this, they are not ashamed to mention it.

Homosexual activity is not reported for Siwan females.

The way in which cross-gender behavior is linked to homosexual behavior, and the meaning ascribed to the "homosexual" behavior by participants and significant others, differ between the three categories of societies identified in this study. What is considered homosexuality in one culture may be considered appropriate behavior within prescribed gender roles in another, a homosexual act only on the part of one participant in another, or a ritual act involving growth and masculinity in still another. Care must therefore be taken when judging sexual behavior cross-culturally with such culture-bound labels as "homosexual" and "homosexuality."

From a cultural point of view, deviations from sexual mores in a given society appear most likely to occur as a result of the lack of appropriate sexual partners and/or a result of conditioning in approved sexual behavior which is limited by age or ritual (for example, where homosexual intercourse is only appropriate for a certain age group and/or ritual time period and inappropriate thereafter). Homosexual activity initiated by sociocultural variables may over time through interaction with personality variables, produce an outcome not in accordance with the sexual mores of the society.

The findings presented in this chapter illustrate the profound influence of culture on the structuring of individual patterns of sexual behavior. Whether from biological or psychological causation, cross-gender behaving individuals in many societies must cope with a cultural formulation which equates their behavior with homosexual activity and thus makes it a self-fulfilling prophecy that they become homosexually involved. There are also individuals in many societies who might *prefer* to be exclusively homosexual but are prevented from doing so by cultural edicts. From whatever causes that homosexual impulses originate, whether they be biological or psychological, culture provides an additional dimension that cannot be ignored.

CRITICAL-THINKING QUESTIONS

1. What type of society tends to be accepting of homosexuality? What kind of society is disapproving of this sexual orientation? Why?
2. What insights can be drawn from this article that help to explain violence and discrimination directed toward gay people in U.S. society?
3. Are data about sexuality easily available to researchers? Why not?

NOTES

1. Homosexual behavior or activity will be used here to describe sexual behavior between individuals of the same sex; it may have nothing to do with sexual object choice or sexual orientation of the individual involved. Additionally, the terms "sex role" and "gender role" will be used to describe different behavioral phenomena. As Hooker (1965) points out, they "are often used interchangeably, and with resulting confusion." Following her suggestion the term "sex role," when homosexual practices are described, will refer to typical sexual performance only. "The gender connotations (M-F) of these performances need not then be implicitly assumed." The term "gender role" will refer to the expected attitudes and behavior that distinguish males from females.

2. The Human Relations Area Files (HRAF) contain information on the habits, practices, customs, and behavior of populations in hundreds of societies around the world. These files utilize accounts given not only by anthropologists but also by travelers, writers, missionaries, and explorers. Most cross-cultural surveys of sexual behavior, like those of Ford and Beach and Broude and Greene, have been based on HRAF information. A major criticism of the HRAF information on sexual behavior relates to the difficulty of assessing the reliability of the data collected in different time periods by different people with varying amounts of scientific training as observers.

3. "Preliterate" refers to essentially tribal societies that do not have a written language; "peasant" refers to essentially agrarian literate societies; and "complex modern" refers to highly industrialized societies.

4. In one of the first scholarly surveys of homosexual behavior done by an anthropologist, Westermarck (1908) concluded that: "A very important cause of homosexual practices is absence of the other sex."

5. The confounding of transvestism with homosexuality still occurs. For example, Minturn, Grosse, and Haider (1969) coded male homosexuality with transvestism in a recent study of the patterning of sexual beliefs and behavior, "because it is often difficult to distinguish between the two practices, and because they are assumed to be manifestations of the same psychological processes and to have similar causes."

6. The roles described represent the normative cultural ideals of the mestizoized national culture. Mestizos are Mexican nationals of mixed Indian and Spanish ancestry. They make up a large majority of the population, and their culture is the dominant one.

7. Both societies are small, each totaling less than 1,000 inhabitants. The Siwans live in an oasis in the Libyan desert. The people of East Bay (a pseudonym) live in a number of small coastal villages in an island in Melanesia.

REFERENCES

ALLAH, M. 1917. Siwan customs. *Harvard African Studies,* 1: 7.

ANGELINO, A., and C. SHEDD. 1955. A note on berdache. *American Anthropologist,* 57: 121–25.

Associated Press. 1979. Eunuchs gather for convention in India. *Panipat,* February 6, 1979.

BIALOR, P. 1975. Personal communication.

BOGORES, W. 1904. The Chukchee. *Memoirs of American Museum of Natural History,* 2: 449–51.

BROUDE, G., and S. GREENE. 1976. Cross-cultural codes on twenty sexual attitudes and practices. *Ethnology,* 15(4): 410–11.

BULLOUGH, V. 1976. *Sexual variance in society and history,* 22–49. New York: John Wiley.

CARRIER, J. 1976. Cultural factors affecting urban Mexican male homosexual behavior. *Archives of Sexual Behavior,* 5(2): 103–24.

———. 1977. Sex-role preference as an explanatory variable in homosexual behavior. *Archives of Sexual Behavior,* 6(1): 53–65.

CARSTAIRS, G. 1956. Hinjra and Jiryan: Two derivatives of Hindu attitudes to sexuality. *British Journal of Medical Psychology,* 2: 129–32.

DAVENPORT, W. 1965. Sexual patterns and their regulation in a society of the southwest Pacific. In *Sex and behavior,* 164–207. New York: John Wiley.

DEVEREUX, G. 1937. Institutionalized homosexuality of the Mohave Indians. In *The problem of homosexuality in modern society,* 183–226. New York: E. P. Dutton.

DUNDES, A., J. LEACH, and B. OZKOK. 1972. The strategy of Turkish boys' verbal dueling. In *Directions in sociolinguistics: The ethnography of communication.* New York: Holt.

FORD, C. S., and F. A. BEACH. 1951. *Patterns of sexual behavior.* New York: Harper & Row.

FRY, P. 1974. Male homosexuality and Afro-Brazilian possession cults. Unpublished paper presented to Symposium on Homosexuality in Crosscultural Perspective, 73rd Annual Meeting of the American Anthropological Association, Mexico City.

HOOKER, E. 1965. An empirical study of some relations between sexual patterns and gender identity in male homosexuals. In *Sex research: New developments,* 24–25. New York: Holt.

KARLEN, A. 1971. *Sexuality and homosexuality: A new view.* New York: W. W. Norton.

KROEBER, A. 1940. Psychosis or social sanction. *Character and personality,* 8: 204–15. Reprinted in *The nature of culture,* 313. Chicago: University of Chicago Press, 1952.

LEVY, R. 1973. *Tahitians.* Chicago: University of Chicago Press.

MARSHALL, D., and R. SUGGS. 1971. *Human sexual behavior,* 220–21. New York: Basic Books.

McGINN, N. 1966. Marriage and family in middle-class Mexico. *Journal of Marriage and Family Counseling,* 28: 305–13.

MEAD, M. 1961. Cultural determinants of sexual behavior. In *Sex and internal secretions,* 1433–79. Baltimore: Williams & Wilkins.

MINTURN, L., M. GROSSE, and S. HAIDER. 1969. Cultural patterning of sexual beliefs and behavior. *Ethnology,* 8(3): 3.

MORRISON, J. 1935. *The journal of James Morrison.* London: Golden Cockeral Press.

MUNROE, R., J. WHITING, and D. HALLY. 1969. Institutionalized male transvestism and sex distinctions. *American Anthropologist,* 71: 87–91.

OPLER, M. 1960. The Hijarā (hermaphrodites) of India and Indian national character: A rejoinder. *American Anthropologist,* 62(3): 505–11.

PEÑALOSA, F. 1968. Mexican family roles. *Journal of Marriage and Family Counseling,* 30: 680–89.

ROYCE, A. 1973. Personal communication.

SHAH, A. 1961. A note on the Hijadās of Gujarat. *American Anthropologist,* 63(6): 1325–30.

STOLLER, R. 1976. Two feminized male American Indians. *Archives of Sexual Behavior,* 5(6): 536.

WESTERMARCK, E. 1908. On homosexual love. In *The origin and development of the moral ideas.* London: Macmillan.

WILLIAMS, F. 1936. *Papuans of the trans-fly.* London: Oxford University Press.

YOUNG, A. 1973. Gay gringo in Brazil. In *The gay liberation book,* eds. L. Richmond and G. Noguera, 60–67. San Francisco: Ramparts Press.

CLASSIC

CONTEMPORARY

CROSS-CULTURAL

37 Some Principles of Stratification

KINGSLEY DAVIS AND WILBERT E. MOORE,
WITH A RESPONSE BY MELVIN TUMIN

Why is some degree of social stratification found everywhere? This selection outlines what has become known as the "Davis and Moore thesis": Social stratification is a consequence of the fact that some social positions are more important to the operation of a social system than others. The selection is followed by a critical response by Melvin Tumin, who suggests a number of ways in which social stratification is dysfunctional *for society.*

Starting from the proposition that no society is "classless," or unstratified, an effort is made to explain, in functional terms, the universal necessity which calls forth stratification in any social system. Next, an attempt is made to explain the roughly uniform distribution of prestige as between the major types of positions in every society. Since, however, there occur between one society and another great differences in the degree and kind of stratification, some attention is also given

Sources: "Some Principles of Stratification," by Kingsley Davis and Wilbert E. Moore, in *American Sociological Review,* vol. 10, no. 2 (April, 1945), pp. 242–44.

"Some Principles of Stratification: A Critical Analysis," by Melvin Tumin, in *American Sociological Review,* vol. 10, no. 4 (Aug., 1953), pp. 387–93. Reprinted with permission.

to the varieties of social inequality and the variable factors that give rise to them. . . .

Throughout, it will be necessary to keep in mind one thing—namely, that the discussion relates to the system of positions, not to the individuals occupying those positions. It is one thing to ask why different positions carry different degrees of prestige, and quite another to ask how certain individuals get into those positions. Although, as the argument will try to show, both questions are related, it is essential to keep them separate in our thinking. Most of the literature on stratification has tried to answer the second question (particularly with regard to the ease or difficulty of mobility between strata) without tackling the first. The first question, however, is logically prior and, in the case of any particular individual or group, factually prior.

THE FUNCTIONAL NECESSITY OF STRATIFICATION

Curiously, however, the main functional necessity explaining the universal presence of stratification is precisely the requirement faced by any society of placing and motivating individuals in the social structure. As a functioning mechanism a society must somehow distribute its members in social positions and induce them to perform the duties of these positions. It must thus concern itself with motivation at two different levels: to instill in the proper individuals the desire to fill certain positions, and, once in these positions, the desire to perform the duties attached to them. Even though the social order may be relatively static in form, there is a continuous process of metabolism as new individuals are born into it, shift with age, and die off. Their absorption into the positional system must somehow be arranged and motivated. This is true whether the system is competitive or noncompetitive. A competitive system gives greater importance to the motivation to achieve positions, whereas a noncompetitive system gives perhaps greater importance to the motivation to perform the duties of the positions; but in any system both types of motivation are required.

If the duties associated with the various positions were all equally pleasant to the human organism, all equally important to societal survival, and all equally in need of the same ability or talent, it would make no difference who got into which positions, and the problem of social placement would be greatly reduced. But actually it does make a great deal of difference who gets into which positions, not only because some positions are inherently more agreeable than others, but also because some require special talents or training and some are functionally more important than others. Also, it is essential that the duties of the positions be performed with the diligence that their importance requires. Inevitably, then, a society must have, first, some kind of rewards that it can use as inducements, and, second, some way of distributing these rewards differentially according to positions. The rewards and their distribution become a part of the social order, and thus give rise to stratification.

One may ask what kind of rewards a society has at its disposal in distributing its personnel and securing essential services. It has, first of all, the things that contribute to sustenance and comfort. It has, second, the things that contribute to humor and diversion. And it has, finally, the things that contribute to self respect and ego expansion. The last, because of the peculiarly social character of the self, is largely a function of the opinion of others, but it nonetheless ranks in importance with the first two. In any social system all three kinds of rewards must be dispensed differentially according to positions.

In a sense the rewards are "built into" the position. They consist in the "rights" associated with the position, plus what may be called its accompaniments or perquisites. Often the rights, and sometimes the accompaniments, are functionally related to the duties of the position. (Rights as viewed by the incumbent are usually duties as viewed by other members of the community.) However, there may be a host of subsidiary rights and perquisites that are not essential to the function of the position and have only an indirect and symbolic connection with its duties, but which still may be of considerable importance in inducing people to seek the positions and fulfill the essential duties.

If the rights and perquisites of different positions in a society must be unequal, then the society must be stratified, because that is precisely what stratification means. Social inequality is thus an unconsciously evolved device by which societies insure that the most important positions are conscientiously filled by the most qualified persons. Hence every society, no matter how simple or complex, must differentiate persons in terms of both prestige and esteem, and must therefore possess a certain amount of institutionalized inequality.

It does not follow that the amount or type of inequality need be the same in all societies. This is largely a function of factors that will be discussed presently.

THE TWO DETERMINANTS OF POSITIONAL RANK

Granting the general function that inequality subserves, one can specify the two factors that determine the relative rank of different positions. In general those positions convey the best reward, and hence have the highest rank, which (a) have the greatest importance for the society and (b) require the greatest training or talent. The first factor concerns function and is a matter of relative significance; the second concerns means and is a matter of scarcity.

Differential Functional Importance.   Actually a society does not need to reward positions in proportion to their functional importance. It merely needs to give sufficient reward to them to insure that they will be filled competently. In other words, it must see that less essential positions do not compete successfully with more essential ones. If a position is easily filled, it need not be heavily rewarded, even though important. On the other hand, if it is important but hard to fill, the reward must be high enough to get it filled anyway. Functional importance is therefore a necessary but not a sufficient cause of high rank being assigned to a position.[1]

Differential Scarcity of Personnel.   Practically all positions, no matter how acquired, require some form of skill or capacity for performance. This is implicit in the very notion of position, which implies that the incumbent must, by virtue of his incumbency, accomplish certain things.

There are, ultimately, only two ways in which a person's qualifications come about: through inherent capacity or through training. Obviously, in concrete activities both are always necessary, but from a practical standpoint the scarcity may lie primarily in one or the other, as well as in both. Some positions require innate talents of such high degree that the persons who fill them are bound to be rare. In many cases, however, talent is fairly abundant in the population but the training process is so long, costly, and elaborate that relatively few can qualify. Modern medicine, for example, is within the mental capacity of most individuals, but a medical education is so burdensome and expensive that virtually none would undertake it if the position of the M.D. did not carry a reward commensurate with the sacrifice.

If the talents required for a position are abundant and the training easy, the method of acquiring the position may have little to do with its duties. There may be, in fact, a virtually accidental relationship. But if the skills required are scarce by reason of the rarity of talent or the costliness of training, the position, if functionally important, must have an attractive power that will draw the necessary skills in competition with other positions. This means, in effect, that the position must be high in the social scale—must command great prestige, high salary, ample leisure, and the like.

How Variations Are to Be Understood.   Insofar as there is a difference between one system of stratification and another, it is attributable to whatever factors affect the two determinants of differential reward—namely, functional importance and scarcity of personnel. Positions important in one society may not be important in another, because the conditions faced by the societies, or their degree of internal development, may be different. The same conditions, in turn, may affect the question of scarcity; for in some societies the stage of development, or the external situation, may wholly obviate the necessity of certain kinds of skill or talent. Any particular system of stratification, then, can be understood as a product of the special conditions affecting the two aforementioned grounds of differential reward.

CRITICAL RESPONSE BY MELVIN TUMIN

The fact of social inequality in human society is marked by its ubiquity and its antiquity. Every known society, past and present, distributes its scarce and demanded goods and services unequally. And there are attached to the positions which command unequal amounts of such goods and services certain highly morally-toned evaluations of their importance for the society.

The ubiquity and the antiquity of such inequality has given rise to the assumption that there must be something both inevitable and positively functional about such social arrangements. . . . Clearly, the truth or falsity of such an assumption is a strategic question for any general theory of social organization. It is therefore most curious that the basic premises and implications of the assumption have only been most casually explored by American sociologists. . . .

Let us take [the Davis and Moore] propositions and examine them *seriatim.*

(1) *Certain positions in any society are more functionally important than others and require special skills for their performance.*

The key term here is "functionally important." The functionalist theory of social organization is by no means clear and explicit about this term. The minimum common referent is to something known as the "survival value" of a social structure. This concept immediately involves a number of perplexing questions. Among these are: (a) the issue of minimum versus maximum survival, and the possible empirical referents which can be given to those terms; (b) whether such a proposition is a useless tautology since any *status quo* at any given moment is nothing more and nothing less than everything present in the *status quo*. In these terms, all acts and structures must be judged positively functional in that they constitute essential portions of the *status quo;* (c) what kind of calculus of functionality exists which will enable us, at this point in our development, to add and subtract long and short range consequences, with their mixed qualities, and arrive at some summative judgment regarding the rating an act or structure should receive on a scale of greater or lesser functionality? At best, we tend to make primarily intuitive judgments. Often

enough, these judgments involve the use of value-laden criteria, or, at least, criteria which are chosen in preference to others not for any sociologically systematic reasons but by reason of certain implicit value preferences. . . .

A generalized theory of social stratification must recognize that the prevailing system of inducements and rewards is only one of many variants in the whole range of possible systems of motivation which, at least theoretically, are capable of working in human society. It is quite conceivable, of course, that a system of norms could be institutionalized in which the idea of threatened withdrawal of services, except under the most extreme circumstances, would be considered as absolute moral anathema. In such a case, the whole notion of relative functionality, as advanced by Davis and Moore, would have to be radically revised.

(2) *Only a limited number of individuals in any society have the talents which can be trained into the skills appropriate to these positions (i.e., the more functionally important positions).*

The truth of this proposition depends at least in part on the truth of proposition 1 above. It is, therefore, subject to all the limitations indicated above. But for the moment, let us assume the validity of the first proposition and concentrate on the question of the rarity of appropriate talent.

If all that is meant is that in every society there is a *range* of talent, and that some members of any society are by nature more talented than others, no sensible contradiction can be offered, but a question must be raised here regarding the amount of sound knowledge present in any society concerning the presence of talent in the population.

For, in every society there is some demonstrable ignorance regarding the amount of talent present in the population. *And the more rigidly stratified a society is, the less chance does that society have of discovering any new facts about the talents of its members.* Smoothly working and stable systems of stratification, wherever found, tend to build in obstacles to the further exploration of the range of available talent. This is especially true in those societies where the opportunity to discover talent in any one generation varies with the differential resources of the parent generation. Where, for instance, access to education depends upon the wealth of one's parents, and where wealth is differentially distributed, large segments of the population are likely to be deprived of the chance even to *discover* what are their talents.

Whether or not differential rewards and opportunities are functional in any one generation, it is clear that if those differentials are allowed to be socially inherited by the next generation, then the stratification system is specifically dysfunctional for the discovery of talents in the next generation. In this fashion, systems of social stratification tend to limit the chances available to maximize the efficiency of discovery, recruitment and training of "functionally important talent."

. . . In this context, it may be asserted that there is some noticeable tendency for elites to restrict further access to their privileged positions, once they have sufficient power to enforce such restrictions. This is especially true in a culture where it is possible for an elite to contrive a high demand and a proportionately higher reward for its work by restricting the numbers of the elite available to do the work. The recruitment and training of doctors in modern United States is at least partly a case in point. . . .

(3) *The conversion of talents into skills involves a training period during which sacrifices of one kind or another are made by those undergoing the training.*

Davis and Moore introduce here a concept, "sacrifice," which comes closer than any of the rest of their vocabulary of analysis to being a direct reflection of the rationalizations, offered by the more fortunate members of a society, of the rightness of their occupancy of privileged positions. It is the least critically thought-out concept in the repertoire, and can also be shown to be least supported by the actual facts.

In our present society, for example, what are the sacrifices which talented persons undergo in the training period? The possibly serious losses involve the surrender of earning power and the cost of the training. The latter is generally borne by the parents of the talented youth undergoing training, and not by the trainees themselves. But this cost tends to be paid out of income which the parents were able to earn generally by virtue of *their* privileged positions in the hierarchy of stratification. That is to say, the parents' ability to pay for the training of their children is part of the differential *reward* they, the parents, received for their privileged positions in the society. And to charge this sum up against sacrifices made by the youth is falsely to perpetrate a bill or a debt already paid by the society to the parents. . . .

What tends to be completely overlooked, in addition, are the psychic and spiritual rewards which are available to the elite trainees by comparison with their age peers in the labor force. There is, first, the much higher prestige enjoyed by the college student and the professional-school student as compared with persons in shops and offices. There is, second, the extremely highly valued privilege of having greater opportunity for self-development. There is, third, all the psychic gain involved in being allowed to delay the assumption of adult responsibilities such as earning a living and supporting a family. There is, fourth, the access to leisure and freedom of a kind not likely to be experienced by the persons already at work.

If these are never taken into account as rewards of the training period it is not because they are not concretely present, but because the emphasis in American concepts of reward is almost exclusively placed on the material returns of positions. The emphases on enjoyment, entertainment, ego enhancement, prestige and esteem are introduced only when the differentials in these which accrue to the skilled positions need to be justified. If these other rewards were taken into account, it would be much more difficult to demonstrate that the training period, as presently operative, is really sacrificial. Indeed, it might turn out to be the case that even at this point in their careers, the elite trainees were being differentially rewarded relative to their age peers in the labor force. . . .

(4) In order to induce the talented persons to undergo these sacrifices and acquire the training, their future positions must carry an inducement value in the form of differential, i.e., privileged and disproportionate access to the scarce and desired rewards which the society has to offer.

Let us assume, for the purposes of the discussion, that the training period is sacrificial and the talent is rare in every conceivable human society. There is still the basic problem as to whether the allocation of differential rewards in scarce and desired goods and services is the only or the most efficient way of recruiting the appropriate talent to these positions.

For there are a number of alternative motivational schemes whose efficiency and adequacy ought at least to be considered in this context. What can be said, for instance, on behalf of the motivation which De Man called "joy in work," Veblen termed "instinct for workmanship" and which we latterly have come to identify as "intrinsic work satisfaction"? Or, to what extent could the motivation of "social duty" be institutionalized in such a fashion that self-interest and social interest come closely to coincide? Or, how much prospective confidence can be placed in the possibilities of institutionalizing "social service" as a widespread motivation for seeking one's appropriate position and fulfilling it conscientiously?

Are not these types of motivations, we may ask, likely to prove most appropriate for precisely the "most functionally important positions"? Especially in a mass industrial society, where the vast majority of positions become standardized and routinized, it is the skilled jobs which are likely to retain most of the quality of "intrinsic job satisfaction" and be most readily identifiable as socially serviceable. Is it indeed impossible then to build these motivations into the socialization pattern to which we expose our talented youth? . . .

(5) These scarce and desired goods consist of rights and perquisites attached to, or built into, the positions and can be classified into those things which contribute to (a) sustenance and comfort; *(b) humor and diversion; (c) self-respect and ego expansion.*

(6) This differential access to the basic rewards of the society has as a consequence the differentiation of the prestige and esteem which various strata acquire. This may be said, along with the rights and perquisites, to constitute institutionalized social inequality, i.e., stratification.

With the classification of the rewards offered by Davis and Moore there need be little argument. Some question must be raised, however, as to whether any reward system, built into a general stratification system, must allocate equal amounts of all three types of reward in order to function effectively, or whether one type of reward may be emphasized to the virtual neglect of others. This raises the further question regarding which type of emphasis is likely to prove most effective as a differential inducer. Nothing in the known facts about human motivation impels us to favor one type of reward over the other, or to insist that all three types of reward must be built into the positions in comparable amounts if the position is to have an inducement value.

It is well known, of course, that societies differ considerably in the kinds of rewards they emphasize in their efforts to maintain a reasonable balance between responsibility and reward. There are, for instance, numerous societies in which the conspicuous display of differential economic advantage is considered extremely bad taste. In short, our present knowledge commends to us the possibility of considerable plasticity in the way in which different types of rewards can be structured into a functioning society. This is to say, it cannot yet be demonstrated that it is *unavoidable* that differential prestige and esteem shall accrue to positions which command differential rewards in power and property.

What does seem to be unavoidable is that differential prestige shall be given to those in any society who conform to the normative order as against those who deviate from that order in a way judged immoral and detrimental. On the assumption that the continuity of a society depends on the continuity and stability of its normative order, some such distinction between conformists and deviants seems inescapable.

It also seems to be unavoidable that in any society, no matter how literate its tradition, the older, wiser and more experienced individuals who are charged with the enculturation and socialization of the young must have more power than the young, on the assumption that the task of effective socialization demands such differential power.

But this differentiation in prestige between the conformist and the deviant is by no means the same distinction as that between strata of individuals each of which operates *within* the normative order, and is composed of adults. . . .

(7) *Therefore, social inequality among different strata in the amounts of scarce and desired goods, and the amounts of prestige and esteem which they receive, is both positively functional and inevitable in any society.*

If the objections which have heretofore been raised are taken as reasonable, then it may be stated that the only items which any society *must* distribute unequally are the power and property necessary for the performance of different tasks. If such differential power and property are viewed by all as commensurate with the differential responsibilities, and if they are culturally defined as *resources* and not as rewards, then no differentials in prestige and esteem need follow.

Historically, the evidence seems to be that every time power and property are distributed unequally, no matter what the cultural definition, prestige and esteem differentiations have tended to result as well. Historically, however, no systematic effort has ever been made, under propitious circumstances, to develop the tradition that each man is as socially worthy as all other men so long as he performs his appropriate tasks conscientiously. While such a tradition seems utterly utopian, no known facts in psychological or social science have yet demonstrated its impossibility or its dysfunctionality for the continuity of a society. The achievement of a full institutionalization of such a tradition seems far too remote to contemplate. Some successive approximations at such a tradition, however, are not out of the range of prospective social innovation.

What, then, of the "positive functionality" of social stratification? Are there other, negative, functions of institutionalized social inequality which can be identified, if only tentatively? Some such dysfunctions of stratification have already been suggested in the body of this paper. Along with others they may now be stated, in the form of provisional assertions, as follows:

1. Social stratification systems function to limit the possibility of discovery of the full range of talent available in a society. This results from the fact of unequal access to appropriate motivation, channels of recruitment, and centers of training.

2. In foreshortening the range of available talent, social stratification systems function to set limits upon the possibility of expanding the productive resources of the society, at least relative to what might be the case under conditions of greater equality of opportunity.

3. Social stratification systems function to provide the elite with the political power necessary to procure acceptance and dominance of an ideology which rationalizes the *status quo,* whatever it may be, as "logical," "natural" and "morally right." In this manner, social stratification systems function as essentially conservative influences in the societies in which they are found.

4. Social stratification systems function to distribute favorable self-images unequally throughout a population. To the extent that such favorable self-images are requisite to the development of the creative potential inherent in men, to that extent stratification systems function to limit the development of this creative potential.

5. To the extent that inequalities in social rewards cannot be made fully acceptable to the less privileged in a society, social stratification systems function to encourage hostility, suspicion, and distrust among the various segments of a society and thus to limit the possibilities of extensive social integration.

6. To the extent that the sense of significant membership in a society depends on one's place on the prestige ladder of the society, social stratification systems function to distribute unequally the sense of significant membership in the population.

7. To the extent that loyalty to a society depends on a sense of significant membership in the society, social

stratification systems function to distribute loyalty unequally in the population.

8. To the extent that participation and apathy depend upon the sense of significant membership in the society, social stratification systems function to distribute the motivation to participate unequally in a population.

Each of the eight foregoing propositions contains implicit hypotheses regarding the consequences of unequal distribution of rewards in a society in accordance with some notion of the functional importance of various positions. These are empirical hypotheses, subject to test. They are offered here only as exemplary of the kinds of consequences of social stratification which are not often taken into account in dealing with the problem. They should also serve to reinforce the doubt that social inequality is a device which is uniformly functional for the role of guaranteeing that the most important tasks in a society will be performed conscientiously by the most competent persons.

The obviously mixed character of the functions of social inequality should come as no surprise to anyone. If sociology is sophisticated in any sense, it is certainly with regard to its awareness of the mixed nature of any social arrangement, when the observer takes into account long- as well as short-range consequences and latent as well as manifest dimensions.

CRITICAL-THINKING QUESTIONS

1. Why do Davis and Moore argue that all societies attach greater rewards to some positions than to others?

2. Does the Davis and Moore thesis justify social stratification as it presently exists in the United States (or anywhere else)?

3. In what ways does Tumin argue that social stratification is *dysfunctional* for a social system?

NOTE

1. Unfortunately, functional importance is difficult to establish. To use the position's prestige to establish it, as is often unconsciously done, constitutes circular reasoning from our point of view. There are, however, two independent clues: (a) the degree to which a position is functionally unique, there being no other positions that can perform the same function satisfactorily; and (b) the degree to which other positions are dependent on the one in question. Both clues are best exemplified in organized systems of positions built around one major function. Thus in most complex societies the religious, political, economic, and educational functions are handled by distinct structures not easily interchangeable. In addition each structure possesses many different positions, some clearly dependent on, if not subordinate to, others. In sum, when an institutional nucleus becomes differentiated around one main function, and at the same time organizes a large portion of the population into its relationships, *key* positions in it are of the highest functional importance. The absence of such specialization does not prove functional unimportance, for the whole society may be relatively unspecialized; but it is safe to assume that the more important functions receive the first and clearest structural differentiation.

SOCIAL STRATIFICATION

CLASSIC

CONTEMPORARY

CROSS-CULTURAL

38 Who Has How Much and Why

ANDREW HACKER

*While many economists and politicians have applauded the expansion of the U.S. econ-
omy during the 1990s, a number of sociologists point out that income inequality is
greater now than it was in the 1960s: The rich have gotten richer, the middle class has
been shrinking, and the working class is barely surviving. In this selection, Andrew
Hacker explains why he believes that in terms of income and wealth, the United States is
one of the most stratified nations in the industrialized world.*

YES, THE RICH ARE GETTING RICHER

John F. Kennedy defended the importance of
business prosperity by arguing that "a rising tide
lifts all boats." It was a deft figure of speech: We
imagine tugboats, tankers, and superliners all together on the high water.

However, recent decades have failed to vali-
date Kennedy's thesis. Of course, there can be no
denying that the tide of wealth in America has
swelled. Between 1976 and 1996, the amount of
money in the hands of America's households rose
from $2.9 trillion to $4.8 trillion, after the 1976
figure is adjusted to 1996-value dollars. All told,
the income of the average household went from
$39,415 to $47,123, also in constant dollars,
resulting in a twenty-year gain of 19.6 percent.

[Table 1] shows how various segments of the
society fared during those two decades. Its figures, which come from annual Census Bureau
surveys, simply divide the total number of households into five equal groups, ranging from the
poorest to the best-off. So in 1996, each fifth
contained 20.2 million homes, consisting of families or of individuals living alone or together.
Thus the incomes of those in the middle fifth
ranged from $27,760 to $44,006, with an average
of $35,486. The Census also specifies the in-
comes of the richest 5 percent of all households.
Lastly, figures are given for the share of all
household income received by each segment.
Thus in 1996, the middle fifth ended up with
15.1 percent of the total, or $719 billion from the
$4.8 trillion.

Clearly, all boats did not rise equally with
this tide. Here were the twenty-year percentage
increases—and one decrease—in the average
income for each of the quintiles and also for the
top 5 percent:

Source: Reprinted with the permission of Scribner, an imprint
of Simon & Schuster Adult Publishing Group, from *Money:
Who Has How Much and Why* by Andrew Hacker. Copyright
© 1997 by Andrew Hacker.

Richest 5%	+59.9%	Middle 20%	+5.3%
Top 20%	+35.4%	Fourth 20%	+4.5%
Second 20%	+12.4%	Bottom 20%	−0.9%

While all segments of the population enjoyed an increase in income, the top fifth did thirteen times better than the fourth fifth. And measured by their shares of the aggregate, not just the bottom fifth but the three above it all ended up losing ground. Indeed, the overall share received by those segments, comprising four of every five households, dropped from 56.7 percent to 51.0 percent. At the same time, the average income of the richest 5 percent rose from a comfortable $126,131 to an affluent $201,684.

. . . Two factors intertwine. On the one hand, more of the 1996 households had two or more incomes coming in. Thus the $115,514 average for the top fifth could represent, say, $72,035 from one spouse and $43,479 from the other. But it is noteworthy that while there were also more dual earnings down in the fourth quintile, their income average rose by only $601 during the two decades.

The second factor is that 1976 to 1996 saw the creation of more high individual incomes at one end of the scale and more low incomes at the other. Thus the proportion of men earning more than $50,000—again, computed in constant dollars—grew from 14.9 percent to 17.6 percent. But overall, the median income for men dropped from $24,898 to $23,834, due to declining wages for those in the bottom tiers. All indications are that these disparities will continue in the decades ahead.

CHANGING STATES

If income disparities are on the rise, they are also being compressed. . . . In 1960, income in the richest state (Connecticut) was 2.6 times that of the poorest state (Mississippi). By 1996, the gap (Alaska versus West Virginia) had been reduced to a ratio of 2.0. And if the 1996 comparison stays with the contiguous states (New Jersey versus West Virginia), the richest–poorest ratio declines to 1.8.

Closing the gap has nurtured a national homogeneity. This is illustrated vividly in the shopping mall, which has emerged as America's most distinctive institution. Set down in malls in New Hampshire or New Mexico, we would be hard pressed to say where in the country we are. All have Gaps and Radio Shacks, multiplexes playing the same movies, and though food markets may have regional names, their merchandise is much the same.

Mobility also plays a role. The 1990 Census reported that over half the residents of New Hampshire, Florida, Wyoming, Nevada, Oregon, Arizona, Colorado, California, and Alaska had been born elsewhere. And by now, Maryland, Idaho, Delaware, Washington, Virginia, and New Mexico are likely to have joined the list. New

TABLE 1   How Households Divided the Nation's Income, 1976 and 1996 (in 1996-value dollars)

1976			1996	
Share of All Income	*Segment Average*	*Household Segments*	*Segment Average*	*Share of All Income*
43.3%	$85,335	Top 20%	$115,514	49.0%
24.8%	$48,876	Second 20%	$54,922	23.2%
17.1%	$33,701	Middle 20%	$35,486	15.1%
10.4%	$20,496	Fourth 20%	$21,097	9.0%
4.4%	$8,672	Bottom 20%	$8,596	3.7%
100.0%	$39,416	All Households	$47,123	100.0%
16.0%	$126,131	Richest 5%	$201,684	21.4%

arrivals adapt quite easily, since each year sees more Americans sharing common attitudes and attributes.

Among the more striking developments has been the economic rise of the South. In 1960, the six poorest states were all from that region, while by 1996 only three were. Indeed, household income doubled in Arkansas, Mississippi, and South Carolina. Among the losers, Ohio dropped to nine places behind Virginia, and New York's income fell below the national median [see Table 2].

WOMEN AND CHILDREN LAST?

All parents want their children to have a good start in life, and one underpinning is a family budget ample enough to provide a range of opportunities. Yet a rising proportion of children are growing up in homes without the means even for basic necessities.

In 1995, a third of all youngsters lived in homes with incomes of less than $25,000, and one in five were in homes where the income was below $15,000. At issue is what is required for growing up in modern America. More often than not, low incomes bring inferior local schools and inadequate exposure to the manners demanded by the wider world. As a result, millions of American children are deprived of a chance to develop whatever promise they have. Of course, poverty is not the only factor. We all know of youngsters, especially from immigrant families—who move far beyond the world of their parents. Still, two causes of the increased impoverishment of children should be singled out.

Of America's 70.3 million children aged eighteen or under, 31.3 percent are living with only one parent, or with a relative other than a parent, or in a foster home. The 68.7 percent with both of their parents in their home is an all-time low. In 1970, for example, the proportion was 85.2 percent. While it can be questioned whether two parents are necessary for a child's optimal development, the fact remains that single parents earn a lot less money. For two-parent families, the median income is $49,969, almost double the $26,990 for the relatively small group of single fathers and more than three times the $16,235 for single mothers. (The two-parent and one-parent families do not differ much in size. Those with two parents average 1.49 children; and those with single mothers average 1.34.) Nor is childhood poverty due only to marital breakups. Among today's single mothers, an all-time high of 35.6 percent have never been married. In 1970, the proportion was 7.1 percent.

Racial disparities are also reflected in the changing composition of families. As [Table 3] shows, even when black children are raised by two parents, their households are twice as likely as white two-parent homes to have incomes under $15,000. While the $43,946 median income for two-parent black families is fairly close to the $50,594 for whites, the overall black median is only 52.6 percent of the white figure. Moreover, the typical black woman who is raising children on her own must make do with $12,989, compared with $18,099 for the white single mother. These figures suggest that the United States disproportionately denies opportunities to black children. Stated another way, one reason why America's

TABLE 2   A Dozen Gainers and Losers

Gainers' Rank	1960	1996	Losers' Rank	1960	1996
Wisconsin	14th	7th	Michigan	5th	13th
Colorado	20th	6th	Ohio	7th	23rd
Iowa	30th	24th	New York	9th	27th
Virginia	34th	14th	Indiana	16th	26th
Georgia	40th	31st	New Mexico	25th	49th
North Carolina	46th	28th	West Virginia	37th	50th

TABLE 3   The Coming Generation: Incomes of Families
Where Children Are Being Raised

Incomes of White Families	All White Families	Two Parents (76.3%)	Mother Only (18.7%)*
Over $40,000	54.0%	65.0%	15.6%
$15,000–$40,000	32.6%	29.3%	42.6%
Under $15,000	13.4%	5.7%	41.8%
White Median	$43,091	$50,594	$18,099
Per Black $1,000	$1,901	$1,151	$1,393

Incomes of Black Families	All Black Families	Two Parents (39.7%)	Mother Only (54.0%)*
Over $40,000	28.1%	55.9%	8.5%
$15,000–$40,000	36.6%	35.3%	36.0%
Under $15,000	35.3%	8.8%	55.5%
Black Median	$22,671	$43,946	$12,989
Per White $1,000	$526	$869	$718

*The remaining 6.3 percent of black children and 5.0 percent of white children are living with their fathers or with other relatives or are in foster care.

children are not being allowed to show their true talents is that many of them are of African origin.

THE SALARY SPECTRUM

[Table 4] does not list the incomes of corporate chairmen, medical school professors, or investment firm partners. . . . This table records the wages and salaries of full-time workers in forty-two typical occupations.

Despite its reputation as a high-wage economy, the midpoint pay for America's full-time workers in 1996 was a rather modest $25,480, not really enough to give a family a middle-class living standard. The median for the 51.9 million employed men was $28,964, and for the 39.0 million women it was $21,736. (So an average working couple might bring in $50,700, which explains why there are so many dual-earner households.) The table's figures raise several questions and suggest some partial answers.

Women as a group are paid less, but is that because they are clustered in lower-wage occupations? The earnings of bank tellers, hairdressers, and sewing-machine operators suggest that this is the case. Yet the pay for nurses and elementary school teachers—jobs traditionally held by women—have surpassed that of many occupations dominated by men. (Teachers' unions tend to remain strong, while those of construction workers have lost much of their dominant force.) Moreover, each year finds more women in better-paid positions such as pharmacists, financial managers, and college professors.

Indeed, women now account for 38.9 percent of all pharmacists, compared with 12.1 percent in 1970. For insurance adjusters, the respective figures are 71.9 percent and 29.6 percent. And women now make up 54.2 percent of the nation's bartenders, as against 21.1 percent twenty-six years earlier. Yet these shifts do not always bring better earnings. When insurance adjuster was mainly a man's occupation, it paid well for inspecting dented cars and burned-out buildings. Today, most are women who tap claims into computers.

Many of the amenities we desire depend on a supply of low-wage workers. This is clearly the case with those who launder our linen and park

TABLE 4   Median Pay for Full-time Wage and Salary Workers, 1996
(with percentage of women in each occupation)

Above National Median	Earnings[1]	Women[2]	*Below National Median*	Earnings	Women
Lawyers (salaried)	$59,748	35.3%	Printing operators	$25,168	11.0%
Pharmacists	$51,584	38.9%	Automotive mechanics	$24,856	0.9%
Engineers	$49,348	8.6%	Flight attendants	$21,684	81.4%
Computer analysts	$46,332	28.3%	Secretaries	$21,112	98.5%
College faculty	$45,240	38.0%	Factory assemblers	$19,656	42.0%
Financial managers	$40,664	55.4%	Taxicab drivers	$19,448	8.4%
Computer programmers	$40,144	30.1%	Data entry keyers	$19,032	86.2%
Architects	$39,520	19.4%	Meat cutters	$19,032	21.7%
Registered nurses	$36,244	91.5%	Telephone operators	$18,876	88.9%
High school teachers	$36,244	54.8%	Security guards	$17,316	19.6%
Journalists	$35,776	50.0%	Bakers	$17,004	38.8%
Police officers	$34,684	12.4%	Bank tellers	$16,380	90.7%
Elementary school			Bartenders	$16,120	54.2%
teachers	$34,424	82.8%	Janitors and cleaners	$15,652	27.6%
Librarians	$34,320	82.9%	Hairdressers	$15,184	88.3%
Electricians	$31,772	2.2%	Garage workers	$14,352	3.3%
Realtors	$31,460	51.3%	Waiters and waitresses	$14,092	70.1%
Electronic repairers	$31,304	5.5%	Hotel clerks	$13,884	71.2%
Motor vehicle salespeople	$30,836	8.8%	Cooks and chefs	$13,728	35.2%
Designers	$30,784	48.0%	Laundry workers	$13,208	70.3%
Clergy	$27,768	11.5%	Sewing machine		
Insurance adjusters	$26,312	71.9%	operators	$13,208	83.0%

[1]All workers, median earnings: $25,480

[2]Median percentage of women: 42.9%

our cars. But it is also true of hotel clerks, most of whom are young people who haven't yet chosen a long-term career. Waiters and waitresses also tend to be younger or are older women bringing in a household's second income. Sewing-machine operators, many of whom are recent immigrants, often labor under third-world conditions. Were they to demand more than their current pay, their employers would probably send their work to an actual third-world country.

ARE WE STILL NUMBER ONE?

For most of the twentieth century, the United States has led the world in industrial production, technological innovation, and personal standards of living. In 1970, for example, America ranked first in per capita output. Our nearest rivals were Sweden, Canada, Denmark, and Switzerland, which like us

had escaped being World War II battlegrounds. At that time, even advanced countries such as the Netherlands and Britain were only half as productive as the United States. Yet there were signs that change was under way: A once bomb-scarred Germany had risen to sixth place.

The per capita figures for 1995, the most recent at this writing, show dramatic changes. The United States has fallen to sixth place [see Table 5], a sad descent considering that its primacy once seemed beyond challenge. Three other countries—Austria, France, and Belgium—were less than $100 behind America in per capita GDP. Most striking is that in the quarter-century, Japan tripled its per capita production. Although Sweden and the United Kingdom dropped in the rankings, their output still improved while America's was treading water.

Perhaps embarrassed by the GDP measure, which gave the United States sixth place, American

TABLE 5   Per Capita Gross Domestic Product and Purchasing Power
(per $1,000 for the United States)

GDP per Capita, 1970		GDP per Capita, 1995		Purchasing Power, 1995	
1. UNITED STATES	$1,000	Switzerland	$1,506	UNITED STATES	$1,000
2. Sweden	$857	Japan	$1,469	Switzerland	$958
3. Canada	$776	Norway	$1,158	Japan	$819
4. Denmark	$663	Denmark	$1,108	Norway	$813
5. Switzerland	$662	Germany	$1,020	Belgium	$803
6. Germany*	$641	UNITED STATES	$1,000	Austria	$788
7. Norway	$622	Austria	$997	Denmark	$787
8. France	$613	France	$926	Canada	$783
9. Australia	$572	Belgium	$916	France	$779
10. Belgium	$556	Netherlands	$890	Germany	$744
11. Netherlands	$497	Sweden	$880	Netherlands	$739
12. United Kingdom	$450	Finland	$763	Italy	$736
13. Austria	$409	Canada	$718	United Kingdom	$714
14. Japan	$404	Italy	$705	Sweden	$687
15. Italy	$365	United Kingdom	$693	Finland	$658

*West Germany only.

economists devised an alternative gauge. This index computes "personal purchasing power" for each country, by noting differing price levels. Example: While hourly wages in Britain and America are quite similar ($9.37 versus $9.56), the same basket of goods in Britain costs 42.2 percent more. With this new formula, the United States is once again number one, but not because our economy is more innovative or efficient. Prices are lower here due to a combination of choice and circumstance.

Other countries raise much of their public revenue from some variant of a "value-added tax," which is factored into the price of purchases. This charge tends to be "invisible" since it is seldom put on price tags or sales slips. But it clearly raises prices, as can be seen by what a gallon of gasoline costs here and abroad: Austria, $3.13; Italy, $3.46; Norway, $3.79; Japan, $4.14; United States, $1.24. Other countries tax themselves to provide funds for social services and public amenities. Americans have chosen lower taxes and prices and reduced levels of benefits.

America is the world's largest market, measured by the amount of money available for shopping. With one dominant language, national advertising media, and familiar brand names, economies of scale can be reflected in reduced prices. We have also mastered the delivery of bargains at complexes such as Price Cosco and Wal-Mart, and via mail from Lands' End and L. L. Bean. Other countries are beginning to build supermarkets and shopping centers, but they are still well behind America.

So, yes, the United States has the world's highest living standard—if gauged by the sums we devote to personal purchases. But being the leader in consumption is not necessarily a cause for congratulation. If production is what creates national wealth and the prospect of a prosperous future, America is no longer first and is unlikely to regain its primacy.

CRITICAL-THINKING QUESTIONS

1. What data does Hacker offer to support his argument that in the United States the rich are getting richer and the poor are getting poorer? Why does he predict that such disparities will continue?

2. According to Hacker, how do geographical mobility, sex, race, marital status, and occupation affect families' socioeconomic status?

3. How would you explain the increasing social stratification in the United States?

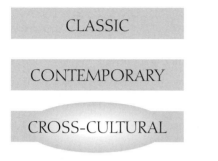

CLASSIC

CONTEMPORARY

CROSS-CULTURAL

39 The Uses of Global Poverty: How Economic Inequality Benefits the West

DAINA STUKULS EGLITIS

Why don't rich nations do more to reduce the severe poverty that paralyzes much of the world? This selection argues that people in rich countries, including the United States, actually benefit from global poverty in a number of ways.

In the global village, there stand a wide variety of homes, from the stately mansion on the hill, to the modest abode blessed with electricity and running water, to the adequate but unheated (or uncooled) hut, to the flood-prone, tattered shanty cobbled together from gathered scrap. Those who live on the hill are aware of their neighbors, as their neighbors are aware of them. Most inhabitants of the global village recognize that wealth and the accompanying opportunities for education, health care, and consumption are not evenly divided and that a substantial gap exists between the more and less materially blessed populations. Not everyone agrees on why that is the case.

Consider the following comparisons of life in the global village: In 1999, the gross national income in purchasing power parity (GNI PPP)[1] in the United States was $31,910. In Germany the figure was $23,510, and in Australia, $23,850. By contrast, the GNI PPP of China was $3,550, in Indonesia it was $2,660, and in Pakistan, $1,860. On the bottom tier of states, we find countries like

Nigeria with a GNI of $770 and Sierra Leone with just $440. If we use the GNI PPP as a yardstick of economic power and the well-being of populations, we may begin to construct a picture of a global system characterized by the massive maldistribution of wealth, economic security, and purchasing power. Our village is one characterized by deep and fundamental stratification.

What have been the responses of well-off states to this global class system with its extremes of wealth and poverty? Not surprisingly, perhaps, political rhetoric has consistently elevated the goal of spreading the prosperity enjoyed by the advanced industrial states of the West around the globe. In remarks made at the United States Coast Guard Academy commencement ceremony in 1989, President George Bush phrased it this way: "What is it that we want to see? It is a growing community of democracies anchoring international peace and stability, and a dynamic free-market system generating prosperity and progress on a global scale. . . . If we succeed, the next decade and the century beyond will be an era of unparalleled growth, an era which sees the flourishing of freedom, peace, and prosperity around the world."

Source: Reprinted by permission of the author.

If shared global prosperity was the goal, it seems safe to say that while there was some modest progress made in areas like Latin America, Eastern Europe, and parts of Asia, "we" did not really succeed, because the global wealth gap is still massive and growing. The rich countries remain rich, and the poor countries, for the most part, remain trapped in desperate, dire poverty. This has not changed.

Another thing that has not changed is the rhetorical commitment to spreading the wealth. In a speech in Coventry, England, in December 2000, President Bill Clinton laid out a "prescription for how the United States might help close the gap between rich and poor nations." And in his farewell address to the nation in January 2001, the President declared that "the global gap requires more than compassion. It requires action."

As of 2002, President George W. Bush has not addressed the question of non-Western development specifically, though it seems relatively safe to say that he too will join the political chorus of support for global prosperity, although his administration seems destined to be defined by a focus on war rather than development.

Western rhetoric, assistance programs, and advice seem to support the goal of global prosperity and its extension to the 1.3 billion who live on less than $1 per day and those millions or even billions more who eke out a sparse existence just above the threshold of absolute poverty. But the reality of prosperity has touched only a relative few countries, while the struggle to meet basic needs touches many more. Social indicators like the GNI PPP highlight the differences we find in our village. But what explains them? Why does global poverty exist and persist? Why does a global class system with a thin layer of rich states and a broad strata of poor countries exist and persist? What explains why some villagers inhabit houses on the mount while others squat in mud huts below? Possible answers are many. This article explores one way of understanding the yawning gap between the planet's wealthiest and poorest states.

In 1971, sociologist Herbert Gans published an article entitled "The Uses of Poverty: The Poor Pay All."[2] In the article, Gans utilized a conservative theoretical perspective in sociology, functionalism, to inquire about the persistence of poverty in America. The functionalist perspective takes as its starting point the position that essentially all institutions and social phenomena that exist in society contribute in some manner to that society—that is, they are functional for society. If they did not contribute to the social order, the functionalists maintain, they would disappear. Using this perspective, functionalists may inquire about, for instance, the functions, both obvious and hidden (or manifest and latent, to use sociologist Robert Merton's terms), of institutions like the education system or the family or social phenomena like punishment for deviance. These social theorists assume that institutions or phenomena exist because they are functional, and hence their guiding question is, What function do they serve?

Gans posed a similar question about poverty, asking, What are the uses of poverty? Clearly, the notion that poverty is functional for society as a whole is ludicrous: Who would suggest that it is functional for those who endure economic deprivation? So Gans offered a modified functionalist analysis: ". . . instead of identifying functions for an entire social system, I shall identify them for the interest groups, socioeconomic classes, and other population aggregates with shared values that 'inhabit' a social system. I suspect that in a modern heterogeneous society, few phenomena are functional or dysfunctional for the society as a whole, and that most result in benefits to some groups and costs to others."

Gans sought to explain the existence and persistence of poverty in modern, wealthy America by highlighting the way that the existence of poverty has benefits for the nonpoor—not just "evil" individuals like the loan shark or the slum lord, but for "normal" members of nonpoor classes. He identified thirteen "uses" of poverty, including the notions that the existence of a poor class "ensures that society's 'dirty work' will be done," that "the poor buy goods others do not want and thus prolong the economic usefulness of such goods," and "the poor can be identified and punished as alleged or real deviants in order to uphold the legitimacy of conventional norms." He was not arguing that poverty is good. He was suggesting that understanding poverty's existence and persistence means recognizing that the poor have positive social and economic functions for the nonpoor. Thus, one would conclude that the elimination of poverty, while elevated as a societal goal, would be, in practice, costly to the nonpoor.

While Gans's theoretically based inquiry into poverty was focused on America's poor, the same question might be asked about the existence of global poverty: What are the "uses" of global poverty for the better-off countries of the world economic system? The purpose of such an inquiry would be, as it was in Gans's inquiry, not to use a functionalist analysis to legitimate poverty or the highly skewed distribution of wealth in the global system, but to contribute to a deeper understanding of why it continues to exist by explaining how its persistence confers benefits on well-off states and their inhabitants.

The argument is not that advanced states are consciously conspiring to keep the poor states destitute: Well-off countries have historically sought to offer help to less developed countries. In reality, however, there are limited incentives for the better-off states to support the full industrial and technological (and even democratic) development of all the states in the global system. To the degree that the existence of a class of poor states is positively functional for wealthy states, we can begin to imagine why development and assistance programs that help ensure survival, but not prosperity, for poor populations are quite characteristic of Western policy.

This article notes eleven "uses" of global poverty. Global poverty is not, from this perspective, functional for the global community as a whole. The notion that the poverty of billions who live in economically marginal states is globally "useful" would be absurd. But it is not absurd to ask how the existence of a class of poor states serves wealthy states. In fact, asking such a question might contribute to a better understanding of the dual phenomena of global poverty and the global "class" system.

Point 1: The existence of global poverty helps ensure the wealth of affordable goods for Western consumers.

The cornucopia of decently priced goods of reasonable quality enjoyed by Western consumers is underpinned by the low-wage work done in low-income countries. The labels on the clothing you are wearing right now likely contain the familiar words "Made in China" or perhaps "Made in Pakistan." Your clothing is probably of reasonable quality, and you likely paid a reasonable (but not necessarily cheap) price for it.

The Western consumer of textiles such as off-the-rack clothing is a beneficiary of a globalized manufacturing process that has seen the movement of manufacturing to low-wage areas located in poor states that provide ready pools of workers needy enough to labor for a pittance. In China, the average hourly wage of apparel workers is about 23 cents. This benefits the consumer of that apparel. The worker herself (workers in this industry are usually female) derives less benefit: The average hourly wage needed to meet basic needs in China, according to Women's Edge, an advocacy group, is 87 cents.[3]

Another way that the impoverished workers of the third world help reduce the cost of goods coming to Western consumers is through their agricultural labor. For instance, the comparably (and sometimes illegally) low wages paid to many poor migrant farm workers from Mexico and Central America in states like California contribute to America's ample and reasonably priced food supply.

Stories about low-wage workers in developing countries have, in recent years, emerged in the Western press and provoked some expressions of outrage and the formation of groups like United

Students Against Sweatshops. These expressions have been small and limited. Imagine, however, the outrage if popular sports shoes, already pricey, climbed another $50 in cost as a result of manufacturers opting for well-paid, unionized labor. Or imagine if the price of a head of iceberg lettuce, America's favorite vegetable, suddenly doubled in price to $3.00. Which outrage would be more potent?

Point 2: The existence of global poverty benefits Western companies and shareholders in the form of increased profit margins.

Labor costs typically constitute a high percentage of a company's expenditures. By reducing labor costs, companies can both keep prices reasonable (which benefits, as noted, the consumer) and raise profit margins. Not surprisingly, then, companies are not likely to locate in—and are more likely to leave—locations where wages are relatively high. The use of poor female workers in the third world is, in this respect, especially "beneficial" to companies. Women comprise about 80 percent of workers in Export Processing Zones and are often paid 20 percent to 50 percent less than male counterparts. The less costly the workforce, the greater the opportunity for profit. Not coincidentally, countries with an ample supply of poor workers willing to work for miserable wages are also countries with lax safety and environmental regulations, which also keeps down the costs to the Western employer and pushes up the profits. Hence, companies benefit directly from the existence of economically deprived would-be workers willing (or not in a position to be unwilling) to work for paltry wages in potentially hazardous, or at least very unpleasant, conditions.

Point 3: The existence of global poverty fosters access to resources in poor states that are needed in or desired by the West.

Poor states may sell raw goods at low prices to Western states, which can transform the resource into a more valuable finished product. The position of the poor states in the world economy makes it less likely that they can derive the full benefit of the resources they possess for the government and people. The case of oil in resource-rich but desperately poor Nigeria is an example. Seven major foreign oil companies operate in Nigeria, all representing interests in wealthy states. The vast majority of benefits from Nigeria's oil has accrued not to the country's people, but to the companies (and consumers) of the wealthy states. There is no attempt to hide this: John Connor, head of Texaco's worldwide exploration and production, talking about a massive oil strike in January 2000, stated that the successful conclusion of the well test "sets the stage for development of a world-class project that will add substantially to the company's resource base."[4] Clearly, the failure of Nigeria's people to benefit from the country's resources is also linked to a succession of corrupt governments, but the poverty of the masses and the powerful position of oil companies help to ensure that resistance to exploitation of resources for the benefit of non-Nigerian interests will be marginal.

Point 4: The existence of global poverty helps support Western medical advances.

The poor provide a pool of guinea pigs for the testing of medicines developed for use primarily in the West. The beneficiaries are not the poor themselves but Western consumers of advanced medicine (60 percent of profits are made in the United States, which leads the world in drug consumption) and the pharmaceutical companies, which stand astride a $350 billion (and growing) industry. A series of reports in the *Washington Post* in December 2000 documents the disturbing practice of conducting drug trials on ill inhabitants of poor states. For instance, an unapproved antibiotic was tested by a major pharmaceutical company on sick children during a meningitis epidemic in Nigeria. The country's lax regulatory oversight, the sense among some doctors that they could not object to experiment conditions for political or economic reasons, the dearth of alternative health care options, combined with the desire of the company to rapidly prepare for the market a potential "blockbuster" drug under-pinned a situation in which disease victims were treated as test subjects rather than patients. This case highlights the way that nonpoor states actu-ally benefit from the existence of poor states with struggling, sick populations. A reporter for the series noted that "companies use the tests to produce new product and revenue streams, but they are also responding to pressure from regula-tors, Congress, and lobbyists for disease victims to develop new medicines quickly. By providing huge pools of human subjects, foreign trials help speed new drugs to the marketplace—where they will be sold mainly to patients in wealthy countries."[5]

Point 5: The existence of global poverty contributes to the advancement of Western economies and societies with the human capital of poor states.

Poorer states like India have become intellec-tual feeders of well-educated and bright individu-als whose skills cannot be fully rewarded in less developed states. The magnetic draw of a better life in economies that amply reward their human capital pulls the brightest minds from their coun-tries of origin, a process referred to as "brain drain." Advanced economies such as the United States and England are beneficiaries of brain drain. The United States has moved to take ad-vantage of the pool of highly educated workers from the developing world: Congress has passed legislation increasing the number of H-1B visas, or "high-tech visas," to bring up to 600,000 work-ers to the United States over the next several years. The United States and England offer attractive op-portunities to highly educated workers from poorer states. Notably, high-tech companies often pay the foreign workers less than their domestic equivalents would demand.

Point 6: The existence of global poverty may contribute to the pacification of the Western proletariat, or "Workers of the world, a blue light special!"

To some degree, the broad availability of good, inexpensive merchandise may help obscure class divisions in the West, at least in the arena of con-sumption. It is clear that those with greater wealth can consume more high-quality goods, but low-end "designer" merchandise is accessible to the less well-off in cathedrals of consumption such as Wal-Mart. At K-Mart, for instance, Martha Stewart peddles her wares, intended to transform "homemaking chores . . . into what we like to call 'domestic art.'" Thanks in part to the low-wage workers in places like China, these goods are available to the unwashed masses (now washed by Martha's smart and cozy towels) as well as to bet-ter-situated homemakers. Consumption appears to be one of the great equalizers of modern society. (It is worth noting, though, that many members of the Western working class are also "victims" of global poverty, since many jobs have gone abroad to low-wage areas, leaving behind, for less edu-cated workers, positions in the less remunerative and less secure service industry or leaving former industrial workers jobless.)

Point 7: Global poverty benefits the West because poor countries make optimal dumping grounds for goods that are dangerous, expired, or illegal.

Wealthy countries and their inhabitants may uti-lize poorer states as repositories for dangerous or unwanted material such as nuclear waste. The des-peration of cash-strapped states benefits better-off countries, which might otherwise have difficulty ridding themselves of the dangerous by-products of their industrial and consumer economies. For in-stance, in December 2000, the Russian Parliament, in an initial vote on the issue, overwhelmingly sup-ported the amendment of an environmental law to permit the importation of foreign nuclear waste. The alteration of the law was supported by the Atomic Ministry of the Russian Federation, which suggested that over the next decade, Russia might earn up to $21 billion from the importation of spent nuclear fuel from states like Japan, Germany, and South Korea. Likely repositories of the radioactive refuse are Mayak and Krasnoyarsk, already among the most contaminated sites on the planet.

India has also emerged as a dumping ground for hazardous junk from the world's industrial giants. The western Indian city of Alang, for instance, is host to the world's largest shipbreaking yard, where Western-owned ships are sent for dismantling and, ostensibly, recycling. The process of "breaking" the old vessels, however, endangers workers and the environment because it releases asbestos, PCBs, and other toxic wastes.[6]

Point 8: The existence of global poverty provides jobs for specialists employed to assist, advise, and study the world's poor and to protect the "better-off" from them.

Within this group of specialists we find people in a variety of professions. There are those who are professional development workers, operating through organizations like the United States Agency for International Development (USAID) to further "America's foreign policy interests in expanding democracy and free markets while improving the lives of the citizens of the developing world."[7] The Peace Corps is also built around the goal of bringing Western "know-how" to the poor with volunteer programs that promote entrepreneurship and agricultural development.

Academics in fields as diverse as economics, sociology, international affairs, political science, and anthropology study, write about, and "decipher" the lives of the poor and the condition of poor states. Texts on development, articles debating why poverty persists, and books from university presses are only some of the products of this research. Journalists and novelists can build careers around bringing colorful, compelling representations of the poor to the warm living rooms of literate, well-off consumers. Still others are charged with the task of protecting wealthy states from "invasions" of the poor: U.S. border patrols, for instance, employ thousands to keep those seeking better fortunes out of U.S. territory.

Point 9: Global poverty benefits inhabitants of wealthy countries, who can feel good about helping the global poor through charitable work and charitable giving.

From the celebrity-studded musical production "We are the World" to trick-or-treating for UNICEF, those who inhabit the wealthy corners of the world feel good about themselves for sharing their good fortune. The Web site of World Vision, a faith-based charity that offers the opportunity to sponsor poor children, features a speak-out area for contributors. On that site, a young Canadian sponsor wrote, "A few days ago I woke up early and turned the TV on . . . looking at those children made me realize I could help them. I thought if I have enough money to pay for the Internet, cell phone, and a couple of other things I didn't need, I said to myself, [then] why not give that money to people who need it instead of spending it all in (*sic*) luxury and things that are not really important. . . . I immediately picked up the phone and called to sponsor a child! I am happy. I can help someone who needs it!"[8]

Apparently, we need not feel guilt about consuming many times what the unfortunate inhabitants of the world's poor states do if only we are willing to give up a few of our luxuries to help them. Indeed, not only do the poor not inspire guilt, they may inspire positive feelings: As the World Vision writer notes, she feels "happy" because she can "help someone who needs it." No less a figure than the world's richest man, Bill Gates, is also "dedicated to improving people's lives by sharing advances in health and learning with the global community" through the Gates Foundation.[9]

A related point is that the poor we see on television or hear about in news or music give those of us in wealthy countries the opportunity to feel good about ourselves, regardless of our position in the socioeconomic structure of our own states. Consider the memorable lines from the 1985 Band-Aid song, "Do They Know It's Christmas?" which was produced by British pop artist Bob Geldorf as a charitable act to raise money for Ethiopia's famine victims: "And the Christmas bells that ring there are the clanging chimes of doom. Well, tonight, thank God, it's them instead of you." Indeed, even the underpaid blue- or pink-collar worker in the West can relate to that sentiment.

Point 10: The poverty of less developed states makes possible the massive flow of resources westward.

Imagine if large and largely poor countries like China, Nigeria, and India consumed at U.S. rates. At present, Americans consume a tremendously disproportionate share of the world's resources. With their profligate use of all manner of resources, most notably fossil fuels, Americans are the greediest consumers of natural resources on the planet. On both an absolute and per capita basis, most world resources flow westward. Notably, an October 4, 2000, article in the *Seattle Times* reported that bicycles, long a characteristic and popular means of transport for Chinese commuters, are losing popularity: "Increasingly, young Chinese are not even bothering to learn to ride bikes, because growing wealth has unleashed a plethora of transportation choices, public and private."[10] The new transportation of choice is still largely public buses or private taxis; the Chinese have not yet graduated to mass private cars. But it is interesting to ponder whether there would be enough (affordable) oil for everyone if the Chinese, with their growing population and prosperity, became a country of two-vehicle families or developed a taste and market for gas-guzzling sports utility vehicles. In this case, the West likely benefits from the fact that few can

afford (at least at present) to consume at the rate its people do.

Point 11: The poorer countries, which reproduce at rates higher than Western states, are useful scapegoats for real and potential global environmental threats.

What is the bigger environmental threat to our planet? Is it the rapid growth of the populations of developing states or the rapid consumption of resources by the much smaller populations of developed states? The overdevelopment of the West may well be the bigger threat, though the growth of populations in third-world countries, which is often linked to conditions of underdevelopment, such as a lack of birth control and the need to have "extra" children as a hedge against high child mortality rates, makes an attractive alternative explanation for those who would not wish to fault the SUV-driving, disposable-diaper using, BBQ-loving American consumer for threats to the global environment. While some Western policymakers express concern about the environmental threats emerging from rapid population growth or the use of "dirty" technology in developing states, there is comparably little serious attention given to the global threat presented by the profligate consumption by Western states. The poor divert attention from the environmental problems caused by Western overconsumption.

I have talked about eleven ways that the continued existence of global poverty benefits those who reside in wealthy states. The argument I have offered to explain the persistence of a strata of poor states and the yawning global gap highlights the idea that while global poverty (and the status quo) is beneficial to the wealthy West, serious steps to alleviate it will not be taken.

It is surely the case that poverty does not have to exist. But while we in the West derive the benefits and bonuses of these economic inequalities, it seems likely that our efforts to support, advise, and assist the less developed states will remain at levels that are financially and politically convenient and feasible, and will target survival rather than true prosperity for those outside our gated, privileged, greedy Western neighborhood. In Gans's words, "Phenomena like poverty can be eliminated only when they become dysfunctional for the affluent or powerful, or when the powerless can obtain enough power to change society."

CRITICAL-THINKING QUESTIONS

1. The author provides a number of ways in which people in rich nations benefit from global poverty. Which do you find most convincing? Why?

2. What weaknesses do you find in the arguments? Explain.

3. From another angle, do you think that rich countries provide assistance to poor countries? In what ways?

NOTES

1. The figures in this paragraph come from the Population Reference Bureau Web site (*http://www.prb.org*), which provides excellent demographic data. According to the PRB, the "GNI PPP per capita is gross national income in purchasing power parity divided by mid-year population. . . . GNI PPP refers to gross national income converted to 'international' dollars using a purchasing power parity conversion factor. International dollars indicate the amount of goods or services one could buy in the United States with a given amount of money. GNI PPP provides an indicator of the welfare of people that is comparable across countries free of price and exchange rate distortions that occur when GNI is converted using market exchange rates."

2. *Social Policy,* July/August 1971.

3. Information on issues of trade and Chinese women is available at *http://www.womensedge.org.* The information cited is from the April 2000 Web issue of *Notes from the Edge.*

4. "Texaco in massive oil strike in Nigeria" in *The Namibian,* available online at *http://www.namibian.com.na/Netstories/2000/January/Marketplace/texaco.html.*

5. Stephens, Joe, "As Drug Testing Spreads, Profits and Lives Hang in Balance," *The Washington Post* 17, (December 2000): A1.

6. Information on both issues is available at the Web site of the environmental group Greenpeace at *http://www.greenpeace.org.*

7. The Web site address is *http://www.usaid.gov.*

8. The charity's Web site address is *http://www.worldvision.org.*

9. The foundation is at *http://www.gatesfoundation.org.*

10. The article is cited at the Web site of the Competitive Enterprise Institute: *http://www.cei.org/CHNReader.asp? ID=1227.*

40 Sex and Temperament in Three Primitive Societies

MARGARET MEAD

The work of anthropologist Margaret Mead laid the foundation for much of our contemporary sociological research and debate on gender. Are "masculine" and "feminine" traits innate or learned? Do men and women differ because of nature (heredity) or nurture (socialization)? Based on her studies of three "primitive peoples" in New Guinea, Margaret Mead argues that cultural conditioning is more important than biology in shaping women's and men's behavior.

We have now considered in detail the approved personalities of each sex among three primitive peoples. We found the Arapesh—both men and women—displaying a personality that, out of our historically limited preoccupations, we would call maternal in its parental aspects, and feminine in its sexual aspects. We found men, as well as women, trained to be cooperative, unaggressive, responsive to the needs and demands of others. We found no idea that sex was a powerful driving force either for men or for women. In marked contrast to these attitudes, we found among the Mundugumor that both men and women

Source: From *Sex and Temperament in Three Primitive Societies,* pp. 279–88, by Margaret Mead, Copyright © 1935, 1950, 1963, by Margaret Mead. Reprinted by permission of HarperCollins Publishers, Inc./ William Morrow.

developed as ruthless, aggressive, positively sexed individuals, with the maternal cherishing aspects of personality at a minimum. Both men and women approximated to a personality type that we in our culture would find only in an undisciplined and very violent male. Neither the Arapesh nor the Mundugumor profit by a contrast between the sexes; the Arapesh ideal is the mild, responsive man married to the mild, responsive woman; the Mundugumor ideal is the violent aggressive man married to the violent aggressive woman. In the third tribe, the Tchambuli, we found a genuine reversal of the sex attitudes of our own culture, with the woman the dominant, impersonal, managing partner, the man the less responsible and the emotionally dependent person. These three situations suggest, then, a very definite conclusion. If those temperamental attitudes which we have traditionally regarded as feminine—such as passivity, responsiveness, and a willingness to cherish children—can so easily be set up as the masculine pattern in one tribe, and in another be outlawed for the majority of women as well as for the majority of men, we no longer have any basis for regarding such aspects of behaviour as sex-linked. And this conclusion becomes even stronger when we consider the actual reversal in Tchambuli of the position of dominance of the two sexes, in spite of the existence of formal patrilineal institutions.

The material suggests that we may say that many, if not all, of the personality traits which we have called masculine or feminine are as lightly linked to sex as are the clothing, the manners, and the form of head-dress that a society at a given period assigns to either sex. When we consider the behaviour of the typical Arapesh man or woman as contrasted with the behaviour of the typical Mundugumor man or woman, the evidence is overwhelmingly in favour of the strength of social conditioning. In no other way can we account for the almost complete uniformity with which Arapesh children develop into contented, passive, secure persons, while Mundugumor children develop as characteristically into violent, aggressive, insecure persons. Only to the impact of the whole of the integrated culture upon the growing child can we lay the formation of the contrasting types. There is no other explanation of race, or diet, or selection that can be adduced to explain them. We are forced to conclude that human nature is almost unbelievably malleable, responding accurately and contrastingly to contrasting cultural conditions. The differences between individuals who are members of different cultures, like the differences between individuals within a culture, are almost entirely to be laid to differences in conditioning, especially during early childhood, and the form of this conditioning is culturally determined. Standardized personality differences between the sexes are of this order, cultural creations to which each generation, male

and female, is trained to conform. There remains, however, the problem of the origin of these socially standardized differences.

While the basic importance of social conditioning is still imperfectly recognized—not only in lay thought, but even by the scientist specifically concerned with such matters—to go beyond it and consider the possible influence of variations in hereditary equipment is a hazardous matter. The following pages will read very differently to one who has made a part of his thinking a recognition of the whole amazing mechanism of cultural conditioning—who has really accepted the fact that the same infant could be developed into a full participant in any one of these three cultures—than they will read to one who still believes that the minutiae of cultural behaviour are carried in the individual germ-plasm. If it is said, therefore, that when we have grasped the full significance of the malleability of the human organism and the preponderant importance of cultural conditioning, there are still further problems to solve, it must be remembered that these problems come *after* such a comprehension of the force of conditioning; they cannot precede it. The forces that make children born among the Arapesh grow up into typical Arapesh personalities are entirely social, and any discussion of the variations which do occur must be looked at against this social background.

With this warning firmly in mind, we can ask a further question. Granting the malleability of human nature, whence arise the differences between the standardized personalities that different cultures decree for all of their members, or which one culture decrees for the members of one sex as contrasted with the members of the opposite sex? If such differences are culturally created, as this material would most strongly suggest that they are, if the newborn child can be shaped with equal ease into an unaggressive Arapesh or an aggressive Mundugumor, why do these striking contrasts occur at all? If the clues to the different personalities decreed for men and women in Tchambuli do not lie in the physical constitution of the two sexes—an assumption that we must reject both for the Tchambuli and for our own society—where can we find the clues upon which the Tchambuli, the Arapesh, the Mundugumor, have built? Cultures are manmade, they are built of human materials; they are diverse but comparable structures within which human beings can attain full human stature. Upon what have they built their diversities?

We recognize that a homogeneous culture committed in all of its gravest institutions and slightest usages to a cooperative, unaggressive course can bend every child to that emphasis, some to a perfect accord with it, the majority to an easy acceptance, while only a few deviants fail to receive the cultural imprint. To consider such traits as aggressiveness or passivity to be sex-linked is not possible in the light of the facts. Have such traits, then, as aggressiveness or passivity, pride or humility, objectivity or a preoccupation with personal relationships, an easy response to the needs of the young and the weak or a hostility to the young and the weak, a tendency to initiate sex-relations or merely to respond to the dictates of a situation or another person's advances—have these traits any basis in temperament at all? Are they potentialities of all human temperaments that can be developed by different kinds of social conditioning and which will not appear if the necessary conditioning is absent?

When we ask this question we shift our emphasis. If we ask why an Arapesh man or an Arapesh woman shows the kind of personality that we have considered in the first section of this book, the answer is: Because of the Arapesh culture, because of the intricate, elaborate, and unfailing fashion in which a culture is able to shape each new-born child to the cultural image. And if we ask the same question about a Mundugumor man or woman, or about a Tchambuli man as compared with a Tchambuli woman, the answer is of the same kind. They display the personalities that are peculiar to the cultures in which they were born and educated. Our attention has been on the differences between Arapesh men and women as a group and Mundugumor men and women as a group. It is as if we had represented the Arapesh personality by a soft yellow, the Mundugumor by a deep red, while the Tchambuli female personality was deep orange, and that of the Tchambuli male, pale green. But if we now ask whence came the original direction in each culture, so that one now shows yellow, another red, the third orange and green by sex, then we must peer more closely. And leaning closer to the picture, it is as if behind the bright consistent yellow of the Arapesh, and the deep equally consistent red of the Mundugumor, behind the orange and green that are Tchambuli, we found in each case the delicate, just discernible outlines of the whole spectrum, differently overlaid in each case by the monotone which covers it. This spectrum is the range of individual differences which lie back of the so much more conspicuous cultural emphases, and it is to this that we must turn to find the explanation of cultural inspiration, of the source from which each culture has drawn.

There appears to be about the same range of basic temperamental variation among the Arapesh and among the Mundugumor, although the violent man is a misfit in the first society and a leader in the second. If human nature were completely homogeneous raw material, lacking specific drives and characterized by no important constitutional differences between individuals, then individuals who display personality traits so antithetical to the social pressure should not reappear in societies of such differing emphases. If the variations between individuals were to be set down to accidents in the genetic process, the same accidents should not be repeated with similar frequency in strikingly different cultures, with strongly contrasting methods of education.

But because this same relative distribution of individual differences does appear in culture after culture, in spite of the divergence between the cultures, it seems pertinent to offer a hypothesis to explain upon what basis the personalities of men and women have been differently standardized so often in the history of the human race. This hypothesis is an extension of that advanced by Ruth Benedict in her *Patterns of Culture*. Let us assume that there are definite temperamental differences between human beings which if not entirely hereditary at least are established on a hereditary base very soon after birth. (Further than this we cannot at present narrow the matter.) These differences finally embodied in the character structure of adults, then, are the clues from which culture works, selecting one temperament, or a combination of related and congruent types, as desirable, and embodying this choice in every thread of the social fabric—in the care of the young child, the games the children play, the songs the people sing, the structure of political organization, the religious observance, the art and the philosophy.

Some primitive societies have had the time and the robustness to revamp all of their institutions to fit one extreme type, and to develop educational techniques which will ensure that the majority of each generation will show a personality congruent with this extreme emphasis. Other societies have pursued a less definitive course, selecting their models not from the most extreme, most highly differentiated individuals, but from the less marked types. In such societies the approved personality is less pronounced, and the culture often contains the types of inconsistencies that many human beings display also; one institution may be adjusted to the uses of pride, another to a casual humility that is congruent neither with pride nor with inverted pride. Such societies, which have taken the more usual and less sharply defined types as models, often show also a less definitely patterned social structure. The culture of such societies may be likened to a house the decoration of which has been informed by no definite and precise taste, no exclusive emphasis upon dignity or comfort or pretentiousness or beauty, but in which a little of each effect has been included.

Alternatively, a culture may take its clues not from one temperament, but from several temperaments. But instead of mixing together into an inconsistent hotchpotch the choices and emphases

of different temperaments, or blending them together into a smooth but not particularly distinguished whole, it may isolate each type by making it the basis for the approved social personality for an age-group, a sex-group, a caste-group, or an occupational group. In this way society becomes not a monotone with a few discrepant patches of an intrusive colour, but a mosaic, with different groups displaying different personality traits. Such specializations as these may be based upon any facet of human endowment—different intellectual abilities, different artistic abilities, different emotional traits. So the Samoans decree that all young people must show the personality trait of unaggressiveness and punish with opprobrium the aggressive child who displays traits regarded as appropriate only in titled middle-aged men. In societies based upon elaborate ideas of rank, members of the aristocracy will be permitted, even compelled, to display a pride, a sensitivity to insult, that would be deprecated as inappropriate in members of the plebeian class. So also in professional groups or in religious sects some temperamental traits are selected and institutionalized, and taught to each new member who enters the profession or sect. Thus the physician learns the bedside manner, which is the natural behaviour of some temperaments and the standard behaviour of the general practitioner in the medical profession; the Quaker learns at least the outward behaviour and the rudiments of meditation, the capacity for which is not necessarily an innate characteristic of many of the members of the Society of Friends.

So it is with the social personalities of the two sexes. The traits that occur in some members of each sex are specially assigned to one sex, and disallowed in the other. The history of the social definition of sex-differences is filled with such arbitrary arrangements in the intellectual and artistic field, but because of the assumed congruence between physiological sex and emotional endowment we have been less able to recognize that a similar arbitrary selection is being made among emotional traits also. We have assumed that because it is convenient for a mother to wish to care for her child, this is a trait with which women have been more generously endowed by a carefully teleological process of evolution. We have assumed that because men have hunted, an activity requiring enterprise, bravery, and initiative, they have been endowed with these useful attitudes as part of their sex-temperament.

Societies have made these assumptions both overtly and implicitly. If a society insists that warfare is the major occupation for the male sex, it is therefore insisting that all male children display bravery and pugnacity. Even if the insistence upon the differential bravery of men and women is not made articulate, the difference in occupation makes this point implicitly. When, however, a society goes further and defines men as brave and women as timorous, when men are forbidden to show fear and women are indulged in the most flagrant display of fear, a more explicit element enters in. Bravery, hatred of any weakness, of flinching before pain or danger—this attitude which is so strong a component of *some human* temperaments has been selected as the key to masculine behaviour. The easy unashamed display of fear or suffering that is congenial to a different temperament has been made the key to feminine behaviour.

Originally two variations of human temperament, a hatred of fear or willingness to display fear, they have been socially translated into inalienable aspects of the personalities of the two sexes. And to that defined sex-personality every child will be educated, if a boy, to suppress fear, if a girl, to show it. If there has been no social selection in regard to this trait, the proud temperament that is repelled by any betrayal of feeling will display itself, regardless of sex, by keeping a stiff upper lip. Without an express prohibition of such behaviour the expressive unashamed man or woman will weep, or comment upon fear or suffering. Such attitudes, strongly marked in certain temperaments, may by social selection be standardized for everyone, or outlawed for everyone, or ignored by society, or made the exclusive and approved behaviour of one sex only.

Neither the Arapesh nor the Mundugumor have made any attitude specific for one sex. All of the energies of the culture have gone towards the creation of a single human type, regardless of class, age, or sex. There is no division into age-classes for which different motives or different moral attitudes are regarded as suitable. There is no class of seers or mediums who stand apart drawing inspiration from psychological sources not available to the majority of the people. The Mundugumor have, it is true, made one arbitrary selection, in that they recognize artistic ability only among individuals born with the cord about their necks, and firmly deny the happy exercise of artistic ability to those less unusually born. The Arapesh boy with a tinea infection has been socially selected to be a disgruntled, antisocial individual, and the society forces upon sunny cooperative children cursed with this affliction a final approximation to the behaviour appropriate to a pariah. With these two exceptions no emotional role is forced upon an individual because of birth or accident. As there is no idea of rank which declares that some are of high estate and some of low, so there is no idea of sex-difference which declares that one sex must feel differently from the other. One possible imaginative social construct, the attribution of different personalities to different members of the community classified into sex-, age-, or caste-groups, is lacking.

When we turn however to the Tchambuli, we find a situation that while bizarre in one respect, seems nevertheless more intelligible in another. The Tchambuli have at least made the point of sex-difference; they have used the obvious fact of sex as an organizing point for the formation of social personality, even though they seem to us to have reversed the normal picture. While there is reason to believe that not every Tchambuli woman is born with a dominating, organizing, administrative temperament, actively sexed and willing to initiate sex-relations, possessive, definite, robust, practical and impersonal in outlook, still most Tchambuli girls grow up to display these traits. And while there is definite evidence to show that all Tchambuli men are not, by native endowment, the delicate responsive actors of a play staged for the women's benefit, still most Tchambuli boys manifest this coquettish play-acting personality most of the time. Because the Tchambuli formulation of sex-attitudes contradicts our usual premises, we can see clearly that Tchambuli culture has arbitrarily permitted certain human traits to women, and allotted others, equally arbitrarily, to men.

CRITICAL-THINKING QUESTIONS

1. How do female and male personality traits differ among the Arapesh, the Mundugumor, and the Tchambuli?

2. How does Mead explain these differences? What does she mean, for example, when she states that "human nature is unbelievably malleable to cultural conditions"?

3. Most people in the United States still describe men as aggressive, strong, confident, and ambitious while characterizing women as emotional, talkative, romantic, and nurturing. Does this mean that biology is more important than environment in shaping our personality and behavior?

CLASSIC

CONTEMPORARY

CROSS-CULTURAL

41 "Night to His Day": The Social Construction of Gender

JUDITH LORBER

Gender is a construction of society that shapes the lives of us all, and defines the world of men and the world of women in opposing terms. Gender is also an important dimension of social stratification.

Talking about gender for most people is the equivalent of fish talking about water. Gender is so much the routine ground of everyday activities that questioning its taken-for-granted assumptions and presuppositions is like wondering about whether the sun will come up. Gender is so pervasive that in our society we assume it is bred into our genes. Most people find it hard to believe that gender is constantly created and re-created out of human interaction, out of social life, and is the texture and order of that social life. Yet gender, like culture, is a human production that depends on everyone constantly "doing gender" (West and Zimmerman 1987).

And everyone "does gender" without thinking about it. Today, on the subway, I saw a well-dressed man with a year-old child in a stroller. Yesterday, on a bus, I saw a man with a tiny baby in a carrier on his chest. Seeing men taking care of small children in public is increasingly common—at least in New York City. But both men were quite obviously

stared at—and smiled at, approvingly. Everyone was doing gender—the men who were changing the role of fathers and the other passengers, who were applauding them silently. But there was more gendering going on that probably fewer people noticed. The baby was wearing a white crocheted cap and white clothes. You couldn't tell if it was a boy or a girl. The child in the stroller was wearing a dark blue T-shirt and dark print pants. As they started to leave the train, the father put a Yankee baseball cap on the child's head. Ah, a boy, I thought. Then I noticed the gleam of tiny earrings in the child's ears, and as they got off, I saw the little flowered sneakers and lace-trimmed socks. Not a boy after all. Gender done. . . .

For the individual, gender construction starts with assignment to a sex category on the basis of what the genitalia look like at birth.[1] Then babies are dressed or adorned in a way that displays the category because parents don't want to be constantly asked whether their baby is a girl or a boy. A sex category becomes a gender status through naming, dress, and the use of other gender markers. Once a child's gender is evident, others treat those in one gender differently from those in the

From "Night to His Day: The Social Construction of Gender," by Judith Lorber, from *Readings for Diversity and Social Justice*, Routledge, 2003.

other, and the children respond to the different treatment by feeling different and behaving differently. As soon as they can talk, they start to refer to themselves as members of their gender. Sex doesn't come into play again until puberty, but by that time, sexual feelings and desires and practices have been shaped by gendered norms and expectations. Adolescent boys and girls approach and avoid each other in an elaborately scripted and gendered mating dance. Parenting is gendered, with different expectations for mothers and for fathers, and people of different genders work at different kinds of jobs. The work adults do as mothers and fathers and as low-level workers and high-level bosses, shapes women's and men's life experiences, and these experiences produce different feelings, consciousness, relationships, skills—ways of being that we call feminine or masculine. All of these processes constitute the social construction of gender.

Gendered roles change—today fathers are taking care of little children, girls and boys are wearing unisex clothing and getting the same education, women and men are working at the same jobs. Although many traditional social groups are quite strict about maintaining gender differences, in other social groups they seem to be blurring. Then why the one-year-old's earrings? Why is it still so important to mark a child as a girl or a boy, to make sure she is not taken for a boy or he for a girl? What would happen if they were? They would, quite literally, have changed places in their social world.

To explain why gendering is done from birth, constantly and by everyone, we have to look not only at the way individuals experience gender but at gender as a social institution. As a social institution, gender is one of the major ways that human beings organize their lives. Human society depends on a predictable division of labor, a designated allocation of scarce goods, assigned responsibility for children and others who cannot care for themselves, common values and their systematic transmission to new members, legitimate leadership, music, art, stories, games, and other symbolic productions.

One way of choosing people for the different tasks of society is on the basis of their talents, motivations, and competence—their demonstrated achievements. The other way is on the basis of gender, race, ethnicity—ascribed membership in a category of people. Although societies vary in the extent to which they use one or the other of these ways of allocating people to work and to carry out other responsibilities, every society uses gender and age grades. Every society classifies people as "girl and boy children," "girls and boys ready to be married," and "fully adult women and men," constructs similarities among them and differences between them, and assigns them to different roles and responsibilities. Personality characteristics, feelings, motivations, and ambitions flow from these different life experiences so that the members of these different groups become different kinds of people. . . .

Western society's values legitimate gendering by claiming that it all comes from physiology—female and male procreative differences. But gender and sex are not equivalent, and gender as a social construction does not flow automatically from genitalia and reproductive organs, the main physiological differences of females and males. . . .

Whatever genes, hormones, and biological evolution contribute to human social institutions is materially as well as qualitatively transformed by social practices. Every social institution has a material base, but culture and social practices transform that base into something with qualitatively different patterns and constraints. The economy is much more than producing food and goods and distributing them to eaters and users; family and kinship are not the equivalent of having sex and procreating; morals and religions cannot be equated with the fears and ecstasies of the brain; language goes far beyond the sounds produced by tongue and larynx. . . .

Similarly, gender cannot be equated with biological and physiological differences between human females and males. The building blocks of gender are *socially constructed statuses*. Western societies have only two genders, "man" and "woman." Some societies have three genders—men, women, and *berdaches* or *hijras* or *xaniths*. Berdaches, hijras, and xaniths are biological males who behave, dress, work, and are treated in most respects as social women; they are therefore not men, nor are they female women; they are, in our language, "male women." There are African and American Indian societies that have a gender status called *manly hearted women*—biological females who work, marry, and parent as men; their social status is "female men" (Amadiume 1987; Blackwood 1984). They do not have to behave or dress as men to have the social responsibilities and prerogatives of husbands and fathers; what makes them men is enough wealth to buy a wife.

Modern Western societies' *transsexuals* and *transvestites* are the nearest equivalent of these crossover genders, but they are not institutionalized as third genders (Bolin 1987). Transsexuals are biological males and females who have sex-change operations to alter their genitalia. They do so in order to bring their physical anatomy in congruence with the way they want to live and with their own sense of gender identity. They do not become a third gender; they change genders. Transvestites are males who live as women and females who live as men but do not intend to have sex-change surgery. Their dress, appearance, and mannerisms fall within the range of what is expected from members of the opposite gender, so that they "pass." They also change genders, sometimes temporarily, some for most of their lives. Transvestite women have fought in wars as men soldiers as recently as the nineteenth century; some married women, and others went back to being women and married men once the war was over. Some were discovered when their wounds were treated; others not until they died. In order to work as a jazz musician, a man's occupation, Billy Tipton, a woman, lived most of her life as a man. She died recently at seventy-four, leaving a wife and three adopted sons for whom she was husband and father, and musicians with whom she had played and traveled, for whom she was "one of the boys" (*New York Times* 1989). There have been

many other such occurrences of women passing as men to do more prestigious or lucrative men's work (Matthaei 1982, 192–93).

Genders, therefore, are not attached to a biological substratum. Gender boundaries are breachable, and individual and socially organized shifts from one gender to another call attention to "cultural, social, or aesthetic dissonances" (Garber 1992, 16). These odd or deviant or third genders show us what we ordinarily take for granted—that people have to learn to be women and men. . . .

Many cultures go beyond clothing, gestures, and demeanor in gendering children. They inscribe gender directly into bodies. In traditional Chinese society, mothers once bound their daughters' feet into three-inch stumps to enhance their sexual attractiveness. Jewish fathers circumcise their infant sons to show their covenant with God. Women in African societies remove the clitoris of prepubescent girls, scrape their labia, and make the lips grow together to preserve their chastity and ensure their marriageability. In Western societies, women augment their breast size with silicone and reconstruct their faces with cosmetic surgery to conform to cultural ideals of feminine beauty. Hanna Papanek (1990) notes that these practices reinforce the sense of superiority or inferiority in the adults who carry them out as well as in the children on whom they are done: The genitals of Jewish fathers and sons are physical and psychological evidence of their common dominant religious and familial status; the genitals of African mothers and daughters are physical and psychological evidence of their joint subordination.

Sandra Bem (1981, 1983) argues that because gender is a powerful "schema" that orders the cognitive world, one must wage a constant, active battle for a child not to fall into typical gendered attitudes and behavior. In 1972, *Ms. Magazine* published Lois Gould's fantasy of how to raise a child free of gender-typing. The experiment calls for hiding the child's anatomy from all eyes except the parents' and treating the child as neither a girl nor a boy. The child, called X, gets to do all the things boys *and* girls do. The experiment is so successful that all the children in X's class at school want to look and behave like X. At the end of the story, the creators of the experiment are asked what will happen when X grows up. The scientists' answer is that by then it will be quite clear what X is, implying that its hormones will kick in and it will be revealed as a female or male. That ambiguous, and somewhat contradictory, ending lets Gould off the hook; neither she nor we have any idea what someone brought up in a totally androgynous manner would be like sexually or socially as an adult. The hormonal input will not create gender or sexuality but will only establish secondary sex characteristics; breasts, beards, and menstruation alone do not produce social manhood or womanhood. Indeed, it is at puberty, when sex characteristics become evident, that most societies put pubescent children through their most important rites of passage, the rituals that officially mark them as fully gendered—that is, ready to marry and become adults.

Most parents create a gendered world for their newborn by naming, birth announcements, and dress. Children's relationships with same-gendered and different-gendered caretakers structure their self-identifications and personalities. Through cognitive development, children extract and apply to their own actions the appropriate behavior for those who belong in their own gender, as well as race, religion, ethnic group, and social class, rejecting what is not appropriate. If their social categories are highly valued, they value themselves highly; if their social categories are of low status, they lose self-esteem (Chodorow 1974). Many feminist parents who want to raise androgynous children soon lose their children to the pull of gendered norms (Gordon 1990, 87–90). My son attended a carefully nonsexist elementary school, which didn't even have girls' and boys' bathrooms. When he was seven or eight years old, I attended a class play about "squares" and "circles" and their need for each other and noticed that all the girl squares and circles wore makeup, but none of the boy squares and circles did. I asked the teacher about it after the play, and she said, "Bobby said he was not going to

wear makeup, and he is a powerful child, so none of the boys would either." In a long discussion about conformity, my son confronted me with the question of who the conformists were, the boys who followed their leader or the girls who listened to the woman teacher. In actuality, they both were, because they both followed same-gender leaders and acted in gender-appropriate ways. (Actors may wear makeup, but real boys don't.)

For human beings there is no essential femaleness or maleness, femininity or masculinity, womanhood or manhood, but once gender is ascribed, the social order constructs and holds individuals to strongly gendered norms and expectations. Individuals may vary on many of the components of gender and may shift genders temporarily or permanently, but they must fit into the limited number of gender statuses their society recognizes. In the process, they re-create their society's version of women and men: "If we do gender appropriately, we simultaneously sustain, reproduce, and render legitimate the institutional arrangements. . . . If we fail to do gender appropriately, we as individuals—not the institutional arrangements—may be called to account (for our character, motives, and predispositions)" (West and Zimmerman 1987, 146).

The gendered practices of everyday life reproduce a society's view of how women and men should act. Gendered social arrangements are justified by religion and cultural productions and backed by law, but the most powerful means of sustaining the moral hegemony of the dominant gender ideology is that the process is made invisible; any possible alternatives are virtually unthinkable (Foucault 1972; Gramsci 1971).

FOR SOCIETY, GENDER MEANS DIFFERENCE

The pervasiveness of gender as a way of structuring social life demands that gender statuses be clearly differentiated. Varied talents, sexual preferences, identities, personalities, interests, and ways of interacting fragment the individual's bodily and social experiences. Nonetheless, these are organized in Western cultures into two and only two socially and legally recognized gender statuses, "man" and "woman." In the social construction of gender, it does not matter what men and women actually do; it does not even matter if they do exactly the same thing. The social institution of gender insists only that what they do is *perceived* as different.

If men and women are doing the same tasks, they are usually spatially segregated to maintain gender separation, and often the tasks are given different job titles as well, such as executive secretary and administrative assistant (Reskin 1988). If the differences between women and men begin to blur, society's "sameness taboo" goes into action (Rubin 1975, 178). At a rock and roll dance at West Point in 1976, the year women were admitted to the prestigious military academy for the first time, the school's administrators "were reportedly perturbed by the sight of mirror-image couples dancing in short hair and dress gray trousers," and a rule was established that women cadets could dance at these events only if they wore skirts (Barkalow and Raab 1990, 53). Women recruits in the U.S. Marine Corps are required to wear makeup—at a minimum, lipstick and eye shadow—and they have to take classes in makeup, hair care, poise, and etiquette. This feminization is part of a deliberate policy of making them clearly distinguishable from men Marines. Christine Williams quotes a twenty-five-year-old woman drill instructor as saying, "A lot of the recruits who come here don't wear makeup; they're tomboyish or athletic. A lot of them have the preconceived idea that going into the military means they can still be a tomboy. They don't realize that you are a *Woman* Marine" (1989, 76–77). . . .

As part of a *stratification* system, gender ranks men above women of the same race and class. Women and men could be different but equal. In practice, the process of creating difference depends to a great extent on differential evaluation. As Nancy Jay (1981) says: "That which is defined, separated out, isolated from all else is A and pure. Not-A is necessarily impure, a random catchall, to

which nothing is external except A and the principle of order that separates it from Not-A" (45). From the individual's point of view, whichever gender is A, the other is Not-A; gender boundaries tell the individual who is like him or her, and all the rest are unlike. From society's point of view, however, one gender is usually the touchstone, the normal, the dominant, and the other is different, deviant, and subordinate. In Western society, "man" is A, "wo-man" is Not-A. (Consider what a society would be like where woman was A and man Not-A.)

The further dichotomization by race and class constructs the gradations of a heterogeneous society's stratification scheme. Thus, in the United States, white is A, African American is Not-A; middle class is A, working class is Not-A, and "African-American women occupy a position whereby the inferior half of a series of these dichotomies converge" (Collins 1990, 70). The dominant categories are the hegemonic ideals, taken so for granted as the way things should be that white is not ordinarily thought of as a race, middle class as a class, or men as a gender. The characteristics of these categories define the Other as that which lacks the valuable qualities the dominants exhibit. . . .

When gender is a major component of structured inequality, the devalued genders have less power, prestige, and economic rewards than the valued genders. In countries that discourage gender discrimination, many major roles are still gendered; women still do most of the domestic labor and child rearing, even while doing full-time paid work; women and men are segregated on the job and each does work considered "appropriate"; women's work is usually paid less than men's work. Men dominate the positions of authority and leadership. . . .

Gender inequality—the devaluation of "women" and the social domination of "men"—has social functions and a social history. It is not the result of sex, procreation, physiology, anatomy, hormones, or genetic predispositions. It is produced and maintained by identifiable social processes and built into the general social structure and individual identities deliberately and purposefully. The social order as we know it in Western societies is organized around racial ethnic, class, and gender inequality. I contend, therefore, that the continuing purpose of gender as a modern social institution is to construct women as a group to be the subordinates of men as a group. The life of everyone placed in the status "woman" is "night to his day—that has forever been the fantasy. Black to his white. Shut out of his system's space, she is the repressed that ensures the system's functioning" (Cixous and Clément [1975] 1986, 67).

CRITICAL-THINKING QUESTIONS

1. After a child is born, how does society transform its sex into gender?
2. How is gender both an important part of how we as individuals experience the world and also an institution of society as a whole?
3. What importance, if any, does the author give to biology in the development of gender?

NOTE

1. In cases of ambiguity in countries with modern medicine, surgery is usually performed to make the genitalia more clearly male or female.

REFERENCES

AMADIUME, IFI. 1987. *Male daughters, female husbands: Gender and sex in an African society*. London: Zed Books.

BARKALOW, CAROL, with ANDREA RAAB. 1990. *In the men's house*. New York: Poseidon Press.

BEM, SANDRA LIPSITZ. 1981. Gender schema theory: A cognitive account of sex typing. *Psychological Review* 88: 354–64.

———. 1983. Gender schema theory and its implications for child development: Raising gender-aschematic children in a gender-schematic society. *Signs: Journal of Women in Culture and Society* 8: 598–616.

BLACKWOOD, EVELYN. 1984. Sexuality and gender in certain Native American tribes: The case of cross-gender females. *Signs: Journal of Women in Culture and Society* 10: 27–42.

BOLIN, ANNE. 1987. Transsexualism and the limits of traditional analysis. *American Behavioral Scientist* 31: 41–65.

CHODOROW, NANCY. 1974. Family structure and feminine personality. In *Women, culture and society*, eds. Rosaldo and Lamphere. Stanford, Calif.: Stanford University Press.

CIXOUS, HÉLÈNE, and CATHERINE CLÉMENT. [1975] 1986. *The newly born woman*, translated by Betsy Wing. Minneapolis: University of Minnesota Press.

COLLINS, PATRICIA HILL. 1990. *Black feminist thought: Knowledge, consciousness, and the politics of empowerment*. Boston: Unwin Hyman.

FOUCAULT, MICHEL. 1972. *The archeology of knowledge and the discourse on language*, translated by A. M. Sheridan Smith. New York: Pantheon.

GARBER, MARJORIE. 1992. *Vested interests: Cross-dressing and cultural anxiety*. New York and London: Routledge.

GORDON, TUULA. 1990. *Feminist mothers*. New York: New York University Press.

GRAMSCI, ANTONIO. 1971. *Selections from the prison notebooks*, translated and edited by Quintin Hoare and Geoffrey Nowell Smith. New York: International Publishers.

JAY, NANCY. 1981. Gender and dichotomy. *Feminist Studies* 7: 38–56.

MATTHAEI, JULIE A. 1982. *An economic history of women's work in America*. New York: Schocken.

PAPANEK, HANNA. 1990. To each less than she needs, from each more than she can do: Allocations, entitlements, and value. In Tinker, ed., *Persistent Inequalities: Women and World Development*, ed. Tinker. New York: Oxford University Press.

RESKIN, BARBARA J. 1988. Bringing the men back in: Sex differentiation and the devaluation of women's work. *Gender and Society* 7: 58–81.

RUBIN, GAYLE. 1975. The traffic in women: Notes on the political economy of sex. In *Toward an Anthropology of Women*, ed. Rayna R[app] Reiter. New York: Monthly Review Press.

WEST, CANDACE, and DON ZIMMERMAN. 1987. Doing gender. *Gender and Society* 1: 125–51.

WILLIAMS, CHRISTINE L. 1989. *Gender differences at work: Women and men in nontraditional occupations*. Berkeley: University of California Press.

CLASSIC

CONTEMPORARY

CROSS-CULTURAL

42 How Subtle Sex Discrimination Works

NIJOLE V. BENOKRAITIS

There are many forms of sex discrimination. Blatant sex discrimination is typically intentional, quite visible, and easily documented. Covert sex discrimination is hidden, purposeful, and difficult to prove. This selection discusses subtle sex discrimination—behavior, often unnoticed, that people have internalized as "normal," "natural," or customary.

Subtle sex discrimination refers to the unequal and harmful treatment of women that is typically less visible and obvious than blatant sex discrimination. It is often not noticed because most people have internalized subtle sexist behavior as "normal," "natural," or acceptable. Subtle sex discrimination can be relatively innocent or manipulative, intentional or unintentional, well-meaning or malicious. Subtle sex discrimination is difficult to document because many people do not perceive it as serious or harmful. In addition, subtle sex discrimination is often more complex than it appears: What is discrimination to many women may not seem discriminatory to many men or even women. . . .

CONDESCENDING CHIVALRY

Condescending chivalry refers to superficially courteous behavior that is protective and paternalistic,

Source: Nijole V. Benokraitis, *Subtle Sexism: Current Practices and Prospects for Change,* pp. 11, 14–24. Copyright © 1997 by Sage Publications, Inc. Reprinted by permission of Sage Publications, Inc.

but treats women as subordinates. Sometimes the chivalry is well-intentioned because it "protects" women from criticism. For example, "A male boss will haul a guy aside and just kick ass if the [male] subordinate performs badly in front of a client" but may not say anything to a female subordinate (Fraker, 1984). Not providing such criticism may seem benevolent in the short term, but it will handicap an employee's performance in the long run. . . .

Thus, chivalrous behavior can signal status inequality. According to some researchers, outmoded attitudes—on the parts of both men and women—are preventing many qualified women from breaking into top jobs as school superintendents. Unlike their male counterparts, female candidates still get such questions from school board members as "How would your husband feel about your moving?" "Can you deal with a district where the administrators are mostly men?" and "Can you handle tough discipline problems?" According to researchers, the oppressive chivalry continues after a woman is hired. Female school superintendents often face greater scrutiny, for example, when it comes to such "masculine" tasks as finances and maintenance issues (see Nakashima, 1996).

SUPPORTIVE DISCOURAGEMENT

Supportive discouragement refers to a form of subtle sex discrimination where women receive mixed messages about their abilities, intelligence, or accomplishments. One form of supportive discouragement involves encouraging women to succeed in general but not rewarding their actual achievements because the latter may not reflect traditionally male interests:

> . . . [H]aving served on several search committees, I'm aware of how often feminist (or even woman-topic) dissertations are dismissed as "jargony," "trendy," etc. . . . I'm not really sure if feminism is still seen as a "fly-by-night" sort of discipline, but the accusation is a difficult one to argue because the people who make it will assure you until they're blue in the face (or you are) that they would love to hire a woman, are not opposed to feminism, etc. But it's only "this" dissertation, you see, they are opposed to. . . . (E-mail correspondence, 1996)

Another form of supportive discouragement encourages women to be ambitious and successful but places numerous obstacles in their paths, which either limit or derail the progress. Consider the following example from a colleague in the United Kingdom:

> One of the largest departments in our College is the Access department which offers part-time courses for people with no formal qualifications who wish to enter higher education or return to work. I would say that about 70 percent of these students are female and intend to go into teaching or similar work. The College refuses to implement a crèche or other day-care on the basis that it would be too expensive; staffing would cost almost nothing as the College runs courses for Nursery Nurses, childcare workers, etc. This despite the fact that of the people who are offered places on the Access course and turn it down, 80 percent give lack of child care as the main reason. Of this 80 percent, 92 percent are women. The courses are also run in some of the worst accommodations on site— "temporary" buildings which have been there for about twenty years and which are in a terrible state.

> The Chemistry department (not many women here) has, however, had at least three major renovations in the last ten years. It certainly makes clear to the many women on the Access course the opinion the College management has of their relative importance. (E-mail correspondence, 1996)

FRIENDLY HARASSMENT

Friendly harassment refers to sexually oriented behavior that, at face value, looks harmless or even playful. If it creates discomfort, embarrassment, or humiliation, however, it is a form of subtle discrimination. According to some female students at Stanford Medical School, for example, it is in such traditionally male-taught courses as those in surgery and internal medicine that many women encounter the most offensive sexual jokes. A fourth-year student said that many of her days "are spent fending off stupid little comments," many of them sexual, from male residents and doctors. She hesitated to complain, however, because good evaluations from professors are essential to get a good residency (Gose, 1995).

When women don't laugh at "stupid little jokes," moreover, they are often accused of not having a sense of humor:

> In response to a question from a friend of mine (a female graduate student) regarding how to comport herself at a job interview, a male faculty adviser responds, "Just flirt!" When I recount the incident to a male friend (junior faculty in another field at another institution), he responds: "Maybe it was a joke. Lighten up!" The primary sexism of the first remark gets echoed in the secondary sexism of the second remark, which trivializes the offense and the indignation ["no sense of humor"]. (E-mail correspondence, 1996)

Humor and jokes serve a number of functions: They reinforce group solidarity; define the defiant/outsider group; educate; save face; ingratiate; express caring for others; provide a safety valve for discussing taboo topics; maintain status inequality; silence or embarrass people; and provide tension release, hostility, and anger toward any group that is seen as marginal, inferior, or threatening. A single joke can serve several of these functions.

Although women's humor can be a powerful tool for changing stereotypes about females, much of men's sexual humor expresses male dominance over women, negates their personhood, and tries to silence women: "There are whole categories of jokes about women for which there are no male parallels: prostitute jokes, mother-in-law jokes, dumb blonde jokes, woman driver jokes, Jewish mother jokes" (Crawford, 1995:138). Women often don't laugh at many of these jokes not because they don't have a sense of humor, but because the "jokes" are hostile, aggressive, and demeaning. . . .

SUBJECTIVE OBJECTIFICATION

Subjective objectification refers to a form of subtle sex discrimination that treats women as children, possessions, or sex objects. Women are often punished like children—their "allowances" may be taken away, they may be forbidden to associate with their friends, their physical mobility may be limited, they may be given curfews, or they may be threatened with punishment similar to that of children. . . .

Our culture is continuously bombarded with images of women as little more than sexual body parts. The Media Action Alliance, which publishes the *Action Agenda* newsletter, is constantly filled with examples of posters, ads, videos, and other media materials that glorify violence against women and exploitation of women's bodies. It has been estimated that the average teenager sees between 1,900 and 2,400 sex-related messages per year on television alone (Brown, Childers, & Waszik, 1990). Many of the images, including those in films targeted at adolescents, treat women's bodies as trophies: Boys compete to be the first to "score," to achieve the most sexual conquests, and to "make it" with the sexiest teenage girls (see Whatley, 1994).

A frightening result of such competition can include rape and other sexual assaults on women. Consider the "Spur Posse" case in California. In 1993 eight members of a suburban high school, many of them top athletes at the school, created a clique called the "Spur Posse." Their primary goal was to "score" with as many girls as possible. They kept track of the girls with whom they had intercourse, and some bragged that their individual tallies ran into the sixties. In at least seven cases, girls from ten to sixteen years old said they had been raped. Some of the parents condoned their sons' behavior. One father, in fact, boasted to reporters that the assaults were not rape but indicators of his son's virility and sexual prowess (Seligmann, 1993).

This bizarre perception of women as possessions and trophies follows many boys into adulthood. According to Brooks (1995:3–4), what he refers to as "the Centerfold Syndrome" represents "one of the most malignant forces in contemporary relationships between men and women." One of the elements of the Centerfold Syndrome is objectification:

Women become objects as men become objectifiers. As the culture has granted men the right and privilege of looking at women, women have been expected to accept the role of stimulators of men's visual interest, with their bodies becoming objects that can be lined up, compared, and rated. . . . Objective physical aspects are critical: Size, shape, and harmony of body parts are more important than a woman's human qualities. . . . Men talk of their attraction to women in dehumanizing terms based on the body part of their obsession—"I'm a leg man," or "I'm an ass man."

Brooks notes that one of the most harmful effects of such objectification is that real women become more complicated, less appealing, and even ugly: "Stretch marks, varicose veins, sagging breasts, and cellulite-marked legs, common phenomena for real female bodies, may be viewed as repugnant by men who see women as objects" (p. 5). As a result, Centerfold Syndrome men may be sexually and emotionally inexpressive with the most important women in their lives.

RADIANT DEVALUATION

Although women are less likely to be openly maligned or insulted than in the past, they are devalued more subtly but just as effectively. Often, the devaluation is done in glowing terms (Benokraitis & Feagin, 1995:102):

A psychologist, one of the most popular instructors in her college, said she would get good teaching evaluations from her male chair but that the positive review would be couched in sex-stereotypical rather than professional terms—she was described as being "mamaish" and as having a "charming" approach to teaching. Being "mama-ish" and "charming" are *not* the criteria used by tenure and promotion committees.

On a much broader scale, some scholars contend that the most recent devaluations have focused on antifeminist intellectual harassment through the use of "vilification and distortion or even violence to repress certain areas of research and forms of inquiry" (Clark et al., 1996:x). Attacks on feminists and feminist scholarship are nothing new. What has changed, however, is that much of the "newest wave of antifeminism cloaks itself in the vestments of feminism: the new antifeminists are women who, claiming to be feminists themselves, now maintain they are rescuing the women's movement from those who have led it astray" (Ginsburg & Lennox, 1996:170). Many of these devaluators have impressive academic credentials, are articulate, have been supported by conservative corporate foundations, and have found a receptive audience in the mainstream media and many publishing companies, which see antifeminism as a "hot commodity" because it is so profitable. Blaming feminism for such (real or imagined) ailments as the deterioration of relationships between the sexes and the presumed dissolution of the family—especially when the criticism comes from well-educated, self-proclaimed feminists—sells a lot of books.

LIBERATED SEXISM

Liberated sexism refers to the process that, at face value, appears to be treating women and men equally but that, in practice, increases men's freedom while placing greater burdens on women. One of the best examples of liberated sexism is work overloads both within the home and at the job site. Since the 1970s, increasing

numbers of women have found themselves with two jobs—one inside and one outside the home. Ironically, women working these "double days" are often referred to as "liberated women." But liberated from what?

Shared parenting reflects more rhetoric than reality. In a national study, Bianchi (1990) found that more than 60 percent of divorced fathers either did not visit their children, or did not visit them and had no telephone or mail contact with them over a one-year period. Employed mothers with preschool-age children spend twenty-four hours more a week in child-care activities than do their husbands. Because the husband's job typically takes priority over his wife's (his salary is usually much higher), nearly nine out of ten mothers care for their children when they are sick, compared with only one out of ten working fathers (DeStefano & Colasanto, 1990). Although in one survey 56 percent of male employees said they were interested in flexible work schedules that would allow them more family time, in reality fewer than 1 percent take advantage of the unpaid paternity leaves that some 30 percent of companies offer today. The Family and Medical Leave Act, which was signed into law by President Clinton in 1993, allows workers of employers with fifty or more employees to take up to twelve weeks of unpaid leave following the birth or adoption of a child. Most men fear the career repercussions of taking paternity leaves or can't afford unpaid leaves financially, however (see Sommer, 1994). . . .

CONSIDERATE DOMINATION

Men often occupy preeminent positions and control important decision-making functions. . . . Men's dominance is built into our language, laws, and customs in both formal and informal ways. The dominance is accepted because it has been internalized and is often portrayed as "collegial," authoritative, or mutually beneficial.

Most of us take for granted that the expert and dominant cast of characters in the media are men.

The media routinely ignore women or present them as second-class citizens. A recent survey of the front-page stories of twenty national and local newspapers found that although women make up 52 percent of the population, they show up just 13 percent of the time in the prime news spots. Even the stories about breast implants quoted men more often than women. Two-thirds of the bylines on front pages were male, and three-quarters of the opinions on op-ed pages were by men. Fewer than a third of the photographs on front pages featured women. Since the old "women's sections" are now more unisex and focus on both men and women, news about and by women has lost space even in these lifestyle sections (Goodman, 1992; see also Overholser, 1996).

Television news is not much better. In a study of the content of evening news programs on CBS, NBC, and ABC, Rakow and Kranich (1991) found that women as on-camera sources of information were used in less than 15 percent of the cases. When women did speak, they were usually passive reactors to public events as housewife or wife of the man in the news rather than participants or experts. Even in critical analyses of issues that affect more women than men, women may not appear on the screen. For example, a lengthy story on CBS on welfare reform did not use any women or feminist sources. . . .

COLLEGIAL EXCLUSION

One of the most familiar forms of subtle sexism is collegial exclusion, whereby women are made to feel invisible or unimportant through physical, social, or professional isolation. When Hall and Sandler's pamphlet, "The Classroom Climate: A Chilly One for Women?" was published in 1982, it was an instant success. Among other reasons, Sandler and Hall articulated the feelings that many women had experienced in higher education of being ignored, not having female role models, or being excluded from classroom discussions and activities. Since then, many studies have documented women's exclusion from classroom discourse, textbooks, and

other academic activities (see, for example, Ginorio, 1995; Lewis, 1990; Maher & Tetreault, 1994; Peterson & Kroner, 1992).

Although there has been greater awareness of exclusion, it's not evident that there has been much change since 1982. At Stanford Medical School, for example, "The male body has been used as the standard, and the woman's body has been seen as a variation on that theme," says a third-year female student. Several women once heard a professor dismiss the clitoris with five words: "like the penis, just shorter" (Gose, 1995:A50). At Yale and American University law schools, female students' complaints are strikingly similar to those that Hall and Sandler described in 1982: Women feel their speech is stifled in class; professors respond more positively to comments by men, even if a woman voiced the same idea first; male students, even friends, ignore women's comments on legal issues and talk around them; male students and faculty devalue women's opinions; and men don't hear what women say (Torry, 1995).

When I asked the subscribers of the Women's Studies e-mail discussion list if they or someone they knew had ever experienced subtle sexism, many of the responses (from both the United States and Europe) described collegial exclusion. Here are a few examples:

Just got back from a national conference and heard a female college president relate her experiences at meetings with other college presidents in the state. She was the only female present at the meetings and found that her suggestions/insights were ignored by her male colleagues. However, when the same suggestions later came from one of them, they were acknowledged. She finally took to writing her suggestions on the chalkboard. They couldn't be ignored that way—or at least not for long.

There was a series of women-only staff development meetings set up by one of the more senior women (there are few), but the "only" time that could be found for this was on Monday at 6:00 p.m. Other staff development meetings are held at lunchtime with time off for anybody who wants to go.

Women often feel they're isolated. . . . Many women begin with great promise but are demoralized and cut off from support . . . I'm referring to women who are cut off from support in ways it's hard to explain . . . often the only women in their departments . . . although some are in departments with other untenured women but the Old White Guys have the power. [The women] often are lacking a real (feminist) community.

CRITICAL-THINKING QUESTIONS

1. Why are the various categories of subtle sex discrimination presented as oxymorons? How does subtle sexism differ from more blatant forms of discrimination?

2. Can you identify situations in which you have experienced subtle sex discrimination? Have you ever discriminated in this way against others?

3. What are the individual and organizational costs of subtle sex discrimination? What remedies might be effective in decreasing this form of inequality?

REFERENCES

BENOKRAITIS, N. V., and J. R. FEAGIN. 1995. *Modern sexism: Blatant, subtle, and covert discrimination.* Englewood Cliffs, N.J.: Prentice Hall.

BIANCHI, S. 1990. America's children: Mixed prospects. *Population Bulletin,* 45: 3–41.

BROOKS, G. R. 1995. *The centerfold syndrome: How men can overcome objectification and achieve intimacy with women.* San Francisco, Calif.: Jossey-Bass.

BROWN, J. D., K. W. CHILDERS, and C. S. WASZIK. 1990. Television and adolescent sexuality. *Journal of Adolescent Health Care,* 11: 62–70.

CLARK, V., S. N. GARNER, M. HIGONNET, and K. H. KATRAK, eds. 1996. *Antifeminism in the academy.* New York: Routledge.

CRAWFORD, M. 1995. *Talking difference: On gender and language.* Thousand Oaks, Calif.: Sage.

DESTEFANO, L., and D. COLASANTO. 1990. Unlike 1975, today most Americans think men have it better. *Gallup Poll Monthly,* (February): 25–36.

FRAKER, S. 1984. Why top jobs elude female executives. *Fortune,* (April 16): 46.

GINORIO, A. B. 1995. *Warming the climate for women in academic science.* Washington, D.C.: Association of American Colleges and Universities.

GINSBURG, E., and S. LENNOX. 1996. Antifeminism in scholarship and publishing. In *Antifeminism in the academy,* eds. V. Clark, S. N. Garner, M. Higonnet, and K. H. Katrak, 169–200. New York: Routledge.

GOODMAN, E. 1992. A woman's place is in the paper. *Baltimore Sun,* (April 7):15A.

GOSE, B. 1995. Women's place in medicine. *Chronicle of Higher Education,* (November 3): A49.

LEWIS, M. 1990. Interrupting patriarchy: Politics, resistance, and transformation in the feminist classroom. *Harvard Educational Review,* 60: 472.

MAHER, F. A., and M. K. T. TETREAULT. 1994. *The feminist classroom.* New York: Basic Books.

NAKASHIMA, E. 1996. When it comes to top school jobs, women learn it's tough to get ahead. *Washington Post,* (April 21): B1, B5.

OVERHOLSER, G. 1996. Front page story: Women. *Washington Post,* (April 21): C6.

PETERSON, S. B., and T. KRONER. 1992. Gender biases in textbooks for introductory psychology and human development. *Psychology of Women Quarterly,* 16: 17–36.

RAKOW, L. F., and K. KRANICH. 1991. Woman as sign in television news. *Journal of Communication,* 41: 8–23.

SELIGMANN, J. 1993. A town's divided loyalties. *Newsweek,* (April 12): 29.

SOMMER, M. 1994. Welcome cribside, Dad. *Christian Science Monitor,* (June 28): 19.

TORRY, S. 1995. Voice of concern grows louder on gender bias issue. *Washington Post,* (November 20): 7.

WHATLEY, M. H. 1994. Keeping adolescents in the picture: Construction of adolescent sexuality in textbook images and popular films. In *Sexual culture and the construction of adolescent identities,* ed. J. M. Irvine, 183–205. Philadelphia: Temple University Press.

CLASSIC

CONTEMPORARY

CROSS-CULTURAL

43 Domestic Violence:
A Cross-Cultural View

ELAINE LEEDER

Domestic violence is a global problem and occurs in both industrialized and developing countries. Elaine Leeder discusses why women and children, especially girls, experience physical abuse in nations as diverse as India, Japan, Vietnam, and Africa. This dark side of family life reflects structural inequality and cultural attitudes about gender.

FAMILY VIOLENCE IN INDIA

The Indian government and feminist organizations are concerned about wife battering, child abuse and neglect, and infanticide, which occur quite regularly there. [Earlier] I mentioned bride burnings in India, called "dowry deaths," which occur as a result of rising demands for the dowry given from the bride's side to the groom's family. I also briefly mentioned female infanticide. Those are extreme forms of gender violence. However, in this [reading] we focus on the regular and daily patterns of domestic violence that take place in India.

Many forms of domestic violence in India occur as a result of rising industrialization and modernization. Families have rising economic expectations, and the problems are acted out at home. Wife battering is a fairly common occurrence (Rao, 1997). Mild forms of wife beating are commonplace, and many men and women

Source: The Family in Global Perspective: A Gendered Journey by Elaine Leeder. Thousand Oaks, Calif.: Sage, 2004, pp. 244–48, 251–54.

admit freely in interviews that it is justified if the woman does not "behave herself." Interestingly, though, in one study only 22 percent of the women admitted on surveys to having been beaten; it is unacceptable to admit abuse, yet it seems to be such a common practice that it is not considered worthy of mention. Only women for whom abuse is a serious or chronic problem are willing to admit it. Otherwise it is such an everyday affair that it is not considered a problem.

In rural India, women believe that alcohol and inadequate dowries provoke the abuse. Some drunken husbands beat their wives without provocation, and women who are beaten complain that the problem is exacerbated by the drunken fits of their husbands. Alcohol is widely available, as it is in the United States, and many of the men say that their drinking is due to a feeling of hopelessness caused by poverty. Their lack of options for breaking out of poverty leads them to drink to "forget their troubles."

Also, as dowry demands have escalated in the past 20 years, many parents have been unable to keep up with the inflation. Some girls are kept hostage by their inlaws in an attempt to extract larger amounts of money from the girls' parents. When those demands are not met, the young bride is beaten, often living in terror of what might become of her. Her power is also diminished in the home after she has been beaten. Sometimes "family resources are transferred away from the wife and her children to other members of the household . . . and the husband and wife are unable to construct a strong marital bond."

It appears that if women have male children they are less likely to be beaten. Having fulfilled societal expectations seems to provide a deterrent to abuse. A rural woman is more likely to be beaten if she has been sterilized. Sterilization is a major form of birth control in rural India; after bearing enough children, a woman often chooses it as contraception. It appears that a man feels freer to beat a woman who has been sterilized, perhaps out of fear of her infidelity.

In rural India, abuse is tolerated under certain circumstances, which include dowry problems, a wife's infidelity, her neglect of household duties, or her disobedience to her husband's dictates. Abuse is also tolerated if a husband beats his wife when he is drunk but is otherwise a good husband. But if a man batters his wife beyond levels considered tolerable for the village, or if he beats her for reasons not considered legitimate by the village, then a village elder or a local monk will intervene to stop the violence.

Finally, we should mention that living outside of marriage is not an option for an Indian woman. There are no alternatives to marriage for Indian women at this time. Although many women work outside of the home, the types of jobs available are limited, pay is quite low, and marriage is considered the norm.

Clearly, wife battering is a prevalent and "normal" family dynamic in India. It is part of the social fabric, so much so that it is not even commented on unless it is extreme. So too is child abuse.

Child abuse has occurred since time immemorial and exists across cultures. Usually it is the poorer classes who get the attention of public health and welfare services. But middle-class practices are more reflective of whether or not abuse is common in a society. In India middle-class families have experienced a greater amount of stress as the country modernizes and industrializes. India is becoming more urban, and this points to a rise in child abuse among Indian families (Segal, 1995). There is intense competition and effort at upward mobility. This also puts stress on the family. In addition, there is a well-established pattern of corporal punishment in raising children. Children are socialized to obey their parents, and there is strict discipline, even though infants are highly indulged. The family is highly hierarchical, and now that families are moving away from the joint family, there is less support for raising children and sharing household tasks. All these factors create an environment that's ripe for an increase in child abuse rates.

The use of corporal punishment is so well entrenched in Indian society that even the middle and upper classes admit to using it. In one study of 319 highly educated, college-graduate parents in three cities in India, a full 56.9 percent reported having used "acceptable" forms of violence, while 41.9 percent engaged in "abusive" violence, and 2.9 percent admitted using "extreme" violence on their children. Unfortunately we have no specific studies of middle- and upper-class parents in the United States with which to compare this data. Suffice it to say that in the United States we have comparably high rates of child abuse, too (Gelles & Straus, 1986). Remember that in the United States *at least* a million children are abused a year.

Female infanticide and child neglect are also major child abuse issues in India, particularly in rural villages. Barbara Miller (1987) has spent years studying abuse in rural north India and has found significant discrimination against girl children there. There is a strong preference for sons. Boys are needed as economic assets, for farming, and for the money they send home if they move away. They are more likely to stay with their families after marriage and maintain their parents in old age. Girls move away when they marry and cannot contribute to the family up-keep. Sons bring dowries and perform rituals among the Hindus when the father dies; therefore boys are important to the maintenance of family life, while girls are seen as a drain economically. This strong preference for sons has led to disappointment when a girl is born, withholding of medical care for girls, and preferential feeding of boy children.

Infanticide is the killing of a child under one year old, and is the most extreme form of child abuse. *Neonaticide* is the killing of an infant up to 24 hours old, and *feticide* is the abortion of a baby in utero, particularly when it is done as sex selection. After a child is 12 months old, the killing is considered a homicide. In north India, the killing of female infants is quite an old phenomenon. The British discovered it as early as 1789 and outlawed it by 1870. In some parts of India during that time, the sex ratio was 118 men to 100 women. Nowadays, systematic, indirect female infanticide still exists. Girls are not actively killed; they are just neglected so badly that they die from lack of care. The numbers seem to cross class and caste, with even wealthier families preferring sons. This is also true for well-educated families.

In India there is also sex-selective abortion. Although there is a lack of definitive data, anecdotal evidence indicates that it is quite widespread. One study found that in one hospital, of the 700 amniocenteses done, 250 were male and 450 were female. A full 430 of the 450 females were aborted, while all the male fetuses were brought to full term.

Now that I have presented this data, I urge a suspension of any ethnocentric value judgments. It is true that these figures are disturbing and certainly are contrary to Western-based humanistic values. Let's try to keep a view that is culturally relative, to understand why people would engage in such behavior. Understanding why it is done, and being aware of one's own bias, might lead us to think of what can be done about it. There are groups working in India and through the United Nations who have declared this problem a public health issue and are trying to prevent or reduce the incidence of these practices.

WIFE BATTERING IN JAPAN

Now let's focus our lens on another part of Asia, this time Japan. In previous chapters we talked about the way the Japanese family is organized, and how unlike it is to families in the United States, even though both countries are highly industrialized. In Japan the incidence of wife battering is quite high. In one study (Yoshihama & Sorenson, 1994), a survey was done of 796 married women, in which more than three-fourths reported at least one type of violence perpetrated by a male intimate partner. This ranged from a slap to an assault with a deadly weapon, from verbal ridicule to restriction of social activities, and from incompliance with contraception to forced, violent sex. About two-thirds of the most serious physically violent incidents resulted in injury.

Unlike the United States, Japan has no specific laws against wife battering as a crime, and there is no governmental funding for services that address the problem. Often, if women get help, it is through services intended for other purposes, like homes established under child welfare laws. Fully one-third of the women who use other services, like shelters that protect prostitutes, were actually battered women seeking protection from their abusers. A husband's violence is one of the primary reasons women list when they are seeking divorce, and contrary to the myths of the quiet, passive Japanese man, violence is an integral part of family life in Japanese society.

Often, when a woman seeks to end a violent marriage, the violence does not end. This is true in the United States as well as Japan. Violence often escalates during the process of separation and divorce. It is as if the man does not want to let go of his property, holding tighter and becoming more abusive as he fears the loss. Male violence in Japan seems to cross all socioeconomic strata and can lead to serious consequences. Women report broken bones, lacerations requiring stitches, ruptured eardrums, and other injuries requiring medical care.

Domestic violence in Japan is still an unrecognized problem. There is not even a word for it in Japanese; language has been adapted from the English to refer to it. An increasing level of media attention is being focused on the problem at the time of the publication of this book, but the level is far below that with which we are familiar in the West. This is a problem that bears watching closely, to see how well Japan deals with a problem that many countries are starting to grapple with. . . .

DOMESTIC VIOLENCE IN VIETNAM

. . . The Socialist Republic of Vietnam is rich in culture, deep in religion, and ancient yet modern. It is beautiful, with pristine beaches, huge rivers, and rice paddies galore. Eighty percent of the population lives in the rural areas, and it has a 94 percent literacy rate. We in the United States think that Vietnam is a place of war, and it was, in fact, for most of the past century. In 1945 Vietnam became independent of France, fought for its freedom, and then fought against the Americans, who established their presence there after the French pulled out.

The war has had a significant impact on family life in Vietnam. With the revolution in 1945 came the first attempts to change the inferior position of women there. Laws were passed to equalize the rights, positions, and interests of women. Unfortunately, today the vestiges of Confucian ideology still linger. Men act as kings in their homes even while the women in the workforce make more money than their husbands (Quy, 1996). Women are employed in the labor market in great numbers, but still do the "second shift" that's common in the United States. After work at the factory, Vietnamese women spend five to six hours a night on housework at home. This has been called

the "invisible violence" of Vietnam, because while there may not be physical violence between men and women, intimidation and fear drive the relationships. This inequity occurs for both urban educated and rural poor women. Many women feel that their situation is predestined, in accordance with Confucian ideology.

Then there is the "visible violence" that recently has led to a large number of divorces in Vietnam. One report indicates that as many as 87.5 percent of the divorces in 1992 were a result of violence or violence-related causes. There are numerous injuries and deaths related to violence in the home, although exact numbers are not available. What is known is that 17.5 percent of the deaths in Vietnam in 1992 were caused by family violence.

One of the reasons given for this problem is low socioeconomic status. Poor men, in particular, feel that it is permissible to take out their frustration and anger on their wives and children. Another reason given is the "feudal attitude": the old Confucian ideas of "thinking highly of men and slightly of women" seem to inform beliefs about hitting one's wife. Sometimes men take lovers, or even concubines, who come to live in the home with the wife, against the wife's will.

Other reasons for violence are drinking, gambling, adultery, and jealousy. Although there are no numbers available on this, the researcher conducted interviews with battered wives who attributed the abusive behavior to a few of these factors. Another reason given was what we would call the "intra-individual theory": that there is "mad blood" in the perpetrator. In Vietnam this means that there are people who always feel anxious and angry and tend to shift the blame onto others, especially their next of kin.

In Vietnamese law, men and women are considered equal. Violence toward wives and children is specifically prohibited and is considered a violation of human rights, and the government has established a series of local and state programs for intervention. There are also laws against the preference for male children, although as we will see, these have certainly not had much of an impact. Interestingly, however, the incidence of rape in Vietnam seems to be low, specifically as compared with the United States (Goodstein, 1996). The Vietnamese Women's Union plays a role at the local level, watching out for the rights of women (Johnson, 1996).

As in many parts of the world, preference for a son remains strong in Vietnam, especially in light of the family planning policy there, which recommends only two children per family (Haughton & Haughton, 1995). Payments must be made to the government should a family have more than two children, although the sanctions are not as strict as they are in neighboring China. Following the Confucian model, in Vietnam there is still the belief that a son will care for you in old age and that a son is an investment, while a daughter will leave. Even though women in Vietnam are well educated (remember, the literacy rate is 94 percent) and well integrated into the workforce, the Vietnamese still prefer male children.

Another problem related to violence in Vietnam is the trafficking in women (Barry, 1996). Vietnam's traditional values, like fate and filial piety, shape the culture and make it ripe for exploitation by the "sex work" industry. Other countries in the region, like Japan, Thailand, and Australia, have well-established sex industries that have begun moving into Vietnam as the country moves toward economic development. Vietnam has a history of sexual exploitation of women, most notably during the Vietnam War, when more than 500,000 women served as prostitutes to the U.S. troops. Many were rape victims or war widows needing to earn a living. Now many women are being forced into prostitution as part of the growing sex trade industry. Because prostitution provides immediate cash incentives for the women when other work is not available, it is becoming an increasingly viable option as the country moves toward a more westernized model of economics.

Vietnam, although a socialist country with some new elements of capitalism, seems to have similar domestic violence problems as other parts of the world: violence against wives, son sex preference, and a growing sex trade. It appears that not many places in the world are free of domestic violence.

DOMESTIC VIOLENCE IN AFRICA

. . . In Uganda, violence against one's wife is accepted as legitimate; when it is mentioned, most men just shrug and say, "It's our culture" (Doro, 1999). If a woman attacks her husband, the violence is considered criminal. The U.S. Department of State Uganda Report on Human Rights Practices for 1998 says that violence against women, including rape, is quite common. There are no specific laws against wife battering, although a law passed in 1997 provides protection for families, including wives and children. But it is hard to implement the law since law enforcement officials view the problem the way the public does, as not a problem.

Families in Uganda endure violence in silence, and violence is worse in the countryside than it is in the city. According to the Human Rights Report, the pattern is similar in other African countries, too. Women have few rights, neighbors don't want to get involved, and the women lie about their injuries if asked about them at medical facilities.

Several women's organizations in coalition are actively pursuing reform and holding public workshops to lobby for a revision of the Domestic Relations Act. Most of the trouble in getting anything done is related to lack of funding. Many of the countries in Africa do not have adequate funds to handle the many social problems they have, like AIDS, and they have put domestic violence issues on the back burner, because they think, after all, "It is our culture."

Other studies done in Africa are also not comprehensive. One study of domestic violence in Nigeria found that polygamy lends itself more to wife battering than do monogamous marriages (Efoghe, 1990). In this study, more polygamous marriages were violent than were monogamous marriages. Another study, of child sexual abuse in Zimbabwe, found that sexual abuse of children is not as prevalent there as it is internationally, with only about 10 percent of the population being victims of this kind of abuse (Khan, 1995). The authors of the study wonder whether this discrepancy reflects underreporting, or if sexual abuse of children is really not a big problem in Zimbabwe.

Finally, let's remember that Africa and parts of Southwest Asia perform ritual circumcision of girls. In Somalia, Kenya, the Sudan, Tanzania, Ethiopia, Egypt, Uganda, Chad, Mali, Senegal, Cameroon, Zaire, Nigeria, to name just a few, girls are cut and scraped to make their bodies more attractive and marriageable. This practice has been framed as a human rights abuse, as well as a form of child abuse that is being taken up as a problem by the United Nations and the World Health Organization.

CRITICAL-THINKING QUESTIONS

1. How is domestic violence similar in India, Japan, Vietnam, and Africa? How does it differ? Also, Leeder notes that rising industrialization and modernization increase the likelihood of family violence. Why, then, is wife battering also common in industrialized countries such as Japan and the United States?

2. Why do most of the women in these countries never complain about domestic violence? What individual, legal, historical, and cultural factors help explain their silence?

3. Leeder urges the reader to suspend "any ethnocentric value judgments" about family violence. What does she mean? And, if we do so, does this

mean that the global community shouldn't interfere with a country's violent practices against women and children?

REFERENCES

BARRY, K. 1996. Industrialization and economic development: The costs to women. In *Vietnam women in transition,* ed. K. Barry. New York: St. Martin's Press.

DORO, M. 1999, August 4. Available on the World Wide Web at End Violence@edc-cit.org.

EFOGHE, G. B. 1990. Nature and type of marriage as predictors of aggressiveness among married men in Ekpoma, Bendel State of Nigeria. *International Journal of Sociology of the Family,* 20 (Spring): 67–78.

GELLES, R., and M. STRAUS. 1986. Societal change and change in family violence from 1975–1985 as revealed in two national surveys. *Journal of Marriage and the Family,* 48 (3): 465–80.

GOODSTEIN, L. 1996. Sexual assessment in the U.S. and Vietnam: Some thoughts and questions. In *Vietnam women in transition,* ed. K. Barry, 275–86. New York: St. Martin's Press.

HAUGHTON, J., and D. HAUGHTON. 1995. Son preference in Vietnam. *Studies in Family Planning,* 26, 6 (Nov/Dec): 325–38.

JOHNSON, M. 1996. Violence against women in the family: The U.S. and Vietnam. In *Vietnam women in transition,* ed. K. Barry. New York: St. Martin's Press.

KHAN, N. 1995. Patterns of child sexual abuse in Zimbabwe: An overview. *Zimbabwe Journal of Educational Research,* 7, 2 (July): 181–208.

MILLER, B. 1987. Female infanticide and child neglect in rural North India. In *Child survival,* ed. N. Scheper-Hughes, 95–112. Dordrecht: D. Reidel Publishing Co.

QUY, L. 1996. Domestic violence in Vietnam. In *Vietnam women in transition,* ed. K. Barry, 263–74. New York: St. Martin's Press.

RAO, V. 1997. Wife beating in rural south India: A qualitative and econometric analysis. *Social Science and Medicine,* 44 (8): 1169–1180.

SEGAL, U. 1995. Child abuse by the middle class: A study of professionals in India. *Child Abuse and Neglect,* 19 (2): 217–31.

YOSHIHAMA, M., and S. SORENSON. 1994. Physical, sexual and emotional abuse by male intimates: Experiences of women in Japan. *Violence and Victims,* 9 (1): 63–77.

CLASSIC

CONTEMPORARY

CROSS-CULTURAL

44 The Souls of Black Folk

W. E. B. DU BOIS

W. E. B. Du Bois, a pioneering U.S. sociologist and the first African American to receive a doctorate from Harvard University, describes how a color-conscious society casts black people as "strangers in their own homes." One result, Du Bois explains, is that African Americans develop a "double consciousness," seeing themselves as Americans but always gazing back at themselves through the eyes of the white majority, as people set below and apart by color.

Between me and the other world there is ever an unasked question: unasked by some through feelings of delicacy; by others through the difficulty of rightly framing it. All, nevertheless, flutter round it. They approach me in a half-hesitant sort of way, eye me curiously or compassionately, and then, instead of saying directly, How does it feel to be a problem? they say, I know an excellent colored man in my town; or, I fought at Mechanicsville; or, Do not these Southern outrages make your blood boil? At these I smile, or am interested, or reduce the boiling to a simmer, as the occasion may require. To the real question, How does it feel to be a problem? I answer seldom a word.

Source: From *The Souls of Black Folk* by W. E. B. Du Bois (New York: Penguin, 1982; orig. 1903), pp. 43–53.

And yet, being a problem is a strange experience—peculiar even for one who has never been anything else, save perhaps in babyhood and in Europe. It is in the early days of rollicking boyhood that the revelation first bursts upon one, all in a day, as it were. I remember well when the shadow swept across me. I was a little thing, away up in the hills of New England, where the dark Housatonic winds between Hoosac and Taghkanic to the sea. In a wee wooden schoolhouse, something put it into the boys' and girls' heads to buy gorgeous visiting-cards—ten cents a package—and exchange. The exchange was merry, till one girl, a tall new-comer, refused my card—refused it peremptorily, with a glance. Then it dawned upon me with a certain suddenness that I was different from the others; or like, mayhap, in heart and life and longing,

261

but shut out from their world by a vast veil. I had thereafter no desire to tear down that veil, to creep through; I held all beyond it in common contempt, and lived above it in a region of blue sky and great wandering shadows. That sky was bluest when I could beat my mates at examination-time, or beat them at a foot-race, or even beat their stringy heads. Alas, with the years all this fine contempt began to fade; for the words I longed for, and all their dazzling opportunities, were theirs, not mine. But they should not keep these prizes, I said; some, all, I would wrest from them. Just how I would do it I could never decide: by reading law, by healing the sick, by telling the wonderful tales that swam in my head—some way. With other black boys the strife was not so fiercely sunny: Their youth shrunk into tasteless sycophancy, or into silent hatred of the pale world about them and mocking distrust of everything white; or wasted itself in a bitter cry, Why did God make me an outcast and a stranger in mine own house? The shades of the prison-house closed round about us all: walls strait and stubborn to the whitest, but relentlessly narrow, tall, and unscalable to sons of night who must plod darkly on in resignation, or beat unavailing palms against the stone, or steadily, half hopelessly, watch the streak of blue above.

After the Egyptian and Indian, the Greek and Roman, the Teuton and Mongolian, the Negro is a sort of seventh son, born with a veil, and gifted with second-sight in this American world—a world which yields him no true self-consciousness, but only lets him see himself through the revelation of the other world. It is a peculiar sensation, this double-consciousness, this sense of always looking at one's self through the eyes of others, of measuring one's soul by the tape of a world that looks on in amused contempt and pity. One ever feels his twoness—an American, a Negro; two souls, two thoughts, two unreconciled strivings; two warring ideals in one dark body, whose dogged strength alone keeps it from being torn asunder.

The history of the American Negro is the history of this strife, this longing to attain self-conscious manhood, to merge his double self into a better and truer self. In this merging he wishes neither of the older selves to be lost. He would not Africanize America, for America has too much to teach the world and Africa. He would not bleach his Negro soul in a flood of white Americanism, for he knows that Negro blood has a message for the world. He simply wishes to make it possible for a man to be both a Negro and an American, without being cursed and spit upon by his fellows, without having the doors of Opportunity closed roughly in his face.

This, then, is the end of his striving: to be a coworker in the kingdom of culture, to escape both death and isolation, to husband and use his best powers and his latent genius. These powers of body and mind have in the past been strangely wasted, dispersed, or forgotten. The shadow of a mighty Negro past flits through the tale of Ethiopia the Shadowy and of Egypt the Sphinx. Through history, the powers of single black men flash here and there like falling stars, and die sometimes before the world has rightly gauged their brightness. Here in America, in the few days since Emancipation, the black man's turning hither and thither in hesitant and doubtful striving has often made his very strength to lose effectiveness, to seem like absence of power, like weakness. And yet it is not weakness—it is the contradiction of double aims. The double-aimed struggle of the black artisan on the one hand to escape white contempt for a nation of mere hewers of wood and drawers of water, and on the other hand to plough and nail and dig for a poverty-stricken horde—could only result in making him a poor craftsman, for he had but half a heart in either cause. By the poverty and ignorance of his people, the Negro minister or doctor was tempted toward quackery and demagogy; and by the criticism of the other world, toward ideals that made him ashamed of his lowly tasks. The would-be black *savant* was confronted by the paradox that the knowledge his people needed was a twice-told tale to his white neighbors, while the knowledge which would teach the white world was Greek to his own flesh and blood. The innate love of harmony and beauty that set the ruder souls of his people a-dancing and a-singing raised but confusion and doubt in the soul of the black artist; for the beauty revealed to him was the soul-beauty of a race which his larger audience despised, and he could not articulate the message of another people. This waste of double aims, this seeking to satisfy two unreconciled ideals, has wrought sad havoc with the courage and faith and deeds of ten thousand thousand people, has sent them often wooing false gods and invoking false means of salvation, and at times has even seemed about to make them ashamed of themselves.

Away back in the days of bondage they thought to see in one divine event the end of all doubt and disappointment; few men ever worshipped Freedom with half such unquestioning faith as did the American Negro for two centuries. To him, so far as he thought and dreamed, slavery was indeed the sum of all villainies, the cause of all sorrow, the root of all prejudice; Emancipation was the key to a promised land of sweeter beauty than ever stretched before the eyes of wearied Israelites. In song and exhortation swelled one refrain—Liberty; in his tears and curses the God he implored had Freedom in his right hand. At last it came, suddenly, fearfully, like a dream. With one wild carnival of blood and passion came the message in his own plaintive cadences:

Shout, O children!
Shout, you're free!
For God has bought your liberty!

Years have passed away since then—ten, twenty, forty; forty years of national life, forty years of renewal and development, and yet the swarthy spectre sits in its accustomed seat at the Nation's feast. In vain do we cry to this our vastest social problem:

Take any shape but that, and my firm nerves
Shall never tremble!

The Nation has not yet found peace from its sins; the freedman has not yet found in freedom his promised land. Whatever of good may have come in these years of change, the shadow of a deep disappointment rests upon the Negro people—a disappointment all the more bitter because the unattained ideal was unbounded save by the simple ignorance of a lowly people.

The first decade was merely a prolongation of the vain search for freedom, the boon that seemed ever barely to elude their grasp, like a tantalizing will-o'-the-wisp, maddening and misleading the headless host. The holocaust of war, the terrors of the Ku Klux Klan, the lies of carpet-baggers, the disorganization of industry, and the contradictory advice of friends and foes, left the bewildered serf with no new watchword beyond the old cry for freedom. As the time flew, however, he began to grasp a new idea. The ideal of liberty demanded for its attainment powerful means, and these the Fifteenth Amendment gave him. The ballot, which before he had looked upon as a visible sign of freedom, he now regarded as the chief means of gaining and perfecting the liberty with which war had partially endowed him. And why not? Had not votes made war and emancipated millions? Had not votes enfranchised the freedmen? Was anything impossible to a power that had done all this? A million black men started with renewed zeal to vote themselves into the kingdom. So the decade flew away, the revolution of 1876 came, and left the half-free serf weary, wondering, but still inspired. Slowly but steadily, in the following years, a new vision began gradually to replace the dream of political power—a powerful movement, the rise of another ideal to guide the unguided, another pillar of fire by night after a clouded day. It was the ideal of "book-learning"; the curiosity, born of compulsory ignorance, to know and test the power of the cabalistic letters of the white man, the longing to know. Here at last seemed to have been discovered the mountain path to Canaan; longer than the highway of Emancipation and law, steep and rugged, but straight, leading to heights high enough to overlook life.

Up the new path the advance guard toiled, slowly, heavily, doggedly; only those who have watched and guided the faltering feet, the misty minds, the dull understandings, of the dark pupils of these schools know how faithfully, how piteously, this people strove to learn. It was weary work. The cold statistician wrote down the inches of progress here and there, noted also where here and there a foot had slipped or someone had fallen. To the tired climbers, the horizon was ever dark, the mists were often cold, the Canaan was always dim and far away. If, however, the vistas disclosed as yet no goal, no resting-place, little but flattery and criticism, the journey at least gave leisure for reflection and self-examination; it changed the child of Emancipation to the youth with dawning self-consciousness, self-realization, self-respect. In those sombre forests of his striving his own soul rose before him, and he saw himself, darkly, as through a veil; and yet he saw in himself some faint revelation of his power, of his mission. He began to have a dim feeling that, to attain his place in the world, he must be himself, and not another. For the first time he sought to analyze the burden he bore upon his back, that dead-weight of social degradation partially masked behind a half-named Negro problem. He felt his poverty; without a cent, without a home, without land, tools, or savings, he had entered into competition with rich, landed, skilled neighbors. To be a man is hard, but to be a poor race in a land of dollars is the very bottom of hardships. He felt the weight of his ignorance, not simply of letters, but of life, of business, of the humanities; the accumulated sloth and shirking and awkwardness of decades and centuries shackled his hands and feet. Nor was his burden all poverty and ignorance. The red stain of bastardy, which two centuries of systematic legal defilement of Negro women had stamped upon his race, meant not only the loss of ancient African chastity, but also the hereditary weight of a mass of corruption from white adulterers, threatening almost the obliteration of the Negro home.

A people thus handicapped ought not to be asked to race with the world, but rather allowed to give all its time and thought to its own social problems. But alas! while sociologists gleefully count his bastards and his prostitutes, the very soul of the toiling, sweating black man is darkened by the shadow of a vast despair. Men call the shadow prejudice, and learnedly explain it as the natural defence of culture against barbarism, learning against ignorance, purity against crime, the "higher" against the "lower" races. To which the Negro cries Amen! and swears that to so much of this strange prejudice as is founded on just homage to civilization, culture, righteousness, and progress, he humbly bows and meekly does obeisance. But before that nameless prejudice that leaps beyond all this he stands helpless, dismayed, and well-nigh speechless; before that personal disrespect and mockery, the ridicule and systematic humiliation, the distortion of fact and wanton license of fancy, the cynical ignoring of the better and the boisterous welcoming of the worse, the all-pervading desire to inculcate disdain for everything black, from Toussaint to the devil—before this there rises a sickening despair that would disarm and discourage any nation save that black host to whom "discouragement" is an unwritten word.

But the facing of so vast a prejudice could not but bring the inevitable self-questioning, self-disparagement, and lowering of ideals which ever accompany repression and breed in an atmosphere of contempt and hate. Whisperings and portents came borne upon the four winds: Lo! we are diseased and dying, cried the dark hosts; we cannot write, our voting is vain; what need of education, since we must always cook and serve? And the Nation echoed and enforced this self-criticism saying: Be content to be servants, and nothing more; what need of higher culture for half-men? Away with the black man's ballot, by force or fraud—and behold the suicide of a race! Nevertheless, out of the evil came something of good— the more careful adjustment of education to real life, the clearer perception of the Negroes' social responsibilities, and the sobering realization of the meaning of progress.

So dawned the time of *Sturm und Drang:* Storm and stress today rocks our little boat on the mad waters of the world-sea; there is within and without the sound of conflict, the burning of body and rending of soul; inspiration strives with doubt, and faith with vain questionings. The bright ideals of the past—physical freedom, political power, the training of brains and the training of hands—all these in turn have waxed and waned, until even the last grows dim and overcast. Are they all wrong, all false? No, not that, but each alone was over-simple and incomplete—the dreams of a credulous race-childhood, or the fond imaginings of the other world which does not know and does not want to know our power. To be really true, all these ideals must be melted and welded into one. The training of the schools we need today more than ever—the training of deft hands, quick eyes and ears, and above all the broader, deeper, higher culture of gifted minds and pure hearts. The power of the ballot we need in sheer self-defence—else what shall save us from a second slavery? Freedom, too, the long-sought, we still seek, the freedom of life and limb, the freedom to work and think, the freedom to love and aspire. Work, culture, liberty—all these we need, not singly but together, not successively but together, each growing and aiding each, and all striving toward that vaster ideal that swims before the Negro people, the ideal of human brotherhood, gained through the unifying ideal of Race; the ideal of fostering and developing the traits and talents of the Negro, not in opposition to or contempt for other races, but rather in large conformity to the greater ideals of the American Republic, in order that some day on American soil two world-races may give each to each those characteristics both so sadly lack. We the darker ones come even now not altogether empty-handed: There are today no truer exponents of the pure human spirit of the Declaration of Independence than the American Negroes; there is no true American music but the wild sweet melodies of the Negro slave, the American fairy tales and folklore are Indian and African; and, all in all, we black men seem the sole oasis of simple faith and reverence in a dusty desert of dollars and smartness. Will America be poorer if she replace her brutal dyspeptic blundering with light-hearted but determined Negro humility? or her coarse and cruel wit with loving jovial good-humor? or her vulgar music with the soul of the Sorrow Songs?

Merely a concrete test of the underlying principles of the great republic is the Negro Problem, and the spiritual striving of the freedmen's sons is in the travail of souls whose burden is almost beyond the measure of their strength, but who bear it in the name of an historic race, in the name of this the land of their fathers' fathers, and in the name of human opportunity.

CRITICAL-THINKING QUESTIONS

1. What does Du Bois mean by the "double consciousness" of African Americans?
2. Du Bois writes that people of color aspire to realizing a "better and truer self." What do you think he imagines such a self to be?
3. What are some of the reasons, according to Du Bois, that Emancipation (from slavery in 1863) brought disappointment to former slaves, at least in the short run?
4. Does this essay seem optimistic or pessimistic about the future of U.S. race relations? Why?

CLASSIC

CONTEMPORARY

CROSS-CULTURAL

45 Controlling Images
and Black Women's
Oppression

PATRICIA HILL COLLINS

*As W. E. B. Du Bois (see Reading 44) noted, many victims of racial prejudice and stereo-
types often experience inevitable self-questioning and self-disparagement. Recently, feminists have argued that women of color typically confront gendered racism—a combination
of both racism and sexism. In the following selection, Patricia Hill Collins shows how negative images of black women have provided an ideological justification for race, gender,
and class inequality.*

"Black women emerged from slavery firmly enshrined in the consciousness of white America as
'Mammy' and the 'bad black woman,'" contends
Cheryl Gilkes (1983:294). The dominant ideology of the slave era fostered the creation of four
interrelated, socially constructed controlling
images of Black womanhood, each reflecting the
dominant group's interest in maintaining Black
women's subordination. Given that both Black
and white women were important to slavery's
continuation, the prevailing ideology functioned
to mask contradictions in social relations affecting all women. According to the cult of true
womanhood, "true" women possessed four cardinal virtues: piety, purity, submissiveness, and do-
mesticity. Elite white women and those of the
emerging middle class were encouraged to aspire

to these virtues. African American women encountered a different set of controlling images.
The sexual ideology of the period as is the case
today "confirmed the differing material circumstances of these two groups of women . . . by balancing opposing definitions of womanhood and
motherhood, each dependent on the other for its
existence" (Carby, 1987:25).

The first controlling image applied to African
American women is that of the mammy—the
faithful, obedient domestic servant. Created to
justify the economic exploitation of house slaves
and sustained to explain Black women's longstanding restriction to domestic service, the
mammy image represents the normative yardstick used to evaluate all Black women's behavior. By loving, nurturing, and caring for her white
children and "family" better than her own, the
mammy symbolizes the dominant group's perception of the ideal Black female relationship to elite
white male power. Even though she may be well
loved and may wield considerable authority in her

Source: Copyright © 1991, from *Black Feminist Thought:
Knowledge, Consciousness, and the Politics of Empowerment*
by Patricia Hill Collins. Reproduced by permission of Routledge, Inc., part of The Taylor and Francis Group.

white "family," the mammy still knows her "place" as obedient servant. She has accepted her subordination.

Black women intellectuals have aggressively deconstructed the image of African American women as contented mammies by challenging traditional views of Black women domestics (Dill, 1980, 1988; Clark-Lewis, 1985; Rollins, 1985). Literary critic Trudier Harris's (1982) volume *From Mammies to Militants: Domestics in Black American Literature* investigates prominent differences in how Black women have been portrayed by others in literature and how they portray themselves. In her work on the difficulties faced by Black women leaders, Rhetaugh Dumas (1980) describes how Black women executives are hampered by being treated as mammies and penalized if they do not appear warm and nurturing. But despite these works, the mammy image lives on in scholarly and popular culture. Audre Lorde's account of a shopping trip offers a powerful example of its tenacity: "I wheel my two-year-old daughter in a shopping cart through a supermarket in . . . 1967, and a little white girl riding past in her mother's cart calls out excitedly, 'Oh look, Mommy, a baby maid!'" (1984:126).[1]

The mammy image is central to interlocking systems of race, gender, and class oppression. Since efforts to control African American family life require perpetuating the symbolic structures of racial oppression, the mammy image is important because it aims to shape Black women's behavior as mothers. As the members of African American families who are most familiar with the skills needed for Black accommodation, Black women are encouraged to transmit to their own children the deference behavior many are forced to exhibit in mammy roles. By teaching Black children their assigned place in white power structures, Black women who internalize the mammy image potentially become effective conduits for perpetuating racial oppression. In addition, employing mammies buttresses the racial superiority of white women employers and weds them more closely to their fathers,

husbands, and sons as sources of elite white male power (Rollins, 1985).

The mammy image also serves a symbolic function in maintaining gender oppression. Black feminist critic Barbara Christian argues that images of Black womanhood serve as a reservoir for the fears of Western culture, "a dumping ground for those female functions a basically Puritan society could not confront" (1985:2). Juxtaposed against the image of white women promulgated through the cult of true womanhood, the mammy image as the Other symbolizes the oppositional difference of mind/body and culture/nature thought to distinguish Black women from everyone else. Christian comments on the mammy's gender significance: "All the functions of mammy are magnificently physical. They involve the body as sensuous, as funky, the part of women that white southern America was profoundly afraid of. Mammy, then, harmless in her position of slave, unable because of her all-giving nature to do harm, is needed as an image, a surrogate to contain all those fears of the physical female" (1985:2). The mammy image buttresses the ideology of the cult of true womanhood, one in which sexuality and fertility are severed. "Good" white mothers are expected to deny their female sexuality and devote their attention to the moral development of their offspring. In contrast, the mammy image is one of an asexual woman, a surrogate mother in blackface devoted to the development of a white family.

No matter how loved they were by their white "families," Black women domestic workers remained poor because they were economically exploited. The restructured post–World War II economy in which African American women moved from service in private homes to jobs in the low-paid service sector has produced comparable economic exploitation. Removing Black women's labor from African American families and exploiting it denies Black extended family units the benefits of either decent wages or Black women's unpaid labor in their homes. Moreover, many white families in both the middle class and working class are able to maintain their class position because they have long used Black women as a source of cheap labor (Rollins, 1985; Byerly, 1986). The mammy image is designed to mask this economic exploitation of social class (King, 1973).

For reasons of economic survival, African American women may play the mammy role in paid work settings. But within African American communities these same women often teach their own children something quite different. Bonnie Thornton Dill's (1980) work on child-rearing patterns among Black domestics shows that while the participants in her study showed deference behavior at work, they discouraged their children from believing that they should be deferent to whites and encouraged their children to avoid domestic work. Barbara Christian's analysis of the mammy in Black slave narratives reveals that, "unlike the white southern image of mammy, she is cunning, prone to poisoning her master, and not at all content with her lot" (1985:5).

The fact that the mammy image cannot control Black women's behavior as mothers is tied to the creation of the second controlling image of Black womanhood. Though a more recent phenomenon, the image of the Black matriarch fulfills similar functions in explaining Black women's placement in interlocking systems of race, gender, and class oppression. Ironically, Black scholars such as William E. B. Du Bois (1969) and E. Franklin Frazier (1948) described the connections among higher rates of female-headed households in African American communities, the importance that women assume in Black family networks, and the persistence of Black poverty. However, neither scholar interpreted Black women's centrality in Black families as a *cause* of African American social class status. Both saw so-called matriarchal families as an *outcome* of racial oppression and poverty. During the eras when Du Bois and Frazier wrote, the oppression of African Americans was so total that control was maintained without the controlling image of matriarch. But what began as a muted

theme in the works of these earlier Black scholars grew into a full-blown racialized image in the 1960s, a time of significant political and economic mobility for African Americans. Racialization involves attaching racial meaning to a previously racially unclassified relationship, social practice, or group (Omi & Winant, 1986). Prior to the 1960s, female-headed households were certainly higher in African American communities, but an ideology racializing female-headedness as a causal feature of Black poverty had not emerged. Moreover, "the public depiction of Black women as unfeminine, castrating matriarchs came at precisely the same moment that the feminist movement was advancing its public critique of American patriarchy" (Gilkes, 1983:296).

While the mammy typifies the Black mother figure in white homes, the matriarch symbolizes the mother figure in Black homes. Just as the mammy represents the "good" Black mother, the matriarch symbolizes the "bad" Black mother. The modern Black matriarchy thesis contends that African American women fail to fulfill their traditional "womanly" duties (Moynihan, 1965). Spending too much time away from home, these working mothers ostensibly cannot properly supervise their children and are a major contributing factor to their children's school failure. As overly aggressive, unfeminine women, Black matriarchs allegedly emasculate their lovers and husbands. These men, understandably, either desert their partners or refuse to marry the mothers of their children. From an elite white male standpoint, the matriarch is essentially a failed mammy, a negative stigma applied to those African American women who dared to violate the image of the submissive, hard-working servant.

Black women intellectuals examining the role of women in African American families discover few matriarchs and even fewer mammies (Hale, 1980; Myers, 1980; Sudarkasa, 1981; Dill, 1988). Instead they portray African American mothers as complex individuals who often show tremendous strength under adverse conditions. In *A Raisin in the Sun*, the first play presented on Broadway written by a Black woman, Lorraine Hansberry (1959) examines the struggles of widow Lena Younger to actualize her dream of purchasing a home for her family. In *Brown Girl, Brownstones*, novelist Paule Marshall (1959) presents Mrs. Boyce, a Black mother negotiating a series of relationships with her husband, her daughters, the women in her community, and the work she must perform outside her home. Ann Allen Shockley's *Loving Her* (1974) depicts the struggle of a lesbian mother trying to balance her needs for self-actualization with the pressures of childrearing in the homophobic community. Like these fictional analyses, Black women's scholarship on Black single mothers also challenges the matriarchy thesis (Ladner, 1972; McCray, 1980; Lorde, 1984; McAdoo, 1985; Brewer, 1988).

Like the mammy, the image of the matriarch is central to interlocking systems of race, gender, and class oppression. Portraying African American women as matriarchs allows the dominant group to blame Black women for the success or failure of Black children. Assuming that Black poverty is passed on intergenerationally via value transmission in families, an elite white male standpoint suggests that Black children lack the attention and care allegedly lavished on white, middle-class children and that this deficiency seriously retards Black children's achievement. Such a view diverts attention from the political and economic inequality affecting Black mothers and children and suggests that anyone can rise from poverty if he or she only received good values at home. Those African Americans who remain poor are blamed for their own victimization. Using Black women's performance as mothers to explain Black economic subordination links gender ideology to explanations of class subordination.

The source of the matriarch's failure is her inability to model appropriate gender behavior. In the post–World War II era, increasing numbers of white women entered the labor market, limited their fertility, and generally challenged their proscribed roles in white patriarchal institutions.

The image of the Black matriarch emerged at that time as a powerful symbol for both Black and white women of what can go wrong if white patriarchal power is challenged. Aggressive, assertive women are penalized—they are abandoned by their men, end up impoverished, and are stigmatized as being unfeminine.

The image of the matriarch also supports racial oppression. Much social science research implicitly uses gender relations in African American communities as one putative measure of Black cultural disadvantage. For example, the Moynihan Report (1965) contends that slavery destroyed Black families by creating reversed roles for men and women. Black family structures are seen as being deviant because they challenge the patriarchal assumptions underpinning the construct of the ideal "family." Moreover, the absence of Black patriarchy is used as evidence for Black cultural inferiority (Collins, 1989). Black women's failure to conform to the cult of true womanhood can then be identified as one fundamental source of Black cultural deficiency. Cheryl Gilkes posits that the emergence of the matriarchal image occurred as a counterideology to efforts by African Americans and women who were confronting interlocking systems of race, gender, and class oppression: "The image of dangerous Black women who are also deviant castrating mothers divided the Black community at the critical period in the Black liberation struggle and created a wider gap between the worlds of Black and white women at a critical period in women's history" (1983:297).

Taken together, images of the mammy and the matriarch place African American women in an untenable position. For Black women workers in domestic work and other occupations requiring long hours and/or substantial emotional labor, becoming the ideal mammy means precious time and energy spent away from husbands and children. But being employed when Black men have difficulty finding steady work exposes African American women to the charge that Black women emasculate Black men by failing to be submissive, dependent, "feminine" women. Moreover, Black women's financial contributions to Black family well-being have also been cited as evidence supporting the matriarchy thesis (Moynihan, 1965). Many Black women are the sole support of their families, and labeling these women "matriarchs" erodes their self-confidence and ability to confront oppression. In essence, African American women who must work are labeled mammies, then are stigmatized again as matriarchs for being strong figures in their own homes.

A third, externally defined, controlling image of Black womanhood—that of the welfare mother—appears tied to Black women's increasing dependence on the post–World War II welfare state. Essentially an updated version of the breeder woman image created during slavery, this image provides an ideological justification for efforts to harness Black women's fertility to the needs of a changing political economy.

During slavery the breeder woman image portrayed Black women as more suitable for having children than white women. By claiming that Black women were able to produce children as easily as animals, this objectification of Black women as the Other provided justification for interference in the reproductive rights of enslaved Africans. Slaveowners wanted enslaved Africans to "breed" because every slave child born represented a valuable unit of property, another unit of labor, and, if female, the prospects for more slaves. The externally defined, controlling image of the breeder woman served to justify slaveowner intrusion into Black women's decisions about fertility (King, 1973; Davis, 1981).

The post–World War II political economy has offered African Americans rights not available in former historical periods (Fusfeld & Bates, 1984; Wilson, 1987). African Americans have successfully acquired basic political and economic protections from a greatly expanded welfare state, particularly Social Security, Aid to Families with Dependent Children, unemployment compensation, affirmative action, voting rights, antidiscrimination legislation, and the

minimum wage. In spite of sustained opposition by Republican administrations in the 1980s, these programs allow many African Americans to reject the subsistence-level, exploitative jobs held by their parents and grandparents. Job export, deskilling, and increased use of illegal immigrants have all been used to replace the loss of cheap, docile Black labor (Braverman, 1974; Gordon et al., 1982; Nash & Fernandez-Kelly, 1983). The large numbers of undereducated, unemployed African Americans, most of whom are women and children, who inhabit inner cities cannot be forced to work. From the standpoint of the dominant group, they no longer represent cheap labor but instead signify a costly threat to political and economic stability.

Controlling Black women's fertility in such a political economy becomes important. The image of the welfare mother fulfills this function by labeling as unnecessary and even dangerous to the values of the country the fertility of women who are not white and middle class. A closer look at this controlling image reveals that it shares some important features with its mammy and matriarch counterparts. Like the matriarch, the welfare mother is labeled a bad mother. But unlike the matriarch, she is not too aggressive—on the contrary, she is not aggressive enough. While the matriarch's unavailability contributed to her children's poor socialization, the welfare mother's accessibility is deemed the problem. She is portrayed as being content to sit around and collect welfare, shunning work and passing on her bad values to her offspring. The image of the welfare mother represents another failed mammy, one who is unwilling to become "de mule uh de world."

The image of the welfare mother provides ideological justifications for interlocking systems of race, gender, and class oppression. African Americans can be racially stereotyped as being lazy by blaming Black welfare mothers for failing to pass on the work ethic. Moreover, the welfare mother has no male authority figure to assist her. Typically portrayed as an unwed mother, she violates one cardinal tenet of Eurocentric masculinist thought: She is a woman alone. As a result, her treatment reinforces the dominant gender ideology positing that a woman's true worth and financial security should occur through heterosexual marriage. Finally, in the post–World War II political economy, one of every three African American families is officially classified as poor. With such high levels of Black poverty, welfare state policies supporting poor Black mothers and their children have become increasingly expensive. Creating the controlling image of the welfare mother and stigmatizing her as the cause of her own poverty and that of African American communities shifts the angle of vision away from structural sources of poverty and blames the victims themselves. The image of the welfare mother thus provides ideological justification for the dominant group's interest in limiting the fertility of Black mothers who are seen as producing too many economically unproductive children (Davis, 1981).

The fourth controlling image—the Jezebel, whore, or sexually aggressive woman—is central in the nexus of elite white male images of Black womanhood because efforts to control Black women's sexuality lie at the heart of Black women's oppression. The image of Jezebel originated under slavery when Black women were portrayed as being, to use Jewelle Gomez's words, "sexually aggressive wet nurses" (Clarke et al., 1983:99). Jezebel's function was to relegate all Black women to the category of sexually aggressive women, thus providing a powerful rationale for the widespread sexual assaults by white men typically reported by Black slave women (Davis, 1981; Hooks, 1981; White, 1985). Yet Jezebel served another function. If Black slave women could be portrayed as having excessive sexual appetites, then increased fertility should be the expected outcome. By suppressing the nurturing that African American women might give their own children which would strengthen Black family networks, and by forcing Black women to work in the field or "wet nurse" white children, slaveowners effectively tied the controlling images of Jezebel and Mammy to the economic exploitation inherent in the institution of slavery.

The fourth image of the sexually denigrated Black woman is the foundation underlying elite white male conceptualizations of the mammy, matriarch, and welfare mother. Connecting all three is the common theme of Black women's sexuality. Each image transmits clear messages about the proper links among female sexuality, fertility, and Black women's roles in the political economy. For example, the mammy, the only somewhat positive figure, is a desexed individual. The mammy is typically portrayed as overweight, dark, and with characteristically African features—in brief, as an unsuitable sexual partner for white men. She is asexual and therefore is free to become a surrogate mother to the children she acquired not through her own sexuality. The mammy represents the clearest example of the split between sexuality and motherhood present in Eurocentric masculinist thought. In contrast, both the matriarch and the welfare mother are sexual beings. But their sexuality is linked to their fertility, and this link forms one fundamental reason they are negative images. The matriarch represents the sexually aggressive woman, one who emasculates Black men because she will not permit them to assume roles as Black patriarchs. She refuses to be passive and thus is stigmatized. Similarly, the welfare mother represents a woman of low morals and uncontrolled sexuality, factors identified as the cause of her impoverished state. In both cases Black female control over sexuality and fertility is conceptualized as antithetical to elite white male interests.

Taken together, these four prevailing interpretations of Black womanhood form a nexus of elite white male interpretations of Black female sexuality and fertility. Moreover, by meshing smoothly with systems of race, class, and gender oppression, they provide effective ideological justifications for racial oppression, the politics of gender subordination, and the economic exploitation inherent in capitalist economies.

CRITICAL-THINKING QUESTIONS

1. Describe the four negative images of Black women. How have these images reinforced an "interlocking system" of Black women's oppression?

2. Collins argues that the controlling images "are designed to make racism, sexism, and poverty appear to be natural, normal, and an inevitable part of everyday life." Do you agree or disagree with this statement? Support your position.

3. Do women of other categories (such as Asians, Latinas, and Native Americans) face similar or different stereotypes?

NOTE

1. Brittan and Maynard (1984) note that ideology (1) is common sense and obvious; (2) appears natural, inevitable, and universal; (3) shapes lived experience and behavior; (4) is sedimented in people's consciousness; and (5) consists of a system of ideas embedded in the social system as a whole. This example captures all dimensions of how racism and sexism function ideologically. The status of Black woman as servant is so "common sense" that even a child knows it. That the child saw a Black female child as a baby maid speaks to the naturalization dimension and to the persistence of controlling images in individual consciousness and the social system overall.

REFERENCES

BRAVERMAN, H. 1974. *Labor and monopoly capital*. New York: Monthly Review Press.

BREWER, R. 1988. Black women in poverty: Some comments on female-headed families. *Signs*, 13(2): 331–39.

BRITTAN, A., and M. MAYNARD. 1984. *Sexism, racism and oppression*. New York: Basil Blackwell.

BYERLY, V. 1986. *Hard times cotton mills girls*. Ithaca, N.Y.: Cornell University Press.

CARBY, H. 1987. *Reconstructing womanhood: The emergence of the Afro-American woman novelist*. New York: Oxford.

CHRISTIAN, B. 1985. *Black feminist criticism: Perspectives on black women writers*. New York: Pergamon.

CLARKE, C., J. L. GOMEZ, E. HAMMONDS, B. JOHNSON, and L. POWELL. 1983. Conversations and questions: Black women on black women writers. *Conditions: Nine*, 3(3): 88–137.

CLARK-LEWIS, E. 1985. *"This work had a' end": The transition from live-in to day work*. Southern Women: The Intersection of Race, Class and Gender. Working Paper #2. Memphis, Tenn.: Center for Research on Women, Memphis State University.

COLLINS, P. H. 1989. A comparison of two works on black family life. *Signs*, 14(4): 875–84.

DAVIS, A. Y. 1981. *Women, race and class*. New York: Random House.

DILL, B. T. 1980. 'The means to put my children through': Child-rearing goals and strategies among black female domestic servants. In *The Black woman*, ed. L. F. Rodgers-Rose, 107–23. Beverly Hills, Calif.: Sage.

———. 1988a. 'Making your job good yourself': Domestic service and the construction of personal dignity. In *Women and the politics of empowerment*, eds. A. Bookman and S. Morgen, 33–52. Philadelphia: Temple University Press.

———. 1988b. Our mothers' grief: Racial ethnic women and the maintenance of families. *Journal of Family History*, 13(4): 415–31.

DU BOIS, W. E. B. 1969. *The Negro American family*. New York: Negro Universities Press.

DUMAS, R. G. 1980. Dilemmas of Black females in leadership. In *The Black woman*, ed. L. F. Rodgers-Rose, 203–15. Beverly Hills, Calif.: Sage.

FRAZIER, E. F. 1948. *The Negro family in the United States*. New York: Dryden Press.

FUSFELD, D. R., and T. BATES. 1984. *The political economy of the urban ghetto*. Carbondale: Southern Illinois University Press.

GILKES, C. T. 1983. From slavery to social welfare: Racism and the control of Black women. In *Class, race, and sex: The dynamics of control*, eds. A. Swerdlow and H. Lessinger, 288–300. Boston: G. K. Hall.

GORDON, D. M., R. EDWARDS, and M. REICH. 1982. *Segmented work, divided workers*. New York: Cambridge University Press.

HALE, J. 1980. The Black woman and child rearing. In *The Black woman*, ed. L. F. Rodgers-Rose, 79–88. Beverly Hills, Calif.: Sage.

HANSBERRY, L. 1959. *A raisin in the sun*. New York: Signet.

HARRIS, T. 1982. *From mammies to militants: Domestics in Black American literature*. Philadelphia: Temple University Press.

HOOKS, B. 1981. *Ain't I a woman: Black women and feminism*. Boston: South End Press.

KING, M. 1973. The politics of sexual stereotypes. *Black Scholar*, 4(6–7): 12–23.

LADNER, J. 1972. *Tomorrow's tomorrow*. Garden City, N.Y.: Doubleday.

LORDE, A. 1984. *Sister outsider*. Trumansberg, N.Y.: The Crossing Press.

MARSHALL, P. 1959. *Brown girl, brownstones*. New York: Avon.

MCADOO, H. P. 1985. Strategies used by Black single mothers against stress. *Review of Black Political Economy*, 14(2–3): 153–66.

MCCRAY, C. A. 1980. The Black woman and family roles. In *The Black woman*, ed. L. F. Rodgers-Rose, 67–78. Beverly Hills, Calif.: Sage.

MOYNIHAN, D. P. 1965. *The negro family: The case for national action.* Washington, D.C.: GPO.

MYERS, L. W. 1980. *Black women: Do they cope better?* Englewood Cliffs, N.J.: Prentice Hall.

NASH, J., and M. P. FERNANDEZ-KELLY, eds. 1983. *Women, men, and the international division of labor.* Albany: State University of New York.

OMI, M., and H. WINANT. 1986. *Racial formation in the United States: From the 1960s to the 1980s.* New York: Routledge.

ROLLINS, J. 1985. *Between women: Domestics and their employers.* Philadelphia: Temple University Press.

SHOCKLEY, A. A. 1974. *Loving her.* Tallahassee, Fla.: Naiad Press.

SUDARKASA, N. 1981. Interpreting the African heritage in Afro-American family organization. In *Black families,* ed. H. P. McAdoo, 37–53. Beverly Hills, Calif.: Sage.

WHITE, D. G. 1985. *Ar'n't I a woman? Female slaves in the plantation south.* New York: W. W. Norton.

WILSON, W. J. 1987. *The truly disadvantaged: The inner city, the underclass, and public policy.* Chicago: University of Chicago Press.

CLASSIC

CONTEMPORARY

CROSS-CULTURAL

46 How Did Jews Become White Folks?

KAREN B. BRODKIN

One way to see how societies construct race and ethnicity is to look at the historical experiences of particular categories of people in the United States. A century ago, the author of this selection explains, Jews and other European immigrants were defined as nonwhite. After World War II, however, Jews were included among "white folks."

The American nation was founded and developed by the Nordic race, but if a few more million members of the Alpine, Mediterranean, and Semitic races are poured among us, the result must inevitably be a hybrid race of people as worthless and futile as the good-for-nothing mongrels of Central America and Southeastern Europe.

> (Kenneth Roberts, quoted in Carlson & Colburn, 1972:312)

It is clear that Kenneth Roberts did not think of my ancestors as white like him. The late nineteenth and early decades of the twentieth centuries saw a steady stream of warnings by scientists, policymakers, and the popular press that "mongrelization" of the Nordic or Anglo-Saxon race—the real Americans—by inferior European races (as well as inferior non-European ones) was destroying the fabric of the nation. I continue to be surprised to read that America did not always regard its immigrant European workers as white,

"How Did Jews Become White Folks?" by Karen Brodkin Sacks, from *How Did Jews Become White Folks & What That Says About Race in America*, by Karen Brodkin Sacks, pp. 79–83, 86–87, 88–92, 96 (New Brunswick, NJ: Rutgers University Press, 1998)

that they thought people from different nations were biologically different. My parents, who are first-generation U.S.-born Eastern European Jews, are not surprised. They expect anti-Semitism to be part of the fabric of daily life, much as I expect racism to be part of it. They came of age in a Jewish world in the 1920s and 1930s at the peak of anti-Semitism in the United States (Gerber, 1986a). . . .

It is certainly true that the United States has a history of anti-Semitism and of beliefs that Jews were members of an inferior race. But Jews were hardly alone. American anti-Semitism was part of a broader pattern of late-nineteenth-century racism against all southern and eastern European immigrants, as well as against Asian immigrants. These views justified all sorts of discriminatory treatment, including closing the doors to immigration from Europe and Asia in the 1920s.[1] This picture changed radically after World War II. Suddenly the same folks who promoted nativism and xenophobia were eager to believe that the Euro-origin people whom they had deported, reviled as members of inferior races, and prevented from immigrating only a few years earlier were now model middle-class white suburban citizens.

It was not an educational epiphany that made those in power change their hearts, their minds, and our race. Instead, it was the biggest and best affirmative action program in the history of our nation, and it was for Euromales. There are similarities and differences in the ways each of the European immigrant groups became "whitened." I want to tell the story in a way that links anti-Semitism to other varieties of anti-European racism, because this foregrounds what Jews shared with other Euroimmigrants and shows changing notions of whiteness to be part of America's larger system of institutional racism.

EURORACES

The U.S. "discovery" that Europe had inferior and superior races came in response to the great waves of immigration from southern and eastern Europe in the late nineteenth century. Before that time, European immigrants—including Jews—had been largely assimilated into the white population. The 23 million European immigrants who came to work in U.S. cities after 1880 were too many and too concentrated to disperse and blend. Instead, they piled up in the country's most dilapidated urban areas, where they built new kinds of working-class ethnic communities. Since immigrants and their children made up more than 70 percent of the population of most of the country's largest cities, urban America came to take on a distinctly immigrant flavor. The golden age of industrialization in the United States was also the golden age of class struggle between the captains of the new industrial empires and the masses of manual workers whose labor made them rich. As the majority of mining and manufacturing workers, immigrants were visibly major players in these struggles (Higham, 1955:226; Steinberg, 1989:36).[2]

The Red Scare of 1919 clearly linked anti-immigrant to anti-working-class sentiment—to the extent that the Seattle general strike of native-born workers was blamed on foreign agitators. The Red Scare was fueled by economic depression, a massive postwar strike wave, the Russian revolution, and a new wave of postwar immigration. Strikers in steel, and the garment and textile workers in New York and New England, were mainly new immigrants. "As part of a fierce counteroffensive, employers inflamed the historic identification of class conflict with immigrant radicalism." Anti-communism and anti-immigrant sentiment came together in the Palmer raids and deportation of immigrant working-class activists. There was real fear of revolution. One of President Wilson's aides feared it was "the first appearance of the soviet in this country" (Higham, 1955:226).

Not surprisingly, the belief in European races took root most deeply among the wealthy U.S.-born Protestant elite, who feared a hostile and seemingly unassimilable working class. By the end of the nineteenth century, Senator Henry Cabot Lodge pressed Congress to cut off immigration to the United States; Teddy Roosevelt raised the alarm of "race suicide" and took Anglo-Saxon women to task for allowing "native" stock to be outbred by inferior immigrants. In the twentieth century, these fears gained a great deal of social legitimacy thanks to the efforts of an influential network of aristocrats and scientists who developed theories of eugenics—breeding for a "better" humanity—and scientific racism. Key to these efforts was Madison Grant's influential *Passing of the Great Race,* in which he shared his discovery that there were three or four major European races ranging from the superior Nordics of northwestern Europe to the inferior southern and eastern races of Alpines, Mediterraneans, and, worst of all, Jews, who seemed to be everywhere in his native New York City. Grant's nightmare was race mixing among Europeans. For him, "the cross between any of the three European races and a Jew is a Jew" (quoted in Higham, 1955:156). He didn't have good things to say about Alpine or Mediterranean "races" either. For Grant, race and class were interwoven: The upper class was racially pure Nordic, and the lower classes came from the lower races.

Far from being on the fringe, Grant's views resonated with those of the nonimmigrant middle class. A *New York Times* reporter wrote of his visit to the Lower East Side:

This neighborhood, peopled almost entirely by the people who claim to have been driven from Poland and Russia, is the eyesore of New York and perhaps the filthiest place on the western continent. It is impossible for a Christian to live there because he will be driven out, either by blows or the dirt and stench. Cleanliness is an unknown quantity to these people. They cannot be lifted up to a higher plane because they do not want to be. If the cholera should ever get among these people, they would scatter its germs as a sower does grain. (quoted in Schoener, 1967:58)[3]

Such views were well within the mainstream of the early twentieth-century scientific community. Grant and eugenicist Charles B. Davenport organized the Galton Society in 1918 in order to foster research and to otherwise promote eugenics and immigration restriction.[4] Lewis Terman, Henry Goddard, and Robert Yerkes, developers of the so-called intelligence test, believed firmly that southeastern European immigrants, African Americans, American Indians, and Mexicans were "feebleminded." And indeed, more than 80 percent of the immigrants whom Goddard tested at Ellis Island in 1912 turned out to be just that. Racism fused with eugenics in scientific circles, and the eugenics circles overlapped with the nativism of WASP aristocrats. During World War I, racism shaped the army's development of a mass intelligence test. Psychologist Robert Yerkes, who developed the test, became an even stronger advocate of eugenics after the war. Writing in the *Atlantic Monthly* in 1923, he noted:

If we may safely judge by the army measurements of intelligence, races are quite as significantly different as individuals. . . [and] almost as great as the intellectual difference between negro and white in the army are the differences between white racial groups. . . .

For the past ten years or so the intellectual status of immigrants has been disquietingly low. Perhaps this is because of the dominance of the Mediterranean races, as contrasted with the Nordic and Alpine. (quoted in Carlson & Colburn, 1972:333–34)

By the 1920s, scientific racism sanctified the notion that real Americans were white and real whites came from northwest Europe. Racism animated laws excluding and expelling Chinese in 1882, and then closing the door to immigration by virtually all Asians and most Europeans in 1924 (Saxton, 1971, 1990). Northwestern European ancestry as a requisite for whiteness was set in legal concrete when the Supreme Court denied Bhagat Singh Thind the right to become a naturalized citizen under a 1790 federal law that allowed whites the right to become naturalized citizens. Thind argued that Asian Indians were the real Aryans and Caucasians, and therefore white. The Court countered that the United States only wanted blond Aryans and Caucasians, "that the blond Scandinavian and the brown Hindu have a common ancestor in the dim reaches of antiquity, but the average man knows perfectly well that there are unmistakable and profound differences between them today" (Takaki, 1989:298–99). A narrowly defined white, Christian race was also built into the 1705 Virginia "Act concerning servants and slaves." This statute stated "that no negroes, mulattos and Indians or other infidels or jews, Moors, Mahometans or other infidels shall, at any time, purchase any christian servant, nor any other except of their own complexion" (Martyn, 1979:111).[5]

The 1930 census added its voice, distinguishing not only immigrant from "native" whites, but also native whites of native white parentage, and native whites of immigrant (or mixed) parentage. In distinguishing immigrant (southern and eastern Europeans) from "native" (northwestern Europeans), the census reflected the racial distinctions of the eugenicist-inspired intelligence tests.[6]

Racism and anti-immigrant sentiment in general and anti-Semitism in particular flourished in higher education. Jews were the first of the Euroimmigrant groups to enter colleges in significant numbers, so it wasn't surprising that they faced the brunt of discrimination there.[7] The Protestant elite complained that Jews were unwashed, uncouth, unrefined, loud, and pushy. Harvard University President A. Lawrence Lowell, who was also a vice president of the Immigration Restriction League, was openly opposed to Jews at Harvard. The Seven Sisters schools had a reputation for "flagrant discrimination." M. Carey Thomas, Bryn Mawr president, may have been a feminist of a kind, but she also was an admirer of scientific racism and an advocate of immigration restriction. She "blocked both the admission of black students and the promotion of Jewish instructors" (Synott, 1986:233, 238–39, 249–50).

Anti-Semitic patterns set by these elite schools influenced standards of other schools, made anti-Semitism acceptable, and "made the aura of exclusivity a desirable commodity for the college-seeking clientele" (Synott, 1986:250; and see Karabel, 1984; Silberman, 1985; Steinberg, 1989: chaps. 5, 9). Fear that colleges "might soon be overrun by Jews" were publicly expressed at a 1918 meeting of the Association of New England Deans. In 1919 Columbia University took steps to decrease the number of entering Jews by a set of practices that soon came to be widely adopted. The school developed a psychological test based on the World War I army intelligence tests to measure "innate ability—and middle-class home environment" and redesigned the admission application to ask for religion, father's name and birthplace, a photo, and a personal interview (Synott, 1986:239–40). Other techniques for excluding Jews, like a fixed class size, a chapel requirement, and preference for children of alumni, were less obvious. Sociologist Jerome Karabel (1984) has argued that these exclusionary efforts provided the basis for contemporary criteria for college admission that mix grades and test scores with criteria for well-roundedness and character, as well as affirmative action for athletes and children of alumni, which allowed schools to select more affluent Protestants. Their proliferation in the 1920s caused the intended drop in the number of Jewish students in law, dental, and medical schools and also saw the imposition of

quotas in engineering, pharmacy, and veterinary schools.[8]. . .

EUROETHNICS INTO WHITES

By the time I was an adolescent, Jews were just as white as the next white person. Until I was eight, I was a Jew in a world of Jews. Everyone on Avenue Z in Sheepshead Bay was Jewish. I spent my days playing and going to school on three blocks of Avenue Z, and visiting my grandparents in the nearby Jewish neighborhoods of Brighton Beach and Coney Island. There were plenty of Italians in my neighborhood, but they lived around the corner. They were a kind of Jew, but on the margins of my social horizons. Portuguese were even more distant, at the end of the bus ride, at Sheepshead Bay. The schul, or temple, was on Avenue Z, and I begged my father to take me like all the other fathers took their kids, but religion wasn't part of my family's Judaism. Just how Jewish my neighborhood was hit me in first grade when I was one of two kids in my class to go to school on Rosh Hashanah. My teacher was shocked—she was Jewish too—and I was embarrassed to tears when she sent me home. I was never again sent to school on Jewish holidays. We left that world in 1949 when we moved to Valley Stream, Long Island, which was Protestant, Republican, and even had farms until Irish, Italian, and Jewish exurbanites like us gave it a more suburban and Democratic flavor. Neither religion nor ethnicity separated us at school or in the neighborhood. Except temporarily. In elementary school years, I remember a fair number of dirt-bomb (a good suburban weapon) wars on the block. Periodically one of the Catholic boys would accuse me or my brother of killing his God, to which we would reply, "Did not" and start lobbing dirt-bombs. Sometimes he would get his friends from Catholic school, and I would get mine from public school kids on the block, some of whom were Catholic. Hostilities lasted no more than a couple of hours and punctuated an otherwise friendly relationship. They ended by junior high years, when other things became more important. Jews, Catholics, and Protestants, Italians, Irish, Poles, and "English" (I don't remember hearing WASP as a kid) were mixed up on the block and in school. We thought of ourselves as middle class and very enlightened because our ethnic backgrounds seemed so irrelevant to high school culture. We didn't see race (we thought), and racism was not part of our peer consciousness, nor were the immigrant or working-class histories of our families.

Like most chicken and egg problems, it's hard to know which came first. Did Jews and other Euroethnics become white because they became middle class? That is, did money whiten? Or did being incorporated in an expanded version of whiteness open up the economic doors to a middle-class status? Clearly, both tendencies were at work. Some of the changes set in motion during the war against fascism led to a more inclusive version of whiteness. Anti-Semitism and anti-European racism lost respectability. The 1940 census no longer distinguished native whites of native parentage from those, like my parents, of immigrant parentage, so that Euroimmigrants and their children were more securely white by submersion in an expanded notion of whiteness. (This census also changed the race of Mexicans to white [U.S. Bureau of the Census, 1940:4].) Theories of nurture and culture replaced theories of nature and biology. Instead of dirty and dangerous races who would destroy U.S. democracy, immigrants became ethnic groups whose children had successfully assimilated into the mainstream and risen to the middle class. In this new myth, Euroethnic suburbs like mine became the measure of U.S. democracy's victory over racism. Jewish mobility became a new Horatio Alger story. In time and with hard work, every ethnic group would get a piece of the pie, and the United States would be a nation with equal opportunity for all its people to become part of a prosperous middle-class majority. And it seemed that Euroethnic immigrants and their children were delighted to join middle America.[9]

This is not to say that anti-Semitism disappeared after World War II, only that it fell from fashion and was driven underground. . . .

Although changing views on who was white made it easier for Euroethnics to become middle class, it was also the case that economic prosperity played a very powerful role in the whitening process. Economic mobility of Jews and other Euroethnics rested ultimately on U.S. postwar economic prosperity with its enormously expanded need for professional, technical, and managerial labor, and on government assistance in providing it. The United States emerged from the war with the strongest economy in the world. Real wages rose between 1946 and 1960, increasing buying power a hefty 22 percent and giving most Americans some discretionary income (Nash et al., 1986:885–86). U.S. manufacturing, banking, and business services became increasingly dominated by large corporations, and these grew into multinational corporations. Their organizational centers lay in big, new urban headquarters that demanded growing numbers of technical and managerial workers. The postwar period was a historic moment for real class mobility and for the affluence we have erroneously come to believe was the U.S. norm. It was a time when the old white and the newly white masses became middle class.

The GI Bill of Rights, as the 1944 Serviceman's Readjustment Act was known, was arguably the most massive affirmative action program in U.S. history. It was created to develop needed labor-force skills, and to provide those who had them with a life-style that reflected their value to the economy. The GI benefits ultimately extended to 16 million GIs (veterans of the Korean War as well) included priority in jobs—that is, preferential hiring, but no one objected to it then—financial support during the job search; small loans for starting up businesses; and, most important, low-interest home loans and educational benefits, which included tuition and living expenses (Brown, 1946; Hurd, 1946; Mosch, 1975; *Postwar Jobs for Veterans,* 1945; Willenz, 1983). This legislation was rightly regarded as one of the most revolutionary postwar programs. I call it affirmative action because it was aimed at and disproportionately helped male, Euro-origin GIs.

GI benefits, like the New Deal affirmative action programs before them and the 1960s affirmative action programs after them, were responses to protest. Business executives and the general public believed that the war economy had only temporarily halted the Great Depression. Many feared its return and a return to the labor strife and radicalism of the 1930s (Eichler, 1982:4; Nash et al., 1986:885). "[M]emories of the Depression remained vivid and many people suffered from what Davis Ross has aptly called 'depression psychosis'—the fear that the war would inevitably be followed by layoffs and mass unemployment" (Wynn, 1976:15).

It was a reasonable fear. The 11 million military personnel who were demobilized in the 1940s represented a quarter of the U.S. labor force (Mosch, 1975:1, 20). In addition, ending war production brought a huge number of layoffs, growing unemployment, and a high rate of inflation. To recoup wartime losses in real wages caused by inflation as well as by the unions' no-strike pledge in support of the war effort, workers staged a massive wave of strikes in 1946. More workers went out on strike that year than ever before, and there were strikes in all the heavy industries: railroads, coal mining, auto, steel, and electrical. For a brief moment, it looked like class struggle all over again. But government and business leaders had learned from the experience of bitter labor struggles after World War I just how important it was to assist demobilized soldiers. The GI Bill resulted from their determination to avoid those mistakes this time. The biggest benefits of this legislation were for college and technical school education, and for very cheap home mortgages.

EDUCATION AND OCCUPATION

It is important to remember that prior to the war, a college degree was still very much a "mark of

the upper class" (Willenz, 1983:165). Colleges were largely finishing schools for Protestant elites. Before the postwar boom, schools could not begin to accommodate the American masses. Even in New York City before the 1930s, neither the public schools nor City College had room for more than a tiny fraction of potential immigrant students.

Not so after the war. The almost 8 million GIs who took advantage of their educational benefits under the GI bill caused "the greatest wave of college building in American history" (Nash et al., 1986:885). White male GIs were able to take advantage of their educational benefits for college and technical training, so they were particularly well positioned to seize the opportunities provided by the new demands for professional, managerial, and technical labor. "It has been well documented that the GI educational benefits transformed American higher education and raised the educational level of that generation and generations to come. With many provisions for assistance in upgrading their educational attainments, veterans pulled ahead of nonveterans in earning capacity. In the long run it was the nonveterans who had fewer opportunities" (Willenz, 1983:165).[10]

Just how valuable a college education was for white men's occupational mobility can be seen in John Keller's study of who benefited from the metamorphosis of California's Santa Clara Valley into Silicon Valley. Formerly an agricultural region, in the 1950s the area became the scene of explosive growth in the semiconductor electronics industry. This industry epitomized the postwar economy and occupational structure. It owed its existence directly to the military and to the National Aeronautics and Space Administration (NASA), who were its major funders and its major markets. It had an increasingly white-collar workforce. White men, who were the initial production workers in the 1950s, quickly transformed themselves into a technical and professional workforce thanks largely to GI benefits and the new junior college training programs designed to meet the industry's growing workforce needs. Keller notes that "62 percent of enrollees at San Jose Junior College (later renamed San Jose City College) came from blue-collar families, and 55 percent of all job placements were as electronics technicians in the industrial and service sectors of the county economy" (1983:363). As white men left assembly work and the industry expanded between 1950 and 1960, they were replaced initially by Latinas and African American women, who were joined after 1970 by new immigrant women. Inmigrating men tended to work in the better-paid unionized industries that grew up in the area.

Postwar expansion made college accessible to the mass of Euromales in general and to Jews in particular. My generation's "Think what you could have been!" answer to our parents became our reality as quotas and old occupational barriers fell and new fields opened up to Jews. The most striking result was a sharp decline in Jewish small businesses and a skyrocketing of Jewish professionals. For example, as quotas in medical schools fell, the numbers of Jewish doctors mushroomed. If Boston is an indication, just over 1 percent of all Jewish men before the war were doctors compared to 16 percent of the postwar generation (Silberman, 1985:124, and see 118–26). A similar Jewish mass movement took place into college and university faculties, especially in "new and expanding fields in the social and natural sciences" (Steinberg, 1989:137).[11] Although these Jewish college professors tended to be sons of businesspersons and professionals, the postwar boom saw the first large-scale class mobility among Jewish men. Sons of working-class Jews now went to college and became professionals themselves; according to the Boston survey, almost two-thirds of them. This compared favorably with three-quarters of the sons of professional fathers (Silberman, 1985: 121–22).[12]

Even more significantly, the postwar boom transformed the U.S. class structure—or at least its status structure—so that the middle class expanded to encompass most of the population. Before the war, most Jews, like most other Americans, were working class. Already upwardly mobile before the war relative to other immigrants, Jews floated high on this rising economic tide, and most of them entered the middle class. Still, even the high tide missed some Jews. As late as 1973, some 15 percent of New York's Jews were poor or near-poor, and in the 1960s, almost 25 percent of employed Jewish men remained manual workers (Steinberg, 1989:89–90).

Educational and occupational GI benefits really constituted affirmative action programs for white males because they were decidedly not extended to African Americans or to women of any race. White male privilege was shaped against the backdrop of wartime racism and postwar sexism. During and after the war, there was an upsurge in white racist violence against black servicemen in public schools, and in the KKK, which spread to California and New York (Dalfiume, 1969:133–34). The number of lynchings rose during the war, and in 1943 there were antiblack race riots in several large northern cities. Although there was a wartime labor shortage, black people were discriminated against in access to well-paid defense industry jobs and in housing. In 1946 there were white riots against African Americans across the South, and in Chicago and Philadelphia as well. Gains made as a result of the wartime Civil Rights movement, especially employment in defense-related industries, were lost with peacetime conversion as black workers were the first fired, often in violation of seniority (Wynn, 1976:114, 116). White women were also laid off, ostensibly to make jobs for demobilized servicemen, and in the long run women lost most of the gains they had made in wartime (Kessler-Harris, 1982). We now know that women did not leave the labor force in any significant numbers but instead were forced to find inferior jobs, largely nonunion, part-time, and clerical.

Theoretically available to all veterans, in practice women and black veterans did not get anywhere near their share of GI benefits. Because women's units were not treated as part of the military, women in them were not considered veterans and were ineligible for Veterans' Administration (VA) benefits (Willenz, 1983:168). The barriers that almost completely shut African American GIs out of their benefits were more complex. In Wynn's portrait (1976:115), black GIs anticipated starting new lives, just like their white counterparts. Over 43 percent hoped to return to school and most expected to relocate, to find better jobs in new lines of work. The exodus from the South toward the North and far West was particularly large. So it wasn't a question of any lack of ambition on the part of African American GIs.

Rather, the military, the Veterans' Administration, the U.S. Employment Service, and the Federal Housing Administration (FHA) effectively denied African American GIs access to their benefits and to the new educational, occupational, and residential opportunities. Black GIs who served in the thoroughly segregated armed forces during World War II served under white officers, usually southerners (Binkin & Eitelberg, 1982; Dalfiume, 1969; Foner, 1974; Johnson, 1967; Nalty & MacGregor, 1981). African American soldiers were disproportionately given dishonorable discharges, which denied them veterans' rights under the GI Bill. Thus between August and November 1946, 21 percent of white soldiers and 39 percent of black soldiers were dishonorably discharged. Those who did get an honorable discharge then faced the Veterans' Administration and the U.S. Employment Service. The latter, which was responsible for job placements, employed very few African Americans, especially in the South. This meant that black veterans did not receive much employment information, and that the offers they did receive were for low-paid and menial jobs. "In one survey of fifty cities, the movement of blacks into peacetime employment was found to be lagging far behind that of white veterans: in Arkansas 95 percent of the placements made by the USES for Afro Americans were in service or unskilled jobs" (Nalty and

MacGregor, 1981:218, and see 60–61). African Americans were also less likely than whites, regardless of GI status, to gain new jobs commensurate with their wartime jobs, and they suffered more heavily. For example, in San Francisco by 1948, Black Americans "had dropped back halfway to their pre-war employment status" (Wynn, 1976:114, 116).[13]

Black GIs faced discrimination in the educational system as well. Despite the end of restrictions on Jews and other Euroethnics, African Americans were not welcome in white colleges. Black colleges were overcrowded, and the combination of segregation and prejudice made for few alternatives. About 20,000 black veterans attended college by 1947, most in black colleges, but almost as many, 15,000, could not gain entry. Predictably, the disproportionately few African Americans who did gain access to their educational benefits were able, like their white counterparts, to become doctors and engineers, and to enter the black middle class (Walker, 1970).

. . . The record is very clear that instead of seizing the opportunity to end institutionalized racism, the federal government did its best to shut and double seal the postwar window of opportunity in African Americans' faces. It consistently refused to combat segregation in the social institutions that were key for upward mobility: education, housing, and employment. Moreover, federal programs that were themselves designed to assist demobilized GIs and young families systematically discriminated against African Americans. Such programs reinforced white/nonwhite racial distinctions even as intrawhite racialization was falling out of fashion. This other side of the coin, that white men of northwestern and southeastern European ancestry were treated equally in theory and in practice with regard to the benefits they received, was part of the larger postwar whitening of Jews and other eastern and southern Europeans.

The myth that Jews pulled themselves up by their own bootstraps ignores the fact that it took federal programs to create the conditions whereby the abilities of Jews and other European immigrants could be recognized and rewarded rather than denigrated and denied. The GI Bill and FHA and VA mortgages were forms of affirmative action that allowed male Jews and other Euro-American men to become suburban homeowners and to get the training that allowed them—but not women vets or war workers—to become professionals, technicians, salesmen, and managers in a growing economy. Jews' and other white ethnics' upward mobility was the result of programs that allowed us to float on a rising economic tide. To African Americans, the government offered the cement boots of segregation, redlining, urban renewal, and discrimination.

Those racially skewed gains have been passed across the generations, so that racial inequality seems to maintain itself "naturally," even after legal segregation ended. Today, in a shrinking economy where downward mobility is the norm, the children and grandchildren of the postwar beneficiaries of the economic boom have some precious advantages. For example, having parents who own their own homes or who have decent retirement benefits can make a real difference in young people's ability to take on huge college loans or to come up with a down payment for a house. Even this simple inheritance helps perpetuate the gap between whites and nonwhites. Sure Jews needed ability, but ability was not enough to make it. The same applies even more in today's long recession.

CRITICAL-THINKING QUESTIONS

1. What specific evidence does the author present to demonstrate that race and ethnicity are socially constructed concepts?

2. How fair is it to say that Jews became successful due to their own abilities and efforts? To what degree did government programs play a part in this upward mobility?

3. According to the author, how do the historical experiences of Jews differ from those of African Americans?

NOTES

This is a revised and expanded version of a paper published in *Jewish Currents* in June 1992 and delivered at the 1992 meetings of the American Anthropological Association in the session *Blacks and Jews, 1992: Reaching across the Cultural Boundaries* organized by Angela Gilliam. I would like to thank Emily Abel, Katya Gibel Azoulay, Edna Bonacich, Angela Gilliam, Isabelle Gunning, Valerie Matsumoto, Regina Morantz-Sanchez, Roger Sanjek, Rabbi Chaim Seidler-Feller, Janet Silverstein, and Eloise Klein Healy's writing group for uncovering wonderful sources and for critical readings along the way.

1. Indeed, Boasian and Du Boisian anthropology developed in active political opposition to this nativism: on Du Bois, see Harrison & Nonini, 1992.

2. On immigrants as part of the industrial workforce, see Steinberg, 1989:36.

3. I thank Roger Sanjek for providing me with this source.

4. It was intended, as Davenport wrote to the president of the American Museum of Natural History, Henry Fairfield Osborne, as "an anthropological society . . . with a central governing body, self-elected and self-perpetuating, and very limited in members, and also confined to native Americans who are anthropologically, socially and politically sound, no Bolsheviki need apply" (Barkan, 1991:67–68).

5. I thank Valerie Matsumoto for telling me about the Thind case and Katya Gibel Azoulay for providing this information to me on the Virginia statute.

6. "The distinction between white and colored" has been "the only racial classification which has been carried through all the 15 censuses." "Colored" consisted of "Negroes" and "other races": Mexican, Indian, Chinese, Japanese, Filipino, Hindu, Korean, Hawaiian, Malay, Siamese, and Samoan. (U.S. Bureau of the Census, 1930:25, 26).

7. For why Jews entered colleges earlier than other immigrants, and for a challenge to views that attribute it to Jewish culture, see Steinberg, 1989.

8. Although quotas on Jews persisted into the 1950s in some of the elite schools, they were much attenuated, as the postwar college-building boom gave the coup-de-grace to the gentleman's finishing school.

9. Indeed, Jewish social scientists were prominent in creating this ideology of the United States as a meritocracy. Most prominent of course was Nathan Glazer, but among them also were Charles Silberman and Marshall Sklare.

10. The belief was widespread that "the GI Bill . . . helped millions of families move into the middle class" (Nash et al., 1986:885). A study that compares mobility among veterans and nonveterans provides a kind of confirmation. In an unnamed small city in Illinois, Havighurst and his colleagues (1951) found no significant difference between veterans and nonveterans, but this was because apparently very few veterans used any of their GI benefits.

11. Interestingly, Steinberg (1989:149) shows that Jewish professionals tended to be children of small-business owners, but their Catholic counterparts tended to be children of workers.

12. None of the Jewish surveys seem to have asked what women were doing. Silberman (1985) claims that Jewish women stayed out of the labor force prior to the 1970s, but if my parents' circle is any indication, there were plenty of working professional women.

13. African Americans and Japanese Americans were the main target of wartime racism (see Murray, 1992). By contrast, there were virtually no anti-German American or anti-Italian American policies in World War II (see Takaki, 1989:357–406).

REFERENCES

BARKAN, ELAZAR. 1991. *The retreat of scientific racism: Changing concepts of race in Britain and the United States between the world wars.* Cambridge: Cambridge University Press.

BINKIN, MARTIN, and MARK J. EITELBERG. 1982. *Blacks and the military.* Washington, D.C.: Brookings.

BROWN, FRANCIS J. 1946. *Educational opportunities for veterans.* Washington, D.C.: Public Affairs Press, American Council on Public Affairs.

CARLSON, LEWIS H., and GEORGE A. COLBURN. 1972. *In their place: White America defines her minorities, 1850–1950.* New York: Wiley.

DALFIUME, RICHARD M. 1969. *Desegregation of the U.S. armed forces: Fighting on two fronts, 1939–1953.* Columbia: University of Missouri Press.

EICHLER, NED. 1982. *The merchant builders.* Cambridge, Mass.: MIT Press.

FONER, JACK. 1974. *Blacks and the military in American history: A new perspective.* New York: Praeger.

GERBER, DAVID. 1986a. Introduction. In *Anti-Semitism in American history,* ed. Gerber, 3–56.

———, ed. 1986b. *Anti-Semitism in American history.* Urbana: University of Illinois Press.

HARRISON, FAYE V., and DONALD NONINI, eds. 1992. *Critique of anthropology* (special issue on W. E. B. Du Bois and anthropology), 12(3).

HAVIGHURST, ROBERT J., JOHN W. BAUGHMAN, WALTER H. EATON, and ERNEST W. BURGESS. 1951. *The American veteran back home: A study of veteran readjustment.* New York: Longmans, Green.

HIGHAM, JOHN. 1955. *Strangers in the land.* New Brunswick: Rutgers University Press.

HURD, CHARLES. 1946. *The veterans' program: A complete guide to its benefits, rights, and options.* New York: McGraw-Hill.

JOHNSON, JESSE J. 1967. *Ebony brass: An autobiography of Negro frustration amid aspiration.* New York: Frederick.

KARABEL, JEROME. 1984. Status-group struggle, organizational interests, and the limits of institutional autonomy. *Theory and Society,* 13: 1–40.

KESSLER-HARRIS, ALICE. 1982. *Out to work: A history of wage-earning women in the United States.* New York: Oxford University Press.

MARTYN, BYRON CURTI. 1979. Racism in the U.S.: A history of anti-miscegenation legislation and litigation. Ph.D. diss., University of Southern California.

MOSCH, THEODORE R. 1975. *The GI bill: A breakthrough in educational and social policy in the United States.* Hicksville, N.Y.: Exposition.

MURRAY, ALICE YANG. 1992. Japanese Americans, redress, and reparations: A study of community, family, and gender, 1940–1990. Ph.D. diss., Stanford University.

NALTY, BERNARD C., and MORRIS J. MACGREGOR, eds. 1981. *Blacks in the military: Essential documents.* Wilmington, Del.: Scholarly Resources.

NASH, GARY B., JULIE ROY JEFFREY, JOHN R. HOWE, ALLEN F. DAVIS, PETER J. FREDERICK, and ALLEN M. WINKLER. 1986. *The American people: Creating a nation and a society.* New York: Harper and Row.

Postwar jobs for veterans. 1945. Annals of the American Academy of Political and Social Science, 238 (March).

SAXTON, ALEXANDER. 1971. *The indispensible enemy.* Berkeley and Los Angeles: University of California Press.

———. 1990. *The rise and fall of the White Republic.* London: Verso.

SCHOENER, ALLON. 1967. *Portal to America: The Lower East Side, 1870–1925.* New York: Holt, Rinehart and Winston.

SILBERMAN, CHARLES. 1985. *A certain people: American Jews and their lives today.* New York: Summit.

STEINBERG, STEPHEN. 1989. *The ethnic myth: Race, ethnicity, and class in America.* 2d ed. Boston: Beacon.

SYNOTT, MARCIA GRAHAM. 1986. Anti-Semitism and American universities: Did quotas follow the Jews? In *Anti-Semitism in American history,* ed. David A. Gerber, 233–74.

TAKAKI, RONALD. 1989. *Strangers from a different shore.* Boston: Little, Brown.

U.S. Bureau of the Census. 1930. *Fifteenth census of the United States.* Vol. 2. Washington, D.C.: U.S. Government Printing Office.

———. 1940. *Sixteenth census of the United States.* Vol. 2. Washington, D.C.: U.S. Government Printing Office.

WALKER, OLIVE. 1970. The Windsor Hills School story. *Integrated Education: Race and Schools,* 8(3): 4–9.

WILLENZ, JUNE A. 1983. *Women veterans: America's forgotten heroines.* New York: Continuum.

WYNN, NEIL A. 1976. *The Afro-American and the Second World War.* London: Elek.

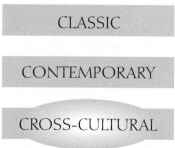

CLASSIC

CONTEMPORARY

CROSS-CULTURAL

47 Out of Harmony: Health Problems and Young Native American Men

JENNIE R. JOE

Despite numerous medical advances, Native American men continue to experience more health problems and shorter life spans than their white counterparts. In this selection, Jennie R. Joe discusses the major health difficulties that confront young Native American men. She maintains that life expectancy rates of Native American men continue to lag behind those of their non-native counterparts because of demographic and historical differences between these groups. According to Joe, colleges can be especially effective in providing intervention strategies that restore the "harmony" in the lives of many Native American men.

The cultural perception and definition of health in most Native American (the term applies to both American Indians and Alaska Natives) communities are based on the concept of balance or harmony: a healthy state in which one is free of pain or discomfort, is at peace with oneself as well as with others, and is in harmony with all other elements of one's environment. Although these are ideal goals, disease, accidents, and misfortunes are also acknowledged as part of the reality of life. Until recently, very few Native Americans traditionally survived to old age. Such an event is considered a special achievement and the individual is honored and respected.

Reaching old age yesterday or today, however, is not easy. Before the mid-1940s, the average life expectancy for Native Americans was less than fifty years. Today, the life expectancy for Native American men continues to lag behind that of white men (*Regional differences,* 1997). Despite a multitude of medical advances, many Native American men at birth face a risk of premature mortality. This premature death and other indicators of poor health dominate the literature on the health of Native American men. Thus, any discussion of their health often emphasizes poor health and early mortality.

Poverty, poor education, high unemployment, unhealthy lifestyles, and voluntary and forced culture change are among the reasons for the premature mortality of Native American men. Although decades have passed since initial European contact, the consequences of colonization that followed this contact have forever altered tribal lifestyles and, in particular, the traditional role once held by young men.

Source: Journal of American College Health, 49 (March, 2001), pp. 237–42. Reprinted with permission of the Helen Dwight Reid Educational Foundation. Published by Heldref Publications, 1319 Eighteenth St., NW, Washington, DC 20036-1802. Copyright © 2001.

METHOD

My review of the health of young Native American men is based on a survey of existing literature as well as my knowledge of health care problems and issues that confront contemporary Native Americans.

RESULTS

Demographics

A majority of the Native American population lives in the American West, albeit Indians are present in all fifty states. Recently, the Native American population has been increasing. For example, the most recent 1995 population projection by the Indian Health Service (IHS) is approximately 2.7 million (*Projected American Indian,* 1994). In the 1990 census, Native American women outnumbered the men, 51 percent to 49 percent (*1990 Census,* 1993; Joe, 1996), and this proportion is not expected to change.

In general, the population profile of Native Americans parallels that of developing countries, namely high birth rates and a young median age. The 1990 census reported that 39 percent of Native Americans were then under the age of twenty years, compared with 29 percent for all races in the United States. The median age reported for the U.S. White population was 33 years, compared with about 27 years for the Native American population (*Projected American Indian,* 1994).

Census data also indicate that in 1990 more than half (56 percent) of Native Americans lived in off-reservation communities. The increased rural-to-urban migration also reflects a change in the pattern of family units (Paisano et al., 1994; Snipp, 1997). For example, Sandefur and Liebler (1997) compared 1990 census data with 1980 data and found an increase in the number of Native American children living with one parent. In 1980, 54.4 percent of these children lived with one parent; in 1990, the percentage increased to 62.9. This 8.5 percent increase for Native Americans was greater than the 6.5 percent increase for the general U.S. population during the same period (Snipp, 1997). Although a majority of the single-parent households among Native Americans are headed by women, it is interesting to note that 9 percent of the single heads of households were fathers (*1990 Census,* 1993).

Most employed Native American men hold low-paying jobs. This low income is further reflected in the $20,025 median family income reported in the 1990 Census, compared with $31,572 for White families. More Native American families also reported incomes below the national poverty level: 27 percent compared with 7 percent of White households (Gregory, Abello, & Johnson, 1997). Single women were heads of household in most of these low-income families, although poverty is also prevalent in two-parent families.

The lack of employment opportunities and poor wages contribute to high rates of unemployment. Even when employed, Native American men are more likely than Native American women to experience financial setbacks in employment. For example, when Gregory and colleagues compared Native American men's and women's earning levels over a ten-year period, they found that the economic deterioration was more devastating for men, whose earnings fell 12 percent between 1979 and 1989. In addition, these researchers noted that the average hourly earning ratio for Native American men, compared with that for Native American women, decreased 9 percent, yet the annual hours worked decreased by 3 percent (Gregory, Abello, & Johnson, 1997).

Economic downturns are especially damaging to those who have not completed high school. According to Gregory and associates (1997), the real income for these men dropped 22 percent, whereas Native American men with a college education experienced income increases.

Thus, the economic picture for Native American men and their families is greatly influenced by their educational attainments. In comparison with Whites, fewer Native Americans complete high school or obtain a college degree. Paisano and colleagues note that only 9 percent of Native

Americans (both men and women) hold a bachelor's degree or higher, compared with 22 percent for Whites. The 1990 Census data (Paisano et al., 1994) revealed that 14 percent of Native Americans between the ages of eighteen and twenty-four years were enrolled in college in 1989. Although this is a significant number, many of these students do not complete college. Family crises or financial difficulties are frequently cited reasons for leaving school.

Research about Native American Men

Although much of what is reported in ongoing studies of men's health generally may have relevance for Native American men, I know of no current efforts to explore where and how some of these findings can be applied to this population. As I have pointed out, there is almost no research on healthy young Native American men of college age, a population that is of special interest for readers of *The Journal of American College Health.*

The focus of most studies on Native American men has been on various deviant behaviors and health problems in this population: alcoholism, delinquency, suicide, homicide, and criminal behavior (Jensen, Strauss, & Harris, 1977; Bachman, 1992). Whereas much is known about the incidence or prevalence of these problems, few researchers have addressed the reasons why the problems exist or why they persist.

Resources

To present a balanced picture of the overall health picture of young Native American men, one must piece together information from many sources. Unfortunately, the data may exist but are often collected in a way that discourages in-depth analyses. For example, health data collected and reported by IHS consist mainly of information from men who use IHS health facilities. Those data contain morbidity and mortality information by age and gender, but they cannot be examined in terms of other important variables such as years of schooling, socioeconomic status, and degree of acculturation.

That the IHS provides service to only a portion of the Indian population contributes to aspects of the data limitation. Despite these drawbacks, the IHS health data are perhaps the only health data collected routinely and reported annually on a significant percentage of Native Americans and are therefore an important resource when one examines the health of this group.

The IHS, funded by the U.S. Congress, offers health care annually to approximately 1.4 million of the estimated 2 million Native Americans who are members of federally recognized tribes (*Regional differences,* 1997) in 35 small hospitals, 2 large hospitals, and 59 health centers. In addition, 12 hospitals and 155 health centers are managed by various tribal entities. Provision of services is based on a set of special federal-tribal treaty relationships. The system includes a variety of medical resources that are often the only health care in isolated rural communities.

The Health Situation

At different times, researchers such as Broudy and May (1983) and Young (1997) have discussed the changing health pattern of Native Americans, using the three-stage epidemiological model proposed by Omran (1983). The first stage in this model proposes an era of health problems caused by pestilence and famine, followed by an era of receding pandemics. In the third era, most health problems are attributed to the emergence of degenerative and manmade diseases. Olshansky and Ault (1986) have proposed a fourth state, the era of delayed degenerative disease.

Whether and for how long ancestors of most contemporary tribal groups experienced periods of pestilence or famine is not clear because most existing archaeological evidence is inconclusive. The era of pandemics, however, is well known. Following European contact, Native Americans experienced waves of contagious diseases such as smallpox that rapidly depopulated most of the Americas (Stearn & Stearn, 1945). The biological consequences of subsequent tuberculosis epidemics continued for Native Americans well into the first half of the 20th century (the incidence of tuberculosis is today once again on the increase among Native Americans) (*Projected American Indian,* 1994; *Regional differences,* 1997). Not until the latter half of the [19th] century did the morbidity and mortality picture for Native Americans shift from infectious diseases to domination by chronic diseases and other health behaviors associated with unhealthy lifestyles (Joe & Young, 1994). The consequences of unhealthy living are perhaps best reflected in the rising mortality and morbidity rates associated with unintentional injuries, especially among young Native American men. Most unintentional injuries, usually the result of automobile accidents, tend to be associated with drinking alcohol. Other accidents may result from high-risk occupations or participation in sports such as rodeos (*Injuries among American Indians,* 1990; *Regional differences,* 1997).

The Health of Young Native American Men

The life expectancy at birth (calculated for the period 1992–1994) for American Indian and Alaska Native men is 67.2 years compared with 72.2 for white men, 75.1 for Native American women, and 78.8 for women of all races (*Regional differences,* 1997). Many Native American men die before reaching the age of 30. For example, between 1992 and 1994, the age-specific death rate for young Native American men aged 15 to 24 years was 202.9 per 100,000, compared with the 1993 rate of 2.1 per 100,000 for U.S. men of all races (*Trends in Indian health,* 1994).

Accidents. Accidents, a majority of which involve motor vehicles and alcohol use (James et al., 1993; Kettl & Bixler, 1993; Sugarman & Grossman, 1996), are a major cause of the shortened life expectancy for many of these young Native American men and a leading cause of

death for Native American men between the ages of 15 to 44 years. Although accident-related deaths are high for native men, the rates fluctuate from year to year; they have nevertheless remained higher than the rates in the general U.S. population. Between 1990 and 1994, the adjusted accident-related mortality rate for Native American men of all ages was 94.5 per 100,000, compared with 30.3 per 100,000 for nonnative American men in 1993 (*Regional differences,* 1997). Alcohol is a major contributor to the high accident rate, and there are indications that, for some men, drinking starts early in life. Mail (1995) notes that alcohol consumption for some of these men started during grade school.

Deaths attributable to accidents are most frequent among younger men in the general population, rather than among men over the age of fifty years. The significance of this problem, however, appears to be greater for young Indian men than for others. For example, between 1992 and 1994, the accident death rate for Native American men aged 15 to 24 years was 150 per 100,000, compared with 57.6 for the same age group of men of all races in the United States. Moreover, the ratio of accident death rates for Native American men and women aged 25 and over is 2.8 to 3. The accident death rates for Native American women, however, are two to three times higher than that for other women in the United States (*Regional differences,* 1997).

Frequently, cultural tolerance for using alcohol, driving on poor roads, driving in unsafe vehicles, and acceptance of laws that prohibit the sale or possession of alcohol on reservations contribute to the high rates of alcohol-related motor vehicle accidents. The prohibition on reservation lands forces those who wish to drink to drive great distances to purchase alcohol, consume it on site, and then attempt the long drive home. Drinking behaviors and drinking styles of Native American men are similar to those of young men in other cultures: They are not afraid to take risks, are willing to test or ignore traffic and drinking laws, and believe that they are immortal.

Suicide. Although suicide rates in the U.S. population tend to be highest among persons over the age of 65 years, suicide is the fifth leading cause of death for Native American men over the age of 10 years. When age is included in the analysis, suicide becomes the second leading cause of death for Native American men between the ages of 10 and 24 years (*Projected American Indian,* 1994; *Regional differences,* 1997). Some suicides occur among boys and adolescents; the overall median age of Native Americans who committed suicide between 1979 and 1992 was 26 years (*Homicide and suicide,* 1996).

In their examination of homicide and suicide rates for Native Americans, researchers at the Centers for Disease Control and Prevention (CDC) found that 64 percent of all suicides between 1979 and 1992 were males, aged 15 to 34. The suicide rates for these men was 62 per 100,000 compared with 10 per 100,000 for Native American women in the same age group (*Homicide and suicide,* 1996). Firearms were used in more than half (57 percent) of the suicides, with poisoning and strangulation as other frequent means of committing suicide.

Although firearms are the weapons of choice for suicides committed by both Native American men and women, hanging is the second choice for men, whereas poisoning ranks second for Native American women (*Homicide and suicide,* 1996). Reasons for these Native Americans choosing to end their lives are not always known, as is true in the general population. Poverty, family difficulties, poor self-esteem, grief, and an overwhelming sense of hopelessness are among the reasons frequently suggested by the victim's families or friends (Joe, 1996).

Homicide. Between 1990 and 1992, homicide was the third leading cause of loss of life for Native Americans less than 65 years of age; 28 was the median age of homicide victims (*Homicide and suicide,* 1996). Seven percent of these cases of lost potential years among Native Americans resulted from homicide, a rate that was exceeded only by two other leading causes of death—unintentional injury and heart disease (*Injuries among American Indians,* 1990; Sugarman & Grossman, 1996).

Data on homicide deaths for Native Americans between 1979 and 1992 indicate that men between the ages of 15 and 44 accounted for 60 percent of all Native American homicides. At highest risk were men aged 25 to 34 years. Rates for this age group between 1979 and 1992 were reported as 47 per 100,000. Forty-eight percent of the Native American homicide deaths involve firearms, primarily handguns, but cutting and stabbing also account for significant numbers of homicides (*Homicide and suicide,* 1996).

Approximately 66 percent of the Native American homicide victims between 1988 and 1991 were killed by persons they knew, and 63 percent of male homicide victims were killed by family members or acquaintances, in contrast to 50 percent for the general U.S. population. Between 1988 and 1991, 51 percent of the Native American victims were killed by other Native Americans, and 39 percent were killed by white persons. A majority of these homicides involved men killing men (*Homicide and suicide,* 1996).

Cancer. Cancer incidence and mortality is increasing among American Indians and Alaskan Natives (Greenwald et al., 1996), as is the case among other minority ethnic groups. The American Cancer Society recently reported that cancer incidence rates between 1988 and 1994 for African American men were 560 per 100,000, compared with 469 per 100,000 for white men (*Cancer facts,* 1997). Although rates of cancer in general are lower for Native Americans than for some other racial groups, rates for specific cancers (nasopharyngeal, gall bladder, and stomach) are higher among Indians and Alaska Natives (Haynes & Smedley, 1999). These lower cancer rates may be attributed, in part, to higher mortality from other causes because Native Americans' lifespans are generally shorter than are those of other ethnic groups.

Many factors—late diagnosis, lack of access to treatment, fear of cancer, a belief that cancer is not a problem for Native Americans—contribute to the high cancer mortality of American Indians and Alaska Natives: Although most cancer prevention programs have been initiated for tribal women, some prevention efforts, especially those emphasizing smoking cessation, have begun to target Native American men. A 1994 national health survey revealed that 54 percent of Native American men and 33 percent of women smoked (*Tobacco use,* 1998). Young men are frequently among the very heavy smokers (Cobb & Paisano, 1997).

Cancer incidence rates for Native Americans are generally lower than those for the U.S. population in general; however, cancer is among the leading causes of death for Indian men. The five major sites of cancers that contributed to high mortality among Native men during the years 1992 and 1994 were the lungs (trachea and bronchi), prostate, colon, stomach, and liver. The most recent IHS report indicates that the overall cancer mortality rate for Native American men aged 14 to 25 years was 3.7 compared with 3.3 per 100,000 for the same age group of U.S. men, all races (Cobb & Paisano, 1997).

The report indicates that the cancer mortality rates for Native American men are approximately 57 percent greater than the rates for Native American women. Although cancer death rates increase with age among Native American women, cancer mortality occurs among younger men (Cobb & Paisano, 1997).

Diseases of the Heart.   Heart disease is the leading cause of death for Native Americans as well as for Asian Americans, Pacific Islanders, and Hispanic Americans (Yu, 1991). One notable exception to these high rates of heart disease death is found among tribal groups in the Southwest, who have low rates of heart disease in spite of a high prevalence of risk factors, including obesity, diabetes mellitus, and hypertension (*Regional differences,* 1997).

According to the IHS, heart disease death rates for U.S. residents of all races have decreased approximately 20 percent since 1984. Although the leading cause of death among Native Americans is heart disease, the IHS reported that their age-adjusted heart disease death rates have been relatively stable since 1984 (*Regional differences,* 1997). Deaths from heart disease, therefore, have not decreased for these Americans as they have for the U.S. population in general.

When Native Americans' heart disease death rates are examined for the years 1990 to 1992, the age-adjusted rate is 157.6 per 100,000, a rate that is 8 percent higher than the rate for all races in the United States. It should also be noted that during this same period, the age-adjusted death rate for heart disease for Native American men in all age groups was higher than it was for Native American women (*Regional differences,* 1997).

Alcohol and Alcohol Abuse.   Alcohol is a frequent confounding factor in many unintended deaths for young Native Americans. During the 1995 fiscal year, alcohol-related hospitalization discharges were 31 per 100,000 of the IHS user population over the age of 15 years, a rate that is 1.6 times greater than the rate for the U.S. population in general (*Regional differences,* 1997).

For many Native American young adults, attitude and perception of alcohol use are established during adolescence, an age when peers are the most powerful determinant of one's behavior (Oetting & Beauvais, 1986; Swaim et al., 1993; Oetting & Donnermeyer, 1998). According to Oetting and Beauvais (1986), the decision of whether to use or not to use alcohol is embedded in adolescents' interactions with close peers. These peer clusters become the setting where "norming" takes place and attitudes and behaviors regarding alcohol use are determined. Beauvais (1998) notes that peer clusters are enmeshed in the larger peer culture and that this larger culture is where certain sociocultural values are learned and parameters are set on how one should behave to fit in with others.

In one earlier study, Swaim and colleagues (1993) found that the dynamic relationship between the influence of peers and parents differs for Native American and other American youth. Peers are important influences for both groups; for Native American youth, the influence of peers is equal to that of their parents.

The problem of alcohol use among the Native American population continues to be studied by researchers in various disciplines. Many theories about alcohol use have evolved from these different perspectives, theories that range from genetic propensity to social deprivation. One explanation held by a number of tribal communities is that the high prevalence of alcohol abuse is a result of the loss of tribal culture or tribal identity, a perspective that has strongly influenced the orientation and intervention strategies offered by prevention and treatment programs.

Beauvais (1998), however, notes that this perspective has not been useful for treating or working with adolescents and young adults. Most of these young people, he writes, have difficulties because they do not yet have the strong cultural identification necessary to want to quit drinking. He therefore concludes that culturally enriched intervention programs may not be meaningful for young Native Americans.

This observation is understandable because colonization either displaced or successfully erased the place for traditional tribal teachings and learning cultural values. Many Native American families, for example, lament that their children or grandchildren do not speak or understand their tribal language (Joe, 1997).

In the past, most Indian parents were purposefully excluded from participating in their children's education and were discouraged from visiting schools where their children were being groomed for the White world. In addition, teachers and administrators made every effort to keep the children from retaining any vestiges of their culture. Students who dared to speak their tribal languages were severely punished; tribal customs were publicly ridiculed, labeled primitive, and were totally unacceptable. It did not take long for many Indian children to become ashamed of their cultural heritage.

COMMENT

The effort to conquer the Americas and its inhabitants displaced and destroyed the culture of many indigenous peoples; the subsequent colonization further altered the traditional lifestyles of those indigenous peoples who survived the warfare, displacement, and repeated waves of devastating communicable diseases. Most of the statistics on poverty, early mortality, and morbidity among young Native American men that I have presented are reminders that significant proportions of each new generation of Native American men continue to suffer long-term consequences of colonization. Unhealthy lifestyles, unintentional accidents, suicide attempts, alcohol abuse, and societal neglect are symptoms of this disenfranchisement.

On the other hand, a significant number of Native American men who enter collegiate communities may be the lucky ones. For a variety of reasons, they have been spared the health problems prevalent in their age group. The collegiate environment, however, does not ensure health. Intense academic, family, or economic stresses have been known to trigger problems that lead to alcohol abuse or other unhealthy lifestyle behaviors.

Some colleges with sizable Native American enrollment have instituted strategies to prevent these problems. Some assist Native American students by designating a space in college residences staffed with peer counselors for incoming students from rural reservation communities. Some colleges and universities promote a Native American resource center, a special place on campus where these students can seek assistance and campus healthcare providers are invited to speak on specific health topics or be available for health discussions. The latter is especially helpful for young Native American men who are less likely than other students are to use campus health services.

Including campus healthcare providers in student orientation programs is also helpful. In some colleges and universities, Native American student organizations have created resource booklets containing information or names of campus healthcare providers. Efforts such as these help support those students who need this type of individual support from their college healthcare providers.

CRITICAL-THINKING QUESTIONS

1. Compare the Native American and White population in terms of median age, income, and employment. How does educational attainment explain some of these variations? Why are such demographic variables inadequate in explaining the overall health picture of Native American men?

2. Researchers have often attributed high and early death rates to "unhealthy lifestyles" during the latter part of the twentieth century. How does unhealthy living increase the mortality rates of young Native American men? Why are car accidents, suicide, homicide, and alcohol abuse higher for Native American men than for their White counterparts?

3. What does Joe mean when she says that the health of most Native American men is "out of harmony"? Out of harmony with what? Why does colonization appear to have had a greater negative impact on the cultural identity and health of Native American men than women? What strategies does Joe propose to restore Native American harmony with themselves and their environment?

REFERENCES

BACHMAN, R. 1992. *Death and violence on the reservation.* New York: Auburn.

BEAUVAIS, F. 1998. American Indian youth and alcohol: A study in perplexity and ambivalence. *Alcoholic Beverage Medical Research Foundation Journal* (suppl. 3), 8(33): 61–65.

BROUDY, D. W., and P. A. MAY. 1983. Demographic and epidemiological transition among the Navajo Indians. *Social Biology,* 30: 1–6.

Cancer facts and figures—1997. 1997. Atlanta, Ga.: American Cancer Society.

COBB, N., and R. E. PAISANO. 1997. *Cancer mortality among American Indians and Alaska Natives in the United States: Regional differences in Indian health, 1989–1993.* Rockville, Md.: USPHS, Indian Health Service.

GREENWALD, J. P., E. F. BORGATTE, R. McCORKLE, and N. POLISSAR. 1996. Explaining reduced cancer survival among the disadvantaged. *Milbank Quarterly,* 74: 215–38.

GREGORY, G. G., A. C. ABELLO, and J. JOHNSON. 1997. The individual economic well-being of Native American men and women during the 1980s: A decade of backwards. *Population Research and Policy Review,* 16: 115–45.

HAYNES, M. A., and B. SMEDLEY, eds. 1999. *The unequal burden of cancer.* Washington, D.C.: National Academy Press.

Homicide and suicide among Native Americans, 1879–1992. 1996. Washington, D.C.: U.S. Dept. of Health and Human Services, Centers for Disease Control, National Center for Injury Prevention and Control.

Injuries among American Indians/Alaska Natives. 1990. Rockville, Md.: USPHS, Indian Health Service.

JAMES, W. H., B. HUTCHINSON, D. MOORE, and A. J. SMITH. 1993. Predictors of driving while intoxicated (DWI) among American Indians in the Northwest. *Journal of Drug Education,* 24(4): 317–24.

JENSEN, G. F., J. H. STRAUSS, and V. W. HARRIS. 1977. Crime, delinquency, and the American Indian. *Human Organization,* 36(3): 252–57.

JOE, J. R. 1996. The health of American Indian and Alaska Native women. *Journal of the American Medical Women's Association,* 51: 141–45.

———. 1997. *Iina ili* (life is valuable): The Hardrock community's efforts to address substance abuse problems. Unpublished report. Tucson: University of Arizona, Native American Research and Training Center.

JOE, J. R., and R. S. YOUNG, eds. 1994. Diabetes as a disease of civilization: The impact of culture change on indigenous peoples. Berlin: Mouton de Gruyter.

KETTL, P. and E. O. BIXLER. 1993. Alcohol and suicide. *American Indian and Alaska Native Mental Health Research,* 5(2): 34–45.

MAIL, P. D. 1995. Early modeling of drinking behavior by Native American elementary school children playing drunk. *International Journal of Addiction,* 30(9): 1187–97.

1990 Census of the population: American Indians and Alaska Native areas. 1993. Washington, D.C.: U.S. Dept. of Commerce, Bureau of the Census.

OETTING, E., and F. BEAUVAIS. 1986. Peer clusters theory: Drugs and the adolescent. *Journal of Counseling and Development,* 65(1): 17–22.

OETTING, E., and J. DONNERMEYER. 1998. Primary socialization theory: The etiology of drugs and deviance. *Substance Abuse and Misuse,* 33: 995–1026.

OLSHANSKY, S. J., and A. G. AULT. 1986. The fourth stage of epidemiological transition: The age of delayed degenerative disease. *Milbank Quarterly,* 64: 390–91.

OMRAN, A. R. 1983. The epidemiology transition theory: A preliminary update. *Journal of Tropical Pediatrics,* 29: 305–16.

PAISANO, E. L., D. L. CAROLL, J. H. COWLES, et al. 1994. *We, the first Americans.* Washington, D.C.: U.S. Dept. of Commerce, Bureau of the Census.

Projected American Indian and Alaska Native population for the United States, 1990–2005. 1994. Rockville, Md.: USPHS, Indian Health Service.

Regional differences in Indian health. 1997. Rockville, Md.: USPHS, Indian Health Service.

SANDEFUR, G. D., and C. A. LIEBLER. 1997. The demography of American Indian family. *Population Research and Policy Review,* 16: 95–114.

SNIPP, C. M. 1997. The size and distribution of the American Indian population: Fertility, mortality, and residence. *Population Research and Policy Review,* 16: 61–93.

STEARN, E. W., and A. E. STEARN. 1945. *The effects of smallpox on the destiny of Amerindians.* Boston: B. Humphries.

SUGARMAN, J. R., and D. C. GROSSMAN. 1996. Trauma among American Indians in an urban county. *Public Health Report,* 111(4): 320.

SWAIM, R. C., E. R. OETTING, P. J. THURMAN, F. BEAUVAIS, and R. W. EDWARDS. 1993. American Indian adolescent drug use and socialization characteristics: A cross-cultural comparison. *Journal of Cross-Cultural Psychology,* 24(1): 53–70.

Tobacco use among U.S. racial/ethnic minority groups: A report of the Surgeon General. 1998. U.S. Dept. of Health and Human Services: Office of Smoking and Health, Centers for Disease Control.

Trends in Indian health, 1994. 1994. Rockville, Md.: USPHS, Indian Health Service.

U.S. CONGRESS. 1986. *Indian health care.* Washington, D.C.: Office of Technology Assessment. U.S. Government Printing Office.

YOUNG, T. K. 1997. Recent health trends in the Native American population. *Population Research and Policy Review,* 16(1, 2): 147–67.

YU, P. N. 1991. Heart disease in Asian and Pacific-Islanders, Hispanics, and Native Americans. *Circulation,* 83(4): 1475–77.

48 The Tragedy of Old Age in America

ROBERT N. BUTLER

The United States has often been described as a "youth culture," in which youth is a measure of personal worth. In this selection, Robert Butler explores the U.S. view of the elderly, which he finds to be fraught with myths and prejudices. He argues that they not only hurt elderly people but also disadvantage everyone.

What is it like to be old in the United States? What will our own lives be like when we are old? Americans find it difficult to think about old age until they are propelled into the midst of it by their own aging and that of relatives and friends. Aging is the neglected stepchild of the human life cycle. Though we have begun to examine the socially taboo subjects of dying and death, we have leaped over that long period of time preceding death known as old age. In truth, it is easier to manage the problem of death than the problem of living as an old person. Death is a dramatic, one-time crisis while old age is a day-by-day and year-by-year confrontation with powerful external and internal forces, a bittersweet coming to terms with one's own personality and one's life.

Those of us who are not old barricade ourselves from discussions of old age by declaring the subject morbid, boring, or in poor taste. Optimism and euphemism are other common devices. People will speak of looking forward to their "retirement years." The elderly are described respectfully as "senior citizens," "golden agers," "our elders," and one hears of old people who are considered inspirations and examples of how to "age well" or "gracefully." There is the popularly accepted opinion that Social Security and pensions provide a comfortable and reliable flow of funds so the elderly have few financial worries. Medicare has lulled the population into reassuring itself that the once terrible financial burdens of late-life illnesses are now eradicated. Advertisements and travel folders show relaxed, happy, well-dressed older people

Source: From *Why Survive? Being Old in America* by Robert N. Butler, M.D., pp. 1–2, 6–12, 15–16, copyright © 1975 by Robert N. Butler, M.D., HarperCollins Publishers, Inc. Reprinted with permission of HarperCollins Publishers, Inc.

enjoying recreation, travel, and their grandchildren. If they are no longer living in the old family home, they are pictured as delighted residents of retirement communities with names like Leisure World and Sun City, with lots of grass, clean air, and fun. This is the American ideal of the "golden years" toward which millions of citizens are expectantly toiling through their workdays.

But this is not the full story. A second theme runs through the popular view of old age. Our colloquialisms reveal a great deal: Once you are old you are "fading fast," "over the hill," "out to pasture," "down the drain," "finished," "out of date," an "old crock," "fogy," "geezer," or "biddy." One hears children saying they are afraid to get old, middle-aged people declaring they want to die after they have passed their prime, and numbers of old people wishing they were dead.

What can we possibly conclude from these discrepant points of view? Our popular attitudes could be summed up as a combination of wishful thinking and stark terror. We base our feelings on primitive fears, prejudice, and stereotypes rather than on knowledge and insight. In reality, the way one experiences old age is contingent upon physical health, personality, earlier-life experiences, the actual circumstances of late-life events (in what order they occur, how they occur, when they occur), and the social supports one receives: adequate finances, shelter, medical care, social roles, religious support, recreation. All of these are crucial and interconnected elements which together determine the quality of late life. . . .

MYTHS AND STEREOTYPES ABOUT THE OLD

In addition to dealing with the difficulties of physical and economic survival, older people are affected by the multitude of myths and stereotypes surrounding old age:

An older person thinks and moves slowly. He does not think as he used to or as creatively. He is bound to himself and to his past and can no longer change or grow.

He can learn neither well nor swiftly and, even if he could, he would not wish to. Tied to his personal traditions and growing conservatism, he dislikes innovations and is not disposed to new ideas. Not only can he not move forward, he often moves backward. He enters a second childhood caught up in increasing egocentricity and demanding more from his environment than he is willing to give to it. Sometimes he becomes an intensification of himself, a caricature of a lifelong personality. He becomes irritable and cantankerous, yet shallow and enfeebled. He lives in his past; he is behind the times. He is aimless and wandering of mind, reminiscing and garrulous. Indeed, he is a study in decline, the picture of mental and physical failure. He has lost and cannot replace friends, spouse, job, status, power, influence, income. He is often stricken by diseases which, in turn, restrict his movement, his enjoyment of food, the pleasures of well-being. He has lost his desire and capacity for sex. His body shrinks, and so too does the flow of blood to his brain. His mind does not utilize oxygen and sugar at the same rate as formerly. Feeble, uninteresting, he awaits his death, a burden to society, to his family and to himself.

In its essentials, this view I have sketched approximates the picture of old age held by many Americans. As in all clichés, stereotypes, and myths there are bits of truth. But many of the current views of old age represent confusions, misunderstandings, or simply a lack of knowledge about old age. Others may be completely inaccurate or biased, reflecting prejudice or outright hostility. Certain prevalent myths need closer examination.

The Myth of "Aging"

The idea of chronological aging (measuring one's age by the number of years one has lived) is a kind of myth. It is clear that there are great differences in the rates of physiological, chronological, psychological, and social aging within the person and from person to person. In fact, physiological indicators show a greater range from the mean in old age than in any other age group, and this is true of personality as well. Older people actually become more diverse rather than more similar with advancing years. There are extraordinarily "young" eighty-year-olds as well as "old" eighty-year-olds. Chronological age, therefore, is a convenient but imprecise indicator of physical, mental, and emotional status. For the purposes of this book, old age may be considered to commence at the conventionally accepted point of sixty-five.

We do know that organic brain damage can create such extensive intellectual impairment that people of all types and personalities may become dull-eyed, blank-faced, and unresponsive. Massive destruction of the brain and body has a "leveling" effect which can produce increasing homogeneity among the elderly. But most older people do not suffer impairment of this magnitude during the greater part of their later life.

The Myth of Unproductivity

Many believe the old to be unproductive. But in the absence of diseases and social adversities, old people tend to remain productive and actively involved in life. There are dazzling examples like octogenarians Georgia O'Keeffe continuing to paint and Pope John XXIII revitalizing his church, and septuagenarians Duke Ellington composing and working his hectic concert schedule and Golda Meir acting as her country's vigorous Prime Minister. Substantial numbers of people become unusually creative for the first time in old age, when exceptional and inborn talents may be discovered and expressed. What is most pertinent to our discussion here, however, is the fact that many old people continue to contribute usefully to their families and community in a variety of ways, including active employment. The 1971 Bureau of Labor Statistics figures show 1,780,000 people over sixty-five working full time and 1,257,000 part time. Since society and business practice do not encourage the continued employment of the elderly, it is obvious that many more would work if jobs were available.

When productive incapacity develops, it can be traced more directly to a variety of losses, diseases, or circumstances than to that mysterious process called aging. Even then, in spite of the presence of severe handicaps, activity and involvement are often maintained.

The Myth of Disengagement

This is related to the previous myth and holds that older people prefer to disengage from life, to withdraw into themselves, choosing to live alone or perhaps only with their peers. Ironically, some gerontologists themselves hold these views. One study, *Growing Old: The Process of Disengagement,* presents the theory that mutual separation of the aged person from his society is a natural part of the aging experience. There is no evidence to support this generalization. Disengagement is only one of many patterns of reaction to old age.

The Myth of Inflexibility

The ability to change and adapt has little to do with one's age and more to do with one's lifelong character. But even this statement has to be qualified. One is not necessarily destined to maintain one's character in earlier life permanently. True, the endurance, the strength, and the stability in human character structure are remarkable and protective. But most, if not all, people change and remain open to change throughout the course of life, right up to its termination. The old notion, whether ascribed to Pope Alexander VI or Sigmund Freud, that character is laid down in final form by the fifth year of life can be confidently refuted. Change is the hallmark of living. The notion that older people become less responsive to innovation and change because of age is not supported by scientific studies of healthy older people living in the community or by everyday observations and clinical psychiatric experience.

A related cliché is that political conservatism increases with age. If one's options are constricted by job discrimination, reduced or fixed income, and runaway inflation, as older people's are, one may become conservative out of economic necessity rather than out of qualities innate in the psyche. Thus an older person may vote against the creation of better schools or an expansion of social services for tax reasons. His property—his home—may be his only equity, and his income is likely to be too low to weather increased taxes. A perfectly sensible self-interest rather than "conservatism" is at work here. Naturally, conservatives do exist among the elderly, but so do liberals, radicals, and moderates. Once again diversity rather than homogeneity is the norm.

The Myth of "Senility"

The notion that old people are senile, showing forgetfulness, confusional episodes, and reduced attention, is widely accepted. "Senility" is a popularized layman's term used by doctors and the public alike to categorize the behavior of the old. Some of what is called senile is the result of brain damage. But anxiety and depression are also frequently lumped within the same category of senility, even though they are treatable and often reversible. Old people, like young people, experience a full range of emotions, including anxiety, grief, depression, and paranoid states. It is all too easy to blame age and brain damage when accounting for the mental problems and emotional concerns of later life.

Drug tranquilization is another frequent, misdiagnosed, and potentially reversible cause of so-called senility. Malnutrition and unrecognized physical illnesses, such as congestive heart failure, may produce "senile behavior" by reducing the supply of blood, oxygen, and food to the brain. Alcoholism, often associated with bereavement, is another cause. Because it has been so convenient to dismiss all these manifestations by lumping them together under an improper and inaccurate diagnostic label, the elderly often do not receive the benefits of decent diagnosis and treatment.

Actual irreversible brain damage,[1] of course, is not a myth, and two major conditions create mental disorders. One is cerebral arteriosclerosis (hardening of the arteries of the brain); the other, unfortunately referred to as senile brain disease, is due to a mysterious dissolution of brain cells. Such conditions account for some 50 percent of the cases of major mental disorders in old age, and the symptoms connected with these conditions are the ones that form the basis for what has come to be known as senility. But, as I wish to emphasize again, similar symptoms can be found in a number of other conditions which *are* reversible through proper treatment.

The Myth of Serenity

In contrast to the previous myths, which view the elderly in a negative light, the myth of serenity portrays old age as a kind of adult fairyland. Now at last comes a time of relative peace and serenity when people can relax and enjoy the fruits of their labors after the storms of active life are over. Advertising slogans, television, and romantic fiction foster the myth. Visions of carefree, cookie-baking grandmothers and rocking-chair grandfathers are cherished by younger generations. But, in fact, older persons experience more stresses than any other age group, and these stresses are often devastating. The strength of the aged to endure crisis is remarkable, and tranquility is an unlikely as well as inappropriate response under these circumstances. Depression, anxiety, psychosomatic illnesses, paranoia, garrulousness, and irritability are some of the internal reactions to external stresses.

Depressive reactions are particularly widespread in late life. To the more blatant psychotic depressions and the depressions associated with organic brain diseases must be added the everyday depressions that stem from long physical illness or chronic discomfort, from grief, despair, and loneliness, and from an inevitably lowered self-esteem that comes from diminished social and personal status.

Grief is a frequent companion of old age—grief for one's own losses and for the ultimate loss of one's self. Apathy and emptiness are a common sequel to the initial shock and sadness that come with the deaths of close friends and relatives. Physical disease and social isolation can follow bereavement.

Anxiety is another common feature. There is much to be anxious about; poverty, loneliness, and illness head the list. Anxiety may manifest itself in many forms: rigid patterns of thinking and behaving, helplessness, manipulative behavior, restlessness and suspiciousness, sometimes to the point of paranoid states.[2]

Anger and even rage may be seen:

Mary Mack, 73, left her doctor's office irritable, depressed, and untreated. She was angry at the doctor's inattention. She charged that he simply regarded her as a complainer and did not take the necessary time to examine her carefully. She had received the same response from other doctors. Meanwhile her doctor entered the diagnosis in his file: hypochondriasis with chronic depression. No treatment was given. The prognosis was evidently considered hopeless.

John Barber, an elderly black man, spent all his life working hard at low wages for his employers. When he was retired he literally went on strike. He refused to do anything. He would sit all day on his front porch, using his family as the substitute victim of his years of pent-up anger. He had always been seen as mild mannered. Now he could afford to let himself go into rages and describe in vicious detail what he was going to do to people. A social worker viewing his behavior declared to his family that he was "psychotic." But Mr. Barber was not insane; he was angry.

AGEISM—THE PREJUDICE AGAINST THE ELDERLY

The stereotyping and myths surrounding old age can be explained in part by lack of knowledge and by insufficient contact with a wide variety of older people. But there is another powerful factor operating—a deep and profound prejudice against the elderly which is found to some degree in all of us. In thinking about how to describe this, I coined the word "ageism" in 1968:

Ageism can be seen as a process of systematic stereotyping of and discrimination against people because they are old, just as racism and sexism accomplish thus with skin color and gender. Old people are categorized as senile, rigid in thought and manner, old-fashioned in morality and skills. . . . Ageism allows the younger generations to see older people as different from themselves; thus they subtly cease to identify with their elders as human beings.

Ageism makes it easier to ignore the frequently poor social and economic plight of older people. We can avoid dealing with the reality that our productivity-minded society has little use for nonproducers—in this case those who have reached an arbitrarily defined retirement age. We can also avoid, for a time at least, reminders of the personal reality of our own aging and death.

Ageism is manifested in a wide range of phenomena, both on individual and institutional levels—stereotypes and myths, outright disdain and dislike, or simply subtle avoidance of contact; discriminatory practices in housing, employment, and services of all kinds; epithets, cartoons, and jokes. At times ageism becomes an expedient method by which society promotes viewpoints about the aged in order to relieve itself of responsibility toward them. At other times ageism serves a highly personal objective, protecting younger (usually middle-aged) individuals—often at high emotional cost—from thinking about things they fear (aging, illness, death). . . .

Older people are not always victims, passive and fated by their environment. They, too, initiate direct actions and stimulate responses. They may exploit their age and its accompanying challenges to gain something they want or need, perhaps to their own detriment (for example, by demanding services from others and thus allowing their own skills to atrophy). Exploitation can backfire; excessive requests to others by an older person may be met at first, but as requests increase they are felt as demands—and may indeed be demands. Younger people who attempt to deal with a demanding older person may find themselves going through successive cycles of rage, guilt, and overprotectiveness without realizing they are being manipulated. In addition to his "age," the older person may exploit his diseases and his impairments, capitalizing upon his alleged helplessness. Invalids of all ages do this, but older people can more easily take on the appearance of frailty when others would not be allowed this behavior. Manipulation by older people is best recognized for what it is—a valuable clue that there is energy available which should be redirected toward greater benefit for themselves and others.

It must also be remembered that the old can have many prejudices against the young. These may be a result of their attractiveness, vigor, and sexual prowess. Older people may be troubled by the extraordinary changes that they see in the world around them and blame the younger generation. They may be angry at the brevity of life and begrudge someone the fresh chance of living out a life span which they have already completed.

Angry and ambivalent feelings flow, too, between the old and the middle-aged, who are caught up in the problems unique to their age and position within the life cycle. The middle-aged bear the heaviest personal and social responsibilities since they are called upon to help support—individually and collectively—both ends of the life cycle: the nurture and education of their young and the financial, emotional, and physical care of the old. Many have not been prepared for their heavy responsibilities and are surprised and overwhelmed by them. Frequently these responsibilities trap them in their careers or life styles until the children grow up or their parents die. A common reaction is anger at both the young and the old. The effects of financial pressures are seen primarily in the middle and lower economic classes. But the middle-aged of all classes are inclined to be ambivalent toward the young and old since both age groups remind them of their own waning youth. In addition—with reason—they fear technological or professional obsolescence as they see what has happened to their elders and feel the pressure of youth pushing its way toward their position in society. Furthermore, their responsibilities are likely to increase in the future as more and more of their parents and grandparents live longer life spans.

CRITICAL-THINKING QUESTIONS

1. Butler presents several themes that shape popular views of old age in the United States. What evidence of these do you find in the mass media? What about in your own attitudes and behavior toward elderly people?

2. Why do you think our society has developed views of aging that are not realistic?

3. How do the elderly themselves sometimes reinforce ageism?

NOTES

1. Human beings react in varying ways to brain disease just as they do to other serious threats to their persons. They may become anxious, rigid, depressed, and hypochondriacal. (Hypochondriasis comprises bodily symptoms or fear of diseases that are not due to physical changes but to emotional concerns. They are no less real simply because they do not have a physical origin.) These reactions can be ameliorated by sensitive, humane concern, talk, and understanding even though the underlying physical process cannot be reversed. Therefore, even the irreversible brain syndromes require proper diagnosis and treatment of their emotional consequences.

2. No less a thinker than Aristotle failed to distinguish between the intrinsic features of aging and the reaction of the elderly to their lives. He considered cowardice, resentment, vindictiveness, and what he called "senile avarice" to be intrinsic to late life. Cicero took a warmer and more positive view of old age. He understood, for example, "If old men are morose, troubled, fretful, and hard to please . . . these are faults of character and not of age." So he explained in his essay *"De Senectute."*

CLASSIC

CONTEMPORARY

CROSS-CULTURAL

49 How the Grandparent Role Is Changing

ROSEANN GIARRUSSO, MERRIL SILVERSTEIN, AND VERN L. BENGSTON

As Reading 50 describes, our world is aging. Increasing numbers of adults—especially in Western nations—are now great-grandparents and even great-great-grandparents. Such unprecedented longevity suggests the growing importance of multigenerational family relations. In this reading, Roseann Giarrusso, Merril Silverstein, and Vern L. Bengston examine how our longevity has already affected intergenerational family structures and why grandparent-grandchild relationships will become more important.

Grandparenthood has changed over the past decades as demographic shifts have increased the complexity of family structures and roles. Increases in longevity, in divorce and remarriage rates, and in old-age migration have simultaneously produced new opportunities and new stresses for grandparents. The longevity revolution has increased the number of three-, four-, and five-generation families, thereby lengthening the time spent in the grandparent role and adding multiple roles of great- and great-great-grandparent. Increases in divorce and remarriage rates have resulted in a high proportion of blended families and step-grandparent relationships. Improved health, stable finances, and early retirement have made geographic mobility possible for retirees. How have these changes in family structure, composition, and living arrangements influenced the role of grandparents? What are the implications of these changes for the psychological well-being and resources available to grandparents?

In this [reading] we first examine how population aging and the changing structure of the intergenerational family highlight the increasing diversity in grandparenting and great-grandparenting styles. Second, we examine how divorce and remarriage in the middle generation influence grandparents' ability to enact their role when custodial parents act as gatekeepers to their children, and we underscore the need for research on grandparents rearing grandchildren in order to determine the psychological costs and rewards to caregiving grandparents. Third, we discuss how household arrangements and geographic mobility of grandparents and grandchildren jointly influence their relationship. We conclude with an overview of some research and policy implications that result from these complex family arrangements and emphasize the need for greater conceptual and theoretical development in grandparenting studies.

Source: Reprinted with permission from *Generations,* 20:1, (Spring, 1996), pp. 17–23. Copyright © The American Society on Aging (San Francisco, CA). *www.asaging.org.*

CHANGING INTERGENERATIONAL FAMILY STRUCTURES

Because of dramatic increases in average longevity over the past century, it has become more likely that grandparents, great-grandparents, and even great-great-grandparents will survive long enough to have relationships with grandchildren, great-grandchildren, or great-great-grandchildren. Where fewer than 50 percent of adolescents in 1900 had two or more grandparents alive, by 1976 that figure had grown to almost 90 percent (Uhlenberg, 1980). Thus, there is an unprecedented number of grandparents in American society today; more than three-quarters of adults can expect to become a grandparent (Barranti, 1985; Hagestad, 1985; Kivnick, 1982).

While historical increases in life expectancy have resulted in families with more generations alive simultaneously, reductions in fertility have resulted in smaller average family size (Bengtson & Treas, 1980; Uhlenberg, 1980; Watkins, Menken, & Bongaarts, 1987). Consequently, the shape of American families has gone from that of a pyramid, with larger numbers of young people at the base, to that of a beanpole. Three, four, and five generations of family members are increasingly present, but with fewer numbers being born in each subsequent generation than in previous eras (Bengtson, Rosenthal, & Burton, 1990).

With fewer family members in each generation, existing *intergenerational* family relations take on added significance. Since there may be more *between*-generation kin than *within*-generation kin available in such a family structure, grandchildren may emerge as potentially more important sources of emotional meaning and practical support for grandparents than in the past. Thus, grandparenthood may be an increasingly significant social role for older people, offering valuable rewards. At the same time, it is important to consider whether a more involved grandparenthood also results in social, economic, and psychological costs—especially for grandparents who

become "surrogate parents" for their grandchildren (Bengtson, Rosenthal, & Burton, 1995).

Elongation of multigenerational families also can occur from age-condensed family patterns: Teenage pregnancy can produce differences of less than twenty years between generations, leading to grandparenthood in one's twenties or thirties, over four or five generations. This kind of intergenerational structure is more common among ethnic minorities than among the white majority. In addition, higher rates of fertility, along with the tendency to include fictive kin in definitions of family, have created a paradox for minority grandparents: Although they have a larger kin network from which they may draw potential support, they also have a larger number of kin to whom they must *provide* support (Bengtson, Rosenthal, & Burton, 1995). . . .

Adult Grandchildren

Not only have relationships with grandparents, great-grandparents, and great-great-grandparents been a neglected topic of research, so too have relationships of grandparents with *adult* grandchildren. Most previous research has tended to focus only on pre-adult grandchildren or those living with the grandparent (Jendrek, 1994; Robertson, 1995). Given the growth recently of studies examining adult parent-child relations, it is surprising that only scant attention has been devoted to studying relationships between grandparents and adult grandchildren.

Because of increases in longevity over the past century, it has become more likely that a grandparent will not only survive, but live long enough to have *long-term* relationships with *adult* grandchildren. As the median age of first grandparenthood has remained relatively constant over the past century at forty-five years (Hagestad, 1985), gains in life expectancy imply that grandparents are spending many more years in the grandparent role: Among women, for example, this status can engage 50 percent of their lives, and the prevalence of grandparents who have adult grandchildren is historically unprecedented (Goldman, 1986). Farkas and Hogan (1994) examined intergenerational family structure in seven economically developed nations (including the United States) during the 1980s and found that more than half (50.6 percent) of people sixty-five years of age and older have a grandchild who is at least eighteen years old. Lawton, Silverstein, and Bengtson (1994) found a slightly higher percentage in a study of intergenerational relations in the United States conducted by the American Association of Retired Persons (AARP), with 56 percent of Americans sixty-five years of age and older having at least one adult grandchild.

In light of the recent expansion in adult grandchild-grandparent relations in the American population, it is unfortunate that little attention has been paid by large-scale survey researchers to these adult intergenerational relationships. For example, most of the major national surveys designed to study social aspects of aging ask no specific questions of older adults about their relationships with grandchildren (or great-grandchildren) or of younger adults about their relationships with grandparents.

Other scholarly analyses concerning the relationships of grandparents with pre-adult grandchildren suggest that grandparents are more involved with their younger grandchildren than ever before. Some researchers have speculated that the grandparent-grandchild bond may be even more significant in adult relations (Hagestad, 1981; Troll, 1980). As yet, however, the trajectory or life-course "career" of grandparent-grandchild relationships, and the contribution of "successful" grandparenting to quality of life of older adults, are issues that are unclear and remain unexamined. . . .

Diversity in the Styles of Grandparenting

Population aging has not only led to the long-term viability of grandparenthood; it has also led to an increasing diversity in the demographic characteristics of individuals holding the roles of grandparent and grandchild. Today grandparents may range in age from 30 to 110, and grandchildren range from newborns to retirees (Hagestad, 1985). With demographic diversity in grandparents has come a corresponding diversity in grandparenting styles (Bengtson, 1985). Consequently, some scholars have suggested that the role of grandparent is ill-defined, that it is a social status without clear normative expectations attached to it. Fischer and Silverman (1982) and Wood (1982) refer to the grandparent role as "tenuous" or "ambiguous," without clear prescriptions regarding the rights and duties of grandparents. In fact, there is no single "grandparent role," but there are multiple ways to be a grandparent. It is important not to confuse variance in styles of role enactment with lack of role definition. What is needed is a classification of the different types of grandparenting since there are a variety of reasons that grandparents do not perform the role in the same way.

Yet there has been little empirical research on the styles of grandparenting and the sources of diversity in those styles. In the only previous attempt to classify grandparent-grandchild relations, Cherlin and Furstenberg (1986) identified five types of grandparenting styles by cross-classifying grandparents on three relationship dimensions: exchange of services with grandchild, influence over grandchild, and frequency of contact with grandchild. They labeled these types as follows: (1) detached, (2) passive, (3) supportive, (4) authoritative, and (5) influential. Their analysis suggested that none of the five styles is dominant, and they conclude that grandparenting styles are quite diverse in contemporary American society.

However, Cherlin and Furstenberg's classification does not take into account several relevant dimensions of grandparent-grandchild relations. One of the most important issues related to grandparenting styles is the extent of bonds, solidarity, or connectedness in multigenerational relationships. The lives of grandparents or great-grandparents and their grandchildren and great-grandchildren are linked in a number of ways: through roles, through interactions, through sentiments, and through exchanges of support. Connectedness between grandparents and grandchildren can also be considered along more social-psychological dimensions. One approach is a typology of grandparenting styles based on six dimensions of intergenerational solidarity (Bengtson & Schrader, 1982) that are comprehensive in describing intergenerational relations and that have been widely used in empirical studies (Atkinson, Kivett, & Campbell, 1986; Roberts & Bengtson, 1990; Rossi & Rossi, 1990). These six dimensions are affection (emotional closeness), association (frequency of contact), consensus (agreement), normative quality (importance of familial obligations to members), structure (geographic proximity), and function (helping behavior).

Silverstein, Lawton, and Bengtson (1994) used data from the AARP national study of intergenerational linkages to create a typology of five categories of adult parent-child relations based on five of the six dimensions of intergenerational solidarity. They found five types of intergenerational relationships: (1) *tight-knit*—connected on all five dimensions of intergenerational solidarity; (2) *sociable*—connected only on associational, structural, affectional, and consensual dimensions of solidarity; (3) *cordial but distant*—connected only on affectional and consensual dimensions of solidarity; (4) *obligatory*—connected on associational, structural, and functional solidarity; and (5) *detached*—connected on none of the five dimensions of intergenerational solidarity. While these dimensions have been used to describe parent-child relations, the same five types of parenting styles may also characterize grandparenting styles and grandparent-grandchild relations—an issue awaiting future research development.

DIVORCE AND REMARRIAGE

The structure of American families has undergone profound changes as a result of increases in divorce and remarriage during the past decade.

Such changes in family composition and living arrangements can interfere with grandparents' ability to perform their role. The parental generation mediates the grandparent-grandchild relationship, since they provide the opportunities for grandparents and grandchildren to socialize together (Barranti, 1985; Hagestad, 1985; Robertson, 1977). When the parents are divorced, the quality of the grandparent-grandchild relationship may suffer—or it may strengthen.

Divorce may weaken grandparent-grandchild relations on the noncustodial (usually paternal) side of the family but strengthen those relations on the custodial (usually maternal) side of the family (Clingempeel et al., 1992; Creasey, 1993; Matthews & Sprey, 1984). Custodial parents can effectively prevent the parents of an estranged spouse from seeing their grandchildren (Gladstone, 1989). Thus, divorce has a particularly harsh effect on the relationship between grandchildren and grandparents whose children have not been given custody. Even though all states now have grandparents' rights legislation, which gives grandparents the power to go to court to secure their right to visit their grandchildren (Wilson & DeShare, 1982), grandparent-grandchild association after divorce will probably become increasingly matrilineal. Further, if the divorced parent remarries, then stepgrandparents may enter with a new role that is fraught with ambiguous expectations (Cherlin, 1978; Henry, Ceglian, & Ostrander, 1993).

The greater their investment in the grandparent role, the more distress grandparents may feel when contact with grandchildren declines following the parental divorce (Myers & Perrin, 1993), and one would expect that reduced contact between grandparent and grandchild will have an enduring effect on the well-being of both generations. The long-term consequence of early parental divorce and remarriage for grandparents and adult grandchildren is a subject that requires further research investigation.

Future research should also examine possible positive outcomes of the increasing complexity of family arrangements; steprelationships, for example, may have taken on added importance. These changes in the family have led to the development of "latent kin networks" (Riley, Kahn, & Foner, 1994), which have the potential of being activated when needed. It is possible that such complex family arrangements have led to new definitions of family, making it necessary to test long-held assumptions about the primacy of biological relationships over other kinship forms. Stepchildren and stepgrandchildren may represent untapped resources for family members in later life.

Most past research on steprelations has focused on the difficulties that exist between preadult stepchildren and their stepparents (Pasley, Ihinger-Tillman, & Lofquist, 1994). We know of no research on how these steprelations develop over the life course, as stepchildren, siblings, parents, grandparents, or great-grandparents age. When stepgrandparents share many years of life with stepgrandchildren, especially during the grandchildren's formative years, the intergenerational bonds that develop may equal or surpass those of biological relations—particularly in cases where custody arrangements preclude contact with biological grandchildren.

GRANDPARENTS AS SURROGATE PARENTS

Increasing numbers of grandparents are rearing their grandchildren because of divorce and other problems such as drug and alcohol addiction, AIDS, incarceration, and unemployment within the parental generation (Chalfie, 1994). Census figures estimate the number of grandchildren living with their grandparents (many without a parent present) to be as high as 3.4 million, with African American grandchildren being slightly more than three times more likely than their white counterparts to be in this type of living arrangement (U.S. Bureau of the Census, 1993). Grandparents caring for grandchildren is such a rapidly growing problem that AARP established the Grandparent Information Center in 1993, which in its first four months of operation received over 2,100 calls and requests for information from grandparents who are rearing a grandchild.

Only recently has research begun to address the role of the grandparents who assume direct, full-time caregiving responsibilities for their grandchildren (Burton, 1995; Chalfie, 1994; Shore & Hayslip, 1994). These studies indicate that caregiving grandparents experience a variety of stresses and strains for which there is little institutional support. They encounter difficulties in such matters as obtaining financial assistance, health insurance coverage, and housing, as well as in gaining legal rights to make decisions regarding the child's education and medical care (Chalfie, 1994). Minority caregiving grandparents, because they tend to have low incomes and multiple caregiving roles, may experience greater stress than similar white grandparents, putting them in "double-jeopardy" of experiencing psychological distress (Dowd & Bengtson, 1978). Many questions on caregiving grandparents need to be addressed in future research: What are the consequences of becoming a parent again in midlife? Does this responsibility lead to lower levels of psychological well-being, or an increase in intergenerational conflict? When grandparents become parents to their grandchildren, who takes over their previous function as safety net in times of family emergencies? And, while providing full-time care for a grandchild may be stressful, grandparent caregivers are also likely to obtain certain rewards and informal support from their intergenerational family relations (Burton, 1995). Future research needs to examine these benefits. . . .

GEOGRAPHIC MOBILITY AND HOUSEHOLD ARRANGEMENTS

Grandparent-grandchild relationships are obviously influenced by how close geographically the generations are to each other, since this factor structures opportunities for interaction (Baranowski,

1987). There is evidence that movement of older people to retirement communities reduces in-person contact between older people and their adult children, and, it may be concluded, with their grandchildren. Developmental approaches to late-life migration have found that return of the elderly to their home community or to the household of an adult child often follows a decline in functioning and death of a spouse (Litwak & Longino, 1988; Silverstein, 1995). However, the role of grandchildren in caregiving to their grandparents following such a move is not known and needs further study.

The role of parent as "gatekeeper" to grandchildren remains a critical factor in regulating grandparent contact. Remarriage of a divorced parent influences the amount of contact between grandparents and their grandchildren when the parent relocates (Gladstone, 1991). The number of adult children moving to the parental home (following divorce or unemployment) with young children in tow has swelled the number of generationally complex households with the older—grandparent—generation as the head of household. At the same time, after leaving the parental nest, adult grandchildren renegotiate their relationships with their grandparents—most commonly reducing the frequency of contact with them (Field & Minkler, 1988). A recent trend may moderate this residential transition: A "boomerang" generation of young adults is moving back to or never leaving the parental nest, to take advantage of a lower cost of living. The result is an increase in the number of three-generational households that have two adult generations. Young-adult "boomerangers" might maintain or strengthen their relationships with grandparents by virtue of living with parents who facilitate extended intergenerational involvement.

In immigrant families, acculturation of adult grandchildren, especially those in ethnic groups with traditional values and orientations, may serve to distance grandparents from their grandchildren. Does assimilation and loss of native language among native-born grandchildren result in reduced intergenerational cohesion with traditional grandparents? There is some evidence that acculturation—the adoption of mainstream values, language, and practices—does create a cultural gulf between generations in the Hispanic family. Schmidt and Padilla (1983) find that Spanish-language compatibility between grandparents and grandchildren predicts the amount of contact between them, underscoring the importance of cultural affinity in structuring intergenerational relations. Research also shows that the better the grandchild speaks the native language of the grandparent, the greater the tendency of grandchildren to live with grandparents (Perez, 1994). Yet, we are unaware of research that formally links acculturation to the propensity of adult grandchildren to move away from grandparents or to leave their ethnic enclave in pursuit of educational or employment opportunities. . . .

POLICY IMPLICATIONS

The results reviewed above concerning increasing family complexity and grandparent-grandchild relations raise new questions not only for researchers but also for program planners and policy makers as well. Recently implemented cuts to government health programs such as Medicare make it clear that federal and state government can go only so far in providing support for old-age dependencies. It is more important than ever to look for alternative solutions to the support and care of the growing population of aging Americans.

The most cost-effective solution may be to develop new programs and policies to shore up or strengthen intergenerational family ties. But before developing such programs, policy makers need to consider the increasing complexity of family arrangements. Successful programs would accommodate the diversity that characterizes the role of grandparent, and also revise traditional definitions of caregiving to conform with changes in the shape of the intergenerational family from pyramid to beanpole. Legislators are familiar with the concept of the "sandwich generation," wherein the middle generation is faced with caring for aging parents while simultaneously raising minor children. However, changes in family structure, coupled with increases in divorce, have resulted in a situation, unparalleled in human history, of fifty-five-year-old children caring for seventy-five-year-old parents and ninety-five-year-old grandparents while rearing adolescent grandchildren—a "club sandwich generation." Policy makers need to develop more programs that provide financial support in such situations—"dependent" care tax credits, for example.

Finally, policy makers must anticipate intergenerational conflict that might result from certain types of geographic mobility or household arrangements and should develop programs that could help families prevent such intergenerational conflicts.

CONCLUSION

In this article we have highlighted three social changes that have increased structural complexity in the intergenerational family, consequently expanding the varieties and contingencies of grandparent-grandchild relationships. Because of the almost exponential rise in the heterogeneity of grandparenting experiences and styles over the last several decades, the investigation of these relationships represents one of the most fertile areas of inquiry in family studies. We predict that social scientists and policy makers will continue to be challenged in their efforts to keep pace with rapid societal changes affecting this ever-evolving and increasingly disparate population of middle-aged and older adults. In the future, intergenerational family structures might become even more diverse. Coupled with shifts in social, political, and economic conditions, such family complexities make even more pressing the need for fresh theoretical perspectives, informed research designs, and innovative

intervention strategies to address the needs of grandparents.

CRITICAL-THINKING QUESTIONS

1. What do Giarrusso and her colleagues mean when they say that the shape of U.S. families has gone from a "pyramid" to a "beanpole"? What are the rewards and costs for grandparents and grandchildren in terms of this changing family structure?

2. Some researchers speculate that grandparent-grandchild relationships in the future may be more significant than in the past. What are the reasons for such predictions? How do divorce, remarriage, and geographical mobility threaten the positive impact of such relationships?

3. Giarrusso and her colleagues propose several economic policies to strengthen intergenerational family ties. Do you think their suggestions are realistic? Also, what role, if any, can families play in addressing the needs of grandparents, adult children, and grandchildren that the authors address?

REFERENCES

Atkinson, M. P., V. R. Kivett, and R. T. Campbell. 1986. Intergenerational solidarity: An examination of a theoretical model. *Journal of Gerontology,* 41: 408–16.

Baranowski, M. D. 1987. The grandfather-grandchild relationship: Patterns and meaning. Paper presented at 40th Annual Scientific Meeting of the Gerontological Society of America, Washington, D.C., Nov. 18–22.

Barranti, C. C. R. 1985. The grandparent/grandchild relationship: Family resources in an era of voluntary bonds. *Family Relations,* 34:43–52.

Bengtson, V. L. 1985. Symbolism and diversity in the grandparenthood role. In *Grandparenthood,* V. L. Bengtson and J. F. Robertson, eds. Beverly Hills, Calif.: Sage.

Bengtson, V. L., C. J. Rosenthal, and L. M. Burton. 1990. Families and aging: Diversity and heterogeneity. In *Handbook of aging and the social sciences,* 3rd ed., eds. R. H. Binstock and L. K. George. San Diego, Calif.: Academic Press.

———. 1995. Paradoxes of families and aging. In *Handbook of aging and the social sciences,* 4th ed., eds. R. H. Binstock and L. K. George. San Diego, Calif.: Academic Press.

Bengtson, V. L., and S. S. Schrader. 1982. Parent-child relations. In *Handbook of research instruments in social gerontology,* vol. 2, eds. D. Mangen and W. Peterson. Minneapolis: University of Minnesota Press.

BENGTSON, V. L., and J. TREAS. 1980. The changing family context of mental health and aging. In *Handbook of mental health and aging,* eds. J. E. Birren and B. Sloane. Englewood Cliffs, N.J.: Prentice-Hall.

BURTON, L. M. 1995. Early and on-time grandmotherhood in multigeneration Black families. Doctoral dissertation. University of Southern California.

CHALFIE, D. 1994. *Going it alone: A closer look at grandparents parenting grandchildren.* Washington, D.C.: AARP Women's Initiative.

CHERLIN, A. 1978. Remarriage as an incomplete institution. *American Journal of Sociology,* 84: 634–50.

CHERLIN, A., and F. FURSTENBERG. 1986. *The new American grandparent: A place in the family.* New York: Basic Books.

CLINGEMPEEL, W. G., et al. 1992. Children's relationships with maternal grandparents: A longitudinal study of family structure and pubertal status effects. *Child Development,* 63: 1404–22.

CREASEY, G. L. 1993. The association between divorce and late adolescent grandchildren's relations with grandparents. *Journal of Youth and Adolescence,* 22(5): 513–29.

DOWD, J. J., and V. L. BENGTSON. 1978. Aging in minority populations: An examination of the double jeopardy hypothesis. *Journal of Gerontology,* 33(3): 427–36.

FARKAS, J. I., and D. P. HOGAN. 1994. The demography of changing intergenerational relationships. In *Adult intergenerational relations: Effects of societal change,* eds. V. L. Bengtson, K. W. Schaie, and L. M. Burton. New York: Springer.

FIELD, D., and M. MINKLER. 1988. Continuity and change in social support between young-old and old-old or very-old age. *Journal of Gerontology,* 43(4): 100–6.

FISCHER, L. R., and J. SILVERMAN. 1982. Grandmothering as a tenuous role relationship. Paper presented at the Annual Meeting of the National Council on Family Relations, Detroit, Mich.

GLADSTONE, J. W. 1989. Grandmother-grandchild contact: The mediating influence of the middle generation following marriage breakdown and remarriage. *Canadian Journal on Aging,* 8: 355–65.

———. 1991. An analysis of changes in grandparent-grandchild visitation following an adult child's remarriage. *Canadian Journal on Aging,* 10(2): 113–26.

GOLDMAN, N. 1986. Effects of mortality levels on kinship. In *Consequences of mortality trends and differentials.* New York: United Nations.

HAGESTAD, G. O. 1981. Problems and promises in the social psychology of intergenerational relations. In *Stability and change in the family,* eds. R. Fogel et al. New York: Academic Press.

———. 1985. Continuity and connectedness. In *Grandparenthood,* eds. V. L. Bengtson and J. F. Robertson. Beverly Hills, Calif.: Sage.

HENRY, C. S., C. P. CEGLIAN, and D. L. OSTRANDER. 1993. The transition to step-grandparenthood. *Journal of Divorce and Remarriage,* 19: 25–44.

JENDREK, M. P. 1994. Grandparents who parent their grandchildren: Circumstances and decisions. *Gerontologist,* 34(2): 206–16.

KIVNICK, H. Q. 1982. Grandparenthood: An overview of meaning and mental health. *Gerontologist,* 22(1): 59–66.

LAWTON, L., M. SILVERSTEIN, and V. L. BENGTSON. 1994. Solidarity between generations in families. In *Hidden connections: Intergenerational linkages in American society,* eds. V. L. Bengtson and R. A. Harootyan. New York: Springer.

LITWAK, E., and C. F. LONGINO. 1988. Migration patterns among the elderly: A developmental perspective. *Gerontologist,* 27: 266–72.

MATTHEWS, S., and J. SPREY. 1984. The impact of divorce on grandparenthood: An exploratory study. *Gerontologist,* 24: 41–47.

MYERS, J. E., and PERRIN, N. 1993. Grandparents affected by parental divorce: A population at risk? *Journal of Counseling and Development,* 22: 62–66.

PASLEY, K., M. IHINGER-TALLMAN, and A. LOFQUIST. 1994. Remarriage and step-families: Making progress in understanding. In *Stepparenting,* eds. K. Pasley and M. Ihinger-Tallman. Westport, Conn.: Greenwood Press.

PEREZ, L. 1994. The household structure of second-generation children: An exploratory study of extended family arrangements. *International Migration Review,* 28(4): 736–47.

RILEY, M. W., R. L. KAHN, and A. FONER, eds. 1994. *Age and structural lag: Society's failure to provide meaningful opportunities in work, family and leisure.* New York: John Wiley.

ROBERTS, R. E. L., and V. L. BENGTSON. 1990. Is intergenerational solidarity a unidimensional construct? A second test of a formal model. *Journal of Gerontology: Social Sciences,* 45: S12–20.

ROBERTSON, J. F. 1977. Grandmotherhood: A study of role conceptions. *Journal of Marriage and the Family,* 39: 165–74.

———. 1995. Grandparenting in an era of rapid change. In *Handbook of aging and the family,* eds. R. Blieszner and V. H. Bedford. Westport, Conn.: Greenwood Press.

ROSSI, A. S., and P. H. ROSSI. 1990. *Of human bonding: Parent-child relationships across the life course.* New York: Aldine de Gruyter.

SCHMIDT, A., and A. M. PADILLA. 1983. Grandparent-grandchild interaction in a Mexican American group. *Hispanic Journal of Behavioral Sciences,* 5(2): 181–98.

SHORE, R. J., and B. HAYSLIP, JR. 1994. Custodial grandparenting: Implications for children's development. In *Redefining families: Implications for children's development,* eds. A. E. Gottfried and A. W. Gottfried. New York: Plenum Press.

SILVERSTEIN, M. 1995. Stability and change in temporal distance between the elderly and their children. *Demography,* 32(1): 29–45.

SILVERSTEIN, M., L. LAWTON, and V. L. BENGTSON. 1994. Types of relations between parents and adult children. In *Hidden connections: Intergenerational linkages in American society,* eds. V. L. Bengtson and R. A. Harootyan. New York: Springer.

TROLL, L. E. 1980. Grandparenting. In *Aging in the 1980s: Psychological issues,* ed. L. W. Poon. Washington, D.C.: American Psychological Association.

UHLENBERG, P. 1980. Death and the family. *Journal of Family History,* 5(3): 313–20.

U.S. BUREAU OF THE CENSUS. 1993. Marital status and living arrangements: March 1993. *Current Population Reports* (Series P-20, No. 478). Washington, D.C.: Government Printing Office.

WATKINS, S. C., J. A. MENKEN, and J. BONGAARTS. 1987. Demographic foundations of family change. *American Sociological Review,* 52: 346–58.

WILSON, K. B., and M. R. DESHARE. 1982. The legal rights of grandparents: A preliminary discussion. *Gerontologist,* 22: 67–71.

WOOD, V. 1982. Grandparenthood: An ambiguous role. *Generations,* 7(2): 18–24.

CLASSIC

CONTEMPORARY

CROSS-CULTURAL

50 Our Aging World

FRANK B. HOBBS AND BONNIE L. DAMON

The average age in societies around the world is rising. Even now, demographers report, the eighty-and-over age group is the fastest-growing portion of the elderly population. Frank B. Hobbs and Bonnie L. Damon describe the growing number of elderly persons worldwide, compare the growth of the elderly population in developed and developing countries, and raise important questions about the future implications of our aging world.

POPULATION AGING IS WORLDWIDE

To set the aging of the United States in context it is useful to look at aging in the rest of the world. Fertility rates and infant and maternal mortality have declined in most nations. Also, mortality from infectious and parasitic diseases has declined. The world's nations generally have improved other aspects of health and education. All of these factors have interacted so that every major region in the world shows an increased proportion of the population that will be sixty-five or older by 2020.

There were 357 million persons aged sixty-five and over in the world in 1994 [see Table 1]. They represent 6 percent of the world's population. By the year 2000, there would be about 418 million elderly. The annual growth rate for the elderly was

2.8 percent in 1993–94 (compared with an average annual rate for the total world population of 1.6 percent). Such growth is expected to continue far into the twenty-first century.

Numerical growth of the elderly population is worldwide. It is occurring in both developed and developing countries. The average annual growth rate in 1993–94 of persons sixty-five years and over was 3.2 percent in developing countries compared with 2.3 percent in the developed world. In absolute numbers, from 1993 to 1994, the net balance of the world's elderly population (sixty-five years and over) increased by over 1,000 persons every hour. Of this increase, 63 percent occurred in developing countries.

Over half (55 percent) of the world's elderly lived in developing nations in 1994. These developing regions could be home to nearly two-thirds (65 percent) of the world's elderly by the year 2020. Thirty nations had elderly populations of at least 2 million in 1994. . . . Current population projections indicate there will be fifty-five such nations by 2020.

Source: From *65+ in the United States.* U.S. Bureau of the Census, Current Population Reports, Special Studies, P23–190 (Washington, D.C.: Government Printing Office, 1996), pp. 24–27.

Among countries with more than 1 million population, Sweden has the highest proportion of people aged sixty-five and over, with 18 percent in 1994—about the same as the state of Florida. Sweden also has the highest proportion aged eighty and over with 5 percent. The Caribbean is the oldest of the major developing regions with 7 percent of its population sixty-five or older in 1994.

By 2020, the elderly will constitute from one-fifth to nearly one-fourth of the population of many European countries. For example, Census Bureau projections indicate that 23 percent of Germany's population would be elderly compared with 22 percent for Italy, Finland, Belgium, Croatia, Denmark, and Greece. The elderly population of twelve additional European countries with more than 1 million population will constitute at least one-fifth of the total country population. The United States would be 16 percent.

Japan's population age sixty-five and over is expected to grow dramatically in the coming decades. According to projections, the percentage of Japan's population that is elderly could grow from 14 percent (17.1 million) in 1994 to 17 percent (21.0 million) in 2000 and to 26 percent (32.2 million) by 2020. . . . This is a rapid rise in a short time. Japan's population eighty years and over also is projected to grow very rapidly, from 3 percent of their total population in 1994 to 7 percent by 2020.

Already the Japanese are reducing retirement benefits and making other adjustments to prepare for the economic and social results of a rapidly aging society.

In 1994, the world had an estimated 61 million persons aged eighty or older. That number is expected to increase to 146 million by the year 2020. Persons eighty years and over constituted only 1 percent of the world's total population in 1994 and more than 20 percent of the world's elderly (28 percent in developed countries, 16 percent in developing nations).

DEVELOPED COUNTRIES NOW HAVE MOST OF THE WORLD'S OLDEST POPULATION

Although the developed countries of the world represented only 22 percent of the total world population in 1994, the majority of the world's population aged eighty and over live in developed countries. However, it is projected that by 2020, the majority will live in developing countries. For many nations, the eighty-and-over age group will be the fastest growing portion of the elderly population. In 2000, 26 percent of the elderly in the United States would be eighty or older, which, among countries with a population size of at least 5 million, would rank sixth, behind Sweden,

TABLE 1   World Population by Age and Sex, 1994 and 2000

Year and Age	Population (millions)			Percentage of Total			Males per 100 Females
	Both Sexes	Male	Female	Both Sexes	Male	Female	
1994							
All ages	5,640	2,841	2,798	100.0%	100.0%	100.0%	101.5
Under 15 years. . .	1,790	917	873	31.7	32.3	31.2	105.1
15 to 64 years . . .	3,492	1,771	1,722	61.9	62.3	61.5	102.9
65 years and over.	357	153	204	6.3	5.4	7.3	75.2
2000							
All ages	6,161	3,103	3,057	100.0	100.0	100.0	101.5
Under 15 years. . .	1,877	962	915	30.5	31.0	29.9	105.2
15 to 64 years . . .	3,866	1,959	1,907	62.7	63.1	62.4	102.8
65 years and over.	418	182	236	6.8	5.9	7.7	77.1

Source: U.S. Bureau of the Census, International Data Base.

TABLE 2   Projected Population for Countries with More than One Million Persons Aged 80 Years and Over, 1994 and 2020

Country/Area	Rank 1994	Rank 2020	Population Aged 80 Years and Over (in thousands, based on rank in 1994) 1994	2020
China, Mainland	1	1	9,010	28,737
United States	**2**	**2**	**7,760**	**13,007**
India	3	3	4,021	12,639
Japan.	4	4	3,597	9,362
Russia	5	5	3,317	7,191
Germany	6	6	3,313	5,889
France	7	8	2,563	3,754
United Kingdom	8	9	2,342	3,400
Italy.	9	7	2,221	4,142
Ukraine	10	12	1,421	2,923
Spain.	11	13	1,287	2,488
Brazil	*	10	*	3,132
Indonesia	*	11	*	3,034
Mexico	*	14	*	2,296
Poland.	*	15	*	1,877
Turkey.	*	16	*	1,751
Canada	*	17	*	1,595
Thailand	*	18	*	1,477
Pakistan.	*	19	*	1,385
Romania	*	20	*	1,264
South Korea	*	21	*	1,221
Vietnam	*	22	*	1,199
Argentina	*	23	*	1,072
Iran	*	24	*	1,039

* Indicates population 80 years and over in 1994 was less than 1 million.

Source: U.S. Bureau of the Census, International Data Base.

Denmark, Switzerland, Cuba, and the United Kingdom.

In 1994, China had the largest number of persons aged eighty or older followed by the United States [see Table 2]. Nine additional countries had over 1 million persons eighty years and over in 1994. By 2020, this list is expected to include thirteen additional countries, ten of which are developing countries. In many developing countries, the population eighty and over in 2020 is likely to at least quadruple from 1994. This highlights the problems governments may have in planning support services for this burgeoning population group.

The rapid growth of the oldest old has various health and economic implications for individuals, families, and governments throughout the world. The oldest old often have severe chronic health problems which demand special attention. The nature and duration of their illnesses are likely to produce a substantial need for prolonged care. Developing nations already have diluted resources. They are the most limited in being able to provide preventive measures and, in future years, supportive services. The United States and other countries face enormous investments and payments to maintain current levels of services for the oldest old.

CRITICAL-THINKING QUESTIONS

1. What are some of the reasons for the growth of aging populations worldwide?

2. In the 1990s, the majority of the world's population aged eighty and over lived in developed countries. How is this expected to change by 2020? As the average length of life continues to increase

in both developed and developing countries, who, if anyone, is responsible for improving the quality of extended life?

3. Hobbs and Damon observe that "The United States and other countries face enormous investments and payments to maintain current levels of services for the old." What, specifically, are examples of such investments and payments? Who will pay for the necessary services for elderly populations—individuals? families? government? corporations? people in the labor force? others?

CLASSIC

CONTEMPORARY

CROSS-CULTURAL

51 Alienated Labor

KARL MARX

The human species, argues Karl Marx, is social by nature and expresses that social nature in the act of production. But within the capitalist economic system, Marx claims, the process of production does not affirm human nature but denies it. The result is what he terms "alienated labor."

[We] have shown that the worker sinks to the level of a commodity, and to a most miserable commodity; that the misery of the worker increases with the power and volume of his production; that the necessary result of competition is the accumulation of capital in a few hands, and thus a restoration of monopoly in a more terrible form; and finally that the distinction between capitalist and landlord, and between agricultural laborer and industrial worker, must disappear, and the whole of society divide into the two classes of property *owners* and *propertyless* workers. . . .

Thus we have now to grasp the real connexion between this whole system of alienation—private property, acquisitiveness,

the separation of labor, capital and land, exchange and competition, value and the devaluation of man, monopoly and competition—and the system of *money*. . . .

We shall begin from a *contemporary* economic fact. The worker becomes poorer the more wealth he produces and the more his production increases in power and extent. The worker becomes an ever cheaper commodity the more goods he creates. The *devaluation* of the human world increases in direct relation with the *increase in value* of the world of things. Labor does not only create goods; it also produces itself and the worker as a *commodity,* and indeed in the same proportion as it produces goods.

This fact simply implies that the object produced by labor, its product, now stands opposed to it as an *alien being,* as a *power independent* of the producer. The product of labor is labor

Source: "Alienated Labor," by Karl Marx from *Karl Marx: Early Writings,* trans. and ed. by T. B. Bottomore. Copyright © 1963, McGraw-Hill Companies. Reprinted with permission.

which has been embodied in an object and turned into a physical thing; this product is an *objectification* of labor. The performance of work is at the same time its objectification. The performance of work appears in the sphere of political economy as a *vitiation*[1] of the worker, objectification as a *loss* and as *servitude to the object,* and appropriation as *alienation.*

So much does the performance of work appear as vitiation that the worker is vitiated to the point of starvation. So much does objectification appear as loss of the object that the worker is deprived of the most essential things not only of life but also of work. Labor itself becomes an object which he can acquire only by the greatest effort and with unpredictable interruptions. So much does the appropriation of the object appear as alienation that the more objects the worker produces the fewer he can possess and the more he falls under the domination of his product, of capital.

All these consequences follow from the fact that the worker is related to the *product of his labor* as to an *alien* object. For it is clear on this presupposition that the more the worker expends himself in work the more powerful becomes the world of objects which he creates in face of himself, the poorer he becomes in his inner life, and the less he belongs to himself. It is just the same as in religion. The more of himself man attributes to God the less he has left in himself. The worker puts his life into the object, and his life then belongs no longer to himself but to the object. The greater his activity, therefore, the less he possesses. What is embodied in the product of his labor is no longer his own. The greater this product is, therefore, the more he is diminished. The *alienation* of the worker in his product means not only that his labor becomes an object, assumes an *external* existence, but that it exists independently, *outside himself,* and alien to him, and that it stands opposed to him as an autonomous power. The life which he has given to the object sets itself against him as an alien and hostile force.

Let us now examine more closely the phenomenon of *objectification;* the worker's production

and the *alienation* and *loss* of the object it produces, which is involved in it. The worker can create nothing without *nature,* without the *sensuous external world.* The latter is the material in which his labor is realized, in which it is active, out of which and through which it produces things.

But just as nature affords the *means of existence* of labor, in the sense that labor cannot *live* without objects upon which it can be exercised, so also it provides the *means of existence* in a narrower sense; namely the means of physical existence for the *worker* himself. Thus, the more the worker *appropriates* the external world of sensuous nature by his labor the more he deprives himself of *means of existence,* in two respects: First, that the sensuous external world becomes progressively less an object belonging to his labor or a means of existence of his labor, and secondly, that it becomes progressively less a means of existence in the direct sense, a means for the physical subsistence of the worker.

In both respects, therefore, the worker becomes a slave of the object; first, in that he receives an *object of work,* i.e., receives *work,* and secondly, in that he receives *means of subsistence.* Thus the object enables him to exist, first as a *worker* and secondly, as a *physical subject.* The culmination of this enslavement is that he can only maintain himself as a *physical subject* so far as he is a *worker,* and that it is only as a *physical subject* that he is a worker.

(The alienation of the worker in his object is expressed as follows in the laws of political economy: The more the worker produces the less he has to consume; the more value he creates the more worthless he becomes; the more refined his product the more crude and misshapen the worker; the more civilized the product the more barbarous the worker; the more powerful the work the more feeble the worker; the more the work manifests intelligence the more the worker declines in intelligence and becomes a slave of nature.)

Political economy conceals the alienation in the nature of labor insofar as it does not examine the direct relationship between the worker (work) *and production.* Labor certainly produces marvels for the rich but it produces privation for the worker. It produces palaces, but hovels for the worker. It produces beauty, but deformity for the worker. It replaces labor by machinery, but it casts some of the workers back into a barbarous kind of work and turns the others into machines. It produces intelligence, but also stupidity and cretinism for the workers.

The direct relationship of labor to its products is the relationship of the worker to the objects of his production. The relationship of property owners to the objects of production and to production itself is merely a *consequence* of this first relationship and confirms it. We shall consider this second aspect later.

Thus, when we ask what is the important relationship of labor, we are concerned with the relationship of the *worker* to production.

So far we have considered the alienation of the worker only from one aspect; namely, *his relationship with the products of his labor.* However, alienation appears not merely in the result but also in the *process of production,* within *productive activity* itself. How could the worker stand in an alien relationship to the product of his activity if he did not alienate himself in the act of production itself? The product is indeed only the *résumé* of activity, of production. Consequently, if the product of labor is alienation, production itself must be active alienation—the alienation of activity and the activity of alienation. The alienation of the object of labor merely summarizes the alienation in the work activity itself.

What constitutes the alienation of labor? First, that the work is *external* to the worker, that it is not part of his nature; and that, consequently, he does not fulfill himself in his work but denies himself, has a feeling of misery rather than well-being, does not develop freely his mental and physical energies but is physically exhausted and mentally debased. The worker, therefore, feels himself at home only during his leisure time, whereas at work he feels homeless. His work is not voluntary but imposed, *forced labor.* It is not

the satisfaction of a need, but only a *means* for satisfying other needs. Its alien character is clearly shown by the fact that as soon as there is no physical or other compulsion it is avoided like the plague. External labor, labor in which man alienates himself, is a labor of self-sacrifice, of mortification. Finally, the external character of work for the worker is shown by the fact that it is not his own work but work for someone else, that in work he does not belong to himself but to another person. . . .

We arrive at the result that man (the worker) feels himself to be freely active only in his animal functions—eating, drinking, and procreating, or at most also in his dwelling and in personal adornment—while in his human functions he is reduced to an animal. The animal becomes human and the human becomes animal.

Eating, drinking, and procreating are of course also genuine human functions. But abstractly considered, apart from the environment of human activities, and turned into final and sole ends, they are animal functions.

We have now considered the act of alienation of practical human activity, labor, from two aspects: (1) the relationship of the worker to the *product of labor* as an alien object which dominates him. This relationship is at the same time the relationship to the sensuous external world, to natural objects, as an alien and hostile world; (2) the relationship of labor to the *act of production* within *labor.* This is the relationship of the worker to his own activity as something alien and not belonging to him, activity as suffering (passivity), strength as powerlessness, creation as emasculation, the *personal* physical and mental energy of the worker, his personal life (for what is life but activity?), as an activity which is directed against himself, independent of him and not belonging to him. This is *self-alienation* as against the [afore]mentioned alienation of the *thing.*

We have now to infer a third characteristic of *alienated labor* from the two we have considered.

Man is a species-being not only in the sense that he makes the community (his own as well as those of other things) his object both practically and theoretically, but also (and this is simply another expression for the same thing) in the sense that he treats himself as the present, living species, as a *universal* and consequently free being.

Species-life, for man as for animals, has its physical basis in the fact that man (like animals) lives from inorganic nature, and since man is more universal than an animal so the range of inorganic nature from which he lives is more universal. Plants, animals, minerals, air, light, etc. constitute, from the theoretical aspect, a part of human consciousness as objects of natural science and art; they are man's spiritual inorganic nature, his intellectual means of life, which he must first prepare for enjoyment and perpetuation. So also, from the practical aspect, they form a part of human life and activity. In practice man lives only from these natural products, whether in the form of food, heating, clothing, housing, etc. The universality of man appears in practice in the universality which makes the whole of nature into his inorganic body: (1) as a direct means of life; and equally (2) as the material object and instrument of his life activity. Nature is the inorganic body of man; that is to say nature, excluding the human body itself. To say that man *lives* from nature means that nature is his *body* with which he must remain in a continuous interchange in order not to die. The statement that the physical and mental life of man, and nature, are interdependent means simply that nature is interdependent with itself, for man is a part of nature.

Since alienated labor (1) alienates nature from man; and (2) alienates man from himself, from his own active function, his life activity; so it alienates him from the species. It makes *species-life* into a means of individual life. In the first place it alienates species-life and individual life, and secondly, it turns the latter, as an abstraction,

into the purpose of the former, also in its abstract and alienated form.

For labor, *life activity, productive life,* now appear to man only as *means* for the satisfaction of a need, the need to maintain his physical existence. Productive life is, however, species-life. It is life creating life. In the type of life activity resides the whole character of a species, its species-character; and free, conscious activity is the species-character of human beings. Life itself appears only as a *means of life.*

The animal is one with its life activity. It does not distinguish the activity from itself. It is *its activity.* But man makes his life activity itself an object of his will and consciousness. He has a conscious life activity. It is not a determination with which he is completely identified. Conscious life activity distinguishes man from the life activity of animals. Only for this reason is he a species-being. Or rather, he is only a self-conscious being, i.e., his own life is an object for him, because he is a species-being. Only for this reason is his activity free activity. Alienated labor reverses the relationship, in that man because he is a self-conscious being makes his life activity, his *being,* only a means for his *existence.*

CRITICAL-THINKING QUESTIONS

1. Does Marx argue that work is inevitably alienating? Why does work within a capitalist economy produce alienation?
2. In what different respects does labor within capitalism alienate the worker?
3. Based on this analysis, under what conditions do you think Marx would argue that labor is not alienating?

NOTE

1. Debasement.

CLASSIC

CONTEMPORARY

CROSS-CULTURAL

52 When Work Disappears

WILLIAM JULIUS WILSON

Many inner-city areas of the United States are facing catastrophic levels of poverty. Why?
In this excerpt, William Julius Wilson offers his assessment of the causes of urban decline
and makes practical suggestions about how we can solve this pressing problem.

The disappearance of work in the ghetto cannot be ignored, isolated or played down. Employment in America is up. The economy has churned out tens of millions of new jobs in the last two decades. In that same period, joblessness among inner-city blacks has reached catastrophic proportions. Yet in this Presidential election year, the disappearance of work in the ghetto is not on either the Democratic or the Republican agenda. There is harsh talk about work instead of welfare but no talk of where to find it.

The current employment woes in the inner city continue to be narrowly defined in terms of race or lack of individual initiative. It is argued that jobs are widely available, that the extent of inner-city poverty is exaggerated. Optimistic policy analysts—and many African Americans—would prefer that more attention be devoted to the successes and struggles of the black working class and the expanding black middle class. This is understandable. These two groups, many of whom

Source: From *When Work Disappears* by William Julius Wilson. Copyright © 1996 by William Julius Wilson, Alfred A. Knopf, Inc. Reprinted by permission of Alfred A. Knopf, Inc.

have recently escaped from the ghetto, represent a majority of the African American population. But ghetto joblessness still afflicts a substantial—and increasing—minority: It's a problem that won't go away on its own. If it is not addressed, it will have lasting and harmful consequences for the quality of life in the cities and, eventually, for the lives of all Americans. Solutions will have to be found—and those solutions are at hand.

For the first time in the twentieth century, a significant majority of adults in many inner-city neighborhoods are not working in a typical week. Inner cities have always featured high levels of poverty, but the current levels of joblessness in some neighborhoods are unprecedented. For example, in the famous black-belt neighborhood of Washington Park on Chicago's South Side, a majority of adults had jobs in 1950; by 1990, only one in three worked in a typical week. High neighborhood joblessness has a far more devastating effect than high neighborhood poverty. A neighborhood in which people are poor but employed is different from a neighborhood in which people are poor and jobless. Many of today's problems in the inner-city neighborhoods—crime, family dissolution, welfare—are fundamentally a consequence of the disappearance of work.

What causes the disappearance of work? There are several factors, including changes in the distribution and location of jobs, and in the level of training and education required to obtain employment. Nor should we overlook the legacy of historic racial segregation. However, the public debate around this question is not productive because it seeks to assign blame rather than recognizing and dealing with the complex realities that have led to economic distress for many Americans. Explanations and proposed solutions to the problem are often ideologically driven.

Conservatives tend to stress the importance of values, attitudes, habits, and styles. In this view, group differences are reflected in the culture. The truth is, cultural factors do play a role; but other, more important variables also have to be taken into account. Although race is clearly a significant variable in the social outcomes of inner-city blacks, it's not the *only* factor. The emphasis on racial differences has obscured the fact that African Americans, whites, and other ethnic groups have many common values, aspirations, and hopes.

An elderly woman who has lived in one inner-city neighborhood on the South Side of Chicago for more than forty years reflects: "I've been here since March 11, 1953. When I moved in, the neighborhood was intact. It was intact with homes, beautiful homes, minimansions, with stores, Laundromats, with Chinese cleaners. We had drugstores. We had hotels. We had doctors over on 39th street. We had doctors' offices in the neighborhood. We had the middle class and upper middle class. It has gone from affluent to where it is today. And I would like to see it come back, that we can have some of the things we had. Since I came in young, and I'm a senior citizen now, I would like to see some of the things come back so I can enjoy them like we did when we first came in."

In the neighborhood of Woodlawn, on the South Side of Chicago, there were more than 800 commercial and industrial establishments in 1950.

Today, it is estimated that only about 100 are left. In the words of Loïc Wacquant, a member of one of the research teams that worked with me over the last eight years: "The once-lively streets—residents remember a time, not so long ago, when crowds were so dense at rush hour that one had to elbow one's way to the train station—now have the appearance of an empty, bombed-out war zone. The commercial strip has been reduced to a long tunnel of charred stores, vacant lots littered with broken glass and garbage, and dilapidated buildings left to rot in the shadow of the elevated train line. At the corner of 63d Street and Cottage Grove Avenue, the handful of remaining establishments that struggle to survive are huddled behind wrought-iron bars. . . . The only enterprises that seem to be thriving are liquor stores and currency exchanges, those 'banks of the poor' where one can cash checks, pay bills and buy money orders for a fee."

The state of the inner-city public schools was another major concern expressed by our urban-poverty study respondents. The complaints ranged from overcrowded conditions to unqualified and uncaring teachers. Sharply voicing her views on these subjects, a twenty-five-year-old married mother of two children from a South Side census tract that just recently became poor stated: "My daughter ain't going to school here. She was going to a nursery school where I paid and of course they took the time and spent it with her, because they was getting the money. But the public schools, no! They are overcrowded and the teachers don't care."

A resident of Woodlawn who had left the neighborhood as a child described how she felt upon her return about the changes that had occurred: "I was really appalled. When I walked down 63d Street when I was younger, everything you wanted was there. But now, coming back as an adult with my child, those resources are just gone, completely. . . . And housing, everybody has moved, there are vacant lots everywhere."

Neighborhoods plagued by high levels of joblessness are more likely to experience low levels of social organization: The two go hand in hand. High rates of joblessness trigger other neighborhood problems that undermine social organization, ranging from crime, gang violence, and drug trafficking to family breakups. And as these controls weaken, the social processes that regulate behavior change.

Industrial restructuring has further accelerated the deterioration of many inner-city neighborhoods. Consider the fate of the West Side black community of North Lawndale in Chicago: Since 1960, nearly half of its housing stock has disappeared; the remaining units are mostly run-down or dilapidated. Two large factories anchored the economy of this neighborhood in its good days—the Hawthorne plant of Western Electric, which employed more than 43,000 workers, and an International Harvester plant with 14,000 workers. But conditions rapidly changed. Harvester closed its doors in the late 1960s. Sears moved most of its offices to the Loop in downtown Chicago in 1973. The Hawthorne plant gradually phased out its operations and finally shut down in 1984.

"Jobs were plentiful in the past," attested a twenty-nine-year-old unemployed black man who lives in one of the poorest neighborhoods on the South Side. "You could walk out of the house and get a job. Maybe not what you want, but you could get a job. Now, you can't find anything. A lot of people in this neighborhood, they want to work but they can't get work. A few, but a very few, they just don't want to work."

The more rapid the neighborhood deterioration, the greater the institutional disinvestment. In the 1960s and 1970s, neighborhoods plagued by heavy abandonment were frequently redlined (identified as areas that should not receive or be recommended for mortgage loans or insurance); this paralyzed the housing market, lowered property values and encouraged landlord abandonment.

As the neighborhood disintegrates, those who are able to leave depart in increasing numbers; among these are many working- and middle-class families. The lower population density in turn creates additional problems. Abandoned buildings increase and often serve as havens for crack use and other illegal enterprises that give criminals—mostly young blacks who are unemployed—footholds in the community. Precipitous declines in density also make it even more difficult to sustain or develop a sense of community. The feeling of safety in numbers is completely lacking in such neighborhoods.

Problems in the new poverty or high-jobless neighborhoods have also created racial antagonism among some of the high-income groups in the city. The high joblessness in ghetto neighborhoods has sapped the vitality of local businesses and other institutions and has led to fewer and shabbier movie theaters, bowling alleys, restaurants, public parks and playgrounds and other recreational facilities. When residents of inner-city neighborhoods venture out to other areas of the city in search of entertainment, they come into brief contact with citizens of markedly different racial or class backgrounds. Sharp differences in cultural style often lead to clashes.

Some behavior on the part of residents from socially isolated ghetto neighborhoods—for instance, the tendency to enjoy a movie in a communal spirit by carrying on a running conversation with friends and relatives or reacting in an unrestrained manner to what they see on the screen—is considered offensive by other groups, particularly black and white members of the middle class. Expressions of disapproval, either overt or with subtle hostile glances, tend to trigger belligerent responses from the ghetto residents, who then purposely intensify the behavior that is the source of irritation. The white and even the black middle-class moviegoers then exercise their option and exit, expressing resentment and experiencing intensified feelings of racial or class antagonism as they depart.

The areas surrendered in such a manner become the domain of the inner-city residents. Upscale businesses are replaced by fast-food chains and other local businesses that cater to the new clientele. White and black middle-class citizens complain bitterly about how certain areas of the central city have changed—and thus become "off limits"—following the influx of ghetto residents.

The negative consequences are clear: Where jobs are scarce, many people eventually lose their feeling of connectedness to work in the formal economy; they no longer expect work to be a regular, and regulating, force in their lives. In the case of young people, they may grow up in an environment that lacks the idea of work as a central experience of adult life—they have little or no labor-force attachment. These circumstances also increase the likelihood that the residents will rely on illegitimate sources of income, thereby further weakening their attachment to the legitimate labor market.

A twenty-five-year-old West Side father of two who works two jobs to make ends meet condemned the attitude toward work of some inner-city black males:

They try to find easier routes and had been conditioned over a period of time to just be lazy, so to speak. Motivation nonexistent, you know, and the society that they're affiliated with really don't advocate hard work and struggle to meet your goals such as education and stuff like that. And they see who's around them and they follow that same pattern, you know. . . . They don't see nobody getting up early in the morning, going to work or going to school all the time. The guys they be with don't do that . . . because that's the crowd that you choose—well, that's been presented to you by your neighborhood.

Work is not simply a way to make a living and support one's family. It also constitutes a framework for daily behavior because it imposes discipline. Regular employment determines where you are going to be and when you are going to be there. In the absence of regular employment, life, including family life, becomes less coherent. Persistent unemployment and irregular employment hinder rational planning in daily life, the necessary condition of adaptation to an industrial economy.

It's a myth that people who don't work don't want to work. One mother in a new poverty neighborhood on the South Side explained her decision to remain on welfare even though she would like to get a job:

I was working and then I had two kids. And I'm struggling. I was making, like, close to $7 an hour. . . . I had to pay a baby-sitter. Then I had to deal with my kids when I got home. And I couldn't even afford medical insurance. . . . I was so scared, when my kids were sick or something, because I have been turned away from a hospital because I did not have a medical card. I don't like being on public aid and stuff right now. But what do I do with my kids when the kids get sick?

Working mothers with comparable incomes face, in many cases, even greater difficulty. Why? Simply because many low-wage jobs do not provide health-care benefits, and most working mothers have to pay for transportation and spend more for child care. Working mothers also have to spend more for housing because it is more difficult for them to qualify for housing subsidies. It is not surprising, therefore, that many welfare-reliant mothers choose not to enter the formal labor market. It would not be in their best economic interest to do so. Given the economic realities, it is also not surprising that many who are working in these low-wage jobs decide to rely on or return to welfare, even though it's not a desirable alternative for many of the black single mothers. As one twenty-seven-year-old welfare mother of three children from an impoverished West Side neighborhood put it: "I want to work. I do not work but I want to work. I don't want to just be on public aid."

As the disappearance of work has become a characteristic feature of the inner-city ghetto, so too has the disappearance of the traditional married-couple family. Only one-quarter of the black families whose children live with them in inner-city neighborhoods in Chicago are husband-wife families today, compared with three-quarters of the inner-city Mexican families, more than one-half of the white families and nearly one-half of the Puerto Rican families. And in census tracts with poverty rates of at least 40 percent, only 16.5 percent of the black families with children in the household are husband-wife families.

There are many factors involved in the precipitous decline in marriage rates and the sharp rise in single-parent families. The explanation most often heard in the public debate associates the increase of out-of-wedlock births and single-parent families with welfare. Indeed, it is widely assumed among the general public and reflected in the recent welfare reform that a direct connection exists between the level of welfare benefits and the likelihood that a young woman will bear a child outside marriage.

However, there is little evidence to support the claim that Aid to Families with Dependent Children plays a significant role in promoting out-of-wedlock births. Research examining the association between the generosity of welfare benefits and out-of-wedlock childbearing and teenage pregnancy indicates that benefit levels have no significant effect on the likelihood that African American girls and women will have children outside marriage. Likewise, welfare rates have either no significant effect or only a small effect on the odds that whites will have children outside marriage. The rate of out-of-wedlock teenage childbearing has nearly doubled since 1975—during years when the value of A.F.D.C., food stamps, and Medicaid fell, after adjusting for inflation. And the smallest increases in the number of out-of-wedlock births have not occurred in states that have had the largest declines in the inflation-adjusted value of A.F.D.C. benefits. Indeed, while the real value of cash welfare benefits has plummeted over the past twenty years, out-of-wedlock childbearing has increased, and postpartum marriages (marriages following the birth of a couple's child) have decreased as well.

It's instructive to consider the social differences between inner-city blacks and other groups, especially Mexicans. Mexicans come to the United States with a clear conception of a traditional family unit that features men as breadwinners. Although extramarital affairs by men are tolerated, unmarried pregnant women are "a source of opprobrium, anguish or great concern," as Richard P. Taub, a member of one of our research teams, put it. Pressure is applied by the kin of both parents to enter into marriage.

The family norms and behavior in inner-city black neighborhoods stand in sharp contrast. The relationships between inner-city black men and women, whether in a marital or nonmarital situation, are often fractious and antagonistic. Inner-city black women routinely say that black men are hopeless as either husbands or fathers and that more of their time is spent on the streets than at home.

The men in the inner city generally feel that it is much better for all parties to remain in a nonmarital relationship until the relationship dissolves rather than to get married and then have to get a divorce. A twenty-five-year-old unmarried West Side resident, the father of one child, expressed this view:

> Well, most black men feel now, why get married when you got six to seven women to one guy, really. You know, because there's more women out here mostly than men. Because most dudes around here are killing each other like fools over drugs or all this other stuff.

The fact that blacks reside in neighborhoods and are engaged in social networks and households that are less conducive to employment than those of other ethnic and racial groups in the inner city clearly has a negative effect on their search for work. In the eyes of employers in metropolitan Chicago, these differences render inner-city blacks less desirable as workers, and therefore are reluctant to hire them. The white chairman of a car transport company, when asked if there were differences in the work ethic of whites, blacks and Hispanics, responded with great certainty:

> Definitely! I don't think, I know: I've seen it over a period of thirty years. Basically, the Oriental is much more aggressive and intelligent and studious than the Hispanic. The Hispanics, except Cubans of course, they have the work ethnic [sic]. The Hispanics are *mañana, mañana, mañana*—tomorrow, tomorrow, tomorrow. As for native-born blacks, they were deemed "the laziest of the bunch."

If some employers view the work ethic of inner-city poor blacks as problematic, many also express concerns about their honesty, cultural attitudes and dependability—traits that are frequently associated with the neighborhoods in which they live. A white suburban retail drugstore manager expressed his reluctance to hire someone from a poor inner-city neighborhood. "You'd be afraid they're going to steal from you," he stated. "They grow up that way. They grow up dishonest and I guess you'd feel like, geez, how are they going to be honest here?"

In addition to qualms about the work ethic, character, family influences, cultural predispositions and the neighborhood milieu of ghetto residents, the employers frequently mentioned concerns about applicants' language skills and educational training. They "just don't have the language skills," stated a suburban employer. The president of an inner-city advertising agency highlighted the problem of spelling:

I needed a temporary a couple months ago, and they sent me a black man. And I dictated a letter to him. He took shorthand, which was good. Something like "Dear Mr. So-and-So, I am writing to ask about how your business is doing." And then he typed the letter, and I read the letter, and it's "I am writing to ax about your business." Now you hear them speaking a different language and all that, and they say "ax" for "ask." Well, I don't care about that, but I didn't say "ax," I said "ask."

Many inner-city residents have a strong sense of the negative attitudes that employers tend to have toward them. A thirty-three-year-old employed janitor from a poor South Side neighborhood had this observation: "I went to a couple jobs where a couple of the receptionists told me in confidence: 'You know what they do with these applications from blacks as soon as the day is over?' They say, 'We rip them and throw them in the garbage.' " In addition to concerns about being rejected because of race, the fears that some inner-city residents have of being denied employment simply because of their inner-city address or neighborhood are not unfounded. A welfare mother who lives in a large public housing project put it this way:

Honestly, I believe they look at the address and the—your attitudes, your address, your surround—you know, your environment has a lot to do with your employment status. The people with the best addresses have the best chances. I feel so, I feel so.

It is instructive to study the fate of the disadvantaged in Europe. There, too, poverty and joblessness are on the increase; but individual deficiencies and behavior are not put forward as the culprits. Furthermore, welfare programs that benefit wide segments of the population like child care, children's allowances (an annual benefit per child), housing subsidies, education, medical care and unemployment insurance have been firmly institutionalized in many Western European democracies. Efforts to cut back on these programs in the face of growing joblessness have met firm resistance from working- and middle-class citizens.

My own belief is that the growing assault on welfare mothers is part of a larger reaction to the mounting problems in our nation's inner cities. When many people think of welfare they think of young, unmarried black mothers having babies. This image persists even though roughly equal numbers of black and white families received A.F.D.C. in 1994, and there were also a good many Hispanics on the welfare rolls. Nevertheless, the rise of black A.F.D.C. recipients was said to be symptomatic of such larger problems as the decline in family values and the dissolution of the family. In an article published in *Esquire,* Pete Hamill wrote:

The heart of the matter is the continued existence and expansion of what has come to be called the Underclass. . . . trapped in cycles of welfare dependency, drugs, alcohol, crime, illiteracy and disease, living in anarchic and murderous isolation in some of the richest cities on the earth. As a reporter, I've covered their miseries for more than a quarter of a century. . . . And in the last decade, I've watched this group of American citizens harden and condense, moving even further away from the basic requirements of a human life: work, family, safety, the law.

One has the urge to shout, "Enough is enough!"

What can be done? I believe that steps must be taken to galvanize Americans from all walks of life who are concerned about human suffering and the public policy direction in which we are now moving. We need to generate a public-private partnership to fight social inequality. The following policy frameworks provide a basis for further discussion and debate. Given the current political climate, these proposals might be dismissed as unrealistic. Nor am I suggesting that we can or should simply import the social policies of the Japanese, the Germans, or other Western Europeans. The question is how we Americans can address the problems of social inequality, including record levels of joblessness in the inner city, that threaten the very fabric of our society.

CREATE STANDARDS FOR SCHOOLS

Ray Marshall, former Secretary of Labor, points out that Japan and Germany have developed policies designed to increase the number of workers with "higher-order thinking skills." These policies require young people to meet high performance standards before they can graduate from secondary schools, and they hold each school responsible for meeting these standards.

Students who meet high standards are not only prepared for work but they are also ready for technical training and other kinds of postsecondary education. Currently, there are no mandatory academic standards for secondary schools in the United States. Accordingly, students who are not in college-preparatory courses have severely limited options with respect to pursuing work after high school. A commitment to a system of performance standards for every public school in the United States would be an important first step in addressing the huge gap in educational performance between the schools in advantaged and disadvantaged neighborhoods.

A system of at least local performance standards should include the kind of support that would enable schools in disadvantaged neighborhoods to meet the standards that are set. State governments, with federal support, not only would have to create equity in local school financing (through loans and scholarships to attract more high-quality teachers, increased support for teacher training and reforms in teacher certification) but would also have to ensure that highly qualified teachers are more equitably distributed in local school districts.

Targeting education would be part of a national effort to raise the performance standards of all public schools in the United States to a desirable level, including schools in the inner city. The support of the private sector should be enlisted in this national effort. Corporations, local businesses, civic clubs, community centers and churches should be encouraged to work with the schools to improve computer-competency training.

IMPROVE CHILD CARE

The French system of child welfare stands in sharp contrast to the American system. In France, children are supported by three interrelated government programs, as noted by Barbara R. Bergmann, a professor of economics at American University: child care, income support, and medical care. The child-care program includes establishments for infant care, high-quality nursery schools (*écoles maternelles*), and paid leave for parents of newborns. The income-support program includes child-support enforcement (so that the absent parent continues to contribute financially to his or her child's welfare), children's allowances, and welfare payments for low-income single mothers. Finally, medical care is provided through a universal system of national health care financed by social security, a preventive-care system for children, and a group of public-health nurses who specialize in child welfare.

ESTABLISH CITY–SUBURBAN PARTNERSHIPS

If the other industrial democracies offer lessons for a long-term solution to the jobs problem involving relationships between employment, education, and family-support systems, they also offer another lesson: the importance of city–suburban integration and cooperation. None of the other industrialized democracies have allowed their city centers to deteriorate as has the United States.

It will be difficult to address growing racial tensions in American cities unless we tackle the problems of shrinking revenue and inadequate social services and the gradual disappearance of work in certain neighborhoods. The city has become a less desirable place in which to live, and the economic and social gap between the cities and suburbs is growing. The groups left behind compete, often along racial lines, for declining resources, including the remaining decent schools, housing, and neighborhoods. The rise of the new urban poverty neighborhoods has worsened these problems. Their high rates of joblessness and social disorganization have created problems that often spill over into other parts of the city. All of these factors aggravate race relations and elevate racial tensions.

Ideally, we would restore the federal contribution to city revenues that existed in 1980 and sharply increase the employment base. Regardless of changes in federal urban policy, however, the fiscal crises in the cities would be significantly eased if the employment base could be substantially increased. Indeed, the social dislocations caused by the steady disappearance of work have led to a wide range of urban social problems, including racial tensions. Increased employment would help stabilize the new poverty neighborhoods, halt the precipitous decline in density, and ultimately enhance the quality of race relations in urban areas.

Reforms put forward to achieve the objective of city–suburban cooperation range from proposals to create metropolitan governments to proposals for metropolitan tax-base sharing (currently in effect in Minneapolis-St. Paul), collaborative metropolitan planning, and the creation of regional authorities to develop solutions to common problems if communities fail to reach agreement. Among the problems shared by many metropolises is a weak public transit system. A commitment to address this problem through a form of city–suburban collaboration would benefit residents of both the city and the suburbs.

The mismatch between residence and the location of jobs is a problem for some workers in America because, unlike the system in Europe, public transportation is weak and expensive. It's a particular problem for inner-city blacks because they have less access to private automobiles and, unlike Mexicans, do not have a network system that supports organized car pools. Accordingly, they depend heavily on public transportation and therefore have difficulty getting to the suburbs, where jobs are more plentiful. Until public transit systems are improved in metropolitan areas, the creation of privately subsidized carpool and van-pool networks to carry inner-city residents to the areas of employment, especially suburban areas, would be a relatively inexpensive way to increase work opportunities.

The creation of for-profit information and placement centers in various parts of the inner city not only could significantly improve awareness of the availability of employment in the metropolitan area but could also serve to refer workers to employers. These centers would recruit or accept inner-city workers and try to place them in jobs. One of their main purposes would be to make persons who have been persistently unemployed or out of the labor force "job ready."

REINTRODUCE THE W.P.A.

The final proposal under consideration here was advanced by the perceptive journalist Mickey Kaus of *The New Republic,* who has long been concerned about the growth in the number of welfare recipients. Kaus's proposal is modeled on the Works Progress Administration (W.P.A.), the large public-works program initiated in 1935 by President Franklin D. Roosevelt. The public-works jobs that Roosevelt had in mind included highway construction, slum clearance, housing construction, and rural electrification. As Kaus points out:

In its eight-year existence, according to official records, the W.P.A. built or improved 651,000 miles of roads, 953 airports, 124,000 bridges and viaducts, 1,178,000 culverts, 8,000 parks, 18,000 playgrounds and athletic fields, and 2,000 swimming pools. It constructed 40,000 buildings (including 8,000 schools) and repaired 85,000 more. Much of New York City—including La Guardia Airport, F.D.R. Drive, plus hundreds of parks and libraries—was built by the W.P.A.

A neo-W.P.A. program of employment, for every American citizen over eighteen who wants it, would provide useful public jobs at wages slightly below the minimum wage. Like the work relief under Roosevelt's W.P.A., it would not carry the stigma of a cash dole. People would be earning their money. Although some workers in the W.P.A.-style jobs "could be promoted to higher-paying public service positions," says Kaus, most of them would advance occupationally by moving to the private sector. "If you have to work anyway," he says, "why do it for $4 an hour?"

Under Kaus's proposal, after a certain date, able-bodied recipients on welfare would no longer receive cash payments. However, unlike the welfare-reform bill that Clinton [signed], Kaus's plan would make public jobs available to those who move off welfare. Also, Kaus argues that to allow poor mothers to work, government-financed day care must be provided for their children if needed. But this service has to be integrated into the larger system of child care for other families in the United States to avoid creating a "day-care ghetto" for low-income children.

A W.P.A.-style jobs program will not be cheap. In the short run, it is considerably cheaper to give people cash welfare than it is to create public jobs. Including the costs of supervisors and materials, each subminimum-wage W.P.A.-style job would cost an estimated $12,000, more than the public cost of staying on welfare. That would represent $12 billion for every 1 million jobs created.

The solutions I have outlined were developed with the idea of providing a policy framework that could be easily adopted by a reform coalition. A broad range of groups would support the long-term solutions—the development of a system of national performance standards in public schools, family policies to reinforce the learning system in the schools, a national system of school-to-work

transition, and the promotion of city-suburban integration and cooperation. The short-term solutions, which range from job information and placement centers to the creation of W.P.A.-style jobs, are more relevant to low-income people, but they are the kinds of opportunity-enhancing programs that Americans of all racial and class backgrounds tend to support.

Although my policy framework is designed to appeal to broad segments of the population, I firmly believe that if adopted, it would alleviate a good deal of the economic and social distress currently plaguing the inner cities. The immediate problem of the disappearance of work in many inner-city neighborhoods would be confronted. The employment base in these neighborhoods would be increased immediately by the newly created jobs, and income levels would rise because of the expansion of the earned-income tax credit. Programs like universal health care and day care would increase the attractiveness of low-wage jobs and "make work pay."

Increasing the employment base would have an enormous positive impact on the social organization of ghetto neighborhoods. As more people become employed, crime and drug use would subside; families would be strengthened and welfare receipt would decline significantly; ghetto-related culture and behavior, no longer sustained and nourished by persistent joblessness, would gradually fade. As more people became employed and gained work experience, they would have a better chance of finding jobs in the private sector when they became available. The attitudes of employers toward inner-city workers would change, partly because the employers would be dealing with job applicants who had steady work experience and would furnish references from their previous supervisors.

This is not to suggest that all the jobless individuals from the inner-city ghetto would take advantage of these employment opportunities. Some have responded to persistent joblessness by abusing alcohol and drugs, and these handicaps will affect their overall job performance, including showing up for work on time or on a consistent basis. But such people represent only a small proportion of inner-city workers. Most of them are ready, willing, able and anxious to hold a steady job.

The long-term solutions that I have advanced would reduce the likelihood that a new generation of jobless workers will be produced from the youngsters now in school and preschool. We must break the cycle of joblessness and improve the youngsters' preparation for the new labor market in the global economy.

My framework for long-term and immediate solutions is based on the notion that the problems of jobless ghettos cannot be separated from those of the rest of the nation. Although these solutions have wide-ranging application and would alleviate the economic distress of many Americans, their impact on jobless ghettos would be profound. Their most important contribution would be their effect on the children of the ghetto, who would be able to anticipate a future of economic mobility and harbor the hopes and aspirations that for so many of their fellow citizens help define the American way of life.

CRITICAL-THINKING QUESTIONS

1. According to Wilson, what is the primary cause of inner-city decline? How does his assessment differ from common notions about this problem?

2. Why have inner-city areas lost so many jobs over the last fifty years?

3. What solutions does Wilson offer? Do you agree with his approach? Why or why not?

CLASSIC

CONTEMPORARY

CROSS-CULTURAL

53 Getting a Job in Harlem: Experiences of African American, Puerto Rican, and Dominican Youth

KATHERINE S. NEWMAN

We often hear that ethnic minorities who live in America's inner cities are society's dregs: They don't want to work, are lazy and immoral, and collect welfare checks at the expense of the average hard-working taxpayer. In contrast, Katherine S. Newman reached very different conclusions in her study of black, Puerto Rican, and Dominican workers in Harlem. In this selection, Newman shows that the working poor—especially the youth in poverty-stricken inner-city neighborhoods—work very hard to get and keep minimum-wage jobs that offer little hope for upward mobility.

If you drive around the suburban neighborhoods of Long Island or Westchester County, you cannot miss the bright orange "Help Wanted" signs hanging in the windows of fast-food restaurants. Teenagers who have the time to work can walk into most of these shops and land a job before they finish filling out the application form. In fact, labor scarcity (for these entry-level jobs) is a problem for employers in these highly competitive businesses. Therefore, though it cuts into their profits, suburban and small-town employers in the more affluent parts of the country are forced to raise wages and redouble their efforts to recruit new employees, often turning to the retiree labor force when the supply of willing youths has run out.

From the vantage point of central Harlem, this "seller's market" sounds like a news bulletin from another planet. Jobs, even lousy jobs, are in such short supply that inner-city teenagers are all but barred from the market, crowded out by adults who are desperate to find work. Burger Barn managers rarely display those orange signs; some have never, in the entire history of their restaurants, advertised for employees. They can depend upon a steady flow of willing applicants coming in the door—and they can be very choosy about whom they sign up. In fact, my research shows that among central Harlem's fast-food establishments, the ratio of applicants to available jobs is fourteen to one. For every fortunate person who lands one of these minimum-wage jobs, there are thirteen others who walk away empty-handed. Since these applicants are also applying to other jobs, we should assume that the overall gap between the supply and demand of workers is not this large. Nonetheless, almost three-quarters of the unsuccessful job-seekers we interviewed were unemployed a year after they applied to Burger Barn,

Source: From *No Shame in My Game,* by Katherine S. Newman, Copyright © 1999 by Russell Sage Foundation. Used by permission of Alfred A. Knopf, a division of Random House, Inc.

suggesting that the majority were no more successful with their other applications.

Statewide estimates of the gap between the number of people who need jobs (the unemployed plus the welfare recipients) and the number of available jobs in New York approach almost 1 million.[1] This is a staggering number—which may indeed be an exaggeration, since it includes many people who are unemployed for only a short time, but it should draw our attention to the acute nature of the job problem, especially for low-skilled workers from the inner city.[2]

Long lines of job-seekers depress the wages of those lucky enough to pass through the initial barriers and find a job. Hamburger flippers in central Harlem generally do not break the minimum wage. Longtime workers, like Kyesha Smith, do not see much of a financial reward for their loyalty. After five years on the job, she was earning $5 an hour, only sixty cents more than the minimum wage at the time. Carmen and Jamal had done no better. And this is not because they are not valued; indeed, they are. It is because the supply-and-demand curves familiar to students of Economics 101 are operating with a vengeance in poor communities, as they are on Long Island or in Madison, Wisconsin, where the same jobs are paying more than $7 an hour.

The long odds of landing a job do not stop thousands of inner city residents from trying. When Disneyland took applications after the Rodney King riot in South-Central Los Angeles, some 6,000 neatly dressed young people—largely black and Latino—waited in line to apply. In January 1992, when a new Sheraton Hotel complex opened in Chicago, 3,000 applicants spent the better part of a day in blowing snow, huddled along the north bank of the Chicago River, hoping for an interview. Four thousand anxious job-seekers stood in lines that wrapped around the block in March 1997 when the Roosevelt Hotel in Manhattan announced it would take applications for 700 jobs.

Why do people seek low-wage jobs in places like Burger Barn? How do they go about the task

in labor markets that are saturated with willing workers? What separates the success stories, the applicants who actually get jobs, from those who are rejected from these entry-level openings? These are questions that require answers if we are to have a clear picture of how the job market operates in poverty-stricken neighborhoods like Harlem.

WHY WORK?

You know, when I was out, when I wasn't working, I used to get into fights. Well, it wasn't really fights, it was like really arguments. . . . [Now, my friends] ask me, "Why don't we see you anymore?" Like, I can't. I don't have time. But, you know, I don't really wanna hang around my block anymore 'cuz it's like getting real bad. You know, it's a lot of people fighting around there for no reason. And they shootin' and stuff like that.

Jessica has worked at a fast-food restaurant in the middle of Harlem since she was seventeen, her first private-sector job following several summers as a city employee in a youth program. During her junior and senior year, Jessie commuted forty-five minutes each way to school, put in a full day at school, and then donned her work uniform for an eight-hour afternoon/evening shift. Exhausted by the regimen, she took a brief break from work toward the end of her senior year, but returned when she graduated from high school. Now, at the age of twenty-one, she is a veteran fast-food employee with an unbroken work record of about three years.

Jessica had several motivations for joining the workforce when she was a teenager, principal among them the desire to be independent of her mother and provide for her own material needs. No less important, however, was her desire to escape the pressures of street violence and what appeared to be a fast track to nowhere among her peers. For in Jessica's neighborhood, many a young person never sees the other side of age twenty. Her own brother was shot in the chest, a victim of mistaken identity. Jessica's mother narrowly escaped a similar fate.

It had to have been like twelve or one o'clock. My mother was in her room and I was in my room. . . . I sleep on the top bunk. We started hearing gunshots, so first thing I did, I jumped from my bed to the floor. I got up after the gunshots stopped and went into my mother's room. She was on the floor. . . . "Are you all right, are you all right?" she said. "Yeah, yeah." The next morning we woke up and it was like a bullet hole in the window in her room. Her bed is like the level of the window. Lucky thing she jumped, I mean went to the floor, because it could have come in through the window.

Incidents of this kind happen every day in Jessica's neighborhood, but contrary to popular opinion, they never become routine, something to be shrugged off as "business as usual." They are the unwelcome and unnatural consequence of a community plagued by a few very troublesome drug dealers, often the only thriving, growth area of the local economy.

Street violence, drive-by shootings, and other sources of terror are obstacles that Jessica and other working-poor people in her community have to navigate around. But Jessica knows that troubles of this kind strike more often among young people who have nothing to do but spend time on the street. Going to work was, for her, a deliberate act of disengagement from such a future.

William, who has worked in the same Burger Barn as Jessica, had the same motivation. A short, stocky African American, who was "a fat, pudgy kid" in his teen years, Will was often the butt of jokes and the object of bullying in the neighborhood. Tougher characters were always giving him a hard time, snatching his belongings, pushing him around. They took a special delight in tormenting the "fat boy." William's ego took a pounding.

As he crested into his teenage years, he wanted some way to occupy his time that would keep him clear of the tensions cropping up in his South Bronx housing project. Lots of boys his age were getting into drugs, but Will says, "Fortunately I was never really into that type of thing." After a stint with a summer youth corps job, he found his "own thing": working for Burger Barn. Having a job took him out of the street and into a safe space.

The job was good. . . . Just having fun that was unadulterated fun. There was no drugs. It was no pretenses, nobody givin' you a hard time. It was just being ourselves. That was cool.

For Stephanie, the trouble wasn't just in the streets, it was in her house. When she was in her teens, Stephanie's mother began taking in boarders in their apartment, young men and their girlfriends who did not always get along with her. The home scene was tense and occasionally violent, with knives flashing. The worse it got, the more Stephanie turned her attention to her job. She focused on what her earnings could do to rescue her from this unholy home life. Because she had her own salary, she was able to put her foot down and insist that her mother get rid of the troublemakers.

By the end of the month, I told my mother, if [that guy's] not gone, I'm not never coming home. You don't even have to worry about me. I have this little job, I can pay for myself. I'll get my cousin [to join me] and we'll get a room. . . . Ever since then, my mother, she trying to do the right thing. She says he's supposed to be out by the end of the month. So by [then] hopefully he'll be gone.

Living where she does, Stephanie is an expert on what happens to people who do not follow the path she has chosen into the legitimate labor market. People she has grown up with, neighbors, and the boyfriends of some of her closest friends have all had brushes with violence and run-ins with the police. It happens alarmingly often in her neighborhood.

[Gary], my girlfriend's boyfriend, just got shot. Gary and his friends . . . always used to stand on this corner. Always, it was their hangout spot. Some other friends was hustlin' [drugs] on our block and they went up to Gary, gave him a high five and just passed by. Some other guys came up to Gary and shot him. Shot him right in the leg. They told him, "Ya'll can't hustle on my block." He's lucky because the bullet grazed him, but it was a hollow-tip bullet, so them bullets explode. Blown off a chunk of his knee.

One of the only positive outcomes of these encounters is the resolution Stephanie feels about taking a completely different approach to her own life. She is hardly ignorant of the consequences of getting too close to the drug trade.

The knowledge has given her confidence, in the face of many obstacles (not the least of which is a chaotic home life), that an honest job for low pay is preferable to getting mixed up with people in the illegal sector.[3]

Because the working poor have little choice but to live in neighborhoods where rents are low, they often find themselves in social settings like Stephanie's. They have lots of friends and neighbors who are working at real jobs for little income, but they also rub shoulders with criminals who headquarter their enterprises in these poor neighborhoods. Exposure to folks who have taken the wrong fork in the road provides good reason for seeking a safe haven like Burger Barn.

There are many "push factors" that prod Harlem youth to look for work. Yet there are many positive inducements as well. Even as young teens, Jessica, William, and Stephanie were anxious to pay their own way, to free their families from the obligation to take care of all their needs. In this, they are typical of the 200 Burger Barn workers I tracked, the majority of whom began their work lives when they were thirteen to fifteen years old. This early experience in the labor force usually involves bagging groceries or working off the books in a local bodega, a menial job under the watchful eye of an adult who, more often than not, was a friend of the family or a relative who happened to have a shop.

Taking a job at the age of thirteen is a familiar path for anyone who lived through or has read about the Great Depression of the 1930s, when working-class families fallen on hard times often sent out their young people to find jobs. It stands in sharp contrast to the prevailing expectations of today's middle-class world, in which young teens are told to concentrate on their homework and their soccer leagues and leave the world of work for later in life.[4]

Yet most of the working poor come from homes where the struggles of the 1930s are all too familiar. Poor parents cannot stretch their resources to take care of their children's needs, much less the demands they make when their better-off peers are buying a new CD or a special kind of jacket—the kinds of frills that middle-class families routinely provide for their teens (along with the second telephone line, access to a car, and many other expensive items). Inner-city kids cannot even dream of such luxuries. Even finding the funds to pay for transportation, basic clothing, books, and other necessary expenses is hard for these families.

While middle-class parents would feel they had abrogated a parental responsibility if they demanded that their kids handle these basic costs (not to mention the frills), many poor parents consider the "demand" perfectly normal. Whether American-born or recent immigrants, these parents often began working at an early age themselves and consequently believe that a "good" kid should not be goofing off in his or her free time—summers, after school, and vacations—but should be bringing in some cash to the family.

Burger Barn earnings will not stretch to cover a poor family's larger items like food and shelter, and in this respect entry-level jobs do not underwrite any real independence. They do make it possible for kids like Kyesha and Carmen to participate in youth culture. Many writers have dismissed teenage workers on these grounds, complaining that their sole (read "trivial") motivation for working (and neglecting school) is to satisfy childish desires for "gold chains and designer sneakers."[5] Jessie and Will do want to look good and be cool. But most of their wages are spent providing for basic expenses. When she was still in high school, Jessica paid for her own books, school transportation, lunches, and basic clothing expenses. Now that she has graduated, she has assumed even more of the cost of keeping herself. Her mother takes care of the roof over their heads, but Jessie is responsible for the rest, as well as for a consistent contribution toward the expense of running a home with other dependent children in it.

Minimum-wage jobs cannot buy real economic independence; they cannot cover the full cost of living, including rent, food, and the rest of an adult's monthly needs. What Jessica can do with her earnings is cover the marginal cost of her presence in the household, leaving something over every week to contribute to the core cost of maintaining the household. Youth workers, particularly those who are parents themselves, generally do turn over part of their pay to the head of the household as a kind of rent. In this fashion, working-poor youth participate in a pooled-income strategy that makes it possible for households—as opposed to individuals—to sustain themselves. Without their contributions, this would become increasingly untenable, especially in families where Mom is receiving public assistance.[6]

This pattern is even more striking among immigrants and native-born minorities who are not incorporated into the state welfare system. In working-poor households with no connection to the state system, survival depends upon multiple workers pooling their resources.[7] Pressures build early for the older children in these communities to take jobs, no matter what the wages, in order to help their parents make ends meet. Ana Gonzales is a case in point. Having reached twenty-one years old, she had been working since she was fifteen. Originally from Ecuador, Ana followed her parents, who emigrated a number of years before and presently work in a factory in New Jersey. Ana completed her education in her home country and got a clerical job. She emigrated at eighteen, joining two younger brothers and a twelve-year-old sister already in New York. Ana has ambitions for going back to college, but for the moment she works full-time in a fast-food restaurant in Harlem, as does her sixteen-year-old brother. Her sister is responsible for cooking and caring for their five-year-old-brother, a responsibility Ana assumes when she is not at work or attending her English as a Second Language class.

The Gonzales family is typical of the immigrant households that participate in the low-wage economy of Harlem and Washington Heights, and it bears a strong resemblance to the Puerto Rican families in other parts of the city.[8] Parents work, adolescent children work, and only the youngest of the children are able to invest themselves in

U.S. schooling. Indeed, it is often the littlest who is deputized to master the English language on behalf of the whole family. Children as young as five or six are designated as interpreters responsible for negotiations between parents and landlords, parents and teachers, parents and the whole English-speaking world beyond the barrio.[9]

The social structure of these households is one that relies upon the contributions of multiple earners for cash earnings, child care, and housework.[10] Parents with limited language skills (and often illegal status) are rarely in a position to support their children without substantial contributions from the children themselves. Jobs that come their way rarely pay enough to organize a "child-centered" household in which education and leisure are the predominant activities of the youth until the age of eighteen. Instead, they must rely upon their children and, at most, can look forward to the eventual upward mobility of the youngest of their kids, who may be able to remain in school long enough to move to better occupations in the future.

Older workers, especially women with children to support, have other motives for entering the low-wage labor market. Like most parents, they have financial obligations: rent, clothes, food, and all the associated burdens of raising kids. Among the single mothers working at Burger Barn, however, the options for better-paying jobs are few and the desire to avoid welfare is powerful.[11] This is particularly true for women who had children when they were in their teens and dropped out of school to take care of them.

Latoya, one of Kyesha Smith's closest friends at Burger Barn, had her first child when she was sixteen. She was married at seventeen and then had another. But the marriage was shaky; her husband was abusive and is in jail now. Latoya learned about being vulnerable, and has made sure she will never become dependent again. She lives with Jason, her common-law husband, a man who is a skilled carpenter, and they have a child between them. Jason makes a good living, a lot more money than Latoya can earn on her own. Now that she has three kids, plus Jason's daughter by his first marriage, she has occasionally been tempted to quit work and just look after them. After all, it is hard to take care of four kids, even with Jason's help, and work a full-time job at the same time. She barely has the energy to crawl into bed at night, and crumbles at the thought of the overnight shifts she is obliged to take.

But Latoya's experience with her first husband taught her that no man is worth the sacrifice of her independence.

This was my first real job. . . . I take it seriously, you know. . . . It means a lot to me. It give you—what's the word I'm lookin' for? Security blanket. 'Cuz, a lot of married women, like when I was married to my husband, when he left, the burden was left on me. If [Jason] leave now, I can deal with the load because I work. [Jason] help me—we split the bills half and half. But if he leaves, I'm not gonna be, well, "Oh my God, I'm stranded. I have no money." No. I have a little bank account; I got my little nest egg. You know, so it does mean a lot to me. I wouldn't just up and leave my job.

For Latoya, as for many other working mothers, working is an insurance policy against dependence on men who may not be around for the long haul.[12]

FINDING A WAY IN

Tiffany was little more than ten years old when she first tried to find work. She was still living with her mother in the Bedford-Stuyvesant area of Brooklyn at that time, but they were in trouble. "Things were bad," she remembers. "Checks weren't coming in. And what would happen is we needed food. . . . So I would pack bags and stuff [in a local store] for spare change. And after a full day, I would make enough to buy groceries." Little Tiffany wasn't saving for gold chains, she was trying to help make ends meet in a family that was falling apart.

But the bagging job wasn't a real, legitimate job. In fact, it was pretty dicey.

We was at the whim of the cashiers. Discretion was with the store owner. 'Cause they would run us out sometimes. It was almost like how you see on a larger scale, big-time [crime] organizations. . . . It was like a

little gang thing going on with the packers. There was a lead packer and even he would extort money from the other packers. One time I got beat up by a guy 'cause I was the only female. I was not gonna give none of my money. And he bullied me around. I was scared. I didn't go back for a while.

Still, Tiffany felt she was doing something useful, something important. When customers gave her a tip, she thought she had earned it, and it was more money than she had ever seen. But the whole day might yield no more than fifty cents.

By the time she was thirteen, Tiffany's mother had given her up to a group home in New York's foster care system. In some ways, she had more stability in her life, facing less pressure to provide the food for the table. Yet group homes are regimented, Spartan places, with many rules and regulations. Once school was out for the summer, Tiffany wanted to escape the military atmosphere—the system of infractions and privileges withdrawn, the searches of personal belongings, the single phone call on the weekends—and find something useful to do. She also wanted to earn some money, since her group home was lean on what it deemed "extras," like funds to take in an occasional movie.

Ironically, because she was in foster care, Tiffany had direct access to the city's employment programs for young minorities, collectively known as "summer youth" by most inner-city kids. Through the good offices of her caseworker, she found a job as a clerical assistant in an office that provided assistance to victims of domestic violence. At the age of thirteen, Tiffany was answering the office phone, taking down information from women who had been battered and were seeking shelter. The job gave Tiffany an appreciation for white-collar work: the clean environment, the comfort of air-conditioning (while her friends working for the parks department were outside sweating the hot summer), and the feeling of importance that comes with a little prestige and the ability to help someone in trouble. It focused her desire to work in a social service agency someday.

Working for summer youth, Tiffany discovered one of the liabilities of a paycheck delivered by the government. Like Social Security checks, these salaries were delivered biweekly, on the same Friday, to thousands of kids working throughout the city. Everyone in her neighborhood knew when those checks would be available.

There was a real element of fear involved. Hundreds of other people were getting their checks. There were many people who would steal your check. People would follow you to the check-cashing place and take your money. Waiting on line, you'd usually take a friend with you to pick up your check. If you were smart, you wouldn't cash it right away. You'd go home. You'd wait and go to a check-cashing place in your neighborhood. But you know the young, they wanted their money right away. They wanted to go shopping. So they'd cash it right there and they get hit.

Despite these problems, Tiffany learned a lot from this job that she could apply to other jobs as she got older. She discovered that work involved taking care of responsibilities that were delegated to her and no one else, that it wasn't always fun but had to be done anyway. It taught her that she had to be on time and that completing her work in a defined period of time was an expectation she had to meet. "I had to stay on top of my duties!" Public employment of the kind Tiffany had is often the first gateway into the full-time labor force that inner-city kids experience.[13] They graduate from bagging groceries for tips into these more regular jobs and learn firsthand what it means to report to work daily, handle responsibilities, and be part of an organization.

Job corps initiatives, like the one Tiffany participated in, were born out of a desire to give inner-city kids something constructive to do in the months between school terms, a prophylactic against petty crime during the long hot summers of the War on Poverty years. But they have a much more important, albeit latent, purpose: They are a proving ground for poor youth who need an introduction to the culture of regular (salaried) work. A summer youth position is often the first regular, on-the-books job that an inner-city kid can find, the first refuge from the temporary, irregular, off-the-books employment that kids find on their own.

Larry's first experience with work was handing out advertising flyers on the sidewalk in front of a drugstore. It wasn't a popular occupation in the wintertime; Larry had to stand outside in the freezing slush, waiting for infrequent customers to come by and reluctantly accept the broadsheet thrust at them. It lasted for only a couple of weeks, for the employer decided it wasn't bringing in much business. So Larry followed the advice of his older friends and applied for a summer youth job. He landed one working for the New York City Parks Council, a jack-of-all trades position. "I basically did everything for them," he noted. "Fixed benches, cleaned the park, helped old people. You know, all kinds of things. Paint, plant, mop, sweep, all that. Whatever they needed done, I'd do it."[14]

Working for the parks and recreation department, Larry learned some basic carpentry skills. He also learned what all newcomers to the world of work must absorb: how to cooperate with other people, show up on time, take directions, and demonstrate initiative. Most important of all, the job gave Larry a track record he could use when he went out to look for a new job when summer was over.

That Park job did get me my job at [Burger Barn], 'cause they could see that I had work experience, you know. They called and they got good reviews on me. I'm a very hard worker and I'm patient. All of the stuff that they was looking for, you know.

Many of the Burger Barn workers in central Harlem got their start in the public sector. They were able to build on this experience: They could prove to the next employer that they had some experience and drive. This alone put them ahead of many other job-seekers who cannot bring these credentials to bear on the task of finding employment.

The experience also gave them a fount of cultural wisdom about what employers are looking for when they make their choices. Much of the literature on the nation's urban ghetto dwellers tells us that this kind of knowledge has disappeared in high-poverty neighborhoods: Young people are said to be ignorant of what work is like, of what the managers on the other side of the counter "see" when job-seekers from communities like Harlem or the South Bronx walk in the door.[15] Do they see a willing worker who should be given a chance, or do they see a street-smart kid in shades and funky clothes who looks like trouble?

High schools in Harlem and elsewhere in New York have turned some attention to this problem by trying to educate young people about the realities of a tough job market. They pound information into the heads of their students: that they have to dress right, speak right, behave with respect and a certain amount of deference. They have to park all the symbolic baggage of their peer culture at home. Whether we consider the success stories, people who have crossed the barrier of finding a job, or the ones who haven't been so fortunate, we find evidence of widespread knowledge of these stylistic hurdles, and recognition that employers hold the upper hand. Decisions will be theirs to make in a highly competitive market, and one must be prepared to meet their expectations.

These very mainstream attitudes are particularly clear in the voices of Harlem youth who have had some experience with youth employment programs. Larry's days in the parks department gave him a chance to see what management's position was.

If you come to an interview talking that street slang, you lost your chances of getting that job. I think if you want a job, you gotta speak appropriately to the owner, to the employer. . . .

CRITICAL-THINKING QUESTIONS

1. What motivates inner-city teenagers to work in "hamburger flipping" jobs (such as the Burger Barn) that many middle-class adolescents avoid?

2. How do applicants who get minimum-wage jobs differ from those who are rejected?

3. How do summer youth jobs sponsored by the government encourage a work ethic and provide inner-city teenagers with "cultural wisdom" about the workplace?

NOTES

1. The Greater Upstate Law Project and NYC-based Housing Works, both welfare rights advocacy organizations, prepared this analysis from Governor Pataki's administrative reports as well as from NYS Department of Social Services and Department of Labor data. These show that 570,100 New Yorkers are unemployed and 618,628 adults are on AFDC or Home Relief (single cases) for a total of 1.2 million potential job-seekers. Department of Labor, *Occupational Outlook Through 1999* (1995), projects that 242,620 jobs will be available every year between 1996 and 1999. The difference between the potential supply and the potential demand is therefore nearly 1 million in the state of New York.

2. New York City is experiencing a moderate recovery from a locally severe recession occurring from 1989 to 1992. The City Office of Management and Budget has forecast a net gain of 92,000 payroll jobs from 1995 through 1999. If this forecast is accurate, there will still be a net loss of 200,000 jobs between 1989 and 1999. See "Work to Be Done: Report of the Borough Presidents' Task Force on Education, Employment and Welfare" (August 1995).

3. Drug dealing tends not to be a woman's business. Crime is generally a male enterprise—and an expanding one at that. We know from youth surveys that a large number of young men from poor urban neighborhoods admit that they participate in criminal activity. Richard B. Freeman, "Why Do So Many Young American Men Commit Crimes and What Might We Do About It?" (NBER Working Paper 5451, 1996), argues that the rise in criminal activity among low-skilled young men over the past twenty years is influenced by the job market disincentives of the 1980s and 1990s.

4. Most young students, those in grades six through eight, who hold jobs are from disadvantaged backgrounds. D. C. Gottfredson, "Youth Employment, Crime and Schooling: A Longitudinal Study of a National Sample," *Developmental Psychology* 21 (1985), pp. 419–32. See also Catherine M. Yamoor and Jaylin T. Mortimer, "Age and Gender Differences in the Effects of Employment on Adolescent Achievement and Well-being," *Youth and Society* 22, no. 2 (December 1990), pp. 225–40. Older teenage workers are just as likely to come from middle-class homes.

5. Academics, too, often focus upon adolescents' expanding interests in acquiring consumer goods as a primary motivation for employment; see Ellen Greenberger and L. Steinberg, *When Teenagers Work* (Basic Books, 1986), and Laurence Steinberg, *Beyond the Classroom* (Simon & Schuster, 1996). This is due, in part, to the changing composition of the teenage workforce, once largely made up of youth from lower classes. See Joseph F. Kett, *Rites of Passage* (Basic Books, 1977).

6. Kathryn Edin's research, based on interviews with 214 AFDC mothers from four cities, makes it exceedingly clear that welfare families cannot make it on state payments alone. Edin found that AFDC, food stamps, and SSI combined make up 63% of the mothers' average total monthly income (which just covers expenses). Contributions from children, family, and friends account for a small but significant 7% of income.

See Kathryn Edin, "Single Mothers and Child Support: The Possibilities and Limits of Child Support Policy," *Children and Youth Services Review* 17, no. 102 (1995), pp. 203–30.

7. See Marta Tienda and Jennifer Glass, "Household Structure and Labor Force Participation of Black, Hispanic, and White Mothers," *Demography* 22, no. 3 (1985), pp. 381–94. Through a statistical analysis of 1980 CPA data, Tienda and Glass found that the number and composition of adults in extended families affects their labor force participation. The extended family arrangement alleviates economic hardships by spreading child care and other domestic obligations among more adults, thus allowing greater proportions of wage earners per household.

8. See Mercer Sullivan, *"Getting Paid": Youth, Crime, and Work in the Inner City* (Cornell University Press, 1989), for an account of Puerto Rican families in Sunset Park, Brooklyn.

9. Very young children in immigrant families are also commonly sent "home" to be cared for by relatives who still reside in the country of origin. Patricia Pessar, "The Role of Households in International Migration and the Case of U.S.-Bound Migration from the Dominican Republic," *International Migration Review* 16, no. 2 (1982), pp. 342–34.

10. For a discussion of the cooperative (and strained) structure of immigrant residence and family, see Sarah J. Mahler, *American Dreaming: Immigrant Life on the Margins* (Princeton University Press, 1995); Sherri Grasmuck and Patricia Pessar, *Between Two Islands: Dominican International Migration* (University of California Press, 1991); Lloyd H. Rogler and Rosemary Santana Cooney, *Puerto Rican Families in New York City: Intergenerational Processes* (Waterfront Press, 1984); Nina Glick Schiller, Linda Basch, and Cristina Szanton Blanc, eds., *Towards a Transnational Perspective on Migration: Race, Class, Ethnicity, and Nationalism Reconsidered* (New York Academy of Sciences, 1992); Alejandro Portes and Ruben G. Rumbaut, *Immigrant America: A Portrait* (University of California Press, 1990); Nancy Foner, ed., *New Immigrants in New York* (Columbia University Press, 1987); and Leo R. Chavez, "Coresidence and Resistance: Strategies for Survival Among Undocumented Mexicans and Central Americans in the United States," *Urban Anthropology* 19, nos. 1–2 (1990), pp. 31–61.

11. Nationwide, unmarried female household heads with children have higher labor force participation rates than married mothers. Tienda and Glass, "Household Structure and Labor Force Participation of Black, Hispanic, and White Mothers," p. 391.

12. This motivation for employment is not uncommon. See Arlie Hochschild, *The Second Shift: Working Parents and the Revolution at Home* (Viking, 1989), pp. 128–41.

13. Currently there are quite a number of demonstration projects around the country that aim to enrich summer youth programs through classroom learning or worksite education, many of which have improved academic outcomes of participants. See Office of the Chief Economist, U.S. Department of Labor, *What's Working (and What's Not): A Summary of Research on the Economic Impacts of Employment and Training Programs* (1995); Jean Baldwin Grossman and Cynthia Sipe, "The Long-Term Impacts of the Summer Training and Education Program" (Philadelphia: Public/Private Ventures); Arnold H. Packer and Marion W. Pines, *School-to-Work* (Princeton: Eye on Education, 1996). Typically, however, participants (a third of whom are 14- and 15-year-olds) in summer programs work for minimum wage in much less structured settings. Many of them get placements at government agencies, schools, and community-based associations doing maintenance or office work while receiving some remedial education.

14. Mayor Giuliani has been an enthusiastic supporter of workfare jobs and has been criticized for substituting these sub-minimum-wage workers for union labor. Funding for summer youth jobs has been progressively curtailed over the years. It is possible that the tasks Larry performed in the parks will become workfare jobs as well. This is important because it may limit the availability of entry-level public-sector positions for young people coming into the labor market.

15. Janice Haaken and Joyce Korschgen, "Adolescents and Conceptions of Social Relations in the Workplace," *Adolescence* 23 (1988), pp. 1–14, reports that adolescents from higher-status backgrounds have a better understanding than adolescents from disadvantaged backgrounds about the workplace expectations of employers. See also James E. Rosenbaum, Takehiko Kariya, Rick Settersten, and Tony Maier, "Market and Network Theories of the Transition from High School to Work: Their Application to Industrialized Societies," *Annual Review of Sociology* 16 (1990), pp. 263–99.

CLASSIC

CONTEMPORARY

CROSS-CULTURAL

54 The Power Elite

C. WRIGHT MILLS

Conventional wisdom suggests that U.S. society operates as a democracy, guided by the "voice of the people." C. Wright Mills argues that above ordinary people—and even above many politicians—are "the higher circles," those who run the corporations, operate the military establishment, and manipulate the machinery of the state. It is this relatively small handful of people whom Mills calls "the power elite."

The powers of ordinary men are circumscribed by the everyday worlds in which they live, yet even in these rounds of job, family, and neighborhood they often seem driven by forces they can neither understand nor govern. "Great changes" are beyond their control, but affect their conduct and outlook nonetheless. The very framework of modern society confines them to projects not their own, but from every side, such changes now press upon the men and women of the mass society, who accordingly feel that they are without purpose in an epoch in which they are without power.

But not all men are in this sense ordinary. As the means of information and of power are centralized,

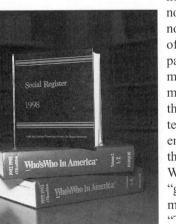

some men come to occupy positions in American society from which they can look down upon, so to speak, and by their decisions mightily affect, the everyday worlds of ordinary men and women. They are not made by their jobs; they set up and break down jobs for thousands of others; they are not confined by simple family responsibilities; they can escape. They may live in many hotels and houses, but they are bound by no one community. They need not merely "meet the demands of the day and hour"; in some part, they create these demands, and cause others to meet them. Whether or not they profess their power, their technical and political experience of it far transcends that of the underlying population. What Jacob Burckhardt said of "great men," most Americans might well say of their elite: "They are all that we are not."

Source: From *The Power Elite, New Edition,* by C. Wright Mills. Copyright © 1956, 2000 by Oxford University Press, Inc.; renewed 1984 by Yaraslava Mills. Reprinted by permission of Oxford University Press, Inc.

The power elite is composed of men whose positions enable them to transcend the ordinary environments of ordinary men and women; they are in positions to make decisions having major consequences. Whether they do or do not make such decisions is less important than the fact that they do occupy such pivotal positions: Their failure to act, their failure to make decisions, is itself an act that is often of greater consequence than the decisions they do make. For they are in command of the major hierarchies and organizations of modern society. They rule the big corporations. They run the machinery of the state and claim its prerogatives. They direct the military establishment. They occupy the strategic command posts of the social structure, in which are now centered the effective means of the power and the wealth and the celebrity which they enjoy.

The power elite are not solitary rulers. Advisers and consultants, spokesmen and opinion-makers are often the captains of their higher thought and decision. Immediately below the elite are the professional politicians of the middle levels of power, in the Congress and in the pressure groups, as well as among the new and old upper classes of town and city and region. Mingling with them, in curious ways which we shall explore, are those professional celebrities who live by being continually displayed but are never, so long as they remain celebrities, displayed enough. If such celebrities are not at the head of any dominating hierarchy, they do often have the power to distract the attention of the public or afford sensations to the masses, or, more directly, to gain the ear of those who do occupy positions of direct power. More or less unattached, as critics of morality and technicians of power, as spokesmen of God and creators of mass sensibility, such celebrities and consultants are part of the immediate scene in which the drama of the elite is enacted. But that drama itself is centered in the command posts of the major institutional hierarchies.

The truth about the nature and the power of the elite is not some secret which men of affairs know but will not tell. Such men hold quite various theories about their own roles in the sequence of event and decision. Often they are uncertain about their roles, and even more often they allow their fears and their hopes to affect their assessment of their own power. No matter how great their actual power, they tend to be less acutely aware of it than of the resistances of others to its use. Moreover, most American men of affairs have learned well the rhetoric of public relations, in some cases even to the point of using it when they are alone, and thus coming to believe it. The personal awareness of the actors is only one of the several sources one must examine in order to understand the higher circles. Yet many who believe that there is no elite, or at any rate none of any consequence, rest their argument upon what men of affairs believe about themselves, or at least assert in public.

There is, however, another view: Those who feel, even if vaguely, that a compact and powerful elite of great importance does now prevail in America often base that feeling upon the historical trend of our time. They have felt, for example, the domination of the military event, and from this they infer that generals and admirals, as well as other men of decision influenced by them, must be enormously powerful. They hear that the Congress has again abdicated to a handful of men decisions clearly related to the issue of war or peace. They know that the bomb was dropped over Japan in the name of the United States of America, although they were at no time consulted about the matter. They feel that they live in a time of big decisions; they know that they are not making any. Accordingly, as they consider the present as history, they infer that at its center, making decisions or failing to make them, there must be an elite of power.

On the one hand, those who share this feeling about big historical events assume that there is an elite and that its power is great. On the other hand, those who listen carefully to the reports of men apparently involved in the great decisions often do not believe that there is an elite whose powers are of decisive consequence.

Both views must be taken into account, but neither is adequate. The way to understand the power of the American elite lies neither solely in recognizing the historic scale of events nor in accepting the personal awareness reported by men of apparent decision. Behind such men and behind the events of history, linking the two, are the major institutions of modern society. These hierarchies of state and corporation and army constitute the means of power; as such they are now of a consequence not before equaled in human history—and at their summits, there are now those command posts of modern society which offer us the sociological key to an understanding of the role of the higher circles in America.

Within American society, major national power now resides in the economic, the political, and the military domains. Other institutions seem off to the side of modern history, and, on occasion, duly subordinated to these. No family is as directly powerful in national affairs as any major corporation; no church is as directly powerful in the external biographies of young men in America today as the military establishment; no college is as powerful in the shaping of momentous events as the National Security Council. Religious, educational, and family institutions are not autonomous centers of national power; on the contrary, these decentralized areas are increasingly shaped by the big three, in which developments of decisive and immediate consequence now occur.

Families and churches and schools adapt to modern life; governments and armies and corporations shape it; and, as they do so, they turn these lesser institutions into means for their ends. Religious institutions provide chaplains to the armed forces where they are used as a means of increasing the effectiveness of its morale to kill. Schools select and train men for their jobs in corporations and their specialized tasks in the armed forces. The extended family has, of course, long been broken up by the industrial revolution, and now the son and the father are removed from the family, by compulsion if need be, whenever the army of the state sends out the call. And the symbols of all these lesser institutions are used to legitimate the power and the decisions of the big three.

The life-fate of the modern individual depends not only upon the family into which he was born or which he enters by marriage, but increasingly upon the corporation in which he spends the most alert hours of his best years; not only upon the school where he is educated as a child and adolescent, but also upon the state which touches him throughout his life; not only upon the church in which on occasion he hears the word of God, but also upon the army in which he is disciplined.

If the centralized state could not rely upon the inculcation of nationalist loyalties in public and private schools, its leaders would promptly seek to modify the decentralized educational system. If the bankruptcy rate among the top 500 corporations were as high as the general divorce rate among the 37 million married couples, there would be economic catastrophe on an international scale. If members of armies gave to them no more of their lives than do believers to the churches to which they belong, there would be a military crisis.

Within each of the big three, the typical institutional unit has become enlarged, has become administrative, and, in the power of its decisions, has become centralized. Behind these developments there is a fabulous technology, for as institutions, they have incorporated this technology and guide it, even as it shapes and paces their developments.

The economy—once a great scatter of small productive units in autonomous balance—has become dominated by two or three hundred giant corporations, administratively and politically interrelated, which together hold the keys to economic decisions.

The political order, once a decentralized set of several dozen states with a weak spinal cord, has become a centralized, executive establishment which has taken up into itself many powers previously scattered, and now enters into each and every cranny of the social structure.

The military order, once a slim establishment in a context of distrust fed by state militia, has become the largest and most expensive feature of government, and, although well-versed in smiling public relations, now has all the grim and clumsy efficiency of a sprawling bureaucratic domain.

In each of these institutional areas, the means of power at the disposal of decision makers have increased enormously; their central executive powers have been enhanced; within each of them modern administrative routines have been elaborated and tightened up.

As each of these domains becomes enlarged and centralized, the consequences of its activities become greater, and its traffic with the others increases. The decisions of a handful of corporations bear upon military and political as well as upon economic developments around the world. The decisions of the military establishment rest upon and grievously affect political life as well as the very level of economic activity. The decisions made within the political domain determine economic activities and military programs. There is no longer, on the one hand, an economy, and, on the other hand, a political order containing a military establishment unimportant to politics and to money-making. There is a political economy linked, in a thousand ways, with military institutions and decisions. On each side of the world-split running through central Europe and around the Asiatic rimlands, there is an ever-increasing interlocking of economic, military, and political structures. If there is government intervention in the corporate economy, so is there corporate intervention in the governmental process. In the structural sense, this triangle of power is the source of the interlocking directorate that is most important for the historical structure of the present.

The fact of the interlocking is clearly revealed at each of the points of crisis of modern capitalist society—slump, war, and boom. In each, men of decision are led to an awareness of the interdependence of the major institutional orders. In the nineteenth century, when the scale of all institutions was smaller, their liberal integration was achieved in the automatic economy, by an autonomous play of market forces, and in the automatic political domain, by the bargain and the vote. It was then assumed that out of the imbalance and friction that followed the limited decisions then possible a new equilibrium would in due course emerge. That can no longer be assumed, and it is not assumed by the men at the top of each of the three dominant hierarchies.

For given the scope of their consequences, decisions—and indecisions—in any one of these ramify into the others, and hence top decisions tend either to become coordinated or to lead to a commanding indecision. It has not always been like this. When numerous small entrepreneurs made up the economy, for example, many of them could fail and the consequences still remain local; political and military authorities did not intervene. But now, given political expectations and military commitments, can they afford to allow key units of the private corporate economy to break down in slump? Increasingly, they do intervene in economic affairs, and as they do so, the controlling decisions in each order are inspected by agents of the other two, and economic, military, and political structures are interlocked.

At the pinnacle of each of the three enlarged and centralized domains, there have arisen those higher circles which make up the economic, the political, and the military elites. At the top of the economy, among the corporate rich, there are the chief executives; at the top of the political order, the members of the political directorate; at the top of the military establishment, the elite of soldier-statesmen clustered in and around the Joint Chiefs of Staff and the upper echelon. As each of these domains has coincided with the others, as decisions tend to become total in their consequence, the leading men in each of the three domains of power—the warlords, the corporation chieftains, the political directorate—tend to come together, to form the power elite of America.

The higher circles in and around these command posts are often thought of in terms of what their members possess: They have a greater share than other people of the things and experiences that are most highly valued. From this point of view, the elite are simply those who have the most of what there is to have, which is generally held to include money, power, and prestige—as well as all the ways of life to which these lead. But the elite are not simply those who have the most, for they could not "have the most" were it not for their positions in the great institutions. For such institutions are the necessary bases of power, of wealth, and of prestige, and at the same time, the chief means of exercising power, of acquiring and retaining wealth, and of cashing in the higher claims for prestige.

By the powerful we mean, of course, those who are able to realize their will, even if others resist it. No one, accordingly, can be truly powerful unless he has access to the command of major institutions, for it is over these institutional means of power that the truly powerful are, in the first instance, powerful. Higher politicians and key officials of government command such institutional power; so do admirals and generals, and so do the major owners and executives of the larger corporations. Not all power, it is true, is anchored in and exercised by means of such institutions, but only within and through them can power be more or less continuous and important.

Wealth also is acquired and held in and through institutions. The pyramid of wealth cannot be understood merely in terms of the very rich; for the great inheriting families, as we shall see, are now supplemented by the corporate institutions of modern society: Every one of the very rich families has been and is closely connected—always legally and frequently managerially as well—with one of the multimillion-dollar corporations.

The modern corporation is the prime source of wealth, but, in latter-day capitalism, the political apparatus also opens and closes many avenues to wealth. The amount as well as the source of income, the power over consumer's goods as well as over productive capital, are determined by position within the political economy. If our interest in the very rich goes beyond their lavish or their miserly consumption, we must examine their relations to modern forms of corporate property as well as to the state; for such relations now determine the chances of men to secure big property and to receive high income.

Great prestige increasingly follows the major institutional units of the social structure. It is obvious that prestige depends, often quite decisively, upon access to the publicity machines that are now a central and normal feature of all the big institutions of modern America. Moreover, one feature of these hierarchies of corporation, state, and military establishment is that their top positions are increasingly interchangeable. One result of this is the accumulative nature of prestige. Claims for prestige, for example, may be initially based on military roles, then expressed in and augmented by an educational institution run by corporate executives, and cashed in, finally, in the political order, where, for General Eisenhower and those he represents, power and prestige finally meet at the very peak. Like wealth and power, prestige tends to be cumulative: The more of it you have, the more you can get. These values also tend to be translatable into one another: The wealthy find it easier than the poor to gain power; those with status find it easier than those without it to control opportunities for wealth.

If we took the 100 most powerful men in America, the 100 wealthiest, and the 100 most celebrated away from the institutional positions they now occupy, away from their resources of men and women and money, away from the media of mass communication that are now focused upon them—then they would be powerless and poor and uncelebrated. For power is not of a man. Wealth does not center in the person of the wealthy. Celebrity is not inherent in any personality. To be celebrated, to be wealthy, to have power requires access to major institutions, for the institutional positions men occupy determine in large part their chances to have and to hold these valued experiences.

The people of the higher circles may also be conceived as members of a top social stratum, as a set of groups whose members know one another, see one another socially and at business, and so, in making decisions, take one another into account. The elite, according to this conception, feel themselves to be, and are felt by others to be, the inner circle of "the upper social classes." They form a more or less compact social and psychological entity; they have become self-conscious members of a social class. People are either accepted into this class or they are not, and there is a qualitative split, rather than merely a numerical scale, separating them from those who are not elite. They are more or less aware of themselves as a social class and they behave toward one another differently from the way they do toward members of other classes. They accept one another, understand one another, marry one another, tend to work and to think if not together at least alike.

Now, we do not want by our definition to prejudge whether the elite of the command posts are conscious members of such a socially recognized class, or whether considerable proportions of the elite derive from such a clear and distinct class. These are matters to be investigated. Yet in order to be able to recognize what we intend to investigate, we must note something that all biographies and memoirs of the wealthy and the powerful and the eminent make clear: No matter what else they may be, the people of these higher circles are involved in a set of overlapping "crowds" and intricately connected "cliques." There is a kind of mutual attraction among those who "sit on the same terrace"—although this often becomes clear to them, as well as to others, only at the point at which they feel the need to draw the line; only when, in their common defense, they come to understand what they have in common, and so close their ranks against outsiders.

The idea of such ruling stratum implies that most of its members have similar social origins, that throughout their lives they maintain a network of informal connections, and that to some degree there is an interchangeability of position between the various hierarchies of money and power and celebrity. We must, of course, note at once that if such an elite stratum does exist, its social visibility and its form, for very solid historical reasons, are quite different from those of the noble cousinhoods that once ruled various European nations.

That American society has never passed through a feudal epoch is of decisive importance to the nature of the American elite, as well as to American society as a historic whole. For it means that no nobility or aristocracy, established before the capitalist era, has stood in tense opposition to the higher bourgeoisie. It means that this bourgeoisie has monopolized not only wealth but prestige and power as well. It means that no set of noble families has commanded the top positions and monopolized the values that are generally held in high esteem; and certainly that no set has done so explicitly by inherited right. It means that no high church dignitaries or court nobilities, no entrenched landlords with honorific accouterments, no monopolists of high army posts have opposed the enriched bourgeoisie and in the name of birth and prerogative successfully resisted its self-making.

But this does *not* mean that there are no upper strata in the United States. That they emerged from a "middle class" that had no recognized aristocratic superiors does not mean they remained middle class when enormous increases in wealth made their own superiority possible. Their origins and their newness may have made the upper strata less visible in America than elsewhere. But in America today there are in fact tiers and ranges of wealth and power of which people in the middle and lower ranks know very little and may not even dream. There are families who, in their well-being, are quite insulated from the economic jolts and lurches felt by the merely prosperous and those farther down the scale. There are also men of power who in quite small groups make decisions of enormous consequence for the underlying population. . . .

CRITICAL-THINKING QUESTIONS

1. What institutions form the "interlocking triangle" in Mills's analysis? Why does he think these are the most powerful social institutions?

2. Explain how Mills argues that the existence of a power elite is not a consequence of *people* per se but a result of the institutions of U.S. society.

3. Does the lack of an aristocratic history mean that power is dispersed throughout U.S. society?

55 Who's Running America?

THOMAS R. DYE

In the previous reading C. Wright Mills asserted that a small group of power elite run U.S. society. Was he right? Thomas Dye contends that some groups are far more powerful than others. He adds that the military establishment and Congress are much less influential than most people (and even Mills) believed.

If there ever was a time when the powers of government were limited—when government did no more than secure law and order, protect individual liberty and property, enforce contracts, and defend against foreign invasion—that time has long passed. Today it is commonplace to observe that governmental institutions intervene in every aspect of our lives—from the "cradle to the grave." Government in America has the primary responsibility for providing insurance against old age, death, dependency, disability, and unemployment; for organizing the nation's health-care system; for providing education at the elementary, secondary, collegiate, and postgraduate levels; for providing public highways and regulating water, rail, and air transportation; for providing police and fire protection; for providing sanitation services and sewage disposal; for financing research in medicine, science, and technology; for delivering the mail; for exploring outer space; for maintaining parks and recreation; for providing housing and adequate food for the poor; for providing job training and

manpower programs; for cleaning the air and water; for rebuilding central cities; for maintaining full employment and a stable money supply; for regulating business practices and labor relations; for eliminating racial and sexual discrimination. Indeed, the list of government responsibilities seems endless, yet each year we manage to find additional tasks for government to do.

THE CONCENTRATION OF GOVERNMENTAL POWER

Government in the United States grew enormously throughout most of the twentieth century, both in absolute terms and in relation to the size of the national economy. The size of the economy is usually measured by the gross domestic product (GDP), the dollar sum of all the goods and services produced in the United States in a year. Governments accounted for only about 8 percent of the GDP at the beginning of the century, and most governmental activities were carried out by state and local governments. Two world wars, the New Deal programs devised during the Great Depression of the 1930s, and the growth of the Great Society

Source: Thomas R. Dye, *Who's Running America? The Bush Restoration,* 7th edition. Upper Saddle River, N.J.: Prentice Hall, 2002, pp. 55–96.

programs of the 1960s and 1970s all greatly expanded the size of government, particularly the federal government. The rise in government growth relative to the economy leveled off during the Reagan presidency (1981–89), and no large new programs were undertaken in the Bush and Clinton years. An economic boom in the 1990s caused the GDP to grow rapidly, while government spending grew only moderately. The result was a modest *decline* in governmental size in relation to the economy. Today, federal expenditures amount to about 20 percent of GDP, and total governmental expenditures are about 30 percent of GDP (see Figure 1).

Not everything that government does is reflected in governmental expenditures. *Regulatory activity,* for example, especially environmental regulations, imposes significant costs on individuals and businesses; these costs are not shown in government budgets.

We have defined our governmental elite as the top executive, congressional, and judicial officers of the *federal* government; the President and Vice-President; secretaries, undersecretaries, and assistant secretaries of executive departments; senior White House presidential advisers; congressional committee chairpersons and ranking minority members; congressional majority and minority party leaders in the House and Senate; Supreme Court Justices; and members of the Federal Reserve Board and the Council of Economic Advisers. And we add to this definition of political elites the "fat cat" contributors who keep them in power.

THE FAT CAT CONTRIBUTORS

More money was spent on political campaigning in 2000 than in any election year in American history. An estimated $3 *billion* was spent by all presidential and congressional candidates, Democratic and Republican parties, political action committees sponsored by interest groups, and independent political organizations in federal, state, and local elections combined. The costs of elections rises in each election cycle. The largest increases in campaign finance came not from regulated "hard money" contributions to candidates, but rather from large unregulated "soft money" contributions to the parties.

Virtually all of the top "fat cat" campaign contributors from the *corporate, banking, and investment* worlds have been previously listed among the nation's largest corporate and monied institutions. AT&T, Philip Morris, Citigroup, and Goldman Sachs regularly appear each election cycle among contributors of $2 to $3 million or more (see Table 1). One notable newcomer among top corporate "fat cat" contributors in 2000 is Bill Gates's Microsoft Corporation. In the past, Gates tried to avoid politics altogether; Microsoft was notably absent from previous lists of top campaign contributors. But Gates learned a hard lesson when Clinton's Justice Department under Attorney General Janet Reno launched its costly antitrust suit against Microsoft.

While contributions from the corporate, banking, and investment institutions are usually divided

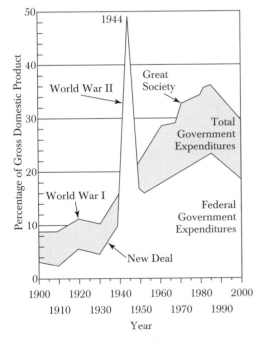

FIGURE 1   The Growth of Government

Source: Budget of the United States Government, 2000.

TABLE 1   The Top Fifty Fat Cat Campaign Contributors, 2000

Rank	Contributor	Total Contributions	To Dems.	To Repubs.
1	American Fedn. of St./Cnty./Munic. Employees	$6,935,989	98%	2%
2	Service Employees International Union	$4,961,010	95%	5%
3	AT&T	$4,667,844	38%	61%
4	Microsoft Corp	$4,309,856	46%	54%
5	Communications Workers of America	$3,871,185	99%	0%
6	National Assn. of Realtors	$3,834,600	41%	59%
7	Goldman Sachs Group	$3,646,382	68%	32%
8	United Food & Commercial Workers Union	$3,578,452	99%	1%
9	Intl. Brotherhood of Electrical Workers	$3,561,860	97%	3%
10	Citigroup Inc.	$3,559,566	53%	47%
11	Philip Morris	$3,460,200	18%	81%
12	SBC Communications	$3,418,466	46%	54%
13	Verizon Communications	$3,357,420	36%	64%
14	Carpenters & Joiners Union	$3,183,383	92%	8%
15	United Parcel Service	$3,133,119	26%	73%
16	American Federation of Teachers	$3,110,055	99%	1%
17	Assn. of Trial Lawyers of America	$3,030,750	88%	12%
18	Laborers Union	$2,929,275	93%	7%
19	National Rifle Assn.	$2,885,377	8%	92%
20	MBNA America Bank	$2,733,000	17%	83%
21	National Education Assn.	$2,584,478	92%	7%
22	Sheet Metal Workers Union	$2,551,584	99%	1%
23	Machinists/Aerospace Workers Union	$2,546,138	99%	1%
24	Teamsters Union	$2,517,240	93%	7%
25	Ernst & Young	$2,497,761	42%	58%
26	National Auto Dealers Assn.	$2,410,200	32%	68%
27	Federal Express Corp.	$2,388,428	34%	66%
28	Enron Corp.	$2,365,458	28%	72%
29	National Assn. of Home Builders	$2,336,799	37%	63%
30	Lockheed Martin	$2,333,794	39%	61%
31	Emily's List	$2,328,840	100%	0%
32	Credit Suisse First Boston	$2,325,705	29%	70%
33	Bristol-Myers Squibb	$2,300,792	14%	86%
34	United Auto Workers	$2,248,755	99%	0%
35	Morgan Stanley, Dean Witter & Co.	$2,225,823	39%	60%
36	BellSouth Corp.	$2,219,752	41%	59%
37	Freddie Mac	$2,198,839	48%	52%
38	AFL-CIO	$2,173,638	96%	4%
39	Global Crossing	$2,142,386	50%	50%
40	Pfizer Inc.	$2,136,647	14%	86%
41	Blue Cross/Blue Shield	$2,125,552	27%	73%
42	American Medical Assn.	$2,077,644	47%	52%
43	National Beer Wholesalers Assn.	$2,059,061	19%	80%
44	Bank of America	$1,889,318	59%	40%
45	Time Warner	$1,860,237	73%	27%
46	National Assn. of Letter Carriers	$1,830,700	86%	13%
47	Union Pacific Corp	$1,805,144	16%	84%
48	General Electric	$1,793,879	39%	61%
49	Joseph E Seagram & Sons	$1,791,060	62%	38%
50	Andersen Worldwide	$1,781,412	29%	70%

between the parties (albeit weighted toward Republicans), contributions from *unions* are almost exclusively directed toward Democrats. Indeed, union contributions are the single largest source of campaign money for the Democratic Party, followed by contributions from Hollywood's entertainment industry.

Contributions from wealthy individuals failed to match institutional contributions. While more than 100 institutions contributed $1 million or more in 2000, only two individuals contributed over this amount. (Peter Buttenwieser of Buttenwieser & Associates of Philadelphia and S. Daniel Abraham of Slim-Fast Foods both contributed over $1 million to Democrats.)

Expenditures for congressional campaigns also reached a new high. The U.S. Senate race in New York, featuring former First Lady Hillary Clinton against relative newcomer Republican Rick Lazio, set a new combined spending record for congressional elections at more than $85 million. A new individual congressional spending record of $65 million was set by multibillionaire investment banker (Goldman Sachs) Democrat Jon Corzine, who dug into his own fortune to win a U.S. Senate seat from New Jersey.

The *average* candidate for a U.S. Senate seat raised and spent over $5 million. And the *average* candidate for a U.S. House seat raised and spent about $800,000. This means that the average incumbent member of Congress must raise about $8,000 *per week,* every week of their term in office.

THE POLITICIANS: AMBITION AND OFFICE SEEKING

Ambition is the driving force in politics. Politics attracts people for whom power and celebrity are more rewarding than money, leisure, or privacy. "Political office today flows to those who want it enough to spend the time and energy mastering its pursuit. It flows in the direction of ambition—and talent.[1]

Political ambition is the most distinguishing characteristic of elected officeholders. The people who run for and win public office are not necessarily the most intelligent, best informed, wealthiest, or most successful business or professional people. At all levels of the political system, from presidential candidates, members of Congress, governors and state legislators, to city councils and school board members, it is the most politically ambitious people who are willing to sacrifice time, family and private life, and energy and effort for the power and celebrity that comes with public office.

Politics is becoming increasingly professionalized. "Citizen-statesmen"—people with business or professional careers who get into politics part-time or for short periods of time—are being driven out of political life by career politicians—people who enter politics early in life as a full-time occupation and expect to make it their career. Politically ambitious young people seek out internships and staff positions with members of Congress, with congressional committees, in state legislators' or governors' offices, or mayors' or council chambers. Others volunteer to work in political campaigns. Many find political mentors, as they learn how to organize campaigns, contact financial contributors, and deal with the media. By their early thirties, they are ready to run for local office or the state legislature. Rather than challenge a strong incumbent, they may wait for an open seat to be created by retirement, reapportionment, or its holder seeking another office. Or they may make an initial attempt against a strong incumbent of the opposition party in order to gain experience and win the appreciation of their own party's supporters for a good effort. Over time, running for and holding elective office becomes their career. They work harder at it than anyone else, in part because they have no real private sector career to return to in case of defeat.

The prevalence of lawyers in politics is an American tradition. Among the nation's Founders—the fifty-five delegates to the Constitutional Convention in 1787—some twenty-five were lawyers. The political dominance of lawyers is even greater today, with lawyers filling nearly two thirds of U.S. Senate seats and nearly half of the seats in the U.S. House of Representatives.

It is sometimes argued that lawyers dominate in politics because of the parallel skills required in law and politics. Lawyering is the representation of clients; a lawyer employs similar skills whether representing clients in private practice or representing constituents in Congress. Lawyers are trained to deal with statutory law, so they may at least know how to find United States Code (the codified laws of the United States government) in a law library when they arrive in Congress to make or amend these laws.

But it is more likely that the people attracted to politics decide to go to law school, fully aware of the tradition of lawyers in American politics. Moreover, political officeholding, at the state and local level as well as in the national government, can help a struggling lawyer's private practice through free public advertising and opportunities to make contacts with potential clients. Finally, there are many special opportunities for lawyers to acquire public office in "lawyers only" posts in federal, state, and local government as judges and prosecuting attorneys. The lawyer-politician is not usually a top professional lawyer. Instead, the typical lawyer-politician uses his or her law career as a means of support—one that is compatible with political office seeking and officeholding.

A significant number of top politicians have inherited great wealth. The Roosevelts, Rockefellers, Kennedys, Bushes, and others have used their wealth and family connections to support their political careers. However, it is important to note that *a majority of the nation's top politicians have climbed the ladder from relative obscurity to political success.* Many have acquired some wealth in the process, but most political leaders started their climb from very middle-class circumstances. Thus, as in the corporate world, we find more "climbers" than "inheritors" at the top in the world of politics. . . .

EXECUTIVE DECISION-MAKERS: THE SERIOUS PEOPLE

The politician is a professional office-seeker. The politician knows how to run for office—but not necessarily how to run the government. After victory at the polls, the prudent politician turns to "serious" people to run the government. The corporate and governmental experience and educational credentials of these "serious" decision-makers greatly exceed those of most members of Congress or other elected officials. When presidents turn from the task of *running for office* to the task of *running a government,* they are obliged to recruit higher quality leadership than is typically found among political officeholders.

The responsibility for the initiation of national programs and policies falls primarily upon the top White House staff and the heads of executive departments. Generally, Congress merely responds to policy proposals initiated by the executive branch. The President and his key advisers and administrators have a strong incentive to fulfill their responsibility for decision-making. In the eyes of the American public, they are responsible for everything that happens in the nation, regardless of whether they have the authority or capacity to do anything about it. There is a general expectation that every administration, even one committed to a "caretaker" role, will put forth some sort of policy program.

The President and Vice-President, White House presidential advisers and ambassadors-at-large, Cabinet secretaries, undersecretaries, and assistant secretaries constitute our executive elite. . . .

THE CONGRESSIONAL ESTABLISHMENT

Although policy initiatives are usually developed outside Congress, Congress is no mere "rubber stamp." Key members of Congress do play an independent role in national decision-making; thus, key congressional leaders must be included in any operational definition of a national elite.

Political scientists have commented extensively on the structure of power *within* the Congress. They generally describe a hierarchical structure in both houses of the Congress—a "congressional establishment"—which largely determines what the

Congress will do. The congressional establishment has survived periodic efforts at decentralization. It is composed of the Speaker of the House and president pro tempore of the Senate; House and Senate majority and minority leaders and whips; and committee chairpersons and ranking minority members of House and Senate standing committees. Party leadership roles in the House and Senate are major sources of power in Washington. The Speaker of the House and the majority and minority leaders of the House and Senate direct the business of Congress. Although they share this task with the standing committee chairpersons, these leaders are generally "first among equals" in their relationships with committee chairpersons. But the committee system also creates powerful congressional figures, the chairpersons of the most powerful standing committees—particularly the Senate Foreign Relations, Appropriations, Judiciary, Finance, Armed Services, and Budget committees, and the House Rules, Appropriations, International Relations, Judiciary, Armed Services, Budget, and Ways and Means committees.

Viewed within the broader context of a *national elite,* congressional leaders appear "folksy," parochial, and localistic. Because of the local constituency of members of Congress, they are predisposed to concern themselves with local interests. Members of Congress are part of local elite structures "back home"; they retain their local businesses and law practices, club memberships, and religious affiliations. Members of Congress represent many small segments of the nation rather than the nation as a whole. Even top congressional leaders from safe districts, with many years of seniority, cannot completely shed their local interests. Their claim to *national* leadership must be safely hedged by attention to their local constituents. Consider, for example, the parochial backgrounds of the following top congressional leaders. . . .

THE JUDGES

Nine people—none of whom is elected and all of whom serve for life—possess ultimate authority over all the other institutions of government. The Supreme Court of the United States has the authority to void the acts of popularly elected Presidents and Congresses. There is no appeal from their decision about what is the "supreme law of the land," except perhaps to undertake the difficult task of amending the Constitution itself. Only the good judgment of the Justices—their sense of "judicial self-restraint"—limits their power. It was the Supreme Court, rather than the President or Congress, that took the lead in important issues such as eliminating segregation from public life, ensuring voter equality in representation, limiting the powers of police, and declaring abortion to be a fundamental right of women.

Social scientists have commented frequently on the class bias of Supreme Court Justices: "White; generally Protestant . . . ; fifty to fifty-five years of age at the time of his appointment; Anglo-Saxon ethnic stock . . . ; high social status; reared in an urban environment; member of a civicminded, politically active, economically comfortable family; legal training; some type of public office; generally well educated."[2] No blacks had served on the Supreme Court until the appointment of Associate Justice Thurgood Marshall in 1967. No women had served until the appointment of Sandra Day O'Connor in 1981. Of course, social background does not necessarily determine judicial philosophy. But as John R. Schmidhauser observes, "If . . . the Supreme Court is the keeper of the American conscience, it is essentially the conscience of the American upper-middle class sharpened by the imperative of individual social responsibility and political activism, and conditioned by the conservative impact of legal training and professional attitudes and associations."[3] . . .

THE MILITARY ESTABLISHMENT

In his farewell address to the nation in 1961, President Dwight D. Eisenhower warned of "an immense military establishment and a large arms industry." He observed: "In the councils of government, we must guard against the acquisition of unwarranted influence, whether sought or unsought, by the military-industrial complex."

The phrase *the military-industrial complex* caught on with many commentators over the years. It implied that a giant network of defense contractors—for example, Lockheed Aircraft, General Dynamics, Rockwell, McDonnell Douglas, Boeing, Litton, Hughes Tool, Grumman Aircraft—together with members of Congress in whose districts their plants were located, conspired with the generals in the Pentagon to create a powerful force in governmental and corporate circles. Indeed, radical social commentators held the military-industrial complex responsible for war and "imperialism."

But whatever the power of defense contractors and the military at the height of the Cold War, their influence today in governing circles is miniscule. Indeed, their goal today is to avoid complete dismantlement. Spending for national defense has declined precipitously from 10 percent of the GNP in the Eisenhower and Kennedy years to less than 3 percent today. Spending on Social Security, Medicare, and welfare, including Medicaid, exceeds 58 percent of the federal budget, compared to 16 percent for national defense.[4] There are 2 million civilian employees of the federal government, compared to only 1.4 million people in the armed forces. The long-term decline of U.S. defense spending suggests that the American military-industrial complex was *not* a very powerful conspiracy.

It seems clear in retrospect that C. Wright Mills placed too much importance on the military in his work, *The Power Elite*.[5] Mills was writing in the early 1950s when military prestige was high following victory in World War II. After the war, a few high-level military men were recruited to top corporate positions to add prestige to corporate boards. But this practice ended in the 1960s. The contrast between the political prestige of the military in the post–World War II years and in the post–Vietnam years is striking: The Supreme

Allied Commander in Europe in World War II, Dwight D. Eisenhower, was elected President of the United States; the U.S. Commander in Vietnam, William Westmoreland, was defeated in his bid to become governor of South Carolina! Moreover, in contrast with corporate and governmental elites, military officers do *not* come from the upper or upper-middle class of society. Military officers are more likely to be recruited from lower- and lower-middle-class backgrounds, and more likely to have rural and southern roots than are corporate or governmental elites.[6]

CRITICAL-THINKING QUESTIONS

1. Why does Dye argue that government has far more power today compared to 1900? Why does he include "fat cat" contributors in his definition of political elites?

2. "Politics attracts the best and brightest people." Would Dye agree with this statement? Do you? In addition, why do lawyers dominate U.S. politics?

3. Consider Congress, the military, and the Supreme Court. According to Dye, which group is the most powerful of all our governing circles? Do you agree with Dye's analysis? Explain why or why not.

NOTES

1. Alan Ehrenhalt, *The United States of Ambition: Politicians' Power and Pursuit of Office* (New York: Random House, 1991), p. 22.

2. Henry Abraham, *The Judicial Process* (New York: Oxford University Press, 1962), p. 58.

3. John R. Schmidhauser, *The Supreme Court* (New York: Holt Rinehart and Winston, 1960), p. 59.

4. *Budget of the United States Government 2001* gives this breakdown by function: Social Security: 23.2%; Medicare: 12.0%; Income Security: 14.2%; Medicaid: 9.1%.

5. C. Wright Mills, *The Power Elite* (New York: Oxford, 1956).

6. Morris Janowitz, *The Professional Soldier* (New York: Free Press, 1960), p. 378.

CLASSIC

CONTEMPORARY

CROSS-CULTURAL

56 The Roots of Terrorism

THE 9/11 COMMISSION REPORT

September 11, 2001, was a day of unprecedented shock and suffering in the United States. Almost 2,800 people died in Manhattan, New York; a field in Pennsylvania; and the Pentagon after multiple terrorist attacks. In this selection, the 9/11 Commission Report *provides some insights into the growth of a "new kind of terrorism" that was responsible for the mass murders.*

A DECLARATION OF WAR

In February 1998, the forty-year-old Saudi exile Usama Bin Ladin and a fugitive Egyptian physician, Ayman al Zawahiri, arranged from their Afghan headquarters for an Arabic newspaper in London to publish what they termed a fatwa issued in the name of a "World Islamic Front." A fatwa is normally an interpretation of Islamic

Source: The 9/11 Commission Report: Final Report of the National Commission on Terrorist Attacks Upon the United States, 47–55. Washington, D.C.: U.S. Government Printing Office, 2004.

Note: Islamic names often do not follow the Western practice of the consistent use of surnames. Given the variety of names we mention, we chose to refer to individuals by the last word in the names by which they are known; Nawaf al Hazmi as Hazmi, for instance, omitting the article "al" that would be part of their name in their own societies. We generally make an exception for the more familiar English usage of "Bin" as part of a last name, as in Bin Ladin. Further, there is no universally accepted way to transliterate Arabic words and names into English. We have relied on a mix of common sense, the sound of the name in Arabic, and common usage in source materials, the press, or government documents. When we quote from a source document, we use its transliteration, e.g., "al Qida" instead of al Qaeda.

law by a respected Islamic authority, but neither Bin Ladin, Zawahiri, nor the three others who signed this statement were scholars of Islamic law. Claiming that America had declared war against God and his messenger, they called for the murder of any American, anywhere on earth, as the "individual duty for every Muslim who can do it in any country in which it is possible to do it."[1]

Three months later, when interviewed in Afghanistan by ABC-TV, Bin Ladin enlarged on these themes.[2] He claimed it was more important for Muslims to kill Americans than to kill other infidels. "It is far better for anyone to kill a single American soldier than to squander his efforts on other activities," he said. Asked whether he approved of terrorism and of attacks on civilians, he replied: "We believe that the worst thieves in the world today and the worst terrorists are the Americans. Nothing could stop you except perhaps retaliation in kind. We do not have to differentiate between military or civilian. As far as we are concerned, they are all targets."

Though novel for its open endorsement of indiscriminate killing, Bin Ladin's 1998 declaration was only the latest in the long series of his public and private calls since 1992 that singled out the United States for attack.

In August 1996, Bin Ladin had issued his own self-styled fatwa calling on Muslims to drive American soldiers out of Saudi Arabia. The long, disjointed document condemned the Saudi monarchy for allowing the presence of an army of infidels in a land with the sites most sacred to Islam, and celebrated recent suicide bombings of American military facilities in the Kingdom. It praised the 1983 suicide bombing in Beirut that killed 241 U.S. Marines, the 1992 bombing in Aden, and especially the 1993 firefight in Somalia after which the United States "left the area carrying disappointment, humiliation, defeat and your dead with you."[3]

Bin Ladin said in his ABC interview that he and his followers had been preparing in Somalia for another long struggle, like that against the Soviets in Afghanistan, but "the United States rushed out of Somalia in shame and disgrace." Citing the Soviet army's withdrawal from Afghanistan as proof that a ragged army of dedicated Muslims could overcome a superpower, he told the interviewer: "We are certain that we shall—with the grace of Allah—prevail over the Americans." He went on to warn that "If the present injustice continues . . . , it will inevitably move the battle to American soil."[4]

Plans to attack the United States were developed with unwavering single-mindedness throughout the 1990s. Bin Ladin saw himself as called "to follow in the footsteps of the Messenger and to communicate his message to all nations,"[5] and to serve as the rallying point and organizer of a new kind of war to destroy America and bring the world to Islam.

BIN LADIN'S APPEAL IN THE ISLAMIC WORLD

It is the story of eccentric and violent ideas sprouting in the fertile ground of political and social turmoil. It is the story of an organization poised to seize its historical moment. How did Bin Ladin—with his call for the indiscriminate killing of Americans—win thousands of followers and some degree of approval from millions more?

The history, culture, and body of beliefs from which Bin Ladin has shaped and spread his message are largely unknown to many Americans. Seizing on symbols of Islam's past greatness, he promises to restore pride to people who consider themselves the victims of successive foreign masters. He uses cultural and religious allusions to the holy Qur'an and some of its interpreters. He appeals to people disoriented by cyclonic change as they confront modernity and globalization. His rhetoric selectively draws from multiple sources—Islam, history, and the region's political and economic malaise. He also stresses grievances against the United States widely shared in the Muslim world. He inveighed against the presence of U.S. troops in Saudi Arabia, the home of Islam's holiest sites. He spoke of the suffering of the Iraqi people as a result of sanctions imposed after the Gulf War, and he protested U.S. support of Israel.

Islam

Islam (a word that literally means "surrender to the will of God") arose in Arabia with what Muslims believe are a series of revelations to the Prophet Mohammed from the one and only God, the God of Abraham and of Jesus. These revelations, conveyed by the angel Gabriel, are recorded in the Qur'an. Muslims believe that these revelations, given to the greatest and last of a chain of prophets stretching from Abraham through Jesus, complete God's message to humanity. The Hadith, which recount Mohammed's sayings and deeds as recorded by his contemporaries, are another fundamental source. A third key element is the Sharia, the code of law derived from the Qur'an and the Hadith.

Islam is divided into two main branches, Sunni and Shia. Soon after the Prophet's death, the question of choosing a new leader, or *caliph,* for the Muslim community, or *Ummah,* arose. Initially, his successors could be drawn from the Prophet's contemporaries, but with time, this was no longer possible. Those who became the Shia held that any leader of the Ummah must be a direct descendant of the Prophet; those who became the Sunni argued that lineal descent was not required if the candidate met other standards of faith and knowledge. After bloody struggles, the Sunni became (and remain) the majority sect. (The Shia are dominant in Iran.) The Caliphate—the institutionalized leadership of the Ummah—thus was a Sunni institution that continued until 1924, first under Arab and eventually under Ottoman Turkish control.

Many Muslims look back at the century after the revelations to the Prophet Mohammed as a golden age. Its memory is strongest among the Arabs. What happened then—the spread of Islam from the Arabian Peninsula throughout the Middle East, North Africa, and even into Europe within less than a century—seemed, and seems, miraculous.[6] Nostalgia for Islam's past glory remains a powerful force.

Islam is both a faith and a code of conduct for all aspects of life. For many Muslims, a good government would be one guided by the moral principles of their faith. This does not necessarily translate into a desire for clerical rule and the abolition of a secular state. It does mean that some Muslims tend to be uncomfortable with distinctions between religion and state, though Muslim rulers throughout history have readily separated the two.

To extremists, however, such divisions, as well as the existence of parliaments and legislation, only prove these rulers to be false Muslims usurping God's authority over all aspects of life. Periodically, the Islamic world has seen surges of what, for want of a better term, is often labeled "fundamentalism."[7] Denouncing waywardness among the faithful, some clerics have appealed for a return to observance of the literal teachings of the Qur'an and Hadith. One scholar from the

fourteenth century from whom Bin Ladin selectively quotes, Ibn Taimiyyah, condemned both corrupt rulers and the clerics who failed to criticize them. He urged Muslims to read the Qur'an and the Hadith for themselves, not to depend solely on learned interpreters like himself but to hold one another to account for the quality of their observance.[8]

The extreme Islamist version of history blames the decline from Islam's golden age on the rulers and people who turned away from the true path of their religion, thereby leaving Islam vulnerable to encroaching foreign powers eager to steal their land, wealth, and even their souls.

Bin Ladin's Worldview

Despite his claims to universal leadership, Bin Ladin offers an extreme view of Islamic history designed to appeal mainly to Arabs and Sunnis. He draws on fundamentalists who blame the eventual destruction of the Caliphate on leaders who abandoned the pure path of religious devotion.[9] He repeatedly calls on his followers to embrace martyrdom since "the walls of oppression and humiliation cannot be demolished except in a rain of bullets."[10] For those yearning for a lost sense of order in an older, more tranquil world, he offers his "Caliphate" as an imagined alternative to today's uncertainty. For others, he offers simplistic conspiracies to explain their world.

Bin Ladin also relies heavily on the Egyptian writer Sayyid Qutb. A member of the Muslim Brotherhood[11] executed in 1966 on charges of attempting to overthrow the government, Qutb mixed Islamic scholarship with a very superficial acquaintance with Western history and thought. Sent by the Egyptian government to study in the United States in the late 1940s, Qutb returned with an enormous loathing of Western society and history. He dismissed Western achievements as entirely material, arguing that Western society possesses "nothing that will satisfy its own conscience and justify its existence."[12]

Three basic themes emerge from Qutb's writings. First, he claimed that the world was beset with barbarism, licentiousness, and unbelief (a condition he called *jahiliyya,* the religious term for the period of ignorance prior to the revelations given to the Prophet Mohammed). Qutb argued that humans can choose only between Islam and jahiliyya. Second, he warned that more people, including Muslims, were attracted to jahiliyya and its material comforts than to his view of Islam; jahiliyya could therefore triumph over Islam. Third, no middle ground exists in what Qutb conceived as a struggle between God and Satan. All Muslims—as he defined them—therefore must take up arms in this fight. Any Muslim who rejects his ideas is just one more nonbeliever worthy of destruction.[13]

Bin Ladin shares Qutb's stark view, permitting him and his followers to rationalize even unprovoked mass murder as righteous defense of an embattled faith. Many Americans have wondered, "Why do 'they' hate us?" Some also ask, "What can we do to stop these attacks?"

Bin Ladin and al Qaeda have given answers to both these questions. To the first, they say that America had attacked Islam; America is responsible for all conflicts involving Muslims. Thus Americans are blamed when Israelis fight with Palestinians, when Russians fight with Chechens, when Indians fight with Kashmiri Muslims, and when the Philippine government fights ethnic Muslims in its southern islands. America is also held responsible for the governments of Muslim countries, derided by al Qaeda as "your agents." Bin Ladin has stated flatly, "Our fight against these governments is not separate from our fight against you."[14] These charges found a ready audience among millions of Arabs and Muslims angry at the United States because of issues ranging from Iraq to Palestine to America's support for their countries' repressive rulers.

Bin Ladin's grievance with the United States may have started in reaction to specific U.S. policies but it quickly became far deeper. To the second question, what America could do, al Qaeda's answer was that America should abandon the Middle East, convert to Islam, and end the immorality and godlessness of its society and culture: "It is saddening to tell you that you are the worst civilization witnessed by the history of mankind." If the United States did not comply, it would be at war with the Islamic nation, a nation that al Qaeda's leaders said "desires death more than you desire life."[15]

History and Political Context

Few fundamentalist movements in the Islamic world gained lasting political power. In the nineteenth and twentieth centuries, fundamentalists helped articulate anticolonial grievances but played little role in the overwhelmingly secular struggles for independence after World War I. Western-educated lawyers, soldiers, and officials led most independence movements, and clerical influence and traditional culture were seen as obstacles to national progress.

After gaining independence from Western powers following World War II, the Arab Middle East followed an arc from initial pride and optimism to today's mix of indifference, cynicism, and despair. In several countries, a dynastic state already existed or was quickly established under a paramount tribal family. Monarchies in countries such as Saudi Arabia, Morocco, and Jordan still survive today. Those in Egypt, Libya, Iraq, and Yemen were eventually overthrown by secular nationalist revolutionaries.

The secular regimes promised a glowing future, often tied to sweeping ideologies (such as those promoted by Egyptian President Gamal Abdel Nasser's Arab Socialism or the Ba'ath Party of Syria and Iraq) that called for a single, secular Arab state. However, what emerged were almost invariably autocratic regimes that were usually unwilling to tolerate any opposition—even in countries, such as Egypt, that had a parliamentary tradition. Over time, their policies—repression, rewards, emigration, and the displacement of popular anger onto scapegoats (generally foreign)—were shaped by the desire to cling to power.

The bankruptcy of secular, autocratic nationalism was evident across the Muslim world by the late 1970s. At the same time, these regimes had closed off nearly all paths for peaceful opposition, forcing their critics to choose silence, exile, or violent opposition. Iran's 1979 revolution swept a Shia theocracy into power. Its success encouraged Sunni fundamentalists elsewhere.

In the 1980s, awash in sudden oil wealth, Saudi Arabia competed with Shia Iran to promote its Sunni fundamentalist interpretation of Islam, Wahhabism. The Saudi government, always conscious of its duties as the custodian of Islam's holiest places, joined with wealthy Arabs from the Kingdom and other states bordering the Persian Gulf in donating money to build mosques and religious schools that could preach and teach their interpretation of Islamic doctrine.

In this competition for legitimacy, secular regimes had no alternative to offer. Instead, in a number of cases their rulers sought to buy off local Islamist movements by ceding control of many social and educational issues. Emboldened rather than satisfied, the Islamists continued to push for power—a trend especially clear in Egypt. Confronted with a violent Islamist movement that killed President Anwar Sadat in 1981, the Egyptian government combined harsh repression of Islamic militants with harassment of moderate Islamic scholars and authors, driving many into exile. In Pakistan, a military regime sought to justify its seizure of power by a pious public stance and an embrace of unprecedented Islamist influence on education and society.

These experiments in political Islam faltered during the 1990s: the Iranian revolution lost momentum, prestige, and public support, and Pakistan's rulers found that most of its population had little enthusiasm for fundamentalist Islam. Islamist revival movements gained followers across the Muslim world, but failed to secure political power except in Iran and Sudan. In Algeria, where in 1991 Islamists seemed almost certain to win power through the ballot box, the military preempted their victory, triggering a brutal civil war that continues today. Opponents of today's rulers have few, if any, ways to participate in the existing political system. They are thus a ready audience for calls to Muslims to purify their society, reject unwelcome modernization, and adhere strictly to the Sharia.

Social and Economic Malaise

In the 1970s and early 1980s, an unprecedented flood of wealth led the then largely unmodernized oil states to attempt to shortcut decades of development. They funded huge infrastructure projects, vastly expanded education, and created subsidized social welfare programs. These programs established a widespread feeling of entitlement without a corresponding sense of social obligations. By the late 1980s, diminishing oil revenues, the economic drain from many unprofitable development projects, and population growth made these entitlement programs unsustainable. The resulting cutbacks created enormous resentment among recipients who had come to see government largesse as their right. This resentment was further stoked by public understanding of how much oil income had gone straight into the pockets of the rulers, their friends, and their helpers.

Unlike the oil states (or Afghanistan, where real economic development has barely begun), the other Arab nations and Pakistan once had seemed headed toward balanced modernization. The established commercial, financial, and industrial sectors in these states, supported by an entrepreneurial spirit and widespread understanding of free enterprise, augured well. But unprofitable heavy industry, state monopolies, and opaque bureaucracies slowly stifled growth. More importantly, these state-centered regimes placed their highest priority on preserving the elite's grip on national wealth. Unwilling to foster dynamic economies that could create jobs attractive to educated young men, the countries became economically stagnant and reliant on the safety valve of worker emigration either to the Arab oil states or to the West. Furthermore, the repression and isolation of women in many Muslim countries have not only seriously limited individual opportunity but also crippled overall economic productivity.[16]

By the 1990s, high birthrates and declining rates of infant mortality had produced a common problem throughout the Muslim world: a large, steadily increasing population of young men without any reasonable expectation of suitable or steady employment—a sure prescription for social turbulence. Many of these young men, such as the enormous number trained only in religious schools, lacked the skills needed by their societies. Far more acquired valuable skills but lived in stagnant economies that could not generate satisfying jobs.

Millions, pursuing secular as well as religious studies, were products of educational systems that generally devoted little if any attention to the rest of the world's thought, history, and culture. The secular education reflected a strong cultural preference for technical fields over the humanities and social sciences. Many of these young men, even if able to study abroad, lacked the perspective and skills needed to understand a different culture.

Frustrated in their search for a decent living, unable to benefit from an education often obtained at the cost of great family sacrifice, and blocked from starting families of their own, some of these young men were easy targets for radicalization.

Bin Ladin's Historical Opportunity

Most Muslims prefer a peaceful and inclusive vision of their faith, not the violent sectarianism of Bin Ladin. Among Arabs, Bin Ladin's followers are commonly nicknamed *takfiri,* or "those who define other Muslims as unbelievers," because of their readiness to demonize and murder those with whom they disagree. Beyond the theology lies the simple human fact that most Muslims, like most other human beings, are repelled by mass murder and barbarism whatever their justification.

"All Americans must recognize that the face of terror is not the true face of Islam," President Bush observed. "Islam is a faith that brings comfort to a billion people around the world. It's a faith that has made brothers and sisters of every race. It's a faith based upon love, not hate."[17] Yet as political, social, and economic problems created flammable societies, Bin Ladin used Islam's most extreme, fundamentalist traditions as his match. All these elements—including religion—combined in an explosive compound.

Other extremists had, and have, followings of their own. But in appealing to societies full of discontent, Bin Ladin remained credible as other leaders and symbols faded. He could stand as a symbol of resistance—above all, resistance to the West and to America. He could present himself and his allies as victorious warriors in the one great successful experience for Islamic militancy in the 1980s: the Afghan jihad against the Soviet occupation.

By 1998, Bin Ladin had a distinctive appeal, as he focused on attacking America. He argued that other extremists, who aimed at local rulers or Israel, did not go far enough. They had not taken on what he called "the head of the snake."[18]

Finally, Bin Ladin had another advantage: a substantial, worldwide organization. By the time he issued his February 1998 declaration of war, Bin Ladin had nurtured that organization for nearly ten years. He could attract, train, and use recruits for ever more ambitious attacks, rallying new adherents with each demonstration that his was the movement of the future.

CRITICAL-THINKING QUESTIONS

1. How does Usama Bin Ladin's perspective differ from that found in Islamic teachings? Why does the 9/11 Commission describe Bin Ladin's world view as an "extremist" position that promotes violence and terrorism?

2. After the 9/11 attacks, many people in the United States wondered, "Why do 'they' hate us?" How does the 9/11 Commission answer this question?

3. What are the historical, political, religious, educational, and economic factors that increase Bin Ladin's following?

NOTES

1. "Text of World Islamic Front's Statement Urging Jihad Against Jews and Crusaders," *Al Quds al Arabi,* Feb. 23, 1998 (trans. Foreign Broadcast Information Service), which was published for a large Arab world audience and signed by Usama Bin Ladin, Ayman al Zawahiri (emir of the Egyptian Islamic Jihad), Abu Yasir Rifa'i Ahmad Taha (leader of the Egyptian Islamic Group), Mir Hamzah (secretary of the Jamiat ul Ulema e Pakistan), and Fazlul Rahman (head of the Jihad Movement in Bangladesh).

2. "Hunting Bin Ladin," PBS *Frontline* broadcast, May 1998 (online at www.pbs.org/wgbh/pages/frontline/shows/binladen/who/interview.html).

3. Usama Bin Ladin, "Declaration of War Against the Americans Occupying the Land of the Two Holy Places," Aug. 23, 1996 (trans., online at www.terrorismfiles.org/individuals/declaration_of_jihad1.html).

4. "Hunting Bin Ladin," PBS *Frontline* broadcast, May 1998.

5. Ibid.

6. For a classic passage conveying the nostalgic view of Islam's spread, see Henri Pirenne, *A History of Europe,* trans. Bernard Miall (University Books, 1956), pp. 25–26.

7. See Martin Marty and R. Scott Appleby, eds., *Fundamentalism Observed,* vol. 1 (Univ. of Chicago Press, 1994).

8. See Emmanuel Sivan, *Radical Islam: Medieval Theology and Modern Politics,* enlarged ed. (Yale Univ. Press, 1990).

9. From the perspective of Islamic, not Arab, history, the Baghdad Caliphate's destruction by the Mongols in 1292 marks the end not of Islamic greatness but of Arab dominance of the Muslim world. Moghul India, Safavid Persia, and, above all, the Ottoman Empire were great Islamic powers that arose long after the Baghdad Caliphate fell.

10. Bin Ladin, "Declaration of War," Aug. 23, 1996.

11. The Muslim Brotherhood, which arose in Egypt in 1928 as a Sunni religious/nationalist opposition to the British-backed Egyptian monarchy, spread throughout the Arab world in the mid–twentieth century. In some countries, its oppositional role is nonviolent; in others, especially Egypt, it has alternated between violent and nonviolent struggle with the regime.

12. Sayyid Qutb, *Milestones* (American Trust Publications, 1990). Qutb found sin everywhere, even in rural mid-western churches. Qutb's views were best set out in Sayyid Qutb, "The America I Have Seen" (1949), reprinted in Kamal Abdel-Malek, ed., *America in an Arab Mirror: Images of America in Arabic Travel Literature: An Anthology* (Palgrave, 2000).

13. For a good introduction to Qutb, see National Public Radio broadcast, "Sayyid Qutb's America," May 6, 2003 (online at www.npr.org/display_pages/features/feature_1253796.html).

14. "Bin Laden's 'Letter to America,'" *Observer Worldview,* Nov. 24, 2002 (trans., online at http://observer.guardian.co.uk/worldview/story/0,11581,845725,00.html). The al Qaeda letter was released in conjunction with the release of an audio message from Bin Ladin himself.

15. Ibid.

16. See *Arab Human Development Report 2003* (United Nations, 2003), a report prepared by Arabs that examines not only standard statistical data but also more sensitive social indicators recently identified by the Nobel Prize–winning economist Amartya Sen. It says little, however, about the political dimensions of economic and social trends. See Mark LeVine, "The UN Arab Human Development Report: A Critique," *Middle East Report,* July 26, 2002 (online at www.merip.org/mero/mer0072602.html).

17. President Bush, remarks at roundtable with Arab- and Muslim-American leaders, Sept. 10, 2002 (online at www.whitehouse.gov/news/releases/2002/09/20020910-7.html).

18. See, e.g., Intelligence report, interrogation of Zubaydah, Oct. 29, 2002; CIA analytic report, "Bin Ladin Terrorist Operations: Meticulous and Adaptable," CTC 00-40017CSH, Nov. 2, 2000.

57 "His" and "Her" Marriage

JESSIE BERNARD

Social scientists have found that men and women are not joined at the hip by a wedding ceremony. Rather, their subsequent lives differ in terms of gender roles, power, and ways of communicating. Bernard was among the first sociologists to point out that marriage has a different meaning for women and men. As this selection shows, spouses rarely define reality in the same way, even with regard to simple routines such as sweeping the floor or mowing the lawn.

. . . [T]here is by now a very considerable body of well-authenticated research to show that there really are two marriages in every marital union, and that they do not always coincide.

"HIS" AND "HER" MARRIAGES

. . . [T]he differences in the marriages of husbands and wives have come under the careful scrutiny of a score of researchers. They have found that when they ask husbands and wives identical questions about the union, they often get quite different replies. There is

Source: From *The Future of Marriage* by Jessie Bernard. Copyright © by Jessie Bernard. Reprinted with permission.

Edward Hopper (1882–1967), *Room in New York,* 1932. Oil on Canvas, 29 × 36 in. Sheldon Memorial Art Gallery, University of Nebraska-Lincoln. F. M. Hall Collection, 1932. H-166.

usually agreement on the number of children they have and a few other such verifiable items, although not, for example, on length of premarital acquaintance and of engagement, on age at marriage, and interval between marriage and birth of first child. Indeed, with respect to even such basic components of the marriage as frequency of sexual relations, social interaction, household tasks, and decision making, they seem to be reporting on different marriages. As, I think, they are.

In the area of sexual relations, for example, Kinsey and his associates found different responses in from one- to two-thirds of the couples they studied. Kinsey interpreted these differences in terms of selective perception.

In the generation he was studying, husbands wanted sexual relations oftener than the wives did, thus "the females may be overestimating the actual frequencies" and "the husbands . . . are probably underestimating the frequencies." The differences might also have been vestiges of the probable situation earlier in the marriage when the desired frequency of sexual relations was about six to seven times greater among husbands than among wives. This difference may have become so impressed on the spouses that it remained in their minds even after the difference itself had disappeared or even been reversed. In a sample of happily married, middle-class couples a generation later, Harold Feldman found that both spouses attributed to their mates more influence in the area of sex than they did to themselves.

Companionship, as reflected in talking together, he found, was another area where differences showed up. Replies differed on three-fourths of all the items studied, including the topics talked about, the amount of time spent talking with each other, and which partner initiated conversation. Both partners claimed that whereas they talked more about topics of interest to their mates, their mates initiated conversations about topics primarily of interest to themselves. Harold Feldman concluded that projection in terms of needs was distorting even simple, everyday events, and lack of communication was permitting the distortions to continue. It seemed to him that "if these sex differences can occur so often among these generally well-satisfied couples, it would not be surprising to find even less consensus and more distortion in other less satisfied couples."

Although, by and large, husbands and wives tend to become more alike with age, in this study of middle-class couples, differences increased with length of marriage rather than decreased, as one might logically have expected. More couples in the later than in the earlier years, for example, had differing pictures in their heads about how often they laughed together, discussed together, exchanged ideas, or worked together on projects, and about how well things were going between them.

The special nature of sex and the amorphousness of social interaction help to explain why differences in response might occur. But household tasks? They are fairly objective and clear-cut and not all that emotion-laden. Yet even here there are his-and-her versions. Since the division of labor in the household is becoming increasingly an issue in marriage, the uncovering of differing replies in this area is especially relevant. Hard as it is to believe, Granbois and Willett tell us that more than half of the partners in one sample disagreed on who kept track of money and bills. On the question, who mows the lawn? more than a fourth disagreed. Even family income was not universally agreed on.

These differences about sexual relations, companionship, and domestic duties tell us a great deal about the two marriages. But power or decision making can cover all aspects of a relationship. The question of who makes decisions or who exercises power has therefore attracted a great deal of research attention. If we were interested in who really had the power or who really made the decisions, the research would be hopeless. Would it be possible to draw any conclusion from a situation in which both partners agree that the husband ordered the wife to make all the decisions? Still, an enormous literature documents the quest of researchers for answers to the question of marital power. The major contribution it has made has been to reveal the existence of differences in replies between husbands and wives.

The presence of such inconsistent replies did not at first cause much concern. The researchers apologized for them but interpreted them as due to methodological inadequacies; if only they could find a better way to approach the problem, the differences would disappear. Alternatively, the use of only the wife's responses, which were more easily available, was justified on the grounds that differences in one direction between the partners in one marriage compensated for differences in another direction between the partners in another marriage and thus canceled them out. As, indeed, they did. For when Granbois and Willett, two market researchers, analyzed the replies of husbands and wives separately, the overall picture was in fact the same for both wives and husbands. Such canceling out of differences in the total sample, however, concealed almost as much as it revealed about the individual couples who composed it. Granbois and Willett concluded, as Kinsey had earlier, that the "discrepancies . . . reflect differing perceptions on the part of responding partners." And this was the heart of the matter.

Differing reactions to common situations, it should be noted, are not at all uncommon. They are recognized in the folk wisdom embedded in the story of the blind men all giving different replies to questions on the nature of the elephant. One of the oldest experiments in juridical psychology demonstrates how different the statements of witnesses of the same act can be. Even in laboratory studies, it takes intensive training of raters to make it possible for them to arrive at agreement on the behavior they observe.

It has long been known that people with different backgrounds see things differently. We know, for example, that poor children perceive coins as larger than do children from more affluent homes. Boys and girls perceive differently. A good deal of the foundation for projective tests rests on the different ways in which individuals see identical stimuli. And this perception—or, as the sociologists put it, definition of the situation—is reality for them. In this sense, the realities of the husband's marriage are different from those of the wife's.

Finally, one of the most perceptive of the researchers, Constantina Safilios-Rothschild, asked the crucial question: Was what they were getting, even with the best research techniques, family sociology or wives' family sociology? She answered her own question: What the researchers who relied on wives' replies exclusively were reporting on was the wife's marriage. The husband's was not necessarily the same. There were, in fact, two marriages present:

One explanation of discrepancies between the responses of husbands and wives may be the possibility of two "realities," the husband's subjective reality and the wife's subjective reality—two perspectives which do not always coincide. Each spouse perceives "facts" and situations differently according to his own needs, values, attitudes, and beliefs. An "objective" reality could possibly exist only in the trained observer's evaluation, if it does exist at all.

Interpreting the different replies of husbands and wives in terms of selective perception, projection of needs, values, attitudes, and beliefs, or different definitions of the situation, by no means renders them trivial or incidental or justifies dismissing or ignoring them. They are, rather, fundamental for an understanding of the two marriages, his and hers, and we ignore them at the peril of serious misunderstanding of marriage, present as well as future.

IS THERE AN OBJECTIVE REALITY IN MARRIAGE?

Whether or not husbands and wives perceive differently or define situations differently, still sexual relations are taking place, companionship is or is not occurring, tasks about the house are being performed, and decisions are being made every day by someone. In this sense, some sort of "reality" does exist. David Olson went to the laboratory to see if he could uncover it.

He first asked young couples expecting babies such questions as these: Which one of them would decide whether to buy insurance for the newborn child? Which one would decide the husband's part in diaper changing? Which one would decide whether the new mother would return to work or to school? When there were differences in the answers each gave individually on the questionnaire, he set up a situation in which together they had to arrive at a decision in his laboratory. He could then compare the results of the questionnaire with the results in the simulated situation. He found neither spouse's questionnaire response any more accurate than the other's; that is, neither conformed better to the behavioral "reality" of the laboratory than the other did.

The most interesting thing, however, was that husbands, as shown on their questionnaire response, perceived themselves as having more power than they actually did have in the laboratory "reality," and wives perceived that they had less. Thus, whereas three-fourths (73 percent) of the husbands overestimated their power in decision making, 70 percent of the wives underestimated theirs. Turk and Bell found similar results in Canada. Both spouses tend to attribute decision-making power to the one who has the "right" to make the decision. Their replies, that is, conform to the model of marriage that has characterized civilized mankind for millennia. It is this model rather than their own actual behavior that husbands and wives tend to perceive.

We are now zeroing in on the basic reality. We can remove the quotation marks. For there is, in fact, an objective reality in marriage. It is a reality that resides in the cultural—legal, moral, and conventional—prescriptions and proscriptions and, hence, expectations that constitute marriage. It is the reality that is reflected in the minds of the spouses themselves. The differences between the marriages of husbands and of wives are structural realities, and it is these structural differences that constitute the basis for the different psychological realities.

THE AUTHORITY STRUCTURE OF MARRIAGE

Authority is an institutional phenomenon; it is strongly bound up with faith. It must be believed in; it cannot be enforced unless it also has power. Authority resides not in the person on whom it is conferred by the group or society, but in the recognition and acceptance it elicits in others. Power, on the other hand, may dispense with the prop of authority. It may take the form of the ability to coerce or to veto; it is often personal, charismatic, not institutional. This kind of personal power is self-enforcing. It does not require shoring up by access to force. In fact, it may even operate subversively. A woman with this kind of

power may or may not know that she possesses it. If she does know she has it, she will probably disguise her exercise of it.

In the West, the institutional structure of marriage has invested the husband with authority and backed it by the power of church and state. The marriages of wives have thus been officially dominated by the husband. Hebrew, Christian, and Islamic versions of deity were in complete accord on this matter. The laws, written or unwritten, religious or civil, which have defined the marital union have been based on male conceptions, and they have undergirded male authority.

Adam came first. Eve was created to supply him with companionship, not vice versa. And God himself had told her that Adam would rule over her; her wishes had to conform to his. The New Testament authors agreed. Women were created for men, not men for women; women were therefore commanded to be obedient. If they wanted to learn anything, let them ask their husbands in private, for it was shameful for them to talk in the church. They should submit themselves to their husbands, because husbands were superior to wives; and wives should be as subject to their husbands as the church was to Christ. Timothy wrapped it all up: "Let the woman learn in silence with all subjection. But I suffer not a woman to teach, nor to usurp authority over the man, but to be in silence." Male Jews continued for millennia to thank God three times a day that they were not women. And the Koran teaches women that men are naturally their superiors because God made them that way; naturally, their own status is one of subordination.

The state as well as the church had the same conception of marriage, assigning to the husband and father control over his dependents, including his wife. Sometimes this power was well-nigh absolute, as in the case of the Roman *patria potestas*—or the English common law, which flatly said, "The husband and wife are as one and that one is the husband." There are rules still lingering today with the same, though less extreme, slant. Diane B. Schulder has summarized the legal framework of the wife's marriage as laid down in the common law:

The legal responsibilities of a wife are to live in the home established by her husband; to perform the domestic chores (cleaning, cooking, washing, etc.) necessary to help maintain that home; to care for her husband and children. . . . A husband may force his wife to have sexual relations as long as his demands are reasonable and her health is not endangered. . . . The law allows a wife to take a job if she wishes. However, she must see that her domestic chores are completed, and, if there are children, that they receive proper care during her absence.

A wife is not entitled to payment for household work; and some jurisdictions in the United States expressly deny payment for it. In some states, the wife's earnings are under the control of her husband, and in four, special court approval and in some cases husband's consent are required if a wife wishes to start a business of her own.

The male counterpart to these obligations includes that of supporting his wife. He may not disinherit her. She has a third interest in property owned by him, even if it is held in his name only. Her name is required when he sells property.

Not only divine and civil law but also rules of etiquette have defined authority as a husband's prerogative. One of the first books published in England was a *Boke of Good Manners,* translated from the French of Jacques Le Grand in 1487, which included a chapter on "How Wymmen Ought to Be Gouerned." The thirty-third rule of Plutarch's *Rules for Husbands and Wives* was that women should obey their husbands; if they "try to rule over their husbands they make a worse mistake than the husbands do who let themselves be ruled." The husband's rule should not, of course, be brutal; he should not rule his wife "as a master does his chattel, but as the soul governs the body, by feeling with her and being linked to her by affection." Wives, according to Richard Baxter, a seventeenth-century English divine, had to obey even a wicked husband, the only exception being that a wife need not obey a husband if he ordered her to change her religion. But, again, like Plutarch, Baxter warned that the husband should love his wife; his authority should not be so coercive or so harsh as to destroy love. Among his twelve rules for carrying out the duties of conjugal love, however, was one to the effect that love must not be so imprudent as to destroy authority.

As late as the nineteenth century, Tocqueville noted that in the United States the ideals of democracy did not apply between husbands and wives:

Nor have the Americans ever supposed that one consequence of democratic principles is the subversion of marital power, or the confusion of the natural authorities in families. They hold that every association must have a head in order to accomplish its objective, and that the natural head of the conjugal association is man. They do not therefore deny him the right of directing his partner; and they maintain, that in the smaller association of husband and wife, as well as in the great social community, the object of democracy is to regulate and legalize the powers which are necessary, not to subvert all power.

This opinion is not peculiar to men and contested by women; I never observed that the women of America consider conjugal authority as an unfortunate usurpation [by men] of their rights, nor that they thought themselves degraded by submitting to it. It appears to me, on the contrary, that they attach a sort of pride to the voluntary surrender of their own will, and make it their boast to bend themselves to the yoke, not to shake it off.

The point here is not to document once more the specific ways (religious, legal, moral, traditional) in which male authority has been built into the marital union—that has been done a great many times—but merely to illustrate how different (structurally or "objectively" as well as perceptually or "subjectively") the wife's marriage has actually been from the husband's throughout history.

THE SUBVERSIVENESS OF NATURE

The rationale for male authority rested not only on biblical grounds but also on nature or natural law, on the generally accepted natural superiority of men. For nothing could be more self-evident than that the patriarchal conception of marriage, in which the husband was unequivocally the boss, was natural, resting as it did on the unchallenged superiority of males.

Actually, nature, if not deity, is subversive. Power, or the ability to coerce or to veto, is widely distributed in both sexes, among women as well as among men. And whatever the theoretical or conceptual picture may have been, the actual, day-by-day relationships between husbands and wives have been determined by the men and women themselves. All that the institutional machinery could do was to confer authority; it could not create personal power, for such power cannot be conferred, and women can generate it as well as men. . . . Thus, keeping women in their place has been a universal problem, in spite of the fact that almost without exception institutional patterns give men positions of superiority over them.

If the sexes were, in fact, categorically distinct, with no overlapping, so that no man was inferior to any woman or any woman superior to any man, or vice versa, marriage would have been a great deal simpler. But there is no such sharp cleavage between the sexes except with respect to the presence or absence of certain organs. With all the other characteristics of each sex, there is greater or less overlapping, some men being more "feminine" than the average woman and some women more "masculine" than the average man. The structure of families and societies reflects the positions assigned to men and women. The bottom stratum includes children, slaves, servants, and outcasts of all kinds, males as well as females. As one ascends the structural hierarchy, the proportion of males increases, so that at the apex there are only males.

When societies fall back on the lazy expedient—as all societies everywhere have done—of allocating the rewards and punishments of life on the basis of sex, they are bound to create a host of anomalies, square pegs in round holes, societal misfits. Roles have been allocated on the basis of sex which did not fit a sizable number of both sexes—women, for example, who chafed at subordinate status and men who could not

master superordinate status. The history of the relations of the sexes is replete with examples of such misfits. Unless a modus vivendi is arrived at, unhappy marriages are the result.

There is, though, a difference between the exercise of power by husbands and by wives. When women exert power, they are not rewarded; they may even be punished. They are "deviant." Turk and Bell note that "wives who . . . have the greater influence in decision making may experience guilt over this fact." They must therefore dissemble to maintain the illusion, even to themselves, that they are subservient. They tend to feel less powerful than they are because they *ought* to be.

When men exert power, on the other hand, they are rewarded; it is the natural expression of authority. They feel no guilt about it. The prestige of authority goes to the husband whether or not he is actually the one who exercises it. It is not often even noticed when the wife does so. She sees to it that it is not.

There are two marriages, then, in every marital union, his and hers. And his . . . is better than hers. The questions, therefore, are these: In what direction will they change in the future? Will one change more than the other? Will they tend to converge or to diverge? Will the future continue to favor the husband's marriage? And if the wife's marriage is improved, will it cost the husband's anything, or will his benefit along with hers?

CRITICAL-THINKING QUESTIONS

1. What evidence does Bernard offer to support her conclusion that there are "his" and "her" marriages rather than "our" marriage?
2. Does the traditional inequality of men and women support or undermine marital roles? How?
3. What are the consequences for marriage of the gradual process by which the two sexes are becoming more socially equal?

58 The Mommy Myth

SUSAN J. DOUGLAS AND MEREDITH W. MICHAELS

Many people feel that women have many more choices today than in the past: They can earn a college degree, forge rewarding careers, and successfully juggle work and domestic responsibilities. In contrast, Susan Douglas and Meredith Michaels contend that the media's obsession with "celebrity moms" and mythical images of motherhood make most mothers feel inadequate and unsure of themselves.

It's 5:22 P.M. You're in the grocery checkout line. Your three-year-old is writhing on the floor, screaming, because you have refused to buy her a Teletubby pinwheel. Your six-year-old is whining, repeatedly, in a voice that could saw through cement, "But mommy, puleeze, puleeze" because you have not bought him the latest "Lunchables," which features, as the four food groups, Cheetos, a Snickers, Cheez Whiz, and Twizzlers. Your teenager, who has not spoken a single word in the past four days except, "You've ruined my life," followed by "Everyone else has one," is out in the car, sulking, with the new rap-metal band Piss on the Parentals blasting through the headphones of a Discman.

To distract yourself, and to avoid the glares of other shoppers who have already deemed you the worst mother in America, you leaf through *People*

magazine. Inside, Uma Thurman gushes "Motherhood Is Sexy."[1] Moving on to *Good Housekeeping,* Vanna White says of her child, "When I hear his cry at six-thirty in the morning, I have a smile on my face, and I'm not an early riser."[2] Another unexpected source of earth-mother wisdom, the newly maternal Pamela Lee, also confides to *People,* "I just love getting up with him in the middle of the night to feed him or soothe him."[3] Brought back to reality by stereophonic whining, you indeed feel as sexy as Rush Limbaugh in a thong.

You drag your sorry ass home. Now, if you were a "good" mom, you'd joyfully empty the shopping bags and transform the process of putting the groceries away into a fun game your kids love to play (upbeat Raffi songs would provide a lilting soundtrack). Then, while you steamed the broccoli and poached the chicken breasts in Vouvray and Evian water, you and the kids would also be doing jigsaw puzzles in the shape of the United Arab Emirates so they learned some geography. Your cheerful teenager would say, "Gee, Mom, you gave me the best advice on that last homework assignment."

Reprinted by permission of The Free Press, a Division of Simon & Schuster Adult Publishing Group, from *The Mommy Myth: The Idealization of Motherhood and How It Has Undermined Women* by Susan J. Douglas and Meredith W. Michaels. Copyright 2004 by Susan Douglas and Meredith W. Michaels. All rights reserved.

When your husband arrives, he is so overcome with admiration for how well you do it all that he looks lovingly into your eyes, kisses you, and presents you with a diamond anniversary bracelet. He then announces that he has gone on flex time for the next two years so that he can split childcare duties with you fifty-fifty. The children, chattering away happily, help set the table, and then eat their broccoli. After dinner, you all go out and stencil the driveway with autumn leaves.

But maybe this sounds slightly more familiar. "I won't unpack the groceries! You can't make me," bellows your child as he runs to his room, knocking down a lamp on the way. "Eewee—gross out!" he yells and you discover that the cat has barfed on his bed. You have fifteen minutes to make dinner because there's a school play in half an hour. While the children fight over whether to watch *Hot Couples* or people eating larvae on *Fear Factor,* you zap some Prego spaghetti sauce in the microwave and boil some pasta. *You* set the table. "Mommy, Mommy, Sam losted my hamster," your daughter wails. Your ex-husband calls to say he won't be taking the kids this weekend after all because his new wife, Buffy, twenty-three, has to go on a modeling shoot in Virgin Gorda for the *Sports Illustrated* swimsuit issue, and "she really needs me with her." You go to the TV room to discover the kids watching transvestites punching each other out on *Jerry Springer.* . . .

If you're like us—mothers with an attitude problem—you may be getting increasingly irritable about this chasm between the ridiculous, honey-hued ideals of perfect motherhood in the mass media and the reality of mothers' everyday lives. And you may also be worn down by media images that suggest that however much you do for and love your kids, it is never enough. The love we feel for our kids, the joyful times we have with them, are repackaged into unattainable images of infinite patience and constant adoration so that we fear, as Kristin van Ogtrop put it movingly in *The Bitch in the House,* "I will love my children, but my love for them will always be imperfect."[4]

From the moment we get up until the moment we collapse in bed at night, the media are out there, calling to us, yelling, "Hey you! Yeah, you! Are you *really* raising your kids right?" Whether it's the cover of *Redbook* or *Parents* demanding "Are You a Sensitive Mother?" "Is Your Child Eating Enough?" "Is Your Baby Normal?" (and exhorting us to enter its pages and have great sex at 25, 35, or 85), the nightly news warning us about missing children, a movie trailer hyping a film about a cross-dressing dad who's way more fun than his stinky, careerist wife (*Mrs. Doubtfire*), or Dr. Laura telling some poor mother who works forty hours a week that she's neglectful, the siren song blending seduction and accusation is there all the time. Mothers are subjected to an onslaught of beatific imagery, romantic fantasies, self-righteous sermons, psychological warnings, terrifying movies about losing their children, even more terrifying news stories about abducted and abused children, and totally unrealistic advice about how to be the most perfect and revered mom in the neighborhood, maybe even in the whole country. (Even *Working Mother*—which should have known better—had a "Working Mother of the Year Contest." When Jill Kirschenbaum became the editor in 2001, one of the first things she did was dump this feature, noting that motherhood should not be a "competitive sport.") We are urged to be fun-loving, spontaneous, and relaxed, yet, at the same time, scared out of our minds that our kids could be killed at any moment. No wonder 81 percent of women in a recent poll said it's harder to be a mother now than it was twenty or thirty years ago, and 56 percent felt mothers were doing a worse job today than mothers back then.[5] Even mothers who deliberately avoid TV and magazines, or who pride themselves on seeing through them, have trouble escaping the standards of perfection, and the sense of threat, that the media ceaselessly atomize into the air we breathe.

We are both mothers, and we adore our kids—for example, neither one of us has ever locked them up in dog crates in the basement (although we have, of course, been tempted). The smell of a new baby's head, tucking a child in at night, receiving homemade, hand-scrawled birthday cards, heart-to-hearts with a teenager after a date, seeing *them* become parents—these are joys parents treasure. But like increasing numbers of women, we are fed up with the myth—shamelessly hawked by the media—that motherhood is eternally fulfilling and rewarding, that it is *always* the best and most important thing you do, that there is only a narrowly prescribed way to do it right, and that if you don't love each and every second of it there's something really wrong with you. At the same time, the two of us still have been complete suckers, buying those black-and-white mobiles that allegedly turn your baby into Einstein Jr., feeling guilty for sending in store-bought cookies to the class bake sale instead of homemade like the "good" moms, staying up until 2:30 A.M. making our kids' Halloween costumes, driving to the Multiplex 18 at midnight to pick up teenagers so they won't miss the latest outing with their friends. We know that building a scale model of Versailles out of mashed potatoes may not be quite as crucial to good mothering as *Martha Stewart Living* suggests. Yet here we are, cowed by that most tyrannical of our cultural icons, Perfect Mom. So, like millions of women, we buy into these absurd ideals at the same time that we resent them and think they are utterly ridiculous and oppressive. After all, our parents—the group Tom Brokaw has labeled "the greatest generation"—had parents who whooped them on the behind, screamed stuff at them like "I'll tear you limb from limb," told them babies came from cabbage patches, never drove them four hours to a soccer match, and yet they seemed to have nonetheless saved the western world.

This book is about the rise in the media of what we are calling the "new momism": the insistence that no woman is truly complete or fulfilled unless she has kids, that women remain the best primary caretakers of children, and that to be a remotely decent mother, a woman has to devote her entire physical, psychological, emotional, and intellectual being, 24/7, to her children. The new momism is a highly romanticized and yet demanding view of motherhood in which the standards for success are impossible to meet. The term "momism" was initially coined by the journalist Philip Wylie in his highly influential 1942 bestseller *Generation of Vipers,* and it was a very derogatory term. Drawing from Freud (who else?), Wylie attacked the mothers of America as being so smothering, overprotective, and invested in their kids, especially their sons, that they turned them into dysfunctional, sniveling weaklings, maternal slaves chained to the apron strings, unable to fight for their country or even stand on their own two feet.[6] We seek to reclaim this term, rip it from its misogynistic origins, and apply it to an ideology that has snowballed since the 1980s and seeks to return women to the Stone Age.

The "new momism" is a set of ideals, norms, and practices, most frequently and powerfully represented in the media, that seem on the surface to celebrate motherhood, but which in reality promulgate standards of perfection that are beyond your reach. The new momism is the direct descendant and latest version of what Betty Friedan famously labeled the "feminine mystique" back in the 1960s. The new momism *seems* to be much more hip and progressive than the feminine mystique, because now, of course, mothers can and do work outside the home, have their own ambitions and money, raise kids on their own, or freely choose to stay at home with their kids rather than being forced to. And unlike the feminine mystique, the notion that women should be subservient to men is not an accepted tenet of the new momism. Central to the new momism, in fact, is the feminist insistence that woman have choices, that they are active agents in control of their own destiny, that they have autonomy. But here's where the distortion of feminism occurs. The only truly enlightened choice to make as a woman, the one that proves, first, that you are a "real" woman, and second, that you are a decent, worthy one, is to become a "mom" and to bring to child rearing a combination of selflessness and

professionalism that would involve the cross clon-
ing of Mother Teresa with Donna Shalala. Thus the
new momism is deeply contradictory: It both
draws from and repudiates feminism.

The fulcrum of the new momism is the rise of
a really pernicious ideal in the late twentieth century that the sociologist Sharon Hays has perfectly labeled "intensive mothering."[7] It is no
longer okay, as it was even during the heyday of
June Cleaver, to let (or make) your kids walk to
school, tell them to stop bugging you and go outside and play, or, God forbid, serve them something like Tang, once the preferred beverage of
the astronauts, for breakfast. Of course many of
our mothers baked us cookies, served as Brownie
troop leaders, and chaperoned class trips to Elf
Land. But today, the standards of good motherhood are really over the top. And they've gone
through the roof at the same time that there has
been a real decline in leisure time for most Americans.[8] The yuppie work ethic of the 1980s, which
insisted that even when you were off the job you
should be working—on your abs, your connections, your portfolio, whatever—absolutely conquered motherhood. As the actress Patricia Heaton
jokes in *Motherhood & Hollywood,* now mothers
are supposed to "sneak echinacea" into the "freshly
squeezed, organically grown orange juice" we've
made for our kids and teach them to "download
research for their kindergarten report on 'My
Family Tree—The Early Roman Years.'"[9]

Intensive mothering insists that mothers acquire
professional-level skills such as those of a thera-
pist, pediatrician ("Dr. Mom"), consumer products
safety inspector, and teacher, and that they lavish
every ounce of physical vitality they have, the
monetary equivalent of the gross domestic product
of Australia, and, most of all, every single bit of
their emotional, mental, and psychic energy on
their kids. We must learn to put on the masquerade
of the doting, self-sacrificing mother and wear it
at all times. With intensive mothering, everyone
watches us, we watch ourselves and other mothers,
and we watch ourselves watching ourselves. How
many of you know someone who swatted her child

on the behind in a supermarket because he was,
say, opening a pack of razor blades in the toiletries
aisle, only to be accosted by someone she never
met who threatened to put her up on child-abuse
charges? In 1997, one mother was arrested for child
neglect because she left a ten-year-old and a four-
year-old home for an hour and a half while she
went to the supermarket.[10] Motherhood has become
a psychological police state.

Intensive mothering is the ultimate female
Olympics: We are all in powerful competition with
each other, in constant danger of being trumped by
the mom down the street, or in the magazine we're
reading. The competition isn't just over who's a
good mother—it's over who's the best. We compete
with each other; we compete with ourselves. The
best mothers always put their kids' needs before
their own, period. The best mothers are the main
caregivers. For the best mothers, their kids are the
center of the universe. The best mothers always
smile. They always understand. They are never
tired. They never lose their temper. They never say,
"Go to the neighbor's house and play while
Mommy has a beer." Their love for their children is
boundless, unflagging, flawless, total. Mothers
today cannot just respond to their kids' needs, they
must predict them—and with the telepathic accuracy of Houdini. They must memorize verbatim the
books of all the child-care experts and know which
approaches are developmentally appropriate at different ages. They are supposed to treat their two-
year-olds with "respect." If mothers screw up and
fail to do this on any given day, they should apolo-
gize to their kids, because any misstep leads to permanent psychological and/or physical damage.
Anyone who questions whether this is *the* best and
the necessary way to raise kids is an insensitive, ignorant brute. This is just common sense, right?[11]

The new momism has become unavoidable,
unless you raise your kids in a yurt on the tundra,
for one basic reason: Motherhood became one of
the biggest media obsessions of the last three
decades, exploding especially in the mid-1980s
and continuing unabated to the present. Women
have been deluged by an ever-thickening mudslide

of maternal media advice, programming, and marketing that powerfully shapes how we mothers feel about our relationships with our own kids and, indeed, how we feel about ourselves. These media representations have changed over time, cutting mothers some real slack in the 1970s, and then increasingly closing the vise in the late 1980s and after, despite important rebellions by Roseanne and others. People don't usually notice that motherhood has been such a major media fixation, revolted or hooked as they've been over the years by other media excesses like the O. J. Simpson trials, the Lewinsky-Clinton imbroglio, the Elian Gonzalez carnival, *Survivor,* or the 2002 Washington-area sniper killings in which "profilers" who knew as much as SpongeBob SquarePants nonetheless got on TV to tell us what the killer was thinking.

But make no mistake about it—mothers and motherhood came under unprecedented media surveillance in the 1980s and beyond. And since the media traffic in extremes, in anomalies—the rich, the deviant, the exemplary, the criminal, the gorgeous—they emphasize fear and dread on the one hand and promote impossible ideals on the other. In the process, *Good Housekeeping, People,* E!, Lifetime, *Entertainment Tonight,* and *NBC Nightly News* built an interlocking, cumulative image of the dedicated, doting "mom" versus the delinquent, bad "mother." There have been, since the early 1980s, several overlapping media frameworks that have fueled the new momism. First, the media warned mothers about the external threats to their kids from abductors and the like. Then the "family values" crowd made it clear that supporting the family was not part of the government's responsibility. By the late 1980s, stories about welfare and crack mothers emphasized the internal threats to children from mothers themselves. And finally, the media brouhaha over the "Mommy Track" reaffirmed that businesses could not or would not budge much to accommodate the care of children. Together, and over time, these frameworks produced a prevailing common sense that only you, the individual mother, are responsible for your

child's welfare: The buck stops with you, period, and you'd better be a superstar.

Of course there has been a revolution in fatherhood over the past thirty years, and millions of men today tend to the details of child rearing in ways their own fathers rarely did. Feminism prompted women to insist that men change diapers and pack school lunches, but it also gave men permission to become more involved with their kids in ways they have found to be deeply satisfying. And between images of cuddly, New Age dads with babies asleep on their chests (think old Folger's ads), movies about hunky men and a baby (or clueless ones who shrink the kids), and sensational news stories about "deadbeat dads" and men who beat up their sons' hockey coaches, fathers too have been subject to a media "dad patrol." But it pales in comparison to the new momism. After all, a dad who knows the name of his kids' pediatrician and reads them stories at night is still regarded as a saint; a mother who doesn't is a sinner.

Once you identify it, you see the new momism everywhere. The recent spate of magazines for "parents" (i.e., mothers) bombard the anxiety-induced mothers of America with reassurances that they can (after a $100,000 raise and a personality transplant) produce bright, motivated, focused, fun-loving, sensitive, cooperative, confident, contented kids just like the clean, obedient ones on the cover. The frenzied hypernatalism of the women's magazines alone (and that includes *People, Us,* and *InStyle*), with their endless parade of perfect, "sexy" celebrity moms who've had babies, adopted babies, been to sperm banks, frozen their eggs for future use, hatched the frozen eggs, had more babies, or adopted a small Tibetan village, all to satisfy their "baby lust," is enough to make you want to get your tubes tied. (These profiles always insist that celebs all love being "moms" much, much more than they do their work, let alone being rich and famous, and that they'd spend every second with their kids if they didn't have that pesky blockbuster movie to finish.) Women without children, wherever they look, are besieged by ridiculously romantic images that insist that having children is the most joyous, fulfilling experience in the galaxy, and if they don't have a small drooling creature who likes to stick forks in electrical outlets, they are leading bankrupt, empty lives. Images of ideal moms and their miracle babies are everywhere, like leeches in the Amazon, impossible to dislodge and sucking us dry.

There is also the ceaseless outpouring of books on toilet training, separating one sibling's fist from another sibling's eye socket, expressing breast milk while reading a legal brief, helping preschoolers to "own" their feelings, getting Joshua to do his homework, and raising teenage boys so they become Sensitive New Age Guys instead of rooftop snipers or Chippendale dancers. Over eight hundred books on motherhood were published between 1970 and 2000; only twenty-seven of these came out between 1970 and 1980, so the real avalanche happened in the past twenty years.[12] We've learned about the perils of "the hurried child" and "hyperparenting," in which we schedule our kids with so many enriching activities that they make the secretary of state look like a couch spud. But the unhurried child probably plays too much Nintendo and is out in the garage building pipe bombs, so you can't underschedule them either.

Then there's the Martha Stewartization of America, in which we are meant to sculpt the carrots we put in our kids' lunches into the shape of peonies and build funhouses for them in the backyard; this has raised the bar to even more ridiculous levels than during the June Cleaver era. Most women know that there was a massive public relations campaign during World War II to get women into the workforce, and then one right after the war to get them to go back to the kitchen. But we haven't fully focused on the fact that another, more subtle, sometimes unintentional, more long-term propaganda campaign began in the 1980s to redomesticate the women of America through motherhood.[13] Why aren't all the mothers of America leaning out their windows yelling "I'm mad as hell and I'm not going to take it anymore"?

CRITICAL-THINKING QUESTIONS

1. What is the "new momism"? According to Douglas and Michaels, why has the new momism been unhealthy for women, men, and children? On the other hand, how does the new momism benefit men and children?

2. Think about the television programs you watch and the ads you see in magazines. How many portray mothers realistically—especially working mothers who aren't "celebrity moms"?

3. Do you think that the authors' views are wrong or offensive because they trivialize motherhood? Or do you agree with Douglas and Michaels that we tend to worship an unrealistic image of the "perfect mother"?

NOTES

1. *People,* September 21, 1998.

2. *Good Housekeeping,* January 1995.

3. *People,* July 8, 1996.

4. Kristin van Ogtrop, "Attila the Honey I'm Home," *The Bitch in the House* (New York: William Morrow, 2002), p. 169.

5. "Motherhood Today—A Tougher Job, Less Ably Done," The Pew Research Center for the People & the Press, March 1997.

6. Philip Wylie, *Generation of Vipers* (New York: Holt, Rinehart and Winston, 1942). See also Ruth Feldstein's excellent discussion of momism in *Motherhood in Black and White: Race and Sex in American Liberalism, 1930–1965* (Ithaca: Cornell University Press, 2000), especially chapter 2.

7. Hays's book is must reading for all mothers, and we are indebted to her analysis of intensive mothering, from which this discussion draws. Sharon Hays, *The Cultural Contradictions of Motherhood* (New Haven: Yale University Press, 1996), p. 4.

8. For an account of the decline in leisure time see Juliet B. Schorr, *The Overworked American* (New York: Basic Books, 1992).

9. Patricia Heaton, *Motherhood & Hollywood* (New York: Villard Books, 2002), pp. 48–49.

10. See Katha Pollitt's terrific piece "Killer Moms, Working Nannies" in *The Nation,* November 24, 1997, p. 9.

11. Hays, pp. 4–9.

12. Based on an On-line Computer Library Center, Inc., search under the word *motherhood,* from 1970–2000.

13. Susan Faludi, in her instant classic *Backlash,* made this point, too, but the book focused on the various and multiple forms of backlash, and we will be focusing only on the use of motherhood here.

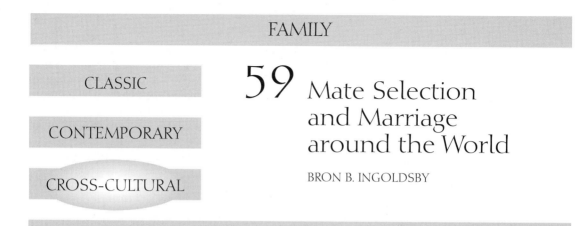

FAMILY

CLASSIC

CONTEMPORARY

CROSS-CULTURAL

59 Mate Selection and Marriage around the World

BRON B. INGOLDSBY

The institution of marriage is very popular throughout the world. Yet, how mates are chosen varies considerably from one culture to another. As Bron B. Ingoldsby shows, free-choice mate selection—which is common in Western countries—is not how couples have been paired with their prospective spouses in most other societies.

MATE SELECTION PROCEDURES

Historically, there have been three general approaches to choosing one's mate: marriage by capture, marriage by arrangement, and free-choice mate selection. I examine each of them in turn.

Marriage by Capture

Although it has probably never been the usual method of obtaining a wife, men have taken women by force in many times and places. This typically occurred in patriarchal societies in which women were often considered property. Often women were seized as part of the spoils of war, and other times a specific woman was forced into marriage because the man wanted her and could not afford the brideprice or obtain the permission of her parents. The capture and marriage of a woman was legal in England until the reign

Source: "Mate Selection and Marriage," by Bron B. Ingoldsby in *Families in Multicultural Perspective,* eds. by Bron B. Ingoldsby and Suzanna Smith, pp. 143–5. Copyright © 1995 Guilford Press, NY. Reprinted by permission of Guilford Press.

of Henry VII, who made it a crime to abduct an heiress (Fielding, 1942).

The ancient Hebrews would seize wives under certain circumstances. A dramatic example is recounted in the Old Testament (Judges, chapter 21), where it was arranged for young women to be kidnapped from two different areas to serve as wives so that the tribe of Benjamin would not die out after a war that they had lost.

There was also a formal procedure for dealing with wives captured in warfare (Deuteronomy 21:10–14):

When thou goest forth to war against thine enemies, and the Lord thy God hath delivered them into thine hands, and thou has taken them captive, And seest among the captives a beautiful woman, and hast a desire unto her, that thou wouldest have her to thy wife; Then thou shalt bring her home to thine house; and she shall shave her head, and pare her nails; And she shall put the raiment of her captivity from off her, and shall remain in thine house, and bewail her father and her mother a full month: and after that thou shalt go in unto her, and be her husband, and she shall be thy wife. And it shall be, if thou have no delight in her, then thou shalt let her go whither she will; but thou shalt not sell her at all for money, thou shalt not make merchandise of her, because thou has humbled her.

At least she was given time to get used to the idea and never sold into slavery! Fielding (1942) cites a number of different cultures, including the Australian aborigines, who frequently resorted to marriage by capture in the recent past. The Yąnomamö of Venezuela (an Amazonian tribe) are reported (Peters, 1987) to use capture as one of their mate selection options. One village is often raided by another for the specific purpose of finding wives. If a man captures a young, attractive female, he must be careful as other men from his own village will try to steal her from him.

In the popular musical *Seven Brides for Seven Brothers,* the concept of marriage by capture is acted out, and one of the songs is based on the historical incident of the rape of the Sabine women. There are many cultures that still have remnants of the old practice of marriage by capture in their wedding ceremonies. In each of them, the match is prearranged, but the husband pretends to take his bride by force, and she feigns resistance.

One example is the Roro of New Guinea. On the wedding day, the groom's party surrounds the bride's home and acts out an assault on it. The bride attempts to run away but is caught. Then a sham battle ensues, with the bride's mother leading the way and crying at the loss of her daughter when she is taken off to the groom (Fielding, 1942).

Marriage by Arrangement

It appears that the most common method of mate selection has been by arrangement. Typically, the parents, often with the aid of certain relatives or professional matchmakers, have chosen the spouse for their child. This form of mate choice is more common when extended kin groups are strong and important. Essentially, marriage is seen as of group, rather than individual, importance, and economics is often the driving force rather than love between the principals.

Arranged marriages have been considered especially important for the rulers of kingdoms and other nobility. Care had to be taken to preserve bloodlines, enhance wealth, and resolve political issues. It is believed, for instance, that the majority of King Solomon's 700 wives and 300 concubines were acquired for the purpose of political alliances.

Stephens (1963) identifies four major reasons that determine mate choice in societies in which marriages are arranged. The first is *price*. The groom's family may need to pay for the bride, with either money or labor. In some cultures, the situation is reversed, with the bride's family paying a dowry to the husband. In other cases, there is a direct exchange, where both families make payments to each other or simply trade women for each other's sons.

The second consideration is *social status*. That is, the reputation of the family from which the spouse for one's child will come is very important. A third determinant is any *continuous marriage arrangement*. This refers to a set pattern for mate selection, which is carried on from generation to generation. For instance, cousin marriages are preferred in many societies.

The final criteria for mate choice are *sororate and levirate* arrangements, which refer to second marriages and tend to be based on brideprice obligations. These terms are more fully explained later in the [reading]. Stephens also notes nineteen societies (including, for example, some large ones such as China and Renaissance Europe) that have practiced child betrothals or child marriages. This means that the marriage is arranged before puberty and can even be worked out before the child is born.

In addition to marriage by capture, the Yąnomamö also practice variety within arranged marriages. The ideal match is between cross-cousins, and the majority of unions fall into this category. Most betrothals are made before the girl is three years of age. Men initiate these arrangements at about the time they become hunters, which is shortly after they turn fifteen. Another acceptable form of mate selection is sister exchange. Two unrelated single males wish to acquire wives and have sisters who are not promised to anyone, so they simply trade sisters (Peters, 1987).

Some societies have provided an "out" for couples who have strong personal preferences that go against the arrangement of their families. This is to permit elopement. Stephens (1963:200) gives this account of the Iban of Borneo:

When a young woman is in love with a man who is not acceptable to her parents, there is an old custom called *nunghop bui,* which permits him to carry her off to his own village. She will meet him by arrangement at the waterside, and step into his boat with a paddle in her hand, and both will pull away as fast as they can. If pursued he will stop every now and then to deposit some article of value on the bank, such as a gun, a jar, or a favor for the acceptance of her family, and when he has exhausted his resources he will leave his own sword. When the pursuers observe this they cease to follow, knowing he is cleared out. As soon as he reaches his own village he tidies up the house and spreads the mats, and when his pursuers arrive he gives them food to eat and toddy to drink, and sends them home satisfied. In the meanwhile he is left in possession of his wife.

Following is a detailed look at some of the specific mechanisms of arranged marriages.

Brideprice. Throughout much of human history, marriage has been seen as chiefly an economic transaction. As an old German saying goes, "It is not man that marries maid, but field marries field, vineyard marries vineyard, cattle marry cattle" (Tober, 1984: p.12). The purpose of a brideprice is to compensate the family of the bride for the loss of her services. It is extremely common and is indicative of the value of women in those societies. Stephens (1963) reports that Murdock's World Ethnographic Sample yields the following breakdown on marriage payments:

Brideprice—260 societies
Bride service—75 societies
Dowry—24 societies
Gift or woman exchange—31 societies
No marriage payment—152 societies

This means that in 62 percent of the world's societies, a man must pay in order to marry a woman. The price is usually paid in animals, shell money, or other valuable commodities and often exceeds one's annual income. Some cultures prefer payment in service, often many years of labor to the bride's parents, or at least permit it for suitors who cannot afford to pay in goods. One famous example from the Old Testament is that of Jacob, who labored seven years for each of Laban's two daughters, Leah and Rachel.

Dowry. The dowry appears to be an inducement for a man to marry a particular woman and therefore relieve her family of the financial burden of caring for her. Although relatively rare, it is a sign of a culture that places a low value on women. Actually, the key purpose of a dowry is probably to stabilize a marriage, because it is not given to the husband but is something that the bride brings with her into the marriage. For example, in Cyprus before the time of English influence, the expected dowry was often a house. If the husband divorced his wife or mistreated her and she left him, the dowry went with her. Like modern-day wedding gifts, or the bride's trousseau, it was an investment in the marriage and intended to reduce the chances of a breakup (Balswick, 1975).

The dowry has been around for a long time. The Babylonian code of Hammurabi (1955 B.C.E.) clearly stated that the wife's property stayed with her if her husband divorced her and passed on to her children when she died. Ancient Greece and Rome also considered the dowry to be essential in any honorable marriage (Fielding, 1942).

. . . [R]esearch in the southern Indian state of Kerala (Billig, 1992) differentiates between the traditional dowry and an actual "groomprice." Groomprice is money paid by the bride's family directly to the husband to use as he sees fit. In the 1950s and 1960s, rapid population growth resulted in more younger women looking for husbands a few (average of seven) years older than themselves. This surplus of potential brides increased the value of husbands. Popular revulsion for the groomprice has resulted in a decrease in the age difference (now five years), women lowering their social status expectations for their husband or increasing their own education, and a government outlawing of the practice.

Sororate and Levirate.   These terms refer to marriage practices designed to control remarriages after the death of the first spouse. In cultures that practice the sororate, a sister replaces a deceased wife. Assume that a man has paid a good brideprice for his wife but some time later she becomes ill and dies. He has lost his wife and the brideprice. Therefore, to make good on the original bargain, the parents who received the brideprice provide the man with a new wife. This new wife is an unmarried sister or other close relative of the first wife. Here we see how marriage is often more of an economic transaction than it is a personal relationship.

Much more widely practiced has been the levirate. Under this system, it is the husband who dies, and his wife must be married to a brother of the deceased man. There are various reasons for this practice. One is that the wife belonged to her husband as part of his property and as such would be inherited along with the other possessions by a near relative. Another is that it is presumed that women need someone to take care of them, and brothers-in-law (which is the meaning of the Latin word *levir*) should assume that responsibility. It has been reported that the levirate has been practiced by the New Caledonians, the Mongols, the Afghans, the Abyssinians, the Hebrews, and the Hindus, as well as certain Native American and African tribes (Fielding, 1942).

The chief reason that the Hindus and Hebrews practiced the levirate was religious and had to do with the importance of having a son in the family. Hindu men needed a son to perform certain sacrifices, so if a man died before having one, a boy born to his former wife and brother would carry out those ceremonies in his name (Fielding, 1942).

For the Hebrews, it was also important that every man have a son, so that his name would not die out. There was a ritualized penalty for men who refused to marry their brother's widow and rear a son in his name (Deuteronomy 25:7–9):

And if the man like not to take his brother's wife, then let his brother's wife go up to the gate unto the elders, and say, My husband's brother refuseth to raise up unto his brother a name in Israel, he will not perform the duty of my husband's brother. Then the elders of his city shall call him, and speak unto him: and if he stand to it, and say, I like not to take her; Then shall his brother's wife come in to him in the presence of the elders, and loose his shoe from his foot, and spit in his face, and shall answer and say, So shall it be done unto that man that will not build up his brother's house.

The punishment for refusing to practice the levirate used to be more severe than the above-quoted ritual. In Genesis, chapter 38, we read of Judah's son Onan and how he was killed by the Lord for refusing to impregnate his dead older brother's wife. The book of Ruth in the Old Testament is also an excellent example of how the levirate worked. It is an account of how Naomi has no more sons for her daughter-in-law Ruth to marry, so she arranges for another male relative, Boaz, to take on the responsibility.

Matchmaking.   There are various ways in which two young people can be brought together. Typically, the parents of both boys and girls will work out the details among themselves and then announce it to their children. The initial go-between in Turkey has been the boy's mother, who would inspect possibilities at the public baths and then give reports to her son (Tober, 1984). The popular musical *Fiddler on the Roof* is about father-arranged marriages. Often, hired go-betweens, or matchmakers, assist in making the arrangement. They might act as intermediaries between the families or suggest potential spouses. Checking for astrological or other religious signs and requirements could also be part of their job.

In the 1800s, bachelor pioneers in the American West would sometimes find a wife by ordering one from a mail-order catalog. Even today, many Asian families publish matrimonial want ads in search of a respectable spouse for their child (Tober, 1984). I recently found the following in the classified section of a Philippine newspaper:

FOREIGNER: video match a decent friendship marriage consultant office introducing a beautiful single educated Filipina view friendship to marriage.

LADIES: Australian European businessmen newly arrive[d] in town sincerely willing to meet decent Filipina view friendship to marriage. Ambassador Hotel suite 216.

Computer dating services in the United States, Japan, and elsewhere manifest the continued utility of professional matchmaking, even in societies in which the individuals involved make the final decisions themselves. There are also magazines designed for singles that include matrimonial or relationship want ads.

There are immigrants to Western societies who are not comfortable with love-based unions and prefer to have their marriages arranged by their parents or through a mediator. It is estimated, for instance, that up to 90 percent of the marriages in the East Indian community in Edmonton, Alberta, are to some degree arranged (Jimenez, 1992). Some ethnic Indians return to the Indian subcontinent to find a spouse, whereas others allow their parents to find a match locally for them. Some place ads in newspapers such as *India Today* or *India Abroad,* which focus on desired background characteristics such as education, religion, and age. In deference to Western customs, the young people can veto any match that does not appeal to them, and a dowry is rarely accepted.

Free-Choice Mate Selection

. . . [L]ove gradually became the principal criterion for marriage in the Western world after the Renaissance. The shift from kinship and economic motives to personal ones in mate selection led to the conclusion that the individuals themselves, rather than their parents or others, were best qualified to make the decision. In societies in which the basic family unit is nuclear, both romantic love and free mate choice are more common. This is because extended kin groups are not important enough to see marriage as needing to be group controlled.

Even though free choice is the mate selection method of the modern United States, one should not conclude that it is the most common approach in the world. In a survey of forty societies, Stephens (1963) found only five in which completely free mate choice is permitted. An additional six allowed the young people to choose their spouse, but subject to parental approval. Twelve other cultures had a mix of arranged marriages and free-choice (usually subject to approval) unions, and the final sixteen allowed only arranged marriages.

Moreover, even free choice does not mean that one can marry anyone. All societies have marital regulations. The rule of *exogamy* declares that a person must marry outside his/her group. Typically, this means that certain relatives are unavailable as marriage partners. Exogamous rules are generally the same as the incest taboos of the society, which prohibit sexual intercourse between close blood relatives. Others go beyond that, however. In classical China, two people with the same surname could not marry even if there was no kinship relation (Hutter, 1981).

The rule of *endogamy* declares that a person must marry within his/her group. This rule applies social pressure to marry someone who is similar to oneself in important ways, including religion, race, or ethnic group; social class; and age. These factors have been found to be related to marital compatibility and are precisely the kinds of things considered by parents in arranged marriages. One reason why the divorce rate seems to be higher in free-choice societies may be that many couples ignore endogamy issues and allow romantic love to be practically the sole consideration in mate selection. There is a tendency for marriages to be fairly homogamous, however, even in free-mate-choice societies.

A final factor is *propinquity* (geographical nearness). It is, of course, impossible to marry someone who lives so far away from you that you never meet. At another level, however, this principle refers to a human tendency to be friends with people with whom it is convenient to interact. Let us say that you leave your hometown to attend college elsewhere. You left a boyfriend or girlfriend back at home and you also meet someone new at college. All other things being equal, which one will you marry? Generally, it will be the one at school simply because it is easier.

Some Examples. Free mate choice is on the rise in China today. However, it is very different from the courtship pattern in North America. Young people gather information about each other first and check for mutual suitability before going public with their relationship. In fact, dating follows, rather than precedes, the decision to marry. Typically, the couple knows each other for well over two years before marrying. This cautious approach is paying off, as the quality of these marriages seems to be higher than that of arranged unions (Liao & Heaton, 1992).

The Igbo are a people living in present-day Nigeria (Okonjo, 1992). About 55 percent of the Igbo have their marriages arranged, while the remaining 45 percent are in free-choice unions. Most of the latter are younger, indicating a move from arranged to free choice, which we see occurring throughout much of the world today. Regardless of type, premarital chastity is very highly valued among the Igbo.

As the Igbo move to free mate choice based on love, their various arranged practices are falling into disfavor. Customs that are quickly disappearing include woman-to-woman marriage. In this situation, an older childless woman pays the brideprice to marry a younger female, usually a cousin. A male mate is chosen for the "wife" to have children with, but they belong to the older female spouse, who has the legal role of "husband."

Another way of securing an heir is *father-to-daughter* marriage. If a man has no sons, he may prohibit a daughter from marrying. She has children from a male mate (not the father) but her sons are considered her father's. Women whose husbands turn out to be impotent are allowed to have a lover from whom to have children, who are considered to be the legal husband's. Other arranged practices seldom practiced anymore are the levirate and child marriages.

CRITICAL-THINKING QUESTIONS

1. What four major issues influence mate choice in societies where marriages are arranged? What societal functions do the specific mechanisms of arranged marriages (such as brideprice, dowry, sororate, levirate, and matchmaking) fulfill?

2. Does marriage by free choice mean that a person can really marry *anyone?* What factors (or rules) considerably narrow the field of eligible mates in societies with free-choice mate selection?

3. What are the advantages and disadvantages of marrying for love (in free-choice societies) rather than economic or political considerations (in societies with arranged marriages)? Would marriages in North America be less likely to end in divorce if marriages were arranged?

REFERENCES

BALSWICK, J. 1975. The function of the dowry system in a rapidly modernizing society: The case of Cyprus. *International Journal of Sociology and the Family,* 5(2): 158–67.

BILLIG, M. 1992. The marriage squeeze and the rise of groomprice in India's Kerala state. *Journal of Comparative Family Studies,* 23(2): 197–216.

FIELDING, W. 1942. *Strange customs of courtship and marriage.* New York: New Home Library.

The Holy Bible. King James Version.

HUTTER, M. 1981. *The changing family: Comparative perspectives.* New York: Wiley.

JIMENEZ, M. 1992. Many Indo-Canadians follow age-old custom. *The Edmonton Journal* (July 26): B3.

LIAO, C., and T. HEATON. 1992. Divorce trends and differentials in China. *Journal of Comparative Family Studies,* 23(3): 413–29.

OKONJO, K. 1992. Aspects of continuity and change in mate selection among the Igbo west of the river Niger. *Journal of Comparative Family Studies,* 23(3): 339–60.

PETERS, J. 1987. Yąnomamö mate selection and marriage. *Journal of Comparative Family Studies,* 18(1): 79–98.

STEPHENS, W. 1963. *The family in cross-cultural perspective.* New York: Holt, Rinehart & Winston.

TOBER, B. 1984. *The bride: A celebration.* New York: Harry N. Abrams.

60 The Protestant Ethic and the Spirit of Capitalism

MAX WEBER

In perhaps his most well-known treatise, Max Weber argues that a major factor in the development of the capitalist economic system was the distinctive world view of early, ascetic Protestantism, especially Calvinism and Puritanism. In this excerpt from his classic analysis, Weber explains that religious ideas about work and materials initially fostered capitalism's growth; ultimately, he concludes, capitalism was able to stand on its own without religious supports.

A product of modern European civilization, studying any problem of universal history, is bound to ask himself to what combination of circumstances the fact should be attributed that in Western civilization, and in Western civilization only, cultural phenomena have appeared which (as we like to think) lie in a line of development having *universal* significance and value. . . . All over the world there have been merchants, wholesale and retail, local and engaged in foreign trade. . . .

But in modern times the Occident has developed, in addition to this, a very different form of capitalism which has appeared nowhere else: the rational capitalistic organization of (formally)

Source: From *The Protestant Ethic and the Spirit of Capitalism* by Max Weber, copyright © 1988, Prentice-Hall, Inc. Reprinted by permission.

free labour. Only suggestions of it are found elsewhere. Even the organization of unfree labour reached a considerable degree of rationality only on plantations and to a very limited extent in the *Ergasteria* of antiquity. In the manors, manorial workshops, and domestic industries on estates with serf labour it was probably somewhat less developed. Even real domestic industries with free labour have definitely been proved to have existed in only a few isolated cases outside the Occident. . . .

Rational industrial organization, attuned to a regular market, and neither to political nor irrationally speculative opportunities for profit, is not, however, the only peculiarity of Western capitalism. The modern rational organization of the capitalistic enterprise would not have been possible without two other important factors in its development: the separation of business from the household, which completely dominates modern economic life, and closely connected with it, rational book-keeping. . . .

Hence in a universal history of culture the central problem for us is not, in the last analysis, even from a purely economic viewpoint, the development of capitalistic activity as such, differing in different cultures only in form: the adventurer type, or capitalism in trade, war, politics, or administration as sources of gain. It is rather the origin of this sober bourgeois capitalism with its rational organization of free labour. Or in terms of cultural history, the problem is that of the origin of the Western bourgeois class and of its peculiarities, a problem which is certainly closely connected with that of the origin of the capitalistic organization of labour, but is not quite the same thing. For the bourgeois as a class existed prior to the development of the peculiar modern form of capitalism, though, it is true, only in the Western Hemisphere.

Now the peculiar modern Western form of capitalism has been, at first sight, strongly influenced by the development of technical possibilities. Its rationality is today essentially dependent on the calculability of the most important technical factors. But this means fundamentally that it is dependent on the peculiarities of modern science, especially the natural sciences based on mathematics and exact and rational experiment. On the other hand, the development of these sciences and of the technique resting upon them now receives important stimulation from these capitalistic interests in its practical economic application. It is true that the origin of Western science cannot be attributed to such interests. Calculation, even with decimals, and algebra have been carried on in India, where the decimal system was invented. But it was only made use of by developing capitalism in the West, while in India it led to no modern arithmetic or bookkeeping. Neither was the origin of mathematics and mechanics determined by capitalistic interests. But

the *technical* utilization of scientific knowledge, so important for the living conditions of the mass of people, was certainly encouraged by economic considerations, which were extremely favourable to it in the Occident. But this encouragement was derived from the peculiarities of the social structure of the Occident. We must hence ask, from *what* parts of that structure was it derived, since not all of them have been of equal importance?

Among those of undoubted importance are the rational structures of law and of administration. For modern rational capitalism has need, not only of the technical means of production, but of a calculable legal system and of administration in terms of formal rules. Without it adventurous and speculative trading capitalism and all sorts of politically determined capitalisms are possible, but no rational enterprise under individual initiative, with fixed capital and certainty of calculations. Such a legal system and such administration have been available for economic activity in a comparative state of legal and formalistic perfection only in the Occident. We must hence inquire where that law came from. Among other circumstances, capitalistic interests have in turn undoubtedly also helped, but by no means alone nor even principally, to prepare the way for the predominance in law and administration of a class of jurists specially trained in rational law. But these interests did not themselves create that law. Quite different forces were at work in this development. And why did not the capitalistic interests do the same in China or India? Why did not the scientific, the artistic, the political, or the economic development there enter upon that path of rationalization which is peculiar to the Occident?

For in all the above cases it is a question of the specific and peculiar rationalism of Western culture. . . . It is hence our first concern to work out and to explain genetically the special peculiarity of Occidental rationalism, and within this field that of the modern Occidental form. Every such attempt at explanation must, recognizing the fundamental importance of the economic factor, above all take account of the economic conditions. But at the same time the opposite correlation must not be left out of consideration. For though the development of economic rationalism is partly dependent on rational technique and law, it is at the same time determined by the ability and disposition of men to adopt certain types of practical rational conduct. When these types have been obstructed by spiritual obstacles, the development of rational economic conduct has also met serious inner resistance. The magical and religious forces, and the ethical ideas of duty based upon them, have in the past always been among the most important formative influences on conduct. In the studies collected here we shall be concerned with these forces.

Two older essays have been placed at the beginning which attempt, at one important point, to approach the side of the problem which is generally most difficult to grasp: the influence of certain religious ideas on the development of an economic spirit, or the *ethos* of an economic system. In this case we are dealing with the connection of the spirit of modern economic life with the rational ethics of ascetic Protestantism. Thus we treat here only one side of the causal chain. . . .

. . .[T]hat side of English Puritanism which was derived from Calvinism gives the most consistent religious basis for the idea of the calling. . . . For the saints' everlasting rest is in the next world; on earth man must, to be certain of his state of grace, "do the works of him who sent him, as long as it is yet day." Not leisure and enjoyment, but only activity serves to increase the glory of God according to the definite manifestations of His will.

Waste of time is thus the first and in principle the deadliest of sins. The span of human life is infinitely short and precious to make sure of one's own election. Loss of time through sociability, idle talk, luxury, even more sleep than is necessary for health, six to at most eight hours, is worthy of absolute moral condemnation. It does not yet hold, with Franklin, that time is money, but the proposition is true in a certain spiritual sense. It is infinitely valuable because every hour lost is lost to

labour for the glory of God. Thus inactive contemplation is also valueless, or even directly reprehensible if it is at the expense of one's daily work. . . .

[T]he same prescription is given for all sexual temptation as is used against religious doubts and a sense of moral unworthiness: "Work hard in your calling." But the most important thing was that even beyond that labour came to be considered in itself the end of life, ordained as such by God. St. Paul's "He who will not work shall not eat" holds unconditionally for everyone. Unwillingness to work is symptomatic of the lack of grace.

Here the difference from the mediæval viewpoint becomes quite evident. Thomas Aquinas also gave an interpretation of that statement of St. Paul. But for him labour is only necessary *naturali ratione* for the maintenance of individual and community. Where this end is achieved, the precept ceases to have any meaning. Moreover, it holds only for the race, not for every individual. It does not apply to anyone who can live without labour on his possessions, and of course contemplation, as a spiritual form of action in the Kingdom of God, takes precedence over the commandment in its literal sense. Moreover, for the popular theology of the time, the highest form of monastic productivity lay in the increase of the *Thesaurus ecclesliæ* through prayer and chant.

. . .For everyone without exception God's Providence has prepared a calling, which he should profess and in which he should labour. And this calling is not, as it was for the Lutheran, a fate to which he must submit and which he must make the best of, but God's commandment to the individual to work for the divine glory. This seemingly subtle difference had far-reaching psychological consequences, and became connected with a further development of the providential interpretation of the economic order which had begun in scholasticism.

It is true that the usefulness of a calling, and thus its favour in the sight of God, is measured primarily in moral terms, and thus in terms of the importance of the goods produced in it for the community. But a further, and, above all, in practice the most important, criterion is found in private profitableness. For if that God, whose hand the Puritan sees in all the occurrences of life, shows one of His elect a chance of profit, he must do it with a purpose. Hence the faithful Christian must follow the call by taking advantage of the opportunity. "If God show you a way in which you may lawfully get more than in another way (without wrong to your soul or to any other), if you refuse this, and choose the less gainful way, you cross one of the ends of your calling, and you refuse to be God's steward, and to accept His gifts and use them for Him when He requireth it: you may labour to be rich for God, though not for the flesh and sin.". . .

The superior indulgence of the *seigneur* and the parvenu ostentation of the *nouveau riche* are equally detestable to asceticism. But, on the other hand, it has the highest ethical appreciation of the sober, middle-class, self-made man. "God blesseth His trade" is a stock remark about those good men who had successfully followed the divine hints. The whole power of the God of the Old Testament, who rewards His people for their obedience in this life, necessarily exercised a similar influence on the Puritan who . . . compared his own state of grace with that of the heroes of the Bible. . . .

Although we cannot here enter upon a discussion of the influence of Puritanism in all . . . directions, we should call attention to the fact that the toleration of pleasure in cultural goods, which contributed to purely aesthetic or athletic enjoyment, certainly always ran up against one characteristic limitation: They must not cost anything. Man is only a trustee of the goods which have come to him through God's grace. He must, like the servant in the parable, give an account of every penny entrusted to him, and it is at least hazardous to spend any of it for a purpose which does not serve the glory of God but only one's own enjoyment. What person, who keeps his eyes open, has not met representatives of this viewpoint even in the present? The idea of a man's duty to his possessions, to which he subordinates himself as an obedient steward, or even as an acquisitive machine, bears with chilling weight on his life. The greater the possessions the heavier, if the ascetic

attitude toward life stands the test, the feeling of responsibility for them, for holding them undiminished for the glory of God and increasing them by restless effort. The origin of this type of life also extends in certain roots, like so many aspects of the spirit of capitalism, back into the Middle Ages. But it was in the ethic of ascetic Protestantism that it first found a consistent ethical foundation. Its significance for the development of capitalism is obvious.

This worldly Protestant asceticism, as we may recapitulate up to this point, acted powerfully against the spontaneous enjoyment of possessions; it restricted consumption, especially of luxuries. On the other hand, it had the psychological effect of freeing the acquisition of goods from the inhibitions of traditionalistic ethics. It broke the bonds of the impulse of acquisition in that it not only legalized it, but (in the sense discussed) looked upon it as directly willed by God. . . .

As far as the influence of the Puritan outlook extended, under all circumstances—and this is, of course, much more important than the mere encouragement of capital accumulation—it favoured the development of a rational bourgeois economic life; it was the most important, and above all the only consistent influence in the development of that life. It stood at the cradle of the modern economic man.

To be sure, these Puritanical ideals tended to give way under excessive pressure from the temptations of wealth, as the Puritans themselves knew very well. With great regularity we find the most genuine adherents of Puritanism among the classes which were rising from a lowly status, the small bourgeois and farmers while the *beati possidentes,* even among Quakers, are often found tending to repudiate the old ideals. It was the same fate which again and again befell the predecessor of this worldly asceticism, the monastic asceticism of the Middle Ages. In the latter case, when rational economic activity had worked out its full effects by strict regulation of conduct and limitation of consumption, the wealth accumulated either succumbed directly to the nobility, as in the time before the Reformation, or monastic discipline threatened to break down, and one of the numerous reformations became necessary.

In fact the whole history of monasticism is in a certain sense the history of a continual struggle with the problem of the secularizing influence of wealth. The same is true on a grand scale of the worldly asceticism of Puritanism. The great revival of Methodism, which preceded the expansion of English industry toward the end of the eighteenth century, may well be compared with such a monastic reform. We may hence quote here a passage from John Wesley himself which might well serve as a motto for everything which has been said above. For it shows that the leaders of these ascetic movements understood the seemingly paradoxical relationships which we have here analysed perfectly well, and in the same sense that we have given them. He wrote:

I fear, wherever riches have increased, the essence of religion has decreased in the same proportion. Therefore I do not see how it is possible, in the nature of things, for any revival of true religion to continue long. For religion must necessarily produce both industry and frugality, and these cannot but produce riches. But as riches increase, so will pride, anger, and love of the world in all its branches. How then is it possible that Methodism, that is, a religion of the heart, though it flourishes now as a green bay tree, should continue in this state? For the Methodists in every place grow diligent and frugal; consequently they increase in goods. Hence they proportionately increase in pride, in anger, in the desire of the flesh, the desire of the eyes, and the pride of life. So, although the form of religion remains, the spirit is swiftly vanishing away. Is there no way to prevent this—this continual decay of pure religion? We ought not to prevent people from being diligent and frugal; *we must exhort all Christians to gain all they can, and to save all they can; that is, in effect, to grow rich.*

As Wesley here says, the full economic effect of those great religious movements, whose significance for economic development lay above all in their ascetic educative influence, generally came only after the peak of the purely religious enthusiasm was past. Then the intensity of the search for the Kingdom of God commenced gradually to pass over into sober economic virtue; the religious roots died out slowly, giving way to utilitarian worldliness. Then, as Dowden puts it, as in *Robinson Crusoe,* the isolated economic man who carries on missionary activities on the side takes the place of the lonely spiritual search for the Kingdom of Heaven of Bunyan's pilgrim, hurrying through the marketplace of Vanity. . . .

A specifically bourgeois economic ethic had grown up. With the consciousness of standing in the fullness of God's grace and being visibly blessed by Him, the bourgeois business man, as long as he remained within the bounds of formal correctness, as long as his moral conduct was spotless and the use to which he put his wealth was not objectionable, could follow his pecuniary interests as he would and feel that he was fulfilling a duty in doing so. The power of religious asceticism provided him in addition with sober, conscientious, and unusually industrious workmen, who clung to their work as to a life purpose willed by God.

Finally, it gave him the comforting assurance that the unequal distribution of the goods of this world was a special dispensation of Divine Providence, which in these differences, as in particular grace, pursued secret ends unknown to men. . . .

One of the fundamental elements of the spirit of modern capitalism, and not only of that but of all modern culture: Rational conduct on the basis of the idea of the calling, was born—that is what this discussion has sought to demonstrate—from the spirit of Christian asceticism. One has only to reread the passage from Franklin, quoted at the beginning of this essay, in order to see that the essential elements of the attitude which was there called the spirit of capitalism are the same as what we have just shown to be the content of the Puritan worldly asceticism, only without the religious basis, which by Franklin's time had died away. . . .

Since asceticism undertook to remodel the world and to work out its ideals in the world, material goods have gained an increasing and finally an inexorable power over the lives of men as at no previous period in history. Today the spirit of religious asceticism—whether finally, who knows?—has escaped from the cage. But victorious capitalism, since it rests on mechanical foundations, needs its support no longer. The rosy blush of its laughing heir, the Enlightenment, seems also to be irretrievably fading, and the idea of duty in one's calling prowls about in our lives like the ghost of dead religious beliefs. Where the fulfilment of the calling cannot directly be related to the highest spiritual and cultural values, or when, on the other hand, it need not be felt simply as economic compulsion, the individual generally abandons the attempt to justify it at all. In the field of its highest development, in the United States, the pursuit of wealth, stripped of its religious and ethical meaning, tends to become associated with purely mundane passions, which often actually give it the character of sport.

No one knows who will live in this cage in the future, or whether at the end of this tremendous development entirely new prophets will arise, or there will be a great rebirth of old ideas and ideals, or, if neither, mechanized petrification, embellished with a sort of convulsive self-importance. For of the last stage of this cultural development, it might well be truly said: "Specialists without spirit, sensualists without heart; this nullity imagines that it has attained a level of civilization never before achieved."

But this brings us to the world of judgments of value and of faith, with which this purely historical discussion need not be burdened. . . .

Here we have only attempted to trace the fact and the direction of its influence to their motives in one, though a very important point. But it would also further be necessary to investigate how Protestant Asceticism was in turn influenced in its development and its character by the totality of social conditions, especsially economic. The modern man is in general, even with the best will, unable to give religious ideas a significance for culture and national character which they deserve. But it is, of course, not my aim to substitute for a one-sided materialistic an equally one-sided spiritualistic causal interpretation of culture and of history. Each is equally possible, but each, if it does not serve as the preparation, but as the conclusion of an investigation, accomplishes equally little in the interest of historical truth.

CRITICAL-THINKING QUESTIONS

1. What are the distinctive characteristics of the religious orientation that Weber called the "Protestant ethic"? In what ways did they promote the development of the capitalist economic system?

2. In what respects do early Calvinists with a sense of "calling" differ from today's "workaholics"?

3. In what sense does Weber's analysis differ from the materialist orientation of Karl Marx (Reading 51), who suggested that productive forces shape the world of ideas?

CLASSIC

CONTEMPORARY

CROSS-CULTURAL

61 How Student Life Is Different at Religious Colleges

NAOMI SCHAEFER RILEY

Religious colleges and universities are thriving. Naomi Schaefer Riley visited twenty of these religious institutions and found that many of the students had fairly traditional and conservative views about politics, drugs, music, and other topics. This selection describes the students' attitudes about premarital sexual behavior, especially while on campus.

In 2003, Yaacov Weinstein and Gil Perl took some time off from their graduate study at Harvard to produce an eleven-page monograph called "A Parent's Guide to Orthodox Assimilation on University Campuses." The two warn that the atmosphere at secular schools—from the classroom, where students are taught that the Torah was not divinely authored and that Israel shouldn't exist, to the dormitory, where the abundance of sex, drugs, and alcohol has now come to include officially sponsored "lingerie study breaks" and "pornography clubs"—encourages young Orthodox Jews to compromise or abandon their faith. Weinstein and Perl observe that even the campus Jewish organizations "often place Orthodox kids in un-*halachic* [contrary to Jewish law] social situations."

Promiscuity, or at least "sexual awareness," has become part of a college education promoted by the administration at secular schools. While she was a student at Williams College, Wendy

Source: Naomi Schaefer Riley, *God on the Quad: How Religious Colleges and the Missionary Generation are Changing America.* New York: St. Martin's Press, 2005, pp. 169–177.

Shalit wrote an article in *Commentary* describing the meeting in which the residents of her dormitory voted to make the bathrooms coed. When Shalit objected to the idea, "The other girls actually seem[ed], for a moment, to take her part, as the poor benighted miss surrounded by a pack of worldlings patting her on the back, flattering and reassuring her. 'Don't worry, I was just like you once,' one of them [began] condescendingly, smiling with the smug authority of the victorious. 'And then . . . I became COMFORTABLE WITH MY BODY.' " After Shalit is embarrassed into going along with the decision, "The resident advisers," she notes, "take this opportunity to announce that if anyone has problems with the coed bathroom, please do come and talk with them—there are any number of good campus counselors at 'Psych Services.' "

And if you're crazy not to want to share a bathroom with a member of the opposite sex, why not a *bedroom?* Several schools, like Haverford College, have recently added the option of coed dorm rooms as a way of accommodating homosexual students who don't feel comfortable living with someone to whom they might be sexually attracted. Of course, since the schools involved would never question students about their sexual orientation, the policy gives a free pass for heterosexual couples to live together. Few administrators feel as though they have any basis for protesting such an arrangement. Tufts University president John DiBiaggio was able to muster only this half-hearted explanation for his rejection of the idea: "I'm not saying that we are prudish. We are not acting in loco parentis. But we are dealing with life-threatening venereal diseases here."

With administrators backed into a corner like this, unable even to seem like they are taking a moral stance, students at secular universities continue to push the envelope. Life on most college campuses remains defined by the 1960s mantra that college is the time for students to get out from under the thumb of their parents and "experiment."

Rich Powers, the dean of students at Wheaton College, who used to work at a public university in Illinois, recalls how, shortly after arriving in his current job, he telephoned one of his former colleagues. "I asked how are things going, and the person I talked to said, 'Oh man, somebody shot off a gun in his apartment the other day and campus police just had to bust a prostitution ring.' " Powers acknowledges that Wheaton is far from perfect, "but the issues here by and large pale by comparison."

Religious college students generally seem to avoid the kind of trouble that puts secular campuses in the headlines. There are certain exceptions, of course, but on the whole, religious campuses are devoid of the alcohol, drugs, sexual activity, and violence that plague many secular universities. "We have our challenges," says Powers. "We want students to think as critically outside classroom as they do inside of it. We want them to make wise decisions which are honoring to the Lord and good for them and the community."

How do they do it? First, and most importantly, religious college kids *want* to be in this environment. Only a small minority of the students I spoke with claimed their parents told them they had to attend a religious college. Carri Jenkins, who is in charge of public relations at Brigham Young, tells me why over lunch with a few other administrators and faculty:

Many of these students have been in a high school where they are the only one who is a member of the Church of Jesus Christ, and they are tired of having to constantly defend who they are. They want to have fun without getting drunk. This is freedom for them. They come here and they can be who they want to be. They can live their principles.

Second, religious college leaders have no problem acting in loco parentis. In fact, the parents themselves often become involved. At Calvin, for instance, there is a parental notification policy for any alcohol use on campus or any other disciplinary infraction. "We've found that to be very effective," says administrator Shirley Hoogstra. "We think that a parent is a partner in the process in terms of discipline."

Administrators at religious colleges, not surprisingly, take a religious approach to discipline. Professor Scott Moore notes that if a Baylor student violates a rule, "any action taken would be redemptive." Most of the adults on these campuses agree that human beings are sinners, prone to make mistakes, and, within limits, it's the job of the college to help set them on the right course, rather than simply kick them out.

Powers explains, "We will hold students accountable for choices, but do it in a gracious fashion, not a punitive fashion." Wheaton's student body president Noel Jabbour finds the administration's attitude useful. "They ask 'How can we help this person to get through what he has done, and explore the reason why he did it?' " Administrators believe the key to successful discipline is creating an environment in which students will come for help before they are caught violating some rule, "when they reach a point where they feel like they are not in control."

Steve Baker, the director of BYU's honor code office, boasts that fewer than 1 percent of students are ever brought to see him. One reason for this is that problems are often handled in a religious context—with a student approaching his bishop or vice versa—before they ever get to the university offices. If a disciplinary infraction does come to the attention of the administration, the student can choose to involve his or her bishop as an advocate. Baker emphasizes that the student is entitled to the "ecclesiastical confidential relationship that no one else is privy to."

Ultimately, religious college administrators are a lot like parents when it comes to the issues of sexuality or the use of alcohol. They offer guidance and help in the process of character formation, which sometimes includes punishment, but more importantly, they are also supposed to prepare their charges for the world outside. Most religious college students do not live in a vacuum. They are aware of how secular culture views dating, sex, marriage, homosexuality, drinking, drugs, and smoking. On some issues their faith may provide clear guidelines regarding what is expected of them in these regards. Mormons, for example, are not allowed to smoke under any circumstances. But in other cases, the gray area is more significant. Are young evangelicals allowed to kiss? To what extent are Catholic students supposed to drink? How are people with homosexual impulses supposed to be treated? It is the job of religious colleges to help their graduates make these decisions.

Administrators and faculty at religious college tend to agree that the place to start addressing these issues is in the dormitories. Most strongly religious schools have stuck with the relic of single-sex dorms. Many students note they are not comfortable sharing their bedrooms and bathrooms with members of the opposite sex. Moreover, they like the fact that they don't have a "third roommate" (the problem created when a roommate's significant other stays over regularly). Lauren Whitnah, a sophomore at Gordon College, was skeptical of the dorm rules, but says she is now grateful for them. "If my roommate was coming in drunk or with her boyfriend, I had recourse to say, 'That's not okay with me and not

okay with the school.' I felt like there would really be someone that would back me up."

Kelly Pascual, a sophomore psychology major at Notre Dame, likes the single-sex dorms because they foster close friendships. Eighty-five percent of the university's student body lives on campus, and there is a general agreement about the positive effects of single-sex dorms. Erica Hayman, a junior, tells me that before she came to Notre Dame, she always wanted to live next door to a guy, and when she arrived freshman year she was irritated to find that on the weekends she could go six or seven hours without seeing one. Since then, though, she has learned to appreciate the value of the living arrangements. She notes, "Notre Dame wouldn't be Notre Dame without single-sex dorms."

The university's visiting hours are, however, some of the most liberal at religious colleges. Members of the opposite sex are allowed in the dorms until midnight on weekdays and two A.M. on weekends.

Few leaders of religious colleges are of the opinion that they can prevent all sexual activity among the students. Instead, most religious college leaders use dorm life as a means of student "formation." What is meant by formation, of course, varies from school to school. At Baylor, it involves a willingness on the part of the administration to adopt behavioral standards, but no one is checking the beds each night.

Some schools have adopted an almost military approach to formation, on the theory that breeding certain habits in students will build character. This has produced mixed results. At Bob Jones, where women and men are not allowed any kind of physical contact, the school's rules may be strict enough to minimize such incidents, but as most administrators will tell you, where there's a will there's a way. Even at Thomas Aquinas College, where students live on a mountaintop, spend almost all their waking hours studying, have a curfew of eleven P.M., and no visitation hours, a young woman was caught having an affair with a married man in a nearby town a few years ago.

At seven thirty on a cold, rainy morning in late April, the chapel at Magdalen, a small Catholic college in rural New Hampshire, is more than half full, most of its students and faculty (all attired, in accordance with the school's dress code, in either coats and ties of muted colors or long skirts and modest blouses) sitting in silence for the fifteen minutes before mass begins. Candles are lit on the altar just as the lights come up in the chapel. Two male students sitting in the third to last row check their voices against a pitch pipe and begin to lead the congregation in song. There is no organ at first, but the congregation's a cappella sounds almost professional. Though the service is slightly more elaborate today because it is the week following Easter, daily mass at Magdalen usually lasts close to an hour.

By the time students leave the chapel to line up for breakfast, where their seats are assigned (differently each day, so as to avoid the formation of cliques), they have made their beds and tidied their rooms. Clothes must be folded neatly, there can be no clutter on desks or dressers, and decorations on the walls are not permitted. Students also carry around an extra pair of shoes with them, and change whenever they walk into a building so that they do not soil the floors. That rule is easily enforced since students themselves do most of the campus cleaning.

"I thought it was crazy, nuts, and bizarre when I came here," says Mark Gillis, who graduated from Magdalen in 1990, and is now a professor there. Gillis, whose parents told him he could either go to Magdalen or be kicked out of the house, remembers his reaction to the school's ten thirty lights-out policy: "I would lie awake for hours. It was like detox." But one day during the spring of his first year, Gillis recalls, "I realized I was happy." Even the students who are forced by their parents to attend, Gillis believes, come to like it eventually. "As you mature, you begin to appreciate things being more or less organized. . . . It's good habits. It's character formation. It's Aristotle."

Magdalen also has the strictest policy with regard to dating—it's not allowed. The rule is actually against "steady company keeping" and most students come to like it after some time. Nancy Carlin, a senior, explains,

> The rule makes perfect sense to me. It has allowed me to have deeper friendships with guys than ever before in my life. There was a sense in high school that if you sit down with a guy you are attached at the hip. They will think, "You are mine and I possess you." It's so freeing to be able to sit at a table with a guy for an hour after lunch and not have people think you must be dating. [The rule against coupling] fosters a sense of self-giving.

"Whereas dating makes your world shrink to about this big," Carlin notes, holding her thumb and forefinger an inch apart, "it seems love should open your world."

Many Magdalen students do get married shortly after graduation, and Carlin thinks they have a better idea of whom they're marrying as a result of the no-dating rule. "It's pretty easy when you're going out to dinner and a movie with a guy that you just put on a front."

But at a place like Magdalen?

"It's much easier here to get to know someone. You are part of a group of friends and you see how they react with other people." Carlin, who grew up in a family with ten children, thinks that the best reason for putting off dating is that you have a better chance of getting into a solid marriage instead of a relationship based only on self-gratification.

Both Bob Jones University and Patrick Henry College have strict rules about dating as well. PHC requires students to get their parents' permission before pursuing a romantic relationship, and BJU requires chaperones for all dates. Though evangelical schools generally allow dating, some of their students have been attracted to the ideas in a recent popular book called *I Kissed Dating Goodbye*—which advocates that young people put off any kind of romantic relationship until they are ready for marriage.

Regardless of their rules on dating, all of the schools in this book try to monitor sexual activity on campus, starting with hugging and kissing. At Thomas Aquinas, students are prohibited from engaging in any public displays of affection because the administrators believe it is harmful to the formation of community. At Brigham Young University, on the other hand, such displays are ubiquitous. Even during the "fireside" talks given by leaders of the church on Sunday evenings in the sports arena, couples are holding hands and men have their arms around their girlfriends' shoulders. There is a strange slow movement everywhere you look as students stroke each other's hair, arms, and faces.

But BYU students do take seriously the rule against premarital sex. Since most of the students live in off-campus housing, the rule is enforced primarily through peer pressure. Minji Cho, who only recently converted to Mormonism and experimented with sex in high school, tells me, "I realized that if I went to a public university there would be a lot of . . . temptation for me. I didn't want to necessarily be around Mormons; anyone with clean morals would have been fine." Knowing how she is struggling, Minji's roommates keep a motherly eye on her.

Like Minji, most religious college students seem thankful they will not have to confront the sorts of sexual pressures they would at secular schools. Rachel Stahl, a sophomore at Gordon, tells me she looks forward to going out with guys there. "I have dated people who aren't Christian and sex is all they want."

But are these students really abstaining from sex? When I asked that question to a gathering of Southern Virginia University faculty about their Mormon students, there was a lot of giggling, and several noted that there would hardly be such an intense obsession with getting married early if students were having sexual contact outside of marriage.

At most of the colleges, though, there is a contingent of students who are not living by the code of sexual conduct. Rev. Mark Poorman, the vice president for student affairs at Notre Dame, is not sure about the percentage of undergrads engaging in sexual activity. He posits that it's rather small, but notes that if the administration finds out about such behavior "from a credible source," they will challenge it.

Indeed, even at schools where students are not watched as closely as they might be at Magdalen or Bob Jones, sexual activity is not flaunted thanks to peer pressure and administrations that are clear about their standards. But an atmosphere where premarital sex is considered shameful and not to be discussed can also encourage what Abby Diepenbrock, a codirector of the Center for Christian Concerns at Westmont, calls "hypocrisy."

"Christian schools and religious schools in general," she says, "have a reputation for saying one thing and then behaving in a different way."

Abby senses that many of her fellow students feel guilty about this disconnect between their words and actions. "You can tell in conversation. People start talking about something that's a little questionable. I hear a lot of people saying, 'Oh, we couldn't do that if Jake were around,' " referring to her codirector. Abby asks, "What does Jake matter? What about the Lord?"

Ben Patterson, Westmont's chaplain, has been surprised by the kinds of things his charges are engaged in.

In areas of [sexual] morality, students are very much affected by their feelings, more than any sense of dogma. . . . It's pretty scary around here how many professing Christian students who are really seriously believers split off there. What they will do . . . in intimate relationships [is] so off the edge. I was at [the evangelical] Hope College for four years and I talked to students periodically who wanted to clean up their sex lives, to get themselves in line with their faith. . . . It took me four years to realize what they meant by that. They weren't having intercourse, but they were doing absolutely anything else. And it just one day dawned on me. Oh heavens. I thought they meant they had very high standards, but they didn't. They went right up to that. That was the only thing left to do. . . . [Westmont students] are in the same place. They'll say, "I feel close. I'm not just doing it with anybody. I care deeply."

The solution to these kinds of moral slip-ups, according to students and faculty, may be early marriage. The median age at which college-educated women marry has increased dramatically in the last few decades. But at most religious schools, getting married young is encouraged, if not expected. (Even at Notre Dame, a number of the seniors remark on their many friends who plan to marry shortly after graduation.) "Ring by spring"—that is, getting engaged by the spring of senior year—is a mantra at almost every school I visit. And there is always a rash of weddings right after graduation.

Because the vast majority of evangelical students do not get married while in college, they use a number of traditions to signify to each other the seriousness of their commitment. Christian Bell and Beth Heinen, the editors of the Calvin newspaper, who are themselves engaged, explain to me the various stages of courtship at Calvin, from the opal, which is the pre-pre-engagement ring, to the pearl, the pre-engagement ring, to the actual engagement ring. (Beth acknowledges that when she heard about the opal, "I was like, 'You've got to be joking.'")

In the Mormon community, courtship does not have so many stages because students often get married while in school, and after a relatively short period of dating. The high rate of marriage among students or recent graduates of religious colleges may be inevitable. Students are, often for the first time, placed in a pool of people their own age who share their beliefs and values.

But with the opportunity comes great anxiety. All of the sexual pressure that students at secular colleges might experience is transformed at religious colleges into the pressure to find a spouse. And it is compounded by the fact that many parents of religious college students found their spouses at such schools. Andrea Ludlow, a senior at BYU, who dates, "but not a ton," explains, some of her classmates "think, 'Oh if I don't get married in college, I'll never get married.'"

Paul Jalsevac, the student body president at the Catholic Christendom College, describes the temptation that arose when he first arrived at school:

You show up, and all of a sudden you discover a whole bunch of people who, well, a whole bunch of girls, who, you know, are pretty beautiful, very nice girls, who share very much the same values and morals as you, the kind of girls you very rarely run into. They are looking for the same things in a relationship and care about the same things. All that groundwork, you know, that you'd have to do back home is not necessary. You have people who actually want a real relationship. They aren't just looking for something physical.

The result, according to Paul, is that freshmen get very serious very quickly. "They think, 'Wow this is the perfect match.'" Laura Johnson, the editor of Gordon College's newspaper, sees a similar phenomenon among her classmates. "The guys think, 'Wow, there are Christian girls here. And they're actually cool.' They haven't seen that. The tendency is 'I have to go get that right away.'"

The pressure is also compounded by the lopsided ratio of women to men at many of these schools. Laura tells me that women often complain to her about the ratio (almost three to one at Gordon). "They say, 'I'm never going to find anyone.'"

But, laughing about the "senior scramble," Laura says, "It doesn't bother me. I know that God is going to provide the right person, here or later on in life."

CRITICAL-THINKING QUESTIONS

1. Most of the students said that they have high moral standards. However, many also admitted to having premarital sexual intercourse. Is there a contradiction between the students' attitudes and behavior? Can you explain this inconsistency?

2. How do religious colleges and universities reinforce beliefs about appropriate sexual behavior? How do the beliefs promote both social control as well as a sense of group solidarity?

3. What are some of the advantages of getting married right after graduation? What are some of the disadvantages?

CLASSIC

CONTEMPORARY

CROSS-CULTURAL

62 Women and Islam

JANE I. SMITH

Many Westerners have a vague notion that women in Iran, Saudi Arabia, and other Islamic societies are subject to relentless control by men. Although there is some truth to this stereotype, a more realistic account of the relationship between Islam and gender must begin with a basic understanding of this unfamiliar religion. In this article, Jane Smith provides an overview of Islamic tenets, explores some of the variations that divide the vast Islamic world, and assesses the relative social standing of the sexes—as Muslims themselves understand it.

To attempt to talk about women in Islam is of course to venture into an area fraught with the perils of overgeneralization, oversimplification, and the almost unavoidable limitations of a Western bias. The first problem is simply one of raw numbers. There are perhaps close to half a billion Muslim women inhabiting all major areas of the world today. Is it possible to say anything that holds true for all of them, let alone for their sisters over the past fourteen centuries of Islam?

Then one must consider all the various elements that comprise the picture of Islamic womanhood. Many of these elements are directly related to the religion of Islam itself, such as past and present legal realities, roles permitted and enforced as a result of Muslim images of women, and the variety of Islamic and hetero-Islamic rites and

Source: Reprinted by permission from *Women in World Religions* by Arvind Sharma (ed.), the State University of New York Press © 1987, State University of New York. All rights reserved.

practices in which Islamic women have traditionally participated. Other elements contributing to the full picture of women in Islam—such as education, political rights, professional employment opportunities, and the like—have less to do with the religion per se but are still influenced by it.

The Holy Qur'an (sometimes transliterated as "Koran") still forms the basis of prevailing family law in most areas of the Muslim world. It has always been and still is considered to be the last in a series of divine revelations from God given in the seventh century C.E. to humanity through the vehicle of his final prophet Muhammad. The Qur'an is therefore the literal and unmitigated word of God, collected and ordered by the young Muslim community but untainted with the thoughts and interpretations of any persons, including Muhammad himself. It is obvious, then, why the regulations formulated by the Qur'an in regard to women have been adhered to with strictness and why changes in Muslim family law are coming about only very slowly in the Islamic world.

The circumstances of women in pre-Islamic Arabia are subject to a variety of interpretations. On the one hand, certain women—soothsayers, priestesses, queens, and even singular individuals—did play powerful roles in society. On the other hand, whatever the earlier realities for women in terms of marriage, divorce, and inheritance of property, it is clear that the Qur'an did introduce very significant changes that were advantageous for women. Contemporary Muslims are fond of pointing out, quite correctly, that Islam brought legal advantages for women quite unknown in corresponding areas of the Western Christian world. What, then, does the Qur'an say about women?

The earliest messages of the Qur'an, and the twin themes that run through all the chapters, are of the realities of the oneness of God and the inevitability of the day of judgment. All persons, men and women, are called upon to testify to those realities. . . . Religiously speaking, then, men and women are fully equal in the eyes of God according to the Qur'an.

Before looking at the specifics of the legal injunctions for women, it is necessary to consider two verses that have caused a great deal of consternation to Westerners. One is 2:228, which says literally that men are a step above women, and the other is 4:34, clarifying that men are the protectors of women (or are in charge of women) because God has given preference to one over the other and because men provide support for women. Perhaps because these verses have been so troublesome for non-Muslims (especially feminists), they have been subject to an enormous amount of explanation and interpretation by contemporary Muslim apologists eager to present a defense of their religion. These writers, men and women, affirm that it is precisely because men are invested with the responsibility of taking care of women, financially and otherwise, that they are given authority over the females of their families. And that, affirm many Muslim women today,

is exactly the way it should be. We will return to this perspective later, particularly in light of what a desire for liberation means—and does not mean—for many Muslim women. . . .

According to the Qur'an, a man may marry up to four wives, so long as he is able to provide for each equally. He may marry a Muslim woman or a member of the Jewish or Christian faith, or a slave woman. A Muslim woman, however, may marry only one husband, and he must be a Muslim. Contemporary Muslim apologists are quick to point out that these restrictions are for the benefit of women, ensuring that they will not be left unprotected. In Islam, marriage is not a sacrament but a legal contract, and according to the Qur'an a woman has clearly defined legal rights in negotiating this contract. She can dictate the terms and can receive the dowry herself. This dowry (*mahr*) she is permitted to keep and maintain as a source of personal pride and comfort.

Polygamy (or more strictly polygyny, plurality of wives) is practiced by only a small percentage of the contemporary Muslim population, and a man with more than two wives is extremely rare. Many countries are now taking steps to modify the circumstances in which a husband may take more than one wife, although only in two countries, Turkey and Tunisia, are multiple marriages actually illegal. Other countries have made such moves as requiring the husband to have the permission of the court (as in Iraq and Syria) or to get the permission of the first wife (as in Egypt), or permitting the wife to write into her marriage contract that she will not allow a cowife (as in Morocco and Lebanon). It seems reasonable to expect that other countries will make changes and modifications. It is interesting to note that while for some finances have dictated monogamy—most husbands have simply not been able to afford more than one wife—changing economic realities may again dictate that a man contemplate the possibility of having several wives to work and supply income for the family.

Muslim women traditionally have been married at an extremely young age, sometimes even before puberty. This practice is related, of course, to the historical fact that fathers and other male relatives generally have chosen the grooms themselves, despite the guarantee of the Qur'an that marriage is a contract into which male and female enter equally. While it is true that technically a girl cannot be forced into a marriage she does not want, pressures from family and the youth of the bride often have made this prerogative difficult to exercise. Today, the right of a male member of the family to contract an engagement for a girl against her wishes has been legally revoked in most places, although it is still a common practice, especially in rural areas. . . .

In the contemporary Islamic world, divorce rates vary considerably from one country to the next. Muslim apologists insist that divorce is not nearly as common in Islamic countries as it is, for example, in the United States. This statement is generally true, although in some countries, such as Morocco, the rate is high and continues to grow. Often what is really only the breaking of the engagement contract is included in divorce statistics, skewing the measure. Many countries are now considering serious changes in divorce procedures. The simultaneous triple repudiation generally has been declared illegal, and in many countries divorce initiated by either party, the man or the woman, must take place in the court of law. Other countries add special stipulations generally favorable to the woman. It remains true, however, that men can divorce for less cause than women, and often divorces hung up in courts with male judges can prove enormously difficult for women to gain.

In accordance with Islamic law, custody of the children traditionally has gone to the father at some time between the age of seven and nine for boys and between seven and puberty for girls, depending on the legal school. This practice too is slowly changing, and in most areas women who have been divorced by their husbands are allowed to keep their sons until puberty and their daughters until they are of an age to be married.

It is considered one of the great innovations of the Qur'an over earlier practices that women are permitted to inherit and own property. Non-Muslims have generally found great difficulty with the Qur'anic stipulation that a woman is allowed to inherit property but that the inheritance should be only half that of a male. According to the Islamic understanding, however, the rationale is precisely that which applies to the verse saying that men are in charge of women. Because women are permitted to keep and maintain their own property without responsibility for taking care of their families financially, it is only reasonable that the male, who must spend his own earning and inheritance for the maintenance of women, should receive twice as much. . . .

According to the Qur'an, women should not expose themselves to public view with lack of modesty. It does not say that they should be covered specifically from head to toe, nor that they should wear face veils or masks or other of the paraphernalia that has adorned many Islamic women through the ages. The Qur'an also suggests that the wives of the Prophet Muhammad, when speaking to other men, should do so from behind a partition, again for purposes of propriety. It has been open to question whether this statement is meant to apply to all women. In the early Islamic community, these verses were exaggerated and their underlying ideas elaborated and defined in ways that led fairly quickly to a seclusion of women which seems quite at odds with what the Qur'an intended or the Prophet wanted. When the community in Medina was established, women participated fully with men in all activities of worship and prayer. Soon they became segregated, however, to the point where an often-quoted *hadith* (no doubt spurious) attributed to Muhammad has him saying that women pray better at home than in the mosque, and best of all in their own closets. Today a number of contemporary Muslim writers are urging a return to the practices of the young Muslim community, with women no longer segregated from the mosque or relegated to certain rear or side portions as they generally have been, but participating fully in worship with men. . . .

What is popularly known as "veiling" is part of the general phenomenon of the segregation of women and yet is also distinctly apart from it. The two are increasingly seen as separate by contemporary Islamic women seeking to affirm a new identity in relation to their religion. Veils traditionally have taken a number of forms: a veil covering the face from just below the eyes down; a *chador* or *burka* covering the entire body, including the face, often with a woven screen in front through which women can see but not be seen; and a full face mask with small slits through the eyes, still worn in some areas of the Arabian Gulf. These costumes, so seemingly oppressive to Western eyes, at least have allowed women to observe without being observed, thus affording their wearers a degree of anonymity that on some occasions has proven useful.

The general movement toward unveiling had its ostensible beginning in the mid-1920s, when the Egyptian feminist Huda Sha'rawi cast off her veil after arriving in Egypt from an international meeting of women. She was followed literally and symbolically by masses of women in the succeeding years, and Egyptian women as well as those in other Middle Eastern countries made great strides in adopting Western dress. At the present time in the history of Islam, however, one finds a quite different phenomenon. Partly in reaction against Western liberation and Western ideals in general, women in many parts of the Islamic world are self-consciously adopting forms of dress by which they can identify with Islam rather than with what they now see as the imperialist West. Islamic dress, generally chosen by Muslim women themselves rather than forced upon them by males, signals for many an identification with a way of life that they are increasingly convinced represents a more viable alternative than that offered by the West. . . .

We see, then, that while legal circumstances for women have undergone some significant changes in the past half-century, the dictates of the Qur'an

continue to be enormously influential in the molding of new laws as well as in the personal choices of Muslim men and women. . . .

I have stressed here the insistence of the Qur'an on the religious and spiritual equality of men and women. And aside from some unfortunate hadith with very weak chains of authority suggesting that the majority of women will be in the Fire on the Day of Judgment because of their mental and physical inferiority, religious literature in general, when talking about human responsibility and concomitant judgment, makes women full partners with men under the divine command to live lives of integrity and righteousness. . . .

Of course, women do participate in many of the activities and duties considered incumbent on all good Muslims, but generally these practices have a somewhat different function for them than for men. Prayer for women, as we have said, is usually in the home rather than in the mosque, and does not necessarily follow the pattern of the regularized five times a day. Participation in the fast itself is normally the same as for the men (except when women are pregnant, nursing, or menstruating), but the particular joys of preparing the fast-breaking meals are for the women alone. While the husband determines the amount of money or goods to be distributed for almsgiving, another responsibility of all Muslims, it is often the wife who takes charge of the actual distribution.

The last duty incumbent on Muslims after the testimony to the oneness of God and prophethood of his apostle Muhammad, the prayer, the fast, and paying the almstax is the pilgrimage once in a lifetime to the holy city of Mecca. Women do participate in this journey, and as transportation becomes easier and the care provided for pilgrims in Saudi Arabia becomes more regularized with modernization, increasing numbers of females join the throngs which gather to circumambulate the Xaaba at Mecca each year. . . .

Saints in Islam are both male and female. One is normally recognized as a saint not by any process of canonization but because of some miraculous deed(s) performed or through a dream communication after death with a living person requesting that a shrine be erected over his or her tomb. Often a woman is favored with these dreams and after the construction of the shrine she becomes the carekeeper of the tomb, a position of some honor and responsibility. . . .

While women in the Islamic world have been segregated and secluded, and historically have been considered second-class citizens by the vast majority of males in the community, they have not been totally without power. They have been able to maintain a degree of control over their own lives and over the men with whom they live through many of the religious practices described above. The fact that they alone have the ability to bear children, the influence they continue to play in the lives of their sons, and the power they have over their sons' wives are subtle indications that there are certain checks and balances on the obvious authority invested by the Qur'an in men. From sexuality to control of the network of communications in the family to manipulation of such external agencies as spirits and supernatural beings, women have had at their control a variety of means to exert their will over the men in their families and over their own circumstances. The subtle means of control available to women throughout the world have of course been exploited: withholding sexual favors (a questionable but often-quoted hadith says that if a woman refuses to sleep with her husband, the angels will curse her until the morning), doing small things to undermine a husband's honor such as embarrassing him in front of guests, indulging in various forms of gossip and social control, and the like. . . .

Until fairly recently, education for women in the Muslim world has been minimal. Girls were given the rudiments of an Islamic education, mainly a little instruction in the Qur'an and the traditions so as to be able to recite their prayers properly. Beyond that their training was not academic but domestic. In the late nineteenth and early twentieth centuries, Islamic leaders awoke with a start to the reality that Muslims were significantly behind the West in a variety of ways, including technology and the education necessary to understand and develop it. Many of these leaders recognized that if Islamic nations were to compete successfully in the contemporary world, it had to be with the aid of a well-educated and responsible female sector. Thus, this century has seen a number of educational advances for women, and in some countries, such as Egypt, Iraq, and Kuwait, women constitute very significant numbers of the university population. Nonetheless, illiteracy in many Muslim nations continues to be high, and the gap between male and female literacy rates is even increasing in some areas. In Saudi Arabia, where at present the economic resources are certainly available, large numbers of Saudi girls are receiving a full education, though separated from boys, and are taught either by men through television transmission or by women.

In education as in most areas of life, the male understanding of women as encouraged by certain parts of the Islamic tradition continues to play an important role. The Qur'an does state, along with the stipulation that women can inherit only half of what men inherit, that the witness (in the court of law) of one man is equal to that of two women. This unfortunately has been interpreted by some in the history of Islam to mean that women are intellectually inferior to men, unstable in their judgment, and too easily swayed by emotion. Such perspectives are certainly not shared by all but nonetheless have been influential (and in some places are increasingly so today) in making it difficult for a woman to have access to the same kinds of educational opportunities that are available to men. Certain subjects are deemed "appropriate" for a woman to study, particularly those geared to make her the best and most productive wife, mother, and female participant in the family structure.

The prevalent view, confirmed by the Qur'an, is that women should be modest and should neither expose themselves to men nor be too much in public places, where they will be subject to men's observation or forced to interact with males not in their immediate families. This view obviously has contributed to the difficulties of receiving a full education and of securing employment outside the home. More employment opportunities are open to women today than in the past, however, and in many countries women hold high-level positions in business, government, civil service, education, and other sectors. Statistics differ greatly across the Islamic world and are difficult to assess because they often fail to take into account the rural woman who may work full time in the fields or other occupation outside the house but does not earn an independent salary. . . .

Saudi Arabia presents an interesting case study of the confrontation of Islamic ideas with contemporary reality. Women are greatly inhibited in the labor arena; because of conservative religious attitudes they must be veiled and covered, are not permitted to drive or even ride in a taxi with a strange man, and in general are unable to participate on the social and professional level with males. However, in a country in which production is both necessary and economically possible and which suffers from a lack of manpower, the use of women in the workforce or increased importation of foreign labor seem the only two (both undesirable) alternatives. Thus more Saudi women are working, and because of their right to inherit, are accumulating very substantial amounts of money. It is interesting to note the rapid rate of construction of new banks exclusively for women in places like Jiddah and Riyadh.

The aforementioned Qur'an verse about the witness of two women being equal to that of one man and the supporting literature attesting to female intellectual, physical (and in fact sometimes moral) inferiority have made it difficult for Muslim women to achieve equal political rights. In most Arab countries (except Saudi Arabia and certain of the Gulf States), as well as in most other parts of the Islamic world, women have now been given the vote. Centuries of passivity in the political realm, however, have made it difficult for women to take advantage of the opportunities now available to them. In some countries, such as Egypt, women are playing major political roles, but generally women politicians find little support from men or even from other women for their aspirations. This is not to underestimate the strong current in Islamic thinking which encourages the full participation of women in politics, as well as in the educational and professional fields.

Like an intricate and complex geometric pattern on a Persian rug or a frieze decorating a mosque, the practices, roles, opportunities, prescriptions, hopes, and frustrations of Islamic women are woven together in a whole. The colors are sometimes bold and striking, at other times muted and subtle. Some contemporary Muslim women are progressive and aggressive, no longer content to fit the traditionally prescribed patterns. Others are passive and accepting, not yet able to discern what new possibilities may be open to them, let alone whether or not they might want to take advantage of such opportunities. Some are Westernized as their mothers and grandmothers were and have every intention of staying that way, while others are increasingly clear in their feelings that the West does not have the answers and that Islam, particularly the Islam of the Qur'an and the community of the Prophet Muhammad, is God's chosen way for humankind. For the latter, their dress, their relationships with their husbands and families, and their verbal assent to Islamic priorities reflect this conviction that the time has come to cease a fruitless preoccupation with things Western and to reaffirm their identity as Muslim women.

It is difficult for Western feminists to grasp exactly what the Muslim woman may mean by "liberation." For many Islamic women, the fruits of liberation in the West are too many broken marriages, women left without the security of men who will provide for them, deteriorating relations between men and women, and sexual license that appears as rank immorality. They see the Islamic system as affirmed by the Qur'an as one in which male authority over them ensures their care and protection and provides a structure in which the family is solid, children are inculcated with lasting values, and the balance of responsibility between man and woman is one in which absolute equality is less highly prized than cooperation and complementarity.

The new Islamic woman, then, is morally and religiously conservative and affirms the absolute value of the true Islamic system for human relationships. She is intolerant of the kind of Islam in which women are subjugated and relegated to roles insignificant to the full functioning of society, and she wants to take full advantage of educational and professional opportunities. She may agree, however, that certain fields of education are more appropriate for women than others, and that certain professions are more natural to males than to females. She participates as a contributor to and decisionmaker for the family, yet recognizes that in any complex relationship final authority must rest with one person. And she is content to delegate that authority to her husband, father, or other male relative in return for the solidarity of the family structure and the support and protection that it gives her and her children.

That not all, or even most, Muslim women subscribe to this point of view is clear. And yet, at the time of this writing, it seems equally clear that if Western observers are to understand women in the contemporary Islamic world, they must appreciate a point of view that is more and more prevalent. The West is increasingly identified with imperialism, and solutions viable for women in the Islamic community are necessarily different from the kinds of solutions that many Western women seem to have chosen for themselves. For the Muslim the words of the Qur'an are divine, and the prescriptions for the roles and rights of females, like the other messages of the holy book, are seen as part of God's divinely ordered plan for all humanity. Change will come slowly, and whatever kinds of liberation ultimately prevail will be cloaked in a garb that is—in one or another of its various aspects—essentially Islamic.

CRITICAL-THINKING QUESTIONS

1. In what formal ways does Islam confer on men authority over women?

2. In what formal and informal ways does Islam give power to women to affect their own lives and those of men?

3. From a Muslim perspective, what are some of the problems with Western living and, particularly, Western feminism?

CLASSIC

CONTEMPORARY

CROSS-CULTURAL

63 Education and Inequality

SAMUEL BOWLES AND HERBERT GINTIS

Education has long been held to be a means to realizing U.S. ideals of equal opportunity. As Lester Ward notes at the beginning of this selection, the promise of education is to allow "natural" abilities to win out over the "artificial" inequalities of class, race, and sex. Samuel Bowles and Herbert Gintis claim that this has happened very little in the United States. Rather, they argue, schooling has more to do with maintaining existing social hierarchy.

Universal education is the power, which is destined to overthrow every species of hierarchy. It is destined to remove all artificial inequality and leave the natural inequalities to find their true level. With the artificial inequalities of caste, rank, title, blood, birth, race, color, sex, etc., will fall nearly all the oppression, abuse, prejudice, enmity, and injustice, that humanity is now subject to. (Lester Frank Ward, *Education* © 1872)

A review of educational history hardly supports the optimistic pronouncements of liberal educational theory. The politics of education are better understood in terms of the need for social control in an unequal and rapidly changing economic order. The founders of the modern U.S.

Source: From *Schooling in Capitalist America: Educational Reform and the Contradictions of Economic Life* by Samuel Bowles and Herbert Gintis. Copyright © 1976 by Basic Books, Inc. (Includes Fig. 1, p. 436). Reprinted with permission.

school system understood that the capitalist economy produces great extremes of wealth and poverty, of social elevation and degradation. Horace Mann and other school reformers of the antebellum period knew well the seamy side of the burgeoning industrial and urban centers. "Here," wrote Henry Barnard, the first state superintendent of education in both Connecticut and Rhode Island, and later to become the first U.S. Commissioner of Education, "the wealth, enterprise and professional talent of the state are concentrated . . . but here also are poverty, ignorance, profligacy and irreligion, and a classification of society as broad and deep as ever divided the plebeian and patrician of ancient Rome."[1] They lived in a world in which, to use de Tocqueville's words, ". . . small aristocratic societies . . . are formed by some manufacturers in the midst of the immense democracy of our age [in which] . . . some men are opulent and a multitude . . . are wretchedly poor."[2] The rapid rise of the factory system, particularly in New England, was celebrated by the early school reformers; yet, the alarming transition from a relatively simple rural society to a highly stratified industrial economy could not be ignored. They shared the fears that de Tocqueville had expressed following his visit to the United States in 1831:

When a workman is unceasingly and exclusively engaged in the fabrication of one thing, he ultimately does his work with singular dexterity; but at the same time he loses the general faculty of applying his mind to the direction of the work. . . . [While] the science of manufacture lowers the class of workmen, it raises the class of masters. . . . [If] ever a permanent inequality of conditions . . . again penetrates into the world, it may be predicted that this is the gate by which they will enter.[3]

While deeply committed to the emerging industrial order, the farsighted school reformers of the mid-nineteenth century understood the explosive potential of the glaring inequalities of factory life. Deploring the widening of social divisions and fearing increasing unrest, Mann, Barnard, and others proposed educational expansion and reform. In his Fifth Report as Secretary of the Massachusetts Board of Education, Horace Mann wrote:

Education, then, beyond all other devices of human origin, is the great equalizer of the conditions of men—the balance wheel of the social machinery. . . . It does better than to disarm the poor of their hostility toward the rich; it prevents being poor.[4]

Mann and his followers appeared to be at least as interested in disarming the poor as in preventing poverty. They saw in the spread of universal and free education a means of alleviating social distress without redistributing wealth and power or altering the broad outlines of the economic system. Education, it seems, had almost magical powers:

The main idea set forth in the creeds of some political reformers, or revolutionizers, is that some people are poor because others are rich. This idea supposed a fixed amount of property in the community . . . and the problem presented for solution is how to transfer a portion of this property from those who are supposed to have too much to those who feel and know that they have too little. At this point, both their theory and their expectation of reform stop. But the beneficent power of education would not be exhausted, even though it should peaceably abolish all the miseries that spring from the coexistence, side by side, of enormous wealth and squalid want. It has a higher function. Beyond the power of diffusing old wealth, it has the prerogative of creating new.[5]

The early educators viewed the poor as the foreign element that they were. Mill hands were recruited throughout New England, often disrupting the small towns in which textile and other rapidly growing industries had located. Following the Irish potato famine of the 1840s, thousands of Irish workers settled in the cities and towns of the northeastern United States. Schooling was seen as a means of integrating this "uncouth and dangerous" element into the social fabric of American life. The inferiority of the foreigner was taken for granted. The editors of the influential *Massachusetts Teacher,* a leader in the educational reform movement, writing in 1851, saw ". . . the increasing influx of foreigners . . ." as a moral and social problem:

Will it, like the muddy Missouri, as it pours its waters into the clear Mississippi and contaminates the whole united mass, spread ignorance and vice, crime and disease, through our native population?

If . . . we can by any means purify this foreign people, enlighten their ignorance and bring them up to our level, we shall perform a work of true and perfect charity, blessing the giver and receiver in equal measure. . . .

With the old not much can be done; but with their children, the great remedy is *education.* The rising generation must be taught as our own children are taught. We say *must be* because in many cases this can only be accomplished by coercion.[6]

Since the mid-nineteenth century the dual objectives of educational reformers—equality of opportunity and social control—have been intermingled, the merger of these two threads sometimes so nearly complete that it becomes impossible to distinguish between the two. Schooling has been at once something done for the poor and to the poor.

The basic assumptions which underlay this commingling help explain the educational reform movement's social legacy. First, educational reformers did not question the fundamental economic institutions of capitalism: Capitalist ownership and control of the means of production and dependent wage labor were taken for granted. In fact, education was to help preserve and extend the capitalist order. The function of the school system was to accommodate workers to its most rapid possible development. Second, it was assumed that people (often classes of people or "races") are differentially equipped by nature or social origins to occupy the varied economic and social levels in the class structure. By providing equal opportunity, the school system was to elevate the masses, guiding them sensibly and fairly to the manifold political, social, and economic roles of adult life.

Jefferson's educational thought strikingly illustrates this perspective. In 1779, he proposed a two-track educational system which would prepare individuals for adulthood in one of the two classes of society: the "laboring and the learned."[7] Even children of the laboring class would qualify for leadership. Scholarships would allow ". . . those persons whom nature hath endowed with genius and virtue . . ." to ". . . be rendered by liberal education worthy to receive and able to guard the sacred deposit of the rights and liberties of their fellow citizens."[8] Such a system, Jefferson asserted, would succeed in ". . . raking a few geniuses from the rubbish."[9] Jefferson's two-tiered educational plan presents in stark relief the outlines and motivation for the stratified structure of U.S. education which has endured up to the present. At the top, there is the highly selective aristocratic tradition, the elite university training future leaders. At the base is mass education for all, dedicated to uplift and control. The two traditions have always coexisted although their meeting point has drifted upward over the years, as mass education has spread upward from elementary school through high school, and now up to the post-high-school level.

Though schooling was consciously molded to reflect the class structure, education was seen as a means of enhancing wealth and morality, which would work to the advantage of all. Horace Mann, in his 1842 report to the State Board of Education, reproduced this comment by a Massachusetts industrialist:

The great majority always have been and probably always will be comparatively poor, while a few will possess the greatest share of this world's goods. And it is a wise provision of Providence which connects so intimately, and as I think so indissolubly, the greatest good of the many with the highest interests in the few.[10]

Much of the content of education over the past century and a half can only be construed as an unvarnished attempt to persuade the "many" to make the best of the inevitable.

The unequal contest between social control and social justice is evident in the total functioning of U.S. education. The system as it stands today provides eloquent testimony to the ability of the well-to-do to perpetuate in the name of equality of opportunity an arrangement which consistently yields to themselves disproportional advantages, while thwarting the aspirations and needs of the working people of the United States. However grating this judgment may sound to the ears of the undaunted optimist, it is by no means excessive in light of the massive statistical data on inequality in the United States. Let us look at the contemporary evidence.

We may begin with the basic issue of inequalities in the years of schooling. As can be seen in [Figure 1], the number of years of schooling attained by an individual is strongly associated with parental socioeconomic status. This figure presents the estimated distribution of years of schooling attained by individuals of varying socioeconomic backgrounds. If we define socio-economic background by a weighted sum of income, occupation, and educational level of the parents, a child from the ninetieth percentile may expect, on the average, five more years of schooling than a child in the tenth percentile.[11]

. . . We have chosen a sample of white males because the most complete statistics are available

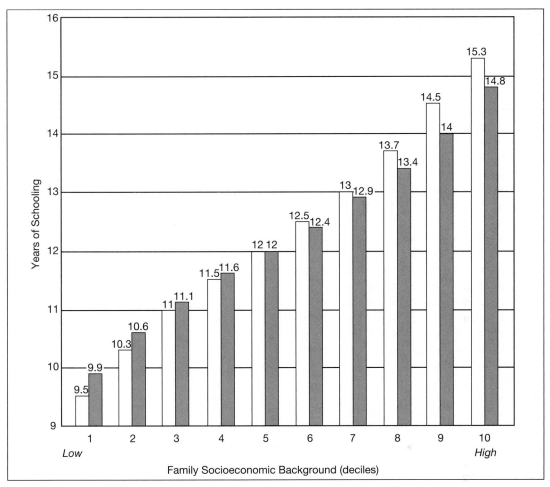

FIGURE 1   Educational Attainments Are Strongly Dependent on Social Background Even for People
of Similar Childhood IQs

Notes: For each socioeconomic group, the left-hand bar indicates the estimated average number of years of schooling attained
by all men from that group. The right-hand bar indicates the estimated average number of years of schooling attained by men
with IQ scores equal to the average for the entire sample. The sample refers to "non-Negro" men of "nonfarm" backgrounds,
aged 35–44 years in 1962. Source: Samuel Bowles and Valerie Nelson, "The 'Inheritance of IQ' and the Intergenerational
Transmission of Economic Inequality," *The Review of Economics and Statistics,* vol. LVI, no. 1 (Feb. 1974).

for this group. Moreover, if inequality for white
males can be documented, the proposition is
merely strengthened when sexual and racial differences are taken into account.

Additional census data dramatize one aspect
of educational inequalities: the relationship between family income and college attendance.
Even among those who had graduated from

high school in the early 1960s, children of families earning less than $3,000 per year were
over six times as likely *not* to attend college as
were the children of families earning over
$15,000.[12] Moreover, children from less well-
off families are *both* less likely to have graduated from high school and more likely to attend
inexpensive, two-year community colleges rather

than a four-year B.A. program if they do make it to college.[13]

Not surprisingly, the results of schooling differ greatly for children of different social backgrounds. Most easily measured, but of limited importance, are differences in scholastic achievement. If we measure the output of schooling by scores on nationally standardized achievement tests, children whose parents were themselves highly educated outperform the children of parents with less education by a wide margin. Data collected for the U.S. Office of Education Survey of Educational Opportunity reveal, for example, that among white high-school seniors, those whose parents were in the top education decile were, on the average, well over three grade levels in measured scholastic achievement ahead of those whose parents were in the bottom decile.[14]

Given these differences in scholastic achievement, inequalities in years of schooling among individuals of different social backgrounds are to be expected. Thus one might be tempted to argue that the close dependence of years of schooling attained on background displayed in the left-hand bars of [Figure 1] is simply a reflection of unequal intellectual abilities, or that inequalities in college attendance are the consequences of differing levels of scholastic achievement in high school and do not reflect any additional social class inequalities peculiar to the process of college admission.

This view, so comforting to the admissions personnel in our elite universities, is unsupported by the data, some of which is presented in [the figure]. The right-hand bars of [the figure] indicate that even among children with identical IQ test scores at ages six and eight, those with rich, well-educated, high-status parents could expect a much higher level of schooling than those with less-favored origins. Indeed, the closeness of the left-hand and right-hand bars in [the figure] shows that only a small portion of the observed social class differences in educational attainment is related to IQ differences across social classes.[15] The dependence of education attained on background is almost as strong for individuals with

the same IQ as for all individuals. Thus, while [the figure] indicates that an individual in the ninetieth percentile in social class background is likely to receive five more years of education than an individual in the tenth percentile, it also indicated that he is likely to receive 4.25 more years schooling than an individual from the tenth percentile with the same IQ. Similar results are obtained when we look specifically at access to college education for students with the same measured IQ. Project Talent data indicates that for "high ability" students (top 25 percent as measured by a composite of tests of "general aptitude"), those of high socioeconomic background (top 25 percent as measured by a composite of family income, parents' education, and occupation) are nearly twice as likely to attend college than students of low socioeconomic background (bottom 25 percent). For "low ability" students (bottom 25 percent), those of high-social background are more than four times as likely to attend college as are their low-social background counterparts.[16]

Inequality in years of schooling is, of course, only symptomatic of broader inequalities in the educational system. Not only do less well-off children go to school for fewer years, they are treated with less attention (or more precisely, less benevolent attention) when they are there. These broader inequalities are not easily measured. Some show up in statistics on the different levels of expenditure for the education of children of different socioeconomic backgrounds. Taking account of the inequality in financial resources for each year in school and the inequality in years of schooling obtained, Jencks estimated that a child whose parents were in the top fifth of the income distribution receives roughly twice the educational resources in dollar terms as does a child whose parents are in the bottom fifth.[17]

The social class inequalities in our school system, then, are too evident to be denied. Defenders of the educational system are forced back on the assertion that things are getting better; the inequalities of the past were far worse.

And, indeed, there can be no doubt that some of the inequalities of the past have been mitigated. Yet new inequalities have apparently developed to take their place, for the available historical evidence lends little support to the idea that our schools are on the road to equality of educational opportunity. For example, data from a recent U.S. Census survey reported in Spady indicate that graduation from college has become no less dependent on one's social background. This is true despite the fact that high-school graduation is becoming increasingly equal across social classes.[18] Additional data confirm this impression. The statistical association (coefficient of correlation) between parents' social status and years of education attained by individuals who completed their schooling three or four decades ago is virtually identical to the same correlation for individuals who terminated their schooling in recent years.[19] On balance, the available data suggests that the number of years of school attained by a child depends upon family background as much in the recent period as it did fifty years ago.

Thus, we have empirical reasons for doubting the egalitarian impact of schooling. . . . We conclude that U.S. education is highly unequal, the chances of attaining much or little schooling being substantially dependent on one's race and parents' economic level. Moreover, where there is a discernible trend toward a more equal educational system—as in the narrowing of the black education deficit, for example—the impact on the structure of economic opportunity is minimal at best.

CRITICAL-THINKING QUESTIONS

1. Describe how the educational system of the United States has historically had two objectives: increasing opportunity on the one hand and stabilizing an unequal society on the other. Which is emphasized in most public discussions of schooling?

2. In what respects, according to Bowles and Gintis, has schooling supported the capitalist economic system? How have such supports shaped the content of the educational system?

3. What are Bowles and Gintis's conclusions about the relationship between schooling and natural ability? Between schooling and social background?

NOTES

1. H. Barnard, *Papers for the Teacher: 2nd Series* (New York: F. C. Brownell, 1866), pp. 293–310.

2. A. de Tocqueville, as quoted in Jeremy Brecher, *Strike!* (San Francisco: Straight Arrow Books, 1972), pp. xi, xii.

3. Ibid., p. 172.

4. Horace Mann as quoted in Michael Katz, ed., *School Reform Past and Present* (Boston: Little, Brown, 1971), p. 141.

5. Ibid., p. 145.

6. *The Massachusetts Teacher* (Oct., 1851), quoted in Katz, pp. 169–70.

7. D. Tyack, *Turning Points in American Educational History* (Waltham, Mass.: Blaisdell, 1967), p. 89.

8. Ibid., p. 10.

9. Ibid., p. 89.

10. Mann, quoted in Katz, p. 147.

11. This calculation is based on data reported in full in Samuel Bowles and Valerie Nelson, "The 'Inheritance of IQ' and the Intergenerational Transmission of Economic Inequality," *The Review of Economics and Statistics,* 56, 1 (Feb., 1974). It refers to non-Negro males from nonfarm backgrounds, aged 35–44 years. The zero-order correlation coefficient between socioeconomic background and years of schooling was estimated at 0.646. The estimated standard deviation of years of schooling was 3.02. The results for other age groups are similar.

12. These figures refer to individuals who were high-school seniors in October 1965, and who subsequently graduated from high school. College attendance refers to both two- and four-year institutions. Family income is for the twelve months preceding October 1965. Data is drawn from U.S. Bureau of the Census, *Current Population Reports,* Series P-60, No. 183 (May, 1969).

13. For further evidence, see ibid.; and Jerome Karabel, "Community Colleges and Social Stratification," *Harvard Educational Review,* 424, 42 (Nov., 1972).

14. Calculation based on data in James S. Coleman et al., *Equality of Educational Opportunity* (Washington, D.C.: U.S. Government Printing Office, 1966), and the authors.

15. The data relating to IQ is from a 1966 survey of veterans by the National Opinion Research Center; and from N. Bayley and E. S. Schaefer, "Correlations of Maternal and Child Behaviors with the Development of Mental Ability: Data from the Berkeley Growth Study," *Monographs of Social Research in Child Development,* 29, 6 (1964).

16. Based on a large sample of U.S. high-school students as reported in John C. Flannagan and William W. Cooley, *Project Talent, One Year Follow-up Study,* Cooperative Research Project, No. 2333 (Pittsburgh: University of Pittsburgh, School of Education, 1966).

17. C. Jencks et al., *Inequality: A Reassessment of the Effects of Family and Schooling in America* (New York: Basic Books, 1972), p. 48.

18. W. L. Spady, "Educational Mobility and Access: Growth and Paradoxes," in *American Journal of Sociology,* 73, 3 (Nov. 1967); and Peter Blau and Otis D. Duncan, *The American Occupational Structure* (New York: John Wiley, 1967). More recent data support the evidence of no trend toward equality. See U.S. Bureau of Census, op. cit.

19. Ibid., Blau and Duncan.

CLASSIC

CONTEMPORARY

CROSS-CULTURAL

64 Savage Inequalities: Children in U.S. Schools

JONATHAN KOZOL

The job of our schools, we like to believe, is to give children a chance to develop their abilities and compete with others for their place in society. But has the game been "fixed" right from the start? Comparing two schools in New York City, Jonathan Kozol points to "savage inequalities" that perpetuate—or even increase—class differences.

"In a country where there is no distinction of class," Lord Acton wrote of the United States 130 years ago, "a child is not born to the station of its parents, but with an indefinite claim to all the prizes that can be won by thought and labor. It is in conformity with the theory of equality . . . to give as near as possible to every youth an equal state in life." Americans, he said, "are unwilling that any should be deprived in childhood of the means of competition."

It is hard to read these words today without a sense of irony and sadness. Denial of "the means of competition" is perhaps the single most consistent outcome of the education offered to poor children in the schools of our large cities; and nowhere is this pattern of denial more explicit or more absolute than in the public schools of New York City.

Average expenditures per pupil in the city of New York in 1987 were some $5,500. In the highest spending suburbs of New York (Great Neck or

Source: From *Savage Inequalities: Children in America's Schools* by Jonathan Kozol. Copyright © 1991 by Jonathan Kozol. Reprinted by permission of Crown Publishers, a division of Random House, Inc.

Manhasset, for example, on Long Island) funding levels rose above $11,000, with the highest districts in the state at $15,000. "Why . . . ," asks the city's Board of Education, "should our students receive less" than do "similar students" who live elsewhere? "The inequity is clear."

But the inequality to which these words refer goes even further than the school board may be eager to reveal. "It is perhaps the supreme irony," says the nonprofit Community Service Society [CSS] of New York, that "the same Board of Education which perceives so clearly the inequities" of funding between separate towns and cities "is perpetuating similar inequities" right in New York. And, in comment on the Board of Education's final statement—"the inequity is clear" the CSS observes, "New York City's poorest . . . districts could adopt that eloquent statement with few changes."

New York City's public schools are subdivided into thirty-two school districts. District 10 encompasses a large part of the Bronx but is, effectively, two separate districts. One of these districts, Riverdale, is in the northwest section of the Bronx. Home to many of the city's most sophisticated and well-educated families, its elementary schools have relatively few low-income students. The other section, to the south and east, is poor and heavily nonwhite.

The contrast between public schools in each of these two neighborhoods is obvious to any visitor. At Public School 24 in Riverdale, the principal speaks enthusiastically of his teaching staff. At Public School 79, serving poorer children to the south, the principal says that he is forced to take the "tenth-best" teachers. "I thank God they're still breathing," he remarks of those from whom he must select his teachers.

Some years ago, District 10 received an allocation for computers. The local board decided to give each elementary school an equal number of computers, even though the schools in Riverdale had smaller classes and far fewer students. When it was pointed out that schools in Riverdale, as a result, had twice the number of computers in proportion to their student populations as the schools in the poor neighborhoods, the chairman of the local board replied, "What is fair is what is determined . . . to be fair."

The superintendent of District 10, Fred Goldberg, tells *The New York Times* that "every effort" is made "to distribute resources equitably." He speculates that some gap might exist because some of the poorer schools need to use funds earmarked for computers to buy basic supplies like pens and paper. Asked about the differences in teachers noted by the principals, he says there are no differences, then adds that next year he'll begin a program to improve the quality of teachers in the poorer schools. Questioned about differences in physical appearances between the richer and the poorer schools, he says, "I think it's demographics."

Sometimes a school principal, whatever his background or his politics, looks into the faces of the children in his school and offers a disarming statement that cuts through official ambiguity. "These are the kids most in need," says Edward Flanery, the principal of one of the low-income schools, "and they get the worst teachers." For children of diverse needs in his overcrowded rooms, he says, "you need an outstanding teacher. And what do you get? You get the worst."

In order to find Public School 261 in District 10, a visitor is told to look for a mortician's office. The funeral home, which faces Jerome Avenue in the North Bronx, is easy to identify by its green awning. The school is next door, in a former roller-skating rink. No sign identifies the building as a school. A metal awning frame without an awning supports a flagpole, but there is no flag.

In the street in front of the school there is an elevated public transit line. Heavy traffic fills the street. The existence of the school is virtually concealed within this crowded city block.

In a vestibule between the outer and inner glass doors of the school there is a sign with these words: "All children are capable of learning."

Beyond the inner doors a guard is seated. The lobby is long and narrow. The ceiling is low. There are no windows. All the teachers that I see at first are middle-aged white women. The principal, who is also a white woman, tells me that the school's "capacity" is 900 but that there are 1,300 children here. The size of classes for fifth and sixth grade children in New York, she says, is "capped" at thirty-two, but she says that class size in the school goes "up to thirty-four." (I later see classes, however, as large as thirty-seven.) Classes for younger children, she goes on, are "capped at twenty-five," but a school can go above this limit if it puts an extra adult in the room. Lack of space, she says, prevents the school from operating a prekindergarten program.

I ask the principal where her children go to school. They are enrolled in private school, she says.

"Lunchtime is a challenge for us," she explains. "Limited space obliges us to do it in three shifts, 450 children at a time."

Textbooks are scarce and children have to share their social studies books. The principal says there is one full-time pupil counselor and another who is here two days a week: a ratio of 930 children to one counselor. The carpets are patched and sometimes taped together to conceal an open space. "I could use some new rugs," she observes.

To make up for the building's lack of windows and the crowded feeling that results, the staff puts plants and fish tanks in the corridors. Some of the plants are flourishing. Two boys, released from class, are in a corridor beside a tank, their noses pressed against the glass. A school of pinkish fish inside the tank are darting back and forth. Farther down the corridor a small Hispanic girl is watering the plants.

Two first grade classes share a single room without a window, divided only by a blackboard. Four kindergartens and a sixth grade class of Spanish-speaking children have been packed into a single room in which, again, there is no window. A second grade bilingual class of thirty-seven children has its own room but again there is no window.

By eleven o'clock, the lunchroom is already packed with appetite and life. The kids line up to get their meals, then eat them in ten minutes. After that, with no place they can go to play, they sit and wait until it's time to line up and go back to class.

On the second floor I visit four classes taking place within another undivided space. The room has a low ceiling. File cabinets and movable blackboards give a small degree of isolation to each class. Again, there are no windows.

The library is a tiny, windowless and claustrophobic room. I count approximately 700 books. Seeing no reference books, I ask a teacher if encyclopedias and other reference books are kept in classrooms.

"We don't have encyclopedias in classrooms," she replies. "That is for the suburbs."

The school, I am told, has twenty-six computers for its 1,300 children. There is one small gym and children get one period, and sometimes two, each week. Recess, however, is not possible because there is no playground. "Head Start," the principal says, "scarcely exists in District 10. We have no space."

The school, I am told, is 90 percent black and Hispanic; the other 10 percent are Asian, white or Middle Eastern.

In a sixth grade social studies class the walls are bare of words or decorations. There seems to be no ventilation system, or, if one exists, it isn't working.

The class discusses the Nile River and the Fertile Crescent.

The teacher, in a droning voice: "How is it useful that these civilizations developed close to rivers?"

A child, in a good loud voice: "What kind of question is that?"

In my notes I find these words: "An uncomfortable feeling—being in a building with no windows. There are metal ducts across the room. Do they give air? I feel asphyxiated. . . ."

On the top floor of the school, a sixth grade of thirty children shares a room with twenty-nine bilingual second graders. Because of the high class size there is an assistant with each teacher. This means that fifty-nine children and four grown-ups—sixty-three in all—must share a room that, in a suburban school, would hold no more than twenty children and one teacher. There are, at least, some outside windows in this room—it is the only room with windows in the school—and the room has a high ceiling. It is a relief to see some daylight.

I return to see the kindergarten classes on the ground floor and feel stifled once again by lack of air and the low ceiling. Nearly 120 children and adults are doing what they can to make the best of things: eighty children in four kindergarten classes, thirty children in the sixth grade class, and about eight grown-ups who are aides and teachers. The kindergarten children sitting on the worn rug, which is patched with tape, look up at me and turn their heads to follow me as I walk past them.

As I leave the school, a sixth grade teacher stops to talk. I ask her, "Is there air conditioning in warmer weather?"

Teachers, while inside the building, are reluctant to give answers to this kind of question.

Outside, on the sidewalk, she is less constrained: "I had an awful room last year. In the winter it was 56 degrees. In the summer it was up to 90. It was sweltering."

I ask her, "Do the children ever comment on the building?"

"They don't say," she answers, "but they know."

I ask her if they see it as a racial message.

"All these children see TV," she says. "They know what suburban schools are like. Then they look around them at their school. This was a roller-rink, you know. . . . They don't comment on it but you see it in their eyes. They understand.". . .

Two months later, on a day in May, I visit an elementary school in Riverdale. The dogwoods and magnolias on the lawn in front of P.S. 24 are in full blossom on the day I visit. There is a well-tended park across the street, another larger park three blocks away. To the left of the school is a playground for small children, with an innovative jungle gym, a slide and several climbing toys. Behind the school there are two playing fields for older kids. The grass around the school is neatly trimmed.

The neighborhood around the school, by no means the richest part of Riverdale, is nonetheless expensive and quite beautiful. Residences in the area—some of which are large, freestanding houses, others condominiums in solid red-brick buildings—sell for prices in the region of $400,000; but some of the larger Tudor houses on the winding and tree-shaded streets close to the school can cost up to $1 million. The excellence of P.S. 24, according to the principal, adds to the value of these homes. Advertisements in *The New York Times* will frequently inform prospective buyers that a house is "in the neighborhood of P.S. 24."

The school serves 825 children in the kindergarten through sixth grade. This is . . . a great deal smaller than the 1,300 children packed into the former skating rink; but the principal of P.S. 24, a capable and energetic man named David Rothstein, still regards it as excessive for an elementary school.

The school is integrated in the strict sense that the middle- and upper-middle-class white children here do occupy a building that contains some Asian and Hispanic and black children; but there is little integration in the classrooms since the vast majority of the Hispanic and black children are assigned to "special" classes on the basis of evaluations that have classified them "EMR"—"educable mentally retarded"—or else, in the worst of cases, "TMR"—"trainable mentally retarded."

I ask the principal if any of his students qualify for free-lunch programs. "About 130 do," he says. "Perhaps another thirty-five receive their lunches at reduced price. Most of these kids are in the special classes. They do not come from this neighborhood."

The very few nonwhite children that one sees in mainstream classes tend to be Japanese or else of other Asian origins. Riverdale, I learn, has been the residence of choice for many years to members of the diplomatic corps.

The school therefore contains effectively two separate schools: one of about 130 children, most of whom are poor, Hispanic, black, assigned to one of the twelve special classes; the other of some 700 mainstream students, almost all of whom are white or Asian.

There is a third track also—this one for the students who are labeled "talented" or "gifted." This is termed a "pull out" program since the children who are so identified remain in mainstream classrooms but are taken out for certain periods each week to be provided with intensive and, in my opinion, excellent instruction in some areas of reasoning and logic often known as "higher-order skills" in the contemporary jargon of the public schools. Children identified as "gifted" are admitted to this program in first grade and, in most cases, will remain there for six years. Even here, however, there are two tracks of the gifted. The regular gifted classes are provided with only one semester of this specialized instruction yearly. Those very few children, on the other hand, who are identified as showing the most promise are assigned, beginning in the third grade, to a program that receives a full-year regimen.

In one such class, containing ten intensely verbal and impressive fourth grade children, nine are white and one is Asian. The "special" class I enter first, by way of contrast, has twelve children of whom only one is white and none is Asian. These racial breakdowns prove to be predictive of the schoolwide pattern.

In a classroom for the gifted on the first floor of the school, I ask a child what the class is doing. "Logic and syllogisms," she replies. The room is fitted with a planetarium. The principal says that all the elementary schools in District 10 were given the same planetariums ten years ago but that certain schools, because of overcrowding, have been forced to give them up. At P.S. 261, according to my notes, there was a domelike space that had been built to hold a planetarium, but the planetarium had been removed to free up space for the small library collection. P.S. 24, in contrast, has a spacious library that holds almost 8,000 books. The windows are decorated with attractive, brightly colored curtains and look out on flowering trees. The principal says that it's inadequate, but it appears spectacular to me after the cubicle that holds a meager 700 books within the former skating rink.

The district can't afford librarians, the principal says, but P.S. 24, unlike the poorer schools of District 10, can draw on educated parent volunteers who staff the room in shifts three days a week. A parent organization also raises independent funds to buy materials, including books, and will soon be running a fund-raiser to enhance the library's collection.

In a large and sunny first grade classroom that I enter next, I see twenty-three children, all of whom are white or Asian. In another first grade, there are twenty-two white children and two others who are Japanese. There is a computer in each class. Every classroom also has a modern fitted sink.

In a second grade class of twenty-two children, there are two black children and three Asian children. Again, there is a sink and a computer. A sixth grade social studies class has only one black child. The children have an in-class research area that holds some up-to-date resources. A set of encyclopedias (World Book, 1985) is in a rack beside a window. The children are doing a Spanish language lesson when I enter. Foreign languages begin in sixth grade at the school, but Spanish is offered also to the kindergarten children. As in every room at P.S. 24, the window shades are clean and new, the floor is neatly tiled in gray and green, and there is not a single light bulb missing.

Walking next into a special class, I see twelve children. One is white. Eleven are black. There are no Asian children. The room is half the size of mainstream classrooms. "Because of overcrowding," says the principal, "we have had to split these rooms in half." There is no computer and no sink.

I enter another special class. Of seven children, five are black, one is Hispanic, one is white. A little black boy with a large head sits in the far corner and is gazing at the ceiling.

"Placement of these kids," the principal explains, "can usually be traced to neurological damage."

In my notes: "How could so many of these children be brain-damaged?"

Next door to the special class is a woodworking shop. "This shop is only for the special classes," says the principal. The children learn to punch in time cards at the door, he says, in order to prepare them for employment.

The fourth grade gifted class, in which I spend the last part of the day, is humming with excitement. "I start with these children in the first grade," says the teacher. "We pull them out of mainstream classes on the basis of their test results and other factors such as the opinion of their teachers. Out of this group, beginning in third grade, I pull out the ones who show the most potential, and they enter classes such as this one."

The curriculum they follow, she explains, "emphasizes critical thinking, reasoning and logic." The planetarium, for instance, is employed not simply for the study of the universe as it exists.

"Children also are designing their own galaxies," the teacher says.

A little girl sitting around a table with her classmates speaks with perfect poise: "My name is Susan. We are in the fourth grade gifted program."

I ask them what they're doing and a child says, "My name is Laurie and we're doing problem-solving."

A rather tall, good-natured boy who is half-standing at the table tells me that his name is David. "One thing that we do," he says, "is logical thinking. Some problems, we find, have more than one good answer. We need to learn not simply to be logical in our own thinking but to show respect for someone else's logic even when an answer may be technically incorrect."

When I ask him to explain this, he goes on, "A person who gives an answer that is not 'correct' may nonetheless have done some interesting thinking that we should examine. 'Wrong' answers may be more useful to examine than correct ones."

I ask the children if reasoning and logic are innate or if they're things that you can learn.

"You know some things to start with when you enter school," Susan says. "But we also learn some things that other children don't."

I ask her to explain this.

"We know certain things that other kids don't know because we're *taught* them."

CRITICAL-THINKING QUESTIONS

1. In principle, what should our schools do for all children?

2. Point to specific differences in schools that Kozol claims amount to "savage inequalities." Do you agree with his argument that schools stack the deck against poor children?

3. What about parents who claim they have earned the right to give their children whatever privileges they can afford to? Would you support a government-imposed equal-funding rule to give children in every neighborhood roughly the same quality of schooling?

CLASSIC

CONTEMPORARY

CROSS-CULTURAL

65 Japanese Mothers as the Best Teachers

KEIKO HIRAO

The Japanese government has tried to encourage fathers to share in their children's up-bringing, including placing advertisements in major newspapers that read "We don't call a man a father if he doesn't participate in childcare." Nonetheless, employed mothers rather than employed fathers are the ones who leave the labor force to devote a major part of their lives to their young children's education.

. . . The intensity and the depth of involvement of many Japanese mothers in their children's education has received considerable attention (Boocock 1991; Ellington 1992; Uno 1993; White 1987). The phenomenon of the *kyōiku mama* (education mother), in which a woman devotes a major part of her life to her child's academic career, is both praised as the source of Japanese students' impressive academic success and criticized for depriving children of their free time. The description of the *kyōiku mama* phenomenon, however, has been limited by a lack of attention to how Japanese education has been privatized in the past twenty years and how the role of *kyōiku mama* has been shaped and influenced by the reality of the educational system in Japan.

According to a survey by the Ministry of Education, over 35 percent of schoolchildren attend

juku (private educational institutions) that provide supplemental academic training (Ministry of Education 1994). The rate of attendance is highest among older children: in 1993, an amazing 67 percent of Japanese ninth graders were enrolled. Between 1985 and 1993, *juku* attendance increased from 17 to 24 percent for elementary school children and from 47 to 60 percent for middle school children. These *juku* statistics, however, tell only a small part of the story, which includes correspondence courses, tutoring services, and various private lessons available to children. When these services are included, 82 percent of all Japanese schoolchildren are enrolled in one or a combination of private educational programs (Ministry of Education 1994).

. . . A recent notable development in educational competition and the *kyōiku mama* phenomenon in Japan is that ever-younger children are becoming involved in educational activities outside of school. Approximately 42 percent of Japanese preschool children are enrolled in some kind of educational program outside of kindergarten and day nurseries

Source: Keiko Hirao, "Mothers as the Best Teachers: Japanese Motherhood and Early Childhood Education." In Mary C. Brinton (Ed.), *Women's Working Lives in East Asia.* Stanford, CA: Stanford University Press, 2001, pp. 180–203.

(Ministry of Health and Welfare 1991). As Norma Field notes, childhood in contemporary Japan has become streamlined as a series of preparatory steps to productive adulthood (Field 1995), and parents—especially mothers—play a vital role as the agents of human capital investment. . . .

DATA

This chapter is based on interviews conducted on the parenting behaviors of mothers in the Tokyo area during 1991–1992 and in Nagoya (Aichi Prefecture) in 1994–1995. The samples for the Tokyo interviews were recruited through three parenting classes sponsored by local governments and playgroup networks. The parenting classes involved approximately eighty participants in total. As I served as the coordinator/instructor, I was able to request the names of participants who were willing to cooperate in the interviews. I then added to the samples through snowball sampling methods. Twenty women from the classes were contacted for the in-depth interviews. I also utilized the discussions in the classes as a means of participant observation. Because the parenting classes were offered in the daytime, the participants were limited to full-time housewives and part-time workers. The format of the interview was mostly open-ended, with some structured questions about personal background. . . .

DEVELOPMENT OF EARLY EDUCATION PROGRAMS: AN OBSESSION WITH PRODIGIES

The educational role played by Japanese mothers starts when children are very young. Kindergartens and nursery schools expect mothers to incorporate an educational agenda into the routine of daily life (Allison 1996). The intensity of this responsibility is illustrated by the recent development of *sōki-kyōiku*, early educational programs that are given either at home or at private, extra-school institutions. These are geared explicitly toward the development of cognitive skills in preschool children.

These programs are "extra-school" in the sense that they are independent from formal kindergartens and accredited day nurseries. Kindergartens and day nurseries operate under the auspices of the Ministry of Education and the Ministry of Health and Welfare, respectively. Because more than 93 percent of preschool children are enrolled in one or the other of these institutions, kindergartens and day nursery programs have now become comparable to formal schools. Private enterprises that provide educational services for preschoolers can be compared to the preschool version of *juku* for school-aged children. *Juku* is distinguished from extracurricular activities as it is administered outside the school system. In the same manner, early education programs function externally to the formal system of kindergarten and nursery schools.

. . . The course content offered in the extra-preschool curriculums varies widely, ranging from music lessons to reading and writing, simple mathematics to foreign languages. Some courses are purely academically oriented, some specialize in preparatory training for entrance examinations for prestigious elementary schools, and others emphasize artistic skills and music lessons. Many boast a combination of some or all of these benefits.

Kumon, a prominent *juku,* for example, invites preschoolers to work on mathematics, English, and Japanese. Founded by Toru Kumon in 1958 in Osaka as a small neighborhood *juku* for school-children, Kumon is now one of the largest *juku* establishments in Japan, with more than 18,000 branch classroom locations all over the country and a total enrollment of 1.5 million (Kumon Kyōiku Kenkyūkai 1998). . . .

During the late 1980s, Kumon expanded its programs to include the enrollment of preschoolers. In 1990, they started a correspondence course through which they delivered monthly educational kits such as videos, flash cards, and workbooks to children between the ages of two and five. In the mid-1980s, Kumon began to commend their high achievers. Among them were preschool children who could work out differential and integral calculus. These youngsters had already finished the high school level mathematics curriculum, and some of their mothers were reported to have started the program while they were pregnant.

The Association of Early Childhood Development, founded by Masaru Ibuka, the founder of Sony, states its mission as assisting in the sound development of the mother-child relationship. Its operation includes developing teaching materials, such as electronically prerecorded flash cards called "talking cards." Courses are offered to children aged 12 to 24 months old. Courses are also available to pregnant women on how to enhance the potential abilities of their unborn children. . . .

The Child Academy, founded by Makoto Shichida, offers comprehensive programs such as storytelling, flash-card learning, haiku, arts and crafts, and music. The Ishii School of Kanji Education focuses on the teaching of reading and writing Chinese characters for preschoolers, offering correspondence courses as well as instruction in classrooms. . . .

The spur for early education began in 1976 when Ibuka published a sensational book titled *Yōchien de wa Ososugiru* ("Kindergarten Is Too Late"). This book became a best-seller and was followed by a flood of publications that advocated early intervention in order to develop the cognitive and verbal skills of infants. Such publications include Shichida's *Miraculous Education for the Zero-Year-Old* (1983) and *Tips on Raising an Intelligent Baby* (1985), Mitsuishi's *Creating Prodigies* (1988), and Ōshima's *Prenatal Education* (1988). The acceleration of early education can be seen through the titles of Ibuka's successive books: *Kindergarten Is Too Late* (1976), followed by *Zero-Year-Old* (1991) and *From Embryo* (1992). We can see the shift in the messages. Kindergarten was too late in the 1970s. But in the 1990s mothers were instructed to be concerned about their children's academic achievements *from conception.*

The accelerated education in Japan parallels, to some extent, the proliferation of educational programs for preschool children in the United States. Programs with heavy educational components for prekindergarten children are also on the increase in the United States. The well-publicized "superkid" practice by Glenn Doman, *How to Teach Your Baby to Read* (1964) and *How to Multiply Your Baby's Intelligence* (1984), for example, resonates with many of the publications by Ibuka, Shichida, and Ishii. They share the common premises that children's IQ is not fixed at birth but is determined by environment and intellectual stimulation, that children's potential for learning has long been underestimated, and that intellectual growth is very rapid during early childhood. In other words, the cognitive potential of children, according to both Doman and Ishii, can be significantly boosted by early intervention programs. . . .

Once education for preschoolers proved to be a profitable business for *juku* industries, other sectors began to enter the market. For example, a company that sells underwear and other home-related products through direct-mail catalogs decided to go into the extra-preschool education business in 1992. They converted their customer list into a mailing list through which they delivered educational materials each month for children under the age of six. It is not unusual, especially in urban areas, for mothers of newborn babies to receive a direct-mail advertisement of courses offered to "enhance the academic ability" of their offspring. The early education "boom" was thus driven by the supply of these services.

Ironically, this development took place outside the public school system just as the Ministry of Education was trying to relax school schedules to remedy the excessive competition for entrance examinations. The public schools have taken to heart the criticism that excessive academic competition causes poor health among children, school violence, and bullying. Contrary to the common belief that Japanese schools are driving their students with relentless pressure for academic success, they are now shifting their emphasis to "creativity," "sociability," and "whole development" and away from rote learning. Approximately one-fourth of the time spent at Japanese schools is now devoted to nonacademic activities, such as recess and club activities (Stevenson 1992). Moreover, the Ministry of Education decided to reduce the time spent in school by seventy hours per year for elementary school students and thirty-five hours for junior high school students. The ministry also stipulates in the new curriculum guidelines that the content be cut by 30 percent, beginning in 2002.

In spite of the ministry's attempt to give children more free time and develop their creativity, the reforms have not extended to broad changes in the entrance examination system for colleges. As a result, many parents feel that school classrooms have become a place to confirm what children already know instead of a center for learning and mastering new subjects. This concern has prompted them to plan ahead out of the fear of having their children fall behind.

For example, Natsuko, who is age 36 and has three school-aged children, comments that

I was too naive when I was raising my first child. You can't believe how smart today's children are. Most first graders already know several *kanji* [Chinese characters], not to mention being able to read and write *hiragana* [the Japanese phonetic syllabary]. My daughter was the only one in the class who could not write her name. Although we are told that teachers don't expect children to have mastered these things by the time they enter school, the fact that all the other children already know them makes the slow starters fall behind.

Another problem with the educational reforms is that all schools must meet minimum standards, but private schools are not bound by the curriculum guidelines stipulated by the Ministry of Education. That is, private schools can use more advanced materials than those used in public schools. They can also allocate more hours to important subjects, such as English, which carries more weight in the college entrance exams. Given that a sizable portion of students admitted to the University of Tokyo, the most prestigious university in the Japanese educational hierarchy, come from private high schools with admission tracks tied to their own attached junior high schools, parents are reminded that educational competition starts at a very young age. Many of these schools push their curricula forward so that students can devote their entire senior

year in high school to preparing for college entrance examinations. Private elementary schools are also attractive to parents who worry that their children will not fare well in the intense competition for junior high schools: many of these private institutions provide an admission track all the way up to high school. Consequently, the age for competition has been lowered, and the competition for a better school career has involved young preschool children.

Chisato is married to a computer engineer and has a three-year-old son. She is planning to send him to a private elementary school. He is attending a weekly preparatory program for the screening test. He also has to do workbook exercises at home with his mother. Chisato comments on their decision as follows:

I know it is a pity that a small boy like him has to work so hard, but it is for his own good. It is much easier to push him now than it will be later. If he can avoid the pressure of the entrance examination for junior high and high school, he can devote more time to developing his talents during the twelve years [he is in school full-time].

Kumiko, who is married to a physician, had a son just three weeks before I interviewed her. When I asked her how she felt about having a baby, she said,

I am glad Satoshi was born in April. Of course it's the best time for having a baby! The weather is nice, and I can take him outside and let him breathe fresh air. You know, oxygen is very important for brain development. Also, he will be one of the oldest in his class [the school year starts in April in Japan], and that will make him ahead of most children. Kids born in spring have better school records. I think that's why children born in April and May are overrepresented among students in the University of Tokyo.

I wish I had asked her where she got this idea about the birth month and the chance of being accepted to the University of Tokyo. When I met her a year later, she had put Satoshi in an enrichment class for infants run by one of the large *juku* establishments. She escorted Satoshi every week and joined an hour-long class with him. She commented bashfully,

Well, I don't mean to raise him as a "super kid." It's just a play group sort of program where children play with toys and listen to songs and so on. I just think it is important to let him play with other babies, because he has to know how to cooperate and socialize with his peers by the time he goes to kindergarten.

Although Kumiko's example may be an extreme case, there are three points that represent the ideas shared by many *kyōiku mama* today. First, a child has to go through keen academic competition in order to obtain a decent educational background. Second, a child's educational success depends on how much the parent puts into it. Third, the younger the child, the better the time for preparation. It is almost always the mother who is responsible for seeing to the provision of these opportunities and who is expected to be closely involved in the process. . . .

JAPANESE WOMEN IN THE COMMUNITY

While the publication trends in popular books set the tenor of public discourse on "good parenting," they also mirror what the public wants to read. The increased demands for parenting advice reflect the social context in which adult socialization takes place for young Japanese mothers.

Adult Socialization and the Role of the Mass Media

Assuming the parental role is a totally fresh endeavor for most Japanese women, who generally become mothers without any firsthand experience of taking care of small children (given that Japanese families typically now have few children). Unlike in the United States, baby-sitting is not a socially accepted way for teenagers to earn money. So it is not unusual for a mother to start parenting with no experience in changing diapers or bathing babies. Parenting, or mothering specifically, is a performance without rehearsal.

Japanese women learn parenting from several socializing agents: parents and in-laws, friends, neighbors, older siblings, books, magazines, television

programs, parenting courses sponsored by local governments, and kindergartens and day-care centers. Among these sources, the mass media is of increasing importance as a socializing agent. When asked where they obtained information on infant care, 35 percent of mothers surveyed in Tokyo named the mass media (books, magazines, and television) as the primary source of information, 34 percent named friends, and 17 percent answered kindergartens and daycare centers (Shirasa 1990). Parents and kin networks still play a major role in providing emotional support, but apparently they are somewhat secondary in the transmission of parenting knowledge.

Given the rapid pace at which childrearing practices have changed over the past decades, it is understandable that what grandmothers did thirty years ago is not often applicable to today's childrearing. For example, women in their 60s raised children when bottle-feeding was predominant; it was regarded as superior and as the "modern" way of feeding. Now the trend has reversed. Today more mothers opt for breast-feeding if it is possible (Katsuura-Cook 1991).

The arrival of parenting magazines is a rational consequence of this "information gap." They began to be published in the early 1980s and now provide detailed, up-to-date information on childrearing practices based on children's ages. Opposite to the decline in the birth rate, the circulation of parenting magazines has steadily increased. The total circulation of the major twelve parenting magazines is estimated to be as high as 2,710,000 (Shiomi 1996). Almost all of these parenting magazines contain advertisements and paid publications by companies that provide extra-preschool curricula and educational materials. No single issue appears without their advertisements and their sponsored articles on early intervention programs.

The effect of the mass media on the early education boom can be seen in a survey that showed a positive relationship between mothers' reliance on published materials for parenting know-how and their attitudes toward extra-preschool curricula. The more they are exposed to parenting information through the mass media, the more they are likely to be influenced to provide enrichment "stimulus" through extra-preschool curricula (Shirasa 1990). These mothers are also more likely to feel uneasy about their child's development if other children of the same age are more advanced in writing Chinese characters and in computations. Thus reliance on the mass media for parenting information seems to go hand in hand with the popularization of early education.

Isolation and Anxiety: Childrearing behind Closed Doors

Another prominent aspect in the lives of Japanese mothers who stay at home full-time is their isolation with their children. Because the social spheres of Japanese men and women tend to be so distinctly separated, there are very few opportunities for full-time housewives of salaried workers to socialize. The husband is busy with long working hours and rarely has spare time to help around the home with chores and childcare. Baby-sitters are not readily available in the neighborhood, and commercialized services are often too expensive. A mother is not qualified to have her baby enrolled in an accredited daycare center if she is not working or does not have another "legitimate" reason, such as illness. Commenting on her days with her baby, Toshiko, a full-time housewife married to a "salaryman," says: "A day, a week, and a month could easily pass without talking to any adult except for people in the market or with a salesperson who comes to our door to sell educational toys and *futon*."

In spite of the great emphasis placed on close mother-child relationships in Japanese families, literature in psychology and sociology has long ignored the situation of young mothers. The focus of attention has always been on *children* and on how the mother-child relationship affects the development of a child's personality, well-being, and so on. Little has been written or known about how the mother-child relationship affects mothers.

The isolation of mothers from other adult interaction is another precondition for the development

of the early education boom. Ironically, extra-preschool courses provide lonely mothers with a place to meet people. Toshiko said that she decided to put her son in an enrichment program because she wanted to meet people and make friends. The "friends" she was talking about were not for her son, but for herself. Kumiko, mentioned earlier in this chapter, also said that chatting with other mothers in the waiting room while their children took classes provided a nice change of pace.

Many mothers are aware of the suffocation of lonely childrearing and many of them do try to get out of the isolation. Ochiai (1989) argues that a new type of network among mothers is emerging in urban areas in response to the lack of support from husbands and kin. They are of a spontaneous nature, usually composed of mothers who meet each other in neighborhood parks or parenting classes sponsored by the local government. These neighborhood networks provide mutual support in parenting and supplement kin networks. However, my observation is that much of what Ochiai calls "networks" tend to be exclusive, rarely involve fathers, and limit concerns to matters revolving around children.

Yoshiko used to work as a secretary at a trading company until she became pregnant. She decided to leave her job and take care of her son at home. The change in her lifestyle and the routines of a full-time housewife were "a kind of culture shock" to her. She described her days as follows:

I usually take my son to a neighborhood park in the morning so that he can play with other children. Mothers chat while children play in the sandbox. If the kids move to the swings, we move with them and chat around the swing, or slides, or whatever. Then we usually go to one of the mothers' houses, order pizza or noodles for lunch, and then chat in the afternoon while the children play in the house. When daddies are on business trips, we sometimes eat supper together. The members are the same and the topic of our conversation is the same. At first I enjoyed being with these people, but I am getting tired of it. It's so suffocating!

After several months, she decided to have her son enroll in Suzuki violin and Kumon so that she could avoid this situation.

I was getting tired of this, but did not want to be ostracized and to be left alone with my kid. Having a private lesson for him gave me a good excuse for keeping some distance from other mothers. They won't feel bad about me if I just say, "I can't join you today because I have to take my kid to a violin lesson."

Again, extra-preschool courses are meeting the demands of their patrons. They provide a place to meet other mothers—and to avoid them.

"A GOOD MOTHER" AS A STATUS: THE CULTURAL CONTRADICTIONS IN WOMEN'S ROLES

Mothers receive mixed and conflicting messages [about] labor force participation: you have to be a good mother, but childrearing will not occupy you for your entire life. On the one hand, mothers are pressed to stay home at least until their children reach the age of three. On the other hand, mothers are aware that they have to be prepared to pursue their "own lives," for their children will grow up and leave the nest. Men and women, especially those who have pursued higher education, have been exposed to contemporary cultural values that emphasize the significance of achievement. . . .

Over 80 percent of Japanese women join the labor force upon graduating from school, but more than 80 percent of these women have withdrawn from the labor force for one year or longer by the time they reach the age of 34. The probability of leaving one's job is not necessarily lower for women with higher education (Brinton 1993; Hirao 1997). That is, highly educated women are as likely to be out of the labor force as their less-educated counterparts during the prime parenting years. Moreover, the probability of coming back to the labor force after initial "retirement" is not necessarily higher for four-year university graduates (Hirao 1998). In other words, Japanese women's human capital is very much underutilized in the labor force.

The most striking thing that I noticed throughout my interviews was the frustration shared by many young mothers. "What depresses me is the social trend that gives praise to career women," said Yuko, a graduate from a prestigious four-year university. She used to work at a large department store as a sales assistant and resigned from her job when she had her second daughter.

They say it's good to be "at the top," pursue your career, and earn money. Super moms who can handle both work and family appear as attractive figures in TV dramas. I used to have self-confidence. I was always at the top both in school and work. My grades were higher than those of my male classmates. I thought I was in a career track until I left it to take care of my kids. Now, I ask myself, "What am I doing here?" I feel trapped and left behind by the rest of the world.

Emiko, who also has two children, expresses her frustration more clearly.

I used to have everything except kids: study, work, travel, and love. I was imbued with the pleasure of achieving what I deserved. But now, I am doing nothing but raising children, feeding them, bathing them, chasing them around, and yelling at them. My speculation is that, in spite of the primacy given to mothering by childcare experts, the perceived value of childrearing is declining.

These women, particularly those with higher education, have experienced an egalitarian school environment and have internalized, to some extent, the idea that it is crucial even for women to have status in society. Upon becoming mothers, however, the role of mother becomes their primary social identity.

Ōhinata (1982) reports changes in mothers' attitudes toward the value of childcare. She compared the attitude of two cohorts of highly educated mothers, one in their 60s and the other in their 30s. Both cohorts shared the idea that childrearing is physically and emotionally demanding. A significant difference was observed, however, in how they viewed the value of childrearing. A majority (74 percent) of the older cohort agreed that childrearing is a worthwhile and wonderful job, while only 40 percent of the younger cohort shared this view. The majority (61 percent) of the younger cohort asserted that their reasons to live exist outside childrearing, while only 20 percent of the older cohort expressed this view.

The ambivalence toward parenting among young mothers is a natural consequence of changing lifestyles. Being a mother no longer necessarily provides a sense of achievement. Becoming a "good mother," however, is a different story. The ideology of the good mother has exerted a strong normative force on Japanese women during the last two decades. This is because mother and child have been seen as an inseparable pair, the mother and child relationship has been conceptualized as an extension of a mother's "self," a substantial proportion of a child's achievement is believed to result from his or her "effort" rather than from innate individual capabilities, and a child's outcomes have become more easily measurable at an early stage of childhood (e.g., school records and results in entrance examinations to prestigious elementary schools).

Mothers can learn where their child stands relative to other children at quite an early stage through various assessments. The results are thought to reflect how hard the child—and the mother—worked. When we take into account the presumably close psychological proximity between mother and child in Japan and the beliefs related to the causal link between maternal care and child outcomes, it is logical to see being a good mother as a status, one that is achievable depending on how much effort one makes.

Natsumi works part-time as a shop clerk in a confectionery store. She feels that her parent-ing is constantly being assessed. In her view, "'a good child' is necessary for becoming 'a good mother.'"

When I talk with other mothers, I often feel that they are evaluating each other's "worth" by the "quality" of the child. A good child is what makes you proud. It isn't your career, your achievement, or what you do as an individual. These things don't count in the world of mothers!

Tomoe, a physician's wife and the full-time mother of one daughter, described early intervention programs as "addictive."

I wasn't serious when I started sending my daughter to a *yōji kyōshitsu.* I was just curious about the program when I saw their flyer in the newspaper. After I enrolled her, however, I soon learned that such a program has an addictive power. She liked going there, and it was exciting to see how quickly and how much a child can learn. This excitement makes you feel as if it was you who took the test and scored so well. Once you feel this excitement, it is very hard to stop; you don't want to feel that you have failed in something.

The *kyōiku mama* syndrome is not an irreversible process: Tomoe began to notice that she was seeking a vicarious sense of achievement.

One day, I was telling my daughter to do her homework. She must have thought I was nagging her too much. She stared at me and said, "Mom, it's my homework, not yours. Don't talk to me like that." I realized that I was pushing her too hard and that being an extreme *kyōiku mama* can be its own form of child abuse.

CRITICAL-THINKING QUESTIONS

1. The Japanese government has tried to reduce the extreme competition to enter college. Why have these efforts been largely unsuccessful?

2. How are Japanese mothers, but not fathers, socialized to be active participants in their children's early education? Also, how is the isolation of mothers one of the reasons for their involvement in the early education boom?

3. What is the cultural contradiction about gender roles that educated mothers encounter in Japanese society? Do you think that U.S. mothers experience the same contradictions? Why or Why not?

REFERENCES

ALLISON, ANNE. 1996. *Permitted and prohibited desires: Mothers, comics, and censorship in Japan.* Boulder, Colo.: Westview Press.

BOOCOCK, SARANE SPENCE. 1991. The Japanese preschool system. In *Windows on Japanese Education,* ed. Edward R. Beauchamp, 97–126. New York: Greenwood Press.

BRINTON, MARY C. 1993. *Women and the economic miracle: Gender and work in postwar Japan.* Berkeley: University of California Press.

DOMAN, GLENN. 1964. *How to teach your baby to read.* New York: Random House.

———. 1984. *How to multiply your baby's intelligence.* New York: Doubleday.

ELLINGTON, LUCIEN. 1992. *Education in the Japanese life-cycle.* Lewiston, N.Y.: E. Mellen Press.

FIELD, NORMA. 1995. The child as laborer and consumer: The disappearance of childhood in contemporary Japan. In *Children and the Politics of Culture,* ed. Sharon Stephens, 51–78. Princeton, N.J.: Princeton University Press.

HIRAO, KEIKO. 1997. Work histories and home investment of married Japanese women. Ph.D. diss., University of Notre Dame, Department of Sociology.

———. 1998. Saishūshoku no taiming: Kekkon/shussan taishokugo no rōdōshijō saisanyū katei no hazādo bunseki (Hazard analyses on the timing of re-entry to the labor force). Paper presented at the Annual Meetings of the Japanese Sociological Society, Kwansei Gakuin University, Nishinomiya, Japan.

IBUKA, MASARU. 1976. *Yōchien dewa ososugiru* (Kindergarten is too late). Tokyo: Goma Shobō.

———. 1991. *Zerosai* (Zero-year-old). Tokyo: Gomashobō.

———. 1992. *Taijikara* (From embryo). Tokyo: Tokumashobō.

KATSUURA-COOK, NORIKO. 1991. *Nihon no kosodate, Amerika no kosodate* (Child-rearing in Japan and the United States). Tokyo: Saiensu.

Kumon Kyōiku Kenkyūkai. 1998. *Company profiles.* Tokyo: Kumon Kyōiku Kenkyūkai.

Ministry of Education, Japan. 1994. *Survey report on Juku and other extra-school programs.* Tokyo: Author.

Ministry of Health and Welfare, Japan. 1991. *Survey on children's environment.* Tokyo: Government Printing Office.

MITSUISHI, YUKIKO. 1988. *Tensaiji o tsukuru!* (Creating prodigies). Tokyo: Fōyu.

OCHIAI, EMIKO. 1989. *Kindai kazoku to feminizumu* (Modern families and feminism). Tokyo: Keisōshobō.

ŌHINATA, MASAMI. 1982. Hahaoya no shinriteki antei to jūsoku o motomete (For the mental stability and fulfillment of mothers). In *Ikuji noirōze* (Childrearing depression). Tokyo: Yūhikaku.

ŌSHIMA, KIYOSHI. 1988. *Taikyō* (Prenatal education). Tokyo: Gomashobō.

SHICHIDA, MAKOTO. 1983. *Kiseki ga okiru shichidashiki zerosai kyōiku* (Miraculous education for zero-year-olds). Tokyo: Homeidō.

———. 1985. *Akachan wo kashikoku sodateru himitsu* (Tips on raising an intelligent baby). Tokyo: Nihon Keizai Shimbunsha.

SHIOMI, TOSHIYUKI. 1996. *Yōji kyōiku sangyō to kosodate* (Education industry and childrearing). Tokyo: Iwanami Shoten.

SHIRASA, IZUMI. 1990. Sōki kyōiku ni kansuru kahaoya no taidō (Attitude of mothers on early education). Master's paper, University of Tokyo.

STEVENSON, HAROLD W. 1992. Learning from Asian schools. *Scientific American* 267 (December): 70–76.

UNO, KATHLEEN S. 1993. The death of 'good wife, wise mother'? In *Postwar Japan as History,* ed. Andrew Gordon. Berkeley: University of California Press.

WHITE, MERRY. 1987. *The Japanese educational challenge: A commitment to children.* New York: Free Press.

CLASSIC

CONTEMPORARY

CROSS-CULTURAL

66 The Social Structure of Medicine

TALCOTT PARSONS

Talcott Parsons, one of the most influential U.S. sociologists during the twentieth century, contributed greatly to the development of structural-functional analysis. In this selection, he examines the significance of health and illness within a social system, with particular attention to the social roles of physicians and patients.

A little reflection will show immediately that the problem of health is intimately involved in the functional prerequisites of the social system. . . . Certainly by almost any definition health is included in the functional needs of the individual member of the society so that from the point of view of functioning of the social system, too low a general level of health, too high an incidence of illness, is dysfunctional. This is in the first instance because illness incapacitates for the effective performance of social roles. It could of course be that this incidence was completely uncontrollable by social action, an independently given condition of social life. But insofar as it is controllable, through rational action or otherwise, it is

clear that there is a functional interest of the society in its control, broadly in the minimization of illness. As one special aspect of this, attention may be called to premature death. From a variety of points of view, the birth and rearing of a child constitute a "cost" to the society, through pregnancy, child care, socialization, formal training, and many other channels. Premature death, before the individual has had the opportunity to play out his full quota of social roles, means that only a partial "return" for this cost has been received.

All this would be true were illness purely a "natural phenomenon" in the sense that, like the vagaries of the weather, it was not, to our knowledge, reciprocally involved in the motivated interactions of human beings. In this case illness would be something which merely "happened to" people, which involved consequences which had to be dealt with and conditions which might or might

Source: Reprinted with the permission of The Free Press, a Division of Simon & Schuster Adult Publishing Group, from *The Social System* by Talcott Parsons. Copyright © 1951, copyright renewed 1979 by Talcott Parsons.

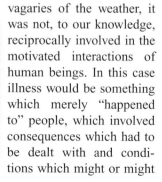

not be controllable but was in no way an expression of motivated behavior.

This is in fact the case for a very important part of illness, but it has become increasingly clear, by no means for all. In a variety of ways motivational factors accessible to analysis in action terms are involved in the etiology of many illnesses, and conversely, though without exact correspondence, many conditions are open to therapeutic influence through motivational channels. To take the simplest kind of case, differential exposure, to injuries or to infection, is certainly motivated, and the role of unconscious wishes to be injured or to fall ill in such cases has been clearly demonstrated. Then there is the whole range of "psychosomatic" illness about which knowledge has been rapidly accumulating in recent years. Finally, there is the field of "mental disease," the symptoms of which occur mainly on the behavioral level. . . .

Summing up, we may say that illness is a state of disturbance in the "normal" functioning of the total human individual, including both the state of the organism as a biological system and of his personal and social adjustments. It is thus partly biologically and partly socially defined. . . .

Medical practice . . . is a "mechanism" in the social system for coping with the illnesses of its members. It involves a set of institutionalized roles. . . . The immediately relevant social structures consist in the patterning of the role of the medical practitioner himself and, though to common sense it may seem superfluous to analyze it, that of the "sick person" himself. . . .

The role of the medical practitioner belongs to the general class of "professional" roles, a subclass of the larger group of occupational roles. Caring for the sick is thus not an incidental activity of other roles though, for example, mothers do a good deal of it—but has become functionally specialized as a full-time "job." This, of course, is by no means true of all societies. As an occupational role it is institutionalized about the technical content of the function which is given a high degree of primacy relative to other status-determinants. It is

thus inevitable both that incumbency of the role should be achieved and that performance criteria by standards of technical competence should be prominent. Selection for it and the context of its performance are to a high degree segregated from other bases of social status and solidarities. . . . Unlike the role of the businessman, however, it is collectivity-oriented not self-oriented.

The importance of this patterning is, in one context, strongly emphasized by its relation to the cultural tradition. One basis for the division of labor is the specialization of technical competence. The role of physician is far along the continuum of increasingly high levels of technical competence required for performance. Because of the complexity and subtlety of the knowledge and skill required and the consequent length and intensity of training, it is difficult to see how the functions could, under modern conditions, be ascribed to people occupying a prior status as one of their activities in that status, following the pattern by which, to a degree, responsibility for the health of her children is ascribed to the mother-status. There is an intrinsic connection between achieved statuses and the requirements of high technical competence. . . .

High technical competence also implies specificity of function. Such intensive devotion to expertness in matters of health and disease precludes comparable expertness in other fields. The physician is not, by virtue of his modern role, a generalized "wise man" or sage—though there is considerable folklore to that effect—but a specialist whose superiority to his fellows is confined to the specific sphere of his technical training and experience. For example, one does not expect the physician as such to have better judgment about foreign policy or tax legislation than any other comparably intelligent and well-educated citizen. There are of course elaborate subdivisions of specialization within the profession. . . . The physician is [also] expected to treat an objective problem in objective, scientifically justifiable terms. For example, whether he likes or dislikes the particular patient as a person is supposed to be irrelevant, as indeed it is to most purely objective problems of how to handle a particular disease.

. . . The "ideology" of the profession lays great emphasis on the obligation of the physician to put the "welfare of the patient" above his personal interests, and regards "commercialism" as the most serious and insidious evil with which it has to contend. The line, therefore, is drawn primarily vis-à-vis "business." The "profit motive" is supposed to be drastically excluded from the medical world. This attitude is, of course, shared with the other professions, but it is perhaps more pronounced in the medical case than in any single one except perhaps the clergy. . . .

An increasing proportion of medical practice is now taking place in the context of organization. To a large extent this is necessitated by the technological development of medicine itself, above all the need for technical facilities beyond the reach of the individual practitioner, and the fact that treating the same case often involves the complex co-operation of several different kinds of physicians as well as of auxiliary personnel. This greatly alters the relation of the physician to the rest of the instrumental complex. He tends to be relieved of much responsibility and hence necessarily of freedom, in relation to his patients other than in his technical role. Even if a hospital executive is a physician himself, he is not in the usual sense engaged in the "practice of medicine" in performing his functions any more than the president of the Miners' Union is engaged in mining coal.

As was noted, for common sense there may be some question of whether "being sick" constitutes a social role at all—isn't it simply a state of fact, a "condition"? Things are not quite so simple as this. The test is the existence of a set of institutionalized expectations and the corresponding sentiments and sanctions.

There seem to be four aspects of the institutionalized expectation system relative to the sick role. First is the exemption from normal social role responsibilities, which of course is relative to the nature and severity of the illness. This exemption requires legitimation by and to the various alters involved and the physician often serves as a court of appeal as well as a direct legitimatizing agent. It is noteworthy that, like all institutionalized patterns, the legitimation of being sick enough to avoid obligations can not only be a right of the sick person but an obligation upon him. People are often resistant to admitting they are sick and it is not uncommon for others to tell them that they *ought* to stay in bed. The word generally has a moral connotation. It goes almost without saying that this legitimation has the social function of protection against "malingering."

The second closely related aspect is the institutionalized definition that the sick person cannot be expected by "pulling himself together" to get well by an act of decision or will. In this sense also he is exempted from responsibility—he is in a condition that must "be taken care of." His "condition" must be changed, not merely his "attitude." Of course the process of recovery may be spontaneous but while the illness lasts he can't "help it." This element in the definition of the state of illness is obviously crucial as a bridge to the acceptance of "help."

The third element is the definition of the state of being ill as itself undesirable with its obligation to want to "get well." The first two elements of legitimation of the sick role thus are conditional in a highly important sense. It is a relative legitimation so long as he is in this unfortunate state which both he and alter hope he can get out of as expeditiously as possible.

Finally, the fourth closely related element is the obligation—in proportion to the severity of the condition, of course—to seek *technically competent* help, namely, in the most usual case, that of a physician and to *cooperate* with him in the process of trying to get well. It is here, of course, that the role of the sick person as patient becomes articulated with that of the physician in a complementary role structure.

It is evident from the above that the role of motivational factors in illness immensely broadens the scope and increases the importance of the institutionalized role aspect of being sick. For then the problem of social control becomes much more than one of ascertaining facts and drawing lines. The privileges and exemptions of the sick role may become objects of a "secondary gain" which the patient is positively motivated, usually unconsciously, to secure or to retain. The problem, therefore, of the balance of motivations to recover becomes of first importance. In general motivational balances of great functional significance to the social system are institutionally controlled, and it should, therefore, not be surprising that this is no exception.

A few further points may be made about the specific patterning of the sick role and its relation to social structure. It is, in the first place, a "contingent" role into which anyone, regardless of his status in other respects, may come. It is, furthermore, in the type case temporary. One may say that it is in a certain sense a "negatively achieved" role, through failure to "keep well," though, of course, positive motivations also operate, which by that very token must be motivations to deviance. . . .

The orientation of the sick role vis-à-vis the physician is also defined as collectively-oriented. It is true that the patient has a very obvious self-interest in getting well in most cases, though this point may not always be so simple. But once he has called in a physician the attitude is clearly marked, that he has assumed the obligation to co-operate with that physician in what is regarded as a common task. The obverse of the physician's obligation to be guided by the welfare of the patient is the latter's obligation to "do his part" to the best of his ability. This point is clearly brought out, for example, in the attitudes of the profession toward what is called "shopping around." By that is meant the practice of a patient "checking" the advice of one physician against that of another without telling physician A that he intends to consult physician B, or if he comes back to A that he has done so or who B is. The medical view is that if the patient is not satisfied with the advice his physician gives him he may properly do one of two things. First he may request

a consultation, even naming the physician he wishes called in, but in that case it is physician A not the patient who must call B in, the patient may not see B independently, and above all not without A's knowledge. The other proper recourse is to terminate the relation with A and become "B's patient." The notable fact here is that a pattern of behavior on the part not only of the physician but also of the patient, is expected which is in sharp contrast to perfectly legitimate behavior in a commercial relationship. If he is buying a car there is no objection to the customer going to a number of dealers before making up his mind, and there is no obligation for him to inform any one dealer what others he is consulting, to say nothing of approaching the Chevrolet dealer only through the Ford dealer.

The doctor-patient relationship is thus focused on these pattern elements. The patient has a need for technical services because he doesn't—nor do his lay associates, family members, etc.—"know" what is the matter or what to do about it, nor does he control the necessary facilities. The physician is a technical expert who by special training and experience, and by an institutionally validated status, is qualified to "help" the patient in a situation institutionally defined as legitimate in a relative sense but as needing help. . . .

CRITICAL-THINKING QUESTIONS

1. Does Parsons understand illness as a biological condition, that is, "something that happens to people"? What are the social elements in health and illness?

2. According to Parsons, what are the distinctive characteristics of the social role of the physician?

3. What are the major elements of "the sick role"? In what respects does Parsons view the social roles of physicians and patients as complementary? Can you see ways in which they may be in conflict?

67 The Slaughterhouse: The Most Dangerous Job

ERIC SCHLOSSER

To prepare for writing his book, Fast Food Nation, *Eric Schlosser conducted research all over the United States and discovered that there is much that consumers don't know about the fast food we eat. In this selection, he describes his visit to a slaughterhouse, which begins the process of turning cattle into hamburgers.*

One night I visit a slaughterhouse somewhere in the High Plains. The slaughterhouse is one of the nation's largest. About five thousand head of cattle enter it every day, single file, and leave in a different form. Someone who has access to the plant, who's upset by its working conditions, offers to give me a tour. The slaughterhouse is an immense building, gray and square, about three stories high, with no windows on the front and no architectural clues to what's happening inside. My friend gives me a chain-mail apron and gloves, suggesting I try them on. Workers on the line wear about eight pounds of chain mail beneath their white coats, shiny steel armor that covers their hands, wrists, stomach, and back. The chain mail's designed to protect workers from cutting themselves and from being cut by other workers. But knives somehow manage to get past it. My host hands me some Wellingtons, the kind of knee-high rubber boots that English gentlemen wear in the countryside. "Tuck your

pants into the boots," he says. "We'll be walking through some blood."

I put on a hardhat and climb a stairway. The sounds get louder, factory sounds, the noise of power tools and machinery, bursts of compressed air. We start at the end of the line, the fabricating room. Workers call it "fab." When we step inside, fab seems familiar: steel catwalks, pipes along the walls, a vast room, a maze of conveyer belts. . . . Some machines assemble cardboard boxes, others vacuum-seal subprimals of beef in clear plastic. The workers look extremely busy, but there's nothing unsettling about this part of the plant. You see meat like this all the time in the back of your local supermarket.

The fab room is cooled to about 40 degrees, and as you head up the line, the feel of the place starts to change. The pieces of meat get bigger. Workers—about half of them women, almost all of them young and Latino—slice meat with long slender knives. They stand at a table that's chest high, grab meat off a conveyer belt, trim away fat, throw meat back on the belt, toss the scraps onto a conveyer belt above them, and then grab more meat, all in a matter of seconds. I'm now struck by

Excerpt from "The Most Dangerous Job," from *Fast Food Nation: The Dark Side of the All-American Meal* by Eric Schlosser. Copyright © 2001 by Eric Schlosser. Reprinted by permission of Houghton Mifflin Company. All rights reserved.

how many workers there are, hundreds of them, pressed close together, constantly moving, slicing. You see hardhats, white coats, flashes of steel. Nobody is smiling or chatting, they're too busy, anxiously trying not to fall behind. An old man walks past me, pushing a blue plastic barrel filled with scraps. A few workers carve the meat with Whizzards, small electric knives that have spinning round blades. The Whizzards look like the Norelco razors that Santa rides in the TV ads. I notice that a few of the women near me are sweating, even though the place is freezing cold.

Sides of beef suspended from an overhead trolley swing toward a group of men. Each worker has a large knife in one hand and a steel hook in the other. They grab the meat with their hooks and attack it fiercely with their knives. As they hack away, using all their strength, grunting, the place suddenly feels different, primordial. The machinery seems beside the point, and what's going on before me has been going on for thousands of years—the meat, the hook, the knife, men straining to cut more meat.

On the kill floor, what I see no longer unfolds in a logical manner. It's one strange image after another. A worker with a power saw slices cattle into halves as though they were two-by-fours, and then the halves swing by me into the cooler. It feels like a slaughterhouse now. Dozens of cattle, stripped of their skins, dangle on chains from their hind legs. My host stops and asks how I feel, if I want to go any further. This is where some people get sick. I feel fine, determined to see the whole process, the world that's been deliberately hidden. The kill floor is hot and humid. It stinks of manure. Cattle have a body temperature of about 101 degrees, and there are a lot of them in the room. Carcasses swing so fast along the rail that you have to keep an eye on them constantly, dodge them, watch your step, or one will slam you and throw you onto the bloody concrete floor. It happens to workers all the time.

I see: a man reach inside cattle and pull out their kidneys with his bare hands, then drop the kidneys down a metal chute, over and over again, as each animal passes by him; a stainless steel rack of tongues; Whizzards peeling meat off decapitated heads, picking them almost as clean as the white skulls painted by Georgia O'Keeffe. We wade through blood that's ankle deep and that pours down drains into huge vats below us. As we approach the start of the line, for the first time I hear the steady *pop, pop, pop* of live animals being stunned.

Now the cattle suspended above me look just like the cattle I've seen on ranches for years, but these ones are upside down swinging on hooks. For a moment, the sight seems unreal; there are so many of them, a herd of them, lifeless. And then I see a few hind legs still kicking, a final reflex action, and the reality comes hard and clear.

For eight and a half hours, a worker called a "sticker" does nothing but stand in a river of blood, being drenched in blood, slitting the neck of a steer every ten seconds or so, severing its carotid artery. He uses a long knife and must hit exactly the right spot to kill the animal humanely. He hits that spot again and again. We walk up a slippery metal stairway and reach a small platform, where the production line begins. A man turns and smiles at me. He wears safety goggles and a hardhat. His face is splattered with gray matter and blood. He is the "knocker," the man who welcomes cattle to the building. Cattle walk down a narrow chute and pause in front of him, blocked by a gate, and then he shoots them in the head with a captive bolt stunner—a compressed-air gun attached to the ceiling by a long hose—which fires a steel bolt that knocks the cattle unconscious. The animals keep strolling up, oblivious to what comes next, and he stands over them and shoots. For eight and a half hours, he just shoots. As I stand there, he misses a few times and shoots the same animal twice. As soon as the steer falls, a worker grabs one of its hind legs, shackles it to a chain, and the chain lifts the huge animal into the air.

I watch the knocker knock cattle for a couple of minutes. The animals are powerful and imposing one moment and then gone in an instant, suspended from a rail, ready for carving. A steer slips from its chain, falls to the ground, and gets its head caught in one end of a conveyer belt. The production line stops as workers struggle to free the steer, stunned but alive, from the machinery. I've seen enough.

I step out of the building into the cool night air and follow the path that leads cattle into the slaughterhouse. They pass me, driven toward the building by workers with long white sticks that seem to glow in the dark. One steer, perhaps sensing instinctively what the other don't, turns and tries to run. But workers drive him back to join the rest. The cattle lazily walk single-file toward the muffled sounds, *pop, pop, pop,* coming from the open door.

The path has hairpin turns that prevent cattle from seeing what's in store and keep them relaxed. As the ramp gently slopes upward, the animals may think they're headed for another truck, another road trip—and they are, in unexpected ways. The ramp widens as it reaches ground level and then leads to a large cattle pen with wooden fences, a corral that belongs in a meadow, not here. As I walk along the fence, a group of cattle approach me, looking me straight in the eye, like dogs hoping for a treat, and follow me out of some mysterious impulse. I stop and try to absorb the whole scene: the cool breeze, the cattle and their gentle lowing, a cloudless sky, steam rising from the plant in the moonlight. And then I notice that the building does have one window, a small square of light on the second floor. It offers a glimpse of what's hidden behind this huge blank façade. Through the little window you can see bright red carcasses on hooks, going round and round.

Knocker, Sticker, Shackler, Rumper, First Legger, Knuckle Dropper, Navel Boner, Splitter Top/Bottom Butt, Feed Kill Chain—the names of job assignments at a modern slaughterhouse convey some of the brutality inherent in the work. Meatpacking is now the most dangerous job in the United States. The injury rate in a slaughterhouse is about three times higher than the rate in a typical American factory. Every year more than one-quarter of the meatpacking workers in this country—roughly forty thousand men and women—suffer an injury or a work-related illness that requires medical attention beyond first aid. There is strong evidence that these numbers,

compiled by the Bureau of Labor Statistics, understate the number of meatpacking injuries that occur. Thousands of additional injuries and illnesses most likely go unrecorded.

Despite the use of conveyer belts, forklifts, dehiding machines, and a variety of power tools, most of the work in the nation's slaughterhouses is still performed by hand. Poultry plants can be largely mechanized, thanks to the breeding of chickens that are uniform in size. The birds in some Tyson factories are killed, plucked, gutted, beheaded, and sliced into cutlets by robots and machines. But cattle still come in all sizes and shapes, varying in weight by hundreds of pounds. The lack of a standardized steer has hindered the mechanization of beef plants. In one crucial respect meatpacking work has changed little in the past hundred years. At the dawn of the twenty-first century, amid an era of extraordinary technological advance, the most important tool in a modern slaughterhouse is a sharp knife.

Lacerations are the most common injuries suffered by meatpackers, who often stab themselves or stab someone working nearby. Tendinitis and cumulative trauma disorders are also quite common. Meatpacking workers routinely develop back problems, shoulder problems, carpal tunnel syndrome, and "trigger finger" (a syndrome in which a finger becomes frozen in a curled position). Indeed, the rate of these cumulative trauma injuries in the meatpacking industry is far higher than the rate in any other American industry. It is roughly thirty-three times higher than the national average in industry. Many slaughterhouse workers make a knife cut every two or three seconds, which adds up to about 10,000 cuts during an eight-hour shift. If the knife has become dull, additional pressure is placed on the worker's tendons, joints, and nerves. A dull knife can cause pain to extend from the cutting hand all the way down the spine.

Workers often bring their knives home and spend at least forty minutes a day keeping the edges smooth, sharp, and sanded, with no pits. One IBP worker, a small Guatemalan woman with graying hair, spoke with me in the cramped kitchen of her mobile home. As a pot of beans cooked on the stove, she sat in a wooden chair, gently rocking, telling the story of her life, of her journey north in search of work, the whole time sharpening big knives in her lap as though she were knitting a sweater.

The "IBP revolution" has been directly responsible for many of the hazards that meatpacking workers now face. One of the leading determinants of the injury rate at a slaughterhouse today is the speed of the disassembly line. The faster it runs, the more likely that workers will get hurt. The old meatpacking plants in Chicago slaughtered about fifty cattle an hour. Twenty years ago, new plants in the High Plains slaughtered about 175 cattle an hour. Today some plants slaughter up to 400 cattle an hour—about half a dozen animals every minute, sent down a single production line, carved by workers desperate not to fall behind. While trying to keep up with the flow of meat, workers often neglect to resharpen their knives and thereby place more stress on their bodies. As the pace increases, so does the risk of accidental cuts and stabbings. "I could always tell the line speed," a former Monfort nurse told me, "by the number of people with lacerations coming into my office." People usually cut themselves; nevertheless, everyone on the line tries to stay alert. Meatpackers often work within inches of each other, wielding large knives. A simple mistake can cause a serious injury. A former IBP worker told me about boning knives suddenly flying out of hands and ricocheting off of machinery. "They're very flexible," she said, "and they'll spring on you . . . zwing, and they're gone."

. . . [B]eef slaughterhouses often operate at profit margins as low as a few pennies a pound. The three meatpacking giants—ConAgra, IBP, and Excel—try to increase their earnings by maximizing the volume of production at each plant. Once a slaughterhouse is up and running, fully staffed, the profits it will earn are directly related to the speed of the line. A faster pace means higher profits. Market pressures now exert a perverse influence on the management of beef plants: the same factors that make these slaughterhouses relatively inefficient (the lack of mechanization, the reliance on human labor) encourage companies to make them even more dangerous (by speeding up the pace).

The unrelenting pressure of trying to keep up with the line has encouraged widespread methamphetamine use among meatpackers. Workers taking "crank" feel charged and self-confident, ready for anything. Supervisors have been known to sell crank to their workers or to supply it free in return for certain favors, such as working a second shift. Workers who use methamphetamine may feel energized and invincible, but are actually putting themselves at much greater risk of having an accident. For obvious reasons, a modern slaughterhouse is not a safe place to be high.

In the days when labor unions were strong, workers could complain about excessive line speeds and injury rates without fear of getting fired. Today only one-third of IBP's workers belong to a union. Most of the nonunion workers are recent immigrants; many are illegals; and they are generally employed "at will." That means they can be fired without warning, for just about any reason. Such an arrangement does not encourage them to lodge complaints. Workers who have traveled a great distance for this job, who have families to support, who are earning ten times more an hour in a meatpacking plant than they could possibly earn back home, are wary about speaking out and losing everything. The line speeds and labor costs at IBP's nonunion plants now set the standard for the rest of the industry. Every other company must try to produce beef as quickly and cheaply as IBP does; slowing the pace to protect workers can lead to a competitive disadvantage.

Again and again workers told me that they are under tremendous pressure not to report injuries. The annual bonuses of plant foremen and supervisors are often based in part on the injury rate of their workers. Instead of creating a safer workplace, these bonus schemes encourage slaughterhouse managers to make sure that accidents and injuries go unreported. Missing fingers, broken bones, deep lacerations, and amputated limbs are difficult to conceal from authorities. But the dramatic and catastrophic injuries in a slaughterhouse are greatly outnumbered by less visible, though no less debilitating, ailments: torn muscles, slipped disks, pinched nerves.

If a worker agrees not to report an injury, a supervisor will usually shift him or her to an easier job for a while, providing some time to heal. If the injury seems more serious, a Mexican worker is often given the opportunity to return home for a while, to recuperate there, then come back to his or her slaughterhouse job in the United States. Workers who abide by these unwritten rules are treated respectfully; those who disobey are likely to be punished and made an example. As one former IBP worker explained, "They're trying to deter you, period, from going to the doctor."

From a purely economic point of view, injured workers are a drag on profits. They are less productive. Getting rid of them makes a good deal of financial sense, especially when new workers are readily available and inexpensive to train. Injured workers are often given some of the most unpleasant tasks in the slaughterhouse. Their hourly wages are cut. And through a wide variety of unsubtle means they are encouraged to quit.

Not all supervisors in a slaughterhouse behave like Simon Legree, shouting at workers, cursing them, belittling their injuries, always pushing them to move faster. But enough supervisors act that way to warrant the comparison. Production supervisors tend to be men in their late twenties and early thirties. Most are Anglos and don't speak Spanish, although more and more Latinos are being promoted to the job. They earn about $30,000 a year, plus bonuses and benefits. In many rural communities, being a supervisor at a meatpacking plant is one of the best jobs in town. It comes with a fair amount of pressure: a supervisor must meet production goals, keep the number of recorded injuries low, and most importantly, keep the meat flowing down the line without interruption. The job also brings enormous power. Each supervisor is like a little dictator in his or her section of the plant, largely free to boss, fire, berate, or reassign workers. That sort of power can lead to all sorts of abuses, especially when the hourly workers being supervised are women.

Many women told me stories about being fondled and grabbed on the production line, and the behavior of supervisors sets the tone for the other male workers. In February of 1999, a federal jury in Des Moines awarded $2.4 million to a female employee at an IBP slaughterhouse. According to the woman's testimony, coworkers had "screamed obscenities and rubbed their bodies against hers while supervisors laughed." Seven months later, Monfort agreed to settle a law-suit filed by the U.S. Equal Employment Opportunity Commission on behalf of fourteen female workers in Texas. As part of the settlement, the company paid the women $900,000 and vowed to establish formal procedures for handling sexual harassment complaints. In their lawsuit the women alleged that supervisors at a Monfort plant in Cactus, Texas, pressured them for dates and sex, and that male coworkers groped them, kissed them, and used animal parts in a sexually explicit manner.

The sexual relationships between supervisors and "hourlies" are for the most part consensual. Many female workers optimistically regard sex with their supervisor as a way to gain a secure place in American society, a green card, a husband—or at the very least a transfer to an easier job at the plant. Some supervisors become meatpacking Casanovas, engaging in multiple affairs. Sex, drugs, and slaughterhouses may seem an unlikely combination, but as one former Monfort employee told me: "Inside those walls is a different world that obeys different laws." . . .

CRITICAL-THINKING QUESTIONS

1. Schlosser claims that one-fourth of all slaughterhouse workers suffer an injury every year. Do you think this record means that the system of processing beef is breaking down or that the system itself is flawed? Why?

2. Do you see parallels between the operation of this slaughterhouse and any other workplace setting you know? If so, explain.

3. Do you think hamburgers would be as popular as they are in this country if people knew more about how beef is processed?

68 Female Genital Mutilation

EFUA DORKENOO AND SCILLA ELWORTHY

In recent decades, numerous women's organizations around the world have focused on a variety of health-related issues and problems, including domestic violence, rape, sexual harassment, and poverty. In this selection, Efua Dorkenoo and Scilla Elworthy examine the complex cultural issues surrounding female genital mutilation, a practice that has received international attention since the early 1990s.

THE FACTS

. . . [F]emale genital mutilation covers four types of operation:

1. *Circumcision*, or cutting of the prepuce or hood of the clitoris, known in Muslim countries as Sunna (tradition). This, the mildest type, affects only a small proportion of the millions of women concerned. It is the only type of mutilation that can correctly be called circumcision, though there has been a tendency to group all kinds of mutilations under the misleading term 'female circumcision.'
2. *Excision*, meaning the cutting of the clitoris and of all or part of the labia minora.
3. *Infibulation*, the cutting of the clitoris, labia minora, and at least part of the labia majora. The two sides of the vulva are then pinned together by silk or catgut sutures, or with thorns, thus obliterating the vaginal introitus except for a very small opening, preserved by the insertion of a tiny piece of wood or a reed for the passage of urine or menstrual blood. These operations are done with special knives, with razor blades or pieces of glass. The girl's legs are then bound together from hip to ankle and she is kept immobile for up to forty days to permit the formation of scar tissue.
4. *Intermediate*, meaning the removal of the clitoris and some parts of the labia minora or the whole of it. Various degrees are done according to the demands of the girl's relatives. . . .

Most frequently these operations are performed by an old woman of the village or by a traditional birth attendant and only rarely by qualified nurses or doctors. The age at which the mutilations are carried out varies from area to area, and according to whether legislation against the practice is foreseen or not. It varies from a few days old (for example, the Jewish Falashas in Ethiopia, and the nomads of the Sudan) to about seven years (as in Egypt and many countries of Central Africa) or—more rarely—adolescence, as among the Ibo of Nigeria. Most experts are agreed that the age of mutilation is becoming younger, and has less and less to do with initiation into adulthood.[1]

Source: "Female Genital Mutilation," by Efua Dorkenoo and Scilla Elworthy from *Female Genital Mutilation: Proposals for Change,* an MRG Report, pp. 92–93. Reprinted with permission.

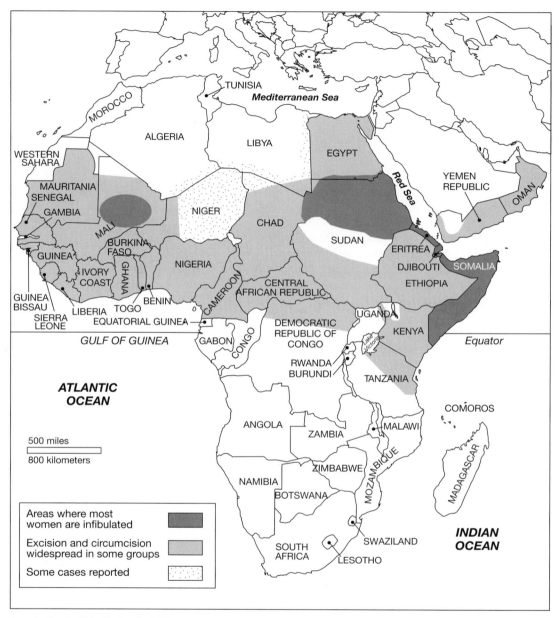

Female Genital Mutilation in Africa

Physical Consequences

Health risks and complications depend on the gravity of the mutilation, hygienic conditions, the skill and eyesight of the operator, and the struggles of the child. Whether immediate or long term, they are grave.[2] Death from bleeding is not uncommon, while long-term complications include chronic infections of the uterus and vagina, painful menstruation, severe pain during intercourse, sterility, and complications during childbirth. Though evidence has yet to be collected, it is also likely that bleeding or open wounds increase the likelihood of HIV transmission and AIDS.

There is great difficulty in obtaining accurate research on the sexual experiences of mutilated women, because the majority are reluctant to speak on the subject and are generally ambivalent on questions of sexual enjoyment.[3] However, in all types of mutilation, even the "mildest" clitoridectomy, a part of a woman's body containing nerves of vital importance to sexual pleasure is amputated.

Psychological Consequences

Even less research has been done to date on the psychological consequences of these traditions. However, many personal accounts and research findings contain repeated references to anxiety prior to the operation, terror at the moment of being seized by an aunt or village matron, unbearable pain, and the subsequent sense of humiliation and of being betrayed by parents, especially the mother. On the other hand, there are references to special clothes and good food associated with the event, to the pride felt in being like everyone else, in being "made clean," in having suffered without screaming.

To be different clearly produces anxiety and mental conflict. An unexcised, non-infibulated girl is despised and made the target of ridicule, and no one in her community will marry her. Thus what is clearly understood to be her life's work, namely marriage and childbearing, is denied her. So, in tight-knit village societies where mutilation is the rule, it will be the exceptional girl who will suffer psychologically, unless she has another very strong identity which she has lost.[4]

There is no doubt that genital mutilation would have overwhelming psychological effects on an unmotivated girl, unsupported by her family, village, peers, and community. To those from other cultures unfamiliar with the force of this particular community identity, the very concept of amputation of the genitals carries a shock value which does not exist for most women in the areas concerned. For them, not to amputate would be shocking.

These observations concern social-psychological factors rather than the central question, namely, what effects do these traumatic operations have on little girls at the moment of operation and as they grow up? The fact is that we simply don't know. We do not know what it means to a girl or woman when her central organ of sensory pleasure is cut off, when her life-giving canal is stitched up amid blood and fear and secrecy, while she is forcibly held down and told that if she screams she will cause the death of her mother or bring shame on the family.

THE PRACTICE

The Area Covered

The countries where one or more forms of female genital mutilation are practised number more than twenty in Africa, from the Atlantic to the Red Sea, the Indian Ocean, and the eastern Mediterranean. Outside Africa, excision is also practised in Oman, South Yemen, and in the United Arab Emirates (UAE). Circumcision is practised by the Muslim populations of Indonesia and Malaysia and by Bohra Muslims in India, Pakistan and East Africa.[5]

On the map of Africa, an uninterrupted belt is formed across the centre of the continent, which then expands up the length of the Nile. This belt, with the exception of the Egyptian buckle, corresponds strikingly with the pattern of countries that have the highest child mortality rates (more than 30 percent for children from one to four years of age).[6] These levels reflect deficiencies of medical care, of clean drinking water, of sanitary infrastructure, and of adequate nutrition in most of the countries.

The gravity of the mutilations varies from country to country. Infibulation is reported to affect nearly all the female population of Somalia, Djibouti, and the Sudan (except the non-Muslim population of southern Sudan), southern

Health and Medicine

Egypt, the Red Sea coast of Ethiopia, northern Kenya, northern Nigeria, and some parts of Mali. The most recent estimate of women mutilated is 74 million.[7]

Ethnic groups closely situated geographically are by no means affected in the same way: For example, in Kenya, the Kikuyu practise excision and the Luo do not; in Nigeria, the Yoruba, the Ibo, and the Hausa do, but not the Nupes or the Fulanis; in Senegal, the Woloff have no practice of mutilation. There are many other examples.

As the subject of female genital mutilation began to be eligible at least for discussion, reports of genital operations on nonconsenting females have appeared from many unexpected parts of the world. During the 1980s, women in Sweden were shocked by accounts of mutilations performed in Swedish hospitals on daughters of immigrants. In France, women from Mali and Senegal have been reported to bring an *exciseuse* to France once a year to operate on their daughters in their apartments.[8] In July 1982 a Malian infant died of an excision performed by a professional circumciser, who then fled to Mali. In the same year, reports appeared in the British press that excision for nonmedical reasons had been performed in a London private clinic.

Legislation

In Africa. Formal legislation forbidding genital mutilation, or more precisely infibulation, exists in the Sudan. A law first enacted in 1946 allows for a term of imprisonment up to five years and/or a fine. However, it is not an offence (under Article 284 of the Sudan Penal Code for 1974) "merely to remove the free and projecting part of the clitoris."

Many references have been made to legislation in Egypt, but after researching the available materials, all that has been traced is a resolution signed by the Minister of Health in 1959, recommending only partial clitoridectomy for those who want an operation, to be performed only by doctors.[9]

In late 1978, largely due to the efforts of the Somali Women's Democratic Organization (SWDO),

Somalia set up a commission to abolish infibulation. In 1988 at a seminar held in Mogadishu, it was recommended that SWDO should propose a bill to the competent authorities to eradicate all forms of female genital mutilation.

In September 1982, President Arap Moi took steps to ban the practices in Kenya, following reports of the deaths of fourteen children after excision. A traditional practitioner found to be carrying out this operation can be arrested under the Chiefs Act and brought before the law.

Official declarations against female genital mutilation were made by the late Captain Thomas Sankara and Abdou Diouf, the heads of state in Burkina Faso and Senegal respectively.

In Western Countries. A law prohibiting female excision, whether consent has been given or not, came into force in Sweden in July 1982, carrying a two-year sentence. In Norway, in 1985, all hospitals were alerted to the practice. Belgium has incorporated a ban on the practice. Several states in the U.S.A. have incorporated female genital mutilation into their criminal code.

In the U.K., specific legislation prohibiting female circumcision came into force at the end of 1985. A person found guilty of an offence is liable to up to five years' imprisonment or to a fine. Female genital mutilation has been incorporated into child protection procedures at local authority levels. As yet no person has been committed in the English courts for female circumcision, but since 1989 there have been at least seven local authority legal interventions which prevented parents from sexually mutilating their daughters or wards.

France does not have specific legislation on female sexual mutilation but under Article 312–3 of the French Penal Code, female genital mutilation can be considered as a criminal offence. Under this code, anybody who exercises violence or seriously assaults a child less than fifteen years old can be punished with imprisonment from ten to twenty years, if the act of violence results in a mutilation, amputation of a limb, the loss of an eye or other parts of the body, or has unintentionally caused the death of the child.

In 1989, a mother who had paid a traditional woman exciser to excise her week-old daughter, in 1984, was convicted and given a three-year suspended jail sentence. In 1991 a traditional exciser was jailed for five years in France.

Contemporary Practices

Opinions are very divided as to whether the practice is disappearing because of legislation or social and economic changes. Esther Ogunmodede, for instance, believes that in Nigeria, Africa's most populous country, the tradition is disappearing but extremely slowly, with millions of excisions still taking place. She reports that in areas where the operations are done on girls of marriageable age, they are "running away from home to avoid the razor." This confirms Fran Hosken's assertion that operations are being done at earlier and earlier ages, in order that the children should be "too young to resist." Fran Hosken does not think that the custom is dying out, and she indisputably has the best published range of information concerning all the countries where the practice is known.

An interesting development took place in Ethiopia during the years of civil warfare which only ended in 1991. When the Eritrean People's Liberation Front (EPLF) occupied large areas from January 1977 to December 1978, among many other reforms they categorically and successfully forbade genital mutilation and forced marriage. In fact, the reason given for the large numbers of young women in the EPLF army was that they were running away from home in other parts of Ethiopia to avoid forced marriage and the knife.[10] Although it appears the practice continues in remote areas, because the consciousness of Eritrean women has changed dramatically during the war years, it is easier to persuade men and women to let go of this practice.

Since 1983, the number of educational programmes initiated to raise public awareness of the health risk associated with female genital mutilation at local, national, and international levels have increased. The media have played a major role in bringing this issue from the domestic to the public domain. As a result of these efforts it can be said that the taboo surrounding even public mention of the practice has at last been broken. There is an increase in public awareness of the harmful effects of female genital mutilation.

It has been noted that female genital mutilation is becoming unpopular amongst the urban elite in some African countries. In Sierra Leone, for example, Koso-Thomas claims that urban men are willing to marry uncircumcised women, in particular when the marriage is not pre-arranged.[11]

In general, among urban educated women, reasons often cited against female genital mutilation include the pointlessness of mutilation, health risks, and reduction of sexual sensitivity. The last reason points to a changing attitude towards women's fundamental human rights amongst urban Africans.

In the main, the practice continues to be widespread among large sectors and groups within Africa. Those in favour of the practice are noted in the 1986 U.N. study to be a passive majority who refer back to traditional society, without necessarily sharing that society's values.[12] In some cases, the practice appears to be spreading to population groups who traditionally never practised female genital mutilation, as observed with city women in Wau, Sudan, who regard it as fashionable, and among converted Muslim women in southern Sudan who marry northern Sudanese men.[13] Furthermore, even in areas where some groups are turning against the practice, the absolute numbers affected may be increasing. Rapid population growth in Africa means greater numbers of female children are born, who in turn are exposed to the risk of mutilation.

THE ISSUES

Female genital mutilation is a complex issue, for it involves deep-seated cultural practices which affect millions of people. However, it can be divided into (at least) four distinct issues.

Rights of Women

Female genital mutilation is an extreme example of the general subjugation of women, sufficiently extreme and horrifying to make women and men question the basis of what is done to women, what women have accepted and why, in the name of society and tradition.

The burning of Indian widows and the binding of the feet of Chinese girl children are other striking examples, sharp enough and strange enough to throw a spotlight on other less obvious ways in which women the world over submit to oppression. It is important to remember that all these practices are, or were, preserved under centuries of tradition, and that foot-binding was only definitively stopped by a massive social and political revolution (replacing the many traditions which it swept away by offering an entirely new social system, revolutionary in many aspects: land ownership, class system, education, sex equality, etc.) which had been preceded by years of patient work by reformers.

Thus, to be successful, campaigns on female genital mutilation should consider carefully not only eliminating but also replacing the custom. (The example of Eritrea, previously quoted, is illuminating here.) Furthermore, such success may be predicated on long-term changes in attitudes and ideologies by both men and women.

A major international expression of the goal of equal rights for women was taken in December 1979, when the U.N. General Assembly adopted the Convention on the Elimination of All Forms of Discrimination Against Women. This came into force in September 1981. The comprehensive convention calls for equal rights for women, regardless of their marital status, in all fields: political, economic, social, cultural and, civil. Article 5(a) obliges states' parties to take:

. . . all appropriate measures to modify the social and cultural patterns of conduct of men and women, with a view to achieving the elimination of prejudices and customary and all other practices which are based on the idea of the inferiority or superiority of either of the sexes or on stereotyped roles for men and women.

To succeed in abolishing such practices will demand fundamental attitudinal shifts in the way that society perceives the human rights of women. The starting point for change should be educational programmes that assist women to recognize their fundamental human rights. This is where UNESCO, the U.N. Centre for Human Rights, and international agencies could help by supporting awareness-building programmes.

Rights of Children

An adult is free to submit her or himself to a ritual or tradition, but a child, having no formed judgement, does not consent but simply undergoes the operation (which in this case is irrevocable) while she is totally vulnerable. The descriptions available of the reactions of children—panic and shock from extreme pain, biting through the tongue, convulsions, necessity for six adults to hold down an eight-year-old, and death—indicate a practice comparable to torture.

Many countries signatory to Article 5 of the Universal Declaration of Human Rights (which provides that no one shall be subjected to torture, or to cruel, inhuman, or degrading treatment) violate that clause. Those violations are discussed and sometimes condemned by various U.N. commissions. Female genital mutilation, however, is a question of torture inflicted not on adults but on girl children, and the reasons given are not concerned with either political conviction or military necessity but are solely in the name of tradition.

The Declaration of the Rights of Children, adopted in 1959 by the General Assembly, asserts that children should have the possibility to develop physically in a healthy and normal way in conditions of liberty and dignity. They should have adequate medical attention and be protected from all forms of cruelty.

It is the opinion of Renée Bridel, of the Fédération Internationale des Femmes de Carrières Juridiques, that "One cannot but consider Member States which tolerate these practices as infringing their obligations as assumed under the terms of the Charter [of the U.N.].[14]

In September 1990, the United Nations Convention on the Rights of the Child went into force. It became part of international human rights law. Under Article 24(3) it states that "States Parties shall take all effective and appropriate measures with a view to abolishing traditional practices prejudicial to the health of children." This crucial article should not merely remain a paper provision, to be given lip service by those entrusted to implement it. Members of the U.N. should work at translating its provisions into specific implementation programmes at grassroots level. Much could be learned (by African states in particular) from countries with established child protection systems.

The Right to Good Health

No reputable medical practitioner insists that mutilation is good for the physical or mental health of girls and women, and a growing number offer research indicating its grave permanent damage to health and underlining the risks of death. Medical facts, carefully explained, may be the way to discourage the practice, since these facts are almost always the contrary of what is believed, and can be shown and demonstrated.

Those U.N. agencies and government departments specifically entrusted with the health needs of women and children must realize that it is their responsibility to support positive and specific preventative programmes against female genital mutilation, for while the practice continues the quality of life and health will inevitably suffer. However, this approach, if presented out of context, ignores the force of societal pressures which drive women to perform these operations, regardless of risk, in order to guarantee marriage for their daughters and to conform to severe codes of female behaviour laid down by male-dominated societies.

The Right to Development

The practice of female genital mutilation must be seen in the context of underdevelopment,[15] and the realities of life for the most vulnerable and exploited sectors—women and children. International political and economic forces have frequently prevented development programmes from meeting the basic needs of rural populations. With no access to education or resources, and with no effective power base, the rural and urban poor cling to traditions as a survival mechanism in time of socioeconomic change.

In societies where marriage for a woman is her only means of survival, and where some form of excision is a prerequisite for marriage, persuading her to relinquish the practice for herself or for her children is an extraordinarily difficult task. Female (and some male) African analysts of development strategies are today constantly urging that the overall deteriorating conditions in which poor women live be made a major focus for change, for unless development affects their lives for the better, traditional practices are unlikely to change.

DIRECTIONS FOR THE FUTURE

The mutilation of female genitals has been practised in many areas for centuries. The greatest determination, combined with sensitivity and understanding of local conditions, will be needed if it is to be abolished. In every country and region where operations are carried out, the situation is different, as is the political will, whether at local or national levels. In Western countries the way forward is relatively clear. In Africa the problem is more profound and the economic and political conditions vastly more difficult, while international agencies have hardly begun to explore their potential role.

What all three have in common is that, to date, nearly all programmes have been individual or *ad hoc* efforts, with little integration into other structures, with minimal evaluation or monitoring, and lacking in long-term goals and strategies. To achieve real change will require more resources, more detailed planning, and more real, sustained commitment from governments and international organizations.

CRITICAL-THINKING QUESTIONS

1. What are the four types of female genital mutilation? How widespread are these practices?

2. What do Dorkenoo and Elworthy mean when they describe female genital mutilation as a "complex" issue? Do they feel that this practice can be abolished or not?

3. Many Western countries have denounced female genital mutilation as barbaric. But what about comparable practices in the United States and other Western nations? Even though they are voluntary, are silicone breast transplants, facelifts, or liposuction more "civilized" in making women's bodies more acceptable to men?

NOTES

1. Fran Hosken, *The Hosken Report—Genital and Sexual Mutilation of Females* (third enlarged/revised edition, Autumn, 1982, published by Women's International Network News, 187 Grant St., Lexington, Mass. 02173, USA). This is the most detailed and comprehensive collection of information available.

2. The consequences of sexual mutilations on the health of women have been studied by Dr. Ahmed Abu-el-Futuh Shandall, Lecturer in the Department of Obstetrics and Gynaecology at the University of Khartoum, in a paper entitled, "Circumcision and Infibulation of Females" (*Sudanese Medical Journal,* Vol. 5, No. 4, 1967); and by Dr. J.A. Verzin, in an article entitled "The Sequelae of Female Circumcision," (*Tropical Doctor,* October, 1975). A bibliography on the subject has been prepared by Dr. R. Cook for the World Health Organization.

3. Readers interested to read more about research on the sexual experience of circumcised women may want to read Hanny Lightfoot-Klein, *Prisoners of Ritual: An Odyssey into Female Genital Mutilation in Africa* (New York: The Haworth Press, 1989).

4. These feelings of rejection are clearly articulated by Kenyan girls in "The Silence over Female Circumcision in Kenya," in *Viva,* August, 1978.

5. Q.R. Ghadially, "Ali for 'Izzat': The Practice of Female Circumcision among Bohra Muslims," *Manushi,* No. 66, New Delhi, India, 1991.

6. See map of Childhood Mortality in the World, 1977 (Health Sector Policy Paper, World Bank, Washington, D.C., 1980).

7. See Hosken for details and estimates of ethnic groups involved.

8. *F Magazine,* No. 4, March, 1979, and No. 31, October, 1980.

9. Marie Assaad, *Female Circumcision in Egypt—Current Research and Social Implications* (American University in Cairo, 1979), p. 12.

10. "Social Transformation of Eritrean Society," paper presented to the People's Tribunal, Milan, 24–26 May 1980, by Mary Dines of Rights and Justice.

11. Koso-Thomas, *The Circumcision of Women: A Strategy for Elimination* (London: Zed Books, 1987).

12. UN Commission on Human Rights, Report of the Working Group on Traditional Practices Affecting Women and Children, 1986.

13. Ellen Ismail et al., *Women of the Sudan* (Bendestorf, Germany: EIS, 1990).

14. *L'enfant mutilé* by Renée Bridel, delegate of the FIFCJ to the UN, Geneva, 1978. See also Raqiya Haji Dualeh Abdalla, Sisters in Affliction (London: Zed Press, 1982) and Asma El Dareer, Woman, Why Do You Weep? (London: Zed Press, 1982).

15. Belkis Woldes Giorgis, *Female Circumcision in Africa,* ST/ECA/ATRCW 81/02.

CLASSIC

CONTEMPORARY

CROSS-CULTURAL

69 The Metropolis and Mental Life

GEORG SIMMEL

In this, one of his best-known essays, Simmel examines what might be called the "spiritual condition" of the modern world. His focus is the city, in which forces of modernity—including anonymity, a detached sophistication, and a preoccupation with commercial matters—are most clearly evident. Note that Simmel finds reason both to praise this new world and to warn of its ability to destroy our humanity.

The deepest problems of modern life derive from the claim of the individual to preserve the autonomy and individuality of his existence in the face of overwhelming social forces, of historical heritage, of external culture, and of the technique of life. The fight with nature which primitive man has to wage for his *bodily* existence attains in this modern form its latest transformation. The eighteenth century called upon man to free himself of all the historical bonds in the state and in religion, in morals and in economics. Man's nature, originally good and common to all, should develop unhampered. In addition to more liberty, the nineteenth century demanded

the functional specialization of man and his work; this specialization makes one individual incomparable to another, and each of them indispensable to the highest possible extent. However, this specialization makes each man the more directly dependent upon the supplementary activities of all others. Nietzsche sees the full development of the individual conditioned by the most ruthless struggle of individuals; socialism believes in the suppression of all competition for the same reason. Be that as it may, in all these positions the same basic motive is at work: The person resists to being leveled down and worn out by a socialtechnological mechanism. An inquiry into the inner meaning of specifically modern life and its products, into the soul of the cultural body, so to speak, must seek to solve the equation which structures like the metropolis set up between

Source: Reprinted and abridged with the permission of The Free Press, a Division of Simon & Schuster from *The Sociology of Georg Simmel,* translated and edited by Kurt H. Wolff. Copyright © 1950, copyright renewed 1978 by The Free Press.

the individual and the superindividual contents of life. Such an inquiry must answer the question of how the personality accommodates itself in the adjustments to external forces. This will be my task today.

The psychological basis of the metropolitan type of individuality consists in the *intensification of nervous stimulation* which results from the swift and uninterrupted change of outer and inner stimuli. Man is a differentiating creature. His mind is stimulated by the difference between a momentary impression and the one which preceded it. Lasting impressions, impressions which differ only slightly from one another, impressions which take a regular and habitual course and show regular and habitual contrasts—all these use up, so to speak, less consciousness than does the rapid crowding of changing images, the sharp discontinuity in the grasp of a single glance, and the unexpectedness of onrushing impressions. These are the psychological conditions which the metropolis creates. With each crossing of the street, with the tempo and multiplicity of economic, occupational and social life, the city sets up a deep contrast with small town and rural life with reference to the sensory foundations of psychic life. The metropolis exacts from man as a discriminating creature a different amount of consciousness than does rural life. Here the rhythm of life and sensory mental imagery flows more slowly, more habitually, and more evenly. Precisely in this connection the sophisticated character of metropolitan psychic life becomes understandable—as over against small town life, which rests more upon deeply felt and emotional relationships. These latter are rooted in the more unconscious layers of the psyche and grow most readily in the steady rhythm of uninterrupted habituations. The intellect, however, has its locus in the transparent, conscious, higher layers of the psyche; it is the most adaptable of our inner forces. In order to accommodate to change and to the contrast of phenomena, the intellect does not require any shocks and inner upheavals; it is only through such upheavals that the more conservative mind could accommodate to the metropolitan rhythm of events. Thus the

metropolitan type of man—which, of course, exists in a thousand individual variants—develops an organ protecting him against the threatening currents and discrepancies of his external environment which would uproot him. He reacts with his head instead of his heart. In this an increased awareness assumes the psychic prerogative. Metropolitan life, thus, underlies a heightened awareness and a predominance of intelligence in metropolitan man. The reaction to metropolitan phenomena is shifted to that organ which is least sensitive and quite remote from the depth of the personality. Intellectuality is thus seen to preserve subjective life against the overwhelming power of metropolitan life, and intellectuality branches out in many directions and is integrated with numerous discrete phenomena.

The metropolis has always been the seat of the money economy. Here the multiplicity and concentration of economic exchange gives an importance to the means of exchange which the scantiness of rural commerce would not have allowed. Money economy and the dominance of the intellect are intrinsically connected. They share a matter-of-fact attitude in dealing with men and with things; and, in this attitude, a formal justice is often coupled with an inconsiderate hardness. The intellectually sophisticated person is indifferent to all genuine individuality, because relationships and reactions result from it which cannot be exhausted with logical operations. In the same manner, the individuality of phenomena is not commensurate with the pecuniary principle. Money is concerned only with what is common to all: It asks for the exchange value, it reduces all quality and individuality to the question: How much? All intimate emotional relations between persons are founded in their individuality, whereas in rational relations man is reckoned with like a number, like an element which is in itself indifferent. Only the objective measurable achievement is of interest. Thus metropolitan man reckons with his merchants and customers, his domestic servants and often even with persons with whom he is obliged to have social intercourse. These features of intellectuality contrast with the nature of the small circle in which the inevitable knowledge of individuality as inevitably produces a warmer tone of behavior, a behavior which is beyond a mere objective balancing of service and return. In the sphere of the economic psychology of the small group it is of importance that under primitive conditions production serves the customer who orders the goods, so that the producer and the consumer are acquainted. The modern metropolis, however, is supplied almost entirely by production for the market, that is, for entirely unknown purchasers who never personally enter the producer's actual field of vision. Through this anonymity the interests of each party acquire an unmerciful matter-of-factness; and the intellectually calculating economic egoisms of both parties need not fear any deflection because of the imponderables of personal relationships. The money economy dominates the metropolis; it has displaced the last survivals of domestic production and the direct barter of goods; it minimizes, from day to day, the amount of work ordered by customers. The matter-of-fact attitude is obviously so intimately interrelated with the money economy, which is dominant in the metropolis, that nobody can say whether the intellectualistic mentality first promoted the money economy or whether the latter determined the former. The metropolitan way of life is certainly the most fertile soil for this reciprocity, a point which I shall document merely by citing the dictum of the most eminent English constitutional historian: Throughout the whole course of English history, London has never acted as England's heart but often as England's intellect and always as her moneybag!

In certain seemingly insignificant traits, which lie upon the surface of life, the same psychic currents characteristically unite. Modern mind has become more and more calculating. The calculative exactness of practical life which the money economy has brought about corresponds to the ideal of natural science: to transform the world into an arithmetic problem, to fix every part of the world by mathematical formulas. Only money economy has filled the days of so many people with weighing, calculating, with numerical determinations, with a reduction of qualitative values to quantitative ones. Through the calculative nature of money a new precision, a certainty in the definition of identities and differences, an unambiguousness in agreements and arrangements has been brought about in the relations of life-elements—just as externally this precision has been effected by the universal diffusion of pocket watches. However, the conditions of metropolitan life are at once cause and effect of this trait. The relationships and affairs of the typical metropolitan usually are so varied and complex that without the strictest punctuality in promises and services the whole structure would break down into an inextricable chaos. Above all, this necessity is brought about by the aggregation of so many people with such differentiated interests, who must integrate their relations and activities into a highly complex organism. If all clocks and watches in Berlin would suddenly go wrong in different ways, even if only by one hour, all economic life and communication of the city would be disrupted for a long time. In addition an apparently mere external factor, long distances, would make all waiting and broken appointments result in an ill-afforded waste of time. Thus, the technique of metropolitan life is unimaginable without the most punctual integration of all activities and mutual relations into a stable and impersonal time schedule. Here again the general conclusions of this entire task of reflection become obvious, namely, that from each point on the surface of existence—however closely attached to the surface alone—one may drop a sounding into the depth of the psyche so that all the most banal externalities of life finally are connected with the ultimate decisions concerning the meaning and style of life. Punctuality, calculability, exactness are forced upon life by the complexity and extension of metropolitan existence and are not only most intimately connected with its money economy and intellectualistic character. These traits must also color the contents of life and favor the exclusion of those irrational, instinctive, sovereign traits and impulses which aim at determining the mode of life from within, instead of receiving the general and precisely schematized form of life from without. . . .

The same factors which have thus coalesced into the exactness and minute precision of the form of life have coalesced into a structure of the highest impersonality; on the other hand, they have promoted a highly personal subjectivity. There is perhaps no psychic phenomenon which has been so unconditionally reserved to the metropolis as has the blasé attitude. The blasé attitude results first from the rapidly changing and closely compressed contrasting stimulations of the nerves. From this, the enhancement of metropolitan intellectuality, also, seems originally to stem. Therefore, stupid people who are not intellectually alive in the first place usually are not exactly blasé. A life in boundless pursuit of pleasure makes one blasé because it agitates the nerves to their strongest reactivity for such a long time that they finally cease to react at all. In the same way, through the rapidity and contradictoriness of their changes, more harmless impressions force such violent responses, tearing the nerves so brutally hither and thither that their last reserves of strength are spent; and if one remains in the same milieu they have no time to gather new strength. An incapacity thus emerges to react to new sensations with the appropriate energy. This constitutes that blasé attitude which, in fact, every metropolitan child shows when compared with children of quieter and less changeable milieus.

This physiological source of the metropolitan blasé attitude is joined by another source which flows from the money economy. The essence of the blasé attitude consists in the blunting of discrimination. This does not mean that the objects are not perceived, as is the case with the half-wit, but rather that the meaning and differing values of things, and thereby the things themselves, are experienced as insubstantial. They appear to the blasé person in an evenly flat and gray tone; no one object deserves preference over any other. This mood is the faithful subjective reflection of the completely internalized money economy. By being the equivalent to all the manifold things in one and the same way, money becomes the most frightful leveler. For money expresses all qualitative differences of things in terms of "how much?" Money, with all its colorlessness and indifference, becomes the common denominator of all values; irreparably it hollows out the core of things, their individuality, their specific value, and their incomparability. All things float with equal specific gravity in the constantly moving stream of money. All things lie on the same level and differ from one another only in the size of the area which they cover. In the individual case this coloration, or rather discoloration, of things through their money equivalence may be unnoticeably minute. However, through the relations of the rich to the objects to be had for money, perhaps even through the total character which the mentality of the contemporary public everywhere imparts to these objects, the exclusively pecuniary evaluation of objects has become quite considerable. The large cities, the main seats of the money exchange, bring the purchasability of things to the fore much more impressively than do smaller localities. That is why cities are also the genuine locale of the blasé attitude. In the blasé attitude the concentration of men and things stimulate the nervous system of the individual to its highest achievement so that it attains its peak. Through the mere quantitative intensification of the same conditioning factors this achievement is transformed into its opposite and appears in the peculiar adjustment of the blasé attitude. In this phenomenon the nerves find in the refusal to react to their stimulation the last possibility of accommodating to the contents and forms of metropolitan life. The self-preservation of certain personalities is brought at the price of devaluating the whole objective world, a devaluation which in the end unavoidably drags one's own personality down into a feeling of the same worthlessness.

Whereas the subject of this form of existence has to come to terms with it entirely for himself, his self-preservation in the face of the large city demands from him a no less negative behavior of a social nature. This mental attitude of metropolitans toward one another we may designate, from a formal point of view, as reserve. If so many inner reactions were responses to the continuous external contacts with innumerable people as are those in the small town, where one knows almost everybody one meets and where one has a positive relation to almost everyone, one would be completely atomized internally and come to an unimaginable psychic state. Partly this psychological fact, partly the right to distrust which men have in the face of the touch-and-go elements of metropolitan life, necessitates our reserve. As a result of this reserve we frequently do not even know by sight those who have been our neighbors for years. And it is this reserve which in the eyes of the small-town people makes us appear to be cold and heartless. Indeed, if I do not deceive myself, the inner aspect of this outer reserve is not only indifference but, more often than we are aware, it is a slight aversion, a mutual strangeness and repulsion, which will break into hatred and fight at the moment of a closer contact, however caused. The whole inner organization of such an extensive communicative life rests upon an extremely varied hierarchy of sympathies, indifferences, and aversions of the briefest as well as of the most permanent nature. The sphere of indifference in this hierarchy is not as large as might appear on the surface. Our psychic activity still responds to almost every impression of somebody else with a somewhat distinct feeling. The unconscious, fluid, and changing character of this impression seems to result in a state of indifference. Actually this indifference would be just as unnatural as the diffusion of indiscriminate mutual suggestion would be unbearable. From both these typical dangers of the metropolis, indifference and indiscriminate suggestibility, antipathy protects us. A latent antipathy and the preparatory stage of practical antagonism affect the distances and aversions without which this mode of life could not at all be led. The extent and the mixture of this style of life, the rhythm of its emergence and disappearance, the forms in which it is satisfied—all these, with the unifying motives

in the narrower sense, form the inseparable whole of the metropolitan style of life. What appears in the metropolitan style of life directly as dissociation is in reality only one of its elemental forms of socialization.

This reserve with its overtone of hidden aversion appears in turn as the form or the cloak of a more general mental phenomenon of the metropolis: It grants to the individual a kind and an amount of personal freedom which has no analogy whatsoever under other conditions. The metropolis goes back to one of the large developmental tendencies of social life as such, to one of the few tendencies for which an approximately universal formula can be discovered. The earliest phase of social formations found in historical as well as in contemporary social structures is this: a relatively small circle firmly closed against neighboring, strange, or in some way antagonistic circles. However, this circle is closely coherent and allows its individual members only a narrow field for the development of unique qualities and free, self-responsible movements. Political and kinship groups, parties and religious associations begin in this way. The self-preservation of very young associations requires the establishment of strict boundaries and a centripetal unity. Therefore they cannot allow the individual freedom and unique inner and outer development. From this stage social development proceeds at once in two different, yet corresponding, directions. To the extent to which the group grows—numerically, spatially, in significance and in content of life—to the same degree the group's direct, inner unity loosens, and the rigidity of the original demarcation against others is softened through mutual relations and connections. At the same time, the individual gains freedom of movement, far beyond the first jealous delimitation. The individual also gains a specific individuality to which the division of labor in the enlarged group gives both occasion and necessity. . . .

It is not only the immediate size of the area and the number of persons which, because of the universal historical correlation between the enlargement of the circle and the personal inner and outer freedom, has made the metropolis the locale of freedom. It is rather in transcending this visible expanse that any given city becomes the seat of cosmopolitanism. The horizon of the city expands in a manner comparable to the way in which wealth develops; a certain amount of property increases in a quasi-automatical way in ever more rapid progression. As soon as a certain limit has been passed, the economic, personal, and intellectual relations of the citizenry, the sphere of intellectual predominance of the city over its hinterland, grow as in geometrical progression. Every gain in dynamic extension becomes a step, not for an equal, but for a new and larger extension. From every thread spinning out of the city, ever new threads grow as if by themselves, just as within the city the unearned increment of ground rent, through the mere increase in communication, brings the owner automatically increasing profits. At this point, the quantitative aspect of life is transformed directly into qualitative traits of character. The sphere of life of the small town is, in the main, self-contained and autarchic. For it is the decisive nature of the metropolis that its inner life overflows by waves into a far-flung national or international area. . . .

The most profound reason, however, why the metropolis conduces to the urge for the most individual personal existence—no matter whether justified and successful—appears to me to be the following: The development of modern culture is characterized by the preponderance of what one may call the "objective spirit" over the "subjective spirit." This is to say, in language as well as in law, in the technique of production as well as in art, in science as well as in the objects of the domestic environment, there is embodied a sum of spirit. The individual in his intellectual development follows the growth of this spirit very imperfectly and at an ever increasing distance. If, for instance, we view the immense culture which for the last hundred years has been embodied in things and in knowledge, in institutions and in comforts, and if we compare all this with the cultural progress of the individual during the same period—at least in high status groups—a frightful disproportion in growth between the two becomes evident. Indeed, at some points we notice a retrogression in the culture of the individual with reference to spirituality, delicacy, and idealism. This discrepancy results essentially from the growing division of labor. For the division of labor demands from the individual an ever more one-sided accomplishment, and the greatest advance in a one-sided pursuit only too frequently means dearth to the personality of the individual. In any case, he can cope less and less with the overgrowth of objective culture. The individual is reduced to a negligible quantity, perhaps less in his consciousness than in his practice and in the totality of his obscure emotional states that are derived from this practice. The individual has become a mere cog in an enormous organization of things and powers which tear from his hands all progress, spirituality, and value in order to transform them from their subjective form into the form of a purely objective life. It needs merely to be pointed out that the metropolis is the genuine arena of this culture which outgrows all personal life. Here in buildings and educational institutions, in the wonders and comforts of space-conquering technology, in the formations of community life, and in the visible institutions of the state, is offered such an overwhelming fullness of crystallized and impersonalized spirit that the personality, so to speak, cannot maintain itself under its impact. On the one hand, life is made infinitely easy for the personality in that stimulations, interests, uses of time, and consciousness are offered to it from all sides. They carry the person as if in a stream, and one needs hardly to swim for oneself. On the other hand, however, life is composed more and more of these impersonal contents and offerings which tend to displace the genuine personal colorations and incomparabilities. This results in the individual's summoning the utmost in uniqueness and particularization, in order to preserve his most personal core. He has to exaggerate this personal element in order to remain audible even to himself.

CRITICAL-THINKING QUESTIONS

1. In what respects does the metropolis symbolize modern society?

2. What does Simmel mean by suggesting that in modern cities, people experience an "intensification of nervous stimulation"? How do we react "with our heads instead of with our hearts"?

3. What does Simmel see as the achievements of modern urban life? What does he think has been lost in the process?

70 Urbanism as a Way of Life

LOUIS WIRTH

For many decades, sociologists in Europe and the United States have commented on the distinctive qualities of urban social life. In 1938, U.S. sociologist Louis Wirth integrated these various insights into a comprehensive theory of urbanism. Although it has been challenged and reformulated over the years, Wirth's theory remains probably the best-known sociological statement on urbanism.

A SOCIOLOGICAL DEFINITION OF THE CITY

Despite the preponderant significance of the city in our civilization, our knowledge of the nature of urbanism and the process of urbanization is meager, notwithstanding many attempts to isolate the distinguishing characteristics of urban life. Geographers, historians, economists, and political scientists have incorporated the points of view of their respective disciplines into diverse definitions of the city. While in no sense intended to supersede these, the formulation of a sociological approach to the city may incidentally serve to call attention to the interrelations between them by emphasizing the peculiar characteristics of the city as a particular form of human association. A sociologically significant definition of the city seeks to select those elements of urbanism which mark it as a distinctive mode of human group life. . . .

Source: From *American Journal of Sociology,* Vol. 44, No. 1, July 1938, pp. 1–24, copyright © 1934 by The University of Chicago Press. Reprinted by permission of the University of Chicago Press.

For sociological purposes a city may be defined as a relatively large, dense, and permanent settlement of socially heterogeneous individuals. On the basis of the postulates which this minimal definition suggests, a theory of urbanism may be formulated in the light of existing knowledge concerning social groups.

A THEORY OF URBANISM

Given a limited number of identifying characteristics of the city, I can better assay the consequences or further characteristics of them in the light of general sociological theory and empirical research. I hope in this manner to arrive at the essential propositions comprising a theory of urbanism. Some of these propositions can be supported by a considerable body of already available research materials; others may be accepted as hypotheses for which a certain amount of presumptive evidence exists, but for which more ample and exact verification would be required. At least such a procedure will, it is hoped, show what in the way of systematic knowledge of the city we now have and what are the crucial and fruitful hypotheses for future research.

The central problem of the sociologist of the city is to discover the forms of social action and organization that typically emerge in relatively permanent, compact settlements of large numbers of heterogeneous individuals. We must also infer that urbanism will assume its most characteristic and extreme form in the measure in which the conditions with which it is congruent are present. Thus the larger, the more densely populated, and the more heterogeneous a community, the more accentuated the characteristics associated with urbanism will be. . . .

Some justification may be in order for the choice of the principal terms comprising our definition of the city, a definition which ought to be as inclusive and at the same time as denotative as possible without unnecessary assumptions. To say that large numbers are necessary to constitute a city means, of course, large numbers in relation to a restricted area or high density of settlement. There are, nevertheless, good reasons for treating large numbers and density as separate factors, because each may be connected with significantly different social consequences. Similarly the need for adding heterogeneity to numbers of population as a necessary and distinct criterion of urbanism might be questioned, since we should expect the range of differences to increase with numbers. In defense, it may be said that the city shows a kind and degree of heterogeneity of population which cannot be wholly accounted for by the law of large numbers or adequately represented by means of a normal distribution curve. Because the population of the city does not reproduce itself, it must recruit its migrants from other cities, the countryside, and— in the United States. . .—from other countries. The city has thus historically been the melting-pot of races, peoples, and cultures, and a most favorable breeding-ground of new biological and cultural hybrids. It has not only tolerated but rewarded individual differences. It has brought together people from the ends of the earth *because* they are different and thus useful to one another, rather than because they are homogeneous and like-minded.

A number of sociological propositions concerning the relationship between (a) numbers of population, (b) density of settlement, (c) heterogeneity of inhabitants and group life can be formulated on the basis of observation and research.

Size of the Population Aggregate

Ever since Aristotle's *Politics,* it has been recognized that increasing the number of inhabitants in a settlement beyond a certain limit will affect the relationships between them and the character of the city. Large numbers involve, as has been pointed out, a greater range of individual variation. Furthermore, the greater the number of individuals participating in a process of interaction, the greater is the *potential* differentiation between them. The personal traits, the occupations, the cultural life, and the ideas of the members of an urban community may, therefore, be expected to range between more widely separated poles than those of rural inhabitants.

That such variations should give rise to the spatial segregation of individuals according to color, ethnic heritage, economic and social status, tastes and preferences, may readily be inferred. The bonds of kinship, of neighborliness, and the sentiments arising out of living together for generations under a common folk tradition are likely to be absent or, at best, relatively weak in an aggregate the members of which have such diverse origins and backgrounds. Under such circumstances competition and formal control mechanisms furnish the substitutes for the bonds of solidarity that are relied upon to hold a folk society together.

Increase in the number of inhabitants of a community beyond a few hundred is bound to limit the possibility of each member of the community knowing all the others personally. Max Weber, in recognizing the social significance of this fact, explained that from a sociological point of view large numbers of inhabitants and density of settlement mean a lack of that mutual acquaintanceship which ordinarily inheres between the inhabitants in a neighborhood.[1] The increase in numbers thus involves a changed character of the social relationships. As Georg Simmel points out: "[If] the unceasing external contact of numbers of persons in the city should be met by the same number of inner reactions as in the small town, in which one knows almost every person he meets and to each of whom he has a positive relationship, one would be completely atomized internally and would fall into an unthinkable mental condition."[2] The multiplication of persons in a state of interaction under conditions which make their contact as full personalities impossible produces that segmentalization of human relationships which has sometimes been seized upon by students of the mental life of the cities as an explanation for the "schizoid" character of urban personality. This is not to say that the urban inhabitants have fewer acquaintances than rural inhabitants, for the reverse may actually be true; it means rather that in relation to the number of people whom they see and with whom they rub elbows in the course of daily life, they know a smaller proportion, and of these they have less intensive knowledge.

Characteristically, urbanites meet one another in highly segmental roles. They are, to be sure, dependent upon more people for the satisfactions of their life-needs than are rural people and thus are associated with a greater number of organized groups, but they are less dependent upon particular persons, and their dependence upon others is confined to a highly fractionalized aspect of the other's round of activity. This is essentially what is meant by saying that the city is characterized by secondary rather than primary contacts. The contacts of the city may indeed be face to face, but they are nevertheless impersonal, superficial, transitory, and segmental. The reserve, the indifference, and the blasé outlook which urbanites manifest in their relationships may thus be regarded as devices for immunizing themselves against the personal claims and expectations of others.

The superficiality, the anonymity, and the transitory character of urban social relations make intelligible, also, the sophistication and the rationality generally ascribed to city-dwellers. Our acquaintances tend to stand in a relationship of utility to us in the sense that the role which each one plays in our life is overwhelmingly regarded as a means for the achievement of our own ends. Whereas the individual gains, on the one hand, a certain degree of emancipation or freedom from the personal and emotional controls of intimate groups, he loses, on the other hand, the spontaneous self-expression, the morale, and the sense of participation that comes with living in an integrated society. This constitutes essentially the state of *anomie,* or the social void, to which Durkheim alludes in attempting to account for the various forms of social disorganization in technological society.

The segmental character and utilitarian accent of interpersonal relations in the city find their institutional expression in the proliferation of specialized tasks which we see in their most developed form in the professions. The operations of the pecuniary nexus lead to predatory relationships, which tend to obstruct the efficient functioning of the social order unless checked by professional codes and occupational etiquette. The premium put upon utility and efficiency suggests the adaptability of the corporate device for the organization of enterprises in which individuals can engage only in groups. The advantage that the corporation has over the individual entrepreneur and the partnership in the urban-industrial world derives not only from the possibility it affords of centralizing the resources of thousands of individuals or from the legal privilege of limited liability and perpetual succession, but from the fact that the corporation has no soul.

The specialization of individuals, particularly in their occupations, can proceed only, as Adam Smith pointed out, upon the basis of an enlarged market, which in turn accentuates the division of labor. This enlarged market is only in part supplied by the city's hinterland; in large measure it is found among the large numbers that the city itself contains. The dominance of the city over the surrounding hinterland becomes explicable in terms of the division of labor which urban life occasions and promotes. The extreme degree of interdependence and the unstable equilibrium of urban life are closely associated with the division of labor and the specialization of occupations. This interdependence and this instability are increased by the tendency of each city to specialize in those functions in which it has the greatest advantage.

In a community composed of a larger number of individuals than can know one another intimately and can be assembled in one spot, it becomes necessary to communicate through indirect media and to articulate individual interests by a process of delegation. Typically in the city, interests are made effective through representation. The individual counts for little, but the voice of the representative is heard with a deference roughly proportional to the numbers for whom he speaks.

While this characterization of urbanism, in so far as it derives from large numbers, does not by any means exhaust the sociological inferences that might be drawn from our knowledge of the relationship of the size of a group to the characteristic behavior of the members, for the sake of brevity the assertions made may serve to exemplify the sort of propositions that might be developed.

Density

As in the case of numbers, so in the case of concentration in limited space certain consequences of relevance in sociological analysis of the city emerge. Of these only a few can be indicated.

As Darwin pointed out for flora and fauna and as Durkheim noted in the case of human societies,[3] an increase in numbers when area is held constant (i.e., an increase in density) tends to produce differentiation and specialization, since only in this way can the area support increased numbers. Density thus reinforces the effect of numbers in diversifying men and their activities and in increasing the complexity of the social structure.

On the subjective side, as Simmel has suggested, the close physical contact of numerous individuals necessarily produces a shift in the media through which we orient ourselves to the urban milieu, especially to our fellow-men. Typically, our physical contacts are close but our social contacts are distant. The urban world puts a premium on visual recognition. We see the uniform which denotes the role of the functionaries, and are oblivious to the personal eccentricities hidden behind the uniform. We tend to acquire and develop a sensitivity to a world of artifacts, and become progressively farther removed from the world of nature.

We are exposed to glaring contrasts between splendor and squalor, between riches and poverty, intelligence and ignorance, order and chaos. The competition for space is great, so that each area generally tends to be put to the use which yields the greatest economic return. Place of work tends to become dissociated from place of residence, for the proximity of industrial and commercial establishments makes an area both economically and socially undesirable for residential purposes.

Density, land values, rentals, accessibility, healthfulness, prestige, aesthetic consideration, absence of nuisances such as noise, smoke, and dirt determine the desirability of various areas of the city as places of settlement for different sections of the population. Place and nature of work, income, racial and ethnic characteristics, social status, custom, habit, taste, preference, and prejudice are among the significant factors in accordance with which the urban population is selected and distributed into more or less distinct settlements. Diverse population elements inhabiting a compact settlement thus become segregated from one another in the degree in which their requirements and modes of life are incompatible and in the measure in which they are antagonistic. Similarly, persons of homogeneous status and needs unwittingly drift into, consciously select, or are forced by circumstances into the same area. The different parts of the city acquire specialized functions, and the city consequently comes to resemble a mosaic of social worlds in which the transition from one to the other is abrupt. The juxtaposition of divergent personalities and modes of life tends to produce a relativistic perspective and a sense of toleration of differences which may be regarded as prerequisites for rationality and which lead toward the secularization of life.[4]

The close living together and working together of individuals who have no sentimental and emotional ties foster a spirit of competition, aggrandizement, and mutual exploitation. Formal controls are instituted to counteract irresponsibility and potential disorder. Without rigid adherence to predictable routines a large compact society would scarcely be able to maintain itself. The clock and the traffic signal are symbolic of the basis of our social order in the urban world. Frequent close physical contact, coupled with great social distance, accentuates the reserve of unattached individuals toward one another and, unless compensated by other opportunities for response, gives rise to loneliness. The necessary frequent movement of great numbers of individuals in a congested habitat causes friction and irritation. Nervous tensions which derive from such personal frustrations are increased by the rapid tempo and the complicated technology under which life in dense areas must be lived.

Heterogeneity

The social interaction among such a variety of personality types in the urban milieu tends to break down the rigidity of caste lines and to complicate the class structure; it thus induces a more ramified and differentiated framework of social stratification than is found in more integrated societies. The heightened mobility of the individual, which brings him within the range of stimulation by a great number of diverse individuals and subjects him to fluctuating status in the differentiated social groups that compose the social structure of the city, brings him toward the acceptance of instability and insecurity in the world at large as a norm. This fact helps to account, too, for the sophistication and cosmopolitanism of the urbanite. No single group

has the undivided allegiance of the individual. The groups with which he is affiliated do not lend themselves readily to a simple hierarchical arrangement. By virtue of his different interests arising out of different aspects of social life, the individual acquires membership in widely divergent groups, each of which functions only with reference to a single segment of his personality. Nor do these groups easily permit a concentric arrangement so that the narrower ones fall within the circumference of the more inclusive ones, as is more likely to be the case in the rural community or in primitive societies. Rather the groups with which the person typically is affiliated are tangential to each other or intersect in highly variable fashion.

Partly as a result of the physical footlooseness of the population and partly as a result of their social mobility, the turnover in group membership generally is rapid. Place of residence, place and character of employment, income, and interests fluctuate, and the task of holding organizations together and maintaining and promoting intimate and lasting acquaintanceship between the members is difficult. This applies strikingly to the local areas within the city into which persons become segregated more by virtue of differences in race, language, income, and social status than through choice or positive attraction to people like themselves. Overwhelmingly the city-dweller is not a home-owner, and since a transitory habitat does not generate binding traditions and sentiments, only rarely is he a true neighbor. There is little opportunity for the individual to obtain a conception of the city as a whole or to survey his place in the total scheme. Consequently he finds it difficult to determine what is to his own "best interests" and to decide between the issues and leaders presented to him by the agencies of mass suggestion. Individuals who are thus detached from the organized bodies which integrate society comprise the fluid masses that make collective behavior in the urban community so unpredictable and hence so problematical.

Although the city, through the recruitment of variant types to perform its diverse tasks and the accentuation of their uniqueness through competition and the premium upon eccentricity, novelty, efficient performance, and inventiveness, produces a highly differentiated population, it also exercises a leveling influence. Wherever large numbers of differently constituted individuals congregate, the process of depersonalization also enters. This leveling tendency inheres in part in the economic basis of the city. The development of large cities, at least in the modern age, was largely dependent upon the concentrative force of steam. The rise of the factory made possible mass production for an impersonal market. The fullest exploitation of the possibilities of the division of labor and mass production, however, is possible only with standardization of processes and products. A money economy goes hand in hand with such a system of production. Progressively as cities have developed upon a background of this system of production, the pecuniary nexus which implies the purchasability of services and things has displaced personal relations as the basis of association. Individuality under these circumstances must be replaced by categories. When large numbers have to make common use of facilities and institutions, those facilities and institutions must serve the needs of the average person rather than those of particular individuals. The services of the public utilities, of the recreational, educational, and cultural institutions, must be adjusted to mass requirements. Similarly, the cultural institutions, such as the schools, the movies, the radio, and the newspapers, by virtue of their mass clientele, must necessarily operate as leveling influences. The political process as it appears in urban life could not be understood unless one examined the mass appeals made through modern propaganda techniques. If the individual would participate at all in the social, political, and economic life of the city, he must subordinate some of his individuality to the demands of the larger community and in that measure immerse himself in mass movements. . . .

On the basis of the three variables, number, density of settlement, and degree of heterogeneity, of the urban population, it appears possible to explain the characteristics of urban life and to account for the differences between cities of various sizes and types.

CRITICAL-THINKING QUESTIONS

1. What basic issue should a sociological theory of urbanism address? Why is Wirth's approach to studying urbanism also termed "ecological"?

2. How does Wirth define a city? How do the three defining factors give rise to an urban way of life?

3. According to Wirth, what are the qualities of social relationships in cities? What moral consequences seem to follow?

NOTES

1. *Wirtschaft und Gesellschaft* (Tübingen, 1925), part I, chap. 8, p. 514.

2. "Die Grossstädte und das Geistesleben," *Die Grossstadt,* ed. Theodor Petermann (Dresden, 1903), pp. 187–206.

3. E. Durkheim, *De la division du travail social* (Paris, 1932), p. 248.

4. The extent to which the segregation of the population into distinct ecological and cultural areas and the resulting social attitude of tolerance, rationality, and secular mentality are functions of density as distinguished from heterogeneity is difficult to determine. Most likely we are dealing here with phenomena which are consequences of the simultaneous operation of both factors.

CLASSIC

CONTEMPORARY

CROSS-CULTURAL

71 Urban Sprawl: The Formation of Edge Cities

JOHN J. MACIONIS AND VINCENT N. PARRILLO

A century ago, industrialization changed the shape of cities by concentrating population and construction in densely packed central cities. In recent years, cities are changing once again, this time spreading outward and creating what analysts call "edge cities."

URBAN SPRAWL: THE FORMATION OF EDGE CITIES

Not since the expansion of small cities into huge metropolises a century ago have we seen as profound a change in our urban world as the emergence of edge cities. An *edge city* is a new, sprawling, middle-class, automobile-dependent center typically located at the fringe of an older urban area, at the intersection of major highways, where little except villages or farmland existed three decades earlier.

In the second half of the twentieth century, North Americans went through three waves of centrifugal movement away from the older cities. First came the suburbanization of North America, most notably after World War II, as people moved into new homes beyond city boundaries. Next came the malling of North America, particularly in the 1960s and 1970s, when we moved our stores out to where we lived. And now, says Joel Garreau (1991), we have moved our means of creating wealth, the essence of urbanism—our jobs—out to where most

of us have lived and shopped for two generations. This has led to the rise of edge cities, resulting in profound changes in the ways we live, work, and play. Garreau (1991:8–9) describes the new urban form this way:

. . . For my sins I once spent a fair chunk of a Christmas season in Tysons Corner, Virginia, stopping people as they hurried about their holiday tasks, asking them what they thought of their brave new world. The words I recorded were searing. They described the area as plastic, a hodgepodge, Disneyland (used as a pejorative), and sterile. They said it lacked livability, civilization, community, neighborhood, and even a soul.

These responses are frightening, if Edge City is the laboratory of how civilized and livable urban Americans will be well into the next century. Right now, it is vertigo-inducing. It may have all the complexity, diversity, and size of a downtown. But it can cover dozens of square miles, and juxtapose schools and freeways and atria and shimmering parking lots with corporate lawns and Day-Glo-orange helicopter wind socks. Its logic takes a while to decode.

Will we ever be proud of this place? Will we ever drag our visiting relatives out to show off our Edge City, our shining city on the hill? Will we ever feel—for this generation and the ones that follow—that it's a good place to be young? To be old? To fall in love? To have a Fourth of July parade? Will it ever be the place we want to call home?

Source: From *Cities and Urban Life* by John J. Macionis and Vincent R. Parrillo, Copyright © 2000. Reprinted by permission of Pearson Education, Inc. Upper Saddle River, N.J.

It is the evolution of edge cities in the past quarter-century that helps explain the increases in population in nonmetropolitan areas, as discussed in the previous chapter. Garreau suggests that North Americans have reinvented the city in the past two decades and that these new urban agglomerations are now the future. Numbering over 200 in the United States, these edge cities with their malls and office parks now dominate the nation's retail trade and office facilities. . . .

Edge cities are appearing in Canada as well as in the United States, but apparently for different reasons. Unlike the United States, the Canadian government does not provide suburb-enhancing tax deductions for home mortgages, and it has greater control over planning and development. In Canada also, there is a greater emphasis on mass transit; a relative lack of freeways; vibrant, bustling urban centers; and a relative lack of racial problems. Nevertheless, edge cities are flourishing. Toronto, for example, has only 46 percent of the area's market. The rest is found in the nine edge cities growing up around it. These are Midtown–Yorkville and North York–North Yonge to the north; Mississauga, the Downsview Airport area, and the Etobicoke–427 area to the west; and the Don Valley Parkway–401 area, Markham–404 area, Eglinton–Don Mills area, and Scarborough to the east.

Joel Garreau (1991:5) points out that attract edge cities have become the dominant form:

By any functional urban standard—tall buildings, bright lights, office space that represents whitecollar jobs, shopping, entertainment, prestigious hotels, corporate headquarters, hospitals with CAT scans, even population—each Edge City is larger than down-town Portland, Oregon, or Portland, Maine, or Tampa, or Tucson. Already, two-thirds of all [North] American office facilities are in Edge Cities, and 80 percent of them have materialized in only the last two decades.

Characteristics and Commonalities

Garreau identified over 200 new edge cities in the United States and Canada, giving him a comparative base for analysis. Garreau (1991:425) concluded that this fledgling urban form, despite a sprawling, apparently chaotic evolution, actually possesses specific characteristics. A full-blown edge city contains

- At least 5 million square feet of leasable office space;
- At least 600,000 square feet of retail space (the equivalent of an average mall of three large stores and 80 to 100 shops and boutiques);
- An increasing population each weekday morning, marking it as primarily a work center, not a residential suburb;
- A local perception as a single-end destination for mixed use—jobs, shopping, and entertainment.

What one cannot find, however, is a clearly defined territorial boundary, for edge cities do not have the same look (the compactness of closely adjacent buildings and high pedestrian traffic), political organization (elected officials or civic codes), or even visual clues of older cities (signs, edges) to mark their perimeters. As Garreau (1991:6) explains:

The reasons these places are tricky to define is that they rarely have a mayor or a city council, and just about never match boundaries on a map. We're still in the process of giving each Edge City its name—a project, incidentally, that could use more flair. In New Jersey, for example, there is one with only the laconic designation "287 and 78." The reason there are no "Welcome to" signs at Edge City is that it is a judgment call where it begins and ends.

A common feature of edge cities is that they have sprouted far from the old downtowns, in locales where, thirty years ago, little existed save villages and farmland. They typically evolve adjacent to two or more major highways, usually with shopping malls serving as anchor points. . . .

Types of Edge Cities

Edge cities fall into one of three major categories: (1) uptowns, built on top of preautomobile settlements, such as Pasadena, California, or Arlington, Virginia; (2) boomers, the typical edge city located at the intersection of two major highways and almost always centered on a mall, and (3) greenfields, a master-planned city by one developer on thousands of farmland acres, such as

Irvine, California, and Las Colinas, near the Dallas-Fort Worth airport (Garreau, 1991:115):

Because boomers, the most common form of edge cities, have grown so profusely throughout North America, urbanists identify three subcategories of them. The strip boomer city is usually only a few hundred yards wide but extends for miles along a major highway. Most representative are the strips along Route 1 in Princeton, Route 128 near the Mass Pike outside Boston, and I-270 in Montgomery County, Maryland, in the Washington, D.C., region. All three suffer severe traffic congestion because of their extended shapes. The node boomer city is relatively dense and contained, such as The Galleria area near Houston, Tysons Corner in Virginia, and the Midtown-Yorkville and North York-North Yonge areas in Toronto. The pig-in-the-python boomer city is a cross between the previous two types. It is a strip that develops one or several nodes along it, such as the Lodge Freeway in Southfield, northwest of Detroit, or King of Prussia, Pennsylvania, northwest of Philadelphia.

Evolving Middle-Class Centers

The majority of metropolitan North Americans now work, shop, and live in and around the 200-plus "new hearths of our civilization." Shopping malls function as the village squares for these new urban centers. Adjacent are the hotels, office buildings, and corporate headquarters, whose tall buildings are not side by side as in a downtown, but instead are located on campuslike settings of grass and trees, gazing at one another at a respectful distance. Surrounding this broad center of employment and shopping are the single-family suburban homes whose occupants now outnumber those living next to the old downtowns.

The rise of edge cities is essentially a function of social class, not race. They are evolving in metropolitan areas with low black populations (Denver, Minneapolis, Seattle, Toronto) as well as in metropolitan areas with high black populations (Atlanta, Chicago, New York, Washington). In the latter, middle-class African Americans (presently about one-third of the total U.S. black population) are just as likely to be part of edge cities as are middle-class whites. Just as the skin of the middle-class North American comes in various

hues—brown, black, shades of tan, and white—so too do edge cities reflect this reality.

The edge city, however, has been criticized as plastic and sterile, lacking in livability, civilization, community, neighborhood—in short, having little urban soul (Garreau, 1991:8). It is, however, an unfinished new city form and we do not yet know if, in its maturity, this ugly duckling will emerge as a splendid swan. Whatever its ultimate shape, we do know that the

Edge City acculturates immigrants, provides child care, and offers safety. It is, on average, an improvement in per capita fuel efficiency over the old suburbia–downtown arrangement, since it moves everything closer to the homes of the middle class.

That is why Edge City is the crucible of [North] America's urban future. Having become the place in which the majority of [North] Americans now live, learn, work, shop, play, pray, and die, Edge City will be the forge of the fabled [North] American way of life well into the twenty-first century.

And edge cities are appearing worldwide as well. They now mark the fringes of Bangkok, Beijing, London, Paris, and Sydney. Increased affluence, the desire for more individual transportation, greater use of computers and telecommunications requiring air climate control, and the existence of world financial centers requiring trading floors of at least 20,000 square feet are some of the important elements shaping the growth of edge cities in urban areas throughout the world.

Three Edge City Variations

Not all edge cities are alike, nor does their evolution occur for the same reasons everywhere. The following examples illustrate how the edge city can serve as its own motivation, emerge as a solution to a problem, or simply become the problem.

Edge City as Motivator. By 1990, Oshawa Centre, one of the oldest shopping malls in Ontario, Canada, was showing its age. Originally built for the town's blue-collar population, the place was dark and ugly, some of the stores had outdoor-facing windows and doors plastered with newspaper and cardboard, and its sales and rental value were declining. Not anymore. The Toronto-based Cambridge Shopping Centres purchased it in 1991 for $145 million. It did so because Garreau had written in *Edge City* that shopping malls usually function as the village squares of the new urban centers. "So, taking that theory," said Ronald Charbon, Cambridge's director of strategic market information, "we said, 'Where are the next edge cities going to occur? Where is the next wave of growth going to occur in the greater metropolitan Toronto area? And are any of our shopping centres sufficiently located to capitalize on that growth?'" (cited in Berman, 1997).

Using census tracts and surveys, Cambridge amassed a population profile of the area, discovering that areas surrounding Oshawa were white-collar and that projections of the area's growth rate were almost three times that in the Greater Toronto Area. So the company took the gamble, invested $40 million in a major facelift, and recruited upscale stores. However, that was only one part of a sophisticated strategy to turn Oshawa Centre (as Garreau described other edge cities) into a village square. Cambridge secured government approval to construct six modest-sized office towers over a twenty-five-year period. The Oshawa Centre is thus in the midst of a massive transformation from a jerry-built suburban mall into a mixed-use development that includes retail, business, government, and community services, all inspired by Garreau's book.

Edge City as the Solution. Since incorporating in 1956, Schaumburg, Illinois, has been what Judy Pasternak (1998) called "the ultimate faceless postwar suburb." Located twenty-six miles northwest of Chicago, the town is home to nearly 74,000 people living in townhouses and subdivisions and shopping in one or more of the sixty-five shopping centers that line its streets. Along its expressway, glassy office towers provide a solid employment base. The one thing lacking in Schaumburg, though, is that it has no center, no downtown, no place to walk to or for people to gather. In fact, it hadn't had a town center since 1875.

That is now changing. The local government tore down a faded strip mall on a thirty-acre site to make way for a downtown center called "Town Square." But this place is no small-town core like the downtowns of older suburbs that developed around train depots generations ago. There are no retail stores lining Main Street. In fact, there is no Main Street. Instead, a supermarket and a cluster of retail stores border a large parking lot, giving this area the look of a shopping center. Nearby is a new library, a brick clock tower, a green wrought-iron gazebo, a pond, curved benches, and a chain restaurant. "It's plastic," grumbled one store owner. Others, however, are more optimistic, hoping that this shopping area—with plenty of parking, strolling amenities, and mixed-use development—will allow community to blossom where none had existed before (Pasternak, 1998).

Edge City as the Problem. The more that Tysons Corner, Virginia—one of Joel Garreau's prime examples of an edge city—continues to grow and thrive economically, the more it remains an object of derisive commentary by architects, city planners, design critics, and urban scholars. Indeed, finding ways to "fix" Tysons Corner has been the goal of several planning studies sponsored by academic institutions, professional groups, and Fairfax County, home to this edge city. Tysons Corner today is larger, in both geographic size and employment, than many U.S. central cities, with over 80,000 jobs and 12,000 residents sharing a few hundred acres of former farmland. Moreover, five new office building projects that will add 10,000 jobs (and perhaps almost as many automobile trips) are under construction, and zoning allows for an additional 20 million square feet of commercial space. Incredibly, though, Metrorail does not go there, making road transit the only means of transportation (Lewis, 1999).

Clearly, mass transit would greatly alleviate the traffic congestion. During weekday rush hours and weekend shopping times, backups are horrendous. Recommendations include creating an elevated rail system looping around Tysons Corner, as well as a link between Tysons and the regional Metro-rail network. But much more is needed. Tysons is not pedestrian-friendly, for there are few sidewalks or signalized crosswalks, which are critical for safely traversing the extraordinarily wide, traffic-choked roads, making walking around Tysons virtually impossible.

Even if traffic congestion could be reduced and pedestrian traffic encouraged, the aesthetic and visual deficiencies, the visual chaos and formlessness would still remain. In the interest of bringing a bit of visual order to Tysons Corner, a county task force developed a plan a few years ago to address streetscapes, pedestrian walkways, site planning of buildings, and open space. Still, Tysons has no civic focus, or heart, and so planners propose a "town center" as a way to "give Tysons more soul." Such an undertaking is still several years away, however. In the meantime, Tysons continues to be emblematic of how poorly we have planned, zoned, and developed much of the landscape girdling our cities since the end of World War II (Lewis, 1999).

CRITICAL-THINKING QUESTIONS

1. What three waves of outward movement from central cities in the United States marked the second half of the twentieth century?
2. In what ways do today's edge cities differ from the old "downtown" cities of a century ago?
3. Why do some critics claim that edge cities are not socially healthy places to live? Do you agree? Why, or why not?

REFERENCES

BERMAN, D. 1997. Shopping on the edge. *Canadian Business,* (October 31): 72–79.

GARREAU, J. 1991. *Edge city.* New York: Doubleday.

LEWIS, R. K. 1999. Saving Tyson's Corner: Plans, but little progress. *Washington Post,* (March 20): G3.

PASTERNAK, J. 1998. "Edge City" is attempting to build a center. *Los Angeles Times,* (January 1): 5.

CLASSIC

CONTEMPORARY

CROSS-CULTURAL

72 Let's *Reduce* Global Population!

J. KENNETH SMAIL

A familiar concern is holding the line on world population increase. But, some people are asking, has population growth already gone too far? In this selection, Ken Smail argues that the long-term "carrying capacity" of the planet may only be half the number of people we have now. And the time left to begin reducing population is running out fast.

The main point of this essay is simply stated. Within the next half-century, it is essential for the human species to have in place a flexible voluntary, equitable, and internationally coordinated plan to dramatically reduce world population by at least two-thirds. This process of voluntary consensus building—local, national, and global—must begin now.

The mathematical inevitability that human numbers will continue their dramatic increase over the next two generations (to perhaps 9 billion or more by the year 2050), the high probability that this numerical increase will worsen the problems that already plague humanity (economic, political, environmental, social, moral, etc.), and the growing realization that the Earth may only be able to support a global human population in the 2 to 3 billion range at an "adequate to comfortable" standard of living, only reinforce this sense of urgency.

Source: The revised version of the essay, "Negative Population Growth" (Smail, 1995), revised and expanded as "Population and Environment" (Smail, 1997a) and "Politics and the Life Sciences" (Smail, 1997b). Reprinted with permission.

There are, however, hopeful signs. In recent years, we have finally begun to come to terms with the fact that the consequences of the twentieth century's rapid and seemingly uncontrolled population growth will soon place us—if it has not done so already—in the greatest crisis our species has yet encountered.

TEN INESCAPABLE REALITIES

In order better to appreciate the scope and ramifications of this still partly hidden crisis, I shall briefly call attention to ten essential and inescapable realities that must be fully understood and soon confronted.

First, during the present century world population will have grown from somewhere around 1.6 billion in 1900 to slightly more than 6 billion by the year 2000, an almost fourfold increase in but 100 years. This is an unprecedented numerical expansion. Throughout human history, world population growth measured over similar 100-year intervals has been virtually nonexistent or, at most, modestly incremental; it has only become markedly exponential within the last few hundred years. To

451

illustrate this on a more easily comprehensible scale, based on the recent rate of increase of nearly 90 million per year, human population growth during the 1990s alone amounted to nearly 1 billion, an astonishing 20 percent increase in but little more than a single decade. Just by itself, this increase is equivalent to the total global population in the year 1800 and is approximately triple the estimated world population (ca. 300 million) at the height of the Roman Empire. It is a chastening thought that even moderate demographic projections suggest that this billion-per-decade rate of increase will continue well into the century, and that the current global total of 6 billion (late 1999 estimate) could easily reach 9 to 10 billion by mid-twenty-first century.

Second, even if a fully effective program of zero population growth (ZPG) were implemented immediately, by limiting human fertility to what demographers term the *replacement rate* (roughly 2.1 children per female), global population would nevertheless continue its rapid rate of expansion. In fact, demographers estimate that it would take at least two to three generations (fifty to seventy-five years) at ZPG fertility levels just to reach a point of population stability, unfortunately at numbers considerably higher than at present. This powerful *population momentum* results from the fact that an unusually high proportion (nearly one-third) of the current world population is under the age of fifteen and has not yet reproduced. Even more broad-based population profiles may be found throughout the developing world, where the under-fifteen age cohort often exceeds 40 percent and where birth rates have remained high even as mortality rates have fallen. While there are some recent indications that fertility rates are beginning to decline, the current composite for the less-developed world—excluding China—is still nearly double (ca. 3.8) that needed for ZPG.

Third, in addition to fertility levels, it is essential to understand that population growth is also significantly affected by changes in mortality rates. In fact, demographic transition theory suggests that the earlier stages of rapid population expansion are typically fueled more by significant reductions

in death rates (i.e., decreased childhood mortality and/or enhanced adult longevity) than by changes in birth rates. Nor does recent empirical data suggest that average human life expectancy has reached anywhere near its theoretical upper limit, in either the developing or developed worlds. Consequently, unless there appears a deadly pandemic, a devastating world war or a massive breakdown in public health (or a combination of all three), it is obvious that ongoing global gains in human longevity will continue to make a major contribution to world population expansion over the next half-century, regardless of whatever progress might be made in reducing fertility.

Fourth, all previous examples of significant human population expansion—and subsequent (occasionally rapid) decline—have been primarily local or, at most, regional phenomena. At the present time, given the current global rate of increase of some 220,000 people per day (more than 9,000 per hour), it is ludicrous to speak of significant empty spaces left on Earth to colonize, certainly when compared with but a century ago. And it is ridiculous to suggest that "off Earth" (extraterrestrial) migration will somehow be sufficient to siphon away excess human population, in either the near or more distant future.

Fifth, given the data and observations presented thus far, it becomes increasingly apparent that the time span available for implementing an effective program of population "control" may be quite limited, with a window of opportunity—even in the more optimistic scenarios—that may not extend much beyond the middle of the next century. As mentioned previously, most middle-of-the-road demographic projections for the year 2050—two generations from now—are in the 8 to 9 billion range. Several observations might help to bring these demographic estimates and the above-mentioned "limited" time span into somewhat better perspective:

- the year 2050 is closer to the present than the year 1950
- an infant born in 2000 will be only fifty years old in the year 2050

- a young person entering the job market in the early twenty-first century will have reached retirement age in the year 2050

These observations also make it quite clear that *those already* born—ourselves, our children, and our grandchildren—will have to confront the overwhelming impact of an additional 3 to 4 billion people.

Sixth, the Earth's long-term carrying capacity, in terms of resources, is indeed finite, despite the continuing use of economic models predicated on seemingly unlimited growth, and notwithstanding the high probability of continued scientific/technological progress. Some further terminological clarification may be useful. "Long-term" is most reasonably defined on the order of several hundred years, at least; it emphatically does not mean the five-to-fifteen-year horizon typical of much economic forecasting or political prognostication. Over this much longer time span, it thus becomes much more appropriate—perhaps even essential to civilizational survival—to define a sustainable human population size in terms of optimums rather than maximums. Further, *what "could" be supported in the short term is not necessarily what "should" be humanity's goal over the longer term.*

As far as resources are concerned, whether these be characterized as renewable or nonrenewable, it is becoming increasingly apparent that the era of inexpensive energy (derived from fossil fuels), adequate food supplies (whether plant or animal), readily available or easily extractable raw materials (from wood to minerals), plentiful fresh water, and readily accessible "open space" is rapidly coming to a close, almost certainly within the next half-century. And finally, the consequences of future scientific/technological advances—whether in terms of energy production, technological efficiency, agricultural productivity, or creation of alternative materials—are much more likely to be incremental than revolutionary, notwithstanding frequent and grandiose claims for the latter.

Seventh, rhetoric about "sustainable growth" is at best a continuing exercise in economic self-deception and at worst a politically pernicious oxymoron. Almost certainly, working toward some sort

of *steady-state sustainability* is much more realistic scientifically, (probably) more attainable economically, and (perhaps) more prudent politically. Assertions that the Earth might be able to support a population of 10, 15, or even 20 billion people for an indefinite period of time at a standard of living superior to the present are not only cruelly misleading but almost certainly false. Rather, extrapolations from the work of a growing number of ecologists, demographers, and numerous others suggest the distinct possibility that *the Earth's true carrying capacity—defined simply as humans in long-term adaptive balance with their ecological setting, resource base, and each other—may already have been exceeded by a factor of two or more.*

To the best of my knowledge, no evidence contradicts this sobering—perhaps even frightening—assessment. Consequently, since at some point in the not-too-distant future the negative consequences and ecological damage stemming from the mutually reinforcing effects of excessive human reproduction and overconsumption of resources could well become irreversible, and because there is only one Earth with which to experiment, it is undoubtedly better for our species to err on the side of prudence, exercising wherever possible a cautious and careful stewardship.

Eighth, only about 20 percent of the current world population (ca. 1.2 billion people) could be said to have a *generally adequate* standard of living, defined here as a level of affluence roughly approximating that of the so-called "developed" world (Western Europe, Japan, and North America). The other 80 percent (ca. 4.8 billion), incorporating most of the inhabitants of what have been termed the "developing nations," live in conditions ranging from mild deprivation to severe deficiency. Despite well-intentioned efforts to the contrary, there is little evidence that this imbalance is going to decrease in any significant way, and a strong likelihood that it may get worse, particularly in view of the fact that more than 90 percent of all future population expansion is projected to occur in these less-developed regions of the world. In fact, there is growing concern that when this burgeoning population growth in the developing world is combined with excessive or wasteful per capita energy and resource consumption in much of the developed world, widespread environmental deterioration (systemic breakdown?) in a number of the Earth's more heavily stressed ecosystems will become increasingly likely. This is especially worrisome in regions already beset by short-sighted or counterproductive economic policies, chronic political instability, and growing social unrest, particularly when one considers that nearly all nations in the less-developed world currently have an understandable desire—not surprisingly expressed as a fundamental right—to increase their standard of living (per capita energy and resource consumption) to something approximating "first world" levels.

Ninth, to follow up on the point just made, the total impact of human numbers on the global environment is often described as the product of three basic multipliers: (1) population size; (2) per capita energy and resource consumption (affluence); and (3) technological efficiency in the production, utilization, and conservation of such energy and resources. This relationship is usually expressed by some variant of the now well-known I = PAT equation: Impact = Population × Affluence × Technology. This simple formula enables one to demonstrate much more clearly the quantitative scope of humanity's dilemma over the next fifty to seventy-five years, particularly if the following projections are anywhere near accurate:

- human population could well *double* by the end of the twenty-first century, from our current 6 billion to perhaps 12 billion or more
- global energy and resource consumption could easily *quadruple* or more during the same period, particularly if (as just indicated in item 8) the less-developed nations are successful in their current efforts to significantly improve their citizens' standard of living to something approaching developed-world norms
- new technologies applied to current energy and resource inefficiencies might be successful in reducing per capita waste or effluence *by half,* or even *two-thirds,* in both the developed and developing worlds

Given these reasonable estimates, the conclusion seems inescapable that the human species' total impact on the Earth's already stressed ecosystem could easily *triple to quadruple* by the middle of the twenty-first century. This impact could be even greater if current (and future) efforts at energy and resource conservation turn out to be less successful than hoped for, or if (as seems likely) the mathematical relationship between these several multipliers is something more than simply linear. It is therefore very important to keep a close watch—for harbingers of future trends and/or problems—on current events in the growing group of nations now experiencing rapid economic development and modernization, with particular attention being given to ongoing changes in India and China, two states whose combined size represents nearly half the population of the less-developed world.

Tenth, and finally, there are two additional considerations—matters not usually factored into the I = PAT equation—that must also be taken into account in any attempt to coordinate appropriate responses to the rapidly increasing global environmental impact described in points 6 through 9. First, given current and likely ongoing scientific uncertainties about environmental limits and ecosystem resilience, not to mention the potential dangers of irreversible damage if such limits are stretched too far (i.e., a permanently reduced carrying capacity), it is extremely important to design into any future planning an adequate safety factor (or sufficient margin for error). In other words, any attempt at "guided social engineering" on the massive scale that will clearly be necessary over the next century will require at least as much attention to safety margins, internal coordination, and systems redundancy as may be found in other major engineering accomplishments—from designing airplanes to building the Channel Tunnel to landing astronauts on the moon.

In addition, such planning must consider yet another seemingly intractable problem. Because the human species not only shares the Earth—but has also co-evolved—with literally millions of other life forms, the closely related issues of wilderness conservation and biodiversity preservation must also be taken fully into account, on several different levels (pragmatic, aesthetic, and moral). In simplest terms, it has now become a matter of critical importance to ask some very basic questions about what proportion of the Earth's surface the human species has the right to exploit or transform—or, conversely, how much of the Earth's surface should be reserved for the protection and preservation of all other life forms. As many have argued, often in eloquent terms, our species will likely be more successful in confronting and resolving these questions—not to mention the other complex problems that are now crowding in upon us—*if we can collectively come to regard ourselves more as the Earth's long-term stewards than its absolute masters.*

To sum up, if the above "inescapable realities" are indeed valid, it is obvious that rational, equitable, and attainable population goals will have to be established in the very near future. It is also obvious that these goals will have to address— and in some fashion resolve—a powerful internal conflict: how to create and sustain an adequate standard of living for *all* the world's peoples, minimizing as much as possible the growing inequities between rich and poor, while simultaneously neither overstressing nor exceeding the Earth's longer-term carrying capacity. *I submit that*

these goals cannot be reached, or this conflict resolved, unless and until world population is dramatically reduced—to somewhere around 2 to 3 billion people—within the next two centuries.

CRITICAL-THINKING QUESTIONS

1. Why, according to this reading, is simply holding the line on population increase not enough?

2. What about the fact that humans share the Earth with millions of other life forms? In facing up to the problem of population increase, what responsibility do we have for other species?

3. All in all, do you agree with Smail that we must find a way to reduce global population? Why or why not?

REFERENCES

SMAIL, J. KENNETH. 1995. Confronting the 21st century's hidden crisis: Reducing human numbers by 80%. *NPG Forum.* Teaneck, N.J.: Negative Population Growth.

———. 1997a. Averting the 21st century's demographic crisis: Can human numbers be reduced by 75%? *Population and Environment,* 18(6): 565–80.

———. 1997b. Beyond population stabilization: The case for dramatically reducing global human numbers. Roundtable: World Population Policy commentary and responses. *Politics and the Life Sciences,* 16, 2 (September, 1997): 183–236.

CLASSIC

CONTEMPORARY

CROSS-CULTURAL

73 Why Humanity Faces Ultimate Catastrophe

THOMAS ROBERT MALTHUS

In this selection, from "An Essay on the Principle of Population," Thomas Robert Malthus foretells human calamity. His dire prediction is based on a single assertion: Human beings will overwhelm the earth's capacity to provide for us. Many of today's environmentalists (sometimes termed "neo-Malthusians") accept this principle and echo his early warning.

STATEMENT OF THE SUBJECT: RATIOS OF THE INCREASE OF POPULATION AND FOOD

In an inquiry concerning the improvement of society, the mode of conducting the subject which naturally presents itself is

1. To investigate the causes that have hitherto impeded the progress of mankind towards happiness
2. To examine the probability of the total or partial removal of the causes in [the] future

To enter fully into this question, and to enumerate all the causes that have hitherto influenced human improvement, would be much beyond the power of an individual. The principal object of the present essay is to examine the

effects of one great cause intimately united with the very nature of man; which, though it has been constantly and powerfully operating since the commencement of society, has been little noticed by the writers who have treated this subject. The facts which establish the existence of this cause have, indeed, been repeatedly stated and acknowledged; but its natural and necessary effects have been almost totally overlooked; though probably among these effects may be reckoned a very considerable portion of that vice and misery, and of that unequal distribution of the bounties of nature, which it has been the unceasing object of the enlightened philanthropist in all ages to correct.

The cause to which I allude is the constant tendency in all animated life to increase beyond the nourishment prepared for it.

Source: From *On the Principle of Population,* Vol. I, by T. R. Malthus (New York: E. P. Dutton & Co., Inc., 1914; orig. 1798).

It is observed by Dr. Franklin that there is no bound to the prolific nature of plants or animals but what is made by their crowding and interfering with each other's means of subsistence. Were the face of the earth, he says, vacant of other plants, it might be gradually sowed and overspread with one kind only, as for instance with fennel: and were it empty of other inhabitants, it might in a few ages be replenished from one nation only, as for instance with Englishmen.[1]

This is incontrovertibly true. Through the animal and vegetable kingdoms Nature has scattered the seeds of life abroad with the most profuse and liberal hand; but has been comparatively sparing in the room and the nourishment necessary to rear them. The germs of existence contained in this earth, if they could freely develop themselves, would fill millions of worlds in the course of a few thousand years. Necessity, that imperious, all pervading law of nature, restrains them within the prescribed bounds. The race of plants and the race of animals shrink under this great restrictive law; and man cannot by any efforts of reason escape from it.

In plants and irrational animals, the view of the subject is simple. They are all impelled by a powerful instinct to the increase of their species; and this instinct is interrupted by no doubts about providing for their offspring. Wherever therefore there is liberty, the power of increase is exerted; and the super-abundant effects are repressed afterwards by want of room and nourishment.

The effects of this check on man are more complicated. Impelled to the increase of his species by an equally powerful instinct, reason interrupts his career, and asks him whether he may not bring beings into the world for whom he cannot provide the means of support. If he attends to this natural suggestion, the restriction too frequently produces vice. If he hear it not, the human race will be constantly endeavouring to increase beyond the mean of subsistence. But as, by the law of our nature which makes food necessary to the life of man, population can never actually increase beyond the lowest nourishment capable of supporting it, a strong check on population, from the difficulty of

acquiring food, must be constantly in operation. This difficulty must fall somewhere, and must necessarily be severely felt in some or other of the various forms of misery, or the fear of misery, by a large portion of mankind.

That population has this constant tendency to increase beyond the means of subsistence, and that it is kept to its necessary level by these causes, will sufficiently appear from a review of the different states of society in which man has existed. But, before we proceed to this review, the subject will, perhaps, be seen in a clearer light if we endeavour to ascertain what would be the natural increase of population if left to exert itself with perfect freedom; and what might be expected to be the rate of increase in the production of the earth under the most favourable circumstances of human industry.

It will be allowed that no country has hitherto been known where the manners were so pure and simple, and the means of subsistence so abundant, that no check whatever has existed to early marriages from the difficulty of providing for a family, and that no waste of the human species has been occasioned by vicious customs, by towns, by unhealthy occupations, or too severe labour. Consequently in no state that we have yet known has the power of population been left to exert itself with perfect freedom.

Whether the law of marriage be instituted, or not, the dictate of nature and virtue seems to be an early attachment to one woman; and where there were no impediments of any kind in the way of a union to which such an attachment would lead, and no causes of depopulation afterwards, the increase of the human species would be evidently much greater than any increase which has been hitherto known. . . .

It may safely be pronounced, . . . that population, when unchecked, goes on doubling itself every twenty-five years, or increases in a geometrical ratio.

The rate according to which the productions of the earth may be supposed to increase, it will not be so easy to determine. Of this, however, we may be perfectly certain, that the ratio of their increase in a limited territory must be of a totally different nature from the ratio of the increase of population. A thousand millions are just as easily doubled every twenty-five years by the power of population as a thousand. But the food to support the increase from the greater number will by no means be obtained with the same facility. Man is necessarily confined in room. When acre has been added to acre till all the fertile land is occupied, the yearly increase of food must depend upon the melioration of the land already in possession. This is a fund, which, from the nature of all soils, instead of increasing, must be gradually diminishing. But population, could it be supplied with food, would go on with unexhausted vigour; and the increase of one period would furnish the power of a greater increase the next, and this without any limit. . . .

Europe is by no means so fully peopled as it might be. In Europe there is the fairest chance that human industry may receive its best direction. The science of agriculture has been much studied in England and Scotland; and there is still a great portion of uncultivated land in these countries. Let us consider at what rate the produce of this island might be supposed to increase under circumstances the most favourable to improvement.

If it be allowed that by the best possible policy, and great encouragements to agriculture, the average produce of the island could be doubled in the first twenty-five years, it will be allowing, probably, a greater increase than could with reason be expected.

In the next twenty-five years, it is impossible to suppose that the produce could be quadrupled. It would be contrary to all our knowledge of the properties of land. The improvement of the barren parts would be a work of time and labour; and it must be evident to those who have the slightest acquaintance with agricultural subjects that, in proportion as cultivation extended, the additions that could yearly be made to the former average produce must be gradually and regularly diminishing. That we may be the better able to compare the increase of population and food, let us make a

supposition, which, without pretending to accuracy, is clearly more favourable to the power of production in the earth than any experience we have had of its qualities will warrant.

Let us suppose that the yearly additions which might be made to the former average produce, instead of decreasing, which they certainly would do, were to remain the same; and that the produce of this island might be increased every twenty-five years by a quantity equal to what it at present produces. The most enthusiastic speculator cannot suppose a greater increase than this. In a few centuries it would make every acre of land in the island like a garden.

If this supposition be applied to the whole earth, and if it be allowed that the subsistence for man which the earth affords might be increased every twenty-five years by a quantity equal to what it at present produces, this will be supposing a rate of increase much greater than we can imagine that any possible exertions of mankind could make it.

It may be fairly pronounced, therefore, that, considering the present average state of the earth, the means of subsistence, under circumstances the most favourable to human industry, could not possibly be made to increase faster than in an arithmetical ratio.

The necessary effects of these two different rates of increase, when brought together, will be very striking. Let us call the population of this island 11 millions; and suppose the present produce equal to the easy support of such a number. In the first twenty-five years the population would be 22 millions, and the food being also doubled, the means of subsistence would be equal to this increase. In the next twenty-five years, the population would be 44 millions, and the means of subsistence only equal to the support of 33 millions. In the next period the population would be 88 millions, and the means of subsistence just equal to the support of half that number. And, at the conclusion of the first century, the population would be 176 millions, and the means of subsistence only equal to the support of 55 millions, leaving a population of 121 millions totally unprovided for.

Taking the whole earth, instead of this island, emigration would of course be excluded; and, supposing the present population equal to a thousand millions, the human species would increase as the numbers, 1, 2, 4, 8, 16, 32, 64, 128, 256, and subsistence as 1, 2, 3, 4, 5, 6, 7, 8, 9. In two centuries the population would be to the means of subsistence as 256 to 9; in three centuries as 4,096 to 13, and in 2,000 years the difference would be almost incalculable.

CRITICAL-THINKING QUESTIONS

1. According to Malthus, at what rate does human population increase? At what rate can the earth's food supplies be increased?

2. Malthus published his essay in 1798; in the two centuries since then, has his dire prediction come to pass? Why, or why not?

3. Following Malthus's thinking, what should be the cornerstone of the world's program to protect the environment? Do you agree with his position or not?

NOTE

1. Franklin's Miscell, p. 9.

CLASSIC

CONTEMPORARY

CROSS-CULTURAL

74 Rich Planet, Poor Planet: Global Environment and Poverty in 2001

CHRISTOPHER FLAVIN

For decades, analysts have pointed to a steady decline in the Earth's natural environment. This troubling trend, they explain, is not simply a technical problem but has much to do with the way societies operate. Moreover, environmental problems are closely linked to another pressing issue—global poverty.

A visit to Brazil's tropical state of Bahia provides contrasting views of the state of the world at the dawn of the new millennium. Bahia's capital, Salvador, has a population of over 3 million and a thoroughly modern veneer. Its downtown is full of large office buildings and busy construction cranes, and its highways are crammed with sport utility vehicles. The state is also rich in natural resources: the wealth provided by gold and sugarcane made Salvador the obvious location for colonial Brazil's leading port and capital for two centuries.[1]

Once a backwater—slavery was not outlawed until the end of the nineteenth century, one of the last regions to ban this practice—Bahia's economy is now booming. The state has a prospering manufacturing sector and has become popular with many leading multinationals, including automobile companies that have put some of their most advanced factories there. The information economy is in a particularly competitive frenzy.

Brazilian Internet service providers are connecting customers for free, and cell phones appear to be almost as common as they are in many European cities.

Scratch the surface, however, and another Bahia is still there. The large favelas that ring Salvador's outskirts are crowded with thousands of poor people who lack more than cell phones and computers: Toilets, running water, and schoolbooks are among the basic services and products that are unavailable to many of Bahia's poor. Similar gaps can be seen in the low hills that run south of Salvador along Bahia's rugged coast: The collapse of many of the country's rich cacao farms due to a devastating pathogen called witches broom and a sharp decline in world chocolate prices have left thousands of farm workers jobless and unable to provide for their families.

Bahia's environmental condition is just as uneven. Considered by ecologists to be one of the world's biological "hot spots," the Atlantic Rain Forest covers more than 2,000 kilometers of Brazil's subtropical coast. In 1993, biologists working in an area south of Salvador identified a world

Source: From *State of the World 2001: A Worldwatch Institute Report on Progress Toward a Sustainable Society* by Lester R. Brown et al., pp. 3–20. Copyright © 2001 by Worldwatch Institute. Reprinted by W. W. Norton & Company, Inc.

record 450 tree species in a single hectare. (A hectare of forest in the northeastern United States typically contains ten species.) In the last decade, Bahia's political and business leaders have come to recognize the extraordinary richness of their biological heritage—wildlands are being protected, ecological research facilities are being set up, and ecotourist resorts are mushrooming. A sign at the airport even warns travelers that removing endemic species from the country is a felony.[2]

And yet, signs of destruction are everywhere: Cattle ranches sprawl where the world's richest forests once stood; 93 percent of the Atlantic forest is already gone, and much of the remainder is fragmented into tiny plots. Pressure on these last bits of forest is enormous—both from powerful landowners and corporations eager to sell forest and agricultural products in the global marketplace, and from poor families desperately seeking a living.[3]

This picture of Bahia in the year 2000 is replicated at scores of locations around the globe. It is the picture of a world undergoing extraordinarily rapid change amid huge and widening disparities. Unprecedented economic prosperity, the emergence of democratic institutions in many countries, and the near instantaneous flow of information and ideas throughout a newly interconnected world allow us to address challenges that have been neglected for decades: meeting the material needs of all 6 billion members of the human race and restoring a sustainable balance between humanity and Earth's ecological systems.

This moment is historic, perhaps even evolutionary, in character. Tragically, it is not being seized. Despite a surge in economic growth in recent years and significant gains in health and education levels in many developing nations, the number of people who survive on less than $1 of income per day—the poverty threshold used by the World Bank—was 1.2 billion in 1998, almost unchanged since 1990. In some parts of the world, including sub-Saharan Africa, South Asia, and the former Soviet Union, the number living in poverty is substantially higher than the figures recorded a decade ago.[4]

The struggle to restore the planet's ecological health presents a similar picture: a number of small battles have been won, but the war itself is still being lost. Double-digit rates of growth in renewable energy markets, plus a two-year decline in global carbon emissions, for example, have failed to slow the rate of global climate change. Indeed, recent evidence, from the rapid melting of glaciers and the declining health of heat-sensitive coral reefs, suggests that climate change is accelerating. The same pattern can be seen in the increased commitment to protection of wild areas and biological diversity: new laws are being passed, consumers are demanding eco-friendly wood products, and ecotourist resorts are sprouting almost as quickly as dotcom companies. But foresters and biologists report that this host of encouraging developments has not reversed the massive loss of forests or the greatest extinction crisis the world has seen in 65 million years.[5]

Long considered distinct issues, consigned to separate government agencies, ecological and social problems are in fact tightly interconnected and mutually reinforcing. The burden of dirty air and water and of decimated natural resources invariably falls on the disadvantaged. And the poor, in turn, are often compelled to tear down the last nearby tree or pollute the local stream in order to survive. Solving one problem without addressing the other is simply not feasible. In fact, poverty and environmental decline are both embedded deeply in today's economic systems. Neither is a peripheral problem that can be considered in isolation. What is needed is what Eduardo Athayde, General Director of Bahia's Atlantic Forest Open University, calls "econology," a synthesis of ecology, sociology, and economics that can be used as the basis for creating an economy that is both socially and ecologically sustainable—the central challenge facing humanity as the new millennium begins.[6]

The challenge is made larger by the fact that it must be met simultaneously at national and global levels, requiring not only cooperation but partnership between North and South. Responsibility for the current health of the planet and its

TABLE 1   The E–9: A Population and Economic Profile

Country or Grouping	Population, 2000	Gross National Product, 1998
	(million)	*(billion dollars)*
China	1,265	924
India	1,002	427
European Union[1]	375	8,312
United States	276	7,903
Indonesia	212	131
Brazil	170	768
Russia	145	332
Japan	127	4,089
South Africa	43	137

[1] Data for European Union do not include Luxembourg.

Source: World Bank, *World Development Indicators 2000* (Washington, D.C.: 2000), 10–12; Population Reference Bureau, "2000 World Population Data Sheet," wall chart (Washington, D.C.: June 2000).

human inhabitants is shared unequally between rich and poor countries, but if these problems are to be resolved, the two groups of nations will need to bring their respective strengths and capabilities to bear. This will require a new form of globalization—one that goes beyond trade links and capital flows to strengthened political and social ties between governments and civil society.

A select group of large industrial and developing countries—a collection that can be called the E–9, given that they are key environmental as well as economic players—could have a central role in closing the North-South gap. Together, this group of countries accounts for 57 percent of the world's population and 80 percent of total economic output (see Table 1). This [reading] uses data on these nine diverse countries and areas to illuminate key economic, social, and ecological trends. But this grouping has more than just analytical value. As argued at the end of the [reading], E–9 cooperation could be a key to achieving accelerated economic and environmental progress in the new century.[7]

A TALE OF TWO WORLDS

Halfway through the year 2000, two stories from the Philippines made headlines around the world.

In June, a computer virus dubbed the "love bug" appeared almost simultaneously on every continent, crashing the computer systems of scores of multinational corporations and government offices, ranging from the U.S. Pentagon to the British Parliament. The estimated total cost of the resulting disruptions: $10 billion. Computer security experts and FBI agents quickly traced the diabolical love bug to a small Manila technical college and a twenty-four-year-old student named Onel de Guzman. For computer experts, this may have been an indication of the vulnerability of the global Internet, but in the Philippines it quickly became a source of national pride. People took the love bug debacle as an encouraging sign that their developing nation was leapfrogging into the top ranks of the global economy's hottest sector.[8]

Across town, a Manila neighborhood called the Promised Land was hit by a different kind of news a month later: more than 200 people were killed in a massive landslide and subsequent fire. Although this tragedy was precipitated by Typhoon Kai Tak, it was anything but a natural disaster. The Promised Land, it turns out, is a combination garbage dump/shantytown that is home to 50,000 people, most of whom make their living by scavenging the food and materials discarded by Manila's growing middle class. When two days of heavy rain loosened the mountain of garbage, it came crashing down on hundreds of homes as well as the dump's electrical lines, starting a massive fire. Scores of Promised Land residents were buried, others were burned alive, and still more were poisoned by toxic chemicals released by the fire.[9]

Economic successes and social failures are now found side by side, not just in the Philippines, but around the world in this supposed time of plenty. The annual output of the world economy has grown from $31 trillion in 1990 to $42 trillion in 2000; by comparison, the total output of the world economy in 1950 was just $6.3 trillion. And in 2000, the growth of the world economy surged to a 4.7 percent annual rate, the highest in the last decade. This increase in economic activity has allowed billions of people to buy new refrigerators, televisions, and computers, and has created millions of jobs. Global telephone connections grew from 520 million in 1990 to 844 million in 1998 (an increase of 62 percent), and mobile phone subscribers went from 11 million to 319 million in that time (up 2,800 percent). The number of "host" computers, a measure of the Internet's expansion, grew from 376,000 in 1990 to 72,398,000 in 1999—an increase of 19,100 percent.[10]

The economic boom of the last decade has not been confined to the rich countries of the North. Much of the growth is occurring in the developing nations of Asia and Latin America, where economic reforms, lowered trade barriers, and a surge in foreign capital have fueled investment and consumption. Between 1990 and 1998, Brazil's economy grew 30 percent, India's expanded 60 percent, and China's mushroomed by a remarkable 130 percent. China now has the world's third largest economy (second if measured in terms of purchasing power parity), and a booming middle class who work in offices, eat fast food, watch color television, and surf the Internet. China alone now has 420 million radios, 344 million television sets, 24 million mobile phones, and 15 million computers.[11]

Still, the global economy remains tarnished by vast disparities (see Table 2). Gross national product (GNP) per person ranges from $32,350 in Japan to $4,630 in Brazil, $2,260 in Russia, and just $440 in India. Even when measured in purchasing power terms, GNP per person among these countries varies by a factor of ten. Per capita income has increased 3 percent annually in forty countries since 1990, but more than eighty nations have per capita incomes that are lower than they were a decade ago. Within countries, the disparities are even more striking. In the United States, the top 10 percent of the population has six times the income of the lowest 20 percent; in Brazil, the ratio is 19 to 1. More than 10 percent of the people living in "rich" countries are still below the poverty line, and in many, inequality has grown over the last two decades.[12]

The boom in global consumption over the past decade has been accompanied by improvements in living standards in many countries and declines in others. The U.N. Development Programme estimates that the share of the world's population suffering from what it calls "low human development" fell from 20 percent in 1975 to 10 percent in 1997. Still, World Bank figures show that 2.8 billion

TABLE 2   Economic Trends in E–9 Nations

| Country | GNP per Person, 1998 | Purchasing Power per Person, 1998 | Population Earning Below $2 per Day, 1993–99[1] | Share of Income or Consumption | |
				Lowest 20 percent, 1993–98[1]	Highest 10 percent, 1993–98[1]
	(dollars)		*(percent)*	*(percent)*	
Japan	32,350	23,592	—	10.6	21.7
United States	29,240	29,240	—	5.2	30.5
Germany[2]	26,570	22,026	—	8.2	23.7
Brazil	4,630	6,460	17.4	2.5	47.6
South Africa	3,310	8,296	35.8	2.9	45.9
Russia	2,260	6,180	25.1	4.4	38.7
China	750	3,051	53.7	5.9	30.4
Indonesia	640	2,407	66.1	8.0	30.3
India	440	2,060	86.2	8.1	33.5

[1]Data are from a single year within the time frame.

[2]Comparable data for European Union not available; Germany is most populous EU member.

Source: World Bank, *World Development Indicators 2000* (Washington, D.C.: 2000), 10–12, 62–64, 66–68.

people, nearly half the world's population, survive on an income of less than $2 per day, while a fifth of humanity, 1.2 billion people, live on less than $1 per day. An estimated 291 million sub-Saharan Africans—46 percent of the region's population— now live on less than $1 a day, while in South Asia, the figure is 522 million. This is a staggering number of people to enter the new century without the income needed to purchase basic necessities such as food, clean water, and health care.[13]

Worldwide, some 1.1 billion people are currently estimated to be malnourished. Most of these are poor people in rural areas who have insufficient land to grow the food they need and not enough income to buy it from others. Many of these people live in countries with food surpluses, but while well-off farmers sell their products to middle-class consumers in distant nations, the proceeds have no benefit for millions of starving children. In some African countries, such as Kenya, Zambia, and Zimbabwe, as much as 40 percent of the population is malnourished.[14]

Roughly 1.2 billion people do not have access to clean water. In China, the portion that fall in this category is 10 percent (125 million people), in India it is 19 percent, and in South Africa, 30 percent. Toilets are even rarer in many

countries: 33 percent of Brazil's population does not have one, nor does 49 percent of Indonesia's or 84 percent of India's.[15]

Polluted water is a major contributor to one of the largest disparities today's world faces: the health gap. Although infant mortality rates have dropped 25 to 50 percent in many countries in the past decade, they still stand at forty-three per thousand live births in China and seventy per thousand in India (see Table 3). Much of the wide difference in this number around the world results from undernutrition and common infectious diseases that remain rampant in many poor countries. More intractable diseases such as cholera and tuberculosis are also becoming epidemic in many areas.

More alarming still is the fact that AIDS, which has been brought under control in some rich countries, is spreading rapidly in many developing nations. The crisis is particularly acute in southern Africa, which a decade ago had relatively low rates of infection. By 2000, HIV infection rates had reached a stunning 20 percent in South Africa, 25 percent in Zimbabwe, and 36 percent in Botswana. Decades of rising life expectancy are being reversed in a matter of years, as hundreds of thousands of young adults and

TABLE 3   Health Indicators in E–9 Nations

Country	Health Expenditures per Person, 1990–98[1]	Infant Mortality		Tuberculosis Incidence, 1997	HIV Prevalence Among Adults, 1997
		1980	1998		
	(dollars of purchasing power)	(per thousand live births)		(per 100,000)	(percent)
United States	4,121	8	4	7	0.76
Germany[2]	2,364	12	5	15	0.08
Japan	1,757	13	7	29	0.01
South Africa	571	42	31	394	12.91
Brazil	503	70	33	78	0.63
Russia	404	22	17	106	0.05
China	142	90	43	113	0.06
India	73	115	70	187	0.82
Indonesia	38	67	51	285	0.05

[1]Data are from the most recent year available.

[2]Comparable data for European Union not available; Germany is most populous EU member.

Source: World Bank, *World Development Indicators 2000* (Washington, D.C.: 2000), 90–92, 102–04, 106–08.

children succumb to the disease. Health care budgets are being overwhelmed, and education undermined by the early deaths of many teachers. It is no accident that the countries most ravaged by AIDS are those with high rates of social disruption and limited government health services. In China, poor people who sell their blood in order to make ends meet are paying a high price in the form of HIV infection from contaminated needles. Ironically, in parts of Africa, it is those who are just emerging from poverty that are being hit the hardest—devastating a generation of educated young workers, a cataclysm that may forestall the growth of an economically secure middle class.[16]

One of the key ingredients of economic progress is education, and on this front, the world is doing better than it was two decades ago (see Table 4). In India, the share of children in secondary school has risen from 41 percent to 60 percent; in China, it has gone from 63 to 70 percent; and in South Africa, from 62 to 95 percent. But even with these improvements, many countries are failing to invest adequately in their young people, who are unlikely to be able to participate in or benefit from today's most vibrant economic sectors, which demand not only basic literacy but often

specialized training. Girls in particular are receiving inadequate education in many countries. Adult female illiteracy rates remain as high as 25 percent in China and 57 percent in India, levels that virtually guarantee a host of social and economic problems—and that make environmental threats more difficult to address.

TESTING THE LIMITS

When the Russian icebreaker *Yamal* reached the North Pole in July 2000, the scientists aboard were confronted with a strange sight: an expanse of open, calm water in place of the two or three meters of pack ice that is common to the region even at the height of summer. In the ninety-one years since Robert Peary and Matthew Henson reached the North Pole by dogsled in 1909, nothing like this had been reported. But human memory is the wrong scale on which to measure this development: Scientists estimate that the last time the polar region was completely ice-free was 50 million years ago.[17]

The dynamic, shifting character of the Arctic ice pack suggests that the open water over the pole itself was, for now, a fleeting phenomenon. But recent scientific evidence confirms the underlying

TABLE 4   Education in E–9 Nations

Country	Adult Illiteracy Rate				Share of Children in Secondary School	
	Female		Male			
	1980	1998	1980	1998	1980	1997
	(percent)				*(percent)*	
Germany[1]	—	—	—	—	82	95
Japan	—	—	—	—	93	100
United States	—	—	—	—	94	96
Russia	2	1	1	0	98	88
Brazil	27	16	23	16	46	66
South Africa	25	16	22	15	62	95
Indonesia	40	20	21	9	42	56
China	48	25	22	9	63	70
India	74	57	45	33	41	60

[1]Comparable data for European Union not available; Germany is most populous EU member.

Source: World Bank, *World Development Indicators 2000* (Washington, D.C.: 2000), 74–76, 82–84.

trend: Earth's frozen top is melting at an extraordinary rate. Submarine sonar measurements indicate a 40 percent decline in the average thickness of summer polar ice since the 1950s, far exceeding the rate of melting previously estimated. Based on these observations, scientists now estimate that by the middle of this century the Arctic could be ice-free in summer.[18]

Among the myriad signs of human-induced global climate change—fossil fuel combustion was recently estimated to have raised atmospheric concentrations of carbon dioxide to their highest levels in 20 million years—this one may be the most dramatic. In late 2000, the Intergovernmental Panel on Climate Change (IPCC), the scientific body that advises government negotiators, produced its latest report. It included the strongest consensus statement yet that societies' release of carbon dioxide and other greenhouse gases "contributed substantially to the observed warming over the last fifty years." By the end of the century, the IPCC concluded, temperatures could be five degrees Celsius higher than in 1990—an increase greater than the change in temperature between the last Ice Age and today.[19]

While the shipping industry is already beginning to view the Arctic meltdown as a potential short-term opportunity—perhaps cutting the transit distance between Europe and the Far East by as much as 5,000 kilometers—the full economic and ecological consequences would be far more extensive and hard to predict. Scientists have recently learned that Arctic ice is a key part of the "engine" that drives the powerful oceanic conveyor belt—the warm Gulf Stream—that provides northern Europe with the relatively temperate and stable climate that allowed European societies to flourish. Shutting it down could change the climate of Europe more than at any time since the last Ice Age. And because the Gulf Stream is a dominant feature in the oceanic circulation system, any major change in its course would have ripple effects globally. Moreover, with less ice to reflect the sun's rays, the warming of Earth that

caused the ice to melt in the first place would accelerate.[20]

Some 10,000 kilometers south of the North Pole lies a very different environment—the world's tropical oceans and their abundant coral reefs, a biologically rich ecosystem that has been described as the rainforest of the ocean (65 percent of fish species are reef dwellers). One of the richest is the Belize Barrier Reef on the Yucatan Peninsula in the Caribbean, the site of a recent diving expedition by marine biologist Jonathan Kelsey and journalist Colin Woodard. What was intended to be an exciting exploration of the region's spectacular, multi-hued marine life turned out to be a disturbing disappointment: "Bright white boulders dotted the seascape in all directions, a sign of severe coral distress," Woodard reported. "A centuries-old stand of elkhorn coral as big as an elephant was now dead and smothered in a thick two-year growth of brown algae. . . . Across the plane, the corals appeared to be dying."[21]

Around the world, from the Caribbean to the Indian Ocean and Australia's Great Barrier Reef, similar observations have been reported in the past two years. Coral polyps are temperature-sensitive, and often sicken or die when ocean surface temperatures rise even slightly. The temporary warming of ocean waters that accompanies El Niño anomalies in the Pacific is generally hard on coral reefs, but the 1998 El Niño was something different: Reports of sick coral were soon being filed by marine biologists around the world, who estimated that more than one quarter of the coral reefs were sick or dying. In some areas of the Pacific, the figure is as high as 90 percent. For many small island nations, the loss in income from fishing and tourism, as well as increased storm damage from the loss of coral reefs, may be enough to trigger the collapse of their economies.[22]

Following another serious episode of coral bleaching just a decade earlier, this recent epidemic of coral disease is another strong indication that the world is warming. But it is more than that: Coral reefs are sort of a marine version of the famous canary in a coalmine—vulnerable to many environmental stresses that now run rampant, including urban sewage, agricultural runoff, and the sedimentation that comes from deforestation. The recent decimation of coral reefs and the growing frequency of such events suggest that the world's ecological balance has been profoundly disturbed.

Whether it is Arctic ice, tropical corals, oceanic fisheries, or old-growth forests, the forces driving ecological destruction are varied, complex, and often dangerously synergistic. Population is one factor. The nearly fourfold expansion in human numbers over the past century has drastically increased demands on natural resources. The combination of population growth and deforestation, for example, has cut the number of hectares of forest per person in half since 1960—increasing pressures on remaining forests and encouraging a rapid expansion in plantation forestry. Demand for water, energy, food, and materials have all been driven up by the unprecedented expansion in human numbers. And increasingly, it is in the world's developing countries that natural systems are declining the fastest and people face the most serious environmentally related stresses (see Table 5).[23]

Population growth alone could not have tested environmental limits this severely, however. The pressures it imposes have been magnified by rising consumption levels as each individual demands more from nature. Meat-based diets and automobile-centered transportation systems are among the highly consumptive practices first adopted by the billion or so people living in rich countries, and now proliferating quickly in many parts of the developing world. Meanwhile, government regulations and emission control technology have lagged well behind the pace of adoption in richer countries. As a consequence, the most serious air pollution is now found in cities such as Jakarta and São Paulo (see Table 6).

The combination of population growth and increased consumption is projected to cause the number of people living in water-deficit countries to jump from 505 million to over 2.4 billion in the next twenty-five years. In countries that already face severe water shortages, such as Egypt, India, and Iran, water scarcity is likely to require large-scale food imports. In northern China, the water table under Beijing fell 2.5 meters in 1999, bringing the total decline since 1965 to 59 meters. Similarly, surging demand for oil—particularly in North

TABLE 5   Ecological Health of E–9 Nations

Country	Share of Land Area That is Forested, 1995[1]	Change of Average Annual Deforestation, 1990–95	Share of Mammals Threatened, 1996	Share of Flowering Plants Threatened, 1997	Share of Land Area Nationally Protected, 1996
		(percent)			
Russia	22	0	11.5	—	3.1
Brazil	16	0.5	18.0	2.4	4.2
United States	6	−0.3	8.2	4.0	13.4
China	4	0.1	19.0	1.0	6.4
Germany[2]	3	0	10.5	0.5	27.0
Indonesia	3	1	29.4	0.9	10.6
India	2	0	23.7	7.7	4.8
Japan	0.7	0.1	22.0	12.7	6.8
South Africa	0.2	0.2	13.4	9.5	5.4

[1]Data may refer to earlier years.

[2]Comparable data for European Union not available; Germany is most populous EU member.

Source: World Bank, *World Development Indicators 2000* (Washington, D.C.: 2000), 126–28.

TABLE 6   Air Pollution in E–9 Nations

Country	Sulfur Dioxide, 1995	Suspended Particulates, 1995	Nitrogen Dioxide, 1995
		(micrograms per cubic meter)	
Germany (Frankfurt)[1]	11	36	45
Japan (Tokyo)	18	49	68
South Africa (Cape Town)	21	—	72
United States (New York)	26	—	79
India (Mumbai)	33	240	39
Brazil (São Paulo)	43	86	83
China (Shanghai)	53	246	73
Russia (Moscow)	109	100	—
Indonesia (Jakarta)	—	271	—

[1]Comparable data for European Union not available; Germany is most populous EU member.
Source: World Bank, *World Development Indicators 2000* (Washington, D.C.: 2000), 162–64.

America and East Asia—contributed in the year 2000 to the highest sustained oil prices the world has seen since the early 1980s. Beyond the proximate political reasons for higher oil prices, the underlying cause is clear: world oil production is nearing its eventual all-time peak, and producers are struggling to meet the combined demands of first-time car owners in China and those who are buying the large SUVs now found in nearly half of U.S. garages.[24]

While the last decade's growth in affluence contributed to many environmental problems, keeping people poor is not the answer—either morally or practically. In impoverished areas around the world, the rural poor are pushed onto marginal, often hilly lands, from which they must hunt bushmeat, harvest trees, or clear land for pasture or crops in order to survive. A 2000 study on the root causes of biodiversity loss, sponsored by the World Wide Fund for Nature (WWF), concluded that together with other forces, poverty often plays a major role.[25]

In the Philippines, for example, the country's rich array of coral reefs, forests, and mangroves—home to an estimated 40,000 species—are shrinking rapidly in area, while the remaining pockets lose much of their original diversity. According to the WWF study, rural poverty and the unequal distribution of land in the Philippines are among the major causes of biodiversity loss that must be remedied if the country's natural wealth is to be preserved for future generations. Similarly, a study in the southern Mexican state of Campeche found that much of the pressure on the Calakmul Biosphere Reserve is coming from the efforts of local indigenous people to meet their material needs. Meeting those needs sustainably is a key component of any effective program to reverse environmental decline.[26] . . .

NORTH MEETS SOUTH

. . . Bridging these gaps between North and South will require a combination of innovative market reforms and a common commitment by governments to fill the gaps left by the private sector. Most of the recent emphasis has been on the market, pointing to developments such as the certified forest products market and booming consumer interest in ecotourism. And even government-negotiated treaties such as the Kyoto Protocol on climate change now rely on market mechanisms as primary tools for achieving their goals. Greenhouse gas trading schemes are being viewed as a way of not only trimming emissions as efficiently as possible, but also distributing the burden of addressing the problem among various countries.

Market mechanisms are often effective, and private innovation is key to solving many problems, but North–South cooperation will have to be based on something more than commercial relationships if the world's current problems are to be surmounted. Cooperation among NGOs, for example, allows innovative social programs and political techniques to be transferred rapidly from one country to another, dramatically speeding the rate of progress. The recent surge in the number of these groups in the developing world is being spurred by the support of foundations in industrial countries, as well as by the spread of democracy in many poor nations. And the Internet is proving a boon to the spread of civil society in countries where it has been weak in the past. The ability of citizens to communicate easily among themselves—and with people in distant lands with similar concerns—is rapidly transforming the political equation in many countries, and is creating more favorable conditions for addressing social and ecological problems.

Government leadership is also key: Governments need to forge strong partnerships and provide sufficient funding to invest in the public infrastructure needed to support a sustainable economy. The failure of many industrial countries to meet the financial commitments they have agreed to under various international agreements and the failure of some developing countries to carry through on political and economic reforms have left a residue of distrust that must be overcome. Although it is unlikely that foreign aid levels will ever return to the figures that were typical in the 1960s and 1970s, a steady flow of well-targeted grants is essential to sustain progress. And with private capital taking up much of the burden of industrial growth and large-scale infrastructure, government aid can be targeted at pressing needs, with multiplier effects on human progress and environmental protection: areas such as education, health care, the status of women, micro-credit, and broad Internet access. One essential step is reducing the developing-country debt burden, which has reached onerous levels in recent years.

The economic and political weakness of many developing countries has prevented them from taking the more central position on the world stage that is now logically theirs. With 80 percent of the world's population, the bulk of its natural resources, and an opportunity to learn from the historical mistakes of today's industrial countries, it seems clear that the South will increasingly dominate the twenty-first century. Today's industrial powers will likely resist this shift, but they will soon find that they cannot achieve their own goals without the cooperation of the South. The summer of 2000 saw an intriguing sign of the changing balance of power when Mexico elected its first president from outside the traditional ruling party. Vicente Fox, a charismatic modern leader, traveled to Washington and called for allowing workers to travel as freely across the Mexico-U.S. border as capital now does.[27]

The existing structure of international institutions such as the World Bank and the World Trade Organization will have to be reformed to allow developing countries to take the more central role that is now essential to solving the world's most difficult problems. With shared power will come shared responsibility—a role that seems far more achievable today than it did two decades ago, when participatory political systems were still rare in the developing world.

One new organizing principle for countries that is particularly appropriate is the E–9 group described earlier—a coalition of northern and southern countries that between them have far greater impact on global social and ecological trends than do the Group of Eight (G–8) industrial countries. Between them, the E–9 have 60 percent of the world's population, 73 percent of the carbon emissions, and 66 percent of higher plant species. (See Table 7.) They have both the ability and the responsibility to lead the world in addressing the main challenges of the twenty-first century.

TABLE 7   The E–9: Leaders for the Twenty-first Century

Country	World Population, 1999	PPP Gross Domestic Product, 1998	Share of World Carbon Emissions, 1999	World Forest Area, 1995	World Vascular Plant Species, 1997
			(percent)		
China	21.0	10.2	13.5	4	11.9
India	16.5	5.4	4.5	2	5.9
European Union	6.3	20.5	14.5	3	—
United States	4.6	21.3	25.5	6	6
Indonesia	3.5	1.3	0.9	3	10.9
Brazil	2.8	2.9	1.5	16	20.8
Russia	2.4	2.4	4.6	22	—
Japan	2.1	8.0	6.0	0.7	2.1
South Africa	0.7	0.9	2.0	0.2	8.7
E–9 Total	**59.9**	**72.9**	**73**	**56.9**	**66.3**

Source: Worldwatch calculations based on Population Reference Bureau, "1999 World Population Data Sheet," wall chart (Washington, D.C.: June 1999); World Bank, *World Development Indicators 2000* (Washington, D.C.: 2000), 10–12; BP Amoco, *BP Amoco: Statistical Review of World Energy* (London: June 2000), 38; U.N. Food and Agriculture Organization, *State of the World's Forests 1999* (New York: 1999), 125–30; World Conservation Union–IUCN, *1997 IUCN Red List of Threatened Plants* (Cambridge, U.K.: 1998), xvii, xxvii–xxxiii.

CRITICAL-THINKING QUESTIONS

1. The article links the problems of environmental decline and poverty. Can you explain how they are connected?

2. What are some of the strategies suggested by the author to protect the planet's natural environment? Which strategies do you find most important? Why?

3. Overall, what do you see as the prospects for halting the decline of the planet's natural environment? Provide reasons for your position.

NOTES

1. Based on author's visit to Bahia, August 2000.

2. James Brooke, "Brazilian Rain Forest Yields Most Diversity for Species of Trees," *New York Times,* 30 March 1993.

3. "Latin America and the Caribbean: Brazil," The Nature Conservancy, <www.tnc.org/brazil/forest.htm>, viewed 12 October 2000.

4. World Bank, *World Development Report 2000/2001* (New York: Oxford University Press, 2000), 21–23.

5. Christopher Flavin, "Wind Power Booms," and idem, "Solar Power Market Jumps," both in Lester R. Brown, Michael Renner, and Brian Halweil, *Vital Signs 2000* (New York: W.W.

Norton & Company, 2000), 56–59; Seth Dunn, "Carbon Emissions Fall Again," in ibid., 66–67; Clive Wilkinson, *Status of Coral Reefs of the World, 2000: Executive Summary,* 9th International Coral Reef Symposium, 23–24 October 2000, Bali, Indonesia; National Snow and Ice Data Center, "Mountain Glacier Fluctuations: Changes in Terminus Location and Mass Balance," <www.nsidc.colorado.edu/NASA/SOTC/glacier_balance.html>, viewed 2 February 2000; Alexander Wood, "An Emerging Consensus on Biodiversity Loss," in Alex Wood, Pamela Stedman-Edwards, and Johanna Meng, eds., *The Root Causes of Biodiversity Loss* (London: Earthscan, 2000), 2.

6. Eduardo Athayde, Atlantic Forest Open University, Salvador, Bahia, Brazil, discussion with author, 10 August 2000.

7. The E–9 concept was first introduced as the E–8 in *State of the World 1997.* This chapter adds South Africa to the group and substitutes the European Union (EU) for Germany, which substantially extends its breadth of economic and ecological coverage. The sector-specific tables that follow, however, use statistics for Germany (the EU's most populous member), due to the lack of comparable data for the EU as a whole.

8. " 'Love Bug' Suspect Charged," *Associated Press,* 29 June 2000; Mark Landler, "A Filipino Linked to 'Love Bug' Talks About His License to Hack," *New York Times,* 21 October 2000.

9. Casualties from "Payatas Relocation Coordination Ordered," Manila Bulletin, <www.mb.com.ph/umain/2000%2D07/mn071805.asp>, viewed 10 September 2000; Typhoon Kai Tak from Roli Ng, "Garbage Slide Kills 46 in Manila's Promised Land," Planet Ark, <www.planetark.com/dailynewsstory.cfm?newsid=7412&newsdate=11-Jul-2000>, viewed 10 September

2000; number of residents from "Manila Urges Payatas Residents to Get Out of Dumpsite," *China Daily Information,* <www.chinadaily.net/cover/storydb/2000/07/15/wnmanila.715.html>, viewed 10 September 2000.

10. Growth of world economy from Angus Maddison, *Monitoring the World Economy 1820–1992* (Paris: Organisation for Economic Co-operation and Development (OECD), 1995), 227, and from Angus Maddison, *Chinese Economic Performance in the Long Run* (Paris: OECD, 1998), 159, using deflators and recent growth rates from International Monetary Fund (IMF), *World Economic Outlook* (Washington, D.C.: October 1999); growth estimate for 2000 from IMF, *World Economic Outlook* (advance copy) (Washington, D.C.: September 2000); International Telecommunications Union (ITU), *World Telecommunication Indicators '98,* Socioeconomic Time-series Access and Retrieval System database, downloaded 24 August 1999, and ITU, *World Telecommunication Development Report 1999* (Geneva: 1999); number of host computers from Internet Software Consortium and Network Wizards, "Internet Domain Surveys," <www.isc.org/ds/>, viewed 20 February 2000.

11. Growth of various economies from World Bank, *World Development Indicators 2000* (Washington, D.C.: 2000), 182–83; China's economy from ibid., 10–12; consumer products in China from ibid., 300, and from Population Reference Bureau, "2000 World Population Data Sheet," wall chart (Washington, D.C.: June 2000), with computers from Ye Di Sheng, "The Development and Market of China's Information Industry and its Investment Opportunity," <www.caspa.com/event/augdin2.htm>, viewed 10 November 2000.

12. Wealth disparities from World Bank, op. cit. note 4, 282–83; trends in per capita income from U.N. Development Programme (UNDP), *Human Development Report 1999* (New York: Oxford University Press, 1999), 2–3; income disparities from World Bank, op. cit. note 11, 66, 68; 10 percent based on UNDP, op. cit. this note, 149, 197; inequality growth from ibid., 3.

13. UNDP, op. cit. note 12, 25; number of people living on less than $1 per day from World Bank, op. cit. note 4, 3, 23.

14. Number of people malnourished is a Worldwatch estimate based on U.N. Administrative Committee on Coordination, Sub-Committee on Nutrition in collaboration with International Food Policy Research Institute (IFPRI), *Fourth Report on the World Nutrition Situation* (Geneva: 1999), and on Rafael Flores, research fellow, IFPRI, Washington, D.C., e-mail to Brian Halweil, Worldwatch Institute, 5 November 1999, and discussion with Gary Gardner, Worldwatch Institute, 3 February 2000; selected countries with chronic hunger from Gary Gardner and Brian Halweil, *Underfed and Overfed: The Global Epidemic of Malnutrition,* Worldwatch Paper 150 (Washington, D.C.: Worldwatch Institute, March 2000), 17.

15. Number without access to clean water from Peter H. Gleick, *The World's Water 1998–1999* (Washington, D.C.: Island Press, 1998), 40; percentages by country from World Bank, op. cit. note 11, 14–16; toilets from World Bank op. cit. note 11, 94–96.

16. Joint United Nations Program on HIV/AIDS, *Report on the Global HIV/AIDS Epidemic—June 2000* (Geneva: June 2000), 124; Elizabeth Rosenthal, "In Rural China, a Steep Price of Poverty: Dying of AIDS," *New York Times,* 28 October 2000.

17. John Noble Wilford, "Ages-Old Polar Ice Cap Is Melting, Scientists Find," *New York Times,* 19 August 2000.

18. D.A. Rothrock, Y. Yu, and G.A. Maykut, "Thinning of the Arctic Sea-Ice Cover," *Geophysical Research Letters,* 1 December 1999, 3469; Ola M. Johannessen, Elena V. Ahalina, and Martin W. Miles, "Satellite Evidence for an Arctic Sea Ice Cover in Transformation," *Science,* 3 December 1999, 1937; Lars H. Smedsrud and Tore Furevik, "Toward an Ice-Free Arctic?" *Cicerone,* February 2000.

19. Paul N. Pearson and Martin R. Palmer, "Atmospheric Carbon Dioxide Concentrations Over the Past 60 Million Years," *Nature,* 17 August 2000, 695; Andrew C. Revkin, "A Shift in Stance on Global Warming Theory," *New York Times,* 26 October 2000.

20. Carsten Rühlemann et al., "Warming of the Tropical Atlantic Ocean and Slowdown of Thermohaline Circulation During the Last Glaciation," *Nature,* 2 December 1999, 511.

21. Percentage of fish species as reef dwellers from Norman Myers, "Synergisms: Joint Effects of Climate Change and Other Forms of Habitat Destruction," in Robert L. Peters and Thomas E. Lovejoy, eds., *Global Warming and Biological Diversity* (New Haven, Conn.: Yale University Press, 1992), 347; Colin Woodard, "Fall of the Magic Kingdom: A Reporter Goes Underwater in the Belize Barrier Reef," *Tuftonia,* summer 2000, 20.

22. Daniel Cooney, "Coral Reefs Disappearing," *Associated Press,* 23 October 2000; Wilkinson, op. cit. note 5; Ove Hoegh-Guldberg et al., *Pacific in Peril,* available at <www.greenpeace.org>.

23. Hectares of forest per person from Robert Engleman et al., *People in the Balance: Population and Natural Resources at the Turn of the Millennium* (Washington, D.C.: Population Action International, 2000), 12.

24. Number of people living in water-deficit countries from ibid., 9; Beijing water table from James Kynge, "China Approves Controversial Plan to Shift Water to Drought-Hit Beijing," *Financial Times,* 7 January 2000; oil prices from U.S. Department of Energy, *Monthly Energy Review,* September 2000; near peak production of oil from Colin J. Campbell and Jean H. Laherrere, "The End of Cheap Oil," *Scientific American,* March 1998, 78–83.

25. Pamela Stedman-Edwards, "A Framework for Analysing Biodiversity Loss," in Wood, Stedman-Edwards, and Meng, op. cit. note 5, 15–16.

26. Wood, Stedman-Edwards, and Meng, op. cit. note 5, 283, 231–54.

27. Developing-country share of population from United Nations, *World Population Prospects: The 1998 Revision* (New York: December 1998); Fox proposal from Mary Jordan, "Mexican Touts Open Borders: Visiting President-Elect Pushes N. American Convergence," *Washington Post,* 25 August 2000.

CLASSIC

CONTEMPORARY

CROSS-CULTURAL

75 Supporting Indigenous Peoples

ALAN THEIN DURNING

A particular concern of many environmentalists (and social scientists) is the steady loss of this planet's cultural diversity as thousands of small societies are pushed aside by the relentless march of economic development. This selection describes the problem and points out that protecting indigenous peoples is not just a matter of justice—the well-being of everyone in the world depends on it.

In July 1992, an aged chief of the Lumad people in the Philippines—a man with a price on his head for his opposition to local energy development—sat at the base of the cloud-covered volcano Mount Apo and made a simple plea.

"Our Christian brothers are enjoying their life here in the plains," said eighty-six-year-old Chief Tulalang Maway, sweeping his arm toward the provincial town of Kidapawan and the agricultural lands beyond, lands his tribe long ago ceded to immigrants from afar. Turning toward the mountain—a Lumad sacred site that he has vowed to defend "to the last drop of blood"—Maway slowly finished his thought, "We only ask them to leave us our last sanctuary."

Chief Maway's words could have been spoken by almost any tribal Filipino, or, for that matter, any Native American, Australian aborigine, African

pygmy, or member of one of the world's thousands of other distinct indigenous cultures. All have ancient ties to the land, water, and wildlife of their ancestral domains, and all are endangered by onrushing forces of the outside world. They have been decimated by violence and plagues. Their cultures have been eroded by missionaries and exploited by wily entrepreneurs. Their subsistence economies have been dismantled in the pursuit of national development. And their homelands have been invaded by commercial resource extractors and overrun by landless peasants.

Chief Maway's entreaty, in its essence, is the call of indigenous peoples everywhere: the plea that their lands be spared further abuse, that their birthright be returned to them. It is a petition that the world's dominant cultures have long ignored, believing the passing of native peoples and their antiquated ways was an inevitable, if lamentable, cost of progress. That view, never morally defensible, is now demonstrably untenable.

Indigenous peoples are the sole guardians of vast, little-disturbed habitats in remote parts of every continent. These territories, which together

Source: "Supporting Indigenous Peoples," by Alan Thein Durning, in *State of the World 1993: A Worldwatch Institute Report on Progress Toward a Sustainable Society,* edited by Lester R. Brown et al. Copyright © 1993 by Worldwatch Institute. Reprinted by permission of W. W. Norton & Company, Inc.

encompass an area larger than Australia, provide important ecological services: They regulate hydrological cycles, maintain local and global climatic stability, and harbor a wealth of biological and genetic diversity. Indeed, indigenous homelands may provide safe haven for more endangered plant and animal species than all the world's nature reserves. Native peoples, moreover, often hold the key to these vaults of biological diversity. They possess a body of ecological knowledge—encoded in their languages, customs, and subsistence practices—that rivals the libraries of modern science.

The human rights enshrined in international law have long demanded that states shield indigenous cultures, but instead these cultures have been dismembered. A more self-interested appeal appears to be in order: Supporting indigenous survival is an objective necessity, even for those callous to the justice of the cause. As a practical matter, the world's dominant cultures cannot sustain the earth's ecological health—a requisite of human advancement—without the aid of the world's endangered cultures. Biological diversity is inextricably linked to cultural diversity.

Around the globe, indigenous peoples are fighting for their ancestral territories. They are struggling in courts and national parliaments, gaining power through new mass movements and international campaigns, and—as on the slopes of Mount Apo—defending their inheritance with their lives. The question is, Who will stand with them?

STATE OF THE NATIONS

Indigenous peoples (or "native" or "tribal" peoples) are found on every continent and in most countries [see Table 1]. The extreme variations in their ways of life and current circumstances defy ready definition. Indeed, many anthropologists insist that indigenous peoples are defined only by the way they define themselves: They think of themselves as members of a distinct people. Still, many indigenous cultures share a number of characteristics that help describe, if not define, them.

They are typically descendants of the original inhabitants of an area taken over by more powerful outsiders. They are distinct from their country's dominant group in language, culture, or religion. Most have a custodial concept of land and other resources, in part defining themselves in relation to the habitat from which they draw their livelihood. They commonly live in or maintain strong ties to a subsistence economy; many are, or are descendants of, hunter-gatherers, fishers, nomadic or seasonal herders, shifting forest farmers, or subsistence peasant cultivators. And their social relations are often tribal, involving collective management of natural resources, thick networks of bonds between individuals, and group decision making, often by consensus among elders.

Measured by spoken languages, the single best indicator of a distinct culture, all the world's people belong to 6,000 cultures; 4,000–5,000 of these are indigenous ones. Of the 5.5 billion humans on the planet, some 190 million to 625 million are indigenous people. (These ranges are wide because of varying definitions of "indigenous." The higher figures include ethnic nations that lack political autonomy, such as Tibetans, Kurds, and Zulus, while the lower figures count only smaller, subnational societies.) In some countries, especially those settled by Europeans in the past five centuries, indigenous populations are fairly easy to count [see Table 2]. By contrast, lines between indigenous peoples and ethnic minorities are difficult to draw in Asia and Africa, where cultural diversity remains greatest.

Regardless of where lines are drawn, however, human cultures are disappearing at unprecedented rates. Worldwide, the loss of cultural diversity is keeping pace with the global loss of biological diversity. Anthropologist Jason Clay of Cultural Survival in Cambridge, Massachusetts, writes, "there have been more . . . extinctions of tribal peoples in this century than in any other in history." Brazil alone lost eighty-seven tribes in the first half of the century. One-third of North American languages and two-thirds of Australian languages have disappeared since 1800—the overwhelming share of them since 1900.

Cultures are dying out even faster than the peoples who belong to them. University of Alaska

TABLE 1   Indigenous Peoples of the World, 1992

Region	Indigenous Peoples
Africa and Middle East	Great cultural diversity throughout continent; "indigenous" share hotly contested lands. Some 25–30 million nomadic herders or pastoralists in East Africa, Sahel, and Arabian peninsula include Bedouin, Dinka, Masai, Turkana. San (Bushmen) of Namibia and Botswana and pygmies of central African rain forest, both traditionally hunter-gatherers, have occupied present homelands for at least 20,000 years (25–350 million indigenous people overall, depending on definitions; 2,000 languages)
Americas	Native Americans concentrated near centers of ancient civilizations: Aztec in Mexico, Mayan in Central America, and Incan in Andes of Bolivia, Ecuador, and Peru. In Latin America, most Indians farm small plots; in North America, 2 million Indians live in cities and on reservations (42 million; 900 languages)
Arctic	Inuit (Eskimo) and other Arctic peoples of North America, Greenland, and Siberia traditionally fishers, whalers, and hunters. Sami (Lapp) of northern Scandinavia are traditionally reindeer herders (2 million; 50 languages)
East Asia	Chinese indigenous peoples, numbering up to 82 million, mostly subsistence farmers such as Bulang of south China or former pastoralists such as ethnic Mongolians of north and west China. Ainu of Japan and aboriginal Taiwanese now largely industrial laborers (12–84 million; 150 languages)
Oceania	Aborigines of Australia and Maoris of New Zealand, traditionally farmers, fishers, hunters, and gatherers. Many now raise livestock. Islanders of South Pacific continue to fish and harvest marine resources (3 million; 500 languages)
South Asia	Gond, Bhil, and other adivasis, or tribal peoples, inhabit forest belt of central India. In Bangladesh, adivasis concentrated in Chittagong hills on Burmese border, several million tribal farmers and pastoralists in Afghanistan, Pakistan, Nepal, Iran, and central Asian republics of former Soviet Union (74–91 million; 700 languages)
Southeast Asia	Tribal Hmong, Karen, and other forest-farming peoples form Asia ethnic mosaic covering up lands. Indigenous population follows distribution of forest: Laos has more forest and tribal peoples, Myanmar and Vietnam have less forest and fewer people, and Thailand and mainland Malaysia have the least. Tribal peoples are concentrated at the extreme ends of the Philippine and Indonesian archipelagos. Island of New Guinea—split politically between Indonesia and Papua New Guinea—populated by indigenous tribes (32–55 million; 1,950 languages)

Source: Worldwatch Institute.

linguist Michael Krauss projects that half the world's languages—the storehouses of peoples' intellectual heritages—will disappear within a century. These languages, and arguably the cultures they embody, are no longer passed on to sufficient numbers of children to ensure their survival. Krauss likens such cultures to animal species doomed to extinction because their populations are below the threshold needed for adequate reproduction. Only 5 percent of all languages, moreover, enjoy the relative safety of having at least a half-million speakers.

To trace the history of indigenous peoples' subjugation is simply to recast the story of the rise of the world's dominant cultures: the spread of Han Chinese into Central and Southeast Asia, the ascent of Aryan empires on the Indian subcontinent,

the southward advance of Bantu cultures across Africa, and the creation of a world economy first through European colonialism and then through industrial development. Surviving indigenous cultures are often but tattered remnants of their predecessors' societies.

When Christopher Columbus reached the New World in 1492, there were perhaps 54 million people in the Americas, almost as many as in Europe at the time; their numbers plummeted, however, as plagues radiated from the landfalls of the conquistadors. Five centuries later, the indigenous peoples of the Americas, numbering some 42 million, have yet to match their earlier population. Similar contractions followed the arrival of Europeans in Australia, New Zealand, and Siberia.

TABLE 2   Estimated Populations of Indigenous
Peoples, Selected Countries, 1992

Country	Population[a]	Share of National Population
	(millions)	(percent)
Papua New Guinea	3.0	77
Bolivia	5.6	70
Guatemala	4.6	47
Peru	9.0	40
Ecuador	3.8	38
Myanmar	14.0	33
Laos	1.3	30
Mexico	10.9	12
New Zealand	0.4	12
Chile	1.2	9
Philippines	6.0	9
India	63.0	7
Malaysia	0.8	4
Canada	0.9	4
Australia	0.4	2
Brazil	1.5	1
Bangladesh	1.2	1
Thailand	0.5	1
United States	2.0	1
Former Soviet Union	1.4	>1

[a]Generally excludes those of mixed ancestry.

Source: Worldwatch Institute.

Worldwide, virtually no indigenous peoples remain entirely isolated from national societies. By indoctrination or brute force, nations have assimilated native groups into the cultural mainstream. As a consequence, few follow the ways of their ancestors unchanged. Just one tenth of the Penan hunter-gatherers continue to hunt in the rain forests of Malaysian Borneo. A similar share of the Sami (Lapp) reindeer-herders of northern Scandinavia accompany their herds on the Arctic ranges. Half of North American Indians and many New Zealand Maori dwell in cities.

Tragically, indigenous peoples whose cultures are besieged frequently end up on the bottom of the national economy. They are often the first sent to war for the state, as in Namibia and the Philippines, and the last to go to work: Unemployment in Canadian Indian communities averages 50 percent. They are overrepresented among migrant laborers in India, beggars in Mexico, and uranium miners in the United States. They are often drawn into the shadow economy: They grow drug crops in northern Thailand, run gambling casinos in the United States, and sell their daughters into prostitution in Taiwan. Everywhere, racism against them is rampant. India's adivasis, or tribal people, endure hardships comparable to the "untouchables," the most downtrodden caste.

Native peoples' inferior social status is sometimes codified in national law and perpetuated by institutionalized abuse. Many members of the hill tribes in Thailand are denied citizenship, and until 1988 the Brazilian constitution legally classified Indians as minors and wards of the state. In the extreme, nation-states are simply genocidal: Burmese soldiers systemically raped, murdered, and enslaved thousands of Arakanese villagers in early 1992. Guatemala has exterminated perhaps 100,000 Mayans in its three-decade counterinsurgency. Similar numbers of indigenous people have died in East Timor and Irian Jaya since 1970 at the hands of Indonesian forces intent on solidifying their power.

In much of the world, the oppression that indigenous peoples suffer has indelibly marked their own psyches, manifesting itself in depression and social disintegration. Says Tamara Gliminova of the Khant people of Siberia, "When they spit into your soul for this long, there is little left."

HOMELANDS

Indigenous peoples not yet engulfed in modern societies live mostly in what Mexican anthropologist Gonzalo Aguirre Beltran called "regions of refuge," places so rugged, desolate, or remote that they have been little disturbed by the industrial economy. They remain in these areas for tragic reasons. Peoples in more fertile lands were eradicated outright to make way for settlers and plantations, or they retreated—sometimes at gun point—into these natural havens. Whereas indigenous peoples exercised de facto control over most of the earth's ecosystems as recently as two centuries ago, the territory they now occupy is reduced to an estimated 12 to 19 percent of the earth's land area—depending, again, on where the line between indigenous peoples and ethnic nations is drawn. And governments recognize their ownership of but a fraction of that area.

Gaining legal protection for the remainder of their subsistence base is most indigenous peoples' highest political priority. If they lose this struggle, their cultures stand little chance of surviving. As the World Council of Indigenous Peoples, a global federation based in Canada, wrote in 1985, "Next to shooting Indigenous Peoples, the surest way to kill us is to separate us from our part of the Earth." Most native peoples are bound to their land through relationships both practical and spiritual, routine and historical. Tribal Filipino Edtami Mansayagan, attempting to communicate the pain he feels at the destruction of the rivers, valleys, meadows, and hillsides of his people's mountain domain, exclaims, "these are the living pages of our un-written history." The question of who shall con-trol resources in the regions of refuge is the crux of indigenous survival.

Indigenous homelands are important not only to endangered cultures; they are also of excep-tional ecological value. Intact indigenous com-munities and little-disturbed ecosystems overlap with singular regularity, from the coastal swamps of South America to the shifting sands of the Sa-hara, from the ice floes of the circumpolar north to the coral reefs of the South Pacific. When, for example, a National Geographic Society team in Washington, D.C., compiled a map of Indian lands and remaining forest cover in Central America in 1992, they confirmed the personal observation of Geodisio Castillo, a Kuna Indian from Panama: "Where there are forests there are indigenous people, and where there are indigenous people there are forests."

Because populations of both indigenous peo-ples and unique plant and animal species are nu-merically concentrated in remnant habitats in the tropics—precisely the regions of refuge that Beltran was referring to—the biosphere's most diverse habitats are usually homes to endangered cultures.

The persistence of biological diversity in these regions is no accident. In the Philippines and Thailand, both representative cases, little more than a third of the land officially zoned as forest remains forest-covered; the tracts that do still stand are largely those protected by tribal people.

The relationship between cultural diversity and biological diversity stands out even in global statistics. Just nine countries together account for 60 percent of human languages. Of these nine cen-ters of cultural diversity, six are also on the roster of biological "megadiversity" countries—nations with exceptional numbers of unique plant and an-imal species. . . . By the same token, two-thirds of all megadiversity countries also rank at the top of the cultural diversity league, with more than 100 languages spoken in each.

Everywhere, the world economy now intrudes on what is left of native lands, as it has for cen-turies. Writes World Bank anthropologist Shelton Davis: "The creation of a . . . global economy . . . has meant the pillage of native peoples' lands, labor and resources and their enforced accultura-tion and spiritual conquest. Each cycle of global economic expansion—the search for gold and spices in the sixteenth century, the fur trade and sugar estate economics of the seventeenth and eigh-teenth centuries, the rise of the great coffee, copra and . . . tropical fruit plantations in the late nine-teenth and early twentieth centuries, the modern search for petroleum, strategic minerals, and trop-ical hardwoods—was based upon the exploitation of natural resources or primary commodities and led to the displacement of indigenous peoples and the undermining of traditional cultures."

The juggernaut of the money economy has not slowed in the late twentieth century; if anything, it has accelerated. Soaring consumer demand among the world's fortunate and burgeoning pop-ulations among the unfortunate fuel the economy's drive into native peoples' territories. Loggers, miners, commercial fishers, small farmers, plan-tation growers, dam builders, oil drillers—all come to seek their fortunes. Governments that equate progress with export earnings aid them, and military establishments bent on controlling far-flung territories back them.

Logging, in particular, is a menace because so many indigenous peoples dwell in woodlands. Japanese builders, for example, are devouring the ancient hardwood forests of tropical Borneo, home of the Penan and other Dayak peoples for disposable concrete molds. Most mahogany exported from Latin America is now logged illegally on Indian reserves and most nonplantation teak cut in Asia currently comes from tribal lands in the war-torn hills of Myanmar.

The consequences of mining on native lands are also ruinous. In the late eighties, for instance, tens of thousands of gold prospectors infiltrated the remote northern Brazilian haven of the Yanomami, the last large, isolated group of indigenous peoples in the Americas. The miners turned streams into sewers, contaminated the environment with the 1,000 tons of toxic mercury they used to purify gold, and precipitated an epidemic of malaria that killed more than a thousand children and elders. Just in time, the Brazilian government recognized and began defending the Yanomami homeland in early 1992, a rare and hopeful precedent in the annals of indigenous history. Still, in Brazil overall, mining concessions overlap 34 percent of Indian lands. . . .

Other energy projects, especially large dams, also take their toll on native habitats. In the north of Canada, the provincial electric utility Hydro Quebec completed a massive project called James Bay I in 1985, inundating vast areas of Cree Indian hunting grounds and unexpectedly contaminating fisheries with naturally occurring heavy metals that had previously been locked away in the soil. The Cree and neighboring Inuit tribes have organized against the project's next gigantic phase, James Bay II. The $60-billion project would tame eleven wild rivers, altering a France-sized area to generate 27,000 megawatts of exportable power. As Matthew Coon-Come, Grand Chief of the Cree, says, "The only people who have the right to build dams on our territory are the beavers." . . .

Commercial producers have also taken over indigenous lands for large-scale agriculture. The Barabaig herders of Tanzania have lost more than 400 square kilometers of dry-season range to a mechanized wheat farm. Private ranchers in Botswana have enclosed grazing lands for their own use, and Australian ranchers have usurped aboriginal lands. In peninsular Malaysia, palm and rubber plantations have left the Orang Asli (Original People) with tiny fractions of their ancient tropical forests.

Less dramatic but more pervasive is the ubiquitous invasion of small farmers onto indigenous lands. Sometimes sponsored by the state but ultimately driven by population growth and maldistribution of farmland, poor settlers encroach on native lands everywhere. In Indonesia during the eighties, for example, the government shifted 2 million people from densely populated islands such as Java to 800,000 hectares of newly cleared plots in sparsely populated indigenous provinces such as Irian Jaya, Kalimantan, and Sumatra. Half the area settled was virgin forest—much of it indigenous territory. . . .

Few states recognize indigenous peoples' rights over homelands, and where they do, those rights are often partial, qualified, or of ambiguous legal force. Countries may recognize customary rights in theory, but enforce common or statutory law against those rights whenever there is a conflict; or they may sanction indigenous rights but refuse to enforce them. Through this cloud of legal contradictions a few countries stand out as exceptional. Papua New Guinea and Ecuador acknowledge indigenous title to large shares of national territory, and Canada and Australia recognize rights over extensive areas. . . . Still, across all the earth's climatic and ecological zones—from the Arctic tundra to the temperate and nontropical forests to the savannahs and deserts—native peoples control slim shares of their ancestral domains. . . .

STEWARDS

Sustainable use of local resources is simple self-preservation for people whose way of life is tied to the fertility and natural abundance of the land. Any community that knows its children and grandchildren will live exactly where it does is more apt to take a longer view than a community without attachments to local places.

Moreover, native peoples frequently aim to preserve not just a standard of living but a way of life rooted in the uniqueness of a local place. Colombian anthropologist Martin von Hildebrand notes, "The Indians often tell me that the difference between a colonist [a non-Indian settler] and an Indian is that the colonist wants to leave money for his children and that the Indians want to leave forests for their children."

Indigenous peoples' unmediated dependence on natural abundance has its parallel in their peerless ecological knowledge. Most forest-dwelling tribes display an utter mastery of botany. One typical group, the Shuar people of Ecuador's Amazonian lowlands, uses 800 species of plants for medicine, food, animal fodder, fuel, construction, fishing, and hunting supplies.

Native peoples commonly know as much about ecological processes that affect the availability of natural resources as they do about those resources' diverse uses. South Pacific islanders can predict to the day and hour the beginning of the annual spawning runs of many fish. Whaling peoples of northern Canada have proved to skeptical western marine biologists that bowhead whales migrate under pack ice. Coastal aborigines in Australia distinguish between eighty different tidal conditions.

Specialists trained in western science often fail to recognize indigenous ecological knowledge because of the cultural and religious ways in which indigenous peoples record and transmit that learning. Ways of life that developed over scores of generations could only thrive by encoding ecological sustainability into the body of practice, myth, and taboo that passes from parent to child. . . .

What are the conditions in which traditional systems of ecological management can persist in the modern world? First, indigenous peoples must have secure rights to their subsistence base—rights that are not only recognized but enforced by the state and, ideally, backed by international law. Latin American tribes such as the Shuar of Ecuador, when threatened with losing their land, have cleared their own forests and taken up cattle ranching, because these actions prove ownership in Latin America. Had Ecuador backed up the Shuar's land rights, the ranching would have been unnecessary.

Second, for indigenous ecological stewardship to survive the onslaught of the outside world, indigenous peoples must be organized politically and the state in which they reside must allow democratic initiatives. The Khant and Mansi peoples of Siberia, just as most indigenous people in the former Soviet Union, were nominally autonomous in their customary territories under Soviet law, but political repression precluded the organized defense of that terrain until the end of the eighties. Since then, the peoples of Siberia have begun organizing themselves to turn paper rights into real local control. In neighboring China, in contrast, indigenous homelands remain pure legal fictions because the state crushes all representative organizations.

Third, indigenous communities must have access to information, support, and advice from friendly sources if they are to surmount the obstacles of the outside world. The tribal people of Papua New Guinea know much about their local environments, for example, but they know little about the impacts of large-scale logging and mining. Foreign and domestic investors have often played on this ignorance, assuring remote groups that no lasting harm would result from leasing parts of their land to resource extractors. If the forest peoples of Papua New Guinea could learn from the experience of indigenous peoples elsewhere—through supportive organizations and indigenous peoples' federations—they might be more careful.

A handful of peoples around the world have succeeded in satisfying all three of these conditions. . . .

RISING FROM THE FRONTIER

From the smallest tribal settlements to the U.N. General Assembly, indigenous peoples' organizations are making themselves felt. Their grassroots movements have spread rapidly since 1970, gaining strength in numbers and through improvement of their political skills. They have pooled their talents in regional, national, and global federations to broaden their influence. This uprising, which like any movement has its share of internal rivalries, may eventually bring fundamental advances in the status of all endangered cultures. . . .

In a world where almost all nations have publicly committed themselves to the goal of sustainable development and most have signed a global treaty for the protection of biological diversity, the questions of cultural survival and indigenous homelands cannot be avoided much longer. As guardians and stewards of remote and fragile ecosystems, indigenous cultures could play a crucial role in safeguarding humanity's planetary home. But they cannot do it alone. They need the support of international law and national policy, and they need the understanding and aid of the world's more numerous peoples.

Giving native peoples power over their own lives raises issues for the world's dominant culture as well—a consumerist and individualist culture born in Europe and bred in the United States. Indeed, indigenous peoples may offer more than a best-bet alternative for preserving the outlying areas where they live. They may offer living examples of cultural patterns that can help revive ancient values within everyone: devotion to future generations, ethical regard for nature, and commitment to community among people. The question may be, then, Are indigenous peoples the past, or are they the future?

CRITICAL-THINKING QUESTIONS

1. How many indigenous cultures are there on this planet? What general traits do they have in common?

2. Why are the world's tribal peoples disappearing?

3. The author asserts that sustaining the world's natural environment depends on assuring the future of indigenous peoples. Why is this so?

CLASSIC

CONTEMPORARY

CROSS-CULTURAL

76 On the Origins of Social Movements

JO FREEMAN

According to Jo Freeman, a "spark of life" sometimes transforms a group of like-minded people into a social movement. In this excerpt from her work, Freeman analyzes this process, illustrating her ideas with an account of the civil rights movement and the women's movement in the United States.

Most movements have inconspicuous beginnings. The significant elements of their origins are usually forgotten or distorted by the time a trained observer seeks to trace them out. Perhaps this is why the theoretical literature on social movements usually concentrates on causes (Gurr, 1970; Davies, 1962; Oberschall, 1973) and motivations (Toch, 1965; Cantril, 1941; Hoffer, 1951; Adorno et al., 1950), while the "spark of life" by which the "mass is to cross the threshold of organizational life" (Lowi, 1971:41) has received scant attention. . . .

From where do the people come who make up the initial, organizing cadre of a movement? How do they come together, and how do they come to share a similar view of the world in circumstances that compel them to

Source: From *Social Movements of the Sixties and Seventies,* ed. Jo Freeman, pp. 8–13, 17–30, copyright © 1983 by Jo Freeman. Reprinted by permission.

political action? In what ways does the nature of the original center affect the future development of the movement?

Before answering these questions, let us first look at data on the origins of [two] social movements prominent in the sixties and seventies: civil rights . . . and women's liberation. These data identify recurrent elements involved in movement formation. The ways in which these elements interact, given a sufficient level of strain, would support the following propositions:

Proposition 1. The need for a *preexisting communications network* or infrastructure within the social base of a movement is a primary prerequisite for "spontaneous" activity. Masses alone do not form movements, however discontented they may be. Groups of previously unorganized individuals may spontaneously form into small local associations—usually along the lines of informal social networks—in response to a specific strain or crisis. If they are not linked in some manner, however, the protest does not become generalized but remains a local irritant or dissolves completely. If a movement is to spread rapidly, the communications network must already exist. If only the rudiments of a network exist, movement formation requires a high input of "organizing" activity.

Proposition 2. Not just any communications network will do. It must be a network that is *cooptable* to the new ideas of the incipient movement. To be cooptable, it must be composed of like-minded people whose backgrounds, experiences, or location in the social structure make them receptive to the ideas of a specific new movement.

Proposition 3. Given the existence of a cooptable communications network, or at least the rudimentary development of a potential one, and a situation of strain, one or more precipitants are required. Here, two distinct patterns emerge that often overlap. In one, a *crisis* galvanizes the network into spontaneous action in a new direction. In the other, one or more persons begin *organizing* a new organization or disseminating a new idea. For spontaneous action to occur, the communications network must be well formed or the initial protest will not survive the incipient stage. If it is not well formed, organizing efforts must occur; that is, one or more persons must specifically attempt to construct a movement. To be successful, organizers must be skilled and must have a fertile field in which to work. If no communications network already exists, there must at least be emerging spontaneous groups that are acutely attuned to the issue, albeit uncoordinated. To sum up, if a cooptable communications network is already established, a crisis is all that is necessary to galvanize it. If it is rudimentary, an organizing cadre of one or more persons is necessary. Such a cadre is superfluous if the former conditions fully exist, but it is essential if they do not.

THE CIVIL RIGHTS MOVEMENT

The civil rights movement has two origins, although one contributed significantly to the other. The first can be dated from December 7, 1955, when the arrest of Rosa Parks for occupying a "white" seat on a bus stimulated both the Montgomery Bus Boycott and the formation of the Montgomery Improvement Association. The second can be dated either from February 1, 1960, when four freshmen at A & T College in Greensboro, North Carolina, sat in at a white lunch counter, or from April 15 to 17, when a conference at Shaw University in Raleigh, North Carolina, resulted in the formation of the Student Non-Violent Coordinating Committee. To understand why there were two origins one has to understand the social structure of the southern black community, as an incipient generation gap alone is inadequate to explain it.

Within this community the two most important institutions, often the only institutions, were the church and the black college. They provided the primary networks through which most southern blacks interacted and communicated with one another on a regular basis. In turn, the colleges and churches were linked in a regional communications network. These institutions were also the source of black leadership, for being a "preacher or a teacher" were the main status positions in black society. Of the two, the church was by far the more important; it touched on more people's lives and was the largest and oldest institution in the black community. Even during slavery there had been an "invisible church." After emancipation, "organized religious life became the chief means by which a structured or organized social life came into existence among the Negro masses" (Frazier, 1963:17). Furthermore, preachers were more economically independent of white society than were teachers.

Neither of these institutions represented all the segments of black society, but the segments they did represent eventually formed the main social base for supplying civil rights activists. The church was composed of a male leadership and a largely middle-aged, lower-class female followership. The black colleges were the homes of black intellectuals and middle-class youth, male and female.

Both origins of the civil rights movement resulted in the formation of new organizations, despite the fact that at least three seemingly potential social movement organizations already existed. The wealthiest of these was the Urban League, founded in 1910. It, however, was not only largely restricted to a small portion of the black and white bourgeoisie but, until 1961, felt itself to be "essentially a social service agency" (Clark, 1966:245).

Founded in 1909, the National Association for the Advancement of Colored People (NAACP) pursued channels of legal change until it finally persuaded the Supreme Court to abolish educational segregation in *Brown* v. *Board of Education*. More than any other single event, this decision created the atmosphere of rising expectations that helped precipitate the movement. The NAACP suffered from its own success, however. Having organized itself primarily to support court cases and utilize other "respectable" means, it "either was not able or did not desire to modify its program in response to new demands. It believed it should continue its important work by using those techniques it had already perfected" (Blumer, 1951:199).

The Congress of Racial Equality, like the other two organizations, was founded in the North. It began "in 1942 as the Chicago Committee of Racial Equality, which was composed primarily of students at the University of Chicago. An offshoot of the pacifist Fellowship of Reconciliation, its leaders were middle-class intellectual reformers, less prominent and more alienated from the mainstream of American society than the founders of the NAACP. They regarded the NAACP's legalism as too gradualist and ineffective, and aimed to apply Gandhian techniques of non-violent direct action to the problem of race relations in the United States. A year later, the Chicago Committee joined with a half dozen other groups that had emerged across the country, mostly

under the encouragement of the F. O. R. to form a federation known as the Congress of Racial Equality" (Rudwick & Meier, 1970:10).

CORE's activities anticipated many of the main forms of protest of the civil rights movement, and its attitudes certainly seemed to fit CORE for the role of a major civil rights organization. But though it became quite influential, at the time the movement actually began, CORE had declined almost to the point of extinction. Its failure reflects the historical reality that organizations are less likely to create social movements than be created by them. More important, CORE was poorly situated to lead a movement of southern blacks. Northern-based and composed primarily of pacifist intellectuals, it had no roots in any of the existing structures of the black community, and in the North these structures were themselves weak. CORE could be a source of ideas, but not of coordination.

The coordination of a new movement required the creation of a new organization. But that was not apparent until after the Montgomery bus boycott began. That boycott was organized through institutions already existing in the black community of Montgomery.

Rosa Parks's refusal to give up her seat on the bus to a white man was not the first time such defiance of segregation laws had occurred. There had been talk of a boycott the previous time, but after local black leaders had a congenial meeting with the city commissioners, nothing happened—on either side (King, 1958:37–41). When Parks, a former secretary of the local NAACP, was arrested, she immediately called E. D. Nixon, at that time the president of the local chapter. He not only bailed her out but informed a few influential women in the city, most of whom were members of the Women's Political Council. After numerous phone calls between their members, it was the WPC that actually suggested the boycott, and E. D. Nixon who initially organized it (ibid.:44–45).

The Montgomery Improvement Association (MIA) was formed at a meeting of eighteen ministers and civic leaders the Monday after Parks's conviction and a day of successful boycotting, to provide ongoing coordination. No one then suspected that coordination would be necessary for over a year, with car pools organized to provide alternative transportation for seventeen thousand riders a day. During this time the MIA grew slowly to a staff of ten in order to handle the voluminous correspondence, as well as to provide rides and keep the movement's momentum going. The organization, and the car pools, were financed by $250,000 in donations that poured in from all over the world in response to heavy press publicity about the boycott. But the organizational framework for the boycott and the MIA was the church. Most, although not all, of the officers were ministers, and Sunday meetings with congregations continued to be the main means of communicating with members of the black community and encouraging them to continue the protest.

The boycott did not end until the federal courts ruled Alabama's bus segregation laws unconstitutional late in 1956—at the same time that state courts ruled the boycott illegal. In the meantime, black leaders throughout the South had visited Montgomery, and out of the discussions came agreement to continue antisegregation protests regularly and systematically under the aegis of a new organization, the Southern Christian Leadership Conference. The NAACP could not lead the protests because, according to an SCLC pamphlet, "during the late fifties, the NAACP had been driven out of some Southern states. Its branches were outlawed as foreign corporations and its lawyers were charged with barratry, that is, persistently inciting litigation."

On January 10, 1957, over one hundred people gathered in Atlanta at a meeting called by four ministers, including Martin Luther King. Bayard Rustin drew up the "working papers." Initially called the Southern Leadership Conference on Transportation and Nonviolent Integration, the SCLC never developed a mass base even when it changed its name. It established numerous "affiliates" but did most of its work through the churches in the communities to which it sent its fieldworkers.

The church was not just the only institution available for a movement to work through; in many ways it was ideal. It performed "the central organizing function in the Negro community" (Holloway, 1969:22), providing both access to large masses of people on a regular basis and a natural leadership. As Wyatt Tee Walker, former executive director of SCLC, commented, "The Church today is central to the movement. If a Negro's going to have a meeting, where's he going to have it? Mostly he doesn't have a Masonic lodge, and he's not going to get the public schools. And the church is the primary means of communication" (Brink & Harris, 1964:103). Thus the church eventually came to be the center of the voter registration drives as well as many of the other activities of the civil rights movement.

Even the young men and women of SNCC had to use the church, though they had trouble doing so because, unlike most of the officers of SCLC, they were not themselves ministers and thus did not have a "fraternal" connection. Instead they tended to draw many of their resources and people from outside the particular town in which they were working by utilizing their natural organizational base, the college.

SNCC did not begin the sit-ins, but came out of them. Once begun, the idea of the sit-in spread initially by means of the mass media. But such sit-ins almost always took place in towns where there were Negro colleges, and groups on these campuses essentially organized the sit-in activities of their communities. Nonetheless, "CORE, with its long emphasis of nonviolent direct action, played an important part, once the sit-ins began, as an educational and organizing agent" (Zinn, 1964:23). CORE had very few staff in the South, but there were enough to at least hold classes and practice sessions in nonviolence.

It was SCLC, however, that was actually responsible for the formation of SNCC; though it might well have organized itself eventually. Ella Baker, then executive secretary of SCLC, thought something should be done to coordinate the rapidly spreading sit-ins in 1960, and many members of

SCLC thought it might be appropriate to organize a youth group. With SCLC money, Baker persuaded her alma mater, Shaw University, to provide facilities to contact the groups at centers of sit-in activity. Some two hundred people showed up for the meeting, decided to have no official connection with SCLC beyond a "friendly relationship," and formed the Student Non-Violent Coordinating Committee (Zinn, 1964:32–34). It had no members, and its fieldworkers numbered two hundred at their highest point, but it was from the campuses, especially the southern black colleges, that it drew its sustenance and upon which its organizational base rested. . . .

THE WOMEN'S LIBERATION MOVEMENT[1]

Women are not well organized. Historically tied to the family and isolated from their own kind, only in the nineteenth century did women in this country have the opportunity to develop independent associations of their own. These associations took years and years of careful organizational work to build. Eventually they formed the basis for the suffrage movement of the early twentieth century. The associations took less time to die. Today the Women's Trade Union League, the General Federation of Women's Clubs, the Women's Christian Temperance Union, not to mention the powerful National Women's Suffrage Association, are all either dead or a pale shadow of their former selves.

As of 1960, not one organization of women had the potential to become a social movement organization, nor was there any form of "neutral" structure of interaction to provide the base for such an organization. The closest exception to the former was the National Women's Party, which has remained dedicated to feminist concerns since its inception in 1916. However, the NWP has been essentially a lobbying group for the Equal Rights Amendment since 1923. From the beginning, the NWP believed that a small group of women concentrating their efforts in the right places was more effective than a mass appeal, and so was not appalled by the fact that as late as 1969 even the majority of avowed feminists in this country had never heard of the ERA or the NWP.

The one large women's organization that might have provided a base for a social movement was the 180,000-member Federation of Business and Professional Women's Clubs. Yet, while it has steadily lobbied for legislation of importance to women, as late as "1966 BPW rejected a number of suggestions that it redefine . . . goals and tactics and become a kind of 'NAACP for women' . . . out of fear of being labeled 'feminist' " (Hole & Levine, 1971:89).

Before any social movement could develop among women, there had to be created a structure to bring potential feminist sympathizers together. To be sure, groups such as the BPW, and institutions such as the women's colleges, might be a good source of adherents for such a movement. But they were determined not to be the source of leadership.

What happened in the 1960s was the development of two new communications networks in which women played prominent roles that allowed, even forced, an awakened interest in the old feminist ideas. As a result, the movement actually has two origins, from two different strata of society, with two different styles, orientations, values, and forms of organization. The first of these will be referred to as the "older branch" of the movement, partially because it began first and partially because it was on the older side of the "generation gap" that pervaded the sixties. Its most prominent organization is the National Organization for Women (NOW), which was also the first to be formed. The style of its organization tended to be traditional with elected officers, boards of directors, bylaws, and the other trappings of democratic procedure. Conversely, the "younger branch" consisted of innumerable small groups engaged in a variety of activities whose contact with one another was always tenuous (Freeman, 1975:50).

The forces that led to NOW's formation were set in motion in 1961 when President Kennedy established the President's Commission on the Status of Women at the behest of Esther Petersen, then director of the Women's Bureau. Its 1963 report, *American Women,* and subsequent committee publications documented just how thoroughly women were denied many rights and opportunities. The most significant response to the activity of the President's commission was the establishment of some fifty state commissions to do similar research on a state level. The Presidential and State Commission activity laid the groundwork for the future movement in two significant ways: (1) It unearthed ample evidence of women's unequal status and in the process convinced many previously uninterested women that something should be done; (2) It created a climate of expectations that something would be done. The women of the Presidential and State Commissions who were exposed to these influences exchanged visits, correspondence, and staff, and met with one another at an annual commission convention. They were in a position to share and mutually reinforce their growing awareness and concern over women's issues. These commissions thus provided an embryonic communications network.

During this time, two other events of significance occurred. The first was the publication of Betty Friedan's *The Feminine Mystique* in 1963. A quick best seller, the book stimulated many women to question the *status quo* and some women to suggest to Friedan that an organization be formed to do something about it. The second event was the addition of "sex" to the 1964 Civil Rights Act.

Many thought the "sex" provision was a joke, and the Equal Employment Opportunity Commission treated it as one, refusing to enforce it seriously. But a rapidly growing feminist coterie within the EEOC argued that "sex" would be taken more seriously if there were "some sort of NAACP for women" to put pressure on the government.

On June 30, 1966, these three strands of incipient feminism came together, and NOW was tied from the knot. At that time, government officials running the Third National Conference of Commissions on the Status of Women, ironically titled "Targets for Action," forbade the presentation of a suggested resolution calling for the EEOC to treat sex discrimination with the same consideration as race discrimination. The officials said one government agency could not be allowed to pressure another, despite the fact that the state commissions were not federal agencies. The small group of women who desired such a resolution had met the night before in Friedan's hotel room to discuss the possibility of a civil rights organization for women. Not convinced of its need, they chose instead to propose the resolution. When conference officials vetoed it, they held a whispered conversation over lunch and agreed to form an action organization "to bring women into full participation in the mainstream of American society now, assuming all the privileges and responsibilities thereof in truly equal partnership with men." The name NOW was coined by Friedan who was at the conference doing research on a book. When word leaked out, twenty-eight women paid five dollars each to join before the day was over (Friedan, 1967:4).

By the time the organizing conference was held the following October 29 through 30, over three hundred men and women had become charter members. It is impossible to do a breakdown on the composition of the charter membership, but one of the officers and board is possible. Such a breakdown accurately reflected NOW's origins. Friedan was president, two former EEOC commissioners were vice presidents, a representative of the United Auto Workers Women's Committee was secretary-treasurer, and there were seven past and present members of the State Commissions on the Status of Women on the twenty member board. One hundred twenty-six of the charter members were Wisconsin residents—and Wisconsin had the most active state Commission. Occupationally, the board and officers were primarily from the professions, labor, government, and communications fields. Of these, only those from labor had any experience in organizing, and they resigned a year later in a dispute over support of the Equal Rights

Amendment. Instead of organizational experience, what the early NOW members had was experience in working with and in the media, and it was here that their early efforts were aimed.

As a result, NOW often gave the impression of being larger than it was. It was highly successful in getting in the press; much less successful in either bringing about concrete changes or forming an organization. Thus it was not until 1970, when the national press simultaneously did major stories on the women's liberation movement, that NOW's membership increased significantly.

In the meantime, unaware of and unknown to NOW, the EEOC, or the State Commissions, younger women began forming their own movement. Here, too, the groundwork had been laid some years before. The different social action projects of the sixties had attracted many women, who were quickly shunted into traditional roles and faced with the self-evident contradiction of working in a "freedom movement" but not being very free. No single "youth movement" activity or organization is responsible for forming the younger branch of the women's liberation movement, but together they created a "radical community" in which like-minded people continually interacted or were made aware of one another. This community provided the necessary network of communication and its radical ideas the framework of analysis that "explained" the dismal situation in which radical women found themselves.

Papers had been circulated on women and individual temporary women's caucuses had been held as early as 1964 (see Hayden & King, 1966). But it was not until 1967 and 1968 that the groups developed a determined, if cautious, continuity and began to consciously expand themselves. At least five groups in five different cities (Chicago, Toronto, Detroit, Seattle, and Gainesville, Florida) formed spontaneously, independently of one another. They came at an auspicious moment, for 1967 was the year in which the blacks kicked the whites out of the civil rights movement, student power was discredited by SDS, and the New Left was on the wane. Only draft resistance activities were on the increase,

and this movement more than any other exemplified the social inequities of the sexes. Men could resist the draft. Women could only counsel resistance.

At this point, there were few opportunities available for political work. Some women fit well into the secondary role of draft counseling. Many didn't. For years their complaints of unfair treatment had been forestalled by movement men with the dictum that those things could wait until after the Revolution. Now these political women found time on their hands, but still the men would not listen.

A typical example was the event that precipitated the formation of the Chicago group, the first independent group in this country. At the August 1967 National Conference for New Politics convention a women's caucus met for days, but was told its resolution wasn't significant enough to merit a floor discussion. By threatening to tie up the convention with procedural motions the women succeeded in having their statement tacked to the end of the agenda. It was never discussed. The chair refused to recognize any of the many women standing by the microphone, their hands straining upwards. When he instead called on someone to speak on "the forgotten American, the American Indian," five women rushed the podium to demand an explanation. But the chairman just patted one of them on the head (literally) and told her, "Cool down, little girl. We have more important things to talk about than women's problems."

The "little girl" was Shulamith Firestone, future author of *The Dialectic of Sex,* and she didn't cool down. Instead she joined with another Chicago woman she met there who had unsuccessfully tried to organize a women's group that summer, to call a meeting of the women who had halfheartedly attended those summer meetings. Telling their stories to those women, they stimulated sufficient rage to carry the group for three months, and by that time it was a permanent institution.

Another somewhat similar event occurred in Seattle the following winter. At the University of Washington, an SDS organizer was explaining to a large meeting how white college youth established rapport with the poor whites with whom they were working. "He noted that sometimes after analyzing societal ills, the men shared leisure time by 'balling a chick together.' He pointed out that such activities did much to enhance the political consciousness of the poor white youth. A woman in the audience asked, 'And what did it do for the consciousness of the chick?' " (Hole & Levine, 1971:120). After the meeting, a handful of enraged women formed Seattle's first group.

Subsequent groups to the initial five were largely organized rather than formed spontaneously out of recent events. In particular, the Chicago group was responsible for the formation of many new groups in Chicago and in other cities. Unlike NOW, the women in the first groups had had years of experience as trained organizers. They knew how to utilize the infrastructure of the radical community, the underground press, and the free universities to disseminate women's liberation ideas. Chicago, as a center of New Left activity, had the largest number of politically conscious organizers. Many traveled widely to leftist conferences and demonstrations, and most used the opportunity to talk with other women about the new movement. In spite of public derision by radical men, or perhaps because of it, young women steadily formed new groups around the country.

ANALYSIS

From these data there appear to be four essential elements involved in movement formation: (1) the growth of a preexisting communications network that is (2) cooptable to the ideas of the new movement; (3) a series of crises that galvanize into action people involved in a cooptable network, and/or (4) subsequent organizing effort to weld the spontaneous groups together into a movement. Each of these elements needs to be examined in detail.

COMMUNICATIONS NETWORK

. . . The women's liberation movement . . . illustrates the importance of a network precisely because the conditions for a movement existed *before*

a network came into being, but the movement didn't exist until afterward. Analysts of socioeconomic causes have concluded that the movement could have started anytime within a twenty-year period. Strain for women was as great in 1955 as in 1965 (Ferriss, 1971). What changed was the organizational situation. It was not until new networks emerged among women aware of inequities beyond local boundaries that a movement could grow past the point of occasional, spontaneous uprisings. The fact that two distinct movements, with two separate origins, developed from two networks unaware of each other is further evidence of the key role of preexisting communications networks as the fertile soil in which new movements can sprout.

References to the importance of a preexisting communications network appear frequently in case studies of social movements, though the theoretical writers were much slower to recognize their salience. According to Buck (1920:43–44), the Grange established a degree of organization among American farmers in the nineteenth century that greatly facilitated the spread of future farmers' protests. Lipset has reported that in Saskatchewan, "the rapid acceptance of new ideas and movements . . . can be attributed mainly to the high degree of organization. . . . The role of the social structure of the western wheat belt in facilitating the rise of new movements has never been sufficiently appreciated by historians and sociologists. Repeated challenges and crises forced the western farmers to create many more community institutions (especially cooperatives and economic pressure groups) than are necessary in a more stable area. These groups in turn provided a structural basis for immediate action in critical situations. [Therefore] though it was a new radical party, the C. C. F. did not have to build up an organization from scratch" (1959:206).

Similarly, Heberle (1951:232) reports several findings that Nazism was most successful in small, well-integrated communities. As Lipset put it, these findings "sharply challenge the various interpretations of Nazism as the product of the growth of anomie and the general rootlessness of modern urban industrial society" (1959: 146).

Indirect evidence attesting to the essential role of formal and informal communications networks is found in diffusion theory, which emphasizes the importance of personal interaction rather than impersonal media communication in the spread of ideas (Rogers, 1962; Lionberger, 1960). This personal influence occurs through the organizational patterns of a community (Lionberger, 1960:73). It does not occur through the mass media. The mass media may be a source of information, but they are not a key source of influence.

Their lesser importance in relation to preexisting communications networks was examined in one study on "The Failure of an Incipient Social Movement" (Jackson, Peterson, Bull, Monsen, & Richmond, 1960). In 1957 a potential tax protest movement in Los Angeles generated considerable interest and publicity for a little over a month but was dead within a year. According to the authors, this did not reflect a lack of public notice. They concluded that "mass communication alone is probably insufficient without a network of communication specifically linking those interested in the matter. . . . If a movement is to grow rapidly, it cannot rely upon its own network of communication, but must capitalize on networks already in existence" (p. 37).

A major reason it took social scientists so long to acknowledge the importance of communications networks was because the prevailing theories of the post–World War II era emphasized increasing social dislocation and anomie. Mass society theorists, as they were called, hypothesized that significant community institutions that linked individuals to governing elites were breaking down, that society was becoming a mass of isolated individuals. These individuals were seen as increasingly irresponsible and ungovernable, prone to irrational protests because they had no mediating institutions through which to pursue grievances (Kornhauser, 1959).

In emphasizing disintegrating vertical connections, mass society theorists passed lightly over the role of horizontal ones, only occasionally acknowledging that "the combination of internal contact and external isolation facilitates the work of the mass agitator" (Kornhauser, 1959:218). This focus changed in the early seventies. Pinard's study of the Social Credit Party of Quebec (1971) severely criticized mass society theory, arguing instead that "when strains are severe and widespread a new movement is more likely to meet its early success among the more strongly integrated citizens" (Pinard, 1971:192).

This insight was expanded by Oberschall (1973), who created a six-cell table to predict both the occurrence and type of protest. As did the mass society theorists, Oberschall said that even when there are grievances, protest will not occur outside institutional channels by those who are connected, through their own leadership or patron/client relationships, with governing elites. Among those who are segmented from such elites, the type of protest will be determined by whether there is communal, associational, or little organization. In the latter case, discontent is expressed through riots or other short-lived violent uprisings. "It is under conditions of strong . . . ties and segmentation that the possibility of the rapid spread of opposition movements on a continuous basis exists" (p. 123).

The movements we have studied would confirm Oberschall's conclusions, but not as strongly as he makes them. In all these cases a preexisting communications network was a necessary but insufficient condition for movement formation. Yet the newly formed networks among student radicals, welfare recipients, and women can hardly compare with the longstanding ties provided by the southern black churches and colleges. Their ties were tenuous and may not have survived the demise of their movements.

The importance of segmentation, or lack of connection with relevant elites, is less obvious in the sixties' movements. The higher socioeconomic status of incipient feminists and Movement leaders would imply greater access to elites than is true for blacks or welfare recipients. If Oberschall were correct, these closer connections should either have permitted easier and more rapid grievance solutions or more effective social control. They did neither. Indeed, it was the group most closely connected to decision-making elites— women of the Presidential and State Commission— who were among the earliest to see the need of a protest organization. Women of the younger branch of the movement did have their grievances against the men of the New Left effectively suppressed for several years, but even they eventually rejected this kind of elite control, even when it meant rejecting the men.

Conversely, Piven and Cloward show that the establishment of closer ties between leaders of local welfare rights groups and welfare workers through advisory councils and community coordinators led to a curtailment of militance and the institutionalization of grievances (1977:326–31). They also argue that the development of government-funded community programs effectively coopted many local black movement leaders in the North and that federal channeling of black protest in the South into voter registration projects focused the movement there into traditional electoral politics (ibid.:253). In short, the evidence about the role of segmentation in movement formation is ambiguous. The effect may be varied considerably by the nature of the political system.

COOPTABILITY

A recurrent theme in our studies is that not just any communications network will do. It must be one that is cooptable to the ideas of the new movement. The Business and Professional Women's (BPW) clubs were a network among women, but having rejected feminism, they could not overcome the ideological barrier to new political action until after feminism became established. . . .

On the other hand, the women on the Presidential and State Commissions and the feminist coterie of the EEOC were cooptable largely because their immersion in the facts of female status and the details of sex discrimination cases made them very conscious of the need for change. Likewise, the young women of the "radical community" lived in an atmosphere of questioning,

confrontation, and change. They absorbed an ideology of "freedom" and "liberation" far more potent than any latent "antifeminism" might have been. . . .

Exactly what makes a network cooptable is harder to elucidate. Pinard (1971:186) noted the necessity for groups to *"possess* or *develop* an ideology or simply subjective interests congruent with that of a new movement" for them to "act as mobilizing rather than restraining agents toward that movement," but did not further explore what affected the "primary group climate." More illumination is provided by the diffusion of innovation studies that point out the necessity for new ideas to fit in with already established norms for changes to happen easily. Furthermore, a social system that has as a value "innovativeness" (as the radical community did) will more rapidly adopt ideas than one that looks upon the habitual performance of traditional practices as the ideal (as most organized women's groups did in the fifties). Usually, as Lionberger (1960:91) points out, "people act in terms of past experience and knowledge." People who have had similar experiences are likely to share similar perceptions of a situation and to mutually reinforce those perceptions as well as their subsequent interpretation. A cooptable network, then, is one whose members have had common experiences that predispose them to be receptive to the particular new ideas of the incipient movement and who are not faced with structural or ideological barriers to action. If the new movement as an "innovation" can interpret these experiences and perceptions in ways that point out channels for social action, then participation in a social movement becomes the logical thing to do.

THE ROLE OF CRISES

As our examples have illustrated, similar perceptions must be translated into action. This is often done by a crisis. For blacks in Montgomery, this was generated by Rosa Parks's refusal to give up her seat on a bus to a white man. For women who formed the older branch of the women's movement, the impetus to organize was the refusal of the EEOC to enforce the sex provision of Title VII, precipitated by the concomitant refusal of federal officials at the conference to allow a supportive resolution. For younger women there were a series of minor crises.

While not all movements are formed by such precipitating events, they are quite common as they serve to crystallize and focus discontent. From their own experiences, directly and concretely, people feel the need for change in a situation that allows for an exchange of feelings with others, mutual validation, and a subsequent reinforcement of innovative interpretation. Perception of an immediate need for change is a major factor in predisposing people to accept new ideas (Rogers, 1962:280). Nothing makes desire for change more acute than a crisis. Such a crisis need not be a major one; it need only embody collective discontent.

ORGANIZING EFFORTS

A crisis will only catalyze a well-formed communications network. If such networks are embryonically developed or only partially cooptable, the potentially active individuals in them must be linked together by someone. . . . As Jackson et al. (1960:37) stated, "Some protest may persist where the source of trouble is constantly present. But interest ordinarily cannot be maintained unless there is a welding of spontaneous groups into some stable organization." In other words, people must be organized. Social movements do not simply occur.

The role of the organizer in movement formation is another neglected aspect of the theoretical literature. There has been great concern with leadership, but the two roles are distinct and not always performed by the same individual. In the early stages of a movement, it is the organizer much more than any leader who is important, and such an individual or cadre must often operate behind the scenes. The nature and function of

these two roles was most clearly evident in the Townsend old-age movement of the thirties. Townsend was the "charismatic" leader, but the movement was organized by his partner, real estate promoter Robert Clements. Townsend himself acknowledges that without Clements's help, the movement would never have gone beyond the idea stage (Holzman, 1963).

The importance of organizers is pervasive in the sixties' movements. Dr. King may have been the public spokesperson of the Montgomery Bus Boycott who caught the eye of the media, but it was E. D. Nixon who organized it. Certainly the "organizing cadre" that young women in the radical community came to be was key to the growth of that branch of the women's liberation movement, despite the fact that no "leaders" were produced (and were actively discouraged). The existence of many leaders but no organizers in the older branch of the women's liberation movement readily explains its subsequent slow development. . . .

The function of the organizer has been explored indirectly by other analysts. Rogers (1962) devotes many pages to the "change agent" who, while he does not necessarily weld a group together or "construct" a movement, does many of the same things for agricultural innovation that an organizer does for political change. Mass society theory makes frequent reference to the "agitator," though not in a truly informative way. Interest groups are often organized by single individuals and some of them evolve into social movements. Salisbury's study of farmers' organizations finds this a recurrent theme. He also discovered that "a considerable number of farm groups were subsidized by other, older, groups. . . . The Farm Bureau was organized and long sustained by subsidies, some from federal and state governments, and some by local businessmen" (Salisbury, 1969:13).

These patterns are similar to ones we have found in the formation of social movements. Other organizations, even the government, often serve as training centers for organizers and sources of material support to aid the formation of groups and/or movements. The civil rights movement was the training ground for many an organizer of other movements. . . . The role of the government in the formation of the National Welfare Rights Organization was so significant that it would lead one to wonder if this association should be considered more of an interest group in the traditional sense than a movement "core" organization.

From all this it would appear that training as an organizer or at least as a proselytizer or entrepreneur of some kind is a necessary background for those individuals who act as movement innovators. Even in something as seemingly spontaneous as a social movement, the professional is more valuable than the amateur.

CRITICAL-THINKING QUESTIONS

1. Why has the role of communications networks in the formation of social movements only recently received the attention of researchers?

2. How do leadership roles emerge in social movements? Are "leaders" the same as "organizers"?

3. Cite some similarities and differences in the development of the civil rights movement and the women's movement.

NOTES

1. Data for this section are based on my observations while a founder and participant in the younger branch of the Chicago women's liberation movement from 1967 through 1969 and editor of the first (at that time, only) national newsletter. I was able, through extensive correspondence and interviews, to keep a record of how each group around the country started, where the organizers got the idea from, who they had talked to, what conferences were held and who attended, the political affiliations (or lack of them) of the first members, and so forth. Although I was a member of Chicago NOW, information on the origins of it and the other older branch organizations comes entirely through ex post facto interviews of the principals and examination of early papers in preparation for my dissertation on the women's liberation movement. Most of my informants requested that their contribution remain confidential.

REFERENCES

ADORNO, L. W., et al. 1950. *The authoritarian personality.* New York: Harper & Row.

BLUMER, H. 1951. Social movements. In *New outline of the principles of sociology,* ed. A. M. Lee. New York: Barnes and Noble.

BRINK, W., and L. HARRIS. 1964. *The Negro revolution in America.* New York: Simon & Schuster.

BUCK, S. J. 1920. *The agrarian crusade.* New Haven, Conn.: Yale University Press.

CANTRIL, H. 1941. *The psychology of social movements.* New York: Wiley.

CLARK, K. B. 1966. The civil rights movement: Momentum and organization. *Daedalus,* Winter.

DAVIES, J. C. 1962. Toward a theory of revolution. *American Sociological Review,* 27(1): 5–19.

FERRISS, A. L. 1971. *Indicators of trends in the status of American women.* New York: Russell Sage Foundation.

FIRESTONE, S. 1971. *Dialectics of sex.* New York: Morrow.

FRAZIER, E. F. 1963. *The Negro church in America.* New York: Schocken.

FREEMAN, J. 1975. *The politics of women's liberation.* New York: Longman.

FRIEDAN, B. 1963. *The feminine mystique.* New York: Dell.

———. 1967. NOW: How it began. *Women Speaking,* April.

GURR, T. 1970. *Why men rebel.* Princeton, N.J.: Princeton University Press.

HAYDEN, C., and M. KING. 1966. A kind of memo. *Liberation,* April.

HEBERLE, R. 1951. *Social movements.* New York: Appleton-Century-Crofts.

HOFFER, E. 1951. *The true believer.* New York: Harper & Row.

HOLE, J., and E. LEVINE. 1971. *Rebirth of feminism.* New York: Quadrangle.

HOLLOWAY, H. 1969. *The politics of the Southern Negro.* New York: Random House.

HOLZMAN, A. 1963. *The Townsend movement: A political study.* New York: Bookman.

JACKSON, M., et al. 1960. The failure of an incipient social movement. *Pacific Sociological Review,* 3(1): 40.

KING, M. L., JR. 1958. *Stride toward freedom.* New York: Harper & Row.

KORNHAUSER, W. 1959. *The politics of mass society.* Glencoe, Ill.: Free Press.

LIONBERGER, H. F. 1960. *Adoption of new ideas and practices.* Ames: Iowa State University Press.

LIPSET, S. M. 1959. *Agrarian socialism.* Berkeley: University of California Press.

LOWI, T. J. 1971. *The politics of discord.* New York: Basic Books.

OBERSCHALL, A. 1973. *Social conflict and social movements.* Englewood Cliffs, N.J.: Prentice-Hall.

PINARD, M. 1971. *The rise of a third party: A study in crisis politics.* Englewood Cliffs, N.J.: Prentice-Hall.

PIVEN, F. F., and R. CLOWARD. 1977. *Poor people's movements: Why they succeed, how they fail.* New York: Pantheon.

ROGERS, E. M. 1962. *Diffusion of innovations.* New York: Free Press.

RUDWICK, E., and A. MEIER. 1970. Organizational structure and goal succession: A comparative analysis of the NAACP and CORE, 1964–1968. *Social Science Quarterly,* 51 (June).

SALISBURY, R. H. 1969. An exchange theory of interest groups. *Midwest Journal of Political Science,* 13(1), (February).

TOCH, H. 1965. *The social psychology of social movements.* Indianapolis, Ind.: Bobbs-Merrill.

ZINN, H. 1964. *SNCC: The new abolitionists.* Boston: Beacon Press.

77 The Animal Rights Movement as a Moral Crusade

JAMES M. JASPER AND DOROTHY NELKIN

Although the number of animal rights organizations in the United States is small compared to the membership of other social movements, animal rights activists have enjoyed numerous victories since the 1980s. Why has this small group been so successful? James M. Jasper and Dorothy Nelkin provide some of the answers. They describe the animal rights movement as a "moral crusade" that relies, for example, on sympathetic media coverage, sentimental views about pets, and coalitions with other recent protest movements to achieve their objectives.

On a warm spring day in May, 1980, Henry Spira was on Manhattan's posh Fifth Avenue with a flatbed truck filled with white rabbits. With him were 300 more demonstrators, many of them dressed in bunny suits. On the sidewalk in front of the headquarters of the cosmetics giant Revlon, they were protesting that company's extensive use of white rabbits to test the safety of new products. The demonstrators were angry about procedures in which substances were placed in rabbits' eyes to test if these ingredients caused redness, swelling, or cloudiness. Many demonstrators had been drawn to the protest by full-page advertisements in the *New York Times* and other papers that asked, "How many rabbits does Revlon blind for beauty's sake?"

Source: Reprinted with the permission of The Free Press, a Division of Simon & Schuster Adult Publishing Group, from *The Animal Rights Crusade: The Growth of a Moral Protest* by James M. Jasper and Dorothy Nelkin. Copyright © 1992 by James M. Jasper and Dorothy Nelkin.

After a friend left him a cat in 1973, Spira, a burly man in his early fifties, had become increasingly outraged over humans' treatment of animals, wondering about "the appropriateness of cuddling one animal while sticking a knife and fork into others." He grew more and more critical of such common practices as wearing furs and leather and eating meat. For more than a year he had talked to Revlon officials, hoping to persuade them to contribute several hundred thousand dollars to help develop alternative tests that did not use live animals. When Revlon officials listened politely but then ignored him, he put together a coalition of 400 animal groups, mostly humane societies operating spay clinics and offering cats and dogs for adoption. And he gathered funds for the newspaper ads. He felt public opinion would be on his side: "I think there are very few people on the street who'll say, 'Yeah, go around and blind rabbits to produce another mascara.'"[1]

Following the May rally, public protests continued alongside Spira's private negotiations, and in December 1980 Revlon capitulated, announcing that it would provide Rockefeller University $750,000 for research on alternative tests. Soon other companies followed Revlon's lead; by 1987 many had ended live animal testing; and the cosmetics industry claimed to have contributed about $5 million to alternatives research.

Four years after the Revlon demonstration, another effort to liberate animals unfolded in the laboratories of the University of Pennsylvania Medical School. On Memorial Day weekend in 1984, five members of the Animal Liberation Front (ALF) surreptitiously entered the deserted research lab of Thomas Gennarelli, who headed a team of researchers studying the effects of severe head injuries. Underway for fourteen years, these experiments currently involved severe shocks and injuries—similar to whiplash in car accidents— to the heads of baboons. The intruders destroyed equipment worth $20,000 and removed sixty hours of videotapes made to document the experiments.

The members of the ALF shared Henry Spira's goal of eliminating any use of animals for human needs, but they felt a stronger sense of urgency that compelled them to break the law. In most of their break-ins—Pennsylvania was one of more than 100 entries—the ALF has liberated animals rather than videotapes. Its members value animal lives so highly that they feel a moral obligation to act to save them, even to damage property in doing so. Violence against property, they claim, is justified to stop violence against living beings (the animals they liberate). As one activist put it, "Property laws are artificial constructs. We feel we answer to a higher law."[2]

Perhaps the most important result of the Memorial Day break-in is what then happened to the videotapes. The ALF, an illegal group designated as a "terrorist" organization by the FBI, passed the tapes to another animal rights group, People for the Ethical Treatment of Animals (PETA). PETA edited the tapes into a twenty-minute film called *Unnecessary Fuss,* which portrayed bantering among researchers and joking about the injured animals—"mocking them," as animal activists put

it. It also appeared that the animals were not fully anesthetized. Scientists were painted as callous, even sadistic, and so brutal that discussion with them about their methods would be useless: Direct action against such research was the only appropriate response. The film proved a powerful instrument for PETA in its efforts to recruit new and committed members to an emerging protest movement.

The Revlon and University of Pennsylvania incidents are just two among thousands of recent animal rights protests, lawsuits, break-ins, and other actions that have targeted scientific laboratories, cosmetic and pharmaceutical firms, slaughterhouses and butchers, fur ranchers and retailers, rodeos and circuses, hunters and trappers, carriage drivers, and even zoos. Since the late 1970s, new animal "rights" organizations have rejuvenated the older and larger animal welfare movement, and together they are reshaping public awareness of animals. As many as 10 to 15 million Americans send money to animal protection groups, which have proliferated: By 1990, there were several thousand animal welfare and several hundred animal rights organizations in the United States. Some focus on particular animals (The Beaver Defenders, Bat Conservation International); others have a religious bent (Life for God's Stray Animals, Jews for Animal Rights); some are organized around tactics (the Animal Legal Defense Fund); others protest particular uses or abuses of animals (Students United Protesting Research Experiments on Sentient Subjects); still others represent links with related causes (Feminists for Animal Rights). The pull of these groups was evident in June 1990, when 30,000 people participated in a march on Washington for animal rights, with slogans such as "Fur Is Dead," "No Tax Dollars for Torture," and "Blinding Bunnies Is Not Beautiful."

Renewed concerns about animals have generated a powerful social movement driven by a simple moral position: Animals are similar enough to humans to deserve serious moral consideration. They are sentient beings entitled to dignified lives, and they should be treated as ends, not as means. Protectors ask how we can love our pets, yet experiment on identical animals in laboratories; how we can cuddle one animal, yet eat another. They have themselves mostly given up meat, dairy products, and eggs; they refuse to wear leather shoes or belts; they do not patronize the products of certain corporations; and many will not wear wool—let alone fur—garments. While some would allow occasional animal research if subjects are fully sedated and the benefits outweigh the harm, others say this concession violates the inherent right of animals to a full life independent of human goals. Movement leaders often use the morally charged language of good and evil, and their political actions and rhetorical style often display an absolutism that discourages discussion or negotiation with those who disagree.

The new movement has exploded into Americans' awareness. Animal rights has been the cover story of magazines as diverse as *Newsweek, U.S. News and World Report, New York Magazine,* the *Atlantic Monthly,* the *New Republic,* the *Village Voice,* the *Progressive,* and the lawyers' weekly *National Law Journal;* its issues have been featured in network television series like *L.A. Law, MacGyver,* and *Designing Women;* it has been examined in major news programs such as *48 Hours.* Despite a tendency to focus on secretive and sensationalist ALF commandos, most media coverage has been sympathetic to the ideas of the movement. Typically, the activists are portrayed as eccentric, but their positions are treated with respect. Comic strips such as *Doonesbury* and *Bloom County* have favorably portrayed animal activists and their issues. *Saturday Night Live* at least recognized the controversy over fur coats in a skit titled "They're Better Off Dead." Celebrities such as Bob Barker, Doris Day, Casey Kasem, River Phoenix, and several of *The Golden Girls* have given their support to the cause.

Consumer goods have followed suit. One Barbie Doll is an "animal loving" Barbie, marketed as an animal rights volunteer—even as real-life activists attack the mink stole sold by the Spiegel Company for other Barbie Dolls. Vegetarian food is sold for the dogs of those with strict animal

rights sensibilities. Public opinion polls show a slippage of support for scientific research using animals, even when it generates information about human health. Activists have delivered a crippling blow to the American fur industry—from which it may never recover. Animal protection is not only one of today's fastest-growing protest movements, it is one of the most effective.

The social roots of this movement lie in the changed relationship between humans and their fellow creatures that resulted from urbanization and industrialization in Western societies, as city dwellers began to encounter animals only as family pets, and less and less as instruments of labor and production. Animals have accompanied men and women throughout their history, some as members of the family to be cherished, others as tools to be used. But in modern times the balance between these attitudes—one sentimental, the other instrumental—has been questioned, as more and more people insist that all animals be treated as though they were partners—"companion animals"—rather than objects.

In the United States, the first societies to prevent cruelty to animals were founded in the 1860s as part of the more general humanitarian impulse of the time. While these societies persisted, further expansion of this animal welfare movement took place in the 1950s, with the founding of such organizations as the Humane Society of the United States. Most of these groups concentrated on problems associated with the growing number of pets: overpopulation and frequent abandonment, the issue of shelters, and the frequency of brutality and cruelty. These humane societies and welfare organizations saw animal cruelty coming from poorly educated or abusive individuals, not from the systematic activities of institutions.

A new ideological agenda for animal protection emerged dramatically in the late 1970s, combining ideas from several sources. It retained the animal welfare tradition's concern for animals as sentient beings that should be protected from unnecessary cruelty. But animal activists added a new language of "rights" as the basis for demanding animal liberation. In the individualist culture of America, "rights talk" is often the only way to express moral values and demands. Rights—whether of patients, women, fetuses, or animals—are accepted as a moral trump card that cannot be disputed. Justified in terms of tradition, nature, or fundamental moral principles, rights are considered nonnegotiable. Protectors compare animal rights to human rights, and the charge of "speciesism" takes its place alongside racism and sexism. Wildlife traffickers are engaged in a "monkey slave trade," laboratories become "torture chambers," and animal testing is a "holocaust."

The moral vision of animal rightists is partly drawn from other movements, especially feminism and environmentalism. At the core of these ideologies is a critique of "instrumentalism," the confusion of ends and means said to prevail in contemporary society. According to this critique, instrumental attitudes reduce nature and women, as well as other humans—all with inherent value as ends in themselves—to the status of things and tools. At the same time, instrumentalism promotes technologies, markets, and bureaucracies—all intended to be the means for attaining the good life—to the status of ends. Uneasiness with instrumental attitudes is widespread: Many people feel that there is something wrong with basing all decisions on economic values; that science lacks a human face; that consumer society creates artificial needs rather than satisfying real ones; that humans are treated like cogs in a machine.

Recent protest movements—ranging from Christian fundamentalists to radical feminists—insist that policies and decisions be guided by moral values and social needs, not by profits, technological feasibility, or bureaucratic inertia. Just as environmentalists question the exploitation of nature for commercial purposes, so animal rights advocates demand the end of animal exploitation for human gain. Animals, like human beings or nature, should be treated as ends rather than as means. This view grounded the mistreatment of animals in institutions rather than blaming misguided individuals. Rather than searching for individual

scientists who inflicted unusual pain on their animal subjects, activists condemned all research using live animals, thereby attacking the heart of biomedical science. Instead of criticizing the occasional circus for its cruelty in training animals, they rejected any use of animals to entertain people as exploitation and humiliation. Here was a new view of the relationship between animals and human institutions, one that often condemned the very essence of those institutions. The appeal of this critique helps explain the transformation of animal protection into a radical animal rights movement.

But a fuller explanation lies in common cultural beliefs and implicit understandings about animals in our society, since the treatment of other species often reflects a culture's moral concerns. Animals were the first subject of painting—on the walls of caves—and the first metaphors in human thought—for example, as symbols of tribes and families. They may have been the first objects to be worshiped, perceived as embodiments of spirits. Animals exhibit enough diversity of behavior and attributes to provide an extensive vocabulary for our own thinking. Throughout recorded history, men and women have found that animals were "good to think with," a rich source of symbols that humans could use to impose order on the world. They are blank slates onto which people have projected their beliefs about the state of nature, about "natural" forms of hierarchy and social organization, about language and rationality, and about moral behavior. Lessons are drawn from the supposed behavior of tortoises and hares, from the social organization of ants and grasshoppers, from the territoriality of lions and wolves.

We also project onto animals the characteristics of humans—sensitivity to pain, emotional bonds such as love and loyalty, the ability to plan and communicate. People have long endowed animals with human characteristics—crafty foxes, greedy pigs, lazy cats. Conversely, they use animals to characterize humans—people chatter like magpies, work like mules, and squirrel things away. We speak of male chauvinist pigs; we complain that Uncle Pete hogs the sports section. We use expressions like rat's nest, rat race, dirty rat, and smelling a rat. The sloth was even unlucky enough to be named after one of the seven deadly sins. But we can also romanticize animals, projecting onto them traits that make them better than people: a goodness, innocence, and purity rarely found in human company. Animals often come to represent the best in human nature, those qualities we cherish and try to protect.

If animals share so many human characteristics, what are the essential differences? The distinction between humans and other animals is the key issue in the growing number of disputes over animal protection. "A life is a life," whether human or nonhuman, is a common refrain in animal rights rhetoric. Ironically, science itself has helped to blur the boundaries between humans and other animals. Evolutionary biology, after all, is controversial among Christian fundamentalists precisely because it violates the long assumed distinction between man and the animal world. While religious movements like creationists struggle to maintain boundaries, believing Man was created in God's image, animal rightists have taken biologists literally, denying moral distinctions between species as the "effluvium of a discredited metaphysics."[3]

For most people, the boundaries between animals and humans are intuitively clear. A human life is simply worth more than a nonhuman life, and while animals deserve some moral consideration, they are not to be exempt from human use. Such distinctions, however, remain matters of belief, not of evidence; they are affected by cultural preferences, personal values, and moral sentiments—traits not entirely open to rational persuasion. Rhetoric that compares animal suffering with the holocaust, that equates speciesism with racism, has emotive power for those who blur the boundaries between humans and other species. For others, these metaphors appear outlandish, threatening, dangerously defying accepted categories. The conflict between animal advocates and animal users is far more than a matter of contrasting tastes or interests. Opposing world views, concepts of identity, ideas of community, are all at stake. The animal rights controversy is about the treatment of animals, but it is also about our definition of ourselves and of a moral society. For this reason, it cannot be easily resolved.

Animal rights is a moral crusade. Its adherents act upon explicit moral beliefs and values to pursue a social order consistent with their principles. Their fervent moral vision crowds out other concerns. Most moral crusades focus on single issues: Some focus on abortion; others on drunken driving; still others on the evils of pornography. Their members—moral missionaries—often insist they have no broader partisan agenda. They are less interested in material benefits for themselves than in correcting perceived injustices. Animals are a perfect cause for such a crusade; seen as innocent victims whose mistreatment demands immediate redress, they are an appealing lightning rod for moral concerns.

The symbolic importance of animals in this crusade underscores the importance of ideas in inspiring social movements, shaping their tactics, and enhancing or limiting their effects. To organize a crusade, movement leaders appeal to the moral sentiments of like-minded citizens, inciting their anger with emotive rhetoric and strategies ranging from colorful public rallies to clandestine break-ins that free animals from laboratories. The language of moral crusades is sometimes shrill, self-righteous, and uncompromising, for bedrock principles are nonnegotiable. In the strident style of Old Testament prophets, scolding and condemning their society, organizers point to evils that surround them and to catastrophes that will befall society in the absence of reform. Extreme and even illegal strategies and tactics are seen as justified in order to stop widespread immoral practices. Their sense of moral urgency encourages believers to ignore laws and conventional political processes, and they organize themselves into groups structured for quick action, not participatory debate. Proselytizing and interventionist in their style, such crusades frequently appear dangerous to those who do not share their judgmental and uncompromising views.

Yet animal protection groups vary widely in their aims and thus in their shrillness. Contrasting goals, tactics, and philosophical positions bring forth different organizations that form a continuum from reformist to radical. However, they tend to cluster into three kinds of groups that we label welfarist, pragmatist, and fundamentalist. In the humane tradition of the ASPCA, animal *welfarists* accept most current uses of animals, but seek to minimize their suffering and pain. They view animals as distinct from humans, but as objects entitled to compassion. Their reformist position, advocated through public education and lobbying for protective legislation, has long enjoyed wide public support and continues to do so. Welfarist groups like the SPCAs and the Humane Society of the United States existed before the animal rights movement appeared, and remain the largest, most powerful organizations.

In the late 1970s, however, more radical groups formed on the fringes of the animal welfare movement, redefining the issue of animal welfare as one of animal rights. Some of these new advocates organized around the well-articulated and widely disseminated utilitarian perspective of philosopher Peter Singer. Because animals could feel pain and pleasure, Singer argued that they deserved moral consideration, and he demanded drastic reduction in their use. The *pragmatist* groups feel that certain species deserve greater consideration than others, and would allow humans to use animals when the benefits deriving from their use outweigh their suffering. They seek to reduce animal use through legal actions, political protest, and negotiation. Henry Spira is a prominent example of a pragmatist.

Some of these new advocates, however, demanded the immediate abolition of all exploitation of animals, on the grounds that animals have inherent, inviolable rights. These more extreme animal rights *fundamentalists* believe that people should never use animals for their own pleasures or interests, regardless of the benefits. Some see even the ownership of pets as a distortion of the animals' natural lives. Insisting that increased understanding

of head injuries does not justify harming baboons, the Animal Liberation Front expresses the fundamentalists' position, as well as their compelling sense of urgency. Although far less numerous than pragmatist or welfarist organizations, these groups set the tone of the new animal rights movement. And they are growing in size and wealth.

These distinctions are not absolute or rigid. Some activists, for example, believe in full animal rights, but pursue their goals with pragmatic strategies. Many shift their language and tactics depending on the issue or political arena. And all are tempted to indulge in fundamentalist rhetoric that simplifies the moral issues and demonizes opponents. But these three labels are useful to highlight important differences and tensions within a movement often described in monolithic terms. For the movement itself is divided over many issues: whether the same attention should be given to helping wild animals and domestic ones, whether insects or reptiles should be championed as fervently as furry mammals, and, especially, whether destructive tactics are acceptable.

Nevertheless, welfarists, pragmatists, and fundamentalists cooperate on specific issues, and their interests as well as rhetoric often merge. Together, they form a remarkably powerful animal protection movement, in which the pragmatists and fundamentalists represent the radical wing—the animal rights crusade. These crusaders would like to challenge Americans to rethink their fundamental beliefs about themselves and their connection to the world around them. They wonder if the boundaries we have drawn between ourselves and other animals are as rigid as we suppose. They would force us to extend the rights we promote for humans to other species. They want nothing short of a moral revolution that would change our food and clothing, our science and health care, our entire relationship to the natural world.

CRITICAL-THINKING QUESTIONS

1. In the previous reading, Jo Freeman maintains that social movements develop when (1) there is

an effective communications network, (2) the communications network is cooptable, (3) a crisis propels like-minded people into action, and (4) people are organized to act. Are these characteristics useful or not in explaining the emergence and success of the animal rights movement?

2. Why do Jasper and Nelkin describe the animal rights movement as a "moral crusade" rather than, for example, a "lunatic fringe" or a terrorist group that vandalizes and destroys scientific research laboratories?

3. Jasper and Nelkin propose a continuum of animal rights organizations that includes welfarists, pragmatists, and fundamentalists. Prepare a short typology of these three groups in terms of their (a) beliefs, (b) major goals, and (c) primary strategies to accomplish their goals. Using your typology, describe what you think are the strengths and weaknesses of each group in developing acceptable public policies that protect animals.

NOTES

1. Quoted in "Animals in Testing. How the CPI Is Handling a Hot Issue," *Chemical Week* 135, 23 (December 5, 1984), 38.

2. Quoted in Richard J. Brenneman, "Animal 'liberator' promises more raids on labs," *Sacramento Bee* (July 2, 1984), B1.

3. James Rachels, *Created from Animals* (New York: Oxford University Press, 1990).

CLASSIC

CONTEMPORARY

CROSS-CULTURAL

78 Abortion Movements in Poland, Great Britain, and the United States

JANET HADLEY

Perhaps one of the best-known feminist slogans during the early 1970s was that "A woman has a right to choose" whether or not to terminate a pregnancy. About 38 percent of the world's population live in countries where abortion has been available on request. Although abortion has been legal in the United States and most of Europe for at least twenty-five years, it remains an explosive issue in many countries and has spawned "for" and "against" social movements and collective behavior. In this reading, Janet Hadley examines some of the controversies and campaigns of abortion rights movements in Poland, the United States, and Great Britain.

In recent years in the United States, in Poland, and in Ireland, too, national politics has at times been convulsed by the issue of abortion. In Germany the historic reunification of East and West almost foundered amid wrangling about conflicting abortion laws. How can abortion, hardly an issue comparable to the great affairs of state, such as the economy or national security, have an impact such as this?

This is an account, first, of how post-Communist Poland found itself in the grip of the abortion debate and secondly how the issue came to be such a seemingly permanent shadow on the political landscape in the United States, in the wake of the Supreme Court's 1973 landmark decision on abortion in the case of *Roe* v. *Wade.* It offers some ideas about why.

Source: From "God's Bullies: Attacks on Abortion," by Janet Hadley, *Feminist Review,* Vol. 48 (Fall 1994), pp. 94–113. Reprinted by permission of the author.

The account focuses on abortion, primarily as a method of birth control, which women have always sought out, legally when they can, illegally when they must. The controversies and campaigns recorded and the ideas offered here concentrate on women's access to affordable, safe and legal abortion—an essential part of women's reproductive freedom in a world where 500 women die every day from the complications of unsafe abortion (World Health Organization, 1993).

The way abortion has at times dominated public debate in both Poland and the United States can hardly be exaggerated, but the contexts are very different. At times, during the 1992 American presidential election campaign, it seemed as if the fate of the United States for the next four years hung solely on the thread of the abortion issue. Economic issues, national security, even political scandals were all pushed into the background. But no one was too surprised to encounter this wild card in the United States' electoral politics.

It had been thus, on and off, for around twenty years, since the 1973 Supreme Court judgement which had sanctioned abortion as a woman's constitutional right.

It was, however, probably a lot harder for anyone to have predicted events in Poland where, for more than four years, well before the forty-year-old Communist regime was finally sloughed off, abortion took centre stage. The renascent right in Poland selected abortion as the first block of the social welfare system for demolition. The battle over it highlights the new relationship between the Roman Catholic Church—once the main element of opposition alongside Solidarity—and the state. As the democratization of Eastern Europe got under way, abortion was one of the first laws to come under fire (Einhorn, 1993).

In some ways the abortion debate in Poland, which of all the former Soviet bloc countries has undergone by far the most draconian reversal of its abortion law, is quite straightforward: The opponents of abortion are solidly Roman Catholic and perceive their efforts as part of the task of rescuing Poland from its years of godlessness. The debate in Poland harks back to the relatively straightforward arguments which took place in Britain at the time of the passing of the Abortion Act in 1967.

In the United States, on the other hand, the issue has been linked to a much more extensive catalogue of perceived "social degeneracy." Opposition to abortion in the United States involves a curious alliance of religious and secular New Right groupings and much of the driving force has been provided, not by the Roman Catholic Church, but by evangelical Christians. . . .

POLAND: NO PLACE TO BE A WOMAN

. . . What we have been witnessing in Poland since 1989, according to one observer, is the "Church's colossal efforts to replace a totalitarian state with a theocracy" (Kissling, 1992). Weekly Masses from Rome are broadcast on Polish TV these days. Scientific conferences open with High Mass, blessings and so on, and military personnel are sent on pilgrimages. Classes in religion (i.e., Roman Catholicism) are mandatory for children in state schools. There is little doubt that the bishops of Poland, who behave more like leaders of a political party than as simple guardians of moral values, have their sights set not only on banning abortion but also divorce, provision of contraception, and other hallmarks of a secular society. One commentator wrote in 1991:

From the very beginning until its unexpected culmination in June [1991—when a draft anti-abortion bill was rejected by parliament in the face of huge pro-choice demonstrations] the Polish controversy on abortion was a classic example of political conflict. Nobody cared any more about subtle moral or political arguments. It was clear that who wins the abortion debate will control the political situation in Poland. (Szawarski, 1991)

The irony is that not only was June 1991 far from being the "culmination," but also that nobody today could be said to have won. (Women, of course, lost.)

The final law, signed by President Lech Walesa in February 1993, was seen by opponents of abortion as a compromise. It is much weaker than they would have liked. The original anti-abortion bill, first published in 1989, promised three years' imprisonment for a woman who induced her own abortion, as well for any doctor caught performing an illegal operation. Under the new law, two years' imprisonment awaits an abortionist, but a woman inducing her own abortion will not face gaol [jail].

The new law allows abortion when a woman's life or health is in danger, after rape or incest, or if there is suspected fetal abnormality. But prenatal testing is only permissible if there is a family history of genetic disorder. There are token provisions urging local authorities to provide contraceptive services.

The Church's Power and Influence

The religious context of the abortion row in Poland goes a long way to explaining how it came to be such a passionate, extreme and dominating issue. Around 95 percent of its 39 million people consider themselves Catholic and there is a very strong family tradition of Catholicism, which during the Communist era greatly strengthened the Church as a focus of national identity and a shelter for opposition. Having a Polish Pope helps too; when John Paul II visited in 1991, he urged his fellow Poles to free themselves from a law permitting abortion, which he called a tragic inheritance of Communism.

Even when the Communist grip seemed at its most unyielding, the Church consistently harried the authorities on issues of sexual control. In a recent survey, conducted since the fall of the Communists, and reported in the *Guardian* (9/14/93), 95 percent of Polish women said they rely on personal experience for their sex education and 73 percent said they had had an unplanned pregnancy.

The only sex-education manual ever produced in Poland had to be withdrawn because of Church protest. Roman Catholic opposition to contraception has been effective—76 percent of the urban population and 87 percent of the rural population use only Church-approved 'natural' methods of fertility control (Mrugala, 1991). (Priests often determine what is sold in local pharmacies.) Poland's 1956 abortion law contained no conscience clause, but the Church's success in pressuring doctors can be judged from the fact that in some state hospitals, staff refusal made it impossible to get an abortion. As early as 1973, Church protests over the rising abortion rate and the behaviour of "callous young women" forced the government to set up a commission to consider whether the law needed amending (Okolski, 1988).

But the pressures on women to have abortions were very strong. Even for those who wanted it, contraception has never been easily available, and was of notoriously poor quality. Abortion—which was free in state hospitals after 1959, and easy to obtain—was therefore the main method of birth control. Women only had to report that they were "in a difficult life situation." "Poland's hard life finds more and more women choosing abortions," reported *The New York Times* in 1983, citing families in some cities waiting eighteen years to obtain a small apartment. Despite the Church's

denunciations, there were an estimated 600,000 abortions a year, compared to just 700,000 live births.

Times may have been hard in 1983, but the economic "shock therapy" of post-Communist Poland has brought unimaginable hardship in its wake. Unemployment is now 2.8 million and will be one-fifth of the workforce in three years' time. The bishops have deplored this, by urging *women* to leave the labour market, to ease unemployment and ensure that men's wages increase. They have made no adverse comment on the virtual shutdown of state-financed child care.

The Bishops, the State, and the Medical Profession

The episcopate first floated the idea of outlawing abortion in 1988, deeming it to be a mortal threat to the "biological substance of the nation." In the spring of 1989 an Unborn Child Protection Bill was published and the Pope hurried to send his congratulations.

In 1990, however, long before the legislative battle had got into its stride, the Ministry of Health took its own initiative, saying that women wanting abortion would now need the permission of three physicians and of a psychologist, whose appointment had been approved by the local bishop, and that an abortion for social reasons must be requested in writing (*The New York Times,* 4/21/92). The psychologist's job is to dissuade women, mainly by putting the frighteners on them. Sterilization and the in-vitro fertilization programme were suspended.

As Poland created its first parliament, abortion became the bellwether for fitness to serve. Anyone supporting abortion rights was traduced as a surreptitious advocate for Communism. Throughout 1990 and 1991 the battle raged, overshadowing the upheavals of the new market economy. Huge demonstrations in favour of abortion took place in Warsaw and women's groups began to get organized to defend abortion rights. Solidarity was split on the issue. Bills were proposed and defeated in dizzying succession. Parish priests threatened to withhold sacraments from anyone who did not sign the petitions against "killing innocent children."

The anti-abortion movement targeted not only abortion but family planning provision, too, blocking the launch of an information campaign in the textile city of Lodz, where there has been an unusually high rate of congenital abnormalities among babies born to women working in the textile factories (Rich, 1991). Their activity was partly financed by pro-life organizations from the United States, such as Human Life International. This evangelical group, fired by a vision of "re-Christianized united Europe stretching from the Atlantic to the Urals," vowed to "flood Eastern Europe" with films, videos (such as *The Silent Scream* which has been shown in Polish schools), fetal models and other propaganda. In 1992, Operation Rescue blockaded a clinic in the Baltic port of Gdynia, with protesters from the United States, Canada and the U.K.

Although one smear in circulation was that "only communists and Jews favor abortion," there is little direct evidence that the anti-abortion campaign was fuelled by a nationalist pro-natalism—a desire to demographically overwhelm Poland's minorities. There was, however, a definite bid to appeal to a repressive notion of proper and traditional Polish "womanhood." The term "emancipation for women" is laden with Communist overtones and has often in reality meant the notorious "double burden" or overloading of women, in Poland and Eastern Europe in general, in which they have been expected to shoulder full-time jobs as well as forty hours a week shopping, cooking, cleaning, laundry, with only the aid of very poor-quality preschool child care and medical care (Jankowska, 1993). Against such a reality, a misty vision of womanhood may have a definite allure.

May 1992 brought another turn of the screw. A new code of medical ethics made it professionally unethical for doctors to perform abortions except in cases of rape or incest or when the woman's life was in danger. Violations would lead to suspension of the doctor's license. The code effectively ended hospital abortions and prenatal testing: Some institutions put up signs, "No Abortions."

The issue continued to rock the government, which twice postponed a final vote on abortion. By the end of 1992, the conflict was extreme enough to threaten the fragile coalition government, an improbable seven-party affair. A million people signed a petition for a referendum. Meanwhile, 61 percent of Poles said they favoured the provisions of the 1956 law.

Turning the Clock Back

Nevertheless, when the government could postpone a vote no longer, a law was finally passed early in 1993. Under the new law, only 3 percent of the abortions previously performed in Poland are now deemed legal. Two years in gaol awaits an illegal abortionist, but there is no punishment for a woman who obtains an illegal operation. Although it is the most restrictive abortion law in Europe, apart from Ireland's, pro-choice campaigners comforted themselves with the rueful thought that things could easily have been much worse.

The legislation satisfies no one. Both sides have vowed to fight on. Even before President Lech Walesa signed the new law, the 1992 doctors' code—a *de facto* ban on abortions in Poland—was having its effect. The Warsaw police morgue has begun receiving bodies of women bearing witness to botched abortions. For the last three years, cases of infanticide have steadily increased.

Deaths will be outnumbered by injuries. Romania, where abortion was illegal until the fall of Ceaușescu in 1989, shows the way. Staff at a clinic for women in Bucharest, set up by Marie Stopes International, found that 80 percent of patients were suffering from past incompetent abortions.

A helpline set up in Warsaw by pro-abortion campaigners is receiving calls from men seeking advice because their wives are refusing to have sex any more. Women are phoning for help, reporting that even in circumstances which comply with the new law, they are being refused operations. In Poland's deep Catholic south, a pregnant Cracow woman, furnished with a police report confirming that she had been raped, was refused help at the hospital (Hoell, 1993).

All the desolately familiar symptoms of outlawed abortion are there: police raids on clinics, small ads appearing in the newspapers: "Gynaecologist: Interventions." The price is $350 to $1,000: The average monthly wage is $200. For professional women "medical tours" can be arranged—to the Ukraine, to Kaliningrad, even to Holland. (But not to the Czech Republic, which in the wake of Poland's new law, moved swiftly to outlaw abortions for foreign visitors.)

Paradoxically, the last few years have seen a burgeoning of women's organizations, formed to defend abortion and women's rights. It is an irony, comments Hanna Jankowska, "when the word 'feminist' sounds in this country like an insult" (1993). But sustaining the momentum of such organizations is uphill work. People are consumed by the effort to cope with the effects of 38 percent inflation.

There are signs that the Church may have overplayed its hand in its attempt to introduce a legislative version of "absolute morality" as part of a plan to create a theocratic Poland. There was strong public support for a referendum on abortion, which the Church opposed, and its popularity has dropped by half since Communism collapsed, according to opinion polls *(Catholic Herald,* 9/9/93). The Irish Church found itself in similar trouble after the referendum on abortion in Ireland in 1992, an event which was much reported in the Polish media.

But it is hard to draw sound parallels with Ireland: The Republic is certainly behind the times, but there are signs that slowly things are creeping forward for women in Ireland. Nothing compares with the crudeness with which the clock hands have been wrenched *back* in Poland.

In September 1993, the political coalition which fostered the anti-abortion legislation suffered a crushing defeat in national elections. The pace of reform was thought to be the main culprit, but the unpopularity of the anti-abortion law was also held to blame. Pro-abortion campaigners are preparing a new bill to reverse the law, scarcely before the ink is dry. In January 1994, Polish doctors amended their medical code, somewhat relaxing the abortion guidelines and increasing scope for prenatal diagnosis of fetal abnormalities.

The bishops and their allies intend to press on towards a theocratic state. They have stated: "We must reject the false and harmful belief—which unfortunately is grounded in social consciousness—that a secular state is perceived as the only and fundamental guarantee of freedom and equality of citizens" (Szawarski, 1991). If they succeed in creating a model Roman Catholic state, it will be women who suffer most directly. That is why no one in Poland, on whichever side of the abortion divide, underestimates the importance of the struggle around abortion as a stalking horse for what may yet come.

It is not possible to yoke together the national experience of abortion politics in Poland with that of the United States, only to offer them as two distinct examples of how abortion seemed at times to be the tail that wagged the dog of national politics. It has been quite remarkable to find abortion ricocheting around the political arena in Poland and other Eastern European countries. But the issue has played a crucial part in the politics of the United States for almost twenty years: in itself an astonishing phenomenon.

USA, 1973—THE SUPREME COURT LIGHTS THE FUSE

Until the historic U.S. Supreme Court judgment of 1973, in the case of *Roe* v. *Wade* (which I shall call plain *Roe*), abortion was not a major issue in the United States. In the late 1960s, when campaigners for abortion reform in California asked people to sign petitions, it took so long for people to think and talk before deciding where they stood that no more than four or five signatures could be gathered in an afternoon's work (Luker, 1984).

But the spark of *Roe* caught dry tinder at once and is still burning. Today, everyone has an opinion on abortion: After thousands of opinion polls, hours of TV debating, radio phone-ins and miles of newsprint, people know with certainty whether they are "pro-choice" or "pro-life."

In the late nineteenth century it was doctors who pressed for anti-abortion legislation in the United States, partly to strengthen the delineation of medicine as a regulated, elite profession. Making abortion illegal, unless performed by a doctor, was an effective way of cutting the ground from under the "quacks." The laws granted doctors alone the discretion to decide when a woman's life was sufficiently endangered to justify the loss of fetal life.

For almost seventy years legal abortion was a matter for medical judgement. Its prevalence and the criteria used varied enormously. Women who could not get legal abortions resorted to illegal practitioners and practices. But in the 1950s and 1960s exclusive medical control over abortion began to crumble.

Briefly, women's lives were changing as they entered the labour market in increasing numbers—for a married woman an unintended pregnancy became much more of a disaster than in the past; secondly, the improvements of medicine and obstetrics made pregnancy and childbirth much safer and made it harder for doctors to cloak a decision to perform an abortion for a wealthy patient behind the excuse that continuing the pregnancy would gravely endanger her health. Doctors' work became much more hospital-based and could be more easily scrutinized and regulated than when they worked in private consulting rooms.

Thirdly, women began to question the right of doctors and lawyers, or anyone, to decide whether or not they should have to continue an unintended pregnancy. Finally, the effects of the Thalidomide cases and the advent of effective contraception all played a part in dragging decisions and policies on abortion into the harsh public light of politics.

Some states began to permit abortion. Between 1967 and 1973, seventeen states rescinded their restrictions on abortion. Thousands of women crossed state boundaries to obtain abortions (Gold, 1990). Abortion was happening, despite its continuing prohibition under federal law.

Several decades of Supreme Court decisions—for instance, acknowledging it was no business of the state (or states) to seek to outlaw the use and purchase of contraceptives—had smoothed the path towards the *Roe* judgment, but nonetheless, when it eventually came, it was quite dramatic. The court said that a woman's right to obtain an abortion, like her right to use contraception without government interference, is constitutionally protected, as part of her fundamental right to privacy. And that because the right to privacy is fundamental (rights under the American constitution are ranked, and *fundamental* trumps every other kind of right) states must show a "compelling interest" before they can intervene.

The court stressed that, of course, the decision to abort must be made together with a doctor. But it devised a sliding scale of maternal/fetal rights, practically sanctioning "abortion on demand" in the first trimester and gradually increasing the amount of protection afforded to the fetus as the weeks of pregnancy progressed.

No Room for Compromise

The significance of the Supreme Court ruling in 1973 was that it turned abortion into a constitutional issue, declaring it a fundamental right of the female citizen, and sweeping away all the various state restrictions. In doing so it called into question the deeply held beliefs of people accustomed to thinking that *theirs* was the majority opinion and set the state on a collision course with an indefatigable group of its citizens. As long as abortion had been purely a medical issue, as it is in Britain (see below), it had been much more difficult to challenge, and far less in the public domain.

The absolute divide between right-to-life/pro-life/anti-choice/anti-abortion people, and the rest is the embryo or fetus. If you believe that the embryo or later the fetus is a person, a human being in the fullest sense, the moral equivalent of a woman, everything else falls into place. The Supreme Court questioned this notion and opened the door to the years of court challenge, endless legislative pressure and single-issue pressure-group politics. For those who believe that abortion is the equivalent of homicide there can hardly be a compromise.

The impact of the *Roe* judgement was enormous. Overnight literally, the opposition mobilized.[1] Its attack has had two aims: to upset and overturn the judicial applecart and at the same time to erect as many obstacles as possible between a woman and a legal abortion. It's been a busy twenty years: *Roe* has been harried almost to extinction by state regulations, such as imposed waiting periods, demands for "informed consent," such as making the woman look at images of fetal development—at all stages, no matter how early her own pregnancy. As pro-choice campaigner Lawrence Lader said, after *Roe,* "We thought we had won. We were wrong" (*Family Planning World,* Jan/Feb, 1992).

At first, state attempts to regulate abortion after *Roe* received a cool response in the Supreme Court, but as the new right has gained power and judges appointed to the court became more conservative, so the judgements have hardened against abortion rights.

Wide-Ranging Success for Abortion's Opponents

The cultural and political climate today is of course very different from that surrounding *Roe* in 1973. On the day of the Supreme Court's ruling on *Roe,* newspapers reported an agreement which might bring an end to the war in Vietnam and carried obituaries of former President Lyndon B. Johnson, whose presidency was marked domestically by the civil rights movement, Black Power and the movement against the war in Vietnam. This is not the place to rehearse the cultural "backlash" of the years since then except to highlight how wide-ranging it has been.

Susan Faludi, for instance, recounts the fate of a script for the TV show *Cagney and Lacey.* In "Choices," as the early 1980s' episode was to be called, Cagney—the single woman in the feisty female cop duo—became pregnant. CBS

programming executives went beserk at the mere idea of abortion (even as an option to be rejected). They demanded numerous rewrites until in the final version, Cagney only mistakenly thinks she is pregnant. "Lacey . . . tells her that if she had been pregnant she should have got married. Abortion is never offered as a choice" (Faludi, 1992:186).

The anti-abortion lobby drew comfort not only from *Cagney and Lacey* but also from the White House. As the violence against clinics increased in 1984 after Ronald Reagan's election to a second term as president, he refused to condemn the actions and their perpetrators (Blanchard & Prewitt, 1993).[2]

Opinion polls show that Americans' attitude to abortion was and generally remains "permit but discourage." It was not very hard to convert such ambivalence into support for restrictions on government funding and so on. The most significant curtailment of rights for low-income women was the Hyde Amendment of 1979 which denied Medicaid funding for abortion, except where a woman's life is in danger. There have also been severe and wide-ranging restrictions on the use of public facilities for abortion: It is illegal, for instance, to perform a private abortion in a private building standing on publicly owned land. By 1979 no federal funds could be used to provide abortion or abortion-related services (Petchesky, 1984).

Today, only half the United States' medical schools even offer the option of training in abortion procedures, and fewer and fewer young doctors are willing to perform abortions. Many gynaecologists still performing abortions are reaching retirement, and in a 1985 study, two-thirds of the gynaecologists in the United States stated that they would not terminate pregnancy. Who would choose to conduct their professional working life in a bullet-proof vest, with an armed guard at the clinic door? In 1988, 83 percent of all United States counties lacked any facilities for abortion, and those counties contain 31 percent of U.S. women aged between fifteen and forty-four (Alan Guttmacher Institute, 1993).

A shadowy world of unlicensed, unregulated abortion facilities in private doctors' offices is beginning to emerge. There are estimated to be several dozen in New York City alone, and a doctor there was recently prosecuted for a botched abortion on a twenty-one-year-old immigrant woman, who subsequently gave birth to a severely mutilated infant (*Family Planning World,* May/June, 1993).

And yet, despite all the legislative obstacles and the physical harassment, the anti-abortion movement has made no dent in the number of abortions taking place in the United States. The overall figure has hovered steadily around 1.6 million a year.

Who Opposes Abortion Rights?

The intimidation of anti-abortion activists, such as Operation Rescue, or the Lambs of Christ, and the violence and terrorism against abortion clinics is what immediately comes to mind when thinking about abortion's opponents, but it is not the only face of the opposition.

After the *Roe* judgment, the Catholic Church was the first into action, with plangent denunciation and millions of dollars poured into new anti-abortion organizations. But as the New Right in the Republican party set out deliberately to woo the anti-abortion voters, as part of its efforts to shift the party itself to the right, the anti-abortion alliance became a curious blend—from Catholics to born-again Christian evangelicals, to more secular "New Right" types. It was ultimately to prove a volatile coalition.

Abortion has been and still is the kernel of a protracted campaign against the social trends of the second half of the twentieth century, and for a reinstatement of "traditional family values." The Reagan presidency boosted the legitimacy, power and influence of "God's bullies" as they have been aptly called. Although the specific goal of the anti-abortionists is to outlaw abortions, it is important to see this in a wider context of conservatism, attacks on welfare and so on.

The movement has two faces—first, the lobbyists and court challengers, as well as the image-makers, whose ideological offensive has sought to control the public perception of abortion and the women who seek it (Petchesky, 1984). In 1990 alone there were 465 abortion related bills presented to state legislatures (McKeegan, 1992). The anti-abortion lobby has used its muscle in the ballot box with considerable effect. Single-issue voting can tip the scales when results are close and election turnouts are low. Packing state legislatures and other elected bodies has been a systematic strategy and for twenty years abortion has wracked the United States, from school boards to Congress.

Secondly, there is the face of direct action, some of it peaceful, but nevertheless extremely intimidating, some of it violent and explicitly women-hating. In 1991 in Wichita, south Kansas, there were more than 2,600 arrests as 30,000 anti-abortion protesters blockaded an abortion clinic. In the last fifteen years around a hundred clinics have been bombed or set on fire. Others have had medical equipment wrecked. Clinic staff and their families have been harassed; doctors have been shot at; in March 1993, one was even killed. Pregnant women arriving at abortion clinics have had to run a gauntlet of screaming demonstrators, some hurling plastic fetal models, some videotaping their faces and noting the numbers on their car license plates for subsequent tracing and personal harassment.

A study of men convicted of anti-abortion violence concluded that they are "clearly acting out of a desire to maintain the dependent status of women." Many also favour policies such as capital and corporal punishment (Blanchard & Prewitt, 1993). Somewhat in a grey area of legality lie the fake abortion clinics which have been set up and are listed in the Yellow Pages, which harangue women who turn up hoping to arrange an abortion, and force them to look at often gruesome pictures of fetuses. . . .

WHY HAS BRITAIN'S ABORTION DEBATE BEEN DIFFERENT?

It seems worth briefly comparing the struggle in the United States with that in Britain, whose political process has never been gripped by the throat as it has in the United States. Pro-choice Republican Senator Robert Packwood explained what the attentions of a single-minded group such as the U.S. anti-abortion lobby mean to his daily political life:

[The pro-lifers] are a frightening force. They are people who are with you 99 percent of the time, but if you vote against them on this issue it doesn't matter what else you stand for. (Tribe, 1992)

That's hard to imagine in Britain. Of course, there have been times when abortion has been a hot issue in the U.K., swelling MPs' mailbags and prompting heated exchanges on *Question Time,* but it has at no time been such dynamite, compelling British MPs to refer their every political step to its impact on those of their supporters who oppose abortion. Part of the reason is that Britain is relatively indifferent to religion and has no comparably powerful, organized fundamentalist or Roman Catholic population. Also, laws made in the United States Supreme Court positively invite legal challenge and counter-challenge. Laws made by Parliament are more resilient in general.

What's more, part of the reason is in the abortion law itself. It is for doctors, says Britain's 1967 Abortion Act—two doctors—to decide whether a woman needs an abortion, under the terms specified by the law. The rights of women do not remotely enter into it. Many campaigners who have defended the provisions of the 1967 Act, from no less than sixteen parliamentary attempts to curtail its scope, believe that it is the Act's reliance on doctors that has allowed it to escape relatively unscathed after twenty-five years.

When opponents of abortion in Britain have attacked the Act, its defenders have quite legitimately and cogently been able to point out that it is not *women* who make the final decision, but (respectable) professionals. (Funding cuts in the National Health Service and excessive Department of Health regulations have more stealthily debilitated abortion provision in Britain—that is another story.) Although the inherent paternalism in the framing of the Act is not only demeaning but

has also led to unfair geographical differences in women's access to a sympathetic, prompt abortion service, the pragmatic, defensive value of investing the responsibility in the medical profession is worth noting.

CRITICAL-THINKING QUESTIONS

1. The United States has witnessed numerous murders of physicians who provide abortion services and bombings of Planned Parenthood clinics. Why, in contrast, has Poland not experienced such violent attacks on the medical profession and on women who seek abortions?

2. Why, in contrast to the United States and Poland, has there been little debate about abortion in Great Britain?

3. Opponents of abortion in Europe and the United States often describe abortion as a breakdown of "social values" and the "traditional family." In contrast, proponents of abortion emphasize a woman's reproductive rights. According to Hadley, how do politics, religion, and economics ultimately shape policy and many women's destiny in abortion debates?

NOTES

1. Kristin Luker (Luker, 1984) describes how would-be activists phoned around frantically in the days after the court decision, trying to find an organization to join. Many of them—women, married, housewives with small children, had never joined anything before—not even the school parent-teacher association.

2. Ronald Reagan not only refused to condemn the violence, in 1984 he wrote a bizarre call-to-arms against abortion, with help from Malcolm Muggeridge *(Abortion and the Conscience of the Nation.* Nashville: Thomas Nelson, 1984).

REFERENCES

ALAN GUTTMACHER INSTITUTE. 1993. *Abortion in the United States: Facts in brief.* New York.

BLANCHARD, D., and T. J. PREWITT. 1993. *Religious violence and abortion.* University Press of Florida.

EINHORN, B. 1993. Polish backlash. *Everywoman,* April.

FALUDI, S. 1992. *Backlash.* London: Vintage.

GOLD, R. B. 1990. *Abortion and women's health: The turning point for America.* New York: Alan Guttmacher Institute.

HOELL, S. 1993. Strict new law drives abortion underground in Poland. *Reuters,* 14 December.

JANKOWSKA, H. 1993. The reproductive rights campaign in Poland. *Women's Studies International Forum,* 16, 3: 291–96.

KISSLING, F. 1992. The Church's heavy hand in Poland. *Planned Parenthood in Europe,* 21, 2 (May): 18–19.

LUKER, K. 1984. *Abortion and the politics of motherhood.* Berkeley: University of California Press.

MCKEEGAN, M. 1992. *Mutiny in the ranks of the right.* New York: The Free Press, Maxwell Macmillan International.

MRUGALA, G. 1991. Polish family planning in crisis: The Roman Catholic influence. *Planned Parenthood in Europe,* 20, 2, (September): 4–5.

OKOLSKI, M. 1988. "Poland" in Sachdev, P., *International handbook on abortion.* New York: Greenwood Press.

PETCHESKY, R. 1984. *Abortion and woman's choice.* New York, Longman.

RICH, VERA. 1991. Poland: Abortion and contraception. *Lancet,* 338, 875, (13 July): 108–9.

SZAWARSKI, Z. 1991. Abortion in Poland. *British Journal of Obstetrics and Gynaecology,* 98 (December): 1202–4.

TRIBE, L. 1992. *Abortion: The clash of absolutes.* New York, Norton.

WORLD HEALTH ORGANIZATION. 1993. *Progress in human reproductive research,* No. 25. Geneva.

CLASSIC

CONTEMPORARY

CROSS-CULTURAL

79 Anomy and Modern Life

EMILE DURKHEIM

In this excerpt from his classic study of suicide, Emile Durkheim asserts that human aspiration, which is not bounded by nature as in other creatures, must be framed by limits imposed by society. Modern societies, however, have lost some of their moral power over the individual. The consequence is a societal condition of anomy (or anomie), which people experience as a lack of moral regulation. In the extreme, anomy prompts people to suicide; more generally, an anomic society contains people with weak and vacillating moral values who have difficulty reining in their own ambitions and desires.

No living being can be happy or even exist unless his needs are sufficiently proportioned to his means. In other words, if his needs require more than can be granted, or even merely something of a different sort, they will be under continual friction and can only function painfully. . . .

In the animal, at least in a normal condition, this equilibrium is established with automatic spontaneity because the animal depends on purely material conditions. All the organism needs is that the supplies of substance and

Source: Reprinted and abridged with the permission of The Free Press, a Division of Simon & Schuster, from *Suicide* by Emile Durkheim, translated by John A. Spaulding and George Simpson. Edited by George Simpson. Copyright © 1951; copyright renewed 1979 by The Free Press.

Edvard Munch, *The Scream,* Oslo, National Gallery, Scala/Art Resource, NY. © 2007 The Munch Museum/The Munch-Ellingsen Group/Artists Rights Society (ARS), New York.

energy constantly employed in the vital process should be periodically renewed by equivalent quantities; that replacement be equivalent to use. When the void created by existence in its own resources is filled, the animal, satisfied, asks nothing further. Its power of reflection is not sufficiently developed to imagine other ends than those implicit in its physical nature. . . .

This is not the case with man, because most of his needs are not dependent on his body or not to the same degree. . . . But how determine the quantity of well-being, comfort or luxury legitimately to be craved by a human being? Nothing appears in man's organic nor in his psychological constitution which sets a limit to such tendencies. The functioning of individual life does not require them to cease at one point rather than at another; the proof being that they have constantly increased since the beginnings of history, receiving more and more complete satisfaction, yet with no weakening of average health. . . . It is not human nature which can assign the variable limits necessary to our needs. They are thus unlimited so far as they depend on the individual alone. Irrespective of any external regulatory force, our capacity for feeling is in itself an insatiable and bottomless abyss.

But if nothing external can restrain this capacity, it can only be a source of torment to itself. Unlimited desires are insatiable by definition and insatiability is rightly considered a sign of morbidity. Being unlimited, they constantly and infinitely surpass the means at their command; they cannot be quenched. Inextinguishable thirst is constantly renewed torture. It has been claimed, indeed, that human activity naturally aspires beyond assignable limits and sets itself unattainable goals. But how can such an undetermined state be any more reconciled with the conditions of mental life than with the demands of physical life? All man's pleasure in acting, moving and exerting himself implies the sense that his efforts are not in vain and that by walking he has advanced. However, one does not advance when one walks toward no goal, or—which is the same thing—when his goal is infinity. Since the distance between us and it is always the same, whatever road we take, we might as well have made the motions without progress from the spot. Even our glances behind and our feeling of pride at the distance covered can cause only deceptive satisfaction, since the remaining distance is not proportionately reduced. To pursue a goal which is by definition unattainable is to condemn oneself to a state of perpetual unhappiness. Of course, man may hope contrary to all reason, and hope has its pleasures even when unreasonable. It may sustain him for a time; but it cannot survive the repeated disappointments of experience indefinitely. What more can the future offer him than the past, since he can never reach a tenable condition nor even approach the glimpsed ideal? Thus, the more one has, the more one wants, since satisfactions received only stimulate instead of filling needs. . . .

To achieve any other result, the passions first must be limited. Only then can they be harmonized with the faculties and satisfied. But since the individual has no way of limiting them, this must be done by some force exterior to him. A regulative force must play the same role for moral needs which the organism plays for physical needs. This means that the force can only be moral. The awakening of conscience interrupted the state of equilibrium of the animal's dormant existence; only conscience, therefore, can furnish the means to re-establish it. Physical restraint would be ineffective; hearts cannot be touched by physio-chemical forces. So far as the appetites are not automatically restrained by physiological mechanisms, they can be halted only by a limit that they recognize as just. Men would never consent to restrict their desires if they felt justified in passing the assigned limit. But, for reasons given above, they cannot assign themselves this law of justice. So they must receive it from an authority which they respect, to which they yield spontaneously. Either directly and as a whole, or through the agency of one of its organs, society alone can play this moderating role; for it is the only moral power superior to the individual, the authority of which he accepts. It alone has the power necessary to stipulate law and to set the point beyond which the passions must not go. . . .

. . . Man's characteristic privilege is that the bond he accepts is not physical but moral; that is, social. He is governed not by a material environment brutally imposed on him, but by a conscience superior to his own, the superiority of which he feels. Because the greater, better part of his existence transcends the body, he escapes the body's yoke, but is subject to that of society.

But when society is disturbed by some painful crisis or by beneficent but abrupt transitions, it is momentarily incapable of exercising this influence; thence come the sudden rises in the curve of suicides which we have pointed out above.

In the case of economic disasters, indeed, something like a declassification occurs which suddenly casts certain individuals into a lower state than their previous one. Then they must reduce their requirements, restrain their needs, learn greater self-control. All the advantages of social influence are lost so far as they are concerned; their moral education has to be recommenced. But society cannot adjust them instantaneously to this new life and teach them to practice the increased self-repression to which they are unaccustomed. So they are not adjusted to the condition forced on them, and its very prospect is intolerable; hence the suffering which detaches them from a reduced existence even before they have made trial of it.

It is the same if the source of the crisis is an abrupt growth of power and wealth. Then, truly, as the conditions of life are changed, the standard according to which needs were regulated can no longer remain the same; for it varies with social resources, since it largely determines the share of each class of producers. The scale is upset; but a new scale cannot be immediately improvised. Time is required for the public conscience to reclassify men and things. So long as the social forces thus freed have not regained equilibrium, their respective values are unknown and so all regulation is lacking for a time. The limits are unknown between the possible and the impossible, what is just and what is unjust, legitimate claims and hopes and those which are immoderate. Consequently, there is no restraint upon aspiration. . . . Appetites, not being controlled by a public opinion become disoriented, no longer recognize the limits proper to them. . . . With increased prosperity desires increase. At the very moment when traditional rules have lost their authority, the richer prize offered these appetites stimulates them and makes them more exigent and impatient of control. The state of de-regulation or anomy is thus further heightened by passions being less disciplined, precisely when they need more disciplining. . . .

This explanation is confirmed by the remarkable immunity of poor countries. Poverty protects against suicide because it is a restraint in itself.

No matter how one acts, desires have to depend upon resources to some extent; actual possessions are partly the criterion of those aspired to. So the less one has the less he is tempted to extend the range of his needs indefinitely. Lack of power, compelling moderation, accustoms men to it, while nothing excites envy if no one has superfluity. Wealth, on the other hand, by the power it bestows, deceives us into believing that we depend on ourselves only. Reducing the resistance we encounter from objects, it suggests the possibility of unlimited success against them. The less limited one feels, the more intolerable all limitation appears. Not without reason, therefore, have so many religions dwelt on the advantages and moral value of poverty. It is actually the best school for teaching self-restraint. Forcing us to constant self-discipline, it prepares us to accept collective discipline with equanimity, while wealth, exalting the individual, may always arouse the spirit of rebellion which is the very source of immorality. This, of course, is no reason why humanity should not improve its material condition. But though the moral danger involved in every growth of prosperity is not irremediable, it should not be forgotten.

If anomy never appeared except, as in the above instances, in intermittent spurts and acute crisis, it might cause the social suicide-rate to vary from time to time, but it would not be a regular, constant factor. In one sphere of social life, however—the sphere of trade and industry—it is actually in a chronic state.

For a whole century, economic progress has mainly consisted in freeing industrial relations from all regulation. Until very recently, it was the function of a whole system of moral forces to exert this discipline. First, the influence of religion was felt alike by workers and masters, the poor and the rich. It consoled the former and taught them contentment with their lot by informing them of the providential nature of the social order, that the share of each class was assigned by God himself, and by holding out the hope for just compensation in a world to come in return for the inequalities of this world. It governed the latter, recalling that worldly interests are not man's entire lot, that they must be subordinate to other and higher interests, and that they should therefore not be pursued without rule or measure. Temporal power, in turn, restrained the scope of economic functions by its supremacy over them and by the relatively subordinate role it assigned them. Finally, within the business world proper, the occupational groups by regulating salaries, the price of products and production itself, indirectly fixed the average level of income on which needs are partially based by the very force of circumstances. However, we do not mean to propose this organization as a model. Clearly it would be inadequate to existing societies without great changes. What we stress is its existence, the fact of its useful influence, and that nothing today has come to take its place.

Actually, religion has lost most of its power. And government, instead of regulating economic life, has become its tool and servant. The most opposite schools, orthodox economists and extreme socialists, unite to reduce government to the role of a more or less passive intermediary among the various social functions. The former wish to make it simply the guardian of individual contracts; the latter leave it the task of doing the collective bookkeeping, that is, of recording the demands of consumers, transmitting them to producers, inventorying the total revenue and distributing it according to a fixed formula. But both refuse it any power to subordinate other social organs to itself and to make them converge toward one dominant aim. On both sides nations are declared to have the single or chief purpose of achieving industrial prosperity; such is the implication of the dogma of economic materialism, the basis of both apparently opposed systems. And as these theories merely express the state of opinion, industry, instead of being still regarded as a means to an end transcending itself, has become the supreme end of individuals and societies alike. Thereupon the appetites thus excited have become freed of any limiting authority. By sanctifying them, so to speak, this apotheosis of well-being has placed them above all human law.

Their restraint seems like a sort of sacrilege. For this reason, even the purely utilitarian regulation of them exercised by the industrial world itself through the medium of occupational groups has been unable to persist. Ultimately, this liberation of desires has been made worse by the very development of industry and the almost infinite extension of the market. So long as the producer could gain his profits only in his immediate neighborhood, the restricted amount of possible gain could not much overexcite ambition. Now that he may assume to have almost the entire world as his customer, how could passions accept their former confinement in the face of such limitless prospects?

Such is the source of the excitement predominating in this part of society, and which has thence extended to the other parts. There the state of crisis and anomy is constant and, so to speak, normal. From top to bottom of the ladder, greed is aroused without knowing where to find ultimate foothold. Nothing can calm it, since its goal is far beyond all it can attain. Reality seems valueless by comparison with the dreams of fevered imaginations; reality is therefore abandoned, but so too is possibility abandoned when it in turn becomes reality. A thirst arises for novelties, unfamiliar pleasures, nameless sensations, all of which lose their savor once known. Henceforth one has no strength to endure the least reverse. The whole fever subsides and the sterility of all the tumult is apparent, and it is seen that all these new sensations in their infinite quantity cannot form a solid foundation of happiness to support one during days of trial. The wise man, knowing how to enjoy achieved results without having constantly to replace them with others, finds in them an attachment to life in the hour of difficulty. But the man who has always pinned all his hopes on the future and lived with his eyes fixed upon it, has nothing in the past as a comfort against the present's afflictions, for the past was nothing to him but a series of hastily experienced stages. What blinded him to himself was his expectation always to find further on the happiness he had so far missed. Now he is stopped in his tracks; from now on nothing remains behind or ahead of him to fix his gaze upon. Weariness alone, moreover, is enough to bring disillusionment, for he cannot in the end escape the futility of an endless pursuit.

We may even wonder if this moral state is not principally what makes economic catastrophes of our day so fertile in suicides. In societies where a man is subjected to a healthy discipline, he submits more readily to the blows of chance. The necessary effort for sustaining a little more discomfort costs him relatively little, since he is used to discomfort and constraint. But when every constraint is hateful in itself, how can closer constraint not seem intolerable? There is no tendency to resignation in the feverish impatience of men's lives. When there is no other aim but to outstrip constantly the point arrived at, how painful to be thrown back! Now this very lack of organization characterizing our economic condition throws the door wide to every sort of adventure. Since imagination is hungry for novelty, and ungoverned, it gropes at random. Setbacks necessarily increase with risks and thus crises multiply, just when they are becoming more destructive.

Yet these dispositions are so inbred that society has grown to accept them and is accustomed to think them normal. It is everlastingly repeated that it is man's nature to be eternally dissatisfied, constantly to advance, without relief or rest, toward an indefinite goal. The longing for infinity is daily represented as a mark of moral distinction, whereas it can only appear within unregulated consciences which elevate to a rule the lack of rule from which they suffer. The doctrine of the most ruthless and swift progress has become an article of faith. But other theories appear parallel with those praising the advantages of instability, which, generalizing the situation that gives them birth, declare life evil, claim that it is richer in grief than in pleasure and that it attracts men only by false claims. Since this disorder is greatest in the economic world, it has most victims there.

Industrial and commercial functions are really among the occupations which furnish the greatest number of suicides. . . . Almost on a level with the liberal professions, they sometimes surpass them; they are especially more afflicted than agriculture, where the old regulative forces still make their appearance felt most and where the fever of business has least penetrated. Here is best recalled what was once the general constitution of the economic order. And the divergence would be yet greater if, among the suicides of industry, employers were distinguished from workmen, for the former are probably most stricken by the state of anomy. The enormous rate of those with independent means (720 per million) sufficiently shows that the possessors of most comfort suffer most. Everything that enforces subordination attenuates the effects of this state. At least the horizon of the lower classes is limited by those above them, and for this same reason their desires are more modest. Those who have only empty space above them are almost inevitably lost in it, if no force restrains them.

CRITICAL-THINKING QUESTIONS

1. How do most creatures restrain their desires? How are human beings distinctive in this way?

2. Why does modern society afford to individuals less moral regulation? Why is this especially true of people (such as rock stars) who experience sudden fame and fortune?

3. How would Durkheim explain the relatively high suicide rate among rock stars and other celebrities?

CLASSIC

CONTEMPORARY

CROSS-CULTURAL

80 The Disenchantment of Modern Life

MAX WEBER

In this excerpt from a speech, "Science as a Vocation," delivered at Munich University in 1918, Weber claims that the rise of science has changed our way of thinking about the world. Where, in the past, humans confronted a world of mystical forces beyond our comprehension, now we assume that all things yield to human comprehension. Thus, Weber concludes, the world has become "disenchanted." Notice, however, that something is lost in the process for, unlike the churches of the past, science can provide no answer to questions of ultimate meaning in life.

Scientific progress is a fraction, the most important fraction, of the process of intellectualization which we have been undergoing for thousands of years and which nowadays is usually judged in such an extremely negative way. Let us first clarify what this intellectualist rationalization, created by science and by scientifically oriented technology, means practically.

Does it mean that we, today, for instance, everyone sitting in this hall, have a greater knowledge of the conditions of life under which we exist than has an American Indian or a Hottentot? Hardly. Unless he is a physicist, one who rides on the streetcar has no idea how the car happened to get into motion. And he does not need to know. He is satisfied that he may "count" on the behavior of the streetcar,

Source: Excerpts from *From Max Weber: Essays in Sociology* by Max Weber, edited by H. H. Gerth & C. Wright Mills, translated by H. H. Gerth & C. Wright Mills. Translation copyright © 1946, 1958 by H. H. Gerth and C. Wright Mills. Used by permission of Oxford University Press.

and he orients his conduct according to this expectation; but he knows nothing about what it takes to produce such a car so that it can move. The savage knows incomparably more about his tools. When we spend money today I bet that even if there are colleagues of political economy here in the hall, almost every one of them will hold a different answer in readiness to the question: How does it happen that one can buy something for money—sometimes more and sometimes less? The savage knows what he does in order to get his daily food and which institutions serve him in this pursuit. The increasing intellectualization and rationalization do *not,* therefore, indicate an increased and general knowledge of the conditions under which one lives.

It means something else, namely, the knowledge or belief that if one but wished one *could* learn it at any time. Hence, it means that principally there are no mysterious incalculable forces that come into play, but rather that one can, in principle, master all things by calculation. This means that the world is disenchanted. One need no longer have recourse to magical means in order to master or implore the spirits, as did the savage, for whom such mysterious powers existed. Technical means and calculations perform the service. This above all is what intellectualization means. . . .

Science today is a "vocation" organized in special disciplines in the service of self-clarification and knowledge of interrelated facts. It is not the gift of grace of seers and prophets dispensing sacred values and revelations, nor does it partake of the contemplation of sages and philosophers about the meaning of the universe. This, to be sure, is the inescapable condition of our historical situation. We cannot evade it so long as we remain true to ourselves. And if Tolstoi's question recurs to you: As science does not, who is to answer the question: "What shall we do, and, how shall we arrange our lives?" or, in the words used here tonight: "Which of the warring gods should we serve? Or should we serve perhaps an entirely different god, and who is he?" then one can say that only a prophet or a savior can give the answers. . . .

To the person who cannot bear the fate of the times like a man, one must say: May he rather return silently, without the usual publicity build-up of renegades, but simply and plainly. The arms of the old churches are opened widely and compassionately for him. After all, they do not make it hard for him. One way or another he has to bring his "intellectual sacrifice"—that is inevitable. If he can really do it, we shall not rebuke him. For such an intellectual sacrifice in favor of an unconditional religious devotion is ethically quite a different matter than the evasion of the plain duty of intellectual integrity, which sets in if one lacks the courage to clarify one's own ultimate standpoint and rather facilitates this duty by feeble relative judgments. In my eyes, such religious return stands higher than the academic prophecy, which does not clearly realize that in the lecture-rooms of the university no other virtue holds but plain intellectual integrity: Integrity, however, compels us to state that for the many who today tarry for new prophets and saviors, the situation is the same as resounds in the beautiful Edomite watchman's song of the period of exile that has been included among Isaiah's oracles:

He calleth to me out of Seir, Watchman, what of the night? The watchman said, The morning cometh, and also the night: if ye will enquire, enquire ye: return, come.

The people to whom this was said has enquired and tarried for more than two millennia, and we are shaken when we realize its fate. From this we want to draw the lesson that nothing is gained by yearning and tarrying alone, and we shall act differently. We shall set to work and meet the "demands of the day," in human relations as well as in our vocation. This, however, is plain and simple, if each finds and obeys the demon who holds the fibers of his very life.

CRITICAL-THINKING QUESTIONS

1. In what sense do members of a traditional society know more about their world than we do? In what sense do we know more?

2. What is "Tolstoi's question"? Why can science not answer it?

3. What does Weber see as the great burden of living in a modern society? In other words, what comforts of the past are less available to modern people?

CLASSIC

CONTEMPORARY

CROSS-CULTURAL

81 The American Paradox: Spiritual Hunger in an Age of Plenty

DAVID G. MYERS

Has life in the United States improved over the course of recent decades? According to David Myers, we live in the best of times because there has never been more material affluence. Yet we also live in the worst of times because many indicators of social health— including the rates of divorce, teen suicide, and violent crime—rose dramatically after 1960.

It was the best of times, it was the worst of times, it was the age of wisdom, it was the age of foolishness, it was the epoch of belief, it was the epoch of incredulity, it was the season of Light, it was the season of Darkness, it was the spring of hope, it was the winter of despair, we had everything before us, we had nothing before us, we were all going direct to Heaven, we were all going direct the other way.

—CHARLES DICKENS, *A Tale of Two Cities*

We Americans embody a paradox. We read and hear it all around us. There are those who rightly claim, "We've never had it so good. Things are going *great* in this country!" And they are right. But then there are those who wring their hands and just as rightly worry that our civilization could collapse on its decaying moral infrastructure. The best of times, the worst of times. Wisdom, foolishness. Light, darkness. Hope, despair. Dickens' words fit.

What are we to make of this seeming paradox? How can this be both the best and worst of times? And where do we go from here?

Source: "The Best of Times, the Worst of Times," from *The American Paradox: Spiritual Hunger in an Age of Plenty,* by David G. Myers. Copyright © 2001 by Yale University Press.

IT IS THE BEST OF TIMES

We are fortunate to be living when we do. Moments ago, I made a cup of tea in a microwave oven, sat down in a comfortable ergonomic office chair in my climate-controlled office, turned on my personal computer, and answered electronic mail from friends in Hong Kong and Scotland. Planning for tomorrow's trip, I check the Seattle weather forecast via the Web, then leap to a University of California survey archive to glean information for this [reading]. Gazing through my double-glazed window, I look across a landscaped courtyard to a state-of-the-art library that feeds to my desktop screen information hidden among millions of published articles. What a different world from the one I was born into barely half a century ago—a world without broadcast television, fax machines, computers, jets, or cell phones. . . .

Ethnic strife and hate crimes still haunt humanity, but in our part of the world bigotry is more gauche and diversity more accepted than ever before. The environment is under assault, but we

517

have awakened to the perils of deforestation, ozone depletion, and global warming and are taking steps to contain the damage. (We middle-aged adults drive cars that get twice the mileage and produce a twentieth the pollution of our first cars.) Our economy has produced a growing underclass. Yet our average disposable income in constant dollars is more than double that of the mid-1950s. This enables our having, among the other accouterments of our unprecedented national wealth, twice as many cars per person today as then and our eating out two and a half times as often.

More good news is bursting from all around:

- Although population has doubled since World War II, food production has tripled and food is cheaper than ever before.
- Welfare rolls are shrinking as joblessness reaches a quarter-century low.
- Inflation—the "cruelest tax"—is at a thirty-year low, interest rates have moderated, the dollar rides strong, and the stock market has touched undreamed-of heights.
- The prices of cars, air travel, gasoline, and hamburgers are at record real-dollar lows. The half gallon of milk that cost the average American thirty-nine minutes of work in 1919 now requires only seven minutes.
- The national budget, faster than anyone dared expect, has a substantial *surplus.*
- Since the early 1990s, the AIDS death rate has plummeted.
- Over the past half century, performance on intelligence tests has been rising, and race and class differences have lessened somewhat.
- Heavy drinking rates, hard liquor consumption, and drunken driving fatalities are declining.
- New drugs are shrinking our tumors and enlarging our sexual potency.

And would any of us really wish to have braved the family life of a century ago? Without indoor plumbing? With less electricity generated each year than we now consume in a day? When trivial infections might take a life and when people feared the two leading causes of death—tuberculosis and pneumonia? (From 1900 to the present, life expectancy has risen from forty-seven to seventy-six years.)

In 1999, Joyce and Paul Bowler—a couple with a keen interest in past ways of life—were selected from among 450 applicants to Britain's Channel 4 network to spend three months with four of their children living the middle-class life of 1900 (which at the time must have seemed like a cuppa tea compared to working-class life). After just a week of rising at 5:30 each morning, preparing food like the Victorians, wearing corsets, shampooing with a mixture of egg, lemon, borax, and camphor, and playing parlor games by gaslight at night, they were "close to calling it quits." They endured. But lacking a surrounding community of other "Victorian" families, the realities of life in the early 1900s lacked the romantic appeal of *Upstairs Downstairs.*

In *The Way We Never Were: American Families and the Nostalgia Trap,* Stephanie Coontz reminds us of the way families *really* were.

Children were exploited. In Pennsylvania mines at the turn of the twentieth century, 120,000 children were at work, most of whom started laboring by age eleven. Children were one-fourth of the workers in southern textile mills. Seven-year-olds sometimes worked twelve-hour shifts before falling asleep on the job and being carried to bed unwashed.

Families were often broken—by death. In colonial times, mortality reduced the average length of marriage to a dozen years. Four in ten children lost a parent by age twenty-one. As late as 1940, one in ten children did not live with either parent, more than double today's one in twenty-five. In 1850, when only 2 percent of the population lived past sixty-five and many people were migrating, few children had ties with their grandparents. Today, "for the first time in history," notes sociologist Arlene Skolnick, "the average couple has more parents living than it has children. It is also the first era when most of the parent–child relationship takes place after the child becomes an adult." Before 1900, only four in ten women married, raised children, and enjoyed the empty nest with their spouse—because most women either died before marriage, never married, died before children were born or grown, or were widowed before age fifty.

And consider the poems unwritten, the music never composed, the philosophy never completed, because Keats died at twenty-five, Mozart at thirty-five, Pascal at thirty-nine.

The social safety net had gaping holes. At the beginning of the twentieth century, we had no social security system. Divorced fathers were not obligated to pay child support. One in five children lived in orphanages, often because their impoverished parents could not support them.

Most people had limited educational opportunities. In the bad old days of a century ago, only half of five- to nineteen-year-olds were in school (compared with more than 90 percent today). Only 3.5 percent of eighteen-year-olds were graduating from high school. Today, eight in ten adults have at least a high school education.

Women had restricted opportunities. A half century ago, only one in five Americans approved "of a married woman earning money in business or industry if she has a husband capable of supporting her." Today, 80 percent approve. Thus, six in ten married women are now in the paid workforce—up from four in ten a half century ago and one in seven a century ago. With greater economic independence, today's women are more likely to marry for love and less likely to endure abuse out of economic need. America's married women, whether employed or not, still devote twice as many hours to household tasks as do their husbands. But men's participation has doubled since 1965, putting them more often in front of the stove, behind the vacuum cleaner, and over the diaper-changing table. Today's men and women are more likely to share opportunities, responsibilities, and power.

Minorities were shunned. Within the memory of many living individuals, some public accommodations offered "colored" and "white" toilets, those with disabilities were ignored, and gays and lesbians hid from public loathing. If we have not yet achieved "the Great Society," we have improved upon yesterday's unjust society.

Ergo, however great our present problems, the past is no golden age to which we would willingly return if only we could. Yesterday was not the best of times, *today* is the best of times. Seen in the rose-tinted rearview mirror, yesterday may *seem* like a golden age. But even the wholesome 1950s was the decade of McCarthyism, segregation, the Korean War, and air-raid drills and bomb shelters. Golden ages do happen, notes political scientist John Mueller. "But we are never actually *in* them," because "no matter how much better the present gets, the past gets better faster in reflection."

In his own golden age of life, my optimistic friend Sir John Templeton is one who does see the present as the best of times. In *Is Progress Speeding Up?* he concludes that things are not only getting better, they are getting better faster than ever, making this "a wonderful time to be alive!"

How true. Yet there is more to the story.

IT IS THE WORST OF TIMES

We are better paid, better fed, better housed, better educated, and healthier than ever before, and with more human rights, faster communication, and more convenient transportation than we have ever known. Ironically, however, for thirty-plus years—from 1960 until the early 1990s—America slid into a deepening social recession that dwarfed the comparatively milder and briefer economic recessions that often dominated our news and politics. Had you fallen asleep in 1960 and awakened in the 1990s, would you—overwhelmed by all the good tidings—feel pleased at the cultural shift? Here are some other facts that would greet you. Since 1960, as we will see,

- The divorce rate has doubled.
- The teen suicide rate has tripled.
- The recorded violent crime rate has quadrupled.
- The prison population has quintupled.
- The percentage of babies born to unmarried parents has (excuse the pun) sextupled.
- Cohabitation (a predictor of future divorce) has increased sevenfold.
- Depression has soared—to ten times the pre-World War II level, by one estimate.

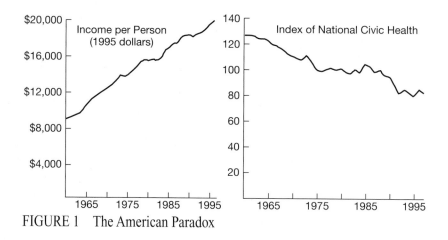

FIGURE 1   The American Paradox

The National Commission on Civic Renewal combined social trends such as these in creating its 1998 "Index of National Civic Health"—which has plunged southward since 1960. Bertrand Russell once said that the mark of a civilized human is the capacity to read a column of numbers and weep. Can we weep for all the crushed lives behind these numbers? It is hard to argue with Al Gore: "The accumulation of material goods is at an all-time high, but so is the number of people who feel an emptiness in their lives."

At the epicenter of America's social recession are children and youth. Writing with Elizabeth Gilman, Yale psychologist Edward Zigler, co-founder of Head Start, reported a consensus among researchers: "In the past thirty years of monitoring the indicators of child well-being, never have the indicators looked so negative." Across America, children are having children and men are fathering children with little commitment to mother or child. In 1960 just over one in ten children did not live with two parents. Today, a third do not. In a recent survey, American Psychological Association members rated "the decline of the nuclear family" as today's number-one threat to mental health. Urie Bronfenbrenner, a respected developmental psychologist, describes the trends starkly: "The present state of children and families in the United States represents the greatest domestic problem our nation has faced since the founding of the Republic.

It is sapping our very roots." Speaking to the National Press Club in late 1998, American Psychological Association president Martin Seligman was struck by a "serious paradox": "Every statistic we have on the 'objective' well-being of young Americans is going north. And every statistic we have on their demoralization, on depression, is going in the other direction."

Facing this cultural erosion, can we—without yearning for an unreal past or squashing basic liberties—expose the corrosive social forces at work and renew our social fabric? And what are the corrosive forces? How is it that things could have gone so well materially and so poorly socially? In other ways, too, these are hardly the best of times, notes Cornell economist Robert Frank in *Luxury Fever*. Americans are spending more hours at work, fewer hours sleeping, and fewer hours with friends and family. "Traffic has grown considerably more congested; savings rates have fallen precipitously; personal bankruptcy filings are at an all-time high; and there is at least a widespread perception that employment security has fallen sharply."

Radical Individualism

Part of the explanation lies in the radical individualism familiar to us in contemporary America's pop psychology and libertarian values. Do your own thing. Seek your own bliss. Challenge authority. If it feels good, do it. Shun conformity. Don't force your values on others. Assert your personal rights (to own guns, sell pornography, do business free of regulations). Protect your privacy. Cut taxes and raise executive pay (personal income takes priority over the common good). To love others, first love yourself. Listen to your own heart. Prefer solo spirituality to communal religion. Be self-sufficient. Expect others likewise to believe in themselves and to make it on their own. Such sentiments define the heart of economic and social individualism, which finds its peak expression in modern America.

The celebration and defense of personal liberty lies at the heart of the old American dream. It drives our free market economy and underlies our respect for the rights of all. In democratic countries that guarantee what Americans consider basic freedoms, people live more happily than in those that don't. Migration patterns testify to this reality. Yet for today's radical individualism, we pay a price: a social recession that imperils children, corrodes civility, and diminishes happiness. When individualism is taken to an extreme, individuals become its ironic casualties.

To cope with the casualties at the base of the social cliffs, we can expand our social ambulance services. Or we can . . . build guardrails at the top. We can dream a new American dream—one that renews our social ecology with values and policies that balance "me thinking" with "we thinking."

What Is the New American Dream?

To counter radical individualism and cultural corrosion, a new, inclusive social renewal movement is emerging: one that affirms liberals' indictment of the demoralizing effects of poverty and conservatives' indictment of toxic media models; one that welcomes liberals' support for family-friendly workplaces and conservatives' support for committed relationships; one that agrees with liberals' advocacy for children in all sorts of families and conservatives' support for marriage and coparenting. Viewing the contest between liberal and conservative ideas, we can

respond like the Dodo in *Alice's Adventures in Wonderland:* "*Everyone* has won and *all* must have prizes!"

Without suppressing our differences do we not—whether self-described liberals or conservatives—share a vision of a better world? Is it not one that rewards initiative but restrains exploitative greed? that balances individual rights with communal well-being? that respects diversity while embracing unifying ideals? that is tolerant of other cultures without being indifferent to moral issues? that protects and heals our degrading physical and social environments? In our utopian social world, adults and children will together enjoy their routines and traditions. They will have close relationships with extended family and with supportive neighbors. Children will live without fear for their safety or the breakup of their families. Fathers and mothers will jointly nurture their children; to say "He fathered the child" will parallel the meaning of "She mothered the child." Free yet responsible media will entertain us with stories and images that exemplify heroism, compassion, and committed love. Reasonable and rooted moral judgments will motivate compassionate acts and enable noble and satisfying lives.

Mapping the Quest

This dreamed-of world is, as yet, far from our real world. Still facing a large gap between the ideal and real, the advent of the new millennium is a fitting time to confront the reality of America's post-1960 social recession, to identify its roots, and to celebrate the quest for a healthier and happier American culture.

CRITICAL-THINKING QUESTIONS

1. In what sense are we in the United States today living in "the best of times"? In what ways has life been getting worse?

2. What role does "radical individualism" play in these trends?

3. What do you think we might do to improve the social health of the United States? Why?

CLASSIC

CONTEMPORARY

CROSS-CULTURAL

82 The Price of Modernization: The Case of Brazil's Kaiapo Indians

MARLISE SIMONS

Among the billions of poor people throughout the Third World, few will have a chance for a better life. But this is exactly what has happened to the Kaiapo, people who live deep in Brazil's rain forest. Has affluence been the blessing that the Kaiapo imagined it would be? To at least some of their number, the modernization of the Kaiapo amounts to little more than the systematic destruction of their traditional way of life.

It is getting dark when Chief Kanhonk sits down in the yard outside his home, ready for a long evening of conversation. Night birds are calling from the bush that sparkles with fireflies. Whooping frogs make a racket by the river. No one seems worried by the squadron of bats sweeping low overhead.

It is that important moment of the day when Indians of the Amazon, who use no written language, meet to talk, pass on information, and tell stories. The night is when they recall ancestral customs, interpret dreams, and comment on changes in nature and other events of the day. But from a nearby home come the sounds of a powerful rival: A television set is screeching cartoons at a group of children. I understand now why, that morning, by way of saying hello, these naked children of the rain forest had shouted things like "He-Man" and "Flintstones."

Three years ago, when money from the sale of gold nuggets and mahogany trees was pouring into Gorotire, Chief Kanhonk agreed to bring in television, or the "big ghost," as it is called here. A shiny satellite dish now stands on the earthen plaza like an alien sculpture, signaling that Gorotire—a small settlement of some 800 people on the Fresco River, a tributary of the Amazon—has become one of the wealthiest Indian villages in Brazil.

Yet Chief Kanhonk appears to regret his decision. "I have been saying that people must buy useful things like knives or fishing hooks," he says darkly. "Television does not fill the stomach. It only shows our children and grandchildren white people's things."

The "big ghost" is just one of the changes that have been sweeping over Gorotire, but it seems to be worrying the elders the most. Some believe it is powerful enough to rob them of their culture. Bebtopup, the oldest medicine man in the village, explains his misgivings: "The night is the time the old people teach the young people. Television has stolen the night."

Source: "The Amazon's Savvy Indians," by Marlise Simons, *The New York Times Magazine,* February 26, 1989, pp. 36–37, 48–52. Copyright © 1989 by The New York Times Company. Reprinted by permission of *The New York Times.*

When I discuss this with Eduardo Viveiros, a Brazilian anthropologist who works with a more isolated Amazonian tribe, he seems less worried. "At least they quickly understood the consequences of watching television," he says. "Many people never discover. Now Gorotire can make a choice."

It was the issue of choice that first drew me to the Kaiapo Indians of the lower Amazon Basin. They seemed to be challenging the widely held notion that forest Indians are defenseless in face of the pressures of the competitive and predatory Western world around them. Unlike most of Brazil's 230,000 Indians, they go out into the white world to defend their interests, and it is no longer unusual to see Kaiapo men—in their stunning body paint and feathered headdresses—showing up in Congress in Brasilia, the nation's capital, or lobbying by doing a war dance outside a government office. They have even bought Western gadgets to record and film their festivals.

Once the masters of immense stretches of forest and savannas, the Kaiapo were for hundreds of years among the most skillful farmers and hunters and fiercest warriors of central Brazil. They terrified other tribes with their raids. From the seventeenth to the nineteenth centuries, they not only resisted the slaving raids of the Portuguese invaders but they also attacked white traders and gold prospectors with such a vengeance that royal orders came from Portugal to destroy the Kaiapo. The white man's wrath and his diseases killed many, yet there are still close to 3,600 Kaiapo in more than a dozen different villages near the Xingu River. They have quarreled and regrouped, but their lands, several vast reservations, are more secure than those of many other tribes.

After many years of isolation in the forest, the Kaiapo now have to deal with the growing encroachments of white society. "They are going through a great transition," says Darrell Posey, an American anthropologist who has worked in Gorotire for more than a decade. "Their survival is a miracle in itself. But I worry whether they can go on making the changes on their own terms."

Colombia, Ecuador, Peru, and Venezuela—four of nine nations in the Amazon Basin, which harbors some 800,000 Indians—each have large numbers of tropical-forest Indians. But nowhere are pressures on Indian land as great as they are in Brazil. As the Amazon is opened up, developers bring in highways, settlers, cattle ranchers, mines, and hydroelectric dams. In Brazil alone, more than ninety tribes have disappeared since the beginning of this century.

The clearing of large areas of the rain forest and the fate of the Indians are also rapidly becoming an issue of international concern. Interest in the region has risen as ecological concerns, such as ozone depletion, the greenhouse effect, and other changes in the global environment become political issues. More attention is paid to scientists who are alarmed at the destruction of the rain forest—a vital flywheel in the world's climate and the nursery of at least half of the world's plant and animal species.

This has also prompted an increasing interest in the highly structured world of the forest Indians and their ancient and intricate knowledge of nature that permits them to survive in the tropical jungle without destroying it. (The Hall of South American Peoples, which includes a life-size model of a Kaiapo warrior, recently opened at the Museum of Natural History in New York City.)

As Indians find greater support among environmentalists, they also get more organized in their fight to protect their habitat. The Kaiapo held their first international congress last week in Altamira, in central Brazil, protesting government plans to build several massive dams that would flood Indian land.

In Brazil, Indian tribes occupy 10 percent of the nation's territory, although much of their land has not been demarcated. Brazil's past military regimes elevated Indian affairs to a national-security issue, because many tribes live in large areas of border land. It is official policy to integrate Indians into the larger society, and the National Indian Foundation, with its 4,900 employees, is in charge of implementing this.

In my eighteen years in Latin America, I have heard many politicians and anthropologists discuss what is usually called "the Indian problem," what to "do" about cultures that have changed little in thousands of years. One school of thought holds that the remote tribes should be kept isolated and protected until they can slowly make their own choices. Another school accepts that the Indian world is on the wane, and talks about "guiding" the Indians toward inevitable change—a process that should take several generations.

But some anthropologists and politicians, including the Brazilian government, believe in still more rapid integration. When Romeo Jucá was head of the Indian Foundation, he said that it was only right for Indians to exploit their wealth, even if it meant acculturation. "We have to be careful how fast we go," he said, "but being Indian does not mean you have to be poor."

Gerardo Reichel-Dolmatoff is one of Latin America's most respected anthropologists. He insists that the Indians are their own best guides into Western society. An Austrian-born Colombian, Reichel-Dolmatoff has worked in Colombia's forests, at the Amazon's headwaters, for almost fifty years. "We cannot choose for them," he insists. "And we cannot put them into reserves, ghettos, ashokas. They are not museum exhibits. . . . If Indians choose the negative aspects of our civilization, we cannot control that. If there is one basic truth in anthropology, it is that cultures change. Static cultures do not exist."

The Indians themselves are pleading for more protection and respect for their cultures. Conrad Gorinsky, son of a Guyana Indian mother and himself a chemist in London, recently said: "We don't want the Indians to change because we have them comfortably in the back of our mind like a kind of Shangri-La, something we can turn to even if we work ourselves to death in New York. But we are hounding and maligning them instead of recognizing them as the guardians of the forests, of the world's genetic banks, of our germ plasm and lifelines."

The aboriginal peoples we call Indians are as different from one another as, say, Europeans are. Even the most isolated groups remain separate

fiefdoms with widely varying experiences, beliefs, and histories. The degree of contact they have with the outside world is just as varied.

I first met Kaiapo tribesmen three years ago in Belém, a large city at the mouth of the Amazon. I saw them again in Brasilia, the capital. In both places, they demonstrated their political skills and capacity to mobilize, showing up in large numbers to protest measures by the government. They seemed particularly adept at commanding the attention of the press. Their body paint, feathers, and other paraphernalia made them appear warlike, exotic, and photogenic.

Back in Gorotire, as it turns out, they are more "ordinary." Wearing feathers and beads, explains Kubei, a chief's son, is for special occasions. "It's our suit and tie." Besides the satellite dish, the Kaiapo also have their own small airplane. Their new wealth has also given them the luxury of hiring non-Indians to help plant new fields. But they remain ready to attack white intruders; some of the adult men have markings on their chests that record the number of outsiders they have killed.

Two roads fan out from the center of Gorotire. A new sand track leads east on a five-hour drive to the town of Redenção. The other road goes south and, in a sense, it leads into the past. Dipping into the forest, it becomes a path that meanders through open patches where the Kaiapo women grow corn, sweet potatoes, bananas, manioc. On the plain ahead, it joins an ancient trail system that once reached for hundreds of miles into northern and western Brazil.

One morning, Beptopup (medicine man, shaman, connoisseur of nature), the anthropologist Darrell Posey (who speaks the Kaiapo language), and I wander into the bush. Beptopup walks past the plants the way you go down a street where you know everyone. Stopping, nodding, his face lighting up with happy recognition, he sometimes goes into a song—a soft, high-pitch chant for a particular plant.

He picks leaves, each one familiar, each one useful. One serves to remove body hair. Another, he says, can prevent pregnancy. The underside of one leaf is so rough it is used to sandpaper wood and file fingernails. Beptopup collects his plants in the morning, he says, because "that is when they have the most strength."

Stopping at a shrub, we look at the large circle around its stem, where nothing grows. "This and other plants have been sent to a laboratory for analysis," says Posey. "We think this one has a natural weedkiller."

Beptopup holds up a branch of what he calls the "eye of the jaguar." "This was our flashlight," he says, showing how to set it afire and swing it gently so its strong glow will light one's path.

One afternoon, when the heat has crept into everything, the women and children come back from the fields to their village. They stop and sit in a creek to escape the swirling gnats and buzzing bees. Others sit outside their homes, going about their age-old business. One woman plucks the radiant feathers of a dead macaw. Another removes her eyebrows and eyelashes, because the Kaiapo women think they are ugly. (A nurse once told me that this custom might have a hygienic origin—to ward off parasites, for instance.) Kaiapo women also deepen their foreheads by shaving the top of their head in a triangle that reaches the crown—a fearsome sight to the unaccustomed eye.

I envy a mother who is clearly enjoying herself fingerpainting her three children. She draws black designs with genipap juice. On the face and the feet she puts red dye from the "urucu," or annatto, plant; Indians say it keeps away chiggers and ticks.

Change has come to Gorotire along the other road, the one leading east to Redenção. Recent Kaiapo history is full of "firsts," but a notable turning point came when prospectors struck gold on Gorotire land in 1980. The Kaiapo raided the camp, twenty miles from the village, but failed to drive away the trespassers. Then they made a deal.

Last fall, when I was visiting Gorotire, about 2,000 gold diggers were stripping the land to the bone farther upstream, and the River Fresco passed the village the color of mud, its water contaminated with oil and mercury. I heard no one complain about that. Gorotire gets 7 percent of the mine's profits—several pounds of gold a week.

In 1984, a lumber company completed the first road. It signed a contract with the Indian Foundation for Gorotire's mahogany (the Indians are wards of the Brazilian government). Most of the mahogany is gone now, and the government agency split the profits with the Kaiapo. Gorotire chose to spend its gold and timber profits on new water and electricity lines and rows of brick houses. Only about half of the inhabitants now live in traditional palm-frond huts.

The young Kaiapo who earn a salary as supervisors at the gold camp have bought their own gas stoves, radios, sofas, and mattresses. For the community, the four tribal chiefs ordered several boats, trucks, and a small plane that ferries people and goods among nearby Kaiapo villages.

One evening, a truck arriving from Redenção—bringing rice, sugar, bottled gas, oil for the generator—is another reminder of how fast Gorotire is adapting to a Western economy. From being a largely self-sufficient community of hunters and farmers, it is now increasingly dependent on outside goods. In Gorotire, it is clearly money, no longer disease or violence, that has become the greatest catalyst for change. Money has given the Kaiapo the means and the confidence to travel and lobby for their rights. At the same time, it is making them more vulnerable.

I have seen other villages where Indians have received large sums of money—for the passage of a railroad or a powerline, or from a mining company. Such money is usually released in installments, through banks, but its arrival has put new strains on the role of the chiefs. Money and goods have introduced a new, materialistic expression of power in societies that have been egalitarian. Among most Indians, a man's prestige has always depended not on what he acquires but on what he gives away.

In Gorotire, some of the young men complain that the chiefs are not distributing community money and goods equally, that the chiefs' relatives and favorites are getting a bigger share and more privileges.

Darrell Posey, the anthropologist, believes the greatest political change came with the road. With it, he says, "the Kaiapo chiefs lost control of which people and what goods would come in." Previously, the chiefs had been the sole distributors. They had also played the vital roles of keeping the peace and leading the ceremonies. Now, the chiefs hardly know the liturgy of the ceremonies; their main task seems to be to deal with the outside world.

The transition is also changing the role of the medicine man. Bebtopup, for example, has an arsenal of remedies for the common ailments—fevers, diarrheas, snake bites, wounds. But he and his colleagues have lost prestige because they do not know how to deal with the diseases brought to Gorotire by white men, such as the pneumonia that strikes the children and the malaria spreading from the gold miners' camp.

Anthropologists sometimes say that when outsiders visit the Indian world, they often focus on themes central not to Indians but to themselves. This might explain why I was so bothered by the garbage, the flotsam of Western civilization.

Gorotire's setting is Arcadian. It lies on a bluff overlooking the River Fresco, with views of the forests across and the mountains behind. Spring rains bring waterfalls and blossoms. But these days the village is awash with rusting cans, plastic wrappers, tapes sprung from their cassettes, discarded mattresses, and clothes. New domestic animals such as dogs, pigs, and ducks have left a carpet of droppings. And giant rats, which suddenly appeared some years ago, seem to be everywhere; some have bitten small children.

"Indians have never had garbage that was not biodegradable," says Sandra Machado, a Brazilian researching Kaiapo farming techniques here. "No one wants to take care of it."

It is a mild moonlit evening, and in the men's house many Kaiapo are watching soccer on television. The bank of the river is a quieter place to talk.

"If you look beyond the garbage and the stone houses, this is still a strong and coherent indigenous culture," says Darrell Posey, speaking of the mixed feelings he has about a decade of developments in Gorotire. "Despite everything, the language is alive, the festivals and initiation rights are observed."

Posey says that the Kaiapo in Gorotire and in other villages continue with their age-old natural farming techniques, using plants to fix nitrogen in the soil, chunks of termite nests instead of chemical fertilizers, plant infusions to kill pests, the nests of ferocious ants to protect fruit trees from other ant predators.

Biologists often complain that there have been many studies of exotic rituals, paraphernalia, and kinships of Indians, but that Western science has paid scant attention to the Indians' use of animals and plants.

Like others working in the Amazon region, Posey worries about the gap between the old and the young. "The old chiefs are turning over decisions to the young because they can drive a truck or operate a video machine or go to the bank," he says. "But the young people don't see the relevance of learning the tribal knowledge and it's being lost."

"You can afford to lose one generation," he adds, "because grandparents do the teaching of their grandchildren. But you cannot afford to lose two generations."

Gorotire has a small Government school, designed to help Indians integrate into the national society. The teacher, who speaks only Portuguese, has started organizing annual Independence Day parades. On the blackboard is a list of patriotic holidays, including Independence Day and the Day of the Soldier. I ask the children later what a soldier is. "Something of white people," one of them says.

Chief Poropot agrees that everyone must learn Portuguese. "The language of the Kaiapo is very ancient and it will never end," he says. "But the women and the children need to learn Portuguese to defend themselves."

Defend themselves?

"If they go to shop in Redenção, they have to talk," he says. "If they get sick, they cannot tell the doctor what they have."

Thirty miles from Gorotire, in the village of Aukre, another Kaiapo tribe is choosing a different strategy for change. Its best-known member is Paiakan, thirty-seven years old, the son of Chief Tikiri.

Calm and articulate, Paiakan has been named to "keep an eye on the whites" in the state capital of Belém. He acts as a kind of roving ambassador for the Kaiapo, even though each village is autonomous. When Kaiapo interests are threatened, he sends out warnings to the communities.

Paiakan's contacts with the outside world and the many pitfalls it holds for Indians have made him more conservative, he says, more so than in the early days, in the 1970s, when he first left home to work on the Trans-Amazonian Highway. As his father's main adviser, he has insisted that Aukre remain a traditional village.

It is built in the age-old circle of mud-and-thatch huts. There is no television, running water, pigs, or piles of garbage. Paiakan and his father have also banned logging and gold digging. This appears to have saved Aukre from the consumerism—and widespread influenza and malaria—of Gorotire.

"The lumber men have come to us with their bags of money," he says. "And we know we have a lot of gold. But we do not want to bring a lot of money in. The Indian still does not know the value of white man's objects or how to treat them." Paiakan cites clothing as an example. "The Indian wears something until it is stiff with dirt, then he throws it out."

But people now want things from the "world of the whites," he continues. "Pressure from the white society is so strong, there is no wall that can stop it." It is the task of the chief to measure the change, provide explanations, he says. "If someone wants to get a radio or a tape recorder, the chiefs cannot stop it."

In Aukre, where two aging chiefs are still in charge of buying goods for the community, they say that they will not buy gadgets. "We explain we cannot buy this thing for you because we do not have the batteries you need and we cannot repair it," Paiakan says.

Of late, Paiakan has been invited abroad to campaign for the protection of the rain forest. He knows the problem only too well. Ranchers have moved almost to the reservation's doorstep, felled trees, and set massive forest fires. Because of deforestation, there have been unusual changes in the water level of the Fresco River.

"Our people are getting very disoriented," says Paiakan. "It would be as if people from another planet came to your cities and started to tear down your houses. The forest is our home." With all the destruction going on, he continues, "the breath of life is drifting up and away from us."

At the age of seventy-eight and retired from teaching at the University of California at Los Angeles, the anthropologist Gerardo Reichel-Dolmatoff lives in Bogotá, Colombia, and is still writing. After studying changes in the Amazon for five decades, he is not optimistic about the prospects for the Indians.

"In Colombia, I don't know of a single case where an aboriginal culture has found a strong adaptive mechanism," he says. "Physical survival is possible. But I have not seen the ancient values replaced by a workable value system. I wish I could be more positive. But in fifty years I have seen too many traditions being lost, too many tribes disappear.

"For 500 years we have witnessed the destruction of the Indians. Now we are witnessing the destruction of the habitat. I suggest more field work, and immediate field work, because soon it will be too late."

At a conference on ethnobiology last fall, Reichel-Dolmatoff urged scientists to insist on spreading the message that Western science has much to learn from Indians, from their well-adapted lives and deeply felt beliefs, their view that whatever man subtracts he must restore by other means.

What suggestions has he made to Indians?

"Indians have to stay in touch with their language—that is absolutely essential," he says. "It embodies their thought patterns, their values, their philosophy." Moreover, he says, talented young Indians should be given a modern academic education, but also the chance to keep in touch with their people. "They come from cultures based on extra ordinary realism and imagery. They should not be forced to enter at the lowest level of our society."

One night, I ask the chiefs in Gorotire: What happens if the gold runs out? After all, most of the mahogany is already gone. Young tribesmen have wanted to invest some of the income, and the chiefs have accepted the idea. Gorotire has bought a home in Belém for Kaiapo who travel there, as well as three houses in Redenção. There is talk of buying a farm, a curious thought, perhaps, for a community that lives on 8 million acres of land. But the Kaiapo, so they say, want it so that white farmers can grow rice for them.

And there is talk of planting new mahogany trees. Soon the conversation turns to a bird that a tribesman explains is very important. It is the bird, he says, that spreads the mahogany seeds.

CRITICAL-THINKING QUESTIONS

1. What have been the short-term consequences of the Kaiapo's new wealth? What are their long-term prospects?

2. What arguments can be made in support of continued effort by the Kaiapo to economically develop their resources? What arguments can be made against doing so?

3. In what ways are other countries involved in the changes taking place in the Amazon Basin?

Photo Credits

p. 1: Alex Colville (1920–), To Prince Edward Island, 1965, acrylic emulsion on masonite, 61.9 × 92.5 cm. National Gallery of Canada, Ottawa. © NGC/MBAC; p. 23: Doranne Jacobson/International Images; p. 35: © CLEO/Jeroboam; p. 55: Corbis/Bettmann; p. 75: Andy Sacks/Getty Images Inc.—Stone Allstock; p. 106: Ed Homonylo © Dorling Kindersley; p. 130: Dan Habib Photography; p. 154: Campbell/Corbis/Sygma; p. 215: Scott Cunningham/Merrill Education; p. 237: Bettmann/Corbis; p. 261: Corbis; p. 293: Michael Kagan; p. 312: U.S. Department of Agriculture; p. 335: Kenneth Meyer/Pearson Education/PH College; p. 356: Edward Hopper (1882–1967) "Room in New York" 1932. Oil on canvas, 29 × 36 in. Sheldon Memorial Art Gallery, University of Nebraska-Lincoln. F.M. Hall Collection. 1932.H-166; p. 375: SP5 Rick Haley/U.S. Army Photo; p. 394: John Giordano/Corbis/SABA Press Photos, Inc.; p. 416: U.S. Department of Health and Human Services; p. 433: New York Convention & Visitors Bureau; p. 456: Bobbie Kingsley/Photo Researchers, Inc.; p. 480: Corbis/Bettmann; p. 510: Edvard Munch, "The Scream." Oslo, National Gallery. Scala/Art Resource, NY. © 2007 The Munch Museum/The Munch-Ellingsen Group/Artists Rights Society (ARS), New York.